r

Pleas

THE GREENWOOD ENCYCLOPEDIA OF
LGBT Issues
WORLDWIDE

THE GREENWOOD ENCYCLOPEDIA OF
LGBT Issues
WORLDWIDE

VOLUME 2

Edited by
Chuck Stewart

GREENWOOD PRESS
An Imprint of ABC-CLIO, LLC

A B C 💿 C L I O

Santa Barbara, California • Denver, Colorado • Oxford, England

Library of Congress Cataloging-in-Publication Data

The Greenwood encyclopedia of LGBT issues worldwide /
edited by Chuck Stewart.
      p. cm.
  Includes bibliographical references and index.
   ISBN 978-0-313-34231-8 (set hard copy : alk. paper) — ISBN 978-0-313-34233-2
(vol 1 hard copy : alk. paper) — ISBN 978-0-313-34235-6 (vol 2 hard copy : alk. paper) —
ISBN 978-0-313-34237-0 (vol 3 hard copy : alk. paper) — ISBN 978-0-313-34232-5
(set ebook) — ISBN 978-0-313-34234-9 (vol 1 ebook) — ISBN 978-0-313-34236-3
(vol 2 ebook) — ISBN 978-0-313-34238-7 (vol 3 ebook)
1. Homosexuality—History—Encyclopedias. 2. Gays—History—Encyclopedias.
3. Bisexuals—History—Encyclopedias. 4. Transgender people—History—
Encyclopedias. I. Stewart, Chuck, 1951– II. Title: Greenwood encyclopedia of
lesbian, gay, bisexual, and transgender issues.
  HQ76.G724   2010
   306.76'609—dc22   2009027698

ISBN: 978-0-313-34231-8
EISBN: 978-0-313-34232-5

14 13 12 11 10   1 2 3 4 5

This book is also available on the World Wide Web as an eBook.
Visit www.abc-clio.com for details.

Greenwood Press
An Imprint of ABC-CLIO, LLC

ABC-CLIO, LLC
130 Cremona Drive, P.O. Box 1911
Santa Barbara, California 93116-1911

This book is printed on acid-free paper ∞

Manufactured in the United States of America

Cartography by Bookcomp, Inc.

CONTENTS

VOLUME 3

Africa and the Middle East

SET PREFACE

The Greenwood Encyclopedia of LGBT Issues Worldwide is a multivolume set presenting comprehensive, authoritative, and current data related to the cultural, social, personal, and political experiences of lesbian, gay, bisexual, and transgendered (LGBT) people. The set encompasses more than 80 countries with each volume covering major populated world regions: Africa and the Middle East, Asia and Oceania, the Americas and the Caribbean, and Europe. Volumes are organized regionally and then alphabetically by country (including Hong Kong and the European Union, the latter because of its importance to European laws) with chapters that reflect LGBT geopolitical and historical context and follow a broad outline of topics—Overview of the country, Overview of LGBT Issues, Education, Employment and Economics, Social/Government Programs, Sexuality/Sexual Practices, Family, Community, Health, Politics and Law, Religion and Spirituality, Violence, and Outlook for the 21st Century. Under these topics, contributors explore a range of contemporary issues including sodomy, antidiscrimination legislation (in employment, child adoption, housing, immigration), marriage and domestic partnerships, speech and association, transsexualism, intersexualism, AIDS, safe-sex educational efforts, and more. As such, the set provides an unparalleled global perspective on LGBT issues and helps facilitate cross-national comparisons.

The term *LGBT* was chosen for this encyclopedia as a shorthand, yet inclusive, notation for the class of people who experience marginalization and discrimination perpetrated by heterosexual norms. In the late 19th century, the word *heterosexual* was invented to denote abnormal sexual behaviors between persons of the opposite sex. Ten years later, the word *homosexual* was invented for the same purpose of medicalizing same-sex behaviors and psychology. Many people found it offensive to categorize their lifestyle as pathology. They also thought that the emphasis on sex restrictive in describing their experiences and, instead, created and used the term *homophile* or *Uranian*. By the mid-20th century, the word *gay* came into common usage. As the gay political movement took roots in the 1950s and 1960s, it became apparent that, in the eyes of the public, gay women were invisible. In response to that phenomenon, many gay organizations changed their names to include women, as in—"lesbian and gay" or "gay and lesbian." Still, bisexuals, the transgendered (which includes transsexuals, transvestites, and intersexed people), and those questioning their sexual orientation believed that "lesbian and gay" was not inclusive enough to describe their experiences and challenged the status quo.

By the 1980s and 1990s, more gay organizations modified their names to include their moniker. However, a backlash occurred with many groups because the names became un-wielding. At the same time, radical street organizations, such as Queer Nation and ACT UP, appropriated the epithet *queer* and embraced its shocking value. This is a common practice by people who are marginalized and discriminated against to defuse the power of hateful words. Further, academia appropriated the word *queer* since it was a concise term denoting all persons outside heteronormative power structures. Still, many community organizations resisted the attempts to include *queer* in their names but rather stuck to some version of lesbian, gay, bisexual, and transgendered (LGBT). In the chapters, readers will encounter many variations of *LGBT*. Sometimes this will be written as "gay community," "lesbian and gay," LGBT, queer, or other terminology. The word usage reveals much about the community's level of understanding concerning LGBT issues.

Contributors were chosen based on their expertise in LGBT issues and knowledge of their country. Every effort was made to find contributors who live, or have lived, in the country in question. This was important, as gay people are often a hidden minority not easily quantified. Some contributors are from countries where gay people are routinely rounded up and killed. Contributors from these countries have taken great personal risk to participate in this encyclopedia and we commend their courage. Each contributor provides an authoritative resource guide that strives to include helpful suggested readings, Web sites, organizations, and film/video sources. The chapters and resources are designed for students, academics, and engaged citizens to study contemporary LGBT issues in depth for specific countries and from a global perspective.

CHUCK STEWART

ACKNOWLEDGMENTS

This ambitious project has been made possible through the work of many scholars. I wish to thank the advisory board—Robert Aldrich of the University of Sydney, David Foster of Arizona State University, John Goss of the Utopia Asian Gay and Lesbian Resources, Jan Lofstrom of the University of Helsinki, Ruth Morgan of the Gay and Lesbian Archives of South Africa, David Paternotte of the University of Brussels, Gerard Sullivan of the University of Sydney, and Walter Williams of the University of Southern California—for their dedicated work and leads to so many wonderful contributors. I want to thank the Institute for the Study of Human Resources (ISHR), D/B/A One for their generous financial support toward completion of this encyclopedia. With so many essays to review, this project could not have been possible without the help of first-level editing by Jessica Chesnutt, Jennafer Collins, Benjamin de Lee, William "B. J." Fleming, Winston Gieseke, Aimee Greenfield, Nicholas Grider, Alice Julier, and Bonnie Stewart. A heartfelt thanks goes to Astrid Cook, Gabriel Molina, Matt Moreno, and Rachel Wexelbaum for their editorial review of many of the essays. A special thanks goes to Wendi Schnaufer of Greenwood Press for her editorial assistance over the entire project.

This project took more than two years to complete. Locating experts on LGBT issues, especially for the smaller countries or in countries where it is dangerous to be gay, was a monumental task. In working with the contributors, I was struck by their dedication to making the world safe for all people. They are much more than just writers; they are people interested in changing the world to make it a better place. They understood that the first step toward reducing heterosexism and homophobia is to educate the public on LGBT culture and issues. To that end, they were eager to participate—even if they faced language difficulties or possible persecution from their governments. I commend each writer for the courage to be part of the solution toward overcoming sexual orientation bias. I hope this encyclopedia will further their vision.

ADVISORY BOARD

EDITOR AND CONTRIBUTORS

EDITOR

Chuck Stewart
Institute for the Study of Human
Resources
Los Angeles, California

CONTRIBUTORS

Tom Ochieng Abongo
Nyanza, Kenya

Brandon L. H. Aultman
Baruch College, City University of
New York

Unoma N. Azuah
International Resource Network for
Sexuality Studies in Africa
Ibadan, Nigeria

Hongwei Bao
The University of Sydney
Australia

Natalie D. A. Bennett
DePaul University
Chicago, Illinois

Martin Blais
Université du Québec à Montréal
Canada

Marianne Blidon
Université Paris 1-Panthéon Sorbonne
Paris, France

Matteo Bonini Baraldi
European Study Centre on
Discrimination
Bologna, Italy

Viachaslau Bortnik
Amnesty International
Gomel, Belarus

Jen Westmoreland Bouchard
Lucidité Writing
Minneapolis, Minnesota

Christopher Burke
University of Otago
Dunedin, Otago, New Zealand

Sinziana Carstocea
Université Libre de Bruxelles
Brussels, Belgium

Line Chamberland
Université du Québec à Montréal
Canada

Beng Chang
University of Minnesota
Minneapolis

Dau-Chuan Chung
University of Sydney
Australia

Donn Colby
Harvard Medical School
Cambridge, Massachusetts

Cristina Corleto
University of Sydney
New South Wales, Australia

Patrice Corriveau
University of Ottawa
Ontario, Canada

Julien Danero Iglesias
Cevipol—Université libre de
   Bruxelles
Brussels, Belgium

Zowie Davy
University of Leeds
United Kingdom

Benjamin de Lee
University of California
Los Angeles

Carmen De Michele
Ludwig-Maximilians University
Munich, Germany

Alexis Dewaele
University of Antwerp, Policy Research
   Centre on Equal Opportunities
Belgium

Marco Díaz-Muñoz
Michigan State University
East Lansing

James Dochterman
University of Southern California

Héctor Domínguez-Ruvalcaba
The University of Texas at Austin

Jesse Field
University of Minnesota
Minneapolis

José Ignacio Pichardo Galán
Universidad Complutense de Madrid
Spain

Jaime Galgani
Universidad Católica de Chile
Santiago

Natalia Gerodetti
Leeds Metropolitan University
United Kingdom

Keith Goddard
GALZ
Milton Park, Harare, Zimbabwe

Kristijan Grđan
Iskorak
Zagreb, Croatia

Michele Grigolo
Italy

Charles Gueboguo
University of Yaounde
Cameroon

Gert Hekma
University of Amsterdam
The Netherlands

Tone Hellesund
Stein Rokkan Center for Social Studies,
   University of Bergen
Norway

Adnan Hossain
University of Hull
Hull, England

Leo Igwe
International Resource Network for
   Sexuality Studies in Africa
Jackson, Tennessee

Hitoshi Ishida
International Christian University
Mitaka-shi, Tokyo, Japan

Frédéric Jörgens
Berlin, Germany

Sanja Juras
KONTRA
Zagreb, Croatia

Krister Karttunen
Helsinki University
Finland

Mark E. King
University of Hong Kong
Hong Kong, China

Anna Kirey
Labrys
Bishkek, Kyrgyzstan

Kurt Krickler
Vienna, Austria

Roman Kuhar
Peace Institute and University
  of Ljubljana
Slovenia

Ann Kristin Lassen
University of Copenhagen
Denmark

Laurence Wai-Teng Leong
Department of Sociology, National
  University of Singapore

Joseph Josy Lévy
Université du Québec à Montréal
Canada

Ed Madden
University of South Carolina
Columbia

Derek Matyszak
GALZ
Milton Park, Harare, Zimbabwe

Eduardo Alfonso Caro Meléndez
Arizona State University
Phoenix

Sukhragchaa Mijidsuren
We Are Family-Mongolia
Ulaanbaatar, Mongolia

Joanna Mizielinska
Warsaw School of Social Psychology
Poland

Nadine Moawad
Rmeyl, Beirut, Lebanon

Maria Federica Moscati
School of Oriental and African Studies
University of London
United Kingdom

Kateřina Nedbálková
Masaryk University
Brno, Czech Republic

Nancy Nteere
Nairobi, Kenya

Caleb Orozco
University of Belize

Emrecan Özen
Lambdaistanbul
Istanbul, Turkey

Evelyne Paradis
IGLA-Europe (Policy Director)
Brussels, Belgium

David Paternotte
Université libre de Bruxelles
Brussels, Belgium

Joseph M. Pierce
The University of Texas at Austin

Monika Pisankaneva
Bilitis Resource Center
Sofia, Bulgaria

Eva Polášková
Masaryk University
Brno, Czech Republic

Álvaro Queiruga
Montevideo, Uruguay

Régis Revenin
Université Paris 1-Panthéon
  Sorbonne / Université Lille
  3-Charles-de-Gaulle
Paris, France

Gabrielle Richard
Université du Québec à Montréal
Canada

Bill Ryan
McGill University
Montreal, Quebec, Canada

Paata Sabelashvili
Inclusive Foundation
Tbilisi, Georgia

Fabiola Fernández Salek
CUNY Department of Humanities
Jamaica, New York

Joel Samper Marbà
Pompeu Fabra University
Andorra la Vella, Andorra

Alexandra Sandels
Menassat
Beirut, Lebanon

Ana Cristina Santos
Birkbeck Institute for Social Research,
    University of London
United Kingdom

Diego Sempol
Universidad Nacional General
Sarmiento-IDES
Montevideo, Uruguay

Fernando Serrano
Bogotá, Colombia

Shivali Shah
Washington, D.C.

Johan H. B. Smuts
AnthroCon RSA Ethnographic
    Research
Port Elizabeth, South Africa

Katsuhiko Suganuma
University of Melbourne
Parkville, Victoria, Australia

Ikuko Sugiura
Chuo University
Hachioji-shi, Tokyo, Japan

Gerard Sullivan
University of Sydney
New South Wales, Australia

Judit Takács
Institute of Sociology of the
    Hungarian Academy of Sciences
Budapest, Hungary

Ferdiansyah Thajib
KUNCI Cultural Studies Center
Yogyakarta, Indonesia

Larry Villegas-Perez
Washington, D.C.

James Daniel Wilets
Nova Southeastern University
Ft. Lauderdale, Florida

Walter L. Williams
University of Southern California
Los Angeles

James A. Wilson Jr.
University of Texas at Austin

Sam Winter
University of Hong Kong
Hong Kong, China

EUROPE

INTRODUCTION

OVERVIEW OF EUROPE

The histories and sociopolitical forces in Europe are deeply complex. With each change in governments or ruling powers, the life experiences of lesbian, gay, bisexual, and transgendered (LGBT) people change. The current status of LGBT rights is dependent upon these forces.

Poland is a prime example of this process. The Polish state is considered to have come into existence in 966 C.E. when the ruler, Mieszko I, converted to Christianity and pulled together regional warlords into one country that approximated the boundaries of modern Poland. Before then, the local religion was an amalgam of various pagan religions, some accepting of homosexuality and some not. Even after the conversion to Christianity, homosexual behaviors were sometimes accepts and at other times they were not, depending on various cultural forces. Over the next 1,000 years, Poland went through periods of empire building; it was later divided between neighboring rulers and then went back to being one country. Poland declared itself a kingdom in 1025 C.E. Five hundred years later, in 1569, it cemented a relationship with the Grand Duchy of Lithuania to form the Polish-Lithuanian Commonwealth. War led to its collapse 200 years later, and it was divided between Russia, Prussia, and Austro-Hungary in 1795. Poland aligned with the French at the beginning of the French expansion into Europe in the late 19th century and adopted the criminal code developed by the French National Constituent Assembly (1789–1791) that decriminalized sodomy. This was further codified under Napoleon in the penal codes of 1810. As such, there was a brief period in which homosexuality was not legally persecuted. Napoleon's march to Russia in the first decade of the 19th century allowed Poland to recapture land that had been taken by Russia. The reunification was brief, as Germany overran Poland in World War I and replaced its government with one friendly to Germany. With the onslaught of Germany, paragraph 175 of the German criminal code that made male homosexual acts a crime was enforced against Polish homosexuals. With the defeat of Germany, Poland reorganized and became an independent state in 1918, but kept the German criminal code and its antigay statutes intact. Unification was short-lived, as Poland was soon divided between Nazi Germany and the Soviet Union. Again, Germany was defeated; this time, the Soviet Union took complete control of Poland, annexing it into the Soviet bloc. The Polish legal system was modified to conform to communist thought. Initially, homosexuality was ignored and not criminalized. However, the medical profession in the Soviet Union reconceptualized homosexuality as a pathology, which influenced all the satellite states, like Poland, to adopt the same view. As a result, Polish homosexuals were in constant fear of being rounded up and sent to reeducation camps or mental hospitals. The collapse of the Soviet Union in 1989, due in part to the Polish Solidarity movement, allowed Poland to regain its independence. The return of freedom of speech and association allowed LGBT people to begin organizing and advocating for equal rights. Poland was interested in joining the European Union (EU). A condition of membership was to implement national antidiscrimination legislation that included a ban on employment discrimination based on sexual orientation. Poland adopted such a policy, met all of the other conditions for membership, and officially joined the EU in 2004. The Polish constitution now officially affords some protection for LGBT people.

War and occupation change societal views concerning homosexuality. For more than 2,000 years, most of Europe has been in a constant state of war and occupation from such sources as the Romans, Christian crusaders, Protestant reformers, border wars, Christian inquisitions and witch hunts, the Ottoman Empire, Napoleon's conquests, World War I and II, and the communist revolution. With each change in government, LGBT people embraced the hope of freedom or the fear of possible extinction. But it does not require full-scale war for conditions to change drastically for LGBT people. Instead, a minor shift in political power within a country can have a major effect on LGBT rights. For example, a majority of EU countries were politically center-left for much of the 1970s through to the late 1990s. The influx of foreign workers from Islamic countries, combined with the fears generated by the terrorist attacks on the United States in 2001, saw a shift in many European countries toward the political right. So far, the rights of LGBT people have not been jeopardized, but there is always the fear that xenophobia and Islamophobia could be applied against homosexuals, and that their hard-fought gains in securing equal rights could be reversed.

The most significant factor that has influenced LGBT rights in modern Europe has been the formation of the European Union. Originating in 1957 with the Treaty of Rome, the European Economic Community (EEC) was established and later renamed the European Community (EC). Its goals were to create internal markets where trade and services could circulate without barriers. By 1992, the EC was expanded to introduce monetary and economic normalization, and its name was changed to the European Union. This allowed for the development of a common currency (the euro) and many other rights such as the right to move and reside in any of the member states. By 2008, 27 countries belonged to the EU as member states, including most of Europe and what used to be the western satellites of the Soviet Union. The EU is approximately half the size of the United States, but with a population that is 50 percent larger, making it the third largest geopolitical center after China and India. Its gross domestic product (GDP) exceeds that of the United States.

The EU has been committed to the active promotion of human rights. In 2000, the Employment Framework Directive was formulated to "take appropriate action to combat discrimination based on sex, racial, or ethnic origin, religion or belief, disability, age, or sexual orientation." The directive obliges all member states to introduce legislation to their governments to implement the directive. As of 2009, most of the member states have passed legislation in their countries implementing the directive. Countries applying to join the EU must also pass legislation implementing the directive. Considering the number of countries and population affected by the Employment Framework Directive, it is arguably the single most important piece of legislation in the history of Europe for protecting the rights of LGBT people.

The impact of the directive has been significant. Many of the early members of the EU were socialist states with liberal values and politically active gay communities. For these countries, it was not a big step to pass antidiscrimination legislation. For other countries, such as the ones that were at one time part of the Soviet Union, the thought of passing antidiscrimination legislation based on sexual orientation was considered a far-off dream for many LGBT people. Most human rights political process requires a bottom-up approach, with community activism slowly creating legal, political, and cultural change. Here, gay rights were affirmed in many cases before there were active LGBT political groups in these countries. Romania is an example. By many estimates, Romania is considered to be the most homophobic country in Europe, and has a highly traumatized and hidden gay community. By joining the EU, it was forced to recognize the existence of LGBT people and legally protect their rights to employment before there was a visible gay community. Romanian activists are scrambling to organize and bring to public attention the employment protections based on sexual orientation. However, LGBT people still need to come out and demand the laws be applied effectively. It will take years of organizing in Romania to make the culture less homophobic.

OVERVIEW OF LGBT ISSUES

Sodomy

For hundreds of years, most European countries had antisodomy laws and customs in place that made male-to-male sexual behaviors illegal. Sodomy was punishable by death in many cases (burning at the stake). This was due to the influence of Christianity. Women, who held a much lower caste than men, were overlooked in the laws. The idea of woman-on-woman sex was incomprehensible for most European cultures. Virtually no European country had antisodomy laws that included women. The French Revolution (1789–1799) instigated a change in the French criminal code by adopting ideas from the 18th-century Enlightenment. Homosexuality was decriminalized along with the offenses of heresy, witchcraft, blasphemy, incest, and bestiality. The 1810 penal code promulgated by Napoleon adopted much of the French criminal code, decriminalizing homosexuality by simply leaving same-sex sexual behaviors out of the legal code. Because of the imperialistic expansion of France into Europe and the Napoleonic Wars, the penal code was adopted throughout most of Europe. Even after the defeat of Napoleon, the penal code remained, and most European countries had no antigay sodomy law.

However, over time, many countries implemented some form of legislation of sexual mores that included phrases such as "unnatural debauchery" (Greece), "offense against nature" (Denmark), and "unnatural fornication" (Croatia). The vague terminology allowed for the prosecution of anyone for behaviors deemed offensive to the ruling power. In some countries, like the Netherlands, although antisodomy statutes dealing with adult men were abolished in 1811, they were later reintroduced by defining sodomy as sex occurring between an adult and minor child. A different strategy used by antigay countries wanting to enter the European Union was to redefine sodomy to include the use of force, or threat of force, in conjunction with male-on-male or female-on-female sex. For example, Moldova replaced "homosexuality" with "forced homosexuality" in its first revision of its antisodomy statutes in 1995 to comply with the Council of Europe's standards. A similar tactic was used by Russia in 1996 to make its legal system appear more modernized when it removed an outright ban on LGBT people.

At this time, no European country has antisodomy laws on its books.

Antidiscrimination Statutes and Violence

The European Parliament has been the primary driving force behind the development of LGBT rights within the European Union. The Roth report, commissioned by the parliament in 1994, recommended full and equal rights for "homosexuals and lesbians" in the European Union. Input was received over the next decade from member states, public meetings, and professionals that reinforced the Roth report. The recommendations were later refined at a summit in Nice (2000) with the creation of the Charter of Fundamental Rights and Freedoms in the EU. Article 21 of the charter explicitly prohibited discrimination on the grounds of sexual orientation. By 2007, the charter acquired the same legally binding character as other European treaties. All member states are required to comply with the charter. A newly established fundamental rights agency was established to oversee compliance with the charter of fundamental rights. Part of the work of the agency is to conduct research on homophobia in the EU.

The adoption of the charter of fundamental rights and establishment of the Fundamental Rights Agency are extremely important for the future of antidiscrimination statutes in Europe. Since the Roth report, it has taken over a decade for all the member states to approve their own antidiscrimination statutes for employment protections based on sexual orientation. If history is any guide, it will probably take another decade or so to fully implement antidiscrimination protections for LGBT people as they relate to housing, services, and public accommodations besides hate crime reporting as specified in the charter of fundamental rights.

Violence against LGBT people has continued to increase across Europe for the past 20 years. Although there are variations in intensity and methodology in specific localities, the general trend has been toward greater and greater violence. As has been observed elsewhere in the world, the act of coming out, organizing, and bringing attention to LGBT people and issues increases acts of violence. Eventually, the violence levels off and then begins to decline as LGBT people become assimilated and LGBT issues are normalized in society. A problem that has spilled over into the LGBT community has been nationalistic hate directed toward immigrants by conservatives. Europe has experienced a massive immigration of workers, many from Islamic countries. As the world economies have entered into recession, the job market has tightened and many people have lost their jobs. The war on terrorism, initiated by the United States, has enlisted the help of many European countries. The synergy between the loss of jobs, tightening economic conditions, and heightening tensions over possible terrorist attacks has given conservative politicians the opportunity to blame Muslims for their problems. Conservatives have traditionally been antigay. There seems to be a convergence between xenophobia and homophobia that has increased the level of hate-motivated crimes against LGBT people.

Marriage and Child Adoption

Of the six countries in the world that allow same-sex marriages, four are found in Europe: Belgium, the Netherlands, Norway, and Spain. The Netherlands led the way by approving same-sex marriages in 2001, becoming the first country in the world to do so in modern times. Initially, there were limitations within same-sex marriages with regards to child adoption and foster care. These have now been lifted. Same-sex marriages in these European countries have been fully harmonized with existing marital laws and are legally equivalent to heterosexual marriages, with exactly the same rights. For many people, both gay and straight, it was thought that gay marriage represented full LGBT emancipation, and that the struggle for equal rights was over. This has not been proven to be true. It has become clear that legal equality does not necessarily translate into social equality. LGBT people still face many acts of discrimination in the workplace, in housing and public accommodations, in medical access, and elsewhere. Legal equality is necessary, but there is still considerable work to be done to break down antigay social barriers.

In a modern context, same-sex marriage may seem new and exotic. Yet there is a long history of different cultures in different times that not only allowed, but also venerated gay marriages. Worldwide, there is considerable evidence of the acceptance of same-sex marriages. For example, during the Ming dynasty period, many women in the southern Chinese province of Fujian bound themselves to younger females in elaborate rituals. The Japanese tradition of Shudo practiced during the medieval period and up to the 19th century instituted age-structured homosexuality analogous to the ancient Greek tradition of pederasty (*paiderastia*). In Europe, the Roman emperor Nero married his slave boy. Same-sex marriages were recorded throughout Europe during the Middle Ages. Legal contracts have been found in France dating from the 14th century that establish a brotherhood between two men. Similar documents are found in many European countries in which the brothers pledged to live as a couple, sharing the joys of life and "one purse" (meaning they shared property jointly). The contracts were sworn before witnesses and legally notarized. Many of these marriages were performed in a church.

Before same-sex marriages were approved in modern Europe, an intermediate step was taken in recognizing same-sex relationships with civil unions and/or domestic partnerships. Many European countries do not provide same-sex couples with the option to marry, but do allow civil unions or partnerships. Currently, Andorra, Croatia, the Czech Republic, Denmark, Finland, France, Germany, Hungary, Iceland, Luxembourg, Portugal, Slovenia, Sweden, Switzerland, and the United Kingdom provide some form of union for same sex couples. How civil unions or domestic partnerships are structured varies from country to country. Sometimes, they are limited to living arrangements and financial entanglement. Other times they include childcare, adoption, and foster care. Within the LGBT community, classifications of civil unions and domestic partnerships are considered one step toward obtaining equality with heterosexuals; ultimately, however, full marriage is desired.

Marriage is problematic for transgendered and intersexual individuals in Europe and elsewhere. For transgendered individuals, changing from one gender to another causes difficulties with identification documents and marriage. In countries such as the United Kingdom, which does not provide for same-sex marriage but does provide for civil partnership, a transgendered person must dissolve his/her civil partnership or marriage before obtaining legal recognition (what is called a gender recognition certificate in the United Kingdom) within the new gender. Once the new gender is established, the person can enter into either marriage or civil partnership, depending on whether the relationship is opposite-sex or same-sex.

Education

Only a few European countries include LGBT issues in their public school curriculum. Typically, they are only addressed within the context of health education and, perhaps, as a safe sex lesson designed to reduce the transmission of HIV. Rarely is homosexuality presented without judgment and as a viable alternative to the heterosexual lifestyle. Most European countries still have state-supported religion, and religious study is required in public education. As such, there is still strong influence of religious thought enforced in public schools. In predominantly Catholic and Protestant countries, an antigay message is still being fostered in elementary and high schools. School is typically a dangerous setting for LGBT students. However, this is slowly being mediated by the greater tolerance shown by society and the changes in antidiscrimination laws that include sexual orientation. Religion, in general, is on the decline in Europe, and its impact on the social discourse is weakening.

Belgium, the Netherlands, Norway, and Spain, the four countries that have approved same-sex marriage, have fairly well-developed antidiscrimination programs in their public schools, even thought they have state-supported religion. These programs include LGBT issues and promote the idea that homosexuality and heterosexuality are equivalent in terms of legal rights and responsibilities, and represent a personal status that does not require justification. In 2006, Spain implemented its new law on education, which explicitly states in its preamble that respect for sexual and familial diversity is to be taught in schools, and that openly gay or lesbian teachers cannot be fired from their jobs.

In many of the previous Western bloc countries of the former Soviet Union, the situation is more complex. They are atheistic states, and religion is not promoted in schools. However, lingering antigay beliefs from the previous communist régime has had a negative affect on LGBT students and teachers. For example, in 2003, the Ministry of Science, Education, and Sport in Croatia implemented curriculum materials that stated that homosexuality was wrong, categorizing it with incest, prostitution, and pedophilia. In the Czech Republic, although textbooks state that homosexuality is not an illness, it is included in a chapter on sexual deviation along with necrophilia and pedophilia. Miroslaw Orzechowski, deputy minister of education in Poland, introduced legislation in 2007 that condemned attempts to bring LGBT topics into schools. He claims that such materials promote sexual deviance. He further advocated the dismissal of openly gay and lesbian teachers.

A few countries like Greece have no sex education in public schools. Likewise, there is no safe sex campaign. Homosexuals are presented in police academies and law schools as criminals and primary suspects related to drug addiction and pedophilia.

AIDS

The health care needs of LGBT people and the issue of AIDS run the gamut from progressive intervention programs to outright denial that there is an AIDS problem. Denmark and a few other European countries not only have extensive safe sex programs, but these programs specifically target male-to-male sexual behaviors in their advertising campaigns. They do not shy away from including homosexuality in their health programs, and health providers are trained to work with the LGBT population. Russia, Croatia, Belarus, and a few of the previous satellite countries of the defunct Soviet Union are at the other extreme. Although they may no longer officially persecute LGBT people, their cultures are extremely antigay. Their medical professionals still see homosexuality as a mental disorder and believe that sexuality can be treated (changed) through medical procedures. They grudgingly admit that some of the population is infected with HIV. AIDS is commonly presented as a Western import, and true citizens of the state have nothing to fear. There are no safe sex campaigns. As can be imagined, it is very difficult to ascertain the true extent of the AIDS problem, and obtaining adequate medical care is difficult. International health organizations believe that AIDS infections are exploding in Russia, faster than almost anywhere else on the planet.

Most European countries fall somewhere between these two extremes, and have implemented safe sex campaigns. In some cases, like in the campaigns found in Italy, the safe sex materials do not mention anything about homosexuality or male-to-male sexual behaviors. In Spain, the Ministry of Health launched its first safe sex advertising campaign targeting men who have sex with men (MSM) in 2007. The minister banned the ads that contained images of two men kissing. Similarly, some countries, like Andorra and Greece, do not allow LGBT people to donate blood. All European countries provide free HIV testing and free HIV medication. However, in the poorer countries, medical services are at a minimum, and the free HIV medications are often unavailable. The international AIDS organizations based in Belgium have seen more gay men engaging in unsafe sexual behaviors and a subsequent rise in HIV infections.

Lesbian health needs are overlooked in virtually all European countries. A few studies of lesbian sexuality and health have been conducted in Denmark, the Netherlands, Belgium, and the United Kingdom, but they have not had a major impact on national health policy.

Religion and Spirituality

Most of the countries of central and western Europe are secular states with a state-recognized and state-supported religion (usually some form of Christianity). Germany typifies this arrangement. Citizens may elect to have 1 percent of their taxes go to their local church. The local churches keep records of who participate in the tax and those who do not. By becoming an official member of the local church, citizens reap additional benefits, including employment opportunities, since the local church controls many sources of employment—schools, hospitals, and social services. Although it is not mandatory to contribute taxes or belong to the local church, the economic benefits of doing so are substantial. Germany is a member of the European Union and has adopted the antidiscrimination statutes related to employment and sexual orientation. This provides LGBT citizens with some level of job protection. However, the law provides exemptions that allow religious groups to discriminate. Within Germany, several million jobs are controlled by the Catholic Church. LGBT people can work at these jobs, but must do so without revealing their sexual orientation; if they do, it is possible that they will be harassed and fired.

The influx of Muslim workers into Europe has created a great deal of tension. The incidence of violence against immigrants has increased. The conservative factions of many political parties have seen an increase in membership and power, primarily due to the controversy over immigration issues. At the same time, antigay Islamic beliefs fuel Muslim violence against LGBT people. In a strange twist of events, the hate crimes being committed against LGBT people by Muslim immigrants are being exploited by conservatives to advocate for immigration restrictions.

The ex-Communist states are all secular countries with no state-recognized religion. With the fall of the Soviet Union and the breakup of the satellite states into independent countries, there has been an increase in the number of people reclaiming their religious heritage. In many cases, this heritage involves orthodox and fundamentalist religions with antigay core beliefs. LGBT people often feel that they are trapped in societies that have not only medicalized homosexuality as a pathology, but ones in which religious condemnation is on the rise. The antidiscrimination laws required by members of the EU give hope in the context of the rising tide of religious hate.

Transgender

Because transgendered individuals cross gender lines, they are often the most visible members of the LGBT community. Not surprisingly, the beginnings of the modern gay rights movement were often led by transgendered people. For example, the Stonewall Bar in New York is where transvestites, transsexuals, and other marginal sexual minorities rioted against police in 1969. This event is often credited with launching the gay civil rights movement in the United States (although it had been already going on for 20 years). This is still true today. In the more repressive European countries (like the ex-Communist countries), transgendered people often found and lead gay rights organizations.

Transsexuals and intersexual people are mostly concerned with gender issues rather than sexual orientation issues. In many cases, they require medical intervention to achieve their gender goals. Because medicine can achieve a certain level of gender and sexual conformity through surgical and hormonal treatments, the community at large often seems to be more accepting of their needs than of homosexuality. For example, in Italy, transgendered individuals obtained the right to sex change operations in 1982. Furthermore, the ex-Communist states seem to be more accepting of a transsexual request for medical intervention than they are to grant equal rights to homosexuals. In contrast, many transgendered people in Demark, Belgium, France, and elsewhere believe there has been too much medicalizing of transgenderism. They advocate a cessation of medical services and call for the acceptance of nonoperative transgenderism (i.e., the choice to forego sexual reassignment surgery).

The European Union has been instrumental in advancing the rights of LGBT people within Europe through the adoption of antidiscrimination resolutions. At this point, the resolutions have focused primarily on sexual orientation and not so much on transgenderism or intersexuality. Expansion in the rights of transgendered and intersexual people has mostly come about through case law developed by the European Court. This process should continue into the foreseeable future.

Intersexuality

Intersexual people are faced with even greater challenges when approaching marriage. Intersexual people, by definition, are between the sexes or of indeterminate sex. Actually, humans are complex and have gender roles (masculinity or femininity), sex roles (biological functioning as male or female), sexual orientation (homosexual or heterosexual), primary and secondary sexual characteristics (hormones, sexual glands, etc.), social roles (mother, father, sister, brother, etc.), and more. Their feelings and identities are very complex and reflect an interplay between biology and social constructs. Most legal systems conflate sex with gender, adding to the confusion. Throughout Europe and elsewhere, many legal systems limit humans to one pole or the other—male or female, gay or straight. As such, birth certificates and driver's licenses are restricted to indicating male or female, with no other option. Intersexual people are often forced into one box or the other at birth, when doctors and parents choose the gender they think is most appropriate for the newborn and perform surgery to obtain outward compliance to societal norms. Many intersexual individuals later feel that the gender and sexual roles assigned to them do not fit. International intersex organizations advocate a cessation of gender assignment surgeries performed on newborn children, leaving such a drastic decision to the individual upon reaching the age of majority. In most European countries, marriage is still limited to opposite-sex couples. An intersexual individual may or may not have legal documents clearly defining the sex to which he or she is assigned, and the documents may or may not reflect how the person feels and identifies. Furthermore, the intersexual individual may be contemplating surgery and hormonal treatments and transitioning from one gender to another. As such, the individual may be unable to conform to legal restrictions related to marriage.

OUTLOOK FOR THE 21ST CENTURY

The primary source of change for LGBT rights in Europe is the people themselves, those who put themselves on the front line, demanding equal treatment under the law and full inclusion in society. Their determination has influenced the European Union and its parliament and courts to champion LGBT rights. Passage of the Employment Framework Directive forces member states to introduce and pass legislation in their countries that provides antidiscrimination employment protection based on sexual orientation. Even countries in which there is limited gay organizing have been forced to adopt antidiscrimination protections, thereby giving hope to a highly marginalized community.

The establishment of the EU Fundamental Rights Agency is very important for the future progress of LGBT rights. The agency's purpose is to assure compliance in implementing antidiscrimination provisions within member states. It is also charged with conducting research concerning LGBT issues. The agency should prove to be very influential throughout Europe in helping LGBT people to gain and maintain their rights.

The world's economies have sustained a major contraction, and Europe has not been exempt from this. Already, there has been a rise in conservative thinking and conservative political leaders. Historically, marginalized people fare poorly under conservative political systems. LGBT people hope that their rights will be maintained and improved through these difficult economic and political times.

ANDORRA

Joel Samper Marbà

OVERVIEW

The Principality of Andorra is a tiny country in southwestern Europe, located in the Pyrenees Mountains between Spain and France. It has a surface of 180 square miles, where only approximately 29 square miles comprise urban space. Its main river is Valira, which is shaped like a Y. One of its valleys is Madriu, which has been declared a World Heritage Site by the United Nations Educational, Scientific and Cultural Organization (UNESCO). Its highest mountain is Comapedrosa, at 9,652 feet. The estimated population is 83,137, and only 37 percent have Andorran nationality. The rest come from Spain (33%), Portugal (16%), France (6%), or elsewhere.[1] Andorra has seven administrative regions: Canillo, Encamp, Ordino,

la Massana, Andorra la Vella, Sant Julià de Lòria, and Escaldes-Engordany. The capital is Andorra la Vella.

Andorra was founded with the signing of the 1278–1288 Pariages by the Bishop of Urgell and the Count of Foix. This agreement established their cosovereignty over the valleys of Andorra after a period of conflict. From that time on, Andorra has never been involved in a war and lacks an army. Always neutral, it has tried to maintain a balance of power between the French side and the Bishop; this was only interrupted for a few years during the French Revolution. Although there are no known cases of prosecution of homosexuals in Andorra, the Spanish Inquisition courts did conduct trials there. The 1419 Council of Land was created as a form of parliament formed by the *heads of house,* that is, the patriarchs of all the families in Andorra. In 1933, universal male suffrage was established; women were not able to vote until 1970.

The 1993 Constitution describes the unique political status of Andorra as a Parliamentary Co-principate, being an independent state. This implies that it has two co-princes as heads of state. One of them is the President of the French Republic, and is known as the French co-prince; the other is the Bishop of La Seu d'Urgell, from the village of La Seu d'Urgell in the bordering Spanish region of Catalunya, known as the Episcopalian co-prince. Also in 1993, Andorra gained wide international recognition when it became a member of the United Nations (UN). Òscar Ribas, then Prime Minister, made the first UN speech in Catalan, the official national language. The currency of Andorra is the euro. Its economy is mainly sustained by tourism. In addition, it is still considered an uncooperative tax haven by the Organization for Economic Cooperation and Development (OECD).

OVERVIEW OF LGBT ISSUES

Andorra belongs to the Council of Europe, but to date is still not a member state of the European Union (EU). Lack of EU membership has been one of the obstacles to improving LGBT rights in areas such as employment. In spite of this, Member of European Parliament (MEP) Raül Romeva of the European Green Party posed a Written Question[2] to the European Commission regarding the rejection of blood donations from homosexuals in Andorra, in terms of the cooperation agreement with the European Community.

Contact with the outside world has not led to a more open-minded society. In fact, 80 percent of the population of Andorra thinks that Andorran society is quite or very conservative, and 50 percent consider it to have little or no tolerance in general. In relation to homosexuality, 28 percent of citizens of Andorra think that their society is tolerant, whereas 55 percent say that it has little or no tolerance for LGBT people.[3]

EDUCATION

Three educational systems coexist in Andorra: the French system, the Spanish system, and the Andorran system. Each is controlled by a different state, so LGBT issues do not receive the same coverage. Lycée Comte de Foix's students organized an NGO (nongovernmental organization) forum that included an LGBT organization. In all Spanish schools, the curriculum includes the subject of education for civic behavior, which addresses the existence and issues of sexual minorities. Educational activities on the subject of sexual minorities have been conducted at the Andorran School of Ordino. The Green Party has been especially active in promoting educational activities and policies dealing with LGBT issues, with the participation of Inclou (Include), a Catalan LGBT association. Several materials are available at the national resource center and the government's public library.

EMPLOYMENT AND ECONOMICS

Discrimination exists against HIV-positive people who apply for residence and work permits. Applicants for such permits must have a medical examination that includes an HIV test. The liberal government—and *liberal* here refers to liberal economic politics—claimed that HIV-positive applicants are not suitable because HIV is considered a "chronic infection which disables one from labor and is a threat to public health."[4] In 1996, however, Andorra had ratified the European Convention on Human Rights, which establishes the universal right to work under the sole condition of required professional competence.

Some doctors have argued that HIV tests are conducted without consent.[5] Furthermore, employment discrimination based on health also affects people under other circumstances. In 2005, 7,960 medical examinations were performed for work permits. At least five of them were denied because of HIV, and four were denied due to diabetes. In 2007, a case was issued to the European Court of Human Rights in Strasbourg when an applicant was denied both work and residence permits based on her medical history. The applicant had an operation on her colon, and another for liver metastasis, but she had completely recovered, as stated by migration services' medical staff. As proof of her recovery, she was already working in Puigcerdà, a town outside of Andorra.

SEXUALITY/SEXUAL PRACTICES

The Ministry of Health has reported that there are fewer AIDS cases in Andorra than in Spain. This may be due to the preference of HIV-positive people from Andorra to move to areas where treatments are more accessible and where there is less prejudice against them. On December 1, 2006, the first campaign aimed at promoting healthy behaviors and the fight against AIDS was announced by the Ministry of Health. The campaign does not mention any specific community, and suggests four ways to prevent sexual transmission: abstaining; engaging in non-penetrative sexual practices, such as petting; using condoms; and "being careful with whom you engage sexual relationships, you never know who is infected."[6] Condoms are available at health centers and other youth centers.

FAMILY

Some parliamentary groups supported the law proposal of De Facto Family Unions presented on October 30, 1997. It included same-sex couples, giving them the same rights as heterosexual couples. It was introduced by Member of Parliament (MP) Rosa Ferrer of New Democracy at the parliamentary session. Yet, this proposal was only included in the National Democratic Initiative's electoral program for the February 1997 general elections. According to the liberal government's criteria, family must be defined as a stable union between a man and woman with the possibility of descendants, so it should be protected as such. Concerns about its implications in obtaining the Andorran nationality were also raised. Former French Co-prince Jacques Chirac made it clear to the Andorran Government that he was reluctant to approve such a law, especially regarding the rights that were to be granted to homosexuals. The law was not passed.

In 2003, the Social Democratic Party resumed political work on the Stable Union of Couples Act,[7] which was enforced two years later. The act establishes duties and benefits for same-sex partners in social security, division of labor, civil service, and inheritance rights. Register officers affirmed that same-sex couples were able to adopt children, a statement that was later denied by Prime Minister Albert Pintat. Same-sex couples in Andorra cannot adopt children.

Same-sex marriage is still not legal in Andorra, and same-sex couples married in Spain have no rights in Andorra. The Episcopalian Co-prince Joan Enric Vives has opposed same-sex marriage. Legally, there is nothing in the Constitution to hinder same-sex couples from marrying.[8] At the same time, the constitution prohibits discrimination, and makes the Universal Declaration of Human Rights binding in Andorra. On April 26, 2004, the Green Party issued a political statement supporting LGBT rights, including same-sex marriage, adoption, civil partnership, and asylum rights. It was the first time a political party supported same-sex marriage. It also proposed a set of public policies aimed to promote nondiscrimination in education, research, civic participation, solidarity, health, old age, and gender identity. One year later, they launched the Marriage for Everybody campaign to raise awareness and explain the importance of supporting LGBT relationships.

COMMUNITY

The homosexual community of Andorra first made itself public when an anonymous group published a press release through a Web site on September 6, 2002. They denounced the unconstitutional discrimination against homosexuals in blood donations. The first and only LGBT organization in Andorra was founded on June 28, 2003. The organization, called Som Com Som (We Are Like We Are), set up an information booth that day in the main square of the capital, Andorra la Vella, and hosted the country's first gay pride celebration, 34 years after the Stonewall riots in New York. Lesbian, gay, and transgender people were present. A presentation ceremony was held at the Congress Hall of the local council (known as Comú) of Andorra la Vella, with the attendance and support of numerous public figures.

Later, a number of contacts were made with political parties, including young members of the Liberal Party currently in power. Som Com Som also ran a Vote Pink campaign before the local elections, consisting of a 33-question survey submitted to political parties. The questionnaire was promptly answered by the Green Party of Andorra (94% affirmative answers), the Democratic Renewal (76%), and the Social Democratic Party (73%), while the Andorran Democratic Center preferred to have a meeting and the Liberal Party delayed responding.[9] The same year, the organization participated in the 25th Andorra la Vella Fair, and received special mention from journalists.[10] On December 2, 2003, Som Com Som organized a conference about AIDS at the main hall of the local council of Escaldes-Engordany. A documentary was screened at the Cultural and Congress Center of Sant Julià de Lòria. Som Com Som has also actively campaigned for gay marriage.

In the first year after the creation of Som Com Som, chaired by Nicolás Pérez, some other Andorran public figures came out. Belén Rojas and Paloma Olea were the first lesbians to come out. Marc Pons of the Social Democratic Party was the first elected politician to come out in 2004. He was a local councilor in Andorra la Vella in the areas of Youth, Culture, Tourism, and Environment between 2003 and 2007. He has been especially active on the blood donations issue. Juli Fernández, Secretary General of the Green Party of Andorra since 2005, member of the Administration Council of the Social Security Fund of Andorra since 2006, and elected Andorran of the Year in 2007,[11] also came out. He has promoted an educational project on LGBT issues and been very active in seeking support from institutions and public representatives.

For the first time, a delegation of four Andorran people of diverse sexual orientations participated in Eurogames Barcelona 2008. The Eurogames are a huge European gay sport event open to everyone. This was also the first time the Eurogames were held in Southern Europe. From July 24 to 28, around 35,000 people enjoyed sports, culture, debates, and fun in Barcelona. The members of the Andorran delegation participated in bowls-*pétanque* and cycling. The Secretary of State of Sports, Youth, and Volunteering from the Government of Andorra, Víctor Filloy, was present at the opening ceremony.

HEALTH

The discrimination against homosexuals in blood donations was the first issue to be denounced by the Andorran gay movement when it first appeared in 2002. Blood donation campaigns are organized by the Red Cross of Andorra, but are performed by the staff of the Établissement Français du Sang (EFS). The EFS has an internal directive not to allow gays to donate blood, as they are considered an at risk group. Meanwhile, the World Health Organization (WHO) and other organizations talk about sexual practices of risk, not groups at risk. Candidates must fill out a form and sit for an interview prior to blood extraction. An Oral Question[12] was posed by MP Maria Pilar Riba of the Social Democratic Party to the government in 2006. The National Ministry of Health claimed that gays were not to be discriminated against, but year after year, gay men are still rejected as blood donors. According to Prime Minister Albert Pintat, this has been for the sake of public health. Historically, the right to donate blood has been, and still is, one of the major demands of the gay community in Andorra.

POLITICS AND LAW

In 2001, the Superior Court dictated in the Nuno case that "the term sex cannot include sexuality or sexual orientation, but the difference between male and female."[13] An aggravating factor for homophobic crime could not be addressed because, at that time, Andorran legislation did not cover this possibility. Som Com Som issued a proposal for reforming the law to the Ombudsman, which was later delivered to the 28-seat parliament (known as the Consell General). In 2005, the reformed penal code[14] prohibited discrimination against sexual orientation in public services, labor, salary, violent acts, murder, and personal data protection.

The co-princes of Andorra, that is, the Bishop of La Seu d'Urgell and the President of the French Republic, are constitutionally recognized figures (as heads of state) with feudal origin. They have membership competences in the Superior Board of Justice and the Constitutional Court. They can hold unconstitutionality appeals, sanction acts, and have the competencies of international representation, ratification of international treaties, and pardon granting. They also have diplomatic bureaus in Andorra. At the same time, Andorran citizens have no power or influence in the election of their co-princes. This means that the co-princes have overwhelming power over national civil institutions. Moreover, both the Catholic Church and French co-prince enjoy privileges such as tax exemption.

Political influence has been used by co-princes. Former French co-prince François Mitterrand did not sign the Nationality Law in 1993. Former Episcopalian co-prince Joan Martí Alanis did not sign the Marriage Law in 1995. Moreover, the

Episcopalian co-prince Joan Enric Vives did not sign the Stable Union of Couples Law in 2005. Laws may be approved by both co-princes, but if one of them holds an unconstitutionality appeal and this appeal fails, then only the approval of the other co-prince is needed. At the same time, "when there may be circumstances preventing one of the co-princes from formalizing the acts,"[15] his or her signature is not needed. In practice, only one signature of either co-prince is needed, so the aforementioned acts could be passed.

Andorra has traditionally been more conservative over controversial issues than its bordering countries. Abortion, prostitution, and panhandling are always illegal and prosecuted. The 2005 penal code made the distribution of pornographic material legal, and some time later, the first sex shops appeared. The age of consent, 16, is the same for same-sex relationships as it is in opposite sex relationships, but is higher than in Spain and France. Currently, sex changes are by no means legally recognized in Andorra, and sex reassignment surgery is not covered under the national health care system.

RELIGION AND SPIRITUALITY

The Constitution of Andorra was written by the Tripartite Commission, formed by representatives of each co-prince and a representative of the citizens. It was approved on March 14, 1993, with 74 percent affirmative votes, but it was not until April 30 that it came into effect, after being ratified by both co-princes. In opposition to the act sanctioning ordinary procedures, any change to the Constitution must be ratified by both co-princes. The representation costs of the co-princes are established by the annual budgets from the public assets. In 2007, they had an overall cost of 428,000 euros each.[16] However, they do not have to justify their expenses.

The Constitution of Andorra states the following:

> Art. 11: 1. The Constitution guarantees the freedom of ideas, religion and cult, and no one is bound to state or disclose his or her ideology, religion or beliefs. 2. Freedom to manifest one's religion or beliefs shall be subject only to such limitations as are prescribed by law and are necessary in the interests of public safety, order, health or morals, or for the protection of the fundamental rights and freedoms of others. 3. The Constitution guarantees the Roman Catholic Church free and public exercise of its activities and the preservation of the relationship of special co-operation with the State in accordance with Andorran tradition.
>
> Art. 20.3: Parents have the right to decide the type of education for their children. They also have the right to moral or religious instruction for their children in accordance with their own convictions.

It is not explicitly stated in the Constitution that Andorra is a lay and nonconfessional state. On one hand, this means that the French co-prince is a prince of a non-lay state; he also has competences that can override what is resolved by the three classic powers, such as pardon granting or act sanctioning. This is totally contradictory to the French tradition. On the other hand, this allows the Vatican to impose political decisions in line with its moral values over Andorran public affairs.

Albert Pintat's liberal government, after 10 years of negotiations and without the intervention of Parliament, agreed on March 17, 2008, on a concordat with the Holy See. Its preamble claims that the agreement is sustained by a tradition of more than 700 years, the Constitution, and the fact that a large portion of the Andorran population professes to be Catholic. It ratifies that the designation of the Episcopalian co-prince lies solely on the jurisdiction of the Holy See, so Andorra still has no power in its designation. Priests practicing in Andorra enjoy Andorran nationality. Catholic Church assets are not subject to taxes, but enjoy state guardianship. The concordat also establishes that Andorran schools must offer lectures on Catholicism. These lectures will be optional for the students, and the lecturers must be authorized by the Church. The definition of lecture contents and the proposal of books and other didactic materials are solely determined by the Church.

In 2005, there was a reform in the Andorran Penal Code concerning abortion or attempted abortion. While this establishes different punishments depending on the case, the law prohibits abortion in all cases. This makes Andorra, besides Malta, the only European state (including Russia, Turkey, and all Eastern European states) with this peculiar status, despite the recommendations of the Council of Europe. Even further, the Episcopalian co-prince declared that he would resign if abortion were to be made legal, which would make the status of the Andorran institutions uncertain.

Only 55 percent of the population of Andorra consider themselves Catholic,[17] compared to 79 percent in Spain. Forty-seven percent of the population of Andorra consider its society quite or very religious, whereas 44 percent consider that it is not or not very religious.[18] In Andorra, there are no religious lobbies outside the Catholic hierarchy like the ones in Spain and other countries. The religion and state issues are more political than civil.

VIOLENCE

Prior to the Andorran gay rights movement, on April 13, 2000, an event of extreme homophobic violence occurred in Andorra la Vella. That night, the 17-year-old Portuguese Nuno Miguel Oliveira died from a brutal beating committed outside a disco by two aggressive young men in their early 20s who looked like skinheads. The young men referred to the sexual orientation of their victim as the reason for their attack.[19] Since this event, several gay clubs have appeared in Andorra, and at least one case of aggression against a same-sex couple has been reported.

OUTLOOK FOR THE 21ST CENTURY

Antisodomy laws have never existed in Andorra. However, the conservative-minded society and small population may make it difficult for LGBT people to come out. The social, political, and historical peculiarities of Andorra could help researchers and the general public to understand why the LGBT rights movement did not appear there until late 2002.

After the rise of the LGBT rights movement in Andorra and the appearance of openly gay people, there has been a wider acceptance of homosexuality. Non-scientific polls conducted by newspapers show that 62 percent of the Andorran population support same-sex marriage.[20] Furthermore, in the 2007 local elections, 13 out of 19 candidates supported it.[21] The fact that same-sex marriage has already been approved in Spain suggests that, sooner or later, this will be a logical step for

Andorra. If so, it remains uncertain whether the French co-prince would sign such a law, or whether the Episcopalian co-prince would resign.

While many nations strive to create a clear distinction between religion and state, Andorra still includes the Catholic Church as part of its public powers. Consequently, the question of the traditional role of co-princes versus the popular democratic will still remains unresolved. However, there is growing public debate over a redefinition of the co-princes' constitutional role, or even a referendum on a Republic of Andorra.

RESOURCE GUIDE

Web Sites/Organizations

INCLOU, www.inclou.org.
   LGBT educational organization of Catalunya.
LGBT Commission of the Green Party of Andorra, www.verds.ad.
Secretariat of LGBT Affairs, Social Democratic Party of Andorra, www.psa.ad.

NOTES

1. Service of Studies, Finance Ministry, Government of Andorra, 2006, http://www. estadistica.ad/indexdee.htm (accessed September 2, 2007).

2. "Does the Commission believe action should be taken, and will it ask for an explanation from the Andorran Government?...Does the Commission believe that the cooperation agreement should be extended in order to include respect for human rights within its scope?," Reference E-2277/06, May 23, 2006, http://www.europarl.europa.eu/sides/get Doc.do?pubRef=-//EP//TEXT+WQ+E-2006–2278+0+DOC+XML+V0//EN (accessed September 2, 2007).

3. Center of Sociological Research of the Institute of Andorran Studies, 2006 Polls, http://www.iea.ad/cres/observatori/temes/valors2semestre2006.htm (accessed September 2, 2007).

4. *Medical Examinations of Migrants Act,* January 28, 1998, Official Bulletin of the Principality of Andorra, Number 4, Year 10, http://www.bopa.ad/bopa/1998/bop10004. pdf (accessed September 14, 2007).

5. Progressive Doctors' organization, http://www.medicos-progresistas.org/mod ules.php?name=News&file=article&sid=264 (accessed September 14, 2007).

6. More Information Less AIDS campaign by the Health and Wellness Ministry, http://www.salutibenestar.ad/VE/sida/sida.html (accessed May 3, 2008).

7. Qualified Law of Stable Union of Couples 4/2005 of February 21st, http://www. bopa.ad/bopa/2005/bop17025.pdf (accessed September 14, 2007).

8. Article 13 states that "Law will regulate marital status of people and forms of marriage...Marital partners have same rights and obligations."

9. *Diari d'Andorra* and *El Periòdic d'Andorra* newspapers, December 12, 2003.

10. "The Present-day Say 'No to war,'" *Diari d'Andorra,* February 18, 2004. Special Mention of the Open Microphone awards in the Present-day Prizes Soiree.

11. "FADEM, Minoves, INAF and Fernández, Andorrans of the Year," *El Periòdic d'Andorra,* April 13, 2007. Fernández was elected by the public in the social category.

12. "Does the Government agree with this clear discrimination against various peoples? If not, what urgent measures will the Government engage in order to make it not happen again?" April 26, 2006, http://www.consellgeneral.ad/micg/webconsell.nsf/0/9371 A21E268F9F87C125739B005922BE (accessed July 7, 2008).

13. Article 313 of the old Andorran Penal Code stated that "Imprisonment of a period less than a year shall be enforced to those who commit acts of vexatory discrimination or attempts against the dignity of someone on grounds of origin, religion, race or sex."

14. *Qualified Law of Penal Code 9/2005,* February 21, 2005, http://www.bopa.ad/bopa/2005/bop17025.pdf (accessed September 14, 2007).

15. Constitution of Andorra, Article 45.3.

16. Finances Ministry, *2007 Budget of the Government of Andorra,* http://www.finances.ad/Web%20Finances/Estructura/Documents/Pressupost_%20liquidacio/Pressupostos/pressupost2007.pdf (accessed May 3, 2008).

17. Center of Sociological Research, Institute of Andorran Studies, *Values Poll, 2005.*

18. Center of Sociological Research, Institute of Andorran Studies, *Values Poll,* 2006, http://www.iea.ad/cres/observatori/temes/valors2semestre2006.htm (accessed September 14, 2007).

19. EFE News Agency, "Murderers of a Young Gay Sentenced to 21 Years in Jail in Andorra," http://chueca.com/actualidad/02/03/2001/andorra-asesinos-anos.html (accessed September 14, 2007).

20. *Diari d'Andorra,* September 4, 2007.

21. *Diari d'Andorra,* November 26, 2007.

AUSTRIA

Kurt Krickler

OVERVIEW

Austria is situated in central Europe. It comprises a total area of 32,000 square miles. It borders Germany and the Czech Republic to the north, Slovakia and Hungary to the east, Slovenia and Italy to the south, and Switzerland and Liechtenstein to the west. It is landlocked, without access to the sea. The capital city is Vienna.

It is a republic composed of nine federal states, and is one of six European countries that have declared neutrality. It has been a member of the European Union (EU) since 1995.

Austria has a population of just above eight million, of which a quarter live in Vienna (more than 1.6 million, 2.2 million with suburbs). The capital is the only city with a population of more than one million. The second largest city, Graz, has 250,000 inhabitants, followed by Linz (190,000), Salzburg (150,000), and Innsbruck (117,000).

German-speaking Austrians are by far the country's largest group (roughly 90%). In addition, there are autochthonous minorities (Slovenes and Croatians). Austria also has a large immigrant population. Around 12 percent of today's population was not born in the country. There are more than 700,000 foreign nationals living in Austria.

OVERVIEW OF LGBT ISSUES

In the European spectrum of countries, Austria's position in terms of the social and political status of LGBT individuals somewhat reflects the country's geographic position in the heart of the continent: Austria is certainly not as advanced as the Nordic countries, England, Spain, or even neighboring Switzerland, but neither is it as conservative as some of the countries in eastern Europe or in the Balkans.

There are a few important historic features that explain why Austria, in comparison with many similar countries, has made less progress in the field of LGBT emancipation and equality. One of these is the fact that Austria's democratic tradition in general is relatively short; it did not really have any liberal revolution deserving this label in the 19th century, and it is a predominantly Catholic country where the Roman Catholic Church continues to have a very strong influence on both politics and society.

Moreover, the Nazis' short but intense antihomosexual brainwash during the years of the Anschluss of Austria to the German (Third) Reich from 1938 to 1945 also left its traces in the minds of people, even long after the end of Nazi rule. This is also reflected by the fact that the Federal Nazi Victims Compensation Act (Opferfürsorgegesetz) was only amended in 2005 to include those Nazi victims persecuted and sent to concentration camps on the grounds of their sexual orientation. It took the LGBT movement more than 20 years of lobbying to achieve this. Until then, the law restricted compensation to persons persecuted on political, religious, or racial grounds, while homosexual victims were considered common criminals, as homosexuality was forbidden both before and after the Anschluss. Therefore, homosexual victims were denied official recognition and, consequently, any legal entitlement to compensation. The amendment in 2005, however, came only at a time when no known Pink Triangle concentration camp survivor was still alive who could make use of the new legislation.

Another important feature of the general LGBT situation is that Austria—between the end of World War II and today—only had a very short period of 13 years (1971–1983) with a left/progressive majority in parliament. Most of the time since 1945, Austria has been governed by a grand coalition between the Socialist (later Social Democratic) Party (SPÖ) and the conservative People's Party (ÖVP). Even when the SPÖ was the stronger and leading coalition partner, the ÖVP could and, indeed, did block any pro-LGBT legal reform with reference to the party's Christian basis and ideology.

However, over the last 30 years, tremendous change has been observed, both in the attitudes of society in general and the media in particular. The change in public opinion is obviously more significant than change at the political level. While homosexuality was a complete taboo up to the 1980s, and was only mentioned in the media in the context of crime—homosexuals had been considered criminals who were topped only by murderers on the hit list of abominable outcasts of society—this has completely changed. Today, the topic of homosexuality is covered and mainstreamed in its many aspects and facets by the mass media. Gays and lesbians are represented in a positive, supportive, or at least neutral and objective way. Hostile media coverage has become an exception.

The change in society's attitudes has coincided with the emergence and growth of a lesbian and gay liberation and emancipation movement and, of course, has been an international phenomenon.

EDUCATION

Austria has a free and public school system, and nine years of education are mandatory. Schools offer a series of vocational-technical and university preparatory tracks, involving one to four additional years of education beyond the minimum mandatory level. Private schools providing primary and secondary education are run mainly, but not exclusively, by the Roman Catholic Church, and account for approximately 10 percent of the 6,800 schools and 120,000 teachers.

There is no tradition of private university education in Austria. Therefore, the state has a quasi monopoly on higher education. This has only been changing slowly in recent years with the establishment of a few private universities.

The positive or at least neutral portrayal of LGBT people and issues in the mass media has actually been the main source of unbiased information for the population at large. In schools, although sexual education is part of the curriculum, homosexuality is not addressed in a systematic and standardized format. In most cases, the topic is ignored by teachers, or at best taken up in a superficial way.

EMPLOYMENT AND ECONOMICS

Austria is one of the 10 richest countries in the world in terms of gross domestic product (GDP) per capita, and has a well-developed social market economy, as well as a very high standard of living. It is a welfare state based on the Scandinavian model. In 2008, the unemployment rate was 4 percent, which, according to the definition of the European Union, is equivalent to full employment.

SOCIAL/GOVERNMENT PROGRAMS

There are no government-funded social programs targeted specifically at LGBT people, but many LGBT initiatives and projects have received subsidies by federal, state, and local governments during the last 25 years.

FAMILY

Traditional family patterns continue to be promoted, although today's reality already paints quite a different picture, illustrated by the following features:

- The divorce rate is 40 percent, meaning that 40 out of 100 marriages are dissolved sooner or later;
- The absolute number of marriages is in decline. While 50,000 couples got married in 1950, only 40,000 couples tied the knot 50 years later, in 2000;
- A third of all children in Austria are born out of wedlock;
- A quarter of all families are single parent families.

COMMUNITY

The first informal gay groups appeared in Austria in the mid-1970s. At that time, lesbians were more likely to be involved in the feminist women's movement. The first gay organization, Homosexuelle Initiative (HOSI) Wien, was founded in 1979, at a time when article 221 of the criminal code (see below) still prohibited the founding of and membership in an association facilitating or promoting homosexuality. In talks between the proponents of the new organization and the competent ministries, it was agreed that article 221 is open to different interpretations: Such an organization would only be illegal if it caused public offence. That is why

HOSI Wien was able to register as the first gay association in January 1980. Today, it is still Austria's largest and leading gay and lesbian organization.

After this precedent, independent regional gay organizations were founded in other cities such as Salzburg, Linz, Graz, and Innsbruck. Soon, the LGBT movement started to diversify. Many informal groups and associations popped up, dealing with specific interests and issues, such as religion and belief, leisure activities, and so on. They also organized around party politics (there are LGBT caucuses within both the Green Party and the SPÖ), cultural activities (film festivals, etc.), and professional interests (for example, gays and lesbians in the medical professions or, most recently, in the police force).

There has also been a growing LGBT community both in Vienna and other major cities, which provides all kinds of services, including free counseling for young lesbians and gays or those who have coming-out problems. More and more commercial businesses serving the LGBT community have sprung up.

Several highlights in the annual calendar of events have been established, attracting more and more participants, including both LGBT people and their heterosexual friends and supporters. The biggest of these events is the annual Rainbow Parade organized by HOSI Wien. This pride parade, along the spectacular scenery of the world famous Ringstrasse in Vienna, attracts more than 100,000 people marching and watching—which is a huge crowd in a city of 1.6 million inhabitants.

Other events of that kind include the Life Ball, the largest HIV/AIDS charity event in Europe, which takes place in the Vienna City Hall every May. Although presented as a mainstream event, it is very much linked to the LGBT community.

HEALTH

Paradoxically, the development regarding the more positive portrayal of homosexuality by the mass media started with the emergence of the AIDS crisis in the mid-1980s. In the context of this disease, the media began to shed light on gay lifestyles and, for the first time, the public was confronted with the fact that homosexuality and homosexuals do exist in society, and not only on its edges.

The AIDS crisis in the 1980s was also the first big probation test for the young LGBT movement that, indeed, passed this test with great bravura. HOSI Wien used the crisis to establish itself as an important player in the fight against AIDS and, together with physicians and other experts, co-founded Austria's first AIDS service organization, offering free and anonymous HIV testing and counseling, as well as doing large-scale prevention campaigns. This turned out to be a great success story. In this context, homosexuality was finally and officially deleted as a diagnosis in Austria's version of the international classification of diseases in 1991.

POLITICS AND LAW

The lack of a democratic tradition, the domination of the Catholic Church, and the oppression of the Nazi years all account for why Austria has had an especially long history of criminalizing and oppressing lesbians and gay men. In 1971, Austria was one of the last countries in Europe to repeal the total ban on homosexuality that also included female homosexuality. The price of this reform, however, that had to be paid to the conservative forces in society and to the powerful Catholic

Church, was the introduction of four antihomosexual law provisions into the penal code in 1971:

- Article 210 (prohibition of male same-sex prostitution): this provision was abolished in 1989 in order to allow the health control of male-to-male prostitutes as part of HIV/AIDS prevention;
- Articles 220 and 221 (ban on positive information about homosexuality and on gay and lesbian associations): the repeal of these articles was voted on by parliament in November 1996 and came into force on March 1, 1997; and
- Article 209, which stipulated a higher age of consent for male-to-male relations (18 years) compared to heterosexual and lesbian relations (14 years) in case one of the partners was of age (18 years; this age of liability for breaches of article 209 was raised to 19 years in 1988; thus, sexual relations between young men were not punishable if both partners were between the ages of 14 and 19).

Contrary to articles 220 and 221, which were hardly ever applied in all the years of their existence and were considered dead law, article 209 had been enforced consistently until its abolition in 2002. Again, Austria was one of the last countries in Europe to equalize the age of consent for heterosexual and homosexual acts.

Antidiscrimination Legislation

Austria also has a very poor record of legal provisions protecting LGBT people from discrimination. It was only in 2004 that antidiscrimination legislation was adopted to ban discrimination based on sexual orientation in the workplace. However, this was not something that the Austrian government—at that time the infamous coalition between the ÖVP and Jörg Haider's right-wing Freedom Party (FPÖ) and later its split-off, the Alliance for the Future of Austria (Bündnis Zukunft Österreich, BZÖ)—was eager to do of its own initiative. The Austrian government and parliament were basically forced to do so, as they had to implement a European Union directive.[1] And although pressured by many civil society organizations to introduce comprehensive antidiscrimination legislation on that occasion, they chose to transpose only the minimum provisions as prescribed by the EU. Thus, LGBT people still wait for efficient and effective legal protection from discrimination in all other areas, such as in access to goods and services.

Partnership Legislation

There is still no same-sex marriage or registered partnership legislation in Austria. However, same-sex couples have the same legal rights as unmarried opposite-sex couples (common-law couples) who, in fact, do already enjoy a wide range of legal rights (and duties), although not exactly the same ones as spouses.

The equal treatment in law of same-sex and opposite-sex domestic partners is owing to a landmark judgment of the European Court of Human Rights (ECtHR) in Strasbourg delivered in July 2003. The case—*Karner versus Austria*—which was supported by HOSI Wien, concerned a gay man who was evicted from the apartment of his deceased partner because, due to the jurisprudence of Austria's supreme court, he was not entitled to take over the lease contract from his deceased partner. While the wording of the Austrian Rent Act is neutral and does not distinguish between same-sex and opposite-sex unmarried domestic partners, the Austrian court argued that the neutral language was for linguistic, but not legal, reasons. The ECtHR, however, ruled that this decision was a violation of the European Human Rights Convention.[2] It also argued that a government must have convincing and weighty reasons to justify a different legal treatment of same-sex and opposite-sex domestic partners. There is hardly any legal area where such weighty reasons could be put forward to exclude same-sex couples from rights granted to opposite-sex unmarried couples.

Since this decision, Austrian courts, therefore, must interpret all laws stipulating rights for domestic partners to cover same-sex partners. And the few laws that explicitly restricted their application to different-sex domestic partners were later ordered to be amended by the Federal Constitutional Court, which indeed, had to change also its own jurisprudence in light of the ECtHR's judgment in *Karner versus Austria*.

In the absence of any registered partnership or marriage legislation for same-sex couples, they have still no access to a lot of rights reserved for spouses. Although many of these legal provisions do not play a significant role in the daily life of most couples, some of these rights are quite important and are highlighted here:

- Inheritance law discriminates against same-sex partners because, if no last will is made, the surviving partner has no right to inherit, as domestic partners, unlike spouses, do not have a legal right of succession;
- The immigration laws only allow privileged treatment for spouses of Austrian citizens or of aliens with legal permission to stay in Austria. Noncitizens, especially those from non-EU countries, have practically no chance of obtaining permission to legally stay and work in Austria by virtue of their same-sex relationship with an Austrian national;
- Widow(er) pension under the state pension schemes, which is the most common basis for retirement pensions in Austria, is restricted to spouses. In the absence of same-sex marriage or registered partnerships, same-sex partners have no legal entitlement to a widow(er) pension;
- There is also discrimination against same-sex partners in income tax provisions.

Adoption and Artificial Insemination

Same-sex partners cannot jointly adopt a child. In theory, a lesbian or a gay man could adopt a child as an individual; in practice, however, the few adoptable children in Austria would be given to couples only—there is a long waiting list of couples wanting to adopt. International adoption by single (homosexual) persons is an alternative, and there has recently been such a case: A man who is living in a same-sex relationship has adopted a black girl from the United States who is growing up with the couple. However, the partner of the adoptive father has no legal relationship to the child. It is also impossible to co-adopt the biological child of one's same-sex partner.

However, in some parts of Austria, children are placed with same-sex couples as foster parents. The city of Vienna, indeed, has run publicity campaigns geared at same-sex couples to enlist them as foster parents.

In some cases, divorcing partners would use the fact that the ex-wife or ex-husband is homosexual as a weapon in the fight for exclusive custody/parenting rights over the couple's children. This has also been used to restrict the right of the divorced partner to visit and see the children on a regular basis, or even to completely deny him or her this right.

The 1992 Reproductive Medicine Act explicitly excludes lesbians (and all single women) from the benefit of artificial insemination or in vitro fertilization methods. These are restricted to married women or women in a long-term, heterosexual partnership.

Asylum Law

Austria has been one of the first countries to recognize gays and lesbians as potentially belonging to a distinct social group that, in case of persecution, would fall under one of the five asylum grounds listed in the Geneva Refugee Convention. In the explanatory notes to the 1991 Asylum Act, the legislator clearly stated that persecution based on sexual orientation could constitute a reason to flee, and thus a reason to be granted political asylum in Austria. Meanwhile, this interpretation of the Geneva Convention has become standard throughout the European Union due to a recent EU directive.[3]

There have been no (known) cases in which asylum was granted to gays and lesbians solely on the grounds of persecution because of their sexuality. However, at least six gay men (five Iranians and one Romanian) have been granted refugee status in the past (the first—Iranian—case dating back to 1984). None of the reasons given in the decisions mentioned persecution because of homosexuality, but this was the only additional reason put forward by those men in their appeals after their initial applications for asylum on other grounds had been rejected.

RELIGION AND SPIRITUALITY

Austria is a predominantly Catholic country. About 74 percent of the population is registered as Roman Catholics, while about 5 percent are Protestants. Both of these groups have been in decline for decades. About 12 percent of the population declares that they have no religion. Of the remaining people, about 180,000 are members of Eastern Orthodox churches and more than 8,000 are Jewish. The influx of people, especially from the former Yugoslav nations, Albania, and particularly from Turkey, have largely contributed to a substantial Muslim minority in Austria. The Muslim community is increasing, comprising around 340,000 people today. Muslims will soon outnumber Protestants. Buddhism, which was legally recognized as a religion in 1983, has around 20,000 followers.

The Roman Catholic Church has a long tradition of interfering in politics and society. Its bishops and its diverse institutions would publish hostile and negative statements on a regular basis regarding all relevant issues of LGBT equality, such as registered partnership.

VIOLENCE

There is no protection whatsoever against hate speech or incitement to hatred on the grounds of sexual orientation or gender identity. There are no legal provisions establishing aggravated circumstances in the case of crimes or violence motivated by homophobia or transphobia.

However, homophobic and transphobic hate speech and violence is no urgent or burning problem in Austria. Most homophobic hate speech originates from reactionary representatives of the Roman Catholic Church or right-wing parties, but is hardly echoed in the media. In most cases, these statements are not taken seriously, and are usually ignored or ridiculed by the mainstream media.

Of course, incidents of homophobic or transphobic violence do occur, but these seem to be single events. In addition, homophobic bullying certainly exists in school, but does not seem to be such a widespread phenomenon as it is in other countries.

Underreporting of cases of homophobic violence or ordinary crimes is certainly a problem, as victims who are not out as gay or lesbian may prefer not to report the crime to the police in order to avoid mentioning this. Such persons, of course, are especially vulnerable victims, and perpetrators may even consider their victims' reluctance to report to the police when choosing them as targets.

Normally, LGBT victims do not need to fear being badly treated or victimized by the police when reporting a crime. In 1993, the current Police Security Act (Sicherheitspolizeigesetz) was adopted. This regulates the competence of the police force and their lawful ways of acting. A decree issued in this context by the minister of the interior provides guidelines and instructions for police interventions, and the nondiscriminatory behavior prescribed by the decree also covers sexual orientation. It reads: "In performing their tasks, members of the police forces must refrain from doing anything that could create the impression of bias or could be perceived as discrimination on the grounds of sex, race or color, national or ethnic origin, religious belief, political conviction or sexual orientation." Moreover, LGBT organizations will also support crime victims when dealing with the police.

OUTLOOK FOR THE 21ST CENTURY

The improvements and progress made over the last 30 years are rooted in society's political awakening in the 1970s, once Bruno Kreisky took over the government in 1970, leading socialist governments until 1983. As one of his first landmark reforms, the total ban on male and female homosexuality was repealed in 1971.

This awakening caught hold of all walks of life and aired a society that had been completely fossilized in the rigidity of traditions and conventions. This development was accompanied by the rejection, to a certain degree, of the suffocating influence of the Catholic Church and its political arm, the conservative Christian Democratic Party, ÖVP.

Another important political element not to be underestimated was the appearance on the political scene of the Green Party. Voted into the national parliament for the first time in 1986, the Green Party has supported and pushed for LGBT rights ever since, keeping these issues unrelentingly on the political agenda.

However, when the ÖVP returned into government (as the junior partner in a coalition with the Social Democratic Party) in 1986, it started to try everything to slow down and completely stop this positive development.

Thus, the ÖVP has been vetoing and blocking any improvement for gays and lesbians over the past 20 years. It has been the clear ideological program of this party to make gays and lesbians second-class citizens and do everything to prevent them from obtaining full equal rights. The repeal in 1996 of the two penal code provisions, articles 220 and 221, was only possible because the SPÖ/ÖVP coalition government had finally agreed on a free vote in parliament; members of parliament (MPs) from the Freedom Party voted in favor of repealing article 221 (ban on gay and lesbian associations), and two MPs missed the vote on article 220 (ban on positive information about homosexuality). While the Freedom Party only voted against the repeal of article 220, the ÖVP voted against the repeal of both provisions.

It is one of the great paradoxes of history that all significant progay reforms have happened during the coalition government between the conservative ÖVP and Jörg Haider's right-wing party at the beginning of the 21st century. In all these cases, the reforms have occurred due to European pressure and against the determination of the ÖVP.

In the case of the repeal of article 209, ÖVP Federal Chancellor Wolfgang Schüssel had defended, in a newspaper interview,[4] the discriminatory age of consent for male homosexuality as late as two weeks before the Federal Constitutional Court declared this provision to be unconstitutional in June 2002. And again, the constitutional court had to correct its own jurisprudence because, in several applications in the 1980s and 1990s, it did not consider article 209 as unconstitutional. But in 1997, the European Human Rights Commission of the Council of Europe in Strasbourg finally found in *Sutherland versus the United Kingdom*[5] that the British higher age of consent provision was in breach of the European Human Rights Convention. In June 2002, several Austrian applications were pending before the Strasbourg court, and it was clear that the ECtHR would rule in favor of the applicants. The Austrian constitutional court obviously did not want to risk being overruled by the Strasbourg court. Thus, it deviated from its previous rulings in article 209 applications and declared the provision to be unconstitutional. And indeed, in January 2003, the Strasbourg court condemned Austria for violating the convention in three article 209 cases.[6]

Granting equal rights to same-sex unmarried partners occurred due to a judgment of the Strasbourg court in July 2003, which was again a slap in the face for the conservative People's Party, which had always defended the different legal treatment of same-sex and opposite-sex domestic partners.

Furthermore, protection from discrimination in the workplace as stipulated in the 2004 Federal Equality Act was imposed on the Austrian government by the European Union. It can be concluded that all recent progress and positive developments for LGBT people in Austria were achieved through pressure from European institutions and against the declared will of the conservative government in Austria.

After its landslide defeat in the 2006 general elections—Wolfgang Schüssel lost the chancellery to the Social Democrats—the ÖVP was trying to determine the causes for their unexpected downfall as, for example, the economic situation was very good at that time. One conclusion that the ÖVP drew, along with many commentators, was that the ÖVP had simply taken a much too conservative course, especially in matters of societal relevance. In the pursuit to become the biggest political party again, a huge internal debate about new political perspectives began within the ÖVP. After a lengthy process, in October 2007, the party came up with some new ideas for a future program, including the proposal to introduce registered partnership for same-sex couples based on the Swiss model. At the same time, however, the ÖVP continued to insist that marriage was a distinct institution for opposite-sex couples and would not be touched. The Swiss registered partnership legislation basically grants the same rights and obligations to same-sex couples as marriage grants to spouses—only adoption and services of reproductive health are excluded. The Swiss legislation, thus, is comparable with the legislation in the five Nordic countries and the United Kingdom. In Europe, only the Netherlands, Belgium, and Spain have gone further in opening up civil marriage for same-sex couples.

It is unclear and, indeed, still doubtful whether this project will become reality. While in April 2008, the federal minister of justice (SPÖ) presented a bill to introduce registered partnership, certain powerful fractions within the ÖVP are still trying to derail the project or water it down to the extent that the LGBT movement would finally say, "No, thanks. If we can only get that little, we prefer to wait and continue to fight for more." In any case, partnership legislation is the last legal challenge of the LGBT movement in the country. The decision to pursue same-sex registered partnership based on the Swiss model was the first time the conservative ÖVP came up with a proactive proposal to improve the situation of LGBT people.

It is generally fair to say that in Austria, LGBT people have finally arrived from the edges to the center of society, although exclusion and discrimination still exist. And of course, there are the usual differences between bigger cities and smaller towns and rural areas, such as differences in terms of exposure to negative reactions in certain professions; these differences certainly make it difficult to generalize. However, on a general note, it can be stated that today, there is a climate in Austria that would allow every gay man and every lesbian woman to come out, provided she or he is equipped with some courage and the will to cope with possible negative reactions. Young gays and lesbians should have fewer and fewer problems when coming out.

RESOURCE GUIDE

Suggested Reading

Andreas Brunner, Ines Rieder, Nadja Schefzig, Hannes Sulzenbacher, and Niko Wahl, eds., *Geheimsache: leben. Schwule und Lesben im Wien des 20. Jahrhunderts* (Vienna: Löcker-Verlag, 2005).

Matti Bunzl, *Symptoms of Modernity: Jews and Queers in Late-Twentieth-Century Vienna* (Berkeley: University of California Press, 1999).

Wolfgang Förster, Tobias G. Natter, and Ines Rieder, eds., *Der andere Blick: Lesbischwules Leben in Österreich* (Vienna: University of Vienna Press, 2001).

Michael Handl, Gudrun Hauer, Kurt Krickler, Friedrich Nussbaumer, and Dieter Schmutzer, eds., *Homosexualität in Österreich* (Vienna: Edition m/Junius, 1989).

Gudrun Hauer, and Dieter Schmutzer, eds., *Das Lambda-Lesebuch—Journalismus andersrum* (Vienna: Edition Regenbogen, 1996).

Barbara Hey, Ronald Pallier, and Roswitha Roth, eds., *Que[e]rdenken. Weibliche/männliche Homosexualität und Wissenschaft* (Innsbruck and Vienna: Studienverlag, 1997).

Kurt Krickler, "Austria," in *Equality for Lesbians and Gay Men—A Relevant Issue in the Civil and Social Dialogue,* ed. Nico J. Beger, Kurt Krickler, Jackie Lewis, and Maren Wuch (Brussels: ILGA-Europe, 1998).

Ulrike Repnik, *Die Geschichte der Lesben- und Schwulenbewegung in Österreich* (Vienna: Milena-Verlag, 2006).

Organizations

HOSI Wien, http://www.hosiwien.at.

http://www.ausdemleben.at.

> HOSI Wien's 2001 Internet exhibition "Die nationalsozialistische Verfolgung der Homosexuellen in Wien 1938–45" ["Lost Lives—Nazi Persecution of Homosexuals in Vienna, 1938–45"] (German/English).

NOTES

1. Council Directive (EC) 2000/78, *Official Journal of the European Union*, L 303 of December 2, 2000.

2. *Karner vs. Austria,* application 40016/98 [2003] ECHR 395 (July 24, 2003).

3. Council Directive (EC) 2004/83, *Official Journal of the European Union*, L 304 of September 30, 2004.

4. *Salzburger Nachrichten,* June 6, 2002.

5. Application 25186/94, opinion of the commission adopted on July 1, 1997.

6. *L. and V. v. Austria,* applications 39392/98 and 39829/98, and *S. L. v. Austria* application 45330/99 (January 9, 2003).

BELARUS

Viachaslau Bortnik

OVERVIEW

Belarus is a landlocked republic located in eastern Europe. It borders Lithuania and Latvia in the north, the Ukraine in the south, the Russian Federation in the east, and Poland in the west. The capital of Belarus is Minsk. The position of the country is of strategic importance for communication between the CIS (Commonwealth of Independent States) member states and the countries of western Europe. It has an area of 80,154 square miles and a population of 9,689,700.[1]

Belarus gained its independence from the Union of Soviet Socialist Republics (USSR) in 1991. It was one of the most affluent parts of the USSR, but since independence it has experienced economic decline. President Alyaksandr Lukashenka has been in power since 1994, and has preserved state control of the economy and civil society, along with all the symbols of Soviet power. This means that Belarus has been sheltered from the worst effects of the painful transition to a market economy that other post-Soviet countries have faced. At the same time, disregard for political freedoms and human rights has led to international condemnation and isolation of the country. Belarus has very close ties with Russia, but relations cooled recently when Russia raised the price of the gas it is supplying to Belarus.

Lukashenka's state-centered economic model is designed to perpetuate tight government control over the political and economic space of Belarus, and to prevent the destabilizing social unrest that he feels has marred the transition to a capitalist economy

in other post-Soviet countries. By ensuring high employment levels, widespread subsidies, and rising real wages, he has retained considerable popular support.[2]

Of all the former Soviet republics, Belarus has suffered the most from the consequences of the Chernobyl nuclear power station failure in 1986. Twenty-three percent of the territory of the country has suffered from radiation. As a result of the radiation release, agriculture was destroyed in a large part of the country, and many villages were abandoned. Resettlement and medical costs were substantial and long term.

Since 1993, the death rate in Belarus has exceeded the birth rate, resulting in the depopulation of urban as well as rural areas.[3]

OVERVIEW OF LGBT ISSUES

While homosexual activity is no longer considered a crime in Belarus, and the age of consent for heterosexual and homosexual relations is equal, LGBT rights still remains a marginal topic in public discourse and does not play any role in national or local politics.

Homophobia remains widespread throughout the country, and instances of harassment and discrimination occur regularly.[4] Many Belarusians consider homosexuality a disease, and some see it as a sin, but few consider it a legitimate sexual orientation. President Lukashenka and members of parliament often make negative statements about homosexuals, strengthening the homophobia in society. Homosexuality is frowned upon in Belarusian society and condemned by the church. Belarus is conservative in this respect, with homosexuals generally being socially stigmatized. Gay life in Belarus remains largely underground, and only a few homosexuals openly declare their sexual orientation.

The government-controlled media often attempts to smear the domestic political opposition by associating it with homosexuality.[5] This strategy is also used against foreign countries; in one two year period, three foreign diplomats were expelled from Belarus on claims of homosexuality.[6] Homosexuality is often seen by the government as allied with Western paths to development.

While the Belarusian constitution says it forbids discrimination, this prohibition has not extended to discrimination based on sexual orientation. Belarusian law does not provide protection for LGBT people against discrimination with regard to employment, housing, or family relationships. Although many people live together outside of marriage, domestic partnership and cohabitation are not recognized by the government and LGBT Belarusian couples do not have any of the rights of heterosexual couples.[7] Gay men are also not allowed to serve in the armed forces.[8]

Although hate crimes against homosexuals are not uncommon, homophobia is not recognized as an independent motive for crimes. LGBT people continue to face harassment and discrimination by the general population; they cannot count on police protection, as the police often refuse to protect the rights of LGBT citizens.[9] There is evidence that LGBT people are targeted for violence; in 2001–2002, five LGBT people were tortured and killed in Minsk.[10] Other countries have granted asylum to Belarusians who claimed discrimination based on sexual orientation.

There is no official recognition of LGBT organizations in Belarus, although many groups continue to operate without registering, which makes them illegal. These groups face difficulties such as armed militia storming into their meetings to threaten and arrest their members; LGBT individuals and groups are also the target of hate crimes. Recent changes to Belarus's criminal code have given the authorities even more latitude to treat the activities of LGBT groups as illegal attempts to discredit or bring harm to Belarus.[11]

Societal Homophobia

Homophobia remains strong within Belarusian society. In 2002, 47 percent of respondents to a survey by the Belarusian Lambda League for Sexual Equality (Lambda Belarus) believed that gay people should be imprisoned.[12] Attitudes such as this continue to keep LGBT people from revealing their sexual orientation.

But the situation is changing. A 2007 poll of young people within the Gomel region conducted by the Tema information center revealed that only 12 percent of respondents think of lesbians and gays as criminals. Forty-eight percent of respondents accept LGBT people.[13] A younger generation is showing increased tolerance and an interest in gay culture, although many critics attribute this to their age and assume that this trend will ultimately be outgrown and forgotten. In spite of the attitudes of young people, common stereotypes and myths, as well as a lack of information on LGBT issues or firsthand experience with LGBT people, affect the general public's attitude toward them.

President Lukashenka has rarely addressed homosexuality. In September 2004, he made a statement about homosexuality at the consultation meeting with the Belarusian Security Council.[14] In April 2005, a new attempt was made to criminalize homosexuality. Speaking in favor of this at a parliamentary session, member of parliament (MP) Viktar Kuchynski stated that "all 'queers' and others are to be punished to the maximum."[15] The measure, to amend the criminal code, did not pass.

There is no serious discussion about LGBT issues in the media, 95 percent of which is controlled by the government. Pro-government media expresses negative views of LGBT people, and has so far served to foster negative attitudes toward LGBT people and issues in Belarusian society. Positive or objective information about homosexuality is often considered promotion of homosexuality. One example occurred with staged footage that purported to show a demonstration by sexual minorities at the Opposition Congress of October 2004. This footage included bystanders' comments that "gays are evil" and a suggestion from the broadcasters that homosexuality is tied to Western development theories.[16] Homosexuality is often viewed as incompatible with the Belarusian identity and threatening to the nation.

Civil society does not provide support to LGBT groups in Belarus. The organizing committee of the First Belarusian Youth Congress voted against the inclusion of delegates from Lambda Belarus. One of the largest youth organizations, Young Front, issued a press release that contained extremely homophobic language. Pavel Severinetz, Young Front's leader, directly referred to homosexuality as "a sin and perversion deserving death," and stated that the very existence of LGBT people was the "result of decay and sinfulness."[17]

EDUCATION

Homosexuality is still not dealt with adequately in the Belarusian education system, and is not presented as an equal alternative to the heterosexual lifestyle. No discussion of sexuality of any kind is included in the curriculum. Besides silencing and ignoring LGBT issues in the school curriculum, teachers and textbooks often present LGBT issues in negative ways, including as a disease, a sin, or an unnatural way of being, which only strengthens old, well-known stereotypes.

School is a dangerous place for many LGBT students. No original publications with any scientific value on this topic are yet available, but some authors stress that homophobia is widespread and instances of harassment occur in public schools.[18] Antibullying policies have not even been considered for discussion.

LGBT studies is still a marginal subject at Belarusian universities. Several students are interested in studies concerning sexual minorities, but the main problem they face is a lack of adequate professors and literature.

EMPLOYMENT AND ECONOMICS

Efforts of the Belarusian government, and some favorable factors such as the Union with Russia, which opened vast markets for Belarusian goods, and also allowed Belarus to buy oil and gas at Russia's internal price. This has allowed Belarus to bypass the severe economic hardships and crises that many former Soviet Union transition economies have encountered, and has resulted in the economic growth seen in recent years. According to the UN *World Economic Situation and Prospects 2006* report, Belarus registers major economic growth: the gross domestic product (GDP) growth rate, as low as 3 percent in 1999, was 11 percent (second place in the CIS) in 2004, and 8.5 percent (fourth place after Azerbaijan and Kazakhstan—oil and gas exporters—and Armenia) in 2005. In terms of the GDP growth rate, Belarus also outperforms neighboring Poland, Latvia, and Lithuania.[19] About 80 percent of all industry remains in state hands.

The Belarusian labor market is highly regulated. Important elements of the central planning system are still in place. The government can affect the structure of wages through the tariff system, a type of centrally determined wage grid. The tariff system is binding in the budget sector, including enterprises and organizations mainly financed and subsidized within state and/or local budgets. The private sector, representing only a small share of employment, has little autonomy.

Current personnel in the armed forces number 72,940, although a reduction to 60,000 is planned. Most soldiers are conscripts serving for a period 12 months (with higher education) or 18 months (without).

The labor code of Belarus prohibits discrimination in employment and in the workplace, but excludes sexual orientation from the list of characteristics against which discrimination is prohibited. Therefore, employers are free to refuse employment to LGBT people, or to dismiss employees because of their sexual orientation or gender identity.

SOCIAL/GOVERNMENT PROGRAMS

Neither the state nor local governments provide funding for any programs specifically for lesbians, gay men, or transgender people in Belarus.

SEXUALITY/SEXUAL PRACTICES

Sexuality and sexual practices are not dealt with on a regular basis in the education system of Belarus. A number of pilot HIV prevention projects have been created by nongovernmental organizations (NGOs) in several public schools around

the country since the mid-1990s. Most of the programs, funded by foreign donors, have been designed to reduce risky sexual behavior through a strong peer-to-
peer intervention component. Educational programs cited male-to-male sex as the
most common transmission route of HIV and AIDS without further discussion.
Implementers of programs often did not illustrate the proper use of condoms. In
Belarus, the distribution of condoms at schools, colleges, and other educational
institutions is illegal.

A 2007 poll of Web site visitors conducted by the Belarusian Web portal Gay.
By revealed that 54 percent of respondents did not use condoms during their last
sexual encounter. Fifteen percent of the visitors never use condoms. Fifty-eight
percent of respondents tested for HIV and/or other sexually transmitted diseases.
According to another poll by Gay. By, 17 percent of respondents have HIV-positive
friends who are gays and lesbians.[20]

FAMILY

The situation of families, women, and children has dramatically worsened during the process of political and economic reform in society. The reforms have
affected the majority of families, reduced their ability to provide economically
for those family members unable to work, had negative effects on consumption
(particularly food), prevented their cultural and educational needs from being
satisfied, and been detrimental to the health of children and adult family members. Against the background of ever-increasing complexities in family life, those
hardest hit have been families with numerous children, single-parent families, and
families with one or more members with physical or mental disabilities. New categories of families needing social support have also appeared, including evacu-
ees, refugees, and the unemployed. The difficulties the family faces in fulfilling its
functions are complicated by the radical stratification of society; the decreasing
social mobility of the majority of citizens; the absence of a legislative base that
would adequately and effectively regulate social relations; the break-up of conven-
tional values, including those of marriage and family; and uncertainty in parents
as to which personal qualities they should develop in their children to help them
achieve success in life.

Lack of social success increases conflicts within the family and frequently leads
to its destruction. Belarus has one of the highest divorce rates in the world. In
the period from January to September 2007, Belarus had 64,410 registered marriages and 26,459 registered divorces. Compared to 2006 figures, the number of
registered marriages had increased by 7.1 percent, but the number of divorces had
increased by 14.8 percent.[21] More than 15 percent of Belarusian families consist of
single mothers with children.

Since the early 1990s the Belarusian family's function of bringing up children
has been significantly distorted because of worsening socioeconomic conditions
in the country. Statistics confirm that parental responsibility for bringing up children
is insufficient. In 1996, parents had 3,600 children taken away from them, including the denial of parental rights in some cases. The term *social orphans* refers to
children abandoned while their parents are still alive, and they are becoming a significant social problem. In 1996, there were 18,200 orphans left without parental
care in the republic (there were 11,200 such children in 1990). Around 90 percent
of these children are social orphans. The numbers of parents indulging in antisocial

behavior (alcoholism, drug abuse, and so on) have risen, as have the cases of especially dangerous violence against children.

The majority of the Belarusian LGBT population is involved in a heterosexual
marriage, or had once been involved in a heterosexual marriage. Often, LGBT
people hide their sexual orientation from spouses and family members. Many also
have children. Very few same-sex couples dare to live together, and even fewer do
so openly. Same-sex couples are frequently the targets of public condemnation, and
sometimes become victims of hate crimes motivated by homophobia.

No information on Belarusian LGBT families is available. Marriage is inacces-
sible to same-sex couples. These issues are not discussed in public debate, and are
not on the agenda of the Belarusian LGBT movement or any political force in
Belarus.

COMMUNITY

During the 70 years of Communism, the Belarusian LGBT community existed
in tight, discreet social networks that were absolutely invisible to the general public. The risk of criminal persecution united people in a secret brotherhood. In the
1990s, Belarus became the first former Soviet state where a popular magazine,
Vstrecha, appeared with a special section on LGBT issues.[22] A few years later, the
first gay bars started to open in Minsk, where the first Belarusian gay activists began
to gather. The emergence of the Belarusian LGBT movement has been connected
with the birth of the nationwide LGBT rights group, Lambda Belarus, in 1998.
Lambda Belarus was quite active between 1998 and 2002, organizing the first
Belarusian gay pride events and conferences, and publishing an LGBT magazine.
After four years of silence, in January 2007 the group came out with fresh initiatives, including the new bimonthly publication *Taboo.*

One of the oldest Belarusian gay groups, Vstrecha (Meeting), is exclusively involved in HIV prevention among men who have sex with men (MSM). They also
serve as a support group for HIV-positive gay men. Funded by large grants from
the Global Fund, Vstrecha operates offices in all regional centers of Belarus. Their
publication of a bulletin for gays of the same name started in February 2007.

Amnesty International's Lesbian, Gay, Bisexual and Transgender Network–
Belarus (AILGBT-Belarus) began its work in 1999 and focuses on advocacy, research, campaigning, and education initiatives. AILGBT-Belarus has co-organized
gay pride events in Minsk in 1999 and 2000, prepared numerous publications on
LGBT issues, run many workshops and seminars in Belarus and abroad, and represented the Belarusian LGBT movement at international conferences. The International Lesbian and Gay Cultural Network awarded the group its Grizzly Bear
Award in 2004 for its attempts to organize an international LGBT conference
in Minsk.

Two new organizations—BelQueer in Minsk, and Volunteers without Borders
in Gomel, were created in 2006. BelQueer was devoted to building gay culture
in Belarusian society. The goal of Volunteers without Borders is to increase the
level of civic engagement within the LGBT population and promote volunteerism
among the LGBT people in Gomel.

The Internet plays the most important role in building community for LGBT
people in Belarus, especially outside of Minsk. For the greater part of the community, the Internet is the main source of information on LGBT life, and very often

the only way of finding a partner as well. Only one gay club exists in all of Belarus, and it is located in Minsk.

In February 2007, AILGBT-Belarus initiated the first meeting of Belarusian LGBT leaders in Minsk. Participants discussed the opportunities for joint projects, information exchange, working with state structures, promotion of LGBT culture, and many other issues. The participants came to some important agreements, including the necessity of maintaining the positive image of the Belarusian LGBT rights movement. In addition, the group discussed strategic approaches to advancing their common cause, including outreach to civil institutions, businesses, and other state structures. This was a historic moment in the movement for LGBT rights in Belarus, and AILGBT is planning more of these meetings in the future. It now works as a permanent forum and is open to newcomers.

HEALTH

The Belarusian health care system is a combination of public and commercial medical services. Basic medical services are provided by the state at no cost to Belarusian citizens. LGBT people do not face any problems in regard to medical care until they disclose their sexual orientation.

Despite the adoption of the 10th revision of the International Classification of Diseases in the late 1990s, Belarusian military doctors still maintain the outdated belief that homosexuality is a kind of personality disorder, and that gay men are unsuitable for military service. According to the list of diseases adopted by the Ministry of Health and Ministry of Defense, homosexuality (along with transsexuality and pedophilia) is classified as "a personality disorder of moderate degree."[23] As a result, homosexuals may not serve in the army during peacetime, but may be enlisted in wartime as partially able. This provision is more than welcome to young gay men who would like to avoid compulsory military service. They are mostly afraid of the physical and psychological harassment they might endure in the army under homophobic military personnel.

AIDS has been a serious health concern for Belarus. The first case of HIV infection involved a foreign citizen, and was registered in 1986. The first HIV-positive Belarusian, who also happened to be the first HIV-positive citizen of the entire USSR, was identified in 1997 in the Gomel region. He happened to be gay. As of December 1, 2007, there were 8,631 cases of HIV infection registered in Belarus. Nearly 35 percent of them were women and over 65 percent were men. Eight hundred and eighty-four new cases of HIV infection were registered between January and November 2007. Intravenous drug use is the most common transmission route, followed by sexual contact. There are no official statistics on cases of HIV infection through same-sex activity in Belarus. According to the nationwide HIV-prevention gay group Vstrecha, 30 of such cases have been registered by the National Center for Public Health, and 14 of these people have already died. Vstrecha believes that real number of HIV-positive gays and lesbians may be higher, but many people hide their sexual orientation.[24]

People suffering from HIV/AIDS still face significant societal discrimination. Reports of this type of discrimination continue, and many of those affected are afraid to disclose their status.

An alarming increase in other sexually transmitted diseases, such as syphilis, was recorded in Belarus in 1996. Although this is now decreasing, there is insufficient data on STD (sexually transmitted disease) cases within MSM. Vstrecha provided approximately 250 MSM with medical treatment for sexually transmitted diseases.[25]

Transsexuals need special attention from medical personnel. The first sex reassignment surgery in Belarus occurred at the National Center for Plastic and Reconstruction Surgeries in 1992. More than 100 surgeries have been performed since that time. As in other post-Soviet states, the number of people who request female-to-male (FTM) transition is five times higher than the number who request male-to-female (MTF) transition.[26] Researchers attribute this phenomenon to conditions imposed by the Soviet model of socialism, where Soviet men enjoyed greater economic opportunities and public respect. Soviet men had traditionally been war heroes, space conquerors, and famous politicians. Although the majority of transsexuals manage to create families, hold down a permanent job, and advance in their careers, Belarusian society at large does not tolerate openly transsexual and transgendered people. Besides experiencing hormone therapy and sex reassignment surgery, they are forced to change their entire lives—their names and surnames, their professions, their place of residence, or even their citizenship status.[27]

No sufficient information is available on intersexual persons in Belarus.

POLITICS AND LAW

In 1994, male homosexual activity in Belarus was decriminalized for the first time under pressure from the Council of Europe and international human rights groups by repealing paragraph 1 of article 119 of the criminal code, which punished homosexual activity between consenting adults. According to the Ministry of Justice, 15 people were sentenced under article 119 during the first six months of 1993, but it was not revealed how many of these sentences were for adult consensual homosexual activity.[28] The current criminal code was passed in 1999, and the only homosexual acts that are still criminalized are those that violate consent.

Chapter 20 of the criminal code, which addresses crimes against sexual inviolability or sexual freedom, contains the sections pertaining to homosexuality. Article 167 addresses forced sexual activities and makes male homosexual behavior (*muzhelozhstvo*), lesbianism, and other forced nonheterosexual acts punishable by 3 to 7 years in prison. If the victim is underage, or if the incident is a repeat offence, the term can rise to 5 to 12 years. Nonconsensual sex with a person under 14 year old, or nonconsensual sex that causes death or serious damage to health, can be punished with a term of 8 to 15 years. Article 168 covers the same crimes, but establishes different penalties when the act is committed by a person over 18 years old on a person under 16 years old. Article 170 covers crimes of coercion, establishing sentences of up to 3 years for crimes committed with coercion by use of "blackmail, threat of destruction, damage or withdrawal of property, etc."[29] When committed against an underage person, these same actions may be punished with sentences up to 4 years of house arrest or 5 years of imprisonment. In these sections, particular sexual acts are not listed, and there is no distinction made between same-sex and opposite-sex crimes. While rape laws specify female victims, all other defined sexual crimes recognize that the victim or perpetrator can be of either gender. The age of consent for participation in sexual activity is 16 years old for both men and women.[30]

Although the Belarusian constitution claims to uphold equality of citizens as a fundamental principle, there is no antidiscrimination law that pertains to LGBT people. Theoretically, article 22 of the constitution provides protection to LGBT people, stating that "All are equal before the law," but this protection is not elaborated upon. In practice, usage of the constitution for the protection of LGBT people is impossible.

Belarusian immigration law does not recognize persecution based on sexual orientation, nor does it recognize same-sex partnerships for immigration purposes. Belarus is a member of the Geneva Refugee Convention, however, and might potentially recognize LGBT people as members of a social group facing persecution. So far, there have been no recorded cases of LGBT people seeking asylum in Belarus on the grounds of persecution because of their sexual orientation or gender identity.

The Belarusian constitution and the marriage and family code affirm that marriage is a specific civil contract between a man and a woman. Belarus does not recognize domestic partnerships, whether homosexual or heterosexual, and confers no rights upon the partners of such relationships. Domestic partnership does not serve as a legal basis for changing one's name or to any claim for material support. Commercial laws can be used when partners have a common business. If cohabitating partners separate, they have no rights similar to spousal rights, such as the right to alimony or other forms of financial support. Cohabitation does not lead to inheritance without a last will and testament. In such cases, the surviving partner will face higher taxes then would a legal spouse, and will not receive the right to claim the other half of the estate. Should cohabitating partners have children, a nonbiological partner has no parental rights unless he or she can legally adopt the biological child of the partner. The adopting partner must not be incapacitated, must be at least 16 years older than the child, and must not have lost parental rights in the past. Cohabitating couples may not adopt orphans, as this right is limited to legally married people.

Although the law in Belarus claims to provide freedom of speech and association, it is in fact severely restricted. Many restrictions attempt to prevent the formation of organizations that are likely to criticize the government. The law requires all NGOs, political parties, and trade unions to register with the government. Any activity on behalf of unregistered organizations is considered illegal. In order to register, applicants must go through a lengthy procedure that includes disclosing the names of the founder and members, a legal address in a nonresidential building, and the payment of a large fee. Activists are hesitant to list their names for fear of retribution. Many organizations cannot afford private space, and are blocked by the government from renting space before they are registered. Thus, organizations are forced to work out of residential spaces, leaving them open to action by the government. Applications for registration are reviewed by the government, which bases its decision largely on the political and ideological compatibility between the goals of the organization and the government's own authoritarian philosophy.

Most LGBT groups in Belarus are unregistered and, therefore, operate illegally. There are a few exceptions to this rule. Yana is registered as an NGO for young women, but focuses its efforts on the needs of lesbians and its membership is primarily, if not entirely, lesbian. The organization organizes social and educational events in several Belarusian cities. The other exception is Vstrecha, a group that registered as an HIV prevention organization that focuses on young people.

In reality, they target men who have sex with men in their outreach, and face regular and ongoing resistance from the authorities. In 1999, Lambda Belarus, which was the most active LGBT group at that time, was denied the opportunity to officially register as an NGO. The government claimed there were technical reasons for denying the application, although it was believed that government rejection was due to their mission of promoting LGBT rights.

In 2002, the only Belarusian publication for sexual minorities, Forum Lambda, had its registration annulled by the State Press Committee. Since 1999, it has been impossible to hold public LGBT events. Earlier attempts to hold gay pride celebrations in 1999 and 2000 were broken up by police, as were attempted international conferences in 2004 and 2006.

Internet censorship is another way in which the government suppresses the LGBT rights movement. In 2002, the Belarusian State University banned access to all online LGBT resources in their computer labs. In 2003, Soyuz Online, the largest Internet café in Minsk, and which once had a significant LGBT customer base, blocked the Belarusian gay site Apagay. In 2004, the Belarusian National Anti-pornography and Violence Commission declared that three Russian LGBT Web sites contained obscene language and pornography, and blocked access to these sites as well.[31] Online dating sites are also prohibited, and LGBT people have even been denied the opportunity to post messages on a televised dating chat room.

Recently, criminal penalties have been introduced to punish any suspended or liquidated organization still in operation. Given the illegal status of most Belarusian LGBT groups, this represents an even larger barrier. Penalties range from a fine and six months' imprisonment to imprisonment for two years for vaguely defined serious cases. Another new regulation prescribes penalties between six months and three years for organizing or funding mass demonstrations. Additionally, organizing group activities that "grossly violate public order" or financing such activities can also lead to a two-year prison term. Providing false information to a foreign organization or government, defined as "information intended to misrepresent or discredit Belarus," is punishable by sentences ranging from six months to two years.[32]

Bisexuals are virtually invisible in Belarusian society, and are stigmatized as much as lesbians and gays.

Only people with the official diagnosis of *transsexualism* (or *sex denial syndrome*) are eligible for passport and biological sex change. A special interdepartmental commission makes decisions on passport sex change, hormonal therapy, and sex reassignment surgery. The commission consists of at least 16 leading specialists from the ministries of health, defense, internal affairs, justice, and education. It takes at least one year from the day of the initial appointment with the secretary of the commission, who serves as a sexologist, and the day of the meeting regarding the passport sex change decision. In the case of a positive decision, the person will receive a new passport, and six months later can apply for authorization of his or her hormone therapy or sex reassignment surgery. At the time of the first appointment with the secretary of the commission, a person who wants to change his or her biological sex should be at least 21 years of age. People with serious "deformation of social adaptation," such as the homeless or unemployed, homosexuals and cross-dressers, people who have their own biological children, and married people are not eligible for sex changes.[33]

RELIGION AND SPIRITUALITY

Approximately 50 percent of Belarusians consider themselves religious. Of persons professing a religious faith, approximately 80 percent belong to the Belarusian Orthodox Church, 14 percent belong to the Catholic Church, 4 percent are members of Eastern religious groups, and 2 percent are Protestant.[34] The predominance of conservative Christians has had a significant impact on general public attitudes towards homosexuality.

None of the mainstream denominations demonstrate acceptance of homosexuality. The Belarusian Orthodox Church considers homosexuality "the gravest of sins," and Lambda Belarus stated that church officials have called for the execution of LGBT people.[35] The European Humanities University prohibited an event sponsored by Amnesty International that included the screening of *Outlawed*, a documentary about discrimination against LGBT people worldwide.[36] The university pointed to pressure from the Orthodox Church as the reason for the ban.

VIOLENCE

The authorities in Belarus do not track data on hate crimes based on homophobia, which makes it difficult to determine the scope of the problem other than through NGO estimates or sporadic media reports. From January 2001 to January 2003, Lambda Belarus documented at least 33 hate crimes based on sexual orientation or gender identity.[37] These crimes ranged from burglary, destruction of property, and dissemination of hate material to threats, assaults, rape, and murder.

Despite the number of such crimes, the police most often refuse to investigate thoroughly, if they register the complaint in the first place. Incidents of police brutality against LGBT people have also been documented.[38] Homosexuals from the Brest region were being entered into a special database following the murder of a homosexual.[39] It is not uncommon for police to collect personal information of those who visit cruising areas, and they have been known to enter bars frequented by LGBT people for the purpose of harassing them. On various occasions, the police have invaded lesbian and gay discos and assaulted partygoers. LGBT persons fear contacting the police in cases of domestic violence, recognizing that they may be arrested and that the offending partner is also at great risk of serious mistreatment in police custody.

OUTLOOK FOR THE 21ST CENTURY

The Belarusian LGBT movement is one of the youngest in Europe. It operates in one of the most repressive political environments, nearly in full international isolation, without public support inside the country. Attempts at consolidation undertaken by LGBT groups in 2007 give vital hope for a growing movement to benefit the Belarusian LGBT community as a whole. The most important step in the near future is seen to be a public campaign to change the legislation affecting the relationship between NGOs and the government; this will allow LGBT groups to work openly and more effectively. The second step is the promotion of antidiscrimination legislation. The Belarusian LGBT movement can only achieve these goals by working in alliance with other organizations that fight for human rights, women's rights, and other progressive causes in the country.

Undoubtedly, gradual change in the political regime and future integration within the European Union will play an important role in the improvement of the situation of LGBT people in Belarus.

RESOURCE GUIDE

Suggested Reading

Viachaslau Bortnik, *Belarusian Legislation about Homosexuals* (Minsk: Belarusian Law Institute, 2003).

Roman Kuhar, and Judit Takács, eds., *Beyond the Pink Curtain: Everyday Life of LGBT People in Eastern Europe* (Ljubljana: Peace Institute, 2007).

Randy O. Solberg, ed., *Let Our Voices Be Heard: Christian Lesbians in Europe Telling Their Stories* (Hamburg: Mein Buch, 2004).

Judit Takács, *Social Exclusion of Young Lesbian, Gay, Bisexual and Transgender (LGBT) People in Europe* (Brussels: ILGA-Europe, 2006).

Videos/Films

They Still Smile (17 min.; 2001). Directed by Irina Sizova. The only existing documentary on the situation of LGBT people in Belarus.

Web Site

Gay.By, http://www.gay.by, e-mail: gay@mail.by.
Gay.By is the best national LGBT news resource in Russian and English, and is updated daily.

Organizations

Belarusian Lambda League for Sexual Equality (Lambda Belarus), http://www.bllambda.org.
    Founded in 1998, Lambda Belarus is a national-level initiative acting in favor of mutually beneficial LGBT and straight communities' integration to overcome homophobia and to promote multiculturalism in Belarusian society.

Belarusian LGBT Network, http://pride.by.
    Formed in 2007, Belarusian LGBT Network serves multiple needs of the Belarusian LGBT community.

Vstrecha (Meeting), http://www.vstrecha.by.
    Formed in the early 1990s, Vstrecha provides information on HIV/AIDS, free testing, telephone support for MSM, and serves as an HIV+ support group.

NOTES

1. Ministry of Statistics and Analysis of the Republic of Belarus, news, January 29, 2008, http://belstat.gov.by/homep/ru/news/news6.htm (accessed February 4, 2008).

2. UNHCR, *Basis of Claims and Background Information on Asylum-Seekers and Refugees from the Republic of Belarus* (UNHCR, 2004), http://www.unhcr.ch/cgi-bin/texis/vtx/home/opendoc.pdf?tbl=RSDLEGAL&id=4166b71a4 (accessed January 4, 2008).

3. CEDAW/C/BLR/4–6, December 19, 2002.

4. U.S. Department of State (DoS), *2006 Country Report on Human Rights Practices in Belarus,* March 6, 2007, http://www.state.gov/g/drl/rls/hrrpt/2006/78802.htm (accessed January 4, 2008).

5. Julie A. Corwin, "A Dirty Trick That Has Proved Exportable" 9, no. 194, part II (2005), Radio Free Europe/Radio Liberty.

6. See the following reports: ILGA, "State Homophobia in Belarus," January 7, 2005, http://www.ilga.org/news_results.asp?LanguageID=1&FileCategory=9&FileID= 491 (accessed January 4, 2008; Radio Free Europe/Radio Liberty, "Analysis: Diplomacy and Debauchery in Belarusian-Czech Relations," January 25, 2005, http://www.rferl.org/featuresarticle/2005/01/83701c0a-3289–404c-8677–10e1c72070ad.html (accessed January 4, 2008); Radio Free Europe/Radio Liberty, "Latvia Accuses Belarus of 'Provocation' over Aired Sex Video," August 1, 2006, http://www.rferl.org/newsline/2006/08/3-cee/cee-010806.asp (accessed January 4, 2008).

7. Viachaslau Bortnik, *Belarusian Legislation about Homosexuals* (Minsk: Belarusian Law Institute, 2003).

8. Vanessa Baird, *The No-Nonsense Guide to Sexual Diversity* (Oxford: New Internationalist Publications, 2001).

9. Roman Kuhar and Judit Takács, eds., *Beyond the Pink Curtain: Everyday Life of LGBT People in Eastern Europe* (Ljubljana: Peace Institute, 2007), 373.

10. Immigration and Refugee Board of Canada, *Belarus: Attitude towards Homosexuals and Lesbians in Belarus; State Protection Available to Non-heterosexuals in Belarus with Special Attention to Minsk (2000–2005)*, Immigration and Refugee Board of Canada, January 16, 2006, http://www.irb-cisr.gc.ca/en/research/rir/?action=record.viewrec&gotorec= 449808 (accessed January 4, 2008).

11. Kuhar and Takács, *Beyond the Pink Curtain*, 366.

12. Randi O. Solberg, *Let Our Voices Be Heard: Christian Lesbians in Europe Telling their Stories* (Hamburg: Mein Buch, 2004), 46.

13. Sonja Dudek, Richard Harnisch, Rupert Haag, Kerstin Hanenkamp, Claudia Körner, and Colin de la Motte-Sherman, *Das Recht, anders zu sein. Menschenrechtsverletzungen an Lesben, Schwulen und Transgender* (Berlin: Querverlag, 2007), 143.

14. "We have to show our society in the near future, what they [European Union and United States] are doing here, how they are trying to turn our girls into prostitutes, how they are feeding our citizens with illicit drugs, how they are spreading disseminating gayness here, which methods they are employing," said President Lukashenka. From Viachaslau Bortnik's report presented at the OSCE Human Dimension Implementation Meeting, Warsaw, October 4–15, 2004; side event "Intolerance, Discrimination and Hate Crimes Based on Sexual Orientation and Gender Identity in the OSCE region."

15. Olga Ulevich, "Deputy Kuchynski Proposed to Imprison Homosexuals," Komsomolskaya Pravda v Byelorussii, April 6, 2005.

16. U.S. Department of State (DoS), *2005 Country Report on Human Rights Practices in Belarus,* March 8, 2006, http://www.state.gov/g/drl/rls/hrrpt/2005/61638.htm (accessed January 4, 2008).

17. Young Front, news release, July 31, 2001, http://www.apagay.com/press/release/2001/2001012e.php (accessed July 24, 2006).

18. Judit Takács, *Social Exclusion of Young Lesbian, Gay, Bisexual and Transgender (LGBT) People in Europe* (Brussels: ILGA-Europe, 2006), 55, 57.

19. United Nations (UN), *World Economic Situation and Prospects,* http://www.un.org/esa/policy/wess/wesp2006files/wesp2006.pdf (accessed April 7, 2008).

20. Gay.by, survey, December 10, 2007, http://www.news.gay.by/news/2007–12– 10–862 (accessed January 4, 2008).

21. Ministry of Statistics and Analysis of the Republic of Belarus, news release, November 16, 2007, http://www.belstat.gov.by/homep/ru/indicators/pressrel/nasel.doc (accessed January 4, 2008).

22. *Vstrecha* was published in 1992–1995.

23. Order of the Ministry of Defense and Ministry of Health of the Republic of Belarus, No. 10/30 (April 26, 2006).

24. Oleg Eryomin (president of *Vstrecha*), interview, Minsk, December 17, 2007.

25. Joint Project of UNDP and Ministry of Health, June 1, 2007, http://www.hiv-aids.by/press_center/news/~page__m41=9~news__m41=233 (accessed March 4, 2008).

26. Oleg Stasevich (leading surgeon at the National Center for Plastic and Reconstruction Surgeries), interview, December 18, 2007.

27. Ibid.

28. Amnesty International, *Report 1994: Belarus* (London: Amnesty International,
1994), 71.

29. *Criminal Code of the Republic of Belarus,* http://www.pravo.by/webnpa/text.
asp?RN=HK9900275 (accessed January 4, 2008).

30. Ibid.

31. DM Europe, *Beltelecom Blocks Russian Gay Websites,* Factiva, February 2, 2005.

32. Zakon Respubliki Belarus, N 71-Z, December 15, 2005.

33. Order of the Ministry of Health of the Republic of Belarus, no. 57, August 4,
2006, http://www.pravo.by/express/arch.asp?typ=7&id=1155883634563 (accessed January 4, 2006).

34. DoS, *International Religious Freedom Report 2007. Belarus,* http://www.state.
gov/g/drl/rls/irf/2007/90165.htm (accessed January 4, 2008).

35. Kuhar and Takács, *Beyond the Pink Curtain,* 364.

36. *Outlawed,* which was produced by the Amnesty International Dutch Section in
1998, tells the stories of lesbians and gay men in five countries (India, Nicaragua, South
Africa, Romania, and the United States), and is an excellent tool for raising awareness about
discrimination and LGBT activism across cultures.

37. Text of the report was included in Solberg, Let Our Voices Be Heard.

38. Kuhar and Takács, *Beyond the Pink Curtain,* 370.

39. UNHCR, *Basis of Claims and Background Information on Asylum-Seekers and
Refugees from the Republic of Belarus,* UNHCR, October 2004, http://www.unhcr.ch/
cgi-bin/texis/vtx/home/opendoc.pdf?tbl=RSDLEGAL&id=4166b71a4 (accessed January 4,
2008).

BELGIUM

David Paternotte and Alexis Dewaele

OVERVIEW

Belgium is a small constitutional monarchy that was founded in 1830. It is situated in the west of Europe, between the North Sea, the Netherlands, Germany, the Grand Duchy of Luxembourg, and France. It covers 12,570 square miles and has about 10 million inhabitants. The main cities are Brussels, Antwerp, Ghent, Charleroi, and Liège. There are three official languages: Dutch, French, and German. Belgium also hosts most of the European Union (EU) institutions (the European Commission, the European Council, and the European Parliament) and the NATO headquarters. The International Lesbian and Gay Association (ILGA) and ILGA-Europe are located in Brussels.

For historical reasons, Belgium is divided along cultural, linguistic, religious, and philosophical lines. However, culture and language are the most relevant cleavages, and the opposition between Dutch-speaking people (60% of the population) and French-speaking people (40%) is one of the main keys to understanding the functioning of the country. In 1993, cultural conflicts and regional disparities led to the federalization of the state, which is now composed of three regions (the Flemish Region, the Walloon Region, and the Brussels Capital Region) and three communities (the Flemish Community, the French Community, and the German Community). Because of a complex distribution of powers, the federal state, communities, regions, and local authorities are all considered relevant actors concerning LGBT policies.

OVERVIEW OF LGBT ISSUES

After many decades of liberal tolerance and moral conservatism, the situation of LGBT people has changed dramatically. In recent years, legal reforms, including those related to same-sex marriage and adoption, have been passed, and public policies dealing with LGBT matters are being implemented. However, LGBT themes remain poorly explored in university, which explains a lack of knowledge about many aspects of the history and the situation of LGBTs in the country.[1]

LGBs are a difficult research population with specific characteristics.[2] They are called a hidden population because of their optional coming out.[3] Only those who choose to come out as gay, lesbian, or bisexual (and thus identify themselves as an LGB) are visible, and the authorities hardly register sexual orientation in research or population surveys, which explicates a scarcity of information. However, several efforts have been recently made to get a better view of the social status of this minority. Transgendered Belgians are even less visible. They have recently begun to organize, and the trans issue is brand new on the political agenda.[4] The first research project investigating the social situation of transgendered people in Belgium has started recently.

EDUCATION

In 1980, a French-speaking lesbian teacher, Eliane Morrissens, was fired because she revealed the professional problems caused by her sexual orientation on television.[5] Since then, the situation of homosexuality and bisexuality at school has noticeably changed, especially in Flanders, where ambitious public policies have been implemented to tackle this issue. However, recent data concerning teenagers' attitudes remain worrying, as many of them do not support equal rights for LGBs.[6]

In Flanders, LGBs appear to be less educated than heterosexuals, even after controlling for age and the educational level of the father. Twice the proportion of LGBs (12%) have no current job compared to heterosexuals (5%).[7] Although it is always difficult to compare a relatively large group of heterosexuals with a small subsample of LGBs, these data might indicate the vulnerability of LGBs at school, as well as during their educational trajectories. It comes as no surprise that several reports refer to the school environment as one dominated by heteronormativity, and point out the invisibility of LGBs. One-fifth of LGB teachers stay closeted within the school environment, and most pupils and LGB teachers do not receive LGB-relevant information and training at school.[8] Although two-thirds of Flemish pupils consider that homosexuality can be discussed at school, they still would not come out if they were homo- or bisexual. Girls appear more tolerant of homo- and bisexuality than boys. The type of schooling also plays a significant role concerning attitudes: art- and theoretical-oriented school environments are more tolerant than technical and professional-oriented schools.[9] Thus, the mental well-being of LGB youth is precarious,[10] and more efforts are required to make them feel secure and accepted.

Notwithstanding these difficulties, several initiatives have been taken by the Flemish community since 1995 to supply helpful information and make educational material available to parents, teachers, and training experts. These efforts encompass the development and distribution of educational brochures, awareness-raising methodologies, and guidelines for LGB volunteers who visit schools.

Methodologies are also aimed at tackling LGB issues with challenging groups (like youngsters with a Muslim background) and within associations for adult education. Finally, lists of LGB-oriented literature and video material are made available.

Fewer initiatives have been taken in French-speaking Belgium, where homophobia at school is a new political issue. In 2003, a survey on health promotion and suicide prevention for LGB youngsters at school, financed by the health minister of the French Community, was published.[11] In 2006, the education minister of the French Community published an educational guidebook on homophobia at school, which has been sent to every primary and high school in French-speaking Belgium.

EMPLOYMENT AND ECONOMICS

Belgium is a modern and open economy, in which services represent more than 65 percent of economic activities. In 2000, the country's gross domestic product (GDP) was approximately 250 billion euros (US$349 billion, almost 3% of the EU total GDP), and productivity is higher than the European average. Per capita income was 62,560 euros (US$87,280, 20% above the EU average). However, public finances are still characterized by a high public debt/GDP ratio (which is now decreasing), and the unemployment rate remains elevated (about 8.6% of the active population in 2000). Belgium is a modern welfare state. The national social security system was established in 1944, and includes retirement pensions and obligatory health insurance.[12]

Diversity at work is becoming an issue in both public and private companies, and is being expanded so that it includes gays and lesbians. In April 2005, the SERV (the socioeconomic board of Flanders) published a note on LGBs and the labor market. It stressed the lack of quantitative data and the invisibility of LGBs, making it impossible to evaluate their participation in the labor market.[13] Although several reports reveal some LGB-specific problems within the work environment (e.g., discrimination, fear of coming out, etc.), little is known about the representation and experiences of LGBs within different sectors and employment segments in Belgium.

In recent years, some reports have provided insight into the barriers experienced by LGBs at work. In 2004, almost 3,000 Flemish LGBs were surveyed about a diverse range of topics (sexual identity, mental well being, experiences of discrimination, etc.), and compared with a representative sample of the Flemish population. On average, LGBs appear to work more hours per week and they more often fulfill a management role. However, even though they have a higher educational level, homo- and bisexual men earn less than heterosexual men. No income difference has been found between lesbian/bisexual and heterosexual women. The same survey results point out that approximately three percent of the respondents were fired, missed a promotion, or did not get a job because of their sexual orientation. Another seven percent think this has been the case, but are not sure. One-fifth of the respondents experienced negative reactions from colleagues or superiors because of their sexual orientation.[14] Finally, compared to Flemish workers in general, LGBs feel less committed to their colleagues.[15]

Another recent survey shows that the attitudes towards LGBs within the federal civil service are quite negative.[16] One-third of roughly 800 surveyed civil servants report that it is rather difficult to come out at work (compared with only 1 out of 10 who think it is not). Forty-six percent state that mocking LGBs is common, and more than one-third have heard their colleagues talking about LGBs in negative terms (e.g., using words such as faggot, sissy, etc.). Ultimately, 31 percent think that talking openly about being LGB at work can damage one's career. These elements might explain why two-thirds of the LGBs surveyed (9% of the total sample) do not come out at work.

This latter study was financed by the Federal Minister of Equal Opportunities. Until now, no initiative has been taken by public authorities to improve the situation of LGBs at work, even though there is a growing awareness that something should be done. A new study concerning discrimination against LGBs in the labor market has been ordered by the Federal Center of Equal Opportunities and Opposition to Racism. This focuses on the specific situation of LGB workers with a low level of education. The results should lead to an adjusted policy within the work environment.

SOCIAL/GOVERNMENT PROGRAMS

Social and government programs that aim to eradicate homophobia and support LGBT people have been implemented in Belgium for more than a decade. A federal minister is responsible for equal opportunity policies, including sexual preferences and gender identity. Furthermore, two specialized bodies, the Center for Equal Opportunities and Opposition to Racism and the Institute for Equality of Women and Men, are in charge of promoting equal opportunities and combating discrimination.

The Flemish government has developed ambitious policies on LGBT matters. Since 1995, there has been a minister for equal opportunities, with a whole administration devoted to these policies. Inspired by the model of gender mainstreaming, sexual orientation is being mainstreamed into all Flemish policies, and an academic study center, the Policy Research Centre on Equal Opportunities, which includes researchers on LGBT issues, has been set up at the universities of Antwerp and Hasselt. This investigates topics related to discrimination and equal opportunities, and gives advice to the minister. There have been fewer initiatives in French-speaking Belgium, even though a dramatic change has been observed in recent years. The minister-president of the French Community is also responsible for equal opportunities, and has taken some measures to combat homophobia at school. The Walloon minister of equal opportunities is explicitly in charge of LGBT issues, and has supported the creation of new LGBT organizations. Up until now, in the region of Brussels Capital, equal opportunity policies have been restricted to gender equality. City councils are increasingly involved in such policies, even in small towns or villages.

SEXUALITY/SEXUAL PRACTICES

No systematic survey of LGBT sexuality has been conducted in Belgium. However, research on HIV/AIDS has revealed some features of Dutch-[17] and French-speaking[18] gay male sexuality (no research has been done on lesbian sexuality).

Research on the knowledge and behavior concerning HIV/AIDS of men who have sex with men (MSM) in French-speaking Belgium shows that a huge majority of respondents (88%) consider themselves homosexuals, seven percent as bisexuals, and five percent do not define themselves. Most of the Belgian MSM are sexually active (96–98%),[19] and most have declared that they have sexual intercourse more than once a month. Only four percent of them have had no sex during the last 12 months. Seven percent have had sexual intercourse with a female partner during the last year. Nineteen percent of the respondents declare 1 male sexual partner in the last year, 57 percent 6 partners or more, and 23 percent more than 20 partners. Most of the French-speaking respondents meet their partners on the Internet, which is followed by meetings at saunas and bars/discos. Seventy-five percent have had a stable relationship with a man in the last 12 months, and half of the respondents were in a stable relationship with a man at the time of the survey. Anal penetration is more common with a stable partner than with casual ones. From the Flemish research, we learn that 42 percent of MSM have never had anal sex, 41 percent have had anal sex with one partner, and 17 percent with several partners. Some data are available on the risky behavior of Flemish MSM. Seventy-five percent of them have had sex while taking some drug (e.g., XTC, cocaine, poppers) in the last three months, and 16 percent have done so a few times. Half of the Flemish MSM with several sex partners (17% of the total sample) do not always use a condom. The same number do not know the serostatus of their sex partners.

Two recent sexual scandals are telling when it comes to sexual morality and the frontiers of legitimate sexual behaviors in Belgium. In 1984, the owners of the main Belgian saunas, Macho I and II, were arrested and charged with incitement to debauchery. They spent several weeks in jail and faced a three-year trial. They were discharged in 1987 because of a lack of evidence. This affair has publicized what is legally considered as debauchery. (Homo)sexual intercourse is only allowed if they involve no more than two consenting adults who share an affective or love bond. Therefore, debauchery includes sexual acts with minors, and those considered promiscuous and/or perverse.[20] Even though it has not been used to penalize homosexual encounters for years, this definition has never been challenged until now.[21]

In 1996, another scandal highlighted some of the frontiers of contemporary Belgian sexual morality. In the context of the Dutroux case, an instance of pedophilia that shook Belgian society, two closeted gay ministers were accused of having sexual intercourse with minors. They were finally discharged, leading to a clear dissociation between pedophilia and homosexuality in public discourse. Nonetheless, by the same token, this affair has contributed to making pedophilia the main sexual taboo in contemporary Belgium.

FAMILY

In recent years, family has become a crucial issue for the Belgian LGBT movement, which mirrors a new social reality. A large quantitative Flemish research project[22] shows that 42 percent of the respondents would like to have a child (36% of the men and 55% of the women). Twelve percent of those who do not want to have a child explain that their choice is due to the lack of a suitable partner, and 11 percent of the sample is already raising a child. More than 80 percent of these children come from a former heterosexual relationship, 16 percent were conceived by in vitro fertilization, 8 percent were adopted, and 3 percent have other origins, such as coparenting or surrogacy.

Most of the children raised by LGBTs in Belgium come from former heterosexual relationships. However, an increasing number of children are being born within an LGBT family.[23] Most of them are raised by a lesbian couple, with one of the partners having been inseminated by an anonymous donor. Indeed, this technique is not restricted to married heterosexual couples, and the Vrije Universiteit Brussel (VUB), the Flemish Free University of Brussels, has developed pioneering and internationally renowned research on assisted reproductive technologies. It has been inseminating lesbians since the early 1980s. All of these medical innovations have been accompanied by a psychological follow-up of these children, which has demonstrated the absence of difference in the psychological development of children raised by same-sex and different-sex partners.[24]

Eight percent of the children raised by LGB parents in Belgium have been adopted. Until 2006, same-sex couples were not allowed to adopt a child jointly. However, a single person could, and some gay men (chiefly) used this legal opportunity to become fathers. It was more common in Flanders, where sexual orientation was not an impediment to adopt, than in French-speaking Belgium, where LGBs were obliged to hide their sexual preference during the adoption process. However, there was no legal bond between the child and the partner of the adoptive parent until 2006. With the new adoption law, same-sex couples are now allowed to adopt as a couple, and an LGB can also adopt his or her partner's child.

Three percent of these children were born in other contexts, such as coparenting or surrogacy. Coparenting projects arise from the decision of nonconjugal couples to conceive together. They may involve more than two persons, as partners may be part of the initial project and also bring up the child. Therefore, coparenting raises the issue of the legal recognition of parenting (which is called *parenté sociale*). Indeed, the two biological parents are the only ones who enjoy rights and obligations towards the offspring, and the introduction of a legal status for nonbiological parents is being discussed in parliament.[25] Surrogacy is characterized by a legal vacuum. As it is not explicitly banned, some gay couples appeal to a surrogate mother. Nonetheless, this reproductive technique does not grant full parental rights over the child.

The paternity or maternity of transgender persons is another burning issue. Some Belgian hospitals have developed techniques that allow transgendered individuals to have children after their sex reassignment operation.[26] However, the new law on transsexuality prevents them from procreating in their former sex, and this might lead to legal controversies in the near future.

Finally, LGBT families cannot be restricted to legal and institutional debates about same-sex partnership and the possibility for same-sex partners to raise children. Families of choice, or chosen families,[27] must also be taken into account. These families reflect the risk for LGBs of having disturbed or broken family relationships because of their sexuality, and are characterized by the significance of friendship ties (friends as family). Flemish research shows that LGBs feel less committed to their family members than average Flemish people. Almost half (48%) of the supportive network of Flemish people (without a partner) is composed of family members, compared to only 17 percent of LGBs (without a partner). Furthermore, the latter group has a support network, which is composed of friends for 64 percent. For the average Flemish (without a partner), only 39 percent of his or her network is composed of friendship relations. Hence, these data prove the importance of friendship networks for LGBs. Nonetheless, these networks do not offer LGBs an equal amount of support when comparing them with the average Flemish: 8 percent of LGBs have no confidants, compared to only 2 percent of Flemish people.[28]

COMMUNITY

The first reliable traces of a gay life in Belgium date back to Antwerp in 1781. At the end of the 19th century and the beginning of the 20th, Brussels, Antwerp, and Liège functioned as venues for Belgians, Dutch, and Germans.[29] Nonetheless, as in many Western countries, a real gay life only emerged after World War II. Nowadays, the Belgian commercial scene is mainly concentrated in Brussels and Antwerp, even though there are some bars, saunas, and discos in Liège, Ghent, Ostend, and Charleroi.

The first Belgian gay and lesbian organization was founded by a woman, Suzan Daniel, in Brussels in 1953. Created after the third Conference of the International Committee for Sexual Equality (ICSE), it was called Centre Culturel Belge—Cultuur Centrum België (CCB) and included both men and women, Flemish and Francophones. Nevertheless, sexual and cultural divisions quickly emerged. A couple of men founded the Centre de Culture et Loisirs—Cultuur- en Ontspanning-scentrum (CCL—COC) in 1954, which became Infor Homo a few years later. Like many other Belgian organizations, this group rapidly split up because of linguistic conflicts, and evolved into a French-speaking association.

In the 1960s and '70s, the Flemish gay and lesbian movement gained its autonomy. In 1968, the first Belgian community services center was launched in Antwerp (the Gesprekscentrum, later Gespreks- en Onthaalcentrum). The first student groups emerged during the same period in Leuven and Ghent. In 1972, the first LGBT coordination, Infoma (Informatie—(Homofilie)—Maatschappij), was set up. Sjaloom, another federation gathered around Christian groups, became the first group to get public funding in 1976. A leftist group, the Rooie Vlinder, was also created in 1976. It later became the Roze Aktie Front. In 1977, Infoma and Sjaloom were obliged to join in a new Flemish federation, the FWH (Federatie Werkgroepen Homofilie/Homoseksualiteit). The FWH, which competed with the Homoliga between 1990 and 2006, quickly became a relevant actor in Flemish civil society. In 2002, it changed its name into Holebifederatie. In 2009, it became Çavaria. Currently, it employs 15 people, has a budget of $1,100,000, and is responsible for more than 100 groups. It was joined by transgendered people in 2005. Moreover, the years 1990 and 2000 were characterized by a tremendous explosion and diversification of LGB groups, which came out in almost every Flemish town. Some are now focused on women, youngsters, the elderly, or migrants. The youth LGBT federation, Wel Jong Niet Hetero, has more than 15 groups and community services centers in Antwerp, Ghent, Hasselt, and Brussels.

In French-speaking Belgium, the CCL, later called Infor Homo, became the main organization of the 1960s and '70s. A more radical group strongly influenced by the French MHAR (Movement Homosexuel d'Action Révolutionnaire) and connected to Flemish groups, the MHAR, appeared in the '70s, but rapidly vanished. At the end of the '70s, a new group called Antenne Rose emerged in Brussels. This became Tels Quels a few years later, and grew into the most important French-speaking association of the '80s and '90s. As in Flanders, the second half of the '90s and first years of the new millennium were characterized by a diversification of the associative landscape. In 1999, a new federation, the Fédération des Associations Gayes et Lesbiennes (FAGL), was founded. Community service centers developed in Brussels, Liège, and Namur. In 2005, the first French-speaking trans group, Trans-Action, was set up, and Arc-en-Ciel Wallonie, the first Walloon LGBT Federation, was constituted in 2007.

The first Belgian lesbian and gay marches, called Roze Zaterdagen (Pink Saturdays), were organized in Flanders by the Rooie Vlinders from 1979 until 1982. After a break of eight years, the Roze Aktie Front revived this tradition in 1990, and LGBT marches occurred every two years in a different Flemish town. Since 1996, Flemish and French-speaking LGBT federations have jointly organized the Belgian lesbian and gay pride parade, which takes place in Brussels every year.

HEALTH

The health of LGBs has mainly been investigated in terms of HIV/AIDS and safe sex–related behavior, as research shows that gay and bisexual men are primarily affected by HIV/AIDS.[30] On the other hand, investigation has focused on the stigmatized status of LGBs.[31] Indeed, the stigma of belonging to a sexual minority goes hand in hand with internal stressors (e.g., internalized homophobia, anxiety, feelings of depression) and external stressors (e.g., experiences of discrimination, bullying). Hence, LGBs who experience a heteronormative or stigmatizing environment suffer from stigma consciousness and internalized homonegativity.[32] Young homosexuals are also more susceptible to depression and suicidal ideation than young heterosexuals.

HIV/AIDS

The first AIDS case was registered in Belgium in 1982. The gay community was the first to be struck by aids, before its spread amongst heterosexuals, African migrants, and drug addicts. Nonetheless, the epidemic has not been as serious as in some other Western countries. From 1982 to December 31, 2005, 19,070 people were diagnosed HIV positive. Among men who have sex with men, an important increase in the number of contaminations has been reported for the period 1997–2005. In 2002, 23.1 percent of the HIV cases were due to homosexual contact. In 2005, this proportion had risen to 32.9 percent.[33]

These recent statistics show a worrying evolution. As in most western European countries, the incidence of HIV and the number of unsafe sex contacts between gay or bisexual men are increasing.[34] Some even speak of a second major health crisis.[35] In 2005, 85 percent of the new HIV positive diagnoses were men, and 75 percent of them were probably infected through homosexual contact.[36] Recently, a new research project has been launched at Ghent University to map the important determinants of risky sex behavior.

Mental Health

In 1999, the results of the first large-scale quantitative and qualitative research project concerning LGBs in Flanders revealed that almost one-fifth of the roughly 1,500 surveyed LGBs had consulted a physician or psychotherapist for a problem related to their sexual orientation at least once in their lifetime. Another groundbreaking study highlighted young LGBs' vulnerable position. LGB youngsters (from 15 to 27 years) have twice the risk of suicidal ideation, and four times the risk for suicide attempts compared to heterosexual youngsters. Young lesbian and bisexual girls seem even more fragile, as they have a six-fold increased risk of suicide attempts.[37] These results and others have opened the eyes of LGB associations and policy actors in Flanders.

A second large-scale quantitative project was ordered by the Flemish Minister of Equal Opportunities in 2003 to explore the impediments that LGBs encounter in their lives. It revealed that one-fifth of the 2,931 respondents feel quite powerless in solving their personal problems, and that more than one-tenth, especially young or less educated respondents, think they have so many problems that they are unable to solve them. Furthermore, twice as many LGB youngsters report severely depressive symptoms compared to heterosexual youngsters, and lesbian and bisexual women score higher than homo- and bisexual men in every age group. However, 77 percent of LGBs perceive their health as good to excellent, a result that does not differ from that of the average Flemish population.[38] Finally, few objective physical health measures are available. Only one Flemish study comparing homo- and bisexuals with heterosexuals indicates that being LGB more than doubles the odds of having a chronic disease.[39]

The health situation of other minorities within the LGBT group remains unclear. Elderly LGBs, for example, are an almost completely invisible group with their own specific health needs.[40] However, the perspective of a future in which an increasing part of the population will be above 60 raises the question of LGBT-friendly health and care facilities. On the other hand, transgendered people constitute an overmedicalized population, as they have mainly been studied from a medical and pathological perspective.[41] At the same time, some empowering initiatives have emerged within medical studies. For instance, the academic hospital of Ghent has had a multidisciplinary *genderteam* since 1985, which helps transsexuals to cope with the process of sex reassignment.

POLITICS AND LAW

Little is known about the legal history of homosexuality in Belgium. Following the research conducted in other European countries, the repression of homosexuality during the ancien régime likely occurred within a broader prohibition of counter-natural, nonmarital, and nonreproductive sexual acts. However, some cases have been documented. The first death and execution on the grounds of sodomy in Europe took place in Ghent in 1292. In 1654, the renowned sculptor Hieronymus Duquesnoy was garroted in the same town, also because of sodomy. In 1618, two women were charged of lesbianism in Bruges and several trials against tribadism occurred in the 18th century.[42]

After the victories of Jemappes (1792) and Fleurus (1794), the French annexed the Belgian territories in 1795. During the French period (1795–1815) and following the 1791 *Code penal révolutionnaire*, the *Code des délits et peines of the 3ème brumaire an IV*, and the 1810 *Code imperial*, the crime of sodomy was abolished. This decision has never been challenged, neither during the Dutch period (1815–1830), nor under the Belgian State (founded in 1830). Moreover, male homosexuals have never been formally banned from the military. However, the absence of explicit criminalization does not imply the disappearance of police molestation and legal prosecution, which occurred under the charges of debauchery, prostitution and procuring, outrage to public decency, or corruption of minors. In 1965, clause 372bis was added to the legal arsenal against homosexuality. Inspired by a French law introduced by the Vichy regime, it increased the legal age of consent for homosexual contact (18 years instead of 16) and attempted to prevent the seduction of boys by homosexual men. This was suppressed in 1985.

The suppression of clause 372bis marked the beginning of a new period in the legal history of homosexuality, characterized by the advocacy and the gaining of new rights. During the second half of the 1980s and the '90s, LGBT associations asked for the removal of legal discrimination against homosexuality, legal protection of sexual orientation, and the recognition of same-sex couples and LGB families. After more than 10 years of political and social debate, most of these requests have been turned into law.

In 1998, the first kind of legal recognition, the *Contrat de Cohabitation légale,* was offered to same-sex couples. It was not specifically designed for same-sex unions, but was accessible to every cohabiting couple regardless of the sexual orientation of its members and the nature of their ties. Hence, it could also be invoked by gay and lesbian couples. This recognizes fewer rights than marriage or civil partnership laws (it mainly concerns property law), and incorporates few obligations (excluding, among others, marital fidelity and consummation). However, it was improved in 2006.

In 2003, an antidiscrimination law, which explicitly mentions sexual orientation as a potential ground to be discriminated on, was passed by the Belgian parliament. This attempts to prevent any form of direct and indirect discrimination in the access to employment and working conditions, the provision of goods and services, and the participation in every economic, social, cultural, and political public activity. The Federal Center for Equal Opportunities and Opposition to Racism is in charge of watching over the application of the law, helping victims of discrimination, engaging legal proceedings on their behalf (like some habilitated LGBT organizations), and advising the Federal Minister of Equal Opportunities on possible improvements. The Federal Institute for the Equality of Women and Men deals with discrimination based on gender identity. In 2007, the 2003 antidiscrimination law was reformed because of a judgment of the constitutional court, and split into three different laws (one dealing with ethnicity, one with gender and transgender, and one with other grounds of discrimination, including sexual orientation).

In 2003, civil marriage was opened up to same-sex couples. Nonetheless, this law did not offer exactly the same rights as are available to different-sex couples. Gay and lesbian unions were denied filiation and adoption rights, and only Belgian or Dutch citizens could marry in Belgium. Since 2003, several legal reforms have been undertaken, and same-sex marriage is now almost identical to different-sex marriage. In 2004, the principle of residence was applied, allowing marriages between a Belgian and a foreigner, as well as the marriage of two foreigners who are Belgian residents. Since 2006, same-sex couples, regardless of their marital status, are also entitled to adopt a child jointly or to adopt their partner's child. Even though the presumption of paternity does not apply to same-sex unions, they have access to filiation law and may thus be recognized as the legal parents of their child.

In 2007, the Belgian parliament passed a law on transsexuality. This allows transsexuals to modify their first name and their picture on their identity card under the condition of hormonal therapy. To change their legal sex, a sex reassignment operation is required. Even if this law improves transsexuals' situation, it attempts to prevent any blurring between sex and gender. It also imposes an implicit obligation of sterilization. Indeed, this law subordinates the change of one's legal sex to the incapability to reproduce in one's biological sex.

These legal reforms have been supported by socialists (Parti Socialiste [PS] and Socialistische Partij Anders [SPA]) and Greens (Ecolo and Agalev/Groen) from both sides of the country, as well as by most Flemish Liberals (Vlaamse Liberalen en Democraten [VLD]) and some Flemish and French-speaking nationalists. French-speaking Liberals (Mouvement Réformateur [MR]), who are composed of both a historic secular and freemason branch and a more recent strong Christian group, are highly divided on LGBT issues. Christian Democrats (Christen-Democratisch en Vlaams [CD&V] and Centre Démocrate Humaniste [CDH]) have historically opposed such rights. However, since 2000, a dramatic shift has occurred in Flanders, where the CD&V, the Flemish Christian Democratic Party, has become more LGBT-friendly. Most of its MPs (members of parliament) voted in favor of same-sex marriage, and some of them wanted to back the opening-up of adoption to same-sex couples. Far-right parties (the French-speaking Front National [FN] and the well-organized Flemish Vlaams Belang) firmly oppose LGBT rights. Even though they are not yet numerous, some prominent politicians are openly gay or lesbian. Among them, the most renowned is Elio Di Rupo, the current president of the French-speaking Socialist Party (PS) and a former federal minister and minister-president of Wallonia.

RELIGION AND SPIRITUALITY

Belgium is a secular state that recognizes and supports the following denominations/faiths: Catholicism, Anglicanism, Protestantism, the Orthodox Churches, Judaism, Islam, Buddhism and the organized laïcité (i.e., a very secularized type of religion).

Although Belgium is a widely secularized country, Catholicism remains the main religion (about 75% of the population). Indeed, most Belgians consider themselves Roman Catholic, and the country has still a wide network of Catholic institutions (e.g., education, the health care sector, etc.). However, only a minority practices its religious beliefs, and religion does not seem to play an important part in the day to day attitudes of Belgians. Confirming this trend, research in different Flemish schools shows that there is no difference in attitudes towards homosexuality between pupils in a Catholic and a non-Catholic school.[43]

Historically, the Catholic Church has always considered homosexuality to oppose its doctrine. In Belgium, too, there has been some commotion about the declarations of some Catholic officials concerning homosexuality. Nonetheless, there seems to be a discrepancy between the more gentle attitudes of the Belgian Catholic Church, which has been comparatively silent on same-sex marriage and adoption, and those of the Vatican hierarchy. The public funding of ministers of religion is probably part of the explanation for this.

Within the Belgian Catholic Church, some homosexual groups have been active for decades, and are among the oldest gay and lesbian associations in the country. Some of the founders of the Flemish gay and lesbian movement were priests, or did not hide being influenced by their Catholic faith. Today, there still is an organized group of LGB priests called holebipastores in Flanders. In the French-speaking part, a Christian gay and lesbian group, La Communauté du Christ Libérateur, was founded in 1974 by a Protestant man, and defends an ecumenical approach.

The organized *laïcité*, which originates from the historical struggles of the secular freemason bourgeoisie and the socialist movement against the Catholic Church, has historically backed LGBT claims. These were regarded as steps towards a more secular society, comparable with issues such as divorce, abortion, or euthanasia (which are all allowed in Belgium).

As in other European countries confronted with immigration by people with a Muslim belief, the question of the compatibility between the Islamic faith and LGBT rights has become a burning issue. Research on the attitudes of 16-year-old Belgian pupils has shown that homonegative attitudes (concerning equal rights for LGBs) are the most widespread amongst boys and pupils with a Muslim background. The latter feel very threatened by homosexuality, and often use religious arguments to motivate their rejection of it.[44]

Combined with increasing Islamophobia, such information sustains the idea that Islam is incompatible with sexual equality, and that the Muslim minorities in western Europe threaten LGBT rights. At least until now, the climate between Muslim and sexual minorities has not polarized. On the contrary, at least in Flanders, action has been undertaken to stimulate the debate between both minorities, and to consult the Muslim community about this issue. The documentary *My Sister Zahra*, about the coming out of LGBs from an ethnic minority, was produced and disseminated successfully by Saddie Choua, someone from within the Muslim community. Other initiatives are promoted by the Flemish equal opportunities policy and executed by LGBT organizations. The Mazumgumzo project aims to make homosexuality debatable within different ethnic communities. The Wadi project is aimed to give educational training related to the specific needs of LGBs from an ethnic minority for social workers and other professionals within the health sector. At the same time, the specific psychotherapeutic needs of LGBs from ethnic minorities are being documented.

VIOLENCE

Homophobic violent acts have rarely been studied in Belgium. The annual report of the Center for Equal Opportunities and Opposition to Racism shows that 7 percent of all the complaints registered in 2006 concerned sexual orientation. Most of them (111 in total) were related to social problems (e.g., fights with neighbors), the denial of access to goods and services, representations of homosexuality in the media, and discrimination in the labor market. Seven complaints also referred to hate crimes.[45]

The first research on violence against LGBs was recently published, and focuses on Brussels. A limited sample of 377 respondents (predominantly male, young, and highly educated) divulges that verbal homophobic aggression is the most commonly experienced crime act (60% of the respondents have experienced this once or several times in their lives). Furthermore, 19 percent have been threatened, 10 percent have been physically attacked, nine percent have been robbed or have had their belongings damaged, and three percent have been raped or assaulted. The offenders were often young (between 18 and 30 years), male, acted in a group (with three or more other offenders) and were unknown to the victim. Ninety percent of the victims have identified the crimes as homophobic because of the language used by the offenders. Few victims have reported these acts to the police because of a lack of confidence in police and justice, the fear of coming out, and/ or bad experiences with the police in the past. The consequences of these aggressions (physical and verbal) can be severe: many felt shocked, reported low levels of perceived personal safety, and started to avoid certain places and intimate behavior in public spaces.[46] Several initiatives have been taken to tackle this problem. A few years ago, the Ministry of Justice started to register homophobic violence, and training is provided for police officers and magistrates.

OUTLOOK FOR THE 21ST CENTURY

In recent years, Belgium has almost achieved complete legal equality for gays, lesbians, and bisexuals. However, LGBs are still discriminated against, and social equality is not yet a reality. Hence, along with an increasing interest in solidarity with LGBs worldwide, the attainment of social equality has become the main target of LGBT organizations and public authorities. This new aim implies a thorough transformation of their strategies, modes of action, and time expectations, as they are confronted with new interlocutors; changing minds requires more time than changing laws.

Diversity within LGBT groups constitutes another emerging issue, as the motto of the 2008 Belgian Lesbian and Gay Pride officially claims (Celebrate Diversity. United Minorities are the Majority). This involves paying more attention to gender, race, disability, faith, or age. It also means considering the political and social significance of sexual diversity—that is, the wide variety of sexual desires, behaviors, and fantasies—a topic that has been left aside over recent years because of the quest for civil rights. Finally, it entails giving more space to transgender issues, as they are barely visible in Belgian society and LGBT organizations' statements.

RESOURCE GUIDE

Organizations

Arc-en-ciel Wallonie, http://www.arcenciel-wallonie.be.
    Walloon LGBT federation.
Fédération des Associations Gayes et Lesbiennes, http://www.fagl.be.
    French-speaking LGBT federation.
Holebifederatie, http://www.holebifederatie.be.
    Flemish LGBT federation.
Tels Quels, http://www.telsquels.be.
    French-speaking LGBT organization.
Wel Jong Niet Hetero, http://www.weljongniethetero.be.
    Flemish LGBT youth federation.

Web Sites

Center for Equal Opportunities and Opposition to Racism, http://www.diversite.be.
Flemish Ministry for Equal Opportunities (*Combattre l'homophobie, pour une école ouverte à la diversité*), http://www.enseignement.be/respel/RespelRech/jd/detailfiche.asp?id= 4851. Educational guide on homosexuality and homophobia produced by the French community of Belgium.
Gelijke Kansen Vlaanderen, http://www.gelijkekansen.be/.

Institute for Equality of Women and Men, http://www.iefh.fgov.be.

Research

Atelier Genre(s) et Sexualité(s) (Université libre de Bruxelles), http://www.ulb.ac.be/is/ags/.
Fonds Suzan Daniel, http://www.fondssuzandaniel.be/.
    Belgian LGBT archives.
Observatoire du sida et des sexualités (Facultés universitaires Saint-Louis), http://centres.
    fusl.ac.be/OBSERVATOIRE/document/Nouveau_site/Home.html.
Steunpunt Gelijkekansebeleid (Universiteiten Antwerpen & Hasselt), http://www.steun-
    puntgelijkekansen.be/.

NOTES

1. Alexis Dewaele, Cathy Herbrand, and David Paternotte, "Études gayes et les-
biennes/holebi-studies: état des savoirs critique et regards croisés entre la Flandre et la
Communauté française de Belgique," in Actes du colloque "*Savoirs de genre/quel genre de
savoir? Genderstudies/ Een genre apart?*" ed. Sandrine Debunne and Sara S'Jegers (Brussels:
Sophia, 2006).

2. Issues concerning sexual orientation and transgender people are sometimes related
but also to be distinguished from one another. The literature we refer to, often only deals
with LGB issues. In that case we use the LGB acronym. Also, when we are not sure if a
statement applies to transgender people, we will use the LGB acronym instead of the LGBT
acronym.

3. John Vincke and Peter Stevens, *Een beleidsgerichte algemene survey van Vlaamse
homoseksuele mannen en vrouwen. Basisrapport* (Brussel/Gent: Ministerie van de Vlaamse
Gemeenschap–Cel Gelijke Kansen/Universiteit Gent–Vakgroep Sociologie, 1999).

4. Annemie Joz Motmans and Joke Denekens, *De transgenderbeweging in Vlaanderen en Brussel in kaart gebracht: organisatiekenmerken, netwerken en strijdpunten* (Antwerpen: Steunpunt Gelijkekansenbeleid, UA–UHasselt, 2006).

5. Bart Hellinck, *Een halve eeuw (in) beweging. Een kroniek van de Vlaamse holebibe-
weging* (Gent: Federatie Werkgroepen Homoseksualiteit, 2002).

6. M. Hooghe, E. Quintelier, E. Claes, Y. Dejaeghere, and A. Harrell, *De houding
van jongeren ten aanzien van holebi-rechten. Een kwantitatieve en kwalitatieve analyse* (Leuven: Center for Citizenship and Democracy, 2007).

7. Steven Lenaers, *Kansen en onkansen in Vlaanderen: Resultaten van de Survey
Gelijke Kansen 2004* (Antwerpen: Steunpunt Gelijkekansenbeleid UA–UHasselt, 2006).

8. See the following reports: Greet De Brauwere, *Onderzoek naar de situatie van
Vlaamse holebi-leerkrachten* (Gent: Hogeschool Gent–Departement Sociaal-Pedagogisch
Werk, Steunpunt Onderzoek en Dienstverlening, 2002); Koen Pelleriaux and Jeff Van
Ouytsel, *De houding van Vlaamse scholieren tegenover holebiseksualiteit* (Antwerpen: Univer-
siteit Antwerpen–Onderzoeksgroep Cultuur & Welzijn/Holebifabriek vzw, 2003).

9. Pelleriaux and Van Ouytsel, *De houding van Vlaamse scholieren tegenover holebiseksualiteit.*

10. John Vincke and Kees van Heeringen, "Confident Support and the Mental Well-
being of Lesbian and Gay Young Adults: A Longitudinal Analysis," *Journal of Community
and Applied Social Psychology* 12 (2002): 181–93.

11. Fédération des Associations Gayes et Lesbiennes (FAGL)—Magenta. *Promotion
de la santé concernant les jeunes d'orientation sexuelle minoritaire (homosexuelle, bisexuelle):
éducation sexuelle et affective en milieu scolaire et prévention du suicide: Recherche exploratoire
et état des lieux au sujet des ESA. Proposition d'un canevas de contenu de formation. Pistes de
travail et recommandations, Étude commanditée par la Ministre de l'Intégration sociale de la
Communauté Française, Nicole Maréchal* (Bruxelles: FAGL, 2003).

12. See http://www.belgium.be/en/index.jsp (accessed July 13, 2009).

13. SERV, "Holebi's en de arbeidsmarkt. Nota van de Sociaal-Economische Raad van Vlaanderen, in opdracht van de Vlaamse Minister van Tewerkstelling en Toerisme," SERV, 2005, http://www.serv.be/Actueel/SERV-nota%20holebis%20en%20de%20arbeidsmarkt.pdf (accessed May 26, 2008).

14. J. Vincke, A. Dewaele, W. Van den Berghe, and N. Cox, *Zzzip—een statistisch onderzoek met het oog op het verzamelen van basismateriaal over de doelgroep holebi's* (Gent: Ugent–Steunpunt Gelijkekansenbeleid [UA–Uhasselt], in opdracht van het Ministerie van de Vlaamse Gemeenschap, Gelijke Kansen in Vlaanderen, 2006).

15. A. Dewaele, N. Cox, W. Van den Berghe, and J. Vincke, *De maatschappelijke positie van holebi's en hun sociale netwerken: over vriendschap en andere bloedbanden* (Antwerpen en Hasselt: Steunpunt Gelijkekansenbeleid, 2006).

16. Inès De Biolley, Melda Aslan, Alexis Dewaele, and Marie-Jo Bonnet, *Recherche exploratoire sur les représentations de l'homosexualité dans la fonction publique,* (Louvain: Cap sciences Humaines, Asbl Associée à l'Université Catholique de Louvain, 2007).

17. John Vincke and Rudi Bleys, *Vitale Vragen 2001: eindrapport* (Antwerpen: Sensoa, 2003).

18. Based on the Flemish or Walloon sample.

19. Vladimir Martens and P. Huynen, "Connaissances et comportements des hommes qui ont des rapports sexuels avec des hommes à l'égard du VIH/SIDA en Communauté Française de Belgique," *Archives of Public Health* 64 (2006):13–26.

20. The following are considered perversions: narcissism, pedophilia, bestiality, incest, necrophilia, fetishism, sadomasochism, exhibitionism, prostitution, public sex.

21. Nicolas Thirion, "Foucault, le droit et la question gay," *Le Banquet* 19 (2004).

22. Vincke, Dewaele, Van den Berghe, and Cox, *Zzzip.*

23. Cathy Herbrand, "La parenté sociale: une réponse à la diversité familiale?" in *Familles plurielles, politique familiale sur mesure?* ed. Marie-Thérèse Casman, Caroline Simaÿs, Riet Bulckens, and Dimitri Mortelmans (Brussels: Luc Pire, 2007), 183–89.

24. Katrien Vanfraussen, "The Childrearing Process in Lesbian Families with Children Created by Means of Donor Insemination," doctoral dissertation, Vrije Universiteit Brussel, 2003.

25. Cathy Herbrand, "La parenté sociale."

26. Petra De Sutter, "Les transparentalités," in *Homoparentalités. Approches scientifiques et politiques,* ed. Anne Cadoret, Martine Gross, Caroline Mécary, and Bruno Perreau (Paris: Presses universitaires de France, 2006).

27. See the following books: Peter M. Nardi, *Gay Men's Friendships—Invincible Communities* (Chicago: University of Chicago Press, 1999); and Kate Weston, *Families We Choose: Lesbians, Gays, Kinship* (New York: Columbia University Press, 1991).

28. Dewaele, Cox, Van den Berghe, and Vincke, *De maatschappelijke positie van holebi's en hun sociale netwerken.*

29. Hellinck, *Een halve eeuw (in) beweging.*

30. See the following: J. Vincke, R. Bolton, and P. De Vleeschouwer, "The Cognitive Structure of the Domain of Safe and Unsafe Gay Sexual Behaviour in Belgium," *AIDS Care* 13, no. 1 (2001): 57–70; François Delor, *Séropositifs. Trajectoires identitaires et rencontres du risque* (Paris: L'Harmattan, 1997); John Vincke and Rudi Bleys, *Vitale Vragen 2001: eindrapport* (Antwerpen: Sensoa, 2003).

31. John Vincke, Lieven De Rycke, and Ralph Bolton, "Gay Identity and the Experience of Gay Social Stress," *Journal of Applied Social Psychology* 29, no. 6 (1999): 1316–31.

32. Dewaele, Cox, Van den Berghe, and Vincke, *De maatschappelijke positie van holebi's en hun sociale netwerken.*

33. A. Sasse and A. Defraye, *Epidémiologie du sida et de l'infection à VIH en Belgique. Situation arrêtée au 31 décembre 2005,* IPH/EPI Reports (33) (Brussels: Institut scientifique de santé publique, 2006).

34. Vincke and Bleys, *Vitale Vragen 2001*.

35. Rudi Bleys, *Een nieuwe 'gezondheidscrisis' bij homomannen: feit of fictie?* unpublished document, 2006.

36. Sensoa, "Nieuwe hiv diagnoses in 2005, 2007," http://www.sensoa.be/pdf/HIV/HIV-diagnose_in_2005.pdf (accessed May 26, 2008).

37. Kees Van Heeringen and John Vincke, "Suicidal Acts and Ideation in Homosexual and Bisexual Young People: A Study of Prevalence and Risk Factors," *Social Psychiatry and Psychiatric Epidemiology* 35, no. 11 (2000): 494–99.

38. Vincke, Dewaele, Van den Berghe, and Cox, *Zzzip*.

39. Steven Lenaers, *Kansen en onkansen in Vlaanderen: Resultaten van de Survey Gelijke Kansen 2004* (Antwerpen: Steunpunt Gelijkekansenbeleid UA–UHasselt, 2006).

40. Jozefien Godemont, Alexis Dewaele, and Jef Breda, *Geen roos zonder doornen: Oudere holebi's, hun sociale omgeving en specifieke behoeften* (Antwerpen: Steunpunt Gelijkekansenbeleid, UA-LUC, 2004).

41. Griet De Cuypere, C. Jannes, and R. Rubens, "Psychosocial Functioning of Transsexuals in Belgium," *Acta Psychiatrica Scandinavica* 91 (1995): 180–84.

42. Hellinck, *Een halve eeuw (in) beweging*.

43. Pelleriaux and Van Ouytsel, *De houding van Vlaamse scholieren tegenover holebiseksualiteit*.

44. Hooghe, Quintelier, Claes, Dejaeghere, and Harrell, *De houding van jongeren ten aanzien van holebi-rechten*.

45. Jozef De Witte, *Jaarverslag 2006* (Brussels: Centrum voor gelijkheid van kansen en voor racismebestrijding, 2007).

46. Marcia Poelman and Dirk Smits, *Agressie tegen holebi's in Brussel-Stad* (Antwerpen/Apeldoorn: Maklu, 2007).

BULGARIA

Monika Pisankaneva

OVERVIEW

Bulgaria is situated on the Balkan Peninsula of southeastern Europe. Its territory of 42,822 square miles is bordered by Romania to the north, Serbia and Macedonia to the west, Greece and Turkey to the south, and the Black Sea to the east.

Bulgaria is one of the oldest states in Europe. It was formed when migrating central Asian Turkic tribes merged with Slavic inhabitants of the Balkans in the 7th century. Historians often describe Bulgaria as a country developing on the periphery of strong empires. In the early centuries of its existence, the Bulgarian state managed to assert its place in the Balkans in spite of constant fighting with the Byzantine Empire. In the 14th century, the country was invaded by the Ottoman Empire and remained under its rule until the end of 19th century. Christianity was introduced to Bulgaria in the 8th century, and historians claim that the preservation of the Christian faith helped Bulgaria to preserve its national identity during the five centuries of Ottoman domination. Today, the largest percentage of the population is Eastern Orthodox Christian (estimated about 82.6%) followed by Muslim (12.2%), other Christian (1.2%), and other religious minorities (about 4%). The country's main ethnic groups are Bulgarians (about 83%), Turks (about 10%), and Roma (about 5%). The remaining estimated 4 percent of the population includes Macedonians, Armenians, Tatars, and other minorities.[1]

At the beginning of 20th century, Bulgaria began developing as a

capitalist country, but its economic development was interrupted by the World War I and II. In both wars, Bulgaria was an ally of Germany. The lost wars caused national catastrophes, which steered the country into the sphere of Soviet influence after a socialist revolution in 1944. From September 1944 to November 1989, Bulgaria functioned as a socialist country, a close ally of the Soviet Union, and a member of the Eastern Bloc. In 1989, there was a political turnover, which led towards gradual democratization, the reintroduction of a multiparty political system, and embracing the goals of a free market economy.

The transition from socialism to capitalism was not an easy one for Bulgaria. There was a prolonged period of economic stagnation that led to hyperinflation in the winter of 1996, and the overturning of the pro-socialist government. In July 1997, the country introduced a currency board, which helped to control the inflation. The reforms after 1997 gradually led to economic stabilization, and a relatively high rate of economic growth (over 5% since 2000; 6.1% for 2006). The country joined NATO in 2004 and the European Union (EU) in January 2007. The gross domestic product (GDP) per capita was $10,700 in 2006.[2] As of 2007, Bulgaria occupied the last position among the EU member states in regard to population income. Today, the main obstacles to Bulgaria's progress are corruption in the public administration, a weak judiciary, and organized crime. Low productivity of labor is often cited as the main economic reason for slow improvement of the standard of living.

Economic and political trends in Bulgaria after 1989 led to a growing gap between the new rich and the poor, as well as an increase in the number of socially marginalized people such as the elderly, the disabled, and the Roma, who were economically segregated for physical or cultural reasons.

OVERVIEW OF LGBT ISSUES

LGBT people are among the least tolerated groups according to the 2007 survey, "Attitude towards Minority Groups and Discriminative Outlook in Bulgarian Society," ordered by the national Commission for Protection from Discrimination, and conducted by Skala Research Agency.[3] The survey involved 1,200 people from 100 different locations in Bulgaria. According to the report, over 50 percent of the respondents would not like to work in the same room with a homosexual person, and 78 percent would not enroll their children at a school where there is a homosexual teacher. Over 70 percent responded that they would never become friends with a homosexual person. At the same time, 53.3 percent of the respondents said that they had never had contact with a homosexual person, which indicates the high level of invisibility of the LGBT population in Bulgaria. The least tolerated group within the LGBT population is the group known as *transvestites,* the term used in Bulgaria to identify men who dress as women, regardless of sexual orientation or gender identity. Fifty-seven percent of all respondents expressed a radically negative attitude towards this group; 53.8 percent of the respondents expressed a total lack of tolerance toward gay men, while 52.8 percent expressed lack of tolerance toward lesbians.

LGBT people in Bulgaria have no restrictions on organizing movements, holding demonstrations, or establishing formal or informal organizations. The first nonprofit nongovernmental organization that openly identified as a "gay rights organization" in its by-laws and founding documents was Bulgarian Gay Organization Gemini

(BGO Gemini), legally registered in 1992. In the past few years, several other organizations that self-identify as LGBT support organizations have been formed: the Queer Bulgaria Foundation, Bilitis Lesbian and Bi-Women Resource Center, and Gay Sports Club Tangra in 2004, and LGBT Idea in 2006. There are also several informal hobby-based clubs for gay men. Most of these organizations and informal groups operate in Sofia, although some of them actively liaise with people from outside the capital.

LGBT issues entered public discourse and the mass media in the second half of the 1990s, when the first generation of gay and lesbian activists came of age. The majority of the activists were people with higher education who had lived or studied in the West, and maintained close contacts with activists from the western European LGBT movement (including the Dutch organization Cultuur en Ontspannings-Centrum [Centre for Culture and Leisure, COC] and the International Lesbian and Gay Association [ILGA]-Europe). They tried to promote LGBT rights in a country in which the double standard between public and private life was widely accepted from the time of socialism. The first media appearances of gay and lesbian activists took place in 1997–1998. They were associated with the work of the first gay organization in the country, BGO Gemini. In the first five years of its existence, this dealt mainly with safe sex among gay men. Towards the end of the 1990s, BGO Gemini developed a wider human rights agenda under theguidance of the Dutch peer organization, the COC.

EDUCATION

Bulgarian school curricula are centrally approved by the Ministry of Education. Primary and secondary education at public schools is fully subsidized by the state. Private schools exist only in the largest urban centers. They have greater freedom in introducing elective subjects and after-school activities, but first of all they need to cover all subjects in the compulsory curricula approved by the Ministry of Education. LGBT people and concerns are not discussed within the compulsory curriculum. Nongovernmental organization (NGO)-piloted programs, mainly those related to sexual health, sometimes touch upon the topic of sexual identities. The problem of such programs is that they last as long as the external funding lasts, and usually do not lead to significant changes in the content of the obligatory subjects.

A recent study conducted by BGO Gemini hints at the basis for homo-, bi-, and transphobia in the Bulgarian schools. It turns out that the diversity of sexual identities is not discussed within the compulsory secondary curriculum. LGBT people and concerns are not mentioned in several subjects dealing directly or indirectly with human sexuality, including psychology, ethics, world and personality, and philosophy. Homosexuality and bisexuality are also never mentioned when students learn about great historical personalities who were known to have same-sex relationships. BGO Gemini evaluated textbooks for 9th to 12th grade students in the subjects of literature, history, ethics, philosophy, world and personality, psychology, and logic. None of these textbooks discuss LGBT people or concerns. The specific chapter "Me and My Sexuality" in the psychology textbook for 9th grade students does not refer to LGBT identities at all; it discusses only heterosexuality. The textbook for the subject world and personality for 12th grade students briefly mentions homosexuality in one of its chapters, providing a neutral comment to the effect that some people develop love relationships with same-sex partners. When differences in society are discussed within any of these subjects, the only differences mentioned are religious and ethnic differences.[4]

Research on discrimination against LGBT students in secondary schools is currently being carried out by BGO Gemini within the scope of the above-mentioned project, but the final report is not yet available. Preliminary findings indicate that students have no one to talk to at school about their sexual orientation. Students do not trust the school psychologists and do not want to reveal their sexual orientation to them. LGBT youth is largely invisible at school except for transvestites, who are often ridiculed by their classmates.

Psychology is a compulsory subject in secondary education, but the curriculum does not include discussion of LGBT people or their concerns. The curricula for psychology courses at universities, on the other hand, include a number of essentialist and constructivist theories of homosexuality, bisexuality, and transsexuality.

Reliable data about the treatment of LGBT students at schools in Bulgaria has not yet been collected. An indication of the lack of special support is the absence of LGBT support groups or LGBT centers at Bulgarian schools.

EMPLOYMENT AND ECONOMICS

Macroeconomic stability and growth have characterized the Bulgarian economy since 1997, when the currency board was introduced. The Bulgarian lev is currently fixed to the euro. The GDP (purchasing power parity) was estimated at $79.05 billion in 2006.[5] Raising the productivity of labor, the main reason for low income levels, is still considered a challenge. The public sector is relatively large in size and scope compared to the best performers among the EU member states. The regulatory environment for the economy is often characterized by analysts as one that relies too much on controls rather than on incentives.

The main law that protects the rights of LGBT people at the workplace is the antidiscrimination law of 2004, which bans discrimination at work on the basis of gender and sexual orientation (among other grounds). The law obliges employers to follow the principles of equal opportunity employment and to have written policies for a tolerant workplace, but no state monitoring of the implementation of this regulation has taken place so far.

In 2006, BGO Gemini implemented a project funded by the Democracy Commission of the U.S. Embassy in Sofia that analyzed employment practices with regards to tolerance in the workplace. Thirty companies and five nonprofit organizations from around the country participated in the project; fifteen of them agreed to be mentioned in the final report. This project had a twofold effect: it helped interested employers to create a tolerant workplace, and it gathered statistics on the current level of intolerance towards LGBT in the job market. The findings demonstrated that, up to this point, the antidiscrimination law has not exercised a considerable influence on employment practices. A survey of 951 employers and employees from around the country indicated that 79 percent of the homosexual employees are hiding their sexual orientation in the workplace. Sixty-seven percent of the homosexual respondents shared that they have occasionally felt subjected to psychological harassment at the workplace, and 34 percent of them have felt systematically harassed. Twenty-nine percent of the interviewed employers said that they would never employ an openly gay person, or one who is suspected by them to be gay.[6] One explanation for the lack of effect of the antidiscrimination law on employment practices could be sought in the low fines that employers have to pay if they are convicted of discrimination—the maximum amount of the fine is 2,000 lev (1,022 euros, or US$1,430).

SOCIAL/GOVERNMENT PROGRAMS

There are a few well-known sexologists with private practices based in Sofia who offer support to LGBT clients. Reparative therapy for LGBT people is not practiced in Bulgaria.

FAMILY

There was a visible backlash of conservatism in Bulgaria after the arrival of democracy in 1990. Socialism could not destroy the traditional patriarchal values within the family, although it promoted equality between men and women. The woman of the socialist family was often overburdened with the roles and responsibilities of worker, mother, and housewife. The procreative nuclear family became a norm during socialism, and remaining single or living as a married couple without children was considered immoral or highly undesirable. Most LGBT people survived this period through marriages of convenience and leading a double life.

After 1990, increased hostility towards minorities, resulting from the growing poverty and insecurity, led to the reemergence and official promotion of conservative values. The double standard between public and private life maintained during socialism remained the main way of hiding personal preferences regarding love and the family. Although the number of unmarried couples and single parents raising children is growing, the nuclear family continues to be the norm.

Today, LGBT people are freer to choose a life with their partner, and are not forced into heterosexual marriages of convenience as frequently as in the socialist past. Nevertheless, most of them prefer to keep their private life a secret. The few visible nonheterosexual couples are pop stars and some leaders of LGBT groups. Sometimes, pop icons who are open about their homosexuality deliver messages to the general public that reinforce stereotypes about gay men. For example, the pop-folk singer Azis, one of the brightest stars of Bulgarian popular music in the early 2000s, appeared on a widely watched TV talk show and disclosed that he is "a woman inside," and his partner is heterosexual. This reinforces the popular stereotype that the gay couple mimics the heterosexual couple and one of the partners plays the role of the husband, and the other one the role of the wife. The one who plays the role of the husband is not perceived to be 100 percent gay. This also reinforces the stereotype that gayness in a man implies femininity.

The availability of private clinics for artificial insemination in the last few years has allowed lesbian women who can afford to pay to get pregnant and give birth. Lesbian couples raising their children together were not a rarity in the recent past, but their children were usually conceived during previous heterosexual marriages. Today, lesbians have more freedom to choose whether to conceive through vaginal intercourse or in an artificial insemination clinic. There is still family pressure on women to have a heterosexual marriage, especially in provincial areas. Lesbians who wish to lead lives without men need to migrate away from their relatives, preferably to one of the largest urban centers, where they will be able to live anonymously with their partners. To a large extent, this holds true for young gay men as well. Most gay men in Bulgaria feel much more comfortable sharing their sexual orientation with anyone other than their parents.

Gay couples involving at least one partner over 35 years old are now looking for informal partnerships with single women or with lesbian couples in order to raise children together, as adopting children is more difficult for single men than for single women as a rule. Although the adoption law does not enumerate restrictions on the gender of the parent, single men in Bulgaria have never successfully adopted children according to the official statistics. The reasons for that are purely moral and not legal. The members of the committees that approve adoption tend to share the patriarchal view that men are worse caregivers than women, and do not believe that a man is able to raise a child on his own. At the same time, there have not been many cases of single men applying to adopt children recorded, which means that the unwritten rules of adoption have largely been left unchallenged.

Second-parent adoption is not yet possible for children raised by lesbian or gay couples, because of the absence of state-recognized domestic partnership and gay marriage laws.

COMMUNITY

The only organized LGBT communities in Bulgaria are the hobby-based groups such as gay sports clubs. Internet-based communities are quite active, but they function mainly as an informal dating service. Leading activists from the existing LGBT rights organizations confess that there is very low interest in any form of political action among LGBT Bulgarians. Equality marches in the capital organized in the years 2005–2007 by BGO Gemini on May 17 (the International Day against Homophobia) have never had more than 20 people in attendance. These were usually the leading activists and the staff of the existing LGBT organizations coming together for the march. Police protection was provided, and there were no hostilities. Most of the people walking by either did not notice, or did not pay much attention to the march.

The first Gay Pride Parade was organized in 2008 by the Bulgarian Gay Organization Gemini and attracted 65 participants and many hate groups. The police arrested 60 people who tried to attack the pride rally. The event received strong media coverage and inspired heated debates about the need for a "public display of homosexuality." Despite the strong opposition to the first gay pride event in 2008, a group of activists came together to organize the second pride parade in 2009. This time the event attracted over 350 people and there were no attacks due to very well-organized security measures. The street parade was protected by over 100 police officers and 70 private security guards. The gay pride event in 2009 marks a new enhanced level of self-organizing of the LGBT communities in Bulgaria. Activists of BGO Gemini and the Bilitis Resource Center for Lesbians and Bisexual Women came together with other active people who were not related to any LGBT organizations. For the first time community interests were well conceptualized and interorganizational tensions were overcome in the name of a common cause. The support from international embassies, including the Dutch, United Kingdom, French, and American, as well as from ILGA-Europe and the Intergroup on LGBT Rights at the European Parliament, helped to increase the political importance of the event. The increased number of participants in 2009 compared to the previous year can be contributed to the better organization and popularization of the event, as well as to its greater commercialization. For the first time the Pride Parade was transformed from a purely political march to an open-air festivity celebrating the visibility and equal rights of LGBT people in Bulgaria.

LGBT night life is quite vigorous in the large urban centers, especially Sofia and Varna, but it is hard to define it as a community life. People go to clubs for pleasure, and are usually not interested in taking part in organized activities with a political purpose. In the last few years, there has been a visible trend of gay night clubs becoming more and more mixed, welcoming all kinds of chic personalities, including heterosexual clients. The same could not be said for the lesbian night clubs. Lesbian clubs demonstrate restrictive entry rules, and are not so open to newcomers unless the latter are introduced by a regular client.

Bisexual people do not form an easily identifiable group. They can travel in gay/lesbian and in straight circles. It is commonly believed that bisexuals are still experimenting with their sexuality, and will sooner or later assume a gay or straight identity. As of 2007, no special programs have been developed by the Bulgarian LGBT organizations oriented exclusively toward bisexuals, and neither have Bulgarian bisexuals organized themselves into an independent organization.

The most visible group among LGBT people is the group of male transvestites. The distinction between a cross-dresser, drag queen, and transgendered person is not usually made in Bulgaria, and all of them are referred to with the common term *transvestite*. Transvestites are the preferred entertainers at night clubs. Some of them are quite famous as pop divas, singers and dancers, or evening talk show hosts. Another visible group of transvestites exists among the street prostitutes in Sofia. They are active at night in one specific downtown area, and sometimes trouble the residents with their behavior.

At the moment, there is no community center operating during the day except for the office of BGO Gemini in Sofia. The staff was hired and equipped using the first large grant provided by the Dutch government program MATRA in 2001.[7] Initially, BGO Gemini was meant to be a safe house for LGBT people, providing space for discussions, movie screenings, and readings. The number of people using this safe house, however, has gradually decreased over the last few years as BGO Gemini transformed from a community-based organization into a professional advocacy group. Today, there are rarely any people aside from professional staff and the board of BGO Gemini visiting this office. The irony of greater professionalization of community-based organizations is that they often lose the intimate contact with the community that created them. BGO Gemini has not escaped this fate. Today, it is the most visible LGBT rights advocacy organization in Bulgaria, with the greatest number of externally funded projects per year, but the number of people within the LGBT groups who actively and visibly support what Gemini is doing is small. The activities of the organization rely primarily on the involvement of the paid staff and occasional volunteers recruited primarily among university students who need to complete an internship at an NGO. At the same time, the nature of projects implemented by the organization has changed over time from ones that are predominantly oriented towards the LGBT people to others that address the society at large and aim to decrease homo-, bi-, and transphobia.

The support organization Bilitis for lesbian and bi women emerged in 2004. It operates on a small scale, predominantly in Sofia. Its work includes the organizing of lesbian leadership camps, lesbian amateur sports, and lesbian and bisexual women's support groups. Occasionally, it supports events that benefit the larger LGBT community, such as the annual gay and lesbian cultural fest organized by the Sofia-based Center for Culture and Debate, the Red House. This was launched for the first time in 2005, and was once again staged in 2006, but with a decreasing audience. In 2007, it was reduced to the screening of a few LGBT-movies over two successive evenings.

Two other LGBT groups were started by former leaders of BGO Gemini after they had left the organization. The Queer Bulgaria Foundation, legally registered in 2004, started as an alternative to BGO Gemini, which many LGBT people criticized for being ineffective in addressing their concerns. However, the organization did not manage to become sustainable. It gradually decreased its activity and closed its office at the end of 2007 after implementing a few donor-driven projects.

LGBT Idea was legally registered in 2006. It operates a virtual cultural center, an online LGBT radio and maintains a detailed online bibliography of all existing publications in the Bulgarian language (articles and books) discussing LGBT people and concerns.

The reasons why LGBT people do not actively respond to the politically oriented initiatives proposed by formal LGBT organizations have often been debated in the circles of activists. The explanation is sought in the overall characteristics of Bulgarian civil society, which is described by social analysts as "a civil society without citizens."[8] Low civic participation in important political processes is a common trend in countries with weak democracies. Civic action is not a major determinant of change in Bulgaria. Advocacy and consultative processes are carried out formally, with the help of small professional groups of experts (usually closely related to the government), and not in broad consultation with the citizens. LGBT Bulgarians are no more or less politically active than the average Bulgarian citizen. This lack of tradition of a mass-scale organized LGBT movement for equal rights seems impossible to comprehend at this stage of political development in the country.

HEALTH

Universal health care in Bulgaria exists only on paper today. The health care reform carried out after 1990 resulted in the deterioration of medical care for the vast majority of the population, especially for low-income groups.

The first empirical survey concerning the health status of LGBT people in Bulgaria was conducted by Queer Bulgaria in 2005, under the project called Improving Access to Health Care of LGBT People in Bulgaria, funded by the Open Society Institute New York.[9] The survey included 280 people who identify as lesbian, gay, bisexual, or transgender from six major Bulgarian cities. The survey was based on in-depth structured interviews, which included not only questions regarding the health status of the people, but also general questions related to their self-identification, acceptance of their sexual identity from parents, colleagues, and friends, and their attitude to gay partnership. A limitation of the survey was that it reached out mainly to people between 19 and 40 years old with secondary or higher education, most of whom were employed. The study did not include the most socially disadvantaged groups. The survey also did not reach out to LGBT people living in small towns or villages. Out of the 280 people who were interviewed, 216 identified as men (gay or bisexual/MSM [men who have sex with men]), 57 as women (lesbian or bisexual) and 7 as transgender (gay, lesbian, or bisexual).

The survey indicated that there are no significant differences between the data gathered from LGBT people and that of heterosexuals in regard to physical activity, smoking, drinking, and general health care. The only difference was in the amount of drug use: the percentage of LGBT people using drugs turned out to be higher than the national average for people within the same age group, although most of the LGBT respondents indicated that their drug usage was a one-time trial usage.

Seventy-six percent of the interviewed women and 44 percent of the interviewed men in the Queer Bulgaria survey of LGBT health status indicated that they have a permanent sexual partner, while 20 percent of the women and 10 percent of the men shared that they have more than one permanent sexual partner. At the same time, 56 percent of the women and 76 percent of the men shared that they have casual sexual encounters. Only 5 percent of the women and 15 percent of the interviewed men disclosed that they have had or currently have a sexually transmitted disease (STD). Forty-six percent of the men and 22 percent of the women have always used STD protection such as condoms or medical gloves during all sexual intercourse, while 15 percent of the men and 2 percent of the women have used protection only with casual partners. For women, these percentages are similar to the national average for using protection during sexual intercourse, while for men— they are higher. None of those surveyed revealed that they are HIV positive.

The survey indicated that the majority of LGBT people are likely to avoid going to the doctor if they fear that they must disclose their sexual orientation. Only 11 percent of the women and 21 percent of the men believed that the medical workers have adequate understanding of the needs of LGBT patients.

Among all other sexual minorities, the needs of intersexual people are most overlooked. The dominant medical paradigm is still one that tries to convert the intersexual person into a man or a woman. The most common form of intersexuality, the androgen insensitivity syndrome among men, is treated by sex change operations, in which the doctors extract the gonads, which are usually hidden in the body, and modify the genitals to take the shape of female genitals. The patient is not given a choice of gender. No representative research of the situation of intersexual persons in Bulgaria has been carried out so far. Single cases can be detected on the Internet, when someone publishes a notice that he or she is looking for contacts with others like him or her.

Sex change operations and gender change at will are implemented in Bulgaria after a court decision to change the individual's personal identification, which is grounded on a supportive statement issued by a commission of psychiatrists and sexologists.

In Bulgaria, AIDS has never been considered a problem initiated by the gay minority. Official statistics of the Ministry of Health since 1986 consistently show that only a small percent of the total number of HIV-infected people in the country have had same-sex contacts.

According to information collected by the Joint United Nations Programme on HIV/AIDS (UNAIDS)-Bulgaria,[10] 803 people infected with HIV lived in the country between 1986 and 2007. These people are officially registered as HIV positive with the Ministry of Health. A leading method of transmission of HIV infection in Bulgaria is sexual intercourse (83%), followed by intravenous use of drugs (13%), and blood transfusion (3%). About 1 percent of HIV-positive people in Bulgaria are born with the disease. The majority of HIV-positive people acquire the disease through heterosexual intercourse, but in the last two years the number of infected men who had acquired HIV through same-sex contact has increased. The number of HIV-positive intravenous drug users has increased tremendously over the last two years as well. The last cases of infection through blood transfusion were detected in 1996. Most of the HIV-positive people live in the four largest Bulgarian cities: Sofia, Varna, Plovdiv, and Burgas. The total number of infected men is 3.5 times greater than the number of infected women.

A national-level HIV/AIDS prevention program has been implemented by the Ministry of Health, funded by the Global Fund for AIDS, and contracted out to NGOs from around the country. The target groups of the program are intravenous drug users, prostitutes, the Roma community, and youth of all backgrounds. Preventive measures for different target groups have been developed. Safe sex programs targeting young people focus on condom usage, and are implemented by youth organizations from around the country. Special safe sex programs for the LGBT groups have been implemented by BGO Gemini in the late 1990s, and in 2007 by the Queer Bulgaria Foundation. A recent project implemented by the Queer Bulgaria Foundation involved AIDS testing by a mobile medical unit at Sofia-based night clubs frequented by relatively affluent gay men. The main criticism of the safe sex and AIDS prevention programs implemented by LGBT organizations is that they do not usually reach out to the people who are really in need of safe sex education, free condoms, or free AIDS testing, such as Roma prostitutes and other low-income people. On the other hand, a number of non-LGBT organizations carry out safe sex and AIDS prevention programs in Roma communities, communities of intravenous drug users, and among young prostitutes. In theory, these programs should reach out to the LGBT members of those groups as well.

POLITICS AND LAW

The overall democratization of the Bulgarian legal and political system after 1990 led to increased freedom of speech and association. Today the Bulgarian laws are compliant with the universal standards for human rights and EU directives.

Until 2002, there was a discriminatory article in the Bulgarian penal code (article 157, paragraph 4) that envisioned sanctions and public censure for people displaying their homosexuality in public or in a scandalous way. Although that was a dead provision that had not been used for starting legal actions in the last few years, the mere existence of such an article in the penal code signaled a discriminatory treatment of homosexuality by the judiciary. The revision of the penal code conducted under the pressure from the European Commission as part of the EU-accession process of Bulgaria led to the abolition of this article.

Two years later, in January 2004, Bulgaria adopted a new antidiscrimination law, which is considered to be one of the best in Europe. Sexual orientation is mentioned among other grounds on which discrimination is prohibited, including race, sex, religion, disability, and age. The law bans discrimination on the grounds of sexual orientation in the fields of employment, health care, and education, recruitment to the military, housing, accommodation, and a range of services available to the public. It also provides protection against harassment and victimization. *Sexual orientation* is explicitly defined in the text of this law as heterosexual, bisexual, or homosexual orientation.

The antidiscrimination law consolidated into one legal text protection against discrimination, victimization, and harassment, which until then was scattered and ineffective. In 2006, the Antidiscrimination Commission was formed as an independent public body guaranteeing maximum enforceability of the new law. This commission is reviewing complaints separately from the courts. It consists of experienced individuals dedicated to human rights.

Since January 2004, four legal cases have been initiated by individuals who have experienced discrimination on the grounds of sexual orientation. All of the cases were won by the claimants. One of the cases became emblematic for the effectiveness of the new law, because it attacked a case of discrimination on the grounds of sexual orientation in Sofia University Saint Kliment Ohridsky, one of the most respected public institutions in the country. The case was started by several gay men, supported by the Queer Bulgaria Foundation, who had been banned from using the university's sauna on the grounds that they were gay. The court compelled Sofia University to pay a fine to the gay claimants and to allow them to use the sauna on equal grounds with all other clients. The case was widely covered in the mass media.

In 2007, some changes to the penal code led to its complete modernization and the abandonment of language that was discriminatory to homosexuals. Texts that envisioned different penalties for the same crimes if committed by heterosexual and homosexual people were abolished (article 157). Sex crimes were no longer differentiated on the basis of the sexual orientation of the perpetrator. A definition of pedophilia was introduced, preventing the comparison of pedophilia with homosexuality. The only recommendation that could be made to the Bulgarian penal code at this stage would be to introduce a general definition of hate crimes instead of listing a few types of hate crimes.

There is still no registered domestic partnership or gay marriage law in Bulgaria. The Bulgarian family code has not been significantly revised since 1985. In 2007, a draft law for registered domestic partnership for only heterosexual couples was submitted, but it did not reach the voting stage in parliament. The introduction of a same sex partnership law will be possible either after a revision of the constitution, which states that marriage is a union between a man and a woman, or after a revision of the family code, which might be modernized to introduce partnership as a new legal form of union between two people (without referring to their gender). Promoters of revision of the family code insist that the gender of the partners should not be mentioned in an amendment referring to registered partnership. Thus, the interests of both heterosexual and homosexual couples will be met.

RELIGION AND SPIRITUALITY

The dominant Orthodox Church displays a lack of acceptance of homosexuality whenever it is called upon to comment on this topic in the mass media. Members of parliament have made use of religious arguments in a recent discussion of proposed changes in the family code that envisioned the introduction of registered partnership law, though only for heterosexual couples. The action of LGBT activists to promote the inclusion of homosexual couples in the new partnership law was confronted by an appeal to traditional Christian values, and not by purely secular judicial arguments. This, however, does not mean that religion plays a major role in forming social attitudes toward LGBT people. Rather, it is an example of the populist use of religious notions by politicians in a secular context to stay on the safe side when discussing a potentially controversial subject.

Some organizations with religious affiliations, such as the online bookstore and publishing house for Christian literature, Memra, recently began to tackle the topic of sexual orientation. As a result of their work, Bulgaria saw the first book on reparative therapy translated from English, *A Parent's Guide to Preventing Homosexuality,* authored by Joseph Nicolosi. Prompted by LGBT activists, the Association of Bulgarian Psychologists provided a critical view of the book and demonstrated that reparative therapy does not have supporters among the leading Bulgarian psychologists.

VIOLENCE

Military

Since January 2007, Bulgaria has had a professional army. Prior to this date, military service was obligatory for men over 18 years old. Before the introduction of the antidiscrimination law in 2004, the Bulgarian military openly discriminated against gay men by treating homosexuality as a psychological disorder. The military recruiting commissions used to ask the sexual orientation of the young men, and those who confessed that they were gay were considered ineligible for military service. In practice, many gay men took advantage of this fact to avoid compulsory military service, because it was widely known that the army could not guarantee protection for gay soldiers. However, a confession was sometimes not enough. The person was asked to prove that he was gay, and usually sent for a series of psychological tests. Eyewitnesses report that the appearance of the person was usually the decisive factor in determining whether he was telling the truth about his sexual orientation in front of the military commission. Many straight-looking gay men have passed their military service without any complications, while non-straight-looking men have had problems in the army regardless of their sexual orientation.

A letter from BGO Gemini certifying that the man is a member of the organization and self-identifies as gay could also serve as a tool for releasing someone form the army by the military doctors. Although BGO Gemini is against the medicalization of homosexuality, it used to provide this form of support to young gay men who wanted to avoid entering the army due to fear of harassment.

OUTLOOK FOR THE 21ST CENTURY

The legal situation of LGBT people in Bulgaria is expected to gradually improve in line with European Union directives. Registered domestic partnership law and same-sex marriage law may come to pass in the 2010s. At the same time, the social attitude towards gay people will not be expected to change for the better in conjunction with the new laws. Recent surveys show a very high level of intolerance among heterosexual Bulgarians towards LGBT groups. The relatively rare reports of LGBT-related violence can be explained by incomplete statistics on hate crimes, and by the low visibility of the groups in question. If the visibility of the average gay, lesbian, bisexual, and transsexual person increases in public places beyond the night clubs and the pop-star environment, violence against such people may also rise, as it has in countries with stronger LGBT movements.

"I have nothing against gay people as long as they do not demonstrate their gayness in front of everybody" is a common saying in Bulgaria these days, which describes the most widespread attitude. Based on this, it could be expected that the LGBT population will remain invisible during the next few years, with occasional appearances of LGBT personalities, mainly in the spheres of art and pop culture.

RESOURCE GUIDE

Organizations/Web Sites

BG-Lesbian, http://www.bg-lesbian.com.
> The only lesbian community Web site in Bulgaria, launched in 2002 by Patricia Vassileva-Elia. Provides enlightening and entertaining reading, forums, personal profiles, and so on.

Bilitis Lesbian and Bi-Women Resource Center, http://www.bg-lesbian.com/bilitis.
> Legally registered in 2004, Bilitis organizes lesbian leadership camps, self-support groups, and some cultural events aimed to improve the visibility of lesbians and bisexual women in society.

Bulgarian Gay Organization Gemini, http://www.bgogemini.org.
> The leading Bulgarian advocacy organization for LGBT rights.

Gay.Bg, http:// www.gay.bg.
> The most frequently visited commercial gay site in Bulgaria.

LGBT Idea, http://www.lgbt-idea.org.
> The most recently formed LGBT support organization in Bulgaria, currently operating an online radio station and a virtual cultural center.

Q Files, http://www.qfiles.net/bg/browse.php.
> The LGBT Idea Association's comprehensive bibliography of articles and books published in the Bulgarian language that discuss LGBT issues. The bibliography contains both articles by Bulgarian authors and that have been translated into Bulgarian.

Sports Group Tangra, http://www.tangra-bulgaria.org.
> The best known gay sports group in Bulgaria, most active in organizing sports events and liaising with international LGBT sports organizations.

NOTES

1. CIA, "Bulgaria," *World Factbook,* https://www.cia.gov/library/publications/the-world-factbook/geos/bu.html.

2. Ibid.

3. Commission for Protection from Discrimination. As printed before its official publication at the Web site of the Commission. State Commission for Protection from Discrimination. Unpublished report used by permission, http://kzd-nondiscrimination.com/.

4. Aksinia Gencheva (director of BGO Gemini), interview conducted by BGO Gemini, November 21, 2007.

5. CIA, "Bulgaria."

6. Gencheva, interview.

7. The Ministry of Foreign Affairs of the Netherlands promotes the strengthening of civil society in Central and Eastern Europe. The name of the MATRA Programme derives from the Dutch for social transformation, "maatschappelijke transformatie." Projects are designed to help strengthen institutions and build the capacity of central government, local authorities, and, above all, civil society organizations. Programs also seek to improve interaction between national and local government and civil society, and to encourage consensus on measures to strengthen democracy and the rule of law. MATRA is based on the philosophy of institution-building by developing and strengthening twinning networks between the Netherlands and the MATRA target countries and encourages "matchmaking"

between Dutch organizations and like-minded "agents of transformation." Dutch Ministry of Foreign Affairs, http://www.minbuza.nl/en/europeancooperation/subsidies,The-Matra-Programme.html.

8. Balkan Assist Association for Partnership and Citizen Activity Support, "Civil Society without the Citizens:/ An Assessment of the Bulgarian Civil Society 2003–2005," report, http://www.balkanassist.bg/Attachments/Doc_47/Civil%20Society%20Index%20 report%20-%20part%201%20(en).pdf (accessed December 14, 2007).

9. Project Report, Queer Bulgaria Foundation, http://www.q-net.or.at/img//004 ae86ae45d6cd8.pdf (accessed September 9, 2009).

10. UNAIDS-Bulgaria, http://www.unaids-bulgaria.org/index.php?magic=1.40.0.0 (accessed December 14, 2007).

CROATIA

Sanja Juras and Kristijan Grđan

OVERVIEW

The Republic of Croatia is located in eastern Europe. It is bordered by the Adriatic Sea to the west, Slovenia and Hungary in the north, Serbia to the east, and Bosnia and Herzegovina to the south. The mainland covers 21,851 square miles, and the surface area of its territorial waters totals 11,995 square miles. According to national statistical data there are 4,437,460 inhabitants in the Republic of Croatia.[1] In the Republic of Croatia, 88 percent of citizens belong to Catholic religion. The Muslim religion is represented at 1.27 percent, and Greek-Catholic at 0.9 percent.[2] The national revenues for 2006 amounted in US$17,972,425,660.[3] According to Ministry of Defence data, the armed forces are composed of 32,886 regular soldiers and 32,360 reservists.

The first appearance of colonists at the geographical territory of Croatia dates from the 7th century. Under the Byzantine Empire, the colonists served in forces against the Avars; that in the first decades of the 7th century, Croatians united to combat the Avars has been established. The first known Croatian duke was Duke Višeslav at the beginning of the 9th century. Croatia was divided into two parts—Pannonia and coastal Croatia. At the beginning of the 10th century, the Croatian Empire was established by Duke Tomislav of the Trpimirović Dynasty. Duke Tomislav unified Pannonia and coastal Croatia. In the year 925, Duke Tomislav became the first king of the Croatian Empire and was confirmed by Pope Ivan X. The history of the Croatian Empire involved a number of conflicts, leading to the

separation of the Dalmatian parts of the territory. In the 10th century, the feudal regime was established. At the end of the 11th century, the Hungarian king Koloman conquered the Croatian Empire and, at the beginning of the 12th century, he made an agreement with 12 elders of the Croatian tribes, who confirmed him as a king of Croatia and Dalmatia. Although Croatia lost its independence and became part of the Hungarian Empire, it still maintained some of its attributes. Croatian remained part of the Hungarian Empire until the 18th century.

From the beginning of the 19th to the beginning of the 20th century, Croatia attempted to establish its independence; however, after 1848, it joined the Habsburg Monarchy. Just before the end of World War I in 1918, the Croatian parliament ended its relationship with the Habsburg Monarchy. The National Council of the State decided to join Serbia and Montenegro. Therefore, the Kingdom of Serbs, Croats, and Slovenians was established. In 1929, King Aleksandar proclaimed a dictatorship and established the Kingdom of Yugoslavia. King Aleksandar died in 1934, and Croatia was granted some autonomy in 1939.

After obtaining support from Germany, Italy, and Japan, the Croatian Party of Radical Rightists took power and established the Independent Republic of Croatia in 1941, led by Ante Pavelić. His regime implemented the Nuremberg Laws, established eight concentration camps, and started a campaign to eliminate Serbs, Jews, and Roma.

After the end of World War I, Croatia joined the Federal Republic of Yugoslavia in 1945, led by Josip Broz Tito, who had established the Communist Yugoslav party in 1941. After Tito died in 1980, political, ethnic, and economic problems appeared.

In 1990, Croatia's first democratic elections were held and the Croatian Democrat Party, led by its president Franjo Tuđman, took power. The first session of the Croatian parliament was held on May 30, 1990, when the Croatian constitution passed. In 1991, after Croatia declared independence from Yugoslavia, the Great Serbian Forces (extremists that were located in Croatia), Yugoslavian National Army, Serbia, and Montenegro formed an alliance to wage war against Croatia.

Some parts of Croatia were occupied by the Yugoslavian National Army, and had to be reintegrated under Croatian authority by military force. The conflicts in the territory of the Republic of Croatia had tremendous impact on the Croatian, Serbian, and Bosnian peoples. As the war progressed, numerous Croatian cities, including Dubrovnik, Zagreb, Karlovac, and Vukovar were bombarded by Serbian military forces. Some sources show that about 550,000 Croats were internally displaced, 150,000 became refugees, 13,233 persons were killed, and 1,149 persons are still missing.

Ethnic cleansing had taken place on both sides. Genocide and other crimes against humanity marked recent Croatian history and influenced political disturbances in regard to the Croatian position in the war. While some considered war to be necessary for Croatian independence and believe that Croatia committed no crimes against humanity, others think that Croatia did commit war crimes and that they should be properly redressed. Such a political situation brought Croatia into conflict with international standards and procedures while considering full collaboration with the International Criminal Tribunal for Yugoslavia. This all had an impact on the international position of the Republic of Croatia, especially in relation to the European Union (EU).

Although Croatia seemed to be developing into a modern democracy, its first president, Franjo Tuđman, ruled by authority. He was head of the Croatian

Democratic Party and had very conservative attitudes. His government promoted Catholic fundamentalism, which made Croatia one of the countries with the strongest international contracts with the Holy See. After President Tuđman died in 1999, parliamentary elections brought in a more leftist-to-centre oriented government in 2001; at that point Croatia started actual democratic reform. This strongly influenced freedom of the press and the separation of the media from governing structures.

In its recent history, Croatia has established good relations with the international community and started the process of obtaining membership in the European Union. Many reforms have been undertaken to change the state administration, strengthen the efficiency of the judiciary, combat corruption, and develop the state economy. The majority of these reforms only exist on paper—while the fundamental legal documents have been drafted and provisions of the Acquis Communitaire for EU accession were followed, there are no efficient mechanisms to enforce the legal provisions. Despite these difficulties, Croatia is currently regarded as a potential member of the European Union.

OVERVIEW OF LGBT ISSUES

Homosexual relations between adults in Croatia were decriminalized in 1977. However, the Croatian penal system has still implemented the criminal offence of *unnatural fornication,* where the age of consent is not equal for heterosexual and homosexual relations. Therefore, the age of consent for heterosexual relations was 14 years, whereas for homosexual relations it was 18 years. Such practices were changed in 1998, when changes in the criminal code came into force.

The first positive legal changes toward the protection of LGBT people from discrimination came in 2003 when Gender Equality Act[4] passed in the Croatian parliament. The Gender Equality Act prohibits discrimination on the grounds of sex, sexual orientation, and family or marital status. In the same year, the Same-Sex Civil Unions Act came in force—it recognizes same-sex union as a legal category, although the scope of rights assigned to same-sex partners is very narrow. From 2003 to the present, nondiscrimination provisions on the ground of sexual orientation were implemented in a number of legal documents—the Labour Act, Media Act, Civil Servants Act, Croatian Radio-Television Act, Electronic Media Act, and so on. In 2007, the Volunteers' Act, prohibiting discrimination on the grounds of gender identity and gender expression, came into force.

The issue of so-called gay marriages appeared mostly after 2002, especially during the procedure of adopting the Same-Sex Civil Unions Act. The passing of that legal document was opposed by the conservative political parties and the Catholic Church. Since this legal document recognized only 2 percent of the rights assigned to married and cohabiting opposite-sex partners, the civil society organizations Iskorak and Kontra initiated parliamentary discussion on a registered partnership act in 2006. However, this legal proposition induced a strong reaction by the leading conservative party, and did not pass in the parliament. The Same-Sex Civil Unions Act remained in force while civil society organizations that provide direct legal help to LGBT people count number of cases where same-sex partners were not treated equally as married couples in rights to inheritance, pension and health insurance, tax benefits, decision making in urgent medical situations, and so on.

In Croatia, there are no restrictions for gay and lesbian people in uniformed services (armed forces, police, and security). Current ordinances on health capability, according to the 10th revised edition of the International Classification of Diseases (ICD) of the World Health Organization (WHO), do not mention homosexuality as a mental disorder. Therefore, homosexuality does not represent a contraindication to working in uniformed services.

However, some Croatian psychiatrists do not follow principles set by the WHO. In 2003, the eminent Croatian psychiatrist, Vladimir Gruden said that homosexuality is a medical disorder; for this statement, he was reprimanded by the Croatian Medical Chamber. Scientific discussions as to whether homosexuality is a psychiatric disorder or not appear quite often in the Croatian academic community. While some accept modern scientific standards, others argue that removing homosexuality from the ICD was the result of political pressure by the homosexual lobby, and that this has no scientific value.

One of the most prominent issues in Croatia has been the debate on sex education. From 1997, Teen STAR, a comprehensive sex education program, has been implemented in public elementary and high schools. The program was negatively assessed by the Office of the Ombudswoman for Children and the Office of the Ombudswoman for Gender Equality because it was determined that the program is discriminatory on the grounds of sex, sexual orientation, and family status. The Ministry of Science, Education, and Sport never implemented comprehensive sex education in public schools, but rather shifted its responsibility to civil society organizations, mainly grounded on Christian principles of morality.

EDUCATION

The Croatian education system does not fulfill the basic conditions for educating children to respect human rights. School textbooks contain gender stereotypes and do not address the rights of sexual or any other minorities.

The Schoolbooks Rules were adopted on January 17, 2007. Under provision 2.4—"Ethical Demands," it is stated that a schoolbook shall contain the richness of diversity of Croatian society, shall enable gaining knowledge on the equality of individuals and social groups, and promote the right to diversity.[5]

Also listed are demands in regard to national, ethnic, and religious minorities, as well as gender equality, but sexual minorities are not specially mentioned and there are no demands listed in regard to that subject. Having in mind that the previous Schoolbooks Rules from the year 2003 contained an antidiscrimination provision that explicitly referred to sexual orientation, this is certainly a step backwards.

Although the National Policy for Gender Equality 2006–2010 (NN, nr. 114/06) elaborates upon gender-sensitive education, but does not address sexual and gender minorities. Furthermore, the policy mentions a need for expanding health education to include human sexuality, with an emphasis on sexually transmitted diseases.

In 2003, the Ministry of Science, Education, and Sport prescribed the program of episcopal subjects, in which it was stated that homosexuality is a wrong aspect of sexuality; it was included in the same category as prostitution, incest, and pedophilia.[6] After the intervention of the Team for Legal Changes, the gender equality ombudswoman advised the ministry to reevaluate such a program. The ministry followed the ombudswoman's recommendation, in a way; it changed the description from wrong to sinful.

There is no sexual education in Croatian public schools as a separate subject. Some aspects of sexuality are discussed in different subjects, mainly biology and catechism. In the subject of biology, human sexuality is explained in relation to the anatomy and physiology of the human organism. Further insight into human sexuality from a biological perspective is given in eighth grade through the themes of the structure and function of reproductive organs, conception and prenatal child development, and responsible sexual behavior, according to the teaching plan and program for elementary school of the Ministry of Science, Education, and Sport. The same program includes elements of sexual education for seventh and eighth grades in catechism through the themes of the dignity of the human body and matrimonial purity, friendship and love, and marriage and celibacy.[7]

A few programs directed toward human sexuality were provided in public schools by nongovernmental organizations (NGOs) with the support of the Ministry of Science, Education, and Sport. The most important is the program Teen STAR, introduced into elementary and high schools on the recommendation of the Croatian Episcopal Conference. In mid-2004, the civil society organizations Iskorak and Kontra evaluated the Teen STAR program and concluded that it is discriminatory toward LGBT people, women, and single-parent families.[8] Such a conclusion was also made by the ombudswoman for children, who found the program to be contrary to the Convention on the Rights of the Child. The same conclusion was made by the gender equality ombudswoman. Meanwhile, Teen STAR is still implemented in Croatian schools.

On September 15, 2006, the Ministry of Science, Education, and Sport introduced the Decision on the Educational Plan and Program for Primary Schools, which also regulates the content of the optional subject Catholic religious teaching.[9] In this program, there is no explicit discriminatory content as there is in the Catholic religious reaching syllabus from 2003. However, the new program emphasizes heterosexuality, making its implementation questionable from the perspective of discrimination against sexual minorities.

The Ministry of Science, Education, and Sport shifted responsibility for creating the program of health education, including a module on human sexuality, to Civil Society Organizations (CSOs). On November 2, 2007, it signed a contract to purchase the proposal of an experimental program of health education from the CSO Citizens Initiative for Democratic Changes (GROZD). The program mentioned was judged by the Office of the Ombudswoman for Gender Equality and the Office of the Ombudswoman for Children to be discriminatory in regards to sexual identity, sexual orientation, and marital status, and therefore contrary to the Constitution of the Republic of Croatia and the Convention on the Rights of the Child. In spite of this, the program will be implemented in both primary and secondary schools. After negotiations with the ministry on November 26, the contract was also signed by the Forum for the Freedom of Education. This program is heteronormative, but it does not contain negative references to sexual minorities or masturbation, and therefore was evaluated as liberal. It will be implemented only in secondary schools, and parents can choose whether or not their child will attend the more liberal program. The program is being implemented in Croatian schools in the 2008–2009 school years.

About 35 percent of children in Croatian schools face some kind of bullying.[10] There is only anecdotal evidence on homophobic bullying in public schools. In such cases, young students have reported abuse from their peers. There are many measures aimed at the prevention of bullying among students; however, no special measures have been undertaken to address homophobic bullying.

EMPLOYMENT AND ECONOMICS

In 2007, the Croatian Institute for Employment recorded more than 250,000 unemployed persons. Generally, the problems of LGBT people do not arise from lack of employment opportunities, but rather from discrimination when it is discovered that the employee or person seeking employment is homosexual.

In 2003, provisions of the Labor Act had been changed in order to ensure protection from discrimination related to sexual orientation in the workplace. Discrimination on the basis of sexual orientation in the workplace was prohibited, and any mistreatment of an employee for that reason was also considered discrimination. The victim of discrimination in the workplace could request compensation for damages through a civil lawsuit. Such discrimination could also be criminally prosecuted.

Generally, victims lack the knowledge about legal mechanisms that could be used to protect their labor rights, and rarely engage in criminal prosecution or civil lawsuits against their employer.

In relation to legal regulations, there are no prohibitions for homosexuals to serve in the police or the army. The only exception is for posts within the organizational structure of the Catholic Church, where it is not illegal to discriminate against someone on the basis of sexual orientation. The person who is discriminated against on the basis of sexual orientation, or on some other grounds, where the Catholic Church is an employer, could not seek legal protection since Croatia has bilateral agreements with the Holy See that allows the Catholic Church to operate independently from national antidiscrimination legislation.

SOCIAL/GOVERNMENT PROGRAMS

There is no government program in Croatia specifically aimed at the protection of the rights of sexual and gender minorities. Some measures regarding the rights of sexual minorities have been implemented in the National Politic for Promotion of Gender Equality 2006–2010 (NN, nr. 114/06) and in the National Program for the Protection and Promotion of Human Rights 2008–2011.

The National Politic for Promotion of Gender Equality contains only two measures aimed at combating discrimination based on sexual orientation. The first measure prescribes conducting research into judicial practice and police conduct in regards to criminal offenses motivated by the sexual orientation of the injured party. The second measure prescribes that representatives of organizations for the rights of sexual and gender minorities will be included in working bodies for adopting laws, programs, and strategies connected to the rights of sexual minorities. Both measures were adopted by the government as a result of advocacy by Kontra, Iskorak, and the Women's Network of Croatia.

The two adopted measures were not implemented in 2007. Nothing in regard to the first measure was made public by implementing institutions, although the deadline for its implementation was 2007. That the second measure would never be implemented became clear during the creation of the proposal of the National Program for the Protection and Promotion of Human Rights, and also during the creation of the proposal for the Anti-discrimination Act, when representatives of organizations for the rights of sexual minorities were not included in working groups, as prescribed in the measure.[11]

The National Program for the Protection and Promotion of Human Rights 2008–2011 contains three measures aimed at the "improvement of legislation" and "increasing tolerance towards sexual and gender minorities."[12] The prescribed measures are not in concordance with the aims. The only effect that can be achieved by the prescribed measures in regard to the first aim is the determination of the existing condition by analysis of the legislation, but without any actions for its improvement. From the government's previous work, it is easy to conclude that the measures aimed at increasing tolerance will result in a few politically harmless events, focused at maintaining the existing conditions in legislation, with little media coverage. Therefore, the aim will not be achieved. Out of three measures, the Governmental Office for Human Rights took the role of the implementing body for only one measure, and that also happened after a critique from Iskorak and Kontra: "98th Aim: To raise tolerance towards sexual and gender minorities, Implementing bodies: The Governmental Office on Gender Equality and the Governmental Office for Human Rights."[13]

One of the main critiques of Croatia by the European Commission was its failure to adopt a national strategic and action plan for combating discrimination. The European Commission, in its progress report on Croatia, notes homophobic incidents and lack of decisiveness of the state in combating the problem of discrimination.

SEXUALITY/SEXUAL PRACTICES

The majority of resources in relation to sexuality refer to young people and women. No research has been conducted to clarify the attitudes of general population in Croatia towards sexuality.

Between 2001 and 2003, the Centre for Education, Counselling, and Research conducted a two-year study on adolescent sexuality. The results showed that young men and women have similar expectations of sexual relationships. Of the respondents, 39.4 percent had had previous sexual experience—50.7 percent of them were young men and 27 percent of them were young women. The young women entered sexual relationships later than young men. While young women have their first sexual experience in a long-term relationship, young men have such an experience in a one-night-stand relationship, usually having consumed alcohol and drugs immediately before. However, more young men than young women responded that they used a condom when they first had sexual intercourse. Forty-eight percent of male respondents and 36 percent of female respondents declared that they always use condoms during sexual intercourse.[14]

In 2005 the Women's Room, a CSO working for the sexual rights of women, conducted a study to determine the status these rights in Croatia (N = 1,491). The results showed that more than 50 percent of women have never participated in any education on sexuality, while the majority of them are actually informed on their sexual rights. More than 60 percent of women had three or fewer sexual partners, and 49 percent of women are generally satisfied with their sexual life. More than 30 percent of women had had sexual experiences involving one night stands. Eighty-four percent of respondents identified as heterosexual and

7 percent had had same-sex experience. In terms of contraception, 66 percent of women did not use any kind of protection the first time they had sexual intercourse. In everyday life, about 45 percent of respondents between the ages of 18 and 50 use contraception—52 percent use condoms and 18 percent use the pill or other hormonal therapies. More than 60 percent of respondents have children, and 31 percent of them have two children. Seventy-seven percent of women planned to become pregnant. In terms of sexual violence, women mostly recognized unwanted physical contact (94%) and forced sexual intercourse (91%). They tended to believe that, in a rape situation, a woman has to engage in strong physical resistance against the sexual perpetrator (36%), that she will have severe physical injuries (32%), and that perpetrator will be an unknown maniac (32%). In 40 percent of women who had experienced sexual violence, however, the perpetrator of sexual violence was partner, in 12 percent it was a family member, in 34 percent a superior at workplace, and in 67 percent an unknown person.[15]

In 2007 the faculties of law and humanities and social sciences, University of Zagreb, published the results of a study aimed to assess negative attitudes towards homosexuality in 31 European countries; the Republic of Croatia was among these. The results showed that, in Croatia, 52.8 percent of respondents would not like to have homosexual neighbor.[16]

In 2008, the Faculty of Humanities and Social Sciences, University of Zagreb, finished a study aimed at exploring a theoretical model relating to the effects of sexually explicit materials (SEM). A survey was conducted that included 650 young Croatian men, aged 15 to 25. The study suggested that "there may be important links between early SEM exposure, sexual socialization and sexual satisfaction— particularly among men with specific SEM preferences." It concluded that "the importance of comprehensive sex education that would address the issue of contemporary pornography should not be disregarded. Inclusion of contents designed to improve media literacy among young people and help them to critically evaluate pornographic images, as well as fantasies and fears they produce, could be invaluable to advancing young people's sexual well being. Neither moral accusations, nor uncritical glorification of contemporary pornography can do the job."[17]

In the context of National Response to HIV/AIDS, a special prevention program for students in elementary and high-schools, MEMOAIDS, has been implemented. The program was created with the support of the Global Fund for HIV/ AIDS, Tuberculosis, and Malaria.[18] At the beginning of 2004, the Croatian Episcopal Conference issued a statement against the program, arguing that it does not follow principles of Christian ethics.

FAMILY

There is no definition of family in Croatian legislation. The Family Act does not contain such a definition. According to article 1 of the act, it regulates marriage, relations between parents and children, adoption, guardianship, effects of the extramarital union between a man and a woman, and procedures of relevant institutions in regards to family relations and guardianship.

Provisions in other acts refer to certain members of the family in terms of prescribing rights and obligations (for example, the Inheritance Act, Asylum Act, Protection of Rights of Patients Act, etc.). Such provisions include married partners in all cases, include unmarried opposite-sex partner almost half of the time, and do not include same-sex partners at all.

The legal provisions follow a traditional perspective regarding family, which is usually recognized as the union of a man and a woman and their children. In 2005, there were 22,138 registered marriages and 4,883 divorces in total.[19] There is evidence of a high prevalence of domestic violence. In the period from 2001 to 2006, 1,807 persons were convicted for domestic violence as a criminal offence, and 719 persons for domestic violence as a misdemeanor.[20]

The Same-Sex Civil Unions Act provides same-sex partners with only two rights: the right to joint ownership of property and the right to financial support. In order to obtain those rights, partners have to prove the existence of their union within three years according to court procedure. There is only one case noted by CSOs Iskorak and Kontra in relation to implementation of the Same-Sex Civil Unions Act since it came into force in 2003. This was a case in which the partners wanted to move to another country and needed written evidence of the existence of their union for visa requirements. For that purpose, they used a contract for the regulation of property rights from the Same-Sex Civil Unions Act. The contract referred to a television and a watch.

According to the Family Act, married heterosexual partners can adopt a child together. A heterosexual partner can also adopt the child of their partner from a previous marriage, provided there is consent from the former partner. A single person can adopt a child only if it is of a special benefit for the child. The adoption procedure in Croatia is long and complicated, and there are few cases where a single person is able to adopt a child. It is not prescribed under the Family Act that same-sex partners can adopt a child. The ombudswoman for children in 2006 made homophobic statements advocating that same-sex couples be denied the right to adopt children.[21]

COMMUNITY

In the late 1970s and early 1980s, the first positive media articles on homosexuality appeared in Croatia. Those articles were written by women involved in the feminist movement. Articles on homosexuality were published in periodicals and student magazines. In Croatia, the lesbian movement emerged directly from the feminist movement. In feminist groups, lesbians first found safe places to gather and discuss specific issues. In 1989, the first lesbian group, Lila Initiative, was founded in Croatia and started with its work as a part of Trešnjevka Women's Group. The daily newspaper *Vjesnik* and two student magazines reported on their work. Their articles were written in an affirmative manner, and for the first time, the rights of lesbians were mentioned, as well as the positions of political parties on homosexuality.

Due to the first democratic elections and the war that lasted from 1990–1995, the 1990s involved great social change for Croatia; it was also a period of strong nationalism and great Catholic influence on state politics. The beginning of the war caused the termination of lesbian activism in 1990. Lila Initiative lost its work facilities. Public discussion was focused exclusively on the war and the political situation in the country.

A breakthrough came in 1992, when the first lesbian and gay group, LIGMA (Lesbian and Gay Men Action), was founded. Members of LIGMA appeared in the media, organized public panels, and published a brochure in the magazine for the Antiwar Campaign of Croatia (AWCC). Nevertheless, in 1993, LIGMA ceased its activities and its publicly known members moved abroad. Until the end of 1990s, the subject of homosexuality was covered in the media in a sensationalistic manner, as something exotic and highly stereotyped.

In 1997, the lesbian group Kontra was founded. This group started the first lesbian emergency information hotline. Since there were no members willing to speak publicly, only the establishment of Kontra and a small number of its events were covered by the media.

In May 2002, Kontra, together with the newly founded group Iskorak started advocating for redrafting the Family Act to alter the definitions of marriage and cohabitation to include same-sex partners. For the first time in many years, representatives of CSOs for the rights of sexual and gender minorities came out in public and advocated for changes in legislation. Public discussion on sexual and gender minorities entered a political context. LORI (Lesbian Organization Rijeka, founded in 2001) also conducted the national awareness campaign Love is Love in 2002.

In June 2002, Kontra and Iskorak organized the first gay pride demonstration as a part of their advocacy activities. The name of the event combined both names of the organizations: Gay Pride 2002: Coming out/Stepping out Against Prejudices (Iskorak Kontra Predrasuda). The minister of the interior, MPs (members of parliament) from different parties, the UN human rights commissioner, and representatives of different human rights organizations from Croatia, the regions of the former Yugoslavia, and abroad, attended the first gay pride demonstration in Croatia on June 29, 2002. Approximately 200–300 people participated. To secure police protection, Kontra and Iskorak put media pressure on the police by publicly asking the minister of the interior how the event would be protected and stated how this would be a test of democracy for Croatia. Participants in Gay Pride 2002 were protected by specially trained police officers in shields and helmets. In fact, there were three policemen for every participant in the event! During the march through the center of Zagreb, citizens and skinheads were shouting and throwing rocks, watermelon, and ashtrays from the cafe bars at the participants. During political speeches held in Zrinjevac Square, a tear gas bomb was thrown. When the event came to an end, the police dispersed, and 27 people were physically attacked while returning home. This demonstration of violence against sexual and gender minorities at the first gay pride march in Croatia was crucial for public recognition of the oppression of sexual and gender minorities in Croatian society. The media reported on the first gay pride march in Croatia by condemning violence against sexual minorities and focusing on LGBT human rights.

Media attention to Gay Pride 2002 and public appearances of activists from Kontra and Iskorak demanding changes in Croatian legislation put pressure on the Croatian government. Cooperation between Iskorak and Kontra and the Ministry of Labor and Social Welfare on the issue of regulating of same-sex civil unions was established. As a result of that cooperation, the Same-Sex Partnerships Bill was drafted, and finally adopted by the Croatian parliament on July 14, 2003.

In the following years, more and more LGBT organizations evolved with different scopes of work.

HEALTH

The HIV/AIDS epidemic is not only a public health problem in Croatia but also the problem of global society. It may have great impact on the economy, especially in countries with a high rate of HIV prevalence among the general population.

People living with HIV and AIDS commonly face stigma and discrimination, and are often on the social margin; this is especially true for gay men who are living with HIV and AIDS.

In Croatia, there is a low prevalence of HIV in the general population. Data from the Croatian Institute of Public Health show that the first people living with HIV in Croatia were detected in 1985.[22] From 1985 to 2006, 608 persons living with HIV and AIDS were registered in the Republic of Croatia, and 137 have since died. According to research conducted in 2006, the prevalence of HIV among gay men was 4.5 percent, therefore confirming the low prevalence of the epidemic in the Croatian gay community. Numbers will increase, however, with the increased ability of men to travel outside of the country, where HIV/AIDS is more widespread, for sexual encounters.

According to results of recent behavioral studies, gay men are inclined to practice risky sexual behavior. Out of 1,120 respondents, 75 percent considered the condom to be effective protection, but 39 percent of them did not use a condom the last time they had anal intercourse.[23]

Unlike in the United States, where the HIV epidemic caused the development of civil organizations advocating for the rights and sexual health of sexual minorities, in Croatia, special preventive health programs for men who have sex with men (MSM) started after advocacy NGOs had been established. More resources and financial support are provided to establish health programs aimed at preventing the spread of HIV than for advocacy or other activities of CSOs dealing with sexual and gender minorities. The majority of preventive health programs for sexually transmitted diseases (STDs) are HIV/AIDS-specific and directed towards MSM, while in regard especially to other STDs lesbians are not covered. Therefore there is lack of reliable data on spread of syphilis, gonorrhea, and other STDs among lesbians.

In regards to MSM, recent studies showed a high prevalence of syphilis, indicating that there is a concentrated epidemic of this disease in this population. However, we have to be very careful while interpreting this data, since there is no accurate information on the prevalence of syphilis among the heterosexual population. Since the Croatian Institute of Public Health records about 20 syphilis cases from the general population annually, many cases might be underreported.

Reparative therapy to cure homosexuality in the Republic of Croatia existed during Soviet times, when homosexuality was considered to be a mental disorder. Although the Diagnostic and Statistical Manual (DSM) of the American Psychiatric Society excluded homosexuality as a mental disorder in 1973, Croatian psychiatrists still saw it as a mental illness. In 1973, homosexual sex was still considered as unnatural fornication and criminally persecuted in Croatia. Homosexuality and lesbianism were commonly treated as psychiatric disorders until 1992, when the WHO changed its ICD. Although homosexuality per se was no longer considered a mental disorder, many psychiatrists still considered it as such, viewing it as the cause of other mental disorders and pathological conditions. Therefore, many eminent Croatian scholars who published in the period after 1992 insisted that homosexuality was a mental disorder and could be effectively treated.

At the end of 2002, Vladimir Gruden, professor of psychiatry of the Faculty of Medicine at the University of Zagreb, publicly stated that homosexuality is a mental disorder.[24] Iskorak and Kontra asked the Croatian Psychologists' Association to issue an opinion as to whether it is or not. In 2003, the same organizations issued a complaint before the Croatian Medical Chamber, requesting disciplinary proceedings against Gruden. The Croatian Psychologists' Association responded that psychologists do not consider homosexuality per se to be mental disorder. The Croatian Medical Chamber agreed with such an opinion, and stated that Gruden only expressed his personal opinion, and that he would emphasize that such an opinion is not in line with scientific truth. However, no disciplinary sanction was declared against Gruden.[25]

In 2007, the eminent child psychology expert Dubravka Kocijan-Hercigonja of the Faculty of Medicine of the University of Zagreb was interviewed about homosexuality by a journalist from the Catholic newspaper *Glas Koncila*. Kocijan-Hercigonja stated that, according to the DSM and ICD classifications, homosexuality is considered a gender identity disorder and could be effectively treated. After Iskorak and Kontra issued a complaint to the Croatian Medical Chamber, the institution responded that they found no violation of the code of medical ethics and deontology.

Iskorak and Kontra's Team for Legal Changes also received some complaints from people who had undergone psychiatric treatment. They were usually minors who complained that their parents forced them to undergo such psychiatric treatment. After changes to the criminal code came into force in October 2006, medically unjustifiable intervention was considered a criminal offense, and the offender could be punished by imprisonment from six months to three years. Psychiatric treatment of the homosexuality of minors, however, was never challenged in that way.

In Croatia, transsexuality is treated as a gender identity disorder according to the ICD classification, and psychiatric treatment is provided for it. The process of transitioning from one gender to another through psychiatric and then surgical procedure remains unclear. It is known that transsexual persons can receive full treatment, including surgery, only after being diagnosed with gender identity disorder.

Transsexuality is usually mixed up with homosexuality, and one of the symptoms of gender identity disorder is so-called homosexual panic. Some public health institutions in Croatia argue that gender identity disorder is, in fact, a reflection of the incapability of a young person to find the ideal of his or her own gender in his or her parents. The similar situation could be applied to girls. Some professionals attribute the cause of homosexuality to the same theory. The national NGOs are not skilled, and have no resources to provide such evaluation and expertise. It can simply be concluded that the Croatian medical profession often perpetuates prejudices and that some basic standards are not generally followed, such as those provided by WHO.

Intersexuality is primarily considered in the Republic of Croatia to be a somatic medical disorder that can be treated by surgical intervention. General health insurance covers surgical correction for congenital anomalies. Following the standard practice in such cases, however, children born with ambiguous sex organs are usually surgically reassigned as females. There is common opinion that the decision to choose his or her sex is rarely left to the child, and usually is made immediately after birth. The exact statistical number of intersexual births is not known.

POLITICS AND LAW

Cooperation between Iskorak and Kontra and the Ministry of Labor and Social Welfare on the issue of regulating of same-sex civil unions has been established. As a result of this, the Same-Sex Partnerships Bill was drafted, and finally adopted by the Croatian parliament on July 14, 2003.

During the advocacy campaign for the Same-Sex Partnership Act, CSOs also advocated for the implementation of antidiscrimination provisions in Croatian legislation. After the success of the advocacy campaign, the majority of the proposed bills and amendments were adopted in July 2003 by the Croatian parliament. For the first time, sexual minorities were explicitly recognized as a group at risk for a specific kind of discrimination. Discrimination on the basis of the sexual orientation was prohibited in the Gender Equality Act, the penal code, the Labor Act, the Act on Scientific Work and Higher Education, and the Schoolbook Rules. Most of the mentioned laws were approved on the same day by the Croatian parliament, and became valid on July 16, 2003. Due to the appearance of CSO representatives in public, there was an increase of social awareness in Croatia, which led to a certain decrease in discrimination.

Cooperation from the Ministry of Work and Social Welfare was crucial for the success of the advocacy campaign. Regional cooperation, especially with Slovenian and Serbian lesbian and gay organizations, was also very helpful to the Croatian LGBT movement. The main opponents to the movement were the conservative parties and the Catholic Church. The only direct international pressure on the Croatian government came from International Lesbian and Gay Association (ILGA)-Europe, which petitioned the government and parliament just before the parliamentary session on the proposed laws, demanding the acceptance of the proposed LGBT-friendly bill. The campaign for the Same-Sex Partnership Act in Croatia was one of the examples of a successful policy change influenced by CSOs. It is practically impossible to imagine that any political party would propose changes in legislation with respect to the protection of sexual and gender minorities in Croatia at that point. There was no pressure from the EU, UN, or the Organization for Security and Co-operation in Europe (OSCE) on the Croatian government regarding the protection of sexual and gender minorities. After the bills were adopted by the Croatian parliament, CSOs continued monitoring further compliance of Croatian laws with EU standards. They immediately started to monitor the implementation of the new antidiscrimination laws.

After parliamentary elections in November 2003, HDZ (the right-wing Croatian Democratic Union) once again became the leading party in Croatia. This severely affected the advocacy efforts of sexual minorities, CSOs, and the implementation of the existing laws. State institutions had intentionally failed to implement the Same-Sex Partnership Act on every single occasion, and had consistently violated the prohibition of discrimination based on same-sex partnership, regulated by section 21 of the act. CSO amendments to draft acts were not adopted, and state institutions failed to provide same-sex partners with the same rights as heterosexual married and common-law partners while adopting the Act on Inheritance and the Act on Protection of the Rights of Patients in 2004, and the Act on State Officials in 2005.

Nevertheless, there were some breakthroughs in several areas of protection of the rights of sexual minorities in those years. The constitutional court of Croatia invalidated the Media Act and the amendment including sexual orientation in the antidiscrimination article of the act was voted on in parliament on May 10, 2004. The Media Act therefore prohibits discrimination on the grounds of sexual education in public reporting. The Croatian constitutional court also invalidated the new criminal code due to procedural mistakes. Iskorak and Kontra successfully advocated for the new article 20 to be included into the Changes to the Criminal Code Bill, which explicitly included sexual orientation in article 174, "Race and Other

Discrimination," of the criminal code. The changes to the criminal code, including this new change, were voted on in parliament on July 13, 2004.

In 2006, after the successful advocacy of Iskorak and Kontra, with the support of the Women's Network and the Serbian Democratic Forum, a definition of hate crime appeared in article 89 of the criminal code:

> Hate crime is any criminal offence, described in this Act that is motivated by hate against the victim due to his/her race, skin colour, sex, sexual orientation, language, religion, political or other belief, national or social origin, property, birth, education, social status, age, medical status, or other characteristics.[26]

There is no specific recognition of gender identity. Gender identity, however, can be interpreted from the term "other characteristics." Also, if a hate crime is committed because a person was perceived to be gay due to his or her gender expression, it can be defined by the court as a hate crime based on the person's perceived sexual orientation. This puts an obligation on the police and courts to document whether the criminal offense was motivated by hatred. Judges would then have the discretionary right to decide whether to increase the penalty due to that fact or not. Iskorak and Kontra also successfully advocated for an amendment to article 91 of the criminal code, which relates to aggravated murder. It now defines murder motivated by hatred as aggravated murder, and prescribes greater penalties for offenders in comparison to regular murder.

Events around the Registered Partnership Bill in 2006 once again revealed the homophobic attitudes of the Croatian government. On June 15, 2005, Iskorak and Kontra presented a registered partnership bill to the public for the first time at a round table discussion held at the European House in Zagreb, and started a new advocacy campaign for the rights of same-sex partners. The bill was supposed to expand the rights of same-sex partners to include all rights enjoyed by married heterosexual couples, except the right to adopt a child. The bill had support from the start from MPs from the Liberal Party, the Social Democratic Party, and the Croatian Social Liberal Party.

In September 2005, MPs Šime Lučin of the Social Democratic Party and Ivo Banac of the Liberal Party put the Registered Partnership Bill forward into parliamentary procedure. The media reported on these events with great interest. On February 15, 2006, the Parliamentary Committee on Gender Equality discussed the Registered Partnership Bill. Representatives of the Team for Legal Changes were present at the discussion and gave their recommendation to MPs Lucin and Banac to use the newly adopted Resolution on Homophobia in Europe as a part of its argumentation in favor of adoption of the bill. The committee adopted the bill and recommended that the Croatian parliament should adopt it as well. The next day, the Parliamentary Committee for Human Rights discussed the bill. This committee consisted mostly of MPs from the Croatian Democratic Union (HDZ), and they voted against the adoption of the bill. Some of the MPs from the HDZ used homophobic hate speech as an argument against the bill. Niko Rebić of HDZ said, "The main message from the Bible on the subject of homosexuality is that it is Sodom and Gomorra."[27] He further stated that "AIDS is one of the signs of what happens in same-sex partnerships."[28] The media reported on this event.

The government did not support the Partnership Bill in parliament. There was a great amount of inflammatory antigay speech during the debates, mostly from representatives of the leading HDZ party. Lucija Čikeš of HDZ said: "The whole Universe is heterosexual, from the fly to the elephant, from atoms to planets. If it was not so, the Sun would not rotate around the earth, it would fall down and we would all burn!"[29] Some MPs from the leading party did not use such explicit hate speech in their argument against the Registered Partnership Bill. They mostly claimed that the bill is too similar to the Family Act, and that same-sex partners are not a family. They claimed that they would support the proposal if it were written in a form of amendments to the Same-Sex Civil Unions Act. This is why the LGBT movement is starting a new campaign for a proposal of amendments to the Same-Sex Civil Unions Act, containing the same rights as in the previous proposal.

Discrimination based on sexual orientation became explicitly prohibited for the first time in Croatia in July 2003, when a set of antidiscrimination laws was adopted by the parliament. The reason for adopting this new national legislation was to comply with the European Union. Prohibitions of discrimination on the basis of sexual orientation were implemented in the Gender Equality Act, the criminal code, the Labor Act, the Scientific Work and Higher Education Act, and the Schoolbooks Rules. In addition, the Same-Sex Civil Unions Act was passed in July 2003. Unfortunately, all of these acts were adopted by parliament according to the wrong procedure. The criminal code adopted in July 2003 was annulled by the constitutional court, and the new criminal code was voted on in 2004 by the correct procedure. The Gender Equality Act was annulled in 2008, and the new act has still not been adopted at the date of writing of this text.

In 2004, a new article was implemented into the Amendments and Modifications of the Criminal Code Act, which explicitly includes sexual orientation in article 174, "Race and Other Discrimination." The Amendments and Modifications of the Criminal Code Act, including this new change, were adopted by the parliament on July 13, 2004. Parliament also adopted the amendment to the Media Act that referred to sexual orientation on May 10, 2004.

The Labour Act defines direct or indirect discrimination against a person seeking employment or a current employee, and in those definitions, sexual orientation is explicitly mentioned. Harassment, including sexual harassment, constitutes discrimination under the act. Shifting the burden of proof is also included as a measure to combat discrimination under the act.

As an exception to the prohibition of discrimination, it is prescribed that any distinction, exclusion, or preference in respect to a particular job will not be considered discrimination when the nature of the job or conditions in which it is performed are such that characteristics related to particular grounds constitute a genuine and determining occupational requirement.

The Act on Scientific Work and Higher Education prescribes that universities, two-year colleges, and other institutions of higher education must define the procedures of admittance of candidates in a manner that guarantees the equal rights of all candidates, regardless of their sexual orientation.

The Civil Servants Act was adopted in 2005. It includes provisions on the prohibition of discrimination and favoritism in the civil service, and explicitly includes sexual orientation in its enactment on equal treatment and equal opportunities.

The definition of a hate crime was included in article 89 of the criminal code in 2006. The definition explicitly mentions sexual orientation. Furthermore, an amendment was introduced into article 91 of the criminal code that relates to aggravated murder. It now defines murder motivated by hatred as aggravated murder and prescribes greater penalties for offenders in comparison to regular murder. The above mentioned amendments were the result of the initiative of Kontra and Iskorak, as well as the Centre for the Rights of Sexual and Gender Minorities, with the support of the Women's Network of Croatia and the Serbian Democratic Forum.

Article 174, paragraph 3 of the criminal code provides sanctions for the criminal offence of racial or other discrimination in relation to identifying a certain characteristic or group affiliation of an individual as inferior, with the aim of spreading hatred. This article includes sanctions for hate speech. From the experience of Kontra and Iskorak with cases of hate speech, it is important to emphasize that all public attorneys considered the existence of direct intent to be crucial for the realization of this criminal offense, and that this interpretation is truly consistent with the formulation from Article 174, paragraph 3. From the point of view of the public attorneys, the existence of this criminal offense cannot be proven unless the suspect literally admits that he or she had the intention of spreading hatred. In all reported cases, the persons charged claimed that they did not intend to spread hatred, and the criminal proceedings were dropped because of that.[30]

Members of parliament, government representatives, and other state officials consistently use hate speech against sexual minorities in public. For example, in 2006, this practice was noted at the session of the Committee for Human Rights and the session of the Croatian parliament during debates on the Registered Partnership Bill. Numerous MPs, mostly from the leading party Croatian Democratic Union (HDZ), and government representatives used homophobic hate speech while addressing the public and their colleagues. Such homophobic language was reported by the media, and therefore had the effect of stigmatizing same sex-couples and people who are living with HIV and AIDS.

On December 9, 2005, the Croatian parliament adopted the new Changes to Public Assembly Act. The amended act prohibited public assembly in an area of 100 meters (300 feet) from the headquarters of the state institutions at Saint Mark's Square. Anyone that approaches within 100 meters of the buildings housing the Croatian parliament, the president of the Republic of Croatia, and the government, regardless of the purpose and the method of the public assembly or number of participants, or anyone that wishes to forward some request, will be punished with a fine of 5,000 HRK–20,000 HRK (675–2,700 euros, US$963–$3850).

This permanent prohibition of public gatherings, regardless of the number of participants, does not satisfy conditions for restriction of the right to freedom of assembly under the Croatian constitution and international law. The provision does not have the purpose of protecting the public and legal order, but is rather meant to protect state officials from having encounters with citizens. This was proven when activists from Kontra and Iskorak faced misdemeanor proceedings for distributing flyers on the rights of same-sex partners under the campaign We Are Not Homophobic, But...to MPs in front of the parliament. Two days after receiving notification on the first hearing at the court, activists tested the implementation of the act. As a part of the organized action, two other activists were sent to distribute flyers under the same conditions at Saint Mark's Square, but this time the flyers contained an advertisement for a hair salon, and the activists were not disturbed. This clearly proved that the act was directed against the expression of political opinion by citizens and CSOs in front of state institutions.

Even if real danger existed in regard to such gatherings, it would be possible to avoid the danger using other security measures, rather than placing restrictions on the right to peaceful assembly. According to the European Convention for Human Rights and Fundamental Freedoms and the practice of the European Court of Human Rights, the right to public assembly should be ensured even if it could represent some danger, because it is possible to prevent such danger by other measures.[31]

In order to be approved, each public assembly in Croatia has to be reported to the police. The application has to include the purpose, place, date, and time of the peaceful assembly or public protest, as well as the number of security guards and number of participants. Therefore, it should be possible to predict dangers and take measures to prevent possible danger, or to reject a public assembly that would present a danger that could not be prevented by other measures. The general prohibition of any peaceful assembly due to its proximity to state institutions, however, cannot be justified. In the last 15 years, there have been no serious incidents related to public gatherings at Saint Mark's Square. Justification of the measure, however, is explained in the act by global security measures against terrorism after the events of 9/11. The explanation of the act does not contain any indication or evidence that Croatia might become a victim of a terrorist attack. Therefore, the general prohibition of public assembly at Saint Mark's Square, regardless of the nature and circumstances of each individual assembly, represents a violation of the right to public assembly.

RELIGION AND SPIRITUALITY

In Croatia, the Catholic Church has great political influence. This is partially due to the international agreements between Croatia and the Holy See, but also to the attitude and religious identity of the majority. The relationship between Croatia and the Catholic Church has great financial value—the Catholic Church has special tax benefits and benefits from health and pension insurance. The international contracts put Catholic Church in a favorable position in relation to other religions.

The Croatian gay and lesbian community could be divided into nonbelievers and true Catholics. While some religious members of the gay and lesbian community practice sexual relationships, some do not. The religious members usually have conservative political attitudes, but as many of them remain in the closet, they do not organize themselves in civil organizations. Most LGBT NGOs in Croatia take a secular point of view in their work; only one of them has opened dialogue with Catholic Church. It is generally believed by Croatian LGBT organizations that the Catholic Church cannot play any role in political life, especially in regard to the human rights of sexual and gender minorities.

In regard to the rights of sexual and gender minorities, as well as the rights of women, the Catholic Church in Croatia has played an important role in creating the policies related to Catholic and sexual education.

In Croatia, episcopal teaching is a separate subject in public schools. It is a facultative program, and not mandatory for non-Catholic students. The classes are scheduled in the middle of the timetable and the majority of children attend episcopal teaching due to the fact that 90 percent of them are Catholics. Other children, regardless their religious views, attend episcopal teaching due to peer pressure. In 2003, the Ministry of Science, Education, and Sport issued the program of episcopal teaching, which made reference to homosexuality. There, it was clearly stated that homosexuality is the wrong type of sexuality and that it is the same as prostitution, incest, and pedophilia. After national NGOs and the ombudswoman for gender equality stated that such provisions are illegal, the Ministry of Science, Education, and Sport changed the wording from wrong to sinful. Although the ombudswoman for gender equality was not satisfied with such intervention, the program has never been changed in an adequate manner.

At the end of 2003, the strong public debate on sexual education in public schools continued. This was due to the fact that the Ministry of Health and Social Welfare, in collaboration with the Zagreb Clinic for Children's Diseases, produced an HIV/AIDS prevention curriculum for elementary and high schools called MEMOAIDS, and implemented it in some public schools. The main resistance to this program came from the Croatian Episcopal Conference, which argued that MEMOAIDS "actually teaches how to use preventive methods while personality of students and educational dimension of school, which purpose is to bring the student in the integrity of life, is neglected....The Episcopal Bishops argue that pressure towards students and teachers who are believers to implement programs that are strictly contrary to the principles of Christian morality is unacceptable."[32] As an alternative, the Croatian Episcopal Conference recommended the Teen STAR program, which was developed by Sister Hanna Klaus in 1988 and implemented by local Croatian NGOs in 1997.

At the beginning of 2004, Iskorak and Kontra attended the Teen STAR training program and found that it has been implemented in some public elementary and high schools in Croatia since 1997. The program was full of discriminatory references. In the program, it was stated that full development of the personality and sexuality of the child is easier to achieve if the mother is unemployed: "the conclusion is that communication on sexuality is not so important as other qualities of family interactions: connectedness, living in family with both biological parents, mother's unemployment."[33] Furthermore, it was stated that one-parent families are not as valuable as families with a father and a mother. The program also put homosexuality in the same category as sexual abuse: "masturbation, homosexuality and sexual abuse." The NGOs issued a complaint before the ombudswoman for children and the ombudswoman for gender equality, arguing that the program is contrary to international and national legal standards. At the end of 2004, the ombudswoman for children warned the Ministry of Science, Education, and Sport that the program is contrary to the Convention on the Rights of the Child, the Croatian constitution, and numerous national legal regulations. She recommended that the ministry redesign the program to be compliant with mentioned legal standards or retract it from public schools. A similar recommendation was given by the ombudswoman for gender equality in 2005, but was never followed by the ministry. At present, the program is still unchanged and implemented in its original form in some public schools in Croatia.

Since public pressure created by national NGOs has been great, the Ministry decided to establish a national committee that would decide which program will be implemented in public schools. The committee consisted of eminent scholars in the field of sexuality, representatives of the Faculty of Law, the ombudswoman for gender equality, and other health experts. The president of this committee, however, was the very same Vladimir Gruden, who was warned in 2002 by the Croatian Medical Chamber for professing his belief that homosexuality is a mental disorder treatable with medical intervention. After a few months of discussion, the

committee concluded that the ministry should adopt a program of health education within which the module on human sexuality could be included.

One year after the conclusion of the committee, nothing was undertaken by
the ministry in regards to sex education. In the middle of 2006, however, the
ministry asked local NGOs to submit their own programs that could be used as
experimental health programs in public schools. The promoters and supporters of
the Teen STAR program established a new NGO called GROZD, and prepared a
health education program based on the same principles as Teen STAR. In relation
to masturbation, for example, it stated that masturbation is sinful and should be
avoided. The program was prepared both for elementary and high schools. The
second NGO was the Forum for Freedom in Education, which prepared a more
liberal program, but only for high schools. Although such a program seemed to be
liberal, it was rather neutral in relation to homosexuality. The Ministry of Science,
Education, and Sport promised the national NGOs that it would buy the selected
programs, then adapt them to conform to international and national standards,
without homophobic attitudes. Furthermore, the ministry stated that it would ask
for the approval of both Ombudswomen and of the Ministry of Health and Social
Welfare before implementing such experimental programs.

At the end of 2006, the Ministry of Health and Social Welfare negatively assessed both programs and recommended that they should not be implemented as
experimental programs in public schools if they were not changed to conform to
professional standards. In terms of GROZD's program, the ombudswoman for
children stated that it does not satisfy professional and legal standards and should
not be implemented in public schools. A similar opinion was given by the ombudswoman for gender equality.

Although the Ministry of Science, Education, and Sport received negative comments from the mentioned institutions, at the end of 2007 it decided to implement
both programs for the following semester.

The Catholic Church in the Republic of Croatia has great influence, not only
in the political sphere, but also in other levels of society. Generally, the attitude of
the Catholic Church toward LGBT people is negative. Although the church states
that it accepts every person, in relation to homosexual people it was stated that they
should not live in line with their sexuality if they want their souls to be safe from
eternal condemnation.

VIOLENCE

According to the statistical data of the Ministry of the Interior, in 2007 there
were 2,158 reported criminal offences against life and body. Of that number, there
were 59 criminal offences of murder and 155 criminal offences of attempted murder.[34] There is no official information on the number of incarcerated persons in the
Croatian prison system. According to the statistical data of the People's Ombudsman, 2,484 people were incarcerated in 2007.

The definition of a hate crime was implemented in the Croatian criminal code in
2006, as a result of the advocacy of Kontra and Iskorak, with the support of the Serbian Democratic Forum and the Croatian Women's Network. Information collected
from the Ministry of the Interior showed that one year after provisions regarding
hate crimes were enforced, police registered 32 cases of hate crimes. Two of the
cases referred to hate crimes committed due to the sexual orientation of the victim.

In spite of this, numerous cases of violent attacks against members of the LGBT community have been reported in past years. After Iskorak and Kontra started to document any case of violence and discrimination reported to them, the numbers started to rise every year. In 2006, there were 16 criminal offenses allegedly committed on the basis of sexual behavior, and in 2007 there were 18 such cases. It is estimated that the exact number of such criminal offenses is much higher; many people do not report violence and other crimes because of fear that their sexual orientation will be publicly disclosed.

In 2002 and 2007, the majority of reported cases were linked to the Gay Pride event in Zagreb. Between 2002 and 2007, there were other cases of violence against members of the LGBT community. Perpetrators often remain unknown due to lack of police investigation and the general inability of the police to conduct criminal investigations in line with the provisions of the Criminal Procedure Act. Only one case has been successfully closed; the perpetrator was sanctioned by a probation sentence. This was the case when a young cadet sent threats by e-mail to Iskorak's official Web address in 2004. The criminal investigation was primarily conducted by the military police of the Ministry of Defense, and perpetrator was rapidly discovered. No such satisfaction has been granted for any victim in other cases of violence. Currently, at the criminal court of Zagreb, there is only one case being tried of a perpetrator who tried to throw a Molotov cocktail at the Zagreb pride march in 2007.

Police misconduct and improper handling of LGBT hate crimes is shown to be a general trend. In cases of violent behavior, the police do not collect evidence for criminal procedure and do not treat such behavior as criminal offenses at all. They only consider violence against members of the LGBT community as misdemeanors against public peace and order. Thus, if the perpetrator attacks the victim on the street, both the perpetrator and the victim will be accused by the police of disturbing public peace and order by fighting and yelling, and both could be punished by fine or imprisonment. Even in 2007, when someone tried to throw a Molotov cocktail at the Zagreb Pride march, the police did not recognize this as a criminal offense, and the head of the police headquarters in Zagreb publicly stated that the police did everything they could and if someone wished to bring criminal charges against the perpetrator they should do that by themselves.[35] Regardless of the police's conduct in this case, the state attorney in Zagreb decided to pursue criminal prosecution against the perpetrator after reading about the case in national newspapers.

RESOURCE GUIDE

Suggested Reading

K. Grđan and S. Juras, *2006 Annual Report on the Status of Human Rights of Sexual and Gender Minorities in Croatia* (Team for Legal Changes of Iskorak and Kontra, 2007).

K. Grđan and S. Juras, *2007 Annual Report on the Status of Human Rights of Sexual and Gender Minorities in Croatia* (Team for Legal Changes of Iskorak and Kontra, 2008).

Organizations/Web Sites

Inqueerzicija—the New Gay Scene, http://www.inqueerzicija.hr.
    Provides space for gay persons to publicize social events and make connections and friendships.

Iskorak—Sexual and Gender Minorities' Rights Center, http://www.iskorak.org.

> Nongovernmental organization established in 2002 to oppose any kind of discrimination and stigma against sexual and gender minorities and to affirm their human rights. Contains basic information on the organization, press releases, publications, telephone numbers, and so on.

Lesbian Group Kontra, http://www.kontra.hr.

> Founded in the summer of 1997 in Zagreb, Kontra operates according to feminist and antimilitaristic principles, and opposes all forms of discrimination. The site contains basic information on the organization, press releases, publications, telephone numbers, and so on.

Lesbian Group Rijeka—LORI, http://www.lori.hr.

> Contains basic information on the organization and its projects.

LGBTIQ Coordination, http://www.lgbtiq-koordinacija.net.

National LGBT portal, http://www.gay.hr.

> First and major LGBTIQ portal, officially established in 2002, with an interactive portal, forum, and user profiles. It represents an active news service for CSO initiatives. It has more than 80,000 visitors per month, and more than 10,000 members.

Queer Zagreb, http://www.queerzagreb.org.

> Nongovernmental, nonprofit organization whose mission is to challenge heteronormative social values through the presentation and production of art, and to raise awareness of and empower queer identity in the region and in the world.

Zagreb Pride, http://www.zagreb-pride.net.

NOTES

1. Central Bureau of Statistics, *2001 Croatian Population Census,* Republic of Croatia.

2. Ibid.

3. Central Bureau of Statistics, *2007 Statistical Information,* Republic of Croatia.

4. *Official Gazette* no. 116/03.

5. *Official Gazette* no. 7/07.

6. "Discussion on comprehensive meaning and inter-relation between terms of 'love' and 'sex' and judgement over wrong types of sexuality (homosexuality, prostitution, incest, transvestites...)," *Official Gazette* no. 156/03.

7. *Official Gazette* no. 102/06.

8. Program of Comprehensive Sexual Education—Teen STAR, 1997.

9. *Official Gazette* no. 102/06

10. According to the data of the ombudswoman for children for 2005.

11. S. Juras and K. Grđan, *2007 Annual Report on the Status of Human Rights of Sexual and Gender Minorities in Croatia,* Team for Legal Changes of Iskorak and Kontra, 2008.

12. According to the data of the ombudswoman for children for 2005.

13. According to the data of the ombudswoman for children for 2005.

14. N. Bijelić, S. Cesar, and A. Hodžić, *Men, Women and Sexuality* (Zagreb, Croatia: Centre for Education, Counselling and Research, 2004).

15. M. Mamula, *Status of Sexual Rights of Women in Croatia—Results of the Research* (Zagreb, Croatia: Women's Room, 2006).

16. A. Štulhofer and I. Rimac, *Determinants of Homonegativity in Europe* (Zagreb, Croatia: University of Zagreb, 2007).

17. A. Štulhofer, V. Buško, and I. Landripet, *Pornography, Sexual Socialization and Satisfaction among Young Men* (Zagreb, Croatia: University of Zagreb, 2008).

18. The program was developed by the Centre for Reproductive Health of the Clinical Hospital Zagreb.

19. Central Bureau of Statistics, *Women and Men in Croatia in 2007,* Republic of Croatia.

20. Central Bureau of Statistics, *Domestic Violence 2001–2006,* Republic of Croatia.

21. S. Juras and K. Grđan, *2006 Annual Report on the Status of Human Rights of Sexual and Gender Minorities in Croatia* (Zagreb, Croatia: Team for Legal Changes of Iskorak and Kontra, 2007).

22. Croatian Institute of Public Health, statistical data, 2008.

23. K. Radić, D. Stanić, L. Bielen, and K. Branko, "Risk for HIV in Croatian Population of Men Having Sex with Men," in *Second Generation of HIV Surveillance in the Republic of Croatia,* ed. I. Gjenero-Margan and B. Kolarić (Zagreb, Croatia: Croatian Institute of Public Health, 2006).

24. Croatian Episcopal Conference, November 20, 2002, Zagreb, Croatia.

25. Decision of the Committee on Medical Ethics and Deontology of the Croatian Medical Chamber no. 09–6/03, May 22, 2003.

26. *Official Gazette* 110/07.

27. Excerpts from the transcript of the meeting of the Parliamentary Meeting on Human Rights and Rights of National Minorities, February 15, 2006.

28. Central Bureau of Statistics, *Domestic Violence 2001–2006.*

29. Nineteenth Parliamentary Assembly, transcript (excerpts), March 19, 2006.

30. Bijelić and Hodžić, *Men, Women and Sexuality.*

31. Rassemblement jurassien and Unité jurassienne v. Switzerland, no. 8191/78, commission decision of October 10, 1979, DR 17, 93.

32. Glas Koncila no. 5(1545) of February 1, 2004.

33. Teen Sexuality Teaching in the Context of Adult Responsibility, 2004.

34. Ministry of Interiors, Department of Analytics and Development, 2007.

35. Juras and Grđan, *2006 Annual Report.*

CZECH REPUBLIC

Eva Polášková and Kateřina Nedbálková

OVERVIEW

The Czech Republic is a land-locked country in Central Europe. It borders Poland in the north, Germany in the west, Austria in the south, and Slovakia in the east. The capital is Prague. The majority of the total area is at an altitude below 1,640 feet above sea level.[1] The Czech Republic has nearly 10.4 million inhabitants, and the average population density is 330 inhabitants per square mile. A large part of the population lives in urban areas (70% in municipalities with a town status). The population in the Czech Republic is nationally homogenous. The most numerous minorities are Ukrainians, Slovaks, Vietnamese, and Roma; however, their total number does not exceed five percent. The Czech Republic is regarded as an atheistic country. Two-thirds of the inhabitants refer to themselves as atheists, and the other third claim to be Christians.[2]

The Czech Republic has existed as an independent country since 1993, when the Federal Republic of Czechoslovakia disintegrated. Since its establishment in 1918 until World War II, Czechoslovakia had belonged to developed democratic countries. After World War II, the Communist party seized power for over 40 years, and Czechoslovakia ranked amongst the totalitarian countries of the Soviet Bloc. The 1989 Velvet Revolution restored parliamentary democracy, and Václav Havel was elected the first democratic president. The country joined the European Union in 2004.

OVERVIEW OF LGBT ISSUES

In comparison with other Central and Eastern European countries, the Czech Republic is relatively more tolerant to same-sex marriages and child adoption.[3] Public perceptions of homosexuality have been associated with medicine and sexology. Homosexuality ceased to be punished by law as early as in the Socialist regime (1961), yet homosexuals were easy victims for the secret police to blackmail and persecute at that time. A significant change took place in 1989 when the first official institutions and organizations for gays and lesbians were founded. In 2006, the Czech Republic was the second of all post-Communist countries to legalize registered partnership for same-sex couples.

EDUCATION

In the Czech Republic, there is multilevel education (preschool, elementary, high school, university, postgraduate, and continuing education). Obligatory school attendance takes nine years. Educational institutions are public or private; public schools do not charge tuition.

The issue of homosexuality is rarely a part of the curriculum at elementary and high schools; whether to include these issues in their teaching is up to teachers or school management. Most frequently, it is discussed as a part of broader subjects, such as family education and civics at the elementary school level. In one of the family education textbooks available, homosexuality is introduced in a chapter on sexual deviations along with pedophilia and necrophilia. Even though the text mentions that homosexuality is not a deviation, it is still symbolically associated with it. At secondary schools, this topic occurs in the social sciences course; here, too, what materials will be used and if and how this topic will be dealt with depend on the skills and competency of the particular teacher. Occasionally, there are explicit homophobic statements on the part of teachers or school management. Concerning the issue of homosexuality, sexuality, or gender, obsolete materials are often used at this type of school. The insufficiency and the stereotypical nature of information is mitigated by occasional lectures and discussions provided by LGBT organizations. However, courses on gay and lesbian studies or queer theory are offered at universities in departments of English studies, as well as in literature and gender studies.

EMPLOYMENT AND ECONOMICS

In the 1990s, crucial changes of propriety ownership took place. State ownership, which made up nearly all ownership (97%) during Socialist rule, was 80 percent privatized 10 years after the Velvet Revolution. The Czech Republic is regarded as a country with a growing economy. The average level of unemployment recently has rested around 5 percent, but is gradually declining.

The Employment Act explicitly refers to and prohibits discrimination in the workplace because of sexual orientation, and a victim has the right to seek judicial protection in these cases. Due to the nonexistence of more extensive research, gay and lesbian discrimination at work is hard to estimate. Existing information suggests that 12 percent of respondents have been discriminated against at work.[4]

By 2004, the obligatory two-year military service in the Czech Republic was abolished, a term of service formerly compulsory for all healthy men. When newcomers joined the armed forces, they were often bullied by soldiers who had been in service longer. If it were revealed, homosexuality was another reason for humiliation. In 2004, the media presented a case of a woman applying for a job in the Czech Army—a job she did not obtain even though she had met all the requirements. The reason for the decision against her was revealed to be a diagnosis of transsexualism.[5]

In 2006 and 2007, the parliament discussed an antidiscrimination law that would establish equal opportunity rights and protect against discrimination due to sexual orientation. The deadline for adopting EU antidiscrimination measurements into the legal system of the Czech Republic was the end of 2006. If there continues to be no redress, the Czech Republic will face negative sanctions, such as a complaint by the European Commission to the European Court of Justice for not meeting the obligations arising from its membership in the EU.

SOCIAL/GOVERNMENT PROGRAMS

As a part of the European Year of Equal Opportunities for All (2007), a Working Group for Sexual Minority Issues was established in the government, which aims at improving the LGBT minority status in the Czech Republic. The members of this team are both activists from nongovernmental, nonprofit organizations focused on the LGBT minority, and academic experts. In 2007, a prominent Czech gay activist became an advisor to the country's minister for human and national minority rights.

SEXUALITY/SEXUAL PRACTICES

Representative research shows that 5 percent of men and 6 percent of women have had sexual experience with the same sex. Ninety-seven percent of inhabitants regard themselves as heterosexuals. Three percent of women and three percent of men refer to themselves as homosexuals or are not sure about their orientation.

The number of people regarding homosexuality as a disease is in decline (22% of men and 27% of women in 2003, as opposed to 33% of men and 41% of women in 1994). Approximately one-third of the population perceives homosexuality as a natural part of life.[6]

As for AIDS, the Czech Republic is one of the least afflicted countries. Since the infection started to spread, the most frequent method of transmission has been via homosexual intercourse (52% of all reported cases). In parts of the gay community, there are still negative attitudes toward people with HIV, and hence it is necessary to promote the establishment of a nondiscriminatory environment.[7]

In Prague, there is a recurrent phenomenon of gay prostitution; in many cases, this is practiced by very young men who identify themselves as heterosexual. In 1995, a special prevention program helping sexually abused children and youth was launched.

FAMILY

The Czech family has undergone a major transformation since 1989. Society experienced changes in the political and economic systems, and began adopting trends characteristic of advanced democratic cultures. These tendencies are markedly

apparent in the structure and dynamics of family, marriage, and reproductive behavior. The marriage rate decreased by half, with people postponing it until their
late twenties. Parents usually have only one child (the Czech Republic has a very
low birth rate). The number of children in incomplete families is increasing—nearly
35 percent of children are born out of wedlock. The divorce rate has increased up to
50 percent. Nevertheless, these trends coexist with a preference for legal marriages
if there are children, and an emphasis on the institution of the traditional family.[8]

The contemporary Czech family is represented by a broad range of family arrangements; however, it is the traditional model comprising a married heterosexual
couple raising children that is being recognized and supported by government
family policy. The existence of gay and lesbian families is not taken into consideration on either legal grounds or in public awareness. The issue of the prevalence
of gay and lesbian families still lacks a detailed examination, yet there is evidence
that such families do exist though they are not commonplace in society. These include both couples raising children from their previous heterosexual relationships
and planned families.[9] In the Czech Republic, there are rather limited official opportunities to establish a family for gay and lesbian people. Gays and lesbians with
registered status are explicitly excluded from the adoption process. Some people
decide to conceal their sexual identity in order to improve their chances in the
adoption evaluation procedure; however, the chance of success is low due to long
waiting lists and a preference for married couples. A similar arrangement also applies to adopting a same-sex partner's biological children; hence, the nonbiological parent-child relationship has little chance of becoming legal and including the
duties and rights pertaining to official adoption. Foster care is available only to
individuals, regardless of their registered status. Only opposite-sex (including unmarried) couples are granted access to assisted reproduction treatment, leaving
out single women and lesbian couples. Based on the data from a pioneering study
on lesbian motherhood, there is an increasing trend of having children within an
already existing same-sex relationship via self-assisted donor insemination or insemination at a clinic (though this is illegal).[10] Public debate over child-rearing by
same-sex couples is affected by a large degree of prejudice; about two-thirds of the
population are against same-sex parenting. In the Czech Republic, a large number
of children are raised in institutional care.

COMMUNITY

Under Communist rule (before 1989), the gay and lesbian community existed
illegally as private gatherings of invited friends. There is also evidence that gays and
lesbians met in psychiatric wards when their situation resulted in hospitalization in
such an institution. The transformation of the regime in late 1980s meant a crucial
change in the extent and form of the gay and lesbian community.

Although there is no geographically concentrated gay and lesbian community
in particular neighborhoods or cities, and there has never been a gay pride march,
Prague tends to be described in LGBT guidebooks as the gay metropolis of the
former Eastern Europe. The public space of the gay and lesbian community is represented by bars, cafes, restaurants, sex clubs, and saunas that are usually situated in
larger cities such as Prague, Brno, and Olomouc. The private space of the subculture is represented by informal groups of friends who meet in private households
and do not opt for official gay and lesbian clubs. A more formally organized part of

the community is represented by nonprofit LGBT organizations; there are several dozen of them in the Czech Republic. These organizations endeavored to put into law a Registered Partnership Act (accomplished in 2006) and organize discussion and support groups, film festivals or lectures, and sport or other leisure events.

Furthermore, the central platform for the formation of an LGBT community is the TV program *Queer* (formerly *Legato*), which has been regularly broadcasted by one state TV channel since 2004. In 2007, the first lesbian publishing house, *Le Press*, was established.

There is practically no bisexual community. Bisexual women very often take part in associations and events devoted primarily to lesbians. The transsexual community is concentrated predominantly in Prague around Transfórum, a single civic association representing trans people's interests. Given the fact that most transsexual individuals, after their sex reassignment, long for assimilation into everyday society, transsexual communities more likely exist online.

HEALTH

Health insurance is provided by law and applies compulsorily to all inhabitants with permanent residence in the Czech Republic. The country has a low incidence of HIV/AIDS. Since 1985, when the National HIV/AIDS Monitoring Program was launched, 1,248 cases have been recorded, with a steady increase of about 10 percent every year. Sexual contact remains the most frequent method of HIV transmission, and gay men are considered the most vulnerable group.

Regarding the incidence of sexually transmitted diseases (STDs) other than HIV, the Czech Republic is comparable with Western European nations. Nevertheless, research indicates that the Czech population's sexual behavior is risky. Research data shows that 9 percent of men and 7 percent of women reported having an STD at some time in their lives.[11] In the 1990s, there was a sudden increase in the prevalence of STDs; currently, the annual growth rate of these STDs is low. The most widespread diseases of this kind are syphilis and gonorrhea. Some STDs must legally be reported to the national registry.

The Czech Republic follows the International Classification of Diseases; as a part of its 10th revision (ICD-10) in 1992, homosexuality was excluded as a disease by the World Health Organization (WHO). Only the persistent rejection of a person's given sexual orientation in favor of heterosexuality is still considered a diagnostic category (ego-dystonic homosexuality).

The prevalence of transsexualism in the Czech Republic is comparable to that of other countries. Among postoperative transsexuals in the Czech Republic, female-to-male transsexuals prevail at a ratio of up to 5:1. This trend is also characteristic of other former Communist countries, while data from Western Europe reveal an opposite trend. Possible explanations for this difference are differing social conditions under socialism, and more difficult self-enforcement of male-to-female gender roles, or differences in diagnostic criteria.[12] The health care system, including health care legislation, is quite favorable to transsexual clients. Sex-reassignment applicants are allowed to change their identity documents and names in accordance with their gender identity as early as before the surgery, which is covered by the public health insurance system. The state officially acknowledges sex reassignment and legal continuity only in individuals who have had the surgery. Those who decide not to or cannot complete the surgery are excluded from this process.[13]

There is scarce data available about intersexuals and their life in the Czech Republic. The topic is discussed exclusively by experts. Related medical procedures are carried out at an early age, so no consent of intersexual individuals themselves is needed, despite the risk of future negative consequences. Parental consent is required; however, the sufficiency of the information offered to them is questionable.[14]

POLITICS AND LAW

In the area of the LGBT minority's rights provision and protection, the Czech Republic is subject to the requirements of the EU legal system. Legal culpability for homosexual behavior was abolished in 1961. In the late 1980s, the legislature cancelled the ban on personal ads aimed at same-sex persons. In a 1990 penal code amendment, the age limit for consensual homosexual intercourse was reduced to the age of 15 (originally it was 18 years for same-sex couples, 15 years for opposite-sex couples). Sexual practices of consenting adult partners are not subject to legal regulations.

Despite the fact that the Czech Republic passed an Act on Registered Partnership for the Same Sex in 2006, the civil status of same-sex couples is still far from being resolved in many aspects. The final form of the act lacks some fundamental partnership rights (e.g., joint property rights, tenancy rights, joint taxation, survivor pension rights) and parenting rights (e.g., the law explicitly excludes any individual with the registered status from the child adoption process).[15] The Czech LGBT community perceives the registration procedure as a symbolic act rather than an opportunity to gain full-fledged partnership rights.

The Czech Republic still lacks unified antidiscrimination legislation; individual regulations are included in separate acts. Yet, the degree of legal protection from discrimination on the grounds of sexual orientation differs substantially within particular regulations. It is solved inadequately in, for example, the labor code, education, social benefits, and health care. Furthermore, new laws do not recognize discrimination based on gender identity, which is essential for the legal protection of transsexuals.

RELIGION AND SPIRITUALITY

Historically, the Czech Republic belongs to countries sharing the European Christian cultural heritage. However, the Communist regime period left indisputable traces on the social milieu of the country. The official ideology until the 1990s was based on an atheistic worldview. About two-thirds of the country's population holds no religious beliefs. Approximately 30 percent declare their membership in one of several faith groups; a prominent position is held by the Roman Catholic Church. Believers are especially prevalent among the older generation, but many of them do not actively practice their religion.

The official approach of the Catholic Church to LGBT issues is traditionally rigid and hostile. Protestant denominations are somewhat less strict; there are even Protestant associations intended for gays and lesbians believing in God. Regarding the passing of the Registered Partnership Act, there have been attempts to include in the wedding ceremony benediction for same-sex couples, which would represent a full-fledged alternative to a the civil ceremony of entering a registered partnership.

Despite the greater openness of some churches, many faith-based organizations contradict their official proclamations, especially in the case of the Catholic Church. For example, it is still legal to treat LGBT individuals differently on the grounds of their sexual orientation (e.g., in the job application process).[16]

VIOLENCE

The 1989 fall of Communism and the change of the social regime had a significant impact on the perception and observance of human rights, which had been rather perfunctory up to then. Since 1989, there has been a crucial liberalization of attitudes toward sexual minorities; nonetheless, a lot of prejudice and stereotypes still remain deeply rooted in society.

The results of the only available research on the subject have shown that Czech sexual minority members are subject to a threat of violent and verbal attacks, and that they encounter discrimination in various areas of their lives.[17] Many cases remain hidden, and they are hardly ever dealt with by court.

The Czech penal code does not distinguish between hate crimes based on sexual orientation and those based on gender identity (although neither qualify as aggravating circumstances). Therefore, there are no statistics available; however, research indicates that 15 percent of respondents have been victims of a violent attack and a third have experienced verbal harassment.[18]

Regarding verbal aggression, bullying at schools is a crucial though often neglected problem. Minorities' rights are guaranteed by the Education Act, yet the Act does not explicitly mention sexual orientation. Based on data from nongovernmental organizations working with children and adolescents, it is clear that bullying represents a serious issue for gay and lesbian youth. Despite the growing number of prevention projects, there is still no unifying policy for both teachers and students. This role is often taken over by NGOs within their peer-to-peer programs.

Very often, the rights of incarcerated LGBT persons are violated. Apart from to the fact that they become an easy target due to their visible distinctness, transsexuals serving their term are also denied proceeding with their medical treatment in order to undergo gender reassignment surgery.

Another problem for transsexuals is the fact that both the authorities and private institutions put postoperative transsexual citizens into a position when they are forced to prove their legal identity repeatedly. Revealing personal information about gender reassignment history interferes with their right to privacy and makes them more vulnerable to possible discrimination in everyday matters (dealing with government authorities, banks, schools, etc.). Another problem is transsexuals' parenting rights—a frequent condition of Czech health institutions is to give up or make contacts with children less frequent in order to obtain approval for the gender reassignment surgery, even though this practice is not a formal part of the legislature.[19]

OUTLOOK FOR THE 21ST CENTURY

One of the future challenges in the Czech Republic is establishing a high-quality network of LGBT-friendly experts (predominantly mental health professionals).

Existing research has shown that many experts are insufficiently educated on LGBT issues and lack experience in working with LGBT clients. However, the greatest insufficiencies in trying to accomplish the equal status of LGBT minorities in the Czech Republic are at the political and legal levels. One major problem is a lack of legal regulation concerning parenting and children's rights (including the possibility of adoption and foster care) for same-sex couples, access to assisted reproduction for lesbian women and couples, and a more comprehensive antidiscrimination law.

RESOURCE GUIDE

Suggested Reading

Human Rights Committee, *The Status of Lesbian, Gay, Bisexual, Transgender and Intersex Rights in the Czech Republic—A Shadow Report* (Office of the United Nations High Commissioner for Human Rights, 2007), http://www.ohchr.org/english/bodies/hrc/docs/ngos/LGBTShadow_CzechRepublic.pdf.

Kateřina Nedbálková, "The Changing Space of the Gay and Lesbian Community in the Czech Republic," in *Beyond the Pink Curtain. Everyday Life of LGBT in Eastern Europe,* ed. R. Kuhar and J. Takács (Ljubljana: Peace Institute, 2007).

Eva Polášková, "The Czech Lesbian Family Study: Investigating Family Practices," in *Beyond the Pink Curtai:. Everyday Life of LGBT in Eastern Europe,* ed. R. Kuhar and J. Takács (Ljubljana: Peace Institute, 2007).

Ivo Procházka, David Janík, and Jiří Hromada, *Social Discrimination of Lesbians, Gay Men and Bisexuals in the Czech Republic* (Prague: Gay iniciativa v ČR, 2003), http://gay.iniciativa.cz/download/diskriminace_en.pdf.

Věra Sokolová, "Representation of Gays and Lesbians in the Mainstream Visual Media," in *Media Image of Lesbians and Gays,* ed. J. Kout, A. Rumpel, and M. Strachoň (Brno: STUD, 2006).

Věra Sokolová, "Representations of Homosexuality and the Separation of Gender and Sexuality in the Czech Republic Before and after 1989," in *Political Systems and Definitions of Gender Roles,* ed. A. K. Isaacs (Pisa, Italy: Edizione Plus, Universita di Pisa, 2001), http://www.stm.unipi.it/Clioh/tabs/libri/2/22-Sokolova_273–288.pdf.

Working Group for the Issues of Sexual Minorities, *Analysis of the Situation of Lesbian, Gay, Bisexual and Transgender Minority in the Czech Republic* (Minister for Human Rights and National Minorities, 2007), http://www.vlada.cz/assets/cs/rvk/rlp/PracSk_sex_mensin/EN_analyza_web.pdf.

Video/Film

S důvorou a láskou [*In Trust and Love*] (52 min.; 2006). Directed and produced by Michal Herz.
    A documentary about the private lives of a popular Czech gay couple and their journey toward registered partnership.

Ted' jsem to konečno já [*Now it's Finally Me*] (28 min.; 2006). Directed by Petr Kaňka. Czech TV, Centre of Musical and Documentary Production.
    A documentary about the personal, health, and social aspects of transsexualism in the Czech Republic. Available online from http://www.ceskatelevize.cz/vysilani/10095359176-ted-jsem-to-konecne-ja/306295350170003.html (Czech version).

Pusinky [*Dolls*] (99 min.; 2007). Directed by Karin Babinská. Czech TV.
    The first Czech feature film with a lesbian main character depicted without traditional stereotypes and clichés. This is an autobiographical film written by the screenwriter about the period of her late teens. Available with English subtitles.

Q: http://www.ceskatelevize.cz/vysilani/10121061347-q.html.

TV queer magazine. Offers a full range of reports and encounters with interesting people.

LeGato: http://www.ceskatelevize.cz/vysilani/1126673688-legato.html.

Q TV magazine predecessor. Available from Czech TV archive.

Andolé nejsou andolé [*Not Angels But Angels*] (77 min.; 1994). Directed by Wiktor Grodecki. MiroFilm.

Tolo bez duše [*Body without Soul*] (94 min.; 1996). Directed by Wiktor Grodecki. MiroFilm.

Mandragora (126 min.; 1997). Directed by Wiktor Grodecki. Prague Film Enterprises.

These three films are Polish director Grodecki's insight into the world of homosexual boy prostitution in Prague in the mid-1990s.

Web Sites

Bengales, http://www.bengales.cz.

DRBNA, http://www.drbna.cz.

This site focuses on parenting issues.

EXODUS, http://www.homosexualita.cz.

Local branch of Exodus International, a Christian organization offering to change homosexual orientation via therapy. In 2003, they sent all Czech elementary and secondary schools the publication *(Self) Therapy of Homosexuality* by the Dutch Catholic writer Gerard J. M. van den Aardweg. The book refers to homosexuality as a disease and to gays and lesbians as handicapped. It received a lot of publicity in the media and the Czech Ministry of Education, Youth, and Sports expressed disapproval of this action.

Gay and bisexual men, http://www.004.cz.

Gejt, http://www.gejt.cz.

This site focuses on teenage gays.

Kluci, http://kluci.info/.

Lesbian and bisexual women, http://www.lesba.cz.

LGBT film festival Mezipatra, http://www.mezipatra.cz/.

The greatest cultural event of the Czech LGBT community, aimed at the general public. The festival's additional program provides information and education.

Trans people (Translidé), http://www.translide.cz.

Information platform for transsexual and transgender people.

Organizations

Česká společnost AIDS pomoc (Czech AIDS Help Society), http://www.aids-pomoc.cz/.

Operating since 1989, it now focuses on school education and prevention and offers anonymous and free testing for HIV. It runs the *Dům svotla* (Home of Light), which also serves as an asylum centre for HIV-positive people in need.

Gay a lesbická liga (Gay and Lesbian League), http://www.glliga.cz.

The only association representing the gay and lesbian community at a political level. It has contributed considerably to the passing of the Registered Partnership Act.

LOGOS Praha, http://www.logos.gl.cz.

Ecumenical Christian community whose aim is to integrate homosexuals into society and churches.

Stejná rodina (The Same Family), Zemodolská 17, http://www.stejnarodina.cz.

The aim of the civic organization *Stejná rodina* is the legislative emancipation of Czech LGBT families. Above all, the organization wants to fight the legislative vacuum surrounding the rights of children born and/or brought up in gay and lesbian families and to help these families obtain the same rights and responsibilities afforded to heterosexual couples. The organization is also trying to become a meeting platform for LGBT families and their children.

STUD Brno, http://www.stud.cz.

One of the most significant Czech LGBT organizations. It was founded in 1996 and is currently involved mainly in organizing the Mezipatra film festival. It has a large library at its disposal open to the public and an archive of material related to LGBT issues. It cooperates with and runs other smaller projects for gays and lesbians.

TransFórum, http://www.transforum.cz.

The only Czech organization representing transgender interests.

NOTES

1. Czech Republic, Ministry of Foreign Affairs, *Czech Republic,* http://www.czech.cz/en/czech-republic/geography/ (accessed November 25, 2007).

2. *Statistical Yearbook of the Czech Republic 2007* (Prague: Czech Statistical Office, 2007), http://www.czso.cz/csu/2007edicniplan.nsf/engpubl/10n1–07–2007 (accessed April 30, 2008).

3. Public Opinion Research Centre of the Institute of Sociology of the Academy of Sciences of the Czech Republic (CVVM), *Češi jsou vůči sňatkům a registrovanému partnerství homosexuálů vstřícnější než Poláci, Maďaři a Slováci,* news release, http://www.cvvm.cas.cz/upl/zpravy/100533s_ov51128.pdf (accessed November 11, 2006).

4. I. Procházka, D. Janík, and J. Hromada, *Společenská diskriminace lesbických žen, gay mužů a bisexuálů v ČR* (Prague: Gay iniciativa v CR, 2003), http://gay.iniciativa.cz/download/diskriminace_en.pdf (accessed November 27, 2006).

5. Case of Jaroslava Brokešová (2004).

6. P. Weiss and J. Zvořina, *Sexuální chování v ČR—situace a trendy* (Prague: Portál, 2001).

7. I. Procházka, J. Novotný, P. Kaňka, and D. Janík, *HIV infekce a homosexualita* (Prague: Česká společnost AIDS pomoc, 2005).

8. *Statistical Yearbook of the Czech Republic 2007.*

9. E. Polášková, "The Czech Lesbian Family Study: Investigating Family Practices," in B*eyond the Pink Curtain: Everyday Life of LGBT in Eastern Europe,* ed. R. Kuhar and J. Takács (Ljubljana: Peace Institute, 2007).

10. E. Polášková, "The Czech Lesbian Family Study."

11. P. Weiss "Zmona sexuálního chování Čechů," *Vesmír* 85, no. 1 (2006): 29–32.

12. H. Fifková, P. Weiss, I. Procházka, J. Jarolím, J. Veselý, and V. Weiss, *Transsexualita: Diagnostika a léčba* (Prague: Grada Publishing, 2002).

13. Human Rights Committee, *The Status of Lesbian, Gay, Bisexual, Transgender and Intersex Rights in the Czech Republic—A Shadow Report* (Office of the United Nations High Commissioner for Human Rights, 2007), http://www.ohchr.org/english/bodies/hrc/docs/ngos/LGBTShadow_CzechRepublic.pdf (accessed October 28, 2007).

14. Ibid.

15. Ibid.

16. *Analýza situace lesbické, gay, bisexuální a transgender menšiny v ČR* (2007). Pracovní skupina pro otázky sexuálních menšin ministryno pro lidská práva a národností menšiny CR, http://www.diskriminace.cz/dt-publikace/analyza_final.pdf (accessed November 8, 2007).

17. Procházka and Hromada, *Společenská diskriminace lesbických žen, gay mužů a bisexuálů v ČR.*

18. Ibid.

19. Human Rights Committee, *The Status of Lesbian, Gay, Bisexual, Transgender and Intersex Rights in the Czech Republic.*

DENMARK

Ann Kristin Lassen

OVERVIEW

Denmark is the smallest and southernmost of the Scandinavian countries. The country borders the North Sea to the west, the Baltic Sea to the east, and, to the south, the peninsula of Jutland is bordered by Germany. Since 1949, Denmark has been a member of NATO and in 1973 the country joined the European Union (EU). Greenland and the Faroe Islands are part of the Kingdom of Denmark. Both are governed by home rule and the Danish parliament has no influence on their domestic legislation. Neither of the two territories are members of the EU.

In 1849, Denmark became a constitutional monarchy, although the role of the monarch is only symbolic and representative. Folketinget, the Danish parliament, consists of 179 seats that are allocated by general elections based on proportional representation at least every fourth year. Greenland and the Faroe Islands have two seats each in the parliament. A liberal-conservative coalition government supported by the nationalist Danish People's Party currently governs Denmark. In total, eight parties won seats in the parliament during the general election in 2007.

Until the 1960s, the Danish population was rather homogenous, but the demand for more labor during the economic progress from the 1960s onward prompted the country to invite foreign nationals to join the labor force. The population of approximately 5.5 million people now consists of 8.8 percent immigrants and their descendants, primarily from Turkey, Iraq, and Poland.[1]

OVERVIEW OF LGBT ISSUES

Since the 1970s, gay and lesbian lifestyles have gradually become more visible in the public space and debate, and the AIDS crisis in the 1980s effectively put homosexuality on the public agenda. The advances made during these years have not come easily, and gay and lesbian persons' ability to form families and enter into registered partnerships have been especially politically contentious issues.[2] These two areas have caused much debate both in society at large and within the gay and lesbian communities, but have nonetheless resulted in new legislation that makes gays and lesbians equal to heterosexuals in many aspects of the law.

In 1981, homosexuality was removed from the National Board of Health's list of diseases. This move has been reflected socially in that it is no longer unusual to see politicians or other public figures being openly gay or lesbian. In general, Denmark is perceived as a tolerant and liberal country when it comes to sexual practices and minorities. However, LGBT persons' rights to adopt or have their marriage blessed in church still meets opposition, primarily from political and religious conservative forces.

Recently, labor unions and employers have begun to focus on LGBT persons' conditions in the workplace, where discrimination still exists, although antidiscrimination legislation protecting the rights of LGBT persons has been passed by the EU and the Danish government.

EDUCATION

The Danish welfare system promises to take care of every citizen from cradle to grave. To a large extent, the educational system is publicly funded, and 88 percent of Danish school children are enrolled in the public primary and lower secondary school system. The central government decides on the general framework for primary and secondary education, thus providing municipal schools with common aims. Each municipality then decides how these should be administered and carried out in practice.

Since 1970, sex education has been a compulsory part of the curriculum. The subject is governed by a principle of neutrality to ensure that no moral judgments are passed in the teaching of the subject. The most recent guideline on how to teach sex education focuses on the positive aspects of sexuality, desire, and quality of life.[3] This opens up the curriculum to include LGBT issues, but with each municipality deciding how to carry out sex education and which aspects to emphasize, the teaching of sex education across the country varies significantly. Teachers can choose to supplement the teaching of sex education with lectures or workshops held by other professionals or organizations. Furthermore, both the Danish Family Planning Association and the Danish National Association of Gays and Lesbians offer sex education programs and workshops to lower and upper secondary pupils. The neutrality principle in sex education thus allows for LGBT issues to be presented to students, but does not ensure that this will be the case in all schools.

EMPLOYMENT AND ECONOMICS

Denmark is a market economy regulated by an extended welfare state. Based on the ideals of universalism and egalitarianism the Danish state is, like the other Scandinavian welfare states, committed to economic redistribution and the provision of extensive social services. With a GDP of $34,207 per capita[4] and a customarily low unemployment rate, Denmark enjoys a high standard of living.

Although labor unions have experienced a decrease in members over the past decades, the Danish market is still to a high degree organized through collective bargaining between labor unions and employers organizations. Collective agreements determine, among other things, the level of pay and access to paid parental leave and additional holidays, but the main pieces of legislation on antidiscrimination stem from the national parliament and the EU. The Act on prohibition against discrimination in respect of employment, passed by the national parliament in 1996, and the Principle of Equal Treatment in Employment and Occupation, passed by the European Union in 2000, protect the rights of nonheterosexuals in the labor market. These apply to employment in both the public and private sectors and make it possible to take legal action when an employee is discriminated against on the grounds of sexual orientation. Despite these laws, gay and lesbian employees still experience such discrimination. Four in 10 homosexuals report being discriminated against in the workplace in relation to lack of promotions, being bullied, receiving inappropriate comments about their sexuality, or being dismissed because of their sexuality.[5] Labor unions have begun to include sexual orientation in their work on equality in the labor market, and provide their LGBT members with legal advice and the opportunity to have their cases tried in a tribunal when experiencing discrimination. Concurrently, employers are starting to address the need for inclusion in the workplace. The two main municipal employers, the Cities of Copenhagen and Aarhus, have now included sexual orientation in their employment policies.

SOCIAL/GOVERNMENT PROGRAMS

Both the central government and the municipalities provide funding to voluntary organizations accommodating a wide range of communities and their needs, including LGBT organizations, but there are no initiatives or programs funded exclusively by the state or municipalities.

SEXUALITY/SEXUAL PRACTICES

The first known case of AIDS in Denmark was identified in 1981. The gay community believed that the authorities responded too slowly to the problem, and that the media reacted too hysterically. This led to the formation of the STOP AIDS organization, which originated from the Danish National Association of Gays and Lesbians but is now an independent organization committed to the prevention of HIV/AIDS and support for those infected.

The central government responded to the AIDS crisis in 1987 by deciding that the national AIDS health care intervention in Denmark should be based on the voluntary corporation of clients, openness, straight and frank information, and antidiscrimination. As a result, safe sex programs and national information campaigns were launched that promoted sex as a good, healthy, and beautiful activity, but also one that called for responsible behavior in the form of safe sex practices.[6]

Gays and other men who have sex with men (MSM) are overrepresented in the figures on HIV infections and AIDS in Denmark.[7] Although the infection rate experienced a decline in the 1990s, it went up again in 2003. The main reasons for this are believed to be the cutback in public funding for information campaigns and the improved treatments for HIV that can give the impression that HIV is yet another treatable STD. As a consequence, new strategies to target groups displaying risky behavior have been implemented, and more municipalities are allocating funds to HIV/AIDS organizations and campaigns.

FAMILY

The idea of a culture of single households has become popular over the past 25 years or so. During this time, however, the composition of Danish households has not changed significantly, and it is estimated that 75 percent of all couples are married[8] and approximately 32 percent of all adults live alone.[9] The marriage rate has been stable over the past decade, with around 36,400 couples getting married every year; the divorce rate has decreased 6.3 percent from 2005 to 2006. There are now 13.3 divorced persons per 1,000 inhabitants[10] and, in spite of this decrease, Denmark still has one of the highest divorce rates in the world.

Although sometimes far from reality, the ideal of the nuclear family has influenced aspects of Danish family law, with severe implications for LGBT persons. Public debate around changes in family laws has especially questioned gays and lesbians' suitability and abilities as parents.[11] No research has yet focused on LGBT families in Denmark, but research from other Scandinavian countries implies that gay and lesbian parents can raise children just as well as heterosexuals can.[12] Gays and lesbians have for a long time opposed the Danish family laws that favor heterosexual couples in this way. Alternative, nonheterosexual family arrangements and their access to adopting a child and receiving publicly funded assisted insemination monitored by doctors has been a politically contentious issue. Prior to 2007, lesbian and single women were not allowed assisted insemination performed by doctors. This restriction applied to public hospitals and private clinics alike, and was seen as an outright discriminatory legislation. Assisted insemination was limited to childless heterosexual couples and was seen by both the left and right political wings as a necessary restriction in the interest of the child. However, the law had a loophole that resulted in midwives setting up a private clinic to accommodate the needs of lesbian and single women who wanted children by the means of assisted insemination. At the same time, these circumstances kept the debate about LGBT parenthood alive.

Nonheterosexual women's right to receive assisted insemination by a doctor was a hotly debated issue throughout the 1990s and the early 21st century, and paved the way for a change in the law in 2006, which was put in effect on January 1, 2007. Thus, a woman's right to receive publicly funded assisted insemination by a qualified doctor thus no longer rests on her relationship with a man, and many alternative family arrangements are expected to benefit from changes in the law.

Despite these changes, gays and lesbians have not been given the same status as heterosexual couples when it comes to adopting a child. When adopting a child in Denmark, government officials need to approve the applicants and their suitability as parents before they can be added to a waiting list to be offered a child to adopt. Gays and lesbians are prohibited by law from adopting and therefore do not have the right to be even considered as adopters. The same argument that was initially used to prohibit lesbian and single women from assisted insemination is now also used to prohibit gays and lesbians from access to adoption, although single women are granted this option. Furthermore, it is argued that most of the countries where children are put up for adoption do not wish to let gays and lesbians adopt, which complicates the matter, as it does not only relate to domestic Danish legislation. As a response to this, some politicians and LGBT interest groups have suggested that Denmark make separate agreements with the countries in question concerning gay and lesbian adopters.

Even though gays and lesbians do not have the right to adopt, LGBT families nevertheless exist in many forms. Some may have children from previous heterosexual relationships, others may have received assisted insemination in private clinics, and some children may have a gay father and a lesbian mother who have chosen to start a family together, with or without respective partners. In any of these cases, a child can only have two parents in a legal sense. In Denmark, LGBT persons are allowed to adopt their partner's child when they have been together for at least 2½ years, provided that the child's other parent is willing to give up his or her legal rights and obligations. However, lesbian couples that have become pregnant by assisted insemination with an anonymous sperm donor have the right to second-parent adoption when the child is three months old.

Family policy in the labor market has yet to adjust to new family arrangements. The legislation concerning the rights to parental leave in the labor market is still gender-specific. This creates problems for parents of the same sex because they lose out on the possibility of caring for their newborn child at home.

COMMUNITY

The Danish National Association of Gays and Lesbians was founded in 1948 (then the Circle of 1948) and, although it has undergone significant changes since its initial formation, it still exists today as the only national organization bringing together gays, lesbians, bisexuals, and transgender people. The organization was inspired by similar organizations in Germany, the Netherlands, and Switzerland, and was founded with the purpose of bringing together gays and lesbians living in isolation in Danish society. Later on, bisexuals were included, and in 2008 it was decided that transgender people would be included in the organization. After only a few years the organization had 1,600 members. During the widespread police harassment and negative public opinion surrounding especially gay men in the 1950s and 1960s, the membership fell to a mere 65 people when the situation for gay men was at its worst.[13] The removal of some of the discriminatory legislation that had been used to target gay men, together with the turn in public opinion, helped change the situation, but radical change was brought about following the Stonewall riots in the United States in 1969. Inspired by the situation in the United States, a group of gay men formed the Gay Liberation Front, which launched a new confrontational style in their campaigning. A few years later, Lesbian Movement was formed by a group of lesbians who neither felt at home in the male-dominated Danish National Association of Gays and Lesbians nor in the heterosexually dominated new feminist movement. Although neither movement lasted more than 10–15 years, they marked a rebellion against what they saw as the older generation's conformity and invisibility in society, and paved the way for change in the campaigning style of the Danish National Association of Gays and Lesbians, who took on a more confrontational approach to bringing about change for gays, lesbians, and bisexuals.

Today, the organization continues to be one of the main platforms in Denmark for political campaigning and activism, as well as cultural activities, sex education workshops, guidance and advice services, and so on, and is also part of the International Lesbian and Gay Association (ILGA). Local grassroots associations and networks exist in all the major cities, organizing social and cultural activities and support groups for people living with HIV/AIDS. The Danish National Association of Gays and Lesbians was until recently the publisher of the longest-surviving magazine for gays, lesbians, and bisexuals, *PAN* magazine.

Immigration from the Middle East and North African countries over the past four decades has introduced ethnic minorities into Danish society. LGBT persons from minority backgrounds face distinct difficulties in Danish society as they struggle with the acceptance of both their sexuality and their ethnic, racial, or religious background. As a response to this situation, Sabaah, meaning *new beginning,* was formed in 2006 as an organization for LGBT persons from minority backgrounds in Denmark. The Danish National Association of Gays and Lesbians also has a branch catering for the needs of gays, lesbians, bisexuals, and transgender people from minority backgrounds.

Trans-Danmark, the National Association of Transvestites and Transsexuals, was initially a group of transgender people loosely connected on the Internet, but is now the main platform for transgender people in the country. The organization is campaigning to change the laws on gender-specific first names and the central person register number (CPR-Number). The organization is the only one representing transgender interests that has the right to attend hearings in the Danish parliament.

In general, the emergence and expansion of Internet use has made it possible for LGBT persons to get together in new ways by joining online networks, forums, or mailing lists. This means that it is no longer necessary to be in or near one of the bigger cities in the country to be a part of the different LGBT communities.

HEALTH

As an extended welfare state, Denmark provides universal health care to all its citizens. In 1983, it was made mandatory for health care personnel to report any incident of AIDS to a central register listing the person's name, CPR-number (which includes details of the persons age and gender), presumed method of transmission, immigration status, and date of first HIV-positive test. Since 1990, HIV infections have been registered as well, although this registration is made anonymously and only includes details of gender, age, presumed method of transmission, immigration status, and dates of previous HIV tests. On this basis, it is estimated that there are currently 5,000 people living with HIV and 550 people suffering from AIDS in Denmark.[14]

Transsexuals make up a small minority, comprising only a few hundred people in Danish society.[15] Their health needs in relation to the alteration of their gender are catered to at the Sexological Clinic in Copenhagen. The clinic is part of a state hospital, and is the only place in the country where transsexuals can receive treatment. Transgender people in the Trans-Danmark organization have opposed the state monopoly on the treatment of transgender persons on several grounds: it is inflexible for those living outside the capital, but most importantly the clinic has a high proportion of interns/younger doctors and a high staff turnover, hindering professional expertise and specialization. Instead, transgender individuals wish to be able to seek treatment and surgery at private clinics and in other hospitals within the EU's internal market, which allows for the free movement of goods, capital, people, and services within EU member states but does not apply to public services such as health provision.

POLITICS AND LAW

Sodomy

Until 1933, sexual relations between men were illegal. Prior to 1933, sodomy laws in which a range of offences against nature were criminalized had regulated men's sexual relations. As offences against nature involved the inappropriate use of the male genitals, women's sexual relations were not punishable and were therefore legal. In 1930, the age of consent for heterosexual relationships was raised from 12 to 15 years, and was set to 18 for homosexuals. This remained the case until 1976, when the age of consent was lowered to 15 for homosexuals as well.

Marriage

In 1989, Denmark became the first country in the world to pass a law making it possible to formally register same-sex partnerships.[16] With few but important exceptions, the law on civil partnership gave same-sex relationships equal status to heterosexual marriages. Political debate on the legal status of other family arrangements than the heterosexual marriage was sparked in 1973, when the Socialist Party proposed a law granting alternative living and family arrangements legal rights in relation to inheritance, adoption, and so on. During the 1970s, members of the Danish Association of Gays and Lesbians debated internally whether or not to conform to heterosexual family life standards and campaign for equal rights to marry. The result was the establishment of a committee to draft a bill legalizing marriage between persons of the same sex. Although a government commission rejected such a bill in 1984, the Danish Association of Gays and Lesbians were successful in their lobbying and in 1989 the bill was proposed in parliament. Following traditional procedures when voting on an ethically delicate matter, all members of parliament were set free from the official party line to vote according to their personal beliefs. The law was passed with 71 votes in favor of and 47 against the bill and on October 1, 1989, cofounder of the Danish Association of Gays and Lesbians Axel Lundahl-Madsen was able to legally register his relationship of many years with Eigil Eskildsen.

Transsexuals

To transgender persons, the law regulating the CPR-number poses specific problems. The CPR-number includes a person's date of birth, but also gives information about the person's sex. People who wish to live as the opposite sex will have to reveal their sex at birth at public or private institutions. For example, libraries, pharmacies, and banks require the CPR-number. Transsexuals who wish to alter their body or change their first name and CPR-number and be recognized as their gender of choice must first undergo treatment at the only public sexological clinic in Denmark. The clinic adheres to the Standards of Care drawn up by the international World Professional Association for Transgender Health.[17]

In order for a transsexual person to change his or her sex, the person must undergo observation and treatment for two years. In this period of time, the person must undergo hormonal treatment for at least one year and live as the gender of choice most of the time. There is no bill specifically addressing transgender surgery; instead. the bill on sterilization and castration regulates this. Permission to undergo surgical procedure to change one's sex is granted by the National Board of Health, which then obtains a statement about the person's suitability for surgery. It is then in the hands of the Medico-Legal Council to decide whether a person is allowed the surgical procedure. Every year, five to ten persons are granted permission to surgically change their sex, most of them being male-to-female. It is commonly assumed that some transsexuals choose to finance surgery abroad, where access is easier and less restricted.[18] A transsexual person who has undergone surgery abroad and afterwards wishes to change his or her gender in a legal sense and thus get a new CPR-number that reflects the new gender of choice can be granted this by applying to the National Board of Health. Applying to the Department of Family Affairs can change gender-specific first names.

Bisexuals

As is the case in many other countries, bisexuals are virtually invisible in Danish legislation. When with a partner of the same sex, bisexuals are viewed as homosexuals; with a partner of the opposite sex, they are perceived as heterosexuals. The only time in Danish legislation when bisexuality is mentioned is in relation to donating blood. MSMs cannot donate blood; neither can a woman who has had sex with a bisexual man. The Danish National Association of Gays and Lesbians has always had bisexual members and, since 2002, has made it a priority to work on increasing the visibility of bisexual people in both the law and society.

RELIGION AND SPIRITUALITY

Denmark enjoys freedom of religion, but the constitution privileges the Evangelical Lutheran church as the state church, and as such, matters of the church are regulated by the Ministry of Ecclesiastical Affairs. Eighty-three percent of the population belongs to the Church of Denmark, but only an estimated 2 percent of the members attend service on a regular basis.[19] The Evangelical Lutheran Church of Denmark does not represent a unified organization, and therefore has no clear or coherent stance toward LGBT issues and people. Some clerics wish to allow for gays and lesbians to marry in their congregations, while others see homosexuality as a sin and therefore incompatible with Christianity.[20] The law on marriage currently prohibits clerics who wish to perform religious wedding ceremonies for same-sex couples from doing so. A change in this will allow for the Church, and not the state, to decide how to proceed in cases where a gay or lesbian couple wishes to marry in the Church of Denmark. Within the Church, this remains a much-debated issue, and the right-wing branch has threatened to leave the Church of Denmark if gays and lesbians are allowed a religious ceremony in the church.

Religious LGBT persons have found different ways to exercise their faith. The Universal Fellowship of Metropolitan Community Churches, which first originated in the United States, also has a congregation in Denmark, bringing together LGBT people from various strands of Christianity to celebrate their faith. The national network Christian and Homosexual invites Christian gays and lesbians to meet likeminded people in an open environment, but does not function as a congregation or perform services.

VIOLENCE

Generally, Denmark has low crime rates, with only 53 homicides in 2005[21] and 7.2 percent of the population reporting incidents or threats of violence in the same year.[22] There are no official surveys documenting the experiences of LGBT persons in relation to hate crimes. Victims of offences who believe the violence to be motivated by bias or prejudice do not have the option to report the incident as a hate crime. Instead, the police decide whether the offence should be investigated as a crime motivated by bias or prejudice. However, bias or prejudice is seen as an aggravating circumstance for an offence, and will result in stricter penalties in cases ruled to be hate crimes. The issue of definitions of hate crime remains a politically contested question and LGBT organizations are lobbying for a change in the law that will make it possible for the victim to define whether he or she has been the victim of a hate crime.

OUTLOOK FOR THE 21ST CENTURY

Since the 1980s, LGBT persons have gained many of the rights that the heterosexual majority of the Danish population enjoys. In particular, gays and lesbians have become an integrated part of much legislation on antidiscrimination and equal rights. Many of the previous laws were changed as a result of extensive lobbying by LGBT interest groups that have put gays and lesbians' equal rights in society at the fore of their political agendas. The LGBT community in Denmark is now experiencing diversification over the issue of integration into the mainstream heterosexual society versus a separatist stance with a focus on difference and the distinct qualities of LGBT people. This may well lead to new subcultures and political debates within LGBT communities and society at large in the future.

RESOURCE GUIDE

Suggested Reading

Henning Bech, *When Men Meet: Homosexuality and Modernity* (Cambridge: Polity Press, 1997).

Nico Beger, Kurt Krickler, Jackie Lewis, and Maren Wuch, eds., *Equality for Lesbians and Gay Men: a Relevant Issue in the Civil and Social Dialogue* (Brussels: ILGA-Europe, 1998).

Jan Löfström, *Scandinavian Homosexualities: Essays on Gay and Lesbian Studies* (New York: Haworth Press, 1998).

Ken Plummer, ed., *Modern Homosexualities: Fragments of Lesbian and Gay Experience* (London: Routledge, 1992).

Robert Wintemute and Mads Andenæs, eds., *Legal Recognition of Same-Sex Partnerships: A Study of National, European and International Law* (Portland: Hart Publishing, 2001).

Films

En Soap (104 min.; 2006). Directed by Pernille Fischer Christensen. Garage Film AB.
   A drama about the friendship between a transgender person and her neighbor.
En Kort, En Lang (98 min.; 2001). Directed by Hella Joof. Angel Films. A film about a gay
   man who finds himself falling in love with his partner's sister-in-law.

Web Sites

Gayguide, http://www.gayguide.dk.
   Provides information on cultural activities for gays, lesbians, and bisexuals.
Kvinfo, http://www.kvinfo.dk.
   Mainly a library and resource center for information on women and gender studies in
   Denmark; also has a section on LGBT issues in Denmark and other Nordic countries.
Mor og Far x 2 (Mom and Dad x 2), http://www.morogfarx2.dk.
   Web-based network for nonheterosexual families.
Regnbuefamilier (Rainbow Families), www.regnbuefamilier.dk.
   Online forum for rainbow families. The Web site provides information on legislation
   and news, as well as advice.

Organizations

AIDS, Phone: +45 39 27 14 40
   Collects funding for patient support, research, and information for the general pub-
   lic on HIV/AIDS
HIV-Danmark, http://www.hiv-danmark.dk.
   Organization for people suffering from HIV in Denmark. Provides support and lob-
   bies in the interest of HIV patients and their relatives.
STOP AIDS—Bøssernes HIV Organisation (Stop AIDS—HIV Organization for HIV-
   positive Gays), http://stopaids.dk.
   The first organization in Denmark to campaign on HIV/AIDS. Provides informa-
   tion on HIV/AIDS and safe sex in gay communities.

Minority Focus

Sabaah, http://www.sabaah.dk.
Salon Oriental, http://www.salonoriental.dk.
   A forum for gays, lesbians, and bisexuals from minority backgrounds. The organiza-
   tion is a part of the Danish Association of Gays and Lesbians.

Political Action

Landsforeningen for Bøsser og Lesbiske (The Danish Association of Gays and Lesbians),
      http://www.lbl.dk.
   The national political platform for gay, lesbian, and bisexual persons. Besides political
   campaigning, the organization has local branches organizing cultural activities, sex
   education workshops, and advice and guidance services.
Lambda, http://www.lambda.dk.
   Organization for gays and lesbians on the island of Funen. The organization is en-
   gaged in political campaigning and also offers an advice service.
The Queer Committee of the Danish Red-Green Alliance, http://www.queer.dk.
   Confronts the heterosexual norms within Danish legislation and politics. The committee also arranges cultural activities for anyone sympathizing with LGBT issues.

Students

BLUS, http://www.blus.dk.
> Organization for gay, lesbian, and bisexual students in the Copenhagen area. Organizes GayDay every Tuesday evening at the Student's House.

Religious

Kristen og Homo (Christian and Homosexual), http://www.kristenoghomo.dk.
> Online network for Christian gay, lesbian, and bisexual persons.

Markens Liljer, http://www.markensliljer.dk.
> The Universal Fellowship of Metropolitan Community Churches branch in Denmark. Performs a ceremony every Sunday at 4 P.M.

Transgender

Alternative Maskuliniteter (Alternative Masculinities), http://www.al-ma.dk.
> Network for alternative expressions of masculinity by persons born as female. Open for all sexual orientations.

Patientforeningen for Transseksuelle (Patient Organization for Transsexuals), http://www.pft.dk.
> Organization that promotes the interests of transsexuals.

Trans-Danmark, Landsforeningen for Transvestitter og Transseksuelle (National Association of Transvestites and Transsexuals), http://www.trans-danmark.dk.
> Internet-based interest group for transvestites and transsexuals. Lobbies for change in the laws on gender-specific first names and CPR-numbers.

NOTES

1. Danish Immigration Service, Ministry for Refugees, Immigration and Integration, *Tal og Fakta—Befolkningsstatistik om Udlændinge* [*Numbers and Facts—Population Survey on Foreign Nationals*] (June 2007), http://www.nyidanmark.dk/da-dk/Statistik/oversigt_statistik.htm (accessed November 27, 2007).

2. See, for example, the articles Mette Liv Mertz, "It Goes Without Saying—The Privilege of Commonplace," *Lambda Nordica* 10, no. 1–2 (2003): 33–38; and Karin Lützen, "Gay and Lesbian Politics: Assimilation or Subversion: A Danish Perspective," *Journal of Homosexuality* 35, no. 3/4 (1998): 233–43.

3. Danish Ministry of Education, *Undervisningsvejledning for Emnet Sundheds- og Seksualundervisning og Familiekundskab* [*Guideline for Teaching the Subject Health, Family and Sex Education*], http://www.faellesmaal.uvm.dk/fag/Sundhed/vejledning.html (accessed October 10, 2007).

4. Organisation for Economic Co-Operation and Development (OECD), *Statistical Profile of Denmark: Figures from 2005,* http://stats.oecd.org/wbos/viewhtml.aspx?queryname=312&querytype=view&lang=zen (accessed October 10, 2007).

5. *Ugebrevet A4* (*A4*), "Bøsser og Lesbiske Diskrimineres på Jobbet" ["Gays and Lesbians Are Discriminated Against in the Workplace"], news release, August 2005, http://www.ugebreveta4.dk/Globals/Temaer/Ligestilling/Bosseroglesbiskediskriminerespajobbet.aspx (accessed December 3, 2007).

6. Henry P. David, Janine M. Morgall, Mogens Osler, Niels K. Rasmussen, and Birgitte Jensen, "United States and Denmark: Different Approaches to Health Care and Family Planning," *Studies in Family Planning* 21, no. 1 (1990): 1–19.

7. Susan A. Cowan and Else Smith, "Forekomsten af HIV/AIDS i Danmark i perioden 1990–2005" ["The Occurence of HIV/AIDS in Denmark in the Period 1990–2005"], *Ugeskrift for Læger* [*Weekly Scientific Journal of the Danish Medical Association*]

168, no. 23 (2006): 2247, http://www.ugeskriftet.dk/portal/page/portal/LAEGERDK/ UGESKRIFT_FOR_LAEGER/TIDLIGERE_NUMRE/2006 (accessed December 13, 2007).

8. Mogens Nygaard Christoffersen, *Familiens Udvikling i det 20. Århundrede: Demografiske Strukturer og Processer* [*The Development of the Family in the 20th Century: Demographic Structures and Processes*], Danish National Centre for Social Research, Report 04:07, 2004, http://www.sfi.dk/sw15159.asp (accessed November 16, 2007).

9. Ibid.

10. Vielser og Skilsmisser [Marriages and Divorces]. Nyt fra Danmarks Statistik [News from Statistics Denmark] Nr. 205 (2006), http://www.dst.dk/Statistik/Nyt/emneopdelt/ nytsingle.aspx?countid=9050&ci=true&pti=1 (accessed December 13, 2007).

11. Christel Stormhøj, "Queering the Family—Critical Reflections on State-Regulated Heteronormativity in Scandinavian Countries," *Lambda Nordica* 9, no. 3–4 (2002): 38–56.

12. Barn i Homosexuella Familjer [Children in Homosexual Families], Statens Offentliga Utredningar [Public Research of the State] 2001:10. Regeringskansliet [Government Offices of Sweden], http://www.regeringen.se/sb/d/108/a/608;jsessionid=a_IhcHF wdxDb (accessed December 2, 2007).

13. Vibeke Nisse and Inge-Lise Paulsen, "Handling Gi'r Forvandling" ["Action Causes Change"], *Lambda Nordica* 6, no.2/3 (2000): 9–41.

14. Cowan and Smith, "Forekomsten af HIV/AIDS i Danmark i perioden 1990–2005."

15. Sexological Clinic, Rigshospitalet, general information on the treatment of transsexuality, http://www.rigshospitalet.dk/rh.nsf/574e4fb13671535fc1256e9100413675/ d0b30b33eee649e4c1256efc003f193d!OpenDocument (accessed November 14, 2007).

16. Ingrid Lund-Andersen, "The Danish Registered Partnership Act, 1989: Has the Act Meant a Change in Attitudes?" in *Legal Recognition of Same-Sex Partnerships—A Study of National, European and International Law,* ed. Robert Wintemute and Mads Andenæs (Portland: Hart Publishing, 2001).

17. Further information can be obtained from the World Professional Association for Transgender Health's Web site, http://www.wpath.org/index.cfm (accessed November 8, 2007).

18. Sexological Clinic, Rigshospitalet, general information on the treatment of transsexuality.

19. Peter Gundelach, Hans Raun Iversen, and Margit Warburg, "Danskernes Nationale Lutherdom" ["The National Lutheranism of the Danes"], *Weekendavisen* [*The Weekly*], September 14, 2007.

20. Church of Denmark, *Bibelen om Homoseksualitet* [*The Bible on Homosexuality*], http://www.folkekirken.dk/aktuelt/temaer/bibelen-ord-fortolkning/bibel-og-homoseksualitet.html (accessed November 29, 2007).

21. Statistics Denmark, *Denmark in Figures* (2007), http://www.denmark.dk/en/ menu/AboutDenmark/DenmarkInBrief/DenmarkAnOverview/DenmarkInWordsAnd-Figures/ (accessed December 13, 2007).

22. Flemming Balvig and Britta Kyvsgaard, *Volden i Danmark 1995 og 2005* [*Violence in Denmark 1995 and 2005*] (University of Copenhagen, Danish Ministry of Justice, Danish Crime Prevention Council, and National Commissioner of Police, 2006), http://www.dkr. dk/sw3415.asp (accessed December 13, 2007).

EUROPEAN UNION

Matteo Bonini Baraldi and Evelyne Paradis

OVERVIEW

Made up of 27 member states (MS), the European Union (EU) is an international entity that has been created and expanded through a number of different international treaties, signed—over the years—by a growing number of European countries. The first signatories of the initial founding treaties were only six (Belgium, Germany, France, Italy, Luxembourg, and the Netherlands); Denmark, Ireland, and the United Kingdom joined in 1973; Greece in 1981; Portugal and Spain in 1986; Austria, Finland, and Sweden in 1995; Cyprus, the Czech Republic, Estonia, Hungary, Latvia, Lithuania, Malta, Poland, Slovakia, and Slovenia in 2004; and Bulgaria and Romania in 2007.

According to the official figures,[1] the majority of citizens in all EU countries believe membership in the EU is a good thing for their country, but the level of support presents remarkable differences throughout the EU, and it has changed over the years. According to the same opinion poll, a majority of people in the EU (54%) consider that their country has actually benefited from its membership in the EU. At present, there are three countries that are negotiating their future membership: Croatia, the former Yugoslav Republic of Macedonia, and Turkey.[2]

Today, the EU is a significant economic and commercial power, and claims to be the world's biggest donor of development aid to poorer countries. As of 2008, the territory of the EU covers more than 4 million square kilometers (approximately 2.5 million square miles). The EU's population is almost half a billion, and it shares a commitment to peace, democracy, the rule of law, and respect for human rights.

The EU is less than half the size of the United States, but its population is over 50 percent larger, the world's third largest after China and India. In terms of birth rates, by 2004 the total fertility rate had fallen to about 1.5 children per woman. The population of young people is lower and the workforce is shrinking; this means that fewer workers will have to support more and more pensioners. The number of people over 80 is forecasted to reach 6.3 percent of the population by 2025.

The EU is performing relatively well in the world's economy. Its gross domestic product (GDP) is steadily growing. As a consequence of the entry of new MS in 2004 and 2007, the EU's GDP is now greater than that of the United States. This is even more striking when one considers that the EU makes up only 7 percent of the world's population, but its trade with the rest of the world accounts for approximately a fifth of global exports and imports.

Europeans seem to be well connected to Europe and to the rest of the world. By 2006, more than 90 percent of businesses and 49 percent of households in the EU-27 had access to the Internet. According to recent statistics, a clear majority of Europeans (56%) say they can hold a conversation in one foreign language. For some of these, it is not a problem to speak two or even three foreign languages. However, almost half of all Europeans have severe difficulties in speaking a language different from their own.

Originally, the Treaty of Rome of 1957 establishing the European Economic Community (EEC)—later the European Community (EC)—was aimed at creating an internal market where people, goods, services, and capital could circulate without barriers. Over time, several other treaties—starting with the European Single Act of 1986—partially changed the face and the substance of the EEC. The EU was formally born in 1992 with the Treaty of Maastricht, which introduced the economic and monetary union and European Union citizenship. Since the adoption of the Maastricht Treaty, every citizen of a MS automatically acquires EU citizenship and the benefits dependent thereon, such as the right to move and reside, the right of petition, the right to vote and stand as a candidate, and to diplomatic protection. Moreover, since 1999, 16 countries—with a total population of over 320 million—have now adopted a single currency, the euro. The Maastricht Treaty was also important because it expressly codified the duty of the EU to respect fundamental rights, a duty arising—up to that point—from the common constitutional traditions of the MS and the European Convention for the Protection of Human Rights and Fundamental Freedoms (ECHR).[3]

In 1997, the Amsterdam Treaty was signed in the attempt to reinforce the project of a political union. While the treaty did not address some of the most important challenges, including decision-making procedures, it did introduce competence of the EC in areas not strictly linked to the economic market, such as visas, asylum, immigration, and other policies concerning the free movement of persons, employment, and customs cooperation. The Treaty of Amsterdam was followed by the adoption of the Nice Treaty in 2000, which further contributed to the process of reforming the EU and was accompanied by the proclamation of the EU Charter of Fundamental Rights. In the following years, the debate over the future of the EU took place in the context of discussions around a draft treaty establishing a constitution for Europe. The entry into force of the new treaty, signed by all MS and ratified by a majority of them, was postponed following the negative outcome of two referenda held in France and the Netherlands. In December 2007, European political leaders launched a new, simplified treaty that should overcome the previous difficulties, the Treaty of Lisbon. This treaty is not yet in force, because not all MS have completed its ratification.

Through the adoption of the various treaties, the EU has acquired varying competencies to legislate and issue regulations in the different political, economic, social, and environmental areas in order to achieve its objectives. According to the recent Treaty of Lisbon, the division of powers and competences now in place in the EU (the three-pillar structure) should be modified. The treaty foresees a renewed division of powers between the EU and the MS: in some areas, the EU has exclusive competence, in some it has a shared competence, and in others it has only a supporting competence (it can only support, coordinate, or supplement the actions of the MS).

A central objective of the European Community, as set in article 14 of the EC treaty, was to establish an internal market, "an area without internal frontiers in which the free movement of goods, persons, services, and capitals is ensured."[4] To this end, many European Community measures are aimed at the approximation of national provisions and mainly address the establishment of a governance regime, rules of exchange, or property rights. Abolition of tariffs in trade, customs union, abolition of quantitative restrictions on imports, prohibition on discrimination against imports and exports, and on discriminatory taxation, were major steps towards an economic union. Since its origins, the EC treaty considered that the internal market should be a system where competition is not distorted. Thus, it provides rules forbidding agreements between undertakings that prevent, restrict, or distort competition, and rules against the abuse of dominant market positions. The EC also regulates both state involvement in business practices and (since 1990) mergers.

As the harmonization of national laws proceeded in these fields, it became increasingly clear that closer economic integration could not function properly without a monetary union. The turning point was the Maastricht Treaty of 1992, which amended the EC treaty to ensure that an economic and monetary union (EMU) could soon be realized. New competencies were added to the EC, such as the management of monetary affairs and the co-ordination and surveillance of national economic policies. These competencies were especially conceived to ensure the realization of one of the four treaty freedoms, the circulation of capital, which had been lagging behind.

Today, European Community policies foreseen by the EC treaty are no longer exclusively connected with the functioning of the common market, but rather testify to the European Community's involvement in social, environmental, and development cooperation policies. In close partnership with MS, the EC can also act—through supporting measures—in such fields as employment, economic and social cohesion, competitiveness, research and technological development, health protection, education and training, and consumer protection. The Treaty of Maastricht also addressed aspects more closely related to the need to ensure more political integration. Alongside economic and monetary powers, new competences were granted to the EC in the fields of visas for third-country nationals, education, culture, public health, and consumer protection.

European Institutions

Apart from the treaties, European Community law takes the form of regulations, directives, and decisions, which are binding, as well as recommendations and opinions. Regulations are general acts directly applicable in the MS, without need of implementing measures. Directives are binding as to the result to be achieved, but MS are free to choose the most appropriate form and means. They need to be transposed by each MS through internal acts of parliament or governmental regulations. Decisions are individual acts that bind only the specific subject to whom they are directed. Recommendations and opinions can be considered instruments of indirect approximation of laws among MS.

The main institutions of the European Community are the European Parliament (EP), the Council of Ministers, the European Commission, and the Court of Justice of the European Communities (ECJ). Legislative power is exercised by the Council alone, or by the Council and the EP together in some matters (the

co-decision procedure). The European Commission has supervisory, decision making, and implementation powers: it is the guardian of the treaties, as it may bring
actions against other European Community institutions and against MS that do
not abide by EU laws and regulations. The European Commission also proposes
new legislation, and implements the rules adopted by the Council. The EP is the
elected body that represents the EU's citizens and takes part in the legislative process. The parliament has developed much since its birth in 1957 with the Treaty of
Rome, from a simple assembly of appointed members to the only directly elected
body of the EU, exercising powers similar to those of the national parliaments.
As for the ECJ, it has the role of interpreting European Community law. It also
delivers judgments on enforcement actions brought by the European Commission
or MS against other MS. The European Council, made up the heads of state and
government of the MS, has developed from an informal meeting to an influentially
guiding and supervisory body.

POLITICS AND LAW

Fundamental Rights

Throughout the past two decades the EU has become increasingly committed
to the active promotion of human rights. A significant manifestation of this commitment was the inclusion in the 1997 Treaty of Amsterdam of article 13, which
empowered the European Community to "take appropriate action to combat discrimination based on sex, racial, or ethnic origin, religion or belief, disability, age,
or sexual orientation." Following from this article, the Employment Framework
Directive was adopted in 2000[5]; this Directive obliges all MS to introduce legislation banning discrimination in employment on a number of grounds, including
sexual orientation. Given the number of countries and the population affected, the
Employment Directive is arguably the most important single legislative initiative in
the history of European lesbian, gay, and bisexual rights. In 2000, the EU also adopted the European Union Charter of Fundamental Rights, which was signed by a
majority of MS in December 2007, conferring the same legally binding character as
the EU treaties themselves. The charter includes sexual orientation discrimination
as a prohibited ground of discrimination in its nondiscrimination article 21, being
the first international human rights charter to do so.

These developments, together with a series of resolutions of the European Parliament, are increasingly establishing a rule that discrimination on the grounds of
sexual orientation is—so far as the EU is concerned—unacceptable. This opens up
the possibility of making progress with eliminating discrimination in all areas of activity that lie within the competence of the European Community, and particularly
in employment, access to goods and service, asylum, and immigration.

At the Nice Summit in 2000, the Charter of Fundamental Rights and Freedoms
in the EU was proclaimed. This charter set out in a single text the whole range
of civil, political, economic, and social rights of European citizens and all persons
residing in the EU, defined as the EU's common values. Its purpose is to make
those principles more visible in order to strengthen the protection of fundamental
rights in the EU. From the point of view of LGBT rights, this is also an important
document because it is the first international human rights instrument to explicitly
include sexual orientation as a prohibited ground of discrimination (article 21).

While proclaimed in 2000, the Charter has still to come into force in the EU. Incorporated in the defunct constitutional treaty rejected by France and the Netherlands in 2005, the Charter's legal status remained unclear until the recent adoption of the most recent EU treaty. With the signature of the Treaty of Lisbon in December 2007, the Charter acquired the same legally binding character as the European treaties themselves. Once the Lisbon Treaty is ratified by MS, the Charter will have the same legal status.

Compliance with the Charter on Fundamental Rights as well as with the European Convention of Human Rights is monitored by the newly established EU Fundamental Rights Agency. The role of the agency, which opened in March 2007, is to provide information and data on fundamental rights in the EU MS in their implementation of EU law. As part of its work program for the first year, the agency conducted both a legal and a sociological study on homophobia and discrimination base on sexual orientation and gender identity in the EU.[6]

The Role of the European Parliament

From an LGBT perspective, the European Parliament has been a principal driving force in bringing LGBT rights onto the European political agenda. A cornerstone in the Parliament's works for LGBT rights was the Roth report and the subsequently adopted "Resolution on equal rights for homosexuals and lesbians in the EC" (February 8, 1994). Although not binding, this resolution was a far reaching text that called upon the European Commission and the MS to secure LGBT rights throughout the European Community.

Since then, the European Parliament's work for LGBT people has steadily increased. members of the European Parliament (MEPs) have been influencing the political agenda by amending Commission proposals to reflect the interests of LGBT people, by organizing public hearings to raise awareness and foster discussion and by drafting reports and resolutions that, although not legally binding, are nonetheless important tools in the EU's political context. In fact, since the Roth report, the Parliament has reiterated its views on LGBT rights in several resolutions on the situation as regards fundamental rights in the EU. Recently, the EP adopted a resolution on homophobia in Europe, where it condemns any discrimination on the basis of sexual orientation (January 18, 2006). The strong stance against homophobia was reiterated in the resolution on the increase in racist and homophobic violence in Europe of June 2006. Another resolution on homophobia in Europe was adopted on April 26, 2007, mainly with a view to expressing deep concern for the homophobic climate that had been escalating in Poland, an EU member state since May 1, 2004. In this resolution, the EP recalled that the EU is a community of values, "with respect for human rights and fundamental freedoms, democracy and the rule of law, equality and non-discrimination among its most cherished values." It also affirmed that "the EU institutions and Member States have a duty to ensure that the human rights of people living in Europe are respected, protected and promoted."[7]

The Parliament has only been partially able to put transgender rights on the European political agenda; much still remains to be done to increase awareness. With the exception of the Parliament's September 12, 1989, resolution on discrimination against transsexuals and the inclusion of gender identity as grounds for asylum, transgender issues continue to be underrepresented. The most groundbreaking advances for transgender people in recent years have come through case law at the European courts, not from the Parliament or the other European institutions.

An important participant in the Parliament has been the Intergroup on Gay and Lesbian Rights. Intergroups bring together MEPs from different political parties who share similar interest on specific issues (e.g. bioethics, disability, etc.). The Intergroup on Gay and Lesbian Rights maintains a European-level watch on issues that affect the LGBT community and ensures that equal rights remain at the forefront of the parliamentary agenda. It also intervenes, whenever possible, in incidents of homophobia, both within the EU and beyond its borders.[8]

The Council of Europe and the European Convention on Human Rights

Created in 1949 in the aftermath of World War II, the Council of Europe (CoE) is an institution completely separated from the EU. It brings together 47 countries with a view to protecting human rights, pluralist democracy, and the rule of law; encouraging the development of Europe's cultural identity and diversity; finding common solutions to the challenges facing European society; and consolidating democratic stability. One of the most prominent achievements of the CoE is the adoption of the European Convention for the Protection of Human Rights and Fundamental Freedoms (ECHR), opened for signature in Rome on November 4, 1950, and in force since September 1953. The ECHR lays down a catalogue of civil and political rights and freedoms and is supplemented by a number of additional protocols. One of its most innovative and useful traits is that it sets up specific enforcement bodies, although the European Court of Human Rights (ECtHR) is the only remaining one after a series of reforms. Decisions of the ECtHR are binding; if left unaddressed, they may trigger action by the Committee of Ministers of the CoE, the body responsible for overseeing that the general or specific obligations arising from the decision are executed.

Among other rights, the ECHR protects the right to respect for private and family file (article 8), freedom of assembly and association (article 11), and the right to marry (article 12). Furthermore, it states that the enjoyment of the rights and freedoms set forth in the European Convention should be secured without discrimination (article14). In order to secure the prohibition of discrimination in the enjoyment of any right set forth by law, and not just European Convention rights, member countries adopted additional protocol 12, which entered into force on April 1, 2005, for the 10 countries that had ratified it by then. As of 2008, only 15 countries have ratified it.[9]

The ECtHR has built a record of decisions whereby it demonstrates increasing support for LGBT issues, albeit it has still to accept that same-sex couples fall within the ambit of the right of respect for family life under article 8. Only in *X, Y, Z v. the United Kingdom* did the ECtHR recognize that the family arrangement of a couple raising a child, where one partner was a female-to-male (FTM) transsexual, did fall within the ambit of family life, although it ruled against the claimant who was trying to have his social tie with the child legally recognized.[10] As regards private life, the ECtHR has ruled that "the object of Article 8 is essentially that of protecting the individual against arbitrary interference by the public authorities," and it added that the provision "does not merely compel the State to abstain from such interference: in addition to this primarily negative undertaking, there may be positive obligations inherent in an effective respect for private or family life" (*Marckx v. Belgium*). During the 1970s, the now defunct European Commission of Human Rights refused several times to accept that cases concerning either criminalizing of sexual conduct between consensual adults of the same sex, or discriminatory age of consent, could fall within the scope of the right of respect for private life; many applications were declared inadmissible or were considered ill-founded.[11] Only in 1981 did the ECtHR find in favor of an applicant who had challenged the criminal prohibition of homosexuality still in force in Northern Ireland (*Dudgeon v. U.K.;* see also *Norris v. Ireland* and *Modinos v. Cyprus*). With this decision, antisodomy laws were declared illegal throughout all Council of Europe countries, more than 20 years earlier than in the United States.

As far as differential age of consent is concerned, the first favorable case came in 1997 (*Sutherland v. U.K.*, decided by the European Commission) and it was confirmed several times by the ECtHR in subsequent cases on grounds that it was discriminatory and thus contrary to articles 8 and 14 of the ECHR.[12] The ECtHR also banned sexual orientation discrimination in (public) employment, by ruling in 1999 that dismissal of members of the armed forces on grounds of homosexuality infringes the right of respect for private life guaranteed by the European Convention.[13]

By now, it is established in case law that "differences based on sexual orientation require particularly serious reasons by way of justification." The first time the prohibition of discrimination was applied by the ECtHR to a case concerning sexual orientation was in 1999 (*Salgueiro da Silva Mouta v. Portugal*); the case concerned custody of a gay father over his child and the ECtHR concluded that denial of custody on grounds of the father's sexual orientation amounts to unacceptable discrimination. Subsequently, several other cases found a violation of article 14, in conjunction with article 8 (*S.L.; L. and V.; R.H.; Ladner; Wolfmeyer; H.G and G.B.; B.B.*).

In 2003, the Court found in favor of a surviving partner who had lost his tenancy rights over the apartment he used to share with his late same-sex partner because Austrian law only granted them to the spouse or the unmarried partner of different sex (*Karner v. Austria;* for a contrary precedent in the Commission, see *Simpson v. U.K.*). In other cases, however, article 8 of the convention did not assist LGBT couples in finding adequate redress: for instance, in *W.J. and D.P. v. the United Kingdom* and in *C. and L.M. v. the United Kingdom,* the Commission found that the deportation of a non-EU citizen without residence permit, although it impinged upon private life and the relationship with his or her same-sex partner, did not constitute a violation of the right of respect for private life (see also *X and Y v. U.K.*). In a 1992 case, the Commission ruled that a stable homosexual relationship between two women does not fall within the scope of the right of respect for family life.[14] The ECtHR has not yet accepted that same-sex couples enjoy a right to respect for their family life or a right to marry. Several statements on the meaning of marriage can be found in cases brought by transgender applicants who could not marry after reassignment. Early case law was repeatedly unfavorable: the ECtHR held that the right to marry foreseen in the convention refers only to traditional marriage between people of a different biological sex (*Rees v. U.K.*), and that domestic laws forbidding marriage of transgender people with a person of the same biological sex cannot be considered an excessive limitation of the right to marry (*Cossey v. U.K.; Sheffield & Horsham v. U.K.*). In these cases, the ECtHR also held that refusal of the government to change the birth certificate after gender reassignment did not constitute a violation of the convention's right to respect of private life. Only in recent times has a more liberal approach developed. In a 2002 landmark decision, the ECtHR finally recognized that the government had to ensure legal recognition of the person's gender reassignment and that there is no justification for "barring the transsexual from enjoying the right to marry under any circumstances" (*Christine Goodwin v. U.K.*).

Finally, in 2007 the ECtHR held that the ban imposed on a pride march and on stationary assemblies by Polish authorities violated both the right to freedom of assembly and the nondiscrimination provision of article 14 (*Bączkowksi v. Poland*). With a landmark decision of January 22, 2008, the ECtHR also held that refusing a lesbian woman the authorization to adopt a child, given "the manner in which certain opinions [of the authorities] were expressed," did mask sexual orientation discrimination, and was thus a conduct in breach of article 14 of the convention taken in conjunction with article 8 (*E.B. v. France*). The ECtHR stressed that "the inescapable conclusion is that her sexual orientation was consistently at the center of deliberations in her regard and omnipresent at every stage of the administrative and judicial proceedings" (paragraph 88). French law did already allow child adoption by single individuals.

EMPLOYMENT AND ECONOMICS

Free Movement

Today, thanks to the development of EU citizenships, all citizens have the right to move, reside, and remain within the territory of the MS. Furthermore, they have the right of equality before the law of other MS: after moving from state to state, they must be treated in the same way as nationals of the MS to which they have moved. More generally, according to recent rules (directive 2004/38/EC), access to social rights by citizens of the EU who move to other MS has been made dependent on the grant of residence by the host state, so as to reflect the contribution of each individual to the society he or she lives in, irrespective of nationality, thus reducing the risk of welfare shopping. Some rights can only be enjoyed after having been granted permanent residence.

Community institutions—and especially the ECJ—have tried to make sure that the benefits descending from national social programs could be afforded to citizens of other MS who were exercising their right to move and reside freely. Several cases brought before the ECJ concerned subsistence allowances, allowances facilitating access to the employment market, and tax breaks. Favorable decisions were reached by virtue of the prohibition of discrimination on grounds of nationality foreseen by the treaty. Furthermore, in the context of equal treatment between men and women, the EC developed a body of laws that has significant social and political repercussions, such as provisions on equal pay; access to employment, vocational training and promotion, and working conditions; social security; occupational social security schemes; and the safety and health at work of pregnant workers.

Originally, guarantees of equal treatment in certain fields were afforded only to those moving from MS to MS for economic purposes: the EC treaty speaks of circulation of *workers,* and affords to migrant workers the right to accept offers of employment, to move freely within the territory of MS for this purpose, to stay in an MS for the purpose of employment, and to remain there after having been employed in that state. Furthermore, the EC treaty guarantees freedom of establishment, which includes the right to take up and pursue activities as self-employed persons and to set up and manage undertakings. Subsequently, rights similar to those given to workers were afforded to other categories of persons, such as students, pensioners, and others. According to a number of old EC regulations and directives, migrant workers had a right to the same social and fiscal benefits as national workers.

Antidiscrimination Legislative Framework

In recent decades, the EU has increasingly taken action to combat discrimination, including discrimination based on sexual orientation. The European Commission maintains that "discrimination seriously undermines EU employment and social protection achievements and that it harms social integration and cohesion," as stated on its Web site. The first EU institution to address LGBT issues in relation to employment was the European Parliament: in 1984, it adopted a Resolution on sexual discrimination at the workplace, where it acknowledged the need to tackle the problems faced by lesbian and gay workers. Subsequently, a European Commission recommendation of 1991 on the protection of the dignity of women and men at work, supplemented by a code of practice on measures to combat sexual harassment, did specifically address harassment against lesbians and gay men. A further positive development (of binding nature) was the amendment of the staff regulations for officials of the Communities in 1998 to foresee sexual orientation as a prohibited ground of discrimination.[15]

A major breakthrough came in 1997 with the inclusion of article 13 in the Treaty of Amsterdam (in force since May 1, 1999), which empowered the European Community to "take appropriate action to combat discrimination based on sex, racial or ethnic origin, religion or belief, disability, age or sexual orientation." This was a unique and vitally important step for gay and lesbian rights in Europe. However, it was not enough in and of itself; it needed to be complemented by concrete measures, both in the legislative and the policy domain. Thanks to various MEPs who kept up the pressure on the European Commission and the respective MS to adopt new legislation, in the year 2000 the Council adopted two landmark directives: the so-called Race Equality Directive (2000/43/EC) combating discrimination on the grounds of racial and ethnic origin in various domains of EC competence, including employment and the provision of goods and services; and the Employment Framework Directive (2000/78/EC), which obliges all MS to introduce legislation banning discrimination in employment on a number of grounds, including sexual orientation.[16]

The Employment Framework Directive represents a significant advance in the progress toward real equality for LGB people in Europe: it prohibits both direct and indirect discrimination based on sexual orientation in access to employment (selection and recruitment) and vocational training, in employment and working conditions (including dismissal and pay), and in membership in employers' organizations or professional bodies. It also protects against harassment and victimization in the workplace.

Because transgender issues are considered to be covered by EC sex discrimination law, gender identity is not mentioned in directive 2000/78. However, discrimination linked to a transgender person's identity was included in the revision of the directive on the equal treatment of men and women (directive 2006/54/EC), which recognizes that the directive also applies to discrimination arising from a person's gender reassignment.

The Employment Framework Directive has been transposed—albeit with a varying degree of accuracy—by all 27 MS of the EU. During negotiations for accession of the MS that joined in 2004 and 2007, the European Commission issued public statements in order to make it clear that antidiscrimination rules need to be considered part of the *acquis communautaire;* this means that antidiscrimination legislation needed to be in place before any country joined the EU. For example, during recent rounds of negotiations, the European Parliament monitored legislative developments in countries that still had discriminatory (often criminal) laws against LGBT people, such as Bulgaria, Cyprus, Hungary, Estonia, Lithuania, and Romania. The implementation of the Employment Framework Directive in national legal systems was first monitored by a group of experts set up by the European Commission who focused specifically on issues of sexual orientation discrimination.[17] Today, implementation of antidiscrimination laws is monitored by the European network of legal experts in the nondiscrimination field, set up by the European Commission in 2004 to cover five grounds of discrimination.

Case Law of the Court of Justice of the EC

In order to have a more complete understanding of the European antidiscrimination legal framework, it is also important to consider the case law on sexual orientation discrimination stemming from European courts, which has not always been favorable to LGBTs. A first noteworthy case was *Grant v. South West Trains Ltd.*[18] In this case, the ECJ was asked to clarify whether the EC provisions on equality between men and women (article 141 of the EC treaty and some secondary law) also covered the case of partner-related employment benefits that had been denied by the British employer of Lisa Grant to her same-sex unmarried partner. The employer's staff regulations granted those benefits to the unmarried partner of an employee, provided that it was of a different sex. The court did not agree with the claimant, and it refused to accept that the differential treatment of the employee, based on the sex of her partner, could be regarded as unlawful (sex) discrimination, because the condition of living with a partner of the opposite sex applied equally to men and women. In contrast, Ms. Grant had argued that she was living with a woman and had been treated less favorably than a man living with a woman, and that this conduct on the part of her employer was sex discrimination forbidden by EC law.

Since then, other cases concerning differences in work-related benefits granted to same-sex registered partners compared to married or registered opposite-sex couples have been brought before the Court of First Instance (CFI) and the ECJ. One case was presented by an official employed by the European Council who had concluded a same-sex registered partnership in his state of origin and claimed the same partner benefits afforded to married officials. Both the CFI and the ECJ rejected his claim on the grounds that legal situations distinct from marriage cannot be treated in the same way as marriage, and that this conclusion did not infringe the principle of equal treatment.[19] Yet, on April 1, 2008, after an ECJ advocate general (Jarabo Colomer Damaso) had delivered his favorable opinion, the court held that Tadao Maruko, the surviving partner of Hans Hettinger, was entitled to the survivor's pension by a pension scheme to which Hettinger had contributed for 45 years.[20] The reason for the refusal was that the two men were parties to a registered life partnership in Germany, rather than to a legal marriage. The court found in favor of Maruko by holding that treating registered same-sex partners differently than married spouses (in relation to pay related benefits) constitutes direct sexual orientation discrimination if the two situations are comparable under the relevant domestic law. *Maruko* has been the ECJ's first judgment in favor of a same-sex couple and a departure from its prior judgment in *D. and Sweden* (2001), which is now overruled.

As regards transgender issues, the case law of the ECJ is conspicuously more favorable. In *P v. S,* the court ruled that discrimination because of gender reassignment is sex discrimination and is, thus, forbidden by EC law.[21] Moreover, in 2004, it concluded that British legislation prohibiting transgender people from marrying a person of a different sex with respect to the acquired sex (because legally it would be a same-sex marriage) was incompatible with EC law insofar as it implied the denial of payment of a survivor's pension to the (unmarried) transgender partner of an employee.[22] Furthermore, the court has recently ruled that the refusal to allow a male-to-female transgender person to retire at age 60, instead of 65 (the retirement age for men in the United Kingdom), is a violation of directive 79/7/EEC on the progressive implementation of the principle of equal treatment for men and women in matters of social security.[23]

POLICIES AND PROGRAMS

EU employment policies and programs that relate to sexual orientation are intrinsically linked to the implementation of the Employment Directive and the mainstreaming of the antidiscrimination principle across the EU's programs and instruments. Recognizing that legislation is not enough, the European Commission has developed programs and projects to support concrete changes in the workplace. First, the European Commission works together with trade unions and employers' associations to support the development of employment practices and workplace policies in line with the directive. For example, the European Commission provided financial support for a project of the European Trade Union Confederation on sexual orientation discrimination. The European Commission has also been working with business by presenting a business case for diversity and good practices by equal opportunity employers, including on sexual orientation. Moreover, the European Commission has supported actions aimed at fighting discrimination in working life through the EQUAL Initiative (European Social Fund), which has fed into the European Employment Strategy. As part of EQUAL, eight projects specifically targeting sexual orientation discrimination were funded.

SOCIAL/GOVERNMENT PROGRAMS

In terms of social policy, the competence of the European Community was originally limited; the EEC Treaty of 1957 only gave a role to the European Community with respect to equal treatment between men and women. However, the development of the internal market in the 1970s was accompanied by an underlying social dimension (see regulation 1408/71 concerning social security for migrant workers), which became more evident with the endorsement of a Community Charter of Basic Social Rights for Workers in 1989. The Amsterdam Treaty contributed to renewed momentum for the European social policy: it introduced the new title on employment and was accompanied by the social protocol. In 2001, the social policy agenda (SPA), prepared by the European Commission after the important Lisbon meeting of the European Council, reflected the new, integrated EU approach aimed at pursuing economic and social renewal through open coordination among MS.

Today, the role of the EC in matters of social solidarity is mainly that of a catalyst. Generally speaking, the European Community does not run its own programs when it comes to social protection and welfare. What it does is to offer additional financial support to national schemes, for instance through the European Social Fund and other programs. Furthermore, it can facilitate cooperation and dialogue with key institutions, agree with MS common objectives, and foster the transfer of best practices. The EU's financial contribution in this field is approximately 10 billion euros per year, which stands out as a very limited budget if compared to the 498 billion euros spent by Germany for social benefits. In this framework, in 2005 the EU adopted a new social agenda, a roadmap for employment and social actions.

More particularly, following the adoption of the Employment Framework Directive, the European Commission launched programs to support the implementation of antidiscrimination legislation. From 2001 to 2006, the European Commission ran its first Community Action Program against discrimination. This was designed to supplement—with awareness-raising and capacity-building actions—the new legislative framework against discrimination in a number of areas. This program involved the expenditure of 100 million euros over a five-year period. Part of this budget was allocated to the European branch of the International Lesbian and Gay Association (ILGA-Europe), as the European umbrella NGO networks representing and defending the rights of people exposed to sexual orientation discrimination. Activities funded under the program include awareness-raising campaigns; training on antidiscrimination legislation for judges, legal practitioners, and NGO representatives; studies on discrimination-related issues (e.g., good practices in the workplace, data collection, etc.); and support for specialized equality bodies.

For the period 2007–2013, the European Commission decided to continue further efforts in this direction by designing a new program called PROGRESS (Program for Employment and Social Solidarity), which combines four former Community action programs. Nondiscrimination is now included in one of PROGRESS's five sections, along with employment, social inclusion and social protection, working conditions, and gender. According to a European Commission leaflet, PROGRESS "will spend its budget of over 700 million on analyzing, networking and sharing of information to improve policy and practice and in campaigns to highlight key employment and social issues over its seven years of implementation." Under PROGRESS, training and awareness-raising activities will continue to be funded, and umbrella networks such as ILGA-Europe will continue to be financially supported.

Another recent EU initiative relevant for LGBT people was the declaration of 2007 as the European Year of Equal Opportunities for All, a year-long concerted effort aimed at making people in the EU more aware of their rights to equal treatment. During this year, MS developed national strategies with priorities for the year on each ground of discrimination included in article 13, and implemented activities and projects addressing all the grounds of discrimination. From a LGBT perspective, the Year of Equal Opportunities allowed LGBT people to gain visibility in many countries and opened up opportunities for national LGBT organizations to establish a sustainable dialogue with policy makers and public officials.

FAMILY

Competence over substantive family law matters, namely the celebration of marriages, conditions to marry, matrimonial property regimes, divorce, maintenance, children, adoption, and all that is related to civil status, is retained by MS. This can be deduced by the fact that no treaty provision enables the EU to adopt substantive measures in these fields. Over the last two decades, MS have each taken their own route as to the recognition of LGBT families. Today, there are various legal schemes ranging from full marriage rights (in Belgium, Spain, the Netherlands, and Sweden) to the possibility of registering very light cohabitation contracts, along with free-standing rights connected to informal, unregistered cohabitation. The following lists provide a simplified overview of developments in national law.

Civil marriage open to same-sex couples:

Belgium
Netherlands
Spain
Sweden

Alternative registration scheme similar to marriage:

Denmark
Finland
Germany
Netherlands
Sweden
United Kingdom

Alternative registration scheme entailing fewer rights and responsibilities than marriage:

Belgium
France
Czech Republic
Luxembourg
Portugal
Slovenia

Although no European Community action has been put in place to ensure coordination or harmonization of national substantive law, there is quite a remarkable EC activism in the field of mutual recognition of judgments among MS, including decisions on matrimonial matters and parental responsibility.

Notwithstanding the predominance of national law as regards family matters, a number of European Community policies confer rights over the individual depending on his or her family status or on his or her family relation with EU citizens. The main problem is to determine who qualifies as a family member for the purposes of European Community law. As already seen, in *D and Sweden v. Council* (see Employment and Economics), the ECJ refused to equate the position of a registered partner with that of a spouse for the purpose of granting a household allowance to a European Council official, although under the national law of the claimant, such equalization was in fact made.[24]

In recent times various directives and regulations have started to define the *family member* in a broader way than the spouse only, but have left unaddressed a number of issues. This is the case, for example, in directive 2004/38/EC on the right of EU citizens and their family members to move and reside freely within the European Union.[25] According to this directive (article 2(2)), family members of EU citizens, irrespective of their nationality, enjoy a number of rights that can be equated to those of EU citizens, such as the right of entry and exit in the territory of a MS of temporary or permanent residence, a right to take up employment or self-employment in the host state, and a right to equal treatment with nationals of that state.

In many ways, this directive epitomizes all the difficulties encountered in the current debate around LGBT families in the EU. It defines as family members not only the spouse and certain descendants or ascendants, but also "the partner with whom the EU citizen has contracted a registered partnership on the basis of the legislation of a MS." This important recognition of national legal schemes akin to marriage and often designed only for same-sex couples is, however, subject to the condition that such registered partnerships are already recognized in the MS to which the couple wishes to move. In other words, if a German couple, registered in Germany, wishes to move to Austria where no recognition exists, Austria may refuse to consider the registered partner of the EU citizen as a family member for the purposes of the directive in question. Although it may well be that the partner can enter the territory of Austria and reside there if he or she is also an EU citizen, the situation is rather different if he or she is a citizen of a country outside the European Union. In this case, it will be very difficult to rely on the directive. Furthermore, it should be added that even if a third-country national (e.g., a Canadian citizen) is allowed entry on grounds that legislation of the host MS (e.g., Sweden) treats registered partnerships "as equivalent to marriage," the directive will still allow differential treatment as compared to the registered partner who has EU citizenship, both at the level of administrative formalities and of consequences of termination of the relationship.

The principle adopted by directive 38—that registered partnerships must be recognized only if the *host* MS already treats them as equivalent to marriage—also inspires other pieces of European legislation, dealing especially with the common asylum system and with immigration.

Mutual Recognition of Judgments in Matrimonial Matters and Parental Responsibility

In 1997, the treaty of Amsterdam inserted the new title IV into the EC treaty, thereby giving competence to the European Community in the field of visas, asylum, immigration, and other policies related to the free movement of persons. The political project behind this transformation was that of ensuring that the EC could progressively become an area of freedom, security, and justice. An integral part of the area of freedom, security, and justice is the so-called judicial cooperation in civil matters, which has cross-border implications. EC measures in this field have the objective of improving and simplifying service of documents, taking of evidence, and the recognition and enforcement of decisions in civil and commercial cases, as well as of promoting the harmonization of laws among MS concerning conflict of laws and jurisdiction. In 1999, at a meeting held in Tampere, the European Council endorsed the principle of mutual recognition of judicial decisions and indicated family litigation among the priority areas to be addressed. Following this indication, in 2000 the Council adopted a program of measures for implementing this principle, where it laid down a series of European Community acts that it considered necessary.[26]

As of now, regulation 44/2001 aims at setting common rules on jurisdiction and on recognition and enforcement of judgments in civil and commercial matters. This regulation does not apply either to rights in property arising out of a matrimonial relationship or to succession. It does, however, apply to judgments concerning maintenance and alimony. As far as matrimonial matters and matters of parental responsibility are concerned, regulation 2201/2003 dictates common rules on jurisdiction and on the recognition and enforcement of judgments. The regulation applies to judgments on divorce, legal separation, or marriage annulment, but does not address their prerequisites or their consequences (such as grounds for divorce, property rights, etc.); furthermore, it covers all decisions on parental responsibility (attribution, exercise, delegation, restriction, or termination) regardless of any link with a matrimonial proceeding, but does not apply to the establishment of parenthood, nor to any other question linked to the status of persons including adoption, name, emancipation, maintenance, trusts, or succession.

Neither of the two regulations modifies substantive or procedural law of the MS or conflict of laws rules. They merely select appropriate and common criteria for establishing which court has international jurisdiction and ensure automatic recognition and enforcement of decisions. After the adoption of the Hague Program in 2004 by the European Council, the Commission has put forward proposals for new legislation on applicable law both in matrimonial matters and in maintenance obligations.

From the perspective of LGBT families, it is unclear whether EU regulations apply to maintenance claims (regulation 44), divorce, separation, or annulments of marriages (regulation 2201) between persons of the same sex contracted in those MS that allow same-sex marriage. As regards matters of parental responsibility, it is even more doubtful that a MS that is the habitual residence of the child but that does not recognize any form of legal link between a child and the partner of the same sex of his or her biological parent or any form of adoption, will consider regulation 2201 applicable to such cases. In addition, it is difficult to assess how MS will deal with matters concerning the termination, separation, or annulment of registered partnerships contracted in other MS. Since regulation 2201 does not apply to such cases, the only viable conclusion is apparently that they will be dealt with by national rules on jurisdiction and on conflicts of laws. In certain cases, however, regulation 44 could apply, especially with respect to all of those schemes that are not considered akin to marriage and, thus, cannot be deemed to be excluded from its scope.

On December 15, 2005, the European Commission published a draft regulation on jurisdiction, applicable law, recognition and enforcement of decisions, and cooperation in matters relating to maintenance obligations,[27] which does include registered partnerships. According to article 1 of the proposal, "this Regulation shall apply to maintenance obligations arising from family relationships or relationships deemed by the law applicable to such relationships as having comparable effects." It is rather clear, thus, that the Commission's proposal does not exclude from its scope those registered partnerships that can be compared to marriage as to their legal consequences, according to the applicable law. A recent proposal of the Commission[28] aims at modifying regulation 2201 with a view to introducing common rules on applicable law in divorce matters, a step that should facilitate the mutual recognition of judgments.

COMMUNITY

While national LGBT organizations have existed in some European countries (e.g., the Netherlands and Denmark) since the 1950s, a European LGBT community emerged over the years, in large part through the action of individual activists who started using the legal and political mechanisms being put in place in Europe. LGBT youth organizations—such as the International Gay and Lesbian Youth Organization (IGLYO) active since the 1980s—trade union based LGBT groups and groups affiliated to political parties, all contributed to the creation of a European LGBT movement.

In 1996, ILGA-Europe was founded, when its parent organization, the International Lesbian and Gay Association (ILGA), established separate regions. As a nongovernmental umbrella organization representing its members, principally organizations of LGBT persons, it took over responsibility for supporting the development of the LGBT movement in Europe and for relationships with the EU, the Council of Europe, and the Organization for Security and Cooperation in Europe. Today, ILGA-Europe has more than 240 member organizations in over 40 European countries; these include national and local organizations, as well as trade union–based groups, political party–based groups, women's groups, and so on. Many of ILGA-Europe's member organizations combine human rights campaigning with providing support services to their community such as telephone help lines, HIV information and advice, and counseling. Initially, ILGA-Europe worked entirely on the basis of volunteer resources. However, the core funding allocated to the organization in 2001 in the context of the EU community antidiscrimination action program enabled ILGA-Europe to set up an office in Brussels and to recruit permanent staff.

HEALTH

The powers of the EU in the field of health care are rather limited. The EU complements the action of MS, whose primary competence in relation to the organization and delivery of health services and medical care is asserted in the EC treaty (article 152). Therefore, the EU can complement national policies by adopting "incentive measures designed to protect and improve human health" (e.g., supporting research into the causes of diseases, and promoting health information, education, and prevention) but it cannot harmonize the laws and regulations of the MS in this area (article 152(4)).

From a legal standpoint, the right to health is recognized in a limited way by the EU. For example, the Charter of Fundamental Rights (article 35) recognizes everyone's right "of access to preventive health care and the right to benefit from medical treatment under the conditions established by national laws and practices."[29] However, extending the scope of EU antidiscrimination legislation to protect against all grounds of discrimination in health care is on the agenda of the European Commission in the context of future legislative proposals implementing the principle of equal treatment outside employment. Adoption of new legislation would considerably extend the protection afforded against discrimination in health in the EU and would open up new opportunities for action in this area.

In this framework, the mainstreaming of nondiscrimination concerns and LGBT issues in EU health policy is progressing at a slow pace. While organizations are raising LGBT issues in the context of debates around an EU mental health strategy, in relation to health and safety at work and the impact of mental illness on employment, and access to health services, EU policies have yet to reflect the needs of LGBT people more specifically. On the other hand, EU programs against AIDS have repeatedly emphasized the importance of nondiscrimination. For example, in its communication on combating HIV/AIDS within the EU and in the neighboring countries (2006–2009), the European Commission says that it will continue to provide leadership to combat stigma and discrimination, identified as barriers to successful prevention.

EDUCATION

According to a Europe-wide survey conducted by ILGA-Europe and IGLYO in 2006, 61 percent of young LGBT people in Europe have experienced forms of discrimination at school.[30] While exclusion, bullying, and marginalizing of LGBT youth in education is a reality in the EU, the competence of the European institutions in this area is mainly related to issues of mobility of students and teachers, mutual recognition of qualifications, and vocational training, as important components of active labor market policies (article 149 of EC treaty).

Indeed, the involvement of the EU in education consists principally in coordination and exchange initiatives. In this context, EU action in relation to issues such as teachers' training, curricular development, and school management, among other areas, is confined to that of fostering cooperation and promoting the exchange of practices and experiences that MS are free to take on board or not as they choose. Indeed, the Treaty states that measures may be taken "excluding any harmonization of the laws and regulations of the MS" (article 149[4]).

In terms of legal protection in this area, it remains to be seen whether the newly adopted Charter of Fundamental Rights (article II-14) that affirms the right to education will have an impact on EU policies in the field of education, and thus offer opportunities to advocate for stronger protection and inclusion of LGBT youth at school, for instance. Moreover, the inclusion of education in the scope of the European antidiscrimination legal framework is under consideration by the European Commission in the context of future proposals to enhance protections against discrimination in areas outside employment (already covered by the Employment Framework Directive) on a number of grounds, including sexual orientation.

Therefore, EU policies related to education and youth have so far covered LGBT issues only marginally. The European Parliament, on the other hand, has highlighted the issue of discrimination and homophobia in education in recent years.

In April 2007, it adopted a resolution voicing concern following an announcement by the Polish education minister of a new draft law to outlaw homosexual propaganda in schools. During the same period, the LGBT Intergroup presented a written declaration on combating homophobic bullying; although the declaration failed to obtain the required number of signatures to become an official document, it was used to raise awareness about the issue among MEPs.

Moreover, EU programs have provided funding opportunities for initiatives aimed at raising awareness of sexual orientation discrimination and building the capacity of LGBT youth organizations. The Youth in Action program has funded exchanges and voluntary service experiences in LGBT organizations in countries like Poland and Lithuania, for instance. A network of youth resources centers funded by the EU, the SALTO-YOUTH centers, also developed resources specifically aimed at promoting the inclusion of young LGB people in the EU youth programs and in international youth work.[31]

VIOLENCE

According to Human Rights First's *2007 Hate Crime Survey,* there is a disturbing rise in hate crimes across Europe. The survey documents dozens of hate crime cases, analyzes trends, and discusses the causes and consequences of hate crime violence; it concludes that only 15 of the 56 participating states of the Organization for Security and Co-operation in Europe (OSCE) are fulfilling their basic commitments to monitor hate crimes, with countries in the EU and North America leading the way. Among other issues, the survey finds that the problem of antigay prejudice and violence has become more visible in many countries, with some of the reported acts of violence in 2006 taking place at gay pride demonstrations.

Most of the work on hate crime and violence in Europe has been carried out by the OSCE[32] (a primary instrument for early warning, conflict prevention, crisis management, and postconflict rehabilitation in its area), and the EU is in the early stages of developing legislation to address hate-motivated violence as a crime. Negotiations over a proposal for a framework decision on combating racism and xenophobia has been taking place for more than five years, and was finally adopted by the European Council in 2007. It has yet to be adopted by all the MS. Unfortunately, this legislation does not cover crimes motivated by homophobia.

Despite the lack of a clear legal framework in the EU to take specific action against homophobic violence, the European Parliament has taken a strong stand to denounce crimes motivated by homophobia and incitement to hatred. In resolutions adopted in 2006 and 2007, the parliament has condemned homophobic hate speech or incitement to hatred and violence, and urged "MS to ensure that lesbian, gay, bisexual and transgender people are protected from homophobic hate speech and violence" (January 18, 2006 and April 26, 2007). The Parliament also requested that the Fundamental Rights Agency conduct a study on homophobia in Europe, which was published in 2008 and calls for European legislation to cover hate speech and homophobic violence.[33] Moreover, a number of MEPs have demonstrated their support for the right to freedom of assembly and protection against violence of LGBT people by attending various pride marches in and outside the EU (in countries like Moldova and Russia), and in particular, pride marches organized in hostile environments.

European Union funding in the area of freedom, security, and justice has in recent years offered opportunities for projects to raise awareness about violence against LGBT people. Through a specific funding scheme that supports actions against all forms of violence, including bullying in schools and discrimination-based violence against vulnerable people (called DAPHNE), projects on bullying and homophobia at school and on supporting families to prevent violence against gay and lesbian youth are receiving financial support from the EU.

OUTLOOK FOR THE 21ST CENTURY

The recognition of rights for LGBT people at the level of the EU has progressed significantly in the past decade. Prohibition of discrimination based on sexual orientation is increasingly enshrined in law at the European level, and a growing number of programs are being developed to support implementation of these legal provisions in practice. However, the protection against discrimination based on sexual orientation only extends to the area of employment in EU legislation. The adoption of a new antidiscrimination directive that would extend the protection against discrimination on a number of grounds of discrimination, including sexual orientation, in areas outside employment (such as access to goods and services, health care, education) is expected to remain on the European agenda over the next few years. Moreover, a number of cases pending before the European Court of Justice and the European Court of Human Rights on issues related to family and partnerships will likely have an impact on developments relating to legal recognition of same-sex couples and of diverse forms of families in Europe.

RESOURCE GUIDE

Suggested Reading

Nico Beger, *Tensions in the Struggle for Sexual Minority Rights in Europe: Que(e)rying Political Practices* (Manchester: Manchester University Press, 2004).

Mark Bell, *Anti-discrimination Law and the European Union* (Oxford: Oxford University Press, 2002).

Mark Bell, "We Are Family? Same-sex Partners and EU Migration Law," *Maastricht Journal of European and Comparative Law* 9 (2002): 335.

Katharina Boele-Woelki, ed., *Perspectives for the Unification and Harmonisation of Family Law in Europe* (Antwerp, Oxford, New York: Intersentia, 2003).

Katharina Boele-Woelki and Angelika Fuchs, eds., *Legal Recognition of Same-Sex Couples in Europe* (Antwerp: Intersentia, 2003).

Matteo Bonini Baraldi, "EU Family Policies between 'Good Old Values' and Fundamental Rights: the Case of Same-Sex Families," *Maastricht Journal of European and Comparative Law* 15, no. 4 (2008): 517.

Matteo Bonini Baraldi, *Freedom and Justice in the EU: Implications of the Hague Programme for Lesbian, Gay, Bisexual and Transgender Families and their Children* (Brussels: ILGA-Europe, 2007).

Damian Chalmers, Christos Hadjiermmanuil, Giorgio Monti, and Adam Tomkins, *European Union Law* (Cambridge: Cambridge University Press, 2006).

Ian Curry-Sumner, *All's Well that Ends Registered? The Substantive and Private International Law Aspects of Non-Marital Registered Relationships in Europe* (Antwerp: Intersentia, 2003).

Helmut Graupner, "Sexuality and Human Rights in Europe," in *Sexuality and Human Rights—A Global Overview,* ed. Helmut Graupner and Phillip Tahmindijs (New York: Harrington Park Press, 2005).

International Commission of Jurists, 1995. *Sexual Orientation and Gender Identity in Human Rights Law: Jurisprudential, Legislative and Doctrinal References from the Council of Europe and the European Union* (Geneva: International Commission of Jurists), http://www.icj.org/IMG/European_Compilation-web.pdf.

Johan Meeusen, Marta Pertegas, Gert Straetmans, and Frederik Swennen, eds., *International Family Law for the European Union* (Antwerp: Intersentia, 2007).

Alastair Mowbray, *Cases and Materials on the European Convention on Human Rights,* 2nd ed. (Oxford: Oxford University Press, 2007).

Clare Ovey and Robin White, *Jacobs and White: The European Convention on Human Rights,* 4th ed. (Oxford: Oxford University Press, 2006).

Sheila Quinn, *Accessing Health: The Context and the Challenges for LGBT People in Central and Eastern Europe* (Brussels: ILGA-Europe, 2006).

Sheila Quinn and Evelyne Paradis, *Going beyond the Law: Promoting Equality in Employment,* 2nd ed. (Brussels: ILGA-Europe, 2007).

Judith Takács, *Social Exclusion of Young Lesbian, Gay, Bisexual and Transgender (LGBT) People in Europe* (Brussels: ILGA-Europe and IGLYO, 2006).

Kees Waaldijk, *More or Less Together: Levels of Legal Consequences of Marriage, Cohabitation and Registered Partnership for Different-sex and Same-sex Partners. A Comparative Study of Nine European Countries,* Documents de travail n. 125 (Paris: Institut National d'Études Démographiques, 2005).

Kees Waaldijk and Matteo Bonini Baraldi, eds., *Combating Sexual Orientation Discrimination in Employment: Legislation in Fifteen EU Member States, Report of the European Group of Experts on Combating Sexual Orientation Discrimination, about the Implementation up to April 2004 of Directive 2000/78/EC Establishing a General Framework for Equal Treatment in Employment and Occupation* (Leiden: Universiteit Leiden, 2004), http://www.emmeijers.nl/experts.

Kees Waaldijk and Matteo Bonini Baraldi, *Sexual Orientation Discrimination in the European Union: National Laws and the Employment Equality Directive* (The Hague: T.M.C. Asser Press, 2006).

Kees Waaldijk and Andrew Clapham, eds., *Homosexuality: A European Community Issue* (Dordrecht: Martinus Nijhoff Publishers, 1993).

Anne Weyembergh and Sinziana Carstocea, eds., *The Gays' and Lesbians' Rights in an Enlarged European Union* (Brussels: Éditions de l'Université de Bruxelles, 2006).

Robert Wintemute, "From 'Sex Rights' to 'Love Rights': Partnership Rights as Human Rights," in *Sex Rights,* ed. Nicholas Bamforth (Oxford: Oxford University Press, 2005).

Robert Wintemute, "Sexual Orientation and Gender Identity," in *Human Rights in the Community: Rights as Agents for Change,* ed. Colin Harvey (Oxford: Hart Publishing, 2005).

Robert Wintemute and Mads Andenaes, eds., *Legal Recognition of Same-Sex Partnerships: A Study on National, European, and International Law* (Oxford: Hart Publishing, 2001).

Web Sites

EQUAL projects on equality at work
> Program that was part of the European Employment Strategy. Financed by the European Social Fund, EQUAL developed and tested new and innovative ideas and practices to combat discrimination and inequality in relation to the labor market. Eight EQUAL projects focused on discrimination based on sexual orientation.

- "Homosexuals and Bisexuals in the Care System" (Sweden): http://www.rfsl.se/?p=566
- Normgiving Diversity on LGB within the Church, the police, and the armed forces (Sweden): http://www.normgivande.nu
- Sexual and Gender Minorities at Work (Finland): http://www.valt.helsinki.fi/sosio/tutkimus/equal/
- Enabling Safety for LesBiGay Teachers (The Netherlands)
- Deledios (France): http://www.autrecercle.org
- Open and Safe at Work (Lithuania): http://www.atviri.lt
- Partnership for Equality (Slovenia): http://www.ljudmila.org/lesbo/
- Beneath the Surface of Discrimination in School (Sweden): http://www.ytan.se

Eurogames, http://www.eurogames.info/
> Eurogames, the European Gay and Lesbian Championships, is an annual European sporting event governed by the European Gay and Lesbian Sport Federation (EGLSF). It is the biggest athletic event for lesbian, gay, bisexual, and transgender people in Europe.

European Commission's Directorate General for Employment, Social Affairs and Equal Opportunities, http://ec.europa.eu/employment_social/fundamental_rights/index_en.htm
> Provides information on all aspects of EU action—both laws and policies—to combat discrimination.

European Commission's Stop Discrimination, http://www.stop-discrimination.info/
> Source of information on the EU-wide campaign For Diversity. Against Discrimination and provides an update on current antidiscrimination issues and activities in all 27 EU member states.

European Gay and Lesbian Managers Association, http://www.egma.eu
> Umbrella organization for national LGBT business associations.

European Gay and Lesbian Sport Federation, http://www.eglsf.info
> Network open to gay, lesbian, straight, and mixed sport groups and organizations that has more than 10,000 members within over 100 organizations and sport groups.

European network of legal experts in the nondiscrimination field, http://ec.europa.eu/employment_social/fundamental_rights/policy/aneval/legnet_en.htm
> Brings together 27 country experts—one for each EU member state—and five coordinators for specific grounds of discrimination, including sexual orientation. The network supports the work of the European Commission by providing independent information and advice on relevant legal developments in the member states, and the implementation of EU antidiscrimination laws.

European Parliament Gay and Lesbian Rights Intergroup, http://www.lgbt-ep.eu/news.php
> Brings together Members of the European Parliament and their support staff wishing to advance LGBT equal rights issues.

European Pride Organisers Association (EPOA), http://www.europride.info
> Network of European gay, lesbian, bisexual, and transgender pride organizations. The purpose of EPOA is to promote lesbian, gay, bisexual, and transgender pride on a pan-European level and to empower and support local and national pride organizations in their efforts of planning and promoting pride celebrations.

Film, http://ec.europa.eu/employment_social/fundamental_rights/movie/film_en.htm
> Introductory film on EU antidiscrimination policies.

Fundamental Rights Agency, http://fra.europa.eu/fra/index.php
> Provides assistance and expertise relating to fundamental rights to the relevant EU institutions and member states when implementing European Community law.

Gay Police European Network, http://www.eurogaypolice.com
> Brings together gay police networks and members of police organizations from different countries.

ILGA-Europe, http://www.ilga-europe.org
> European branch of the International Lesbian and Gay Association (ILGA) that works for human rights and equality for lesbian, gay, bisexual, and transgender people in Europe.

International Gay, Lesbian, Bisexual, Transgender and Queer Youth and Student Organization (IGLYO), http://www.iglyo.com
> Important network meeting point for LGBTQ youth in Europe.

SALTO-Youth Resource Centres, http://www.salto-youth.net/inclusionLGBT/
> Program funded under the European Commission's youth program that provides youth work and training resources and organizes training activities to support youth organizations. One of its projects focused on combating discrimination and promoting the inclusion of young LGBT people.

NOTES

1. All figures in this paragraph are taken from the official EU report "Key Facts and Figures about Europe and the Europeans," http://europa.eu/abc/keyfigures/index_en.htm.

2. See the official Web site of the Commission, Directorate General for Enlargement, http://ec.europa.eu/enlargement/candidate-countries/index_en.htm.

3. Such duty had already been carved out by the Court of Justice of the European Community in more than two decades of case law and the treaty closely replicated the elaborations of the court in the absence of written law.

4. *Official Journal of the European Union* C 321 (December 29, 2006): E/48.

5. Council Directive (EC) 2000/78 of November 27, 2000, establishing a general framework for equal treatment in employment and occupation, *Official Journal of the European Union* L 303 (December 2, 2000): 16.

6. See http://www.fra.europa.eu/fraWebsite/home/pub_cr_homophobia_p2_0309_en.htm.

7. See point 2 of the European Parliament resolution of April 26, 2007 on homophobia in Europe, P6_TA-PROV(2007)0167.

8. More information on the Intergroup is available at http://www.lgbt-ep.eu/news.php.

9. To check the status of ratifications, see conventions.coe.int.

10. All decisions can be found at the Web site of the court: www.echr.coe.int.

11. See Robert Wintemute, *Sexual Orientation and Human Rights. The United States Constitution, the European Convention, and the Canadian Charter* (Oxford: Clarendon Press, 1997).

12. See *L. and V. v. Austria; S.L. v. Austria; R.H. v. Austria; Wolfmeyer v. Austria; Ladner v. Austria; H.G and G.B. v. Austria; B.B. v. U.K.*

13. See *Lustig-Prean and Beckett v. U.K.; Smith and Grady v. U.K.*

14. See *Kerkhoven v. the Netherlands;* see also *Röösli v. Germany; B. v. U.K.*

15. Articles 1a and 27(2) of Council Regulation (EEC, ECSC, Euratom) 781/98 of April 7 1998, *Official Journal of the European Union* L 113 (April 15, 1998): 4.

16. See Kees Waaldijk and Matteo Bonini Baraldi, *Sexual Orientation Discrimination in the European Union: National Laws and the Employment Equality Directive* (The Hague: T.M.C. Asser Press, 2006).

17. Information on the Group, and its report, can be found at www.emmeijers.nl/experts.

18. *Grant v. South West Trains Ltd,* February 17, 1998, case C-249/96, 1998 ECR I-621.

19. *D and Sweden v. Council,* May 31, 2001, joined cases C-122/99 and C-125/99, 2001 ECR I-4319.

20. *Tadao Maruko v. Versorgungswerk der deutschen Bühnen,* case C-267/06, 2008 ECR I-1757.

21. April 30, 1996, case C-13/94, 1996 ECR I-2143.

22. *K.B. v. National Health Service Pensions Agency,* January 7, 2004, case C-117/01, 2004 ECR I-541.

23. *Richards v. Secretary of State for Work and Pensions,* April 27, 2007, case C-423/04, 2006 ECR I-3585.

24. Nowadays, Community Staff regulations have changed and the registered partner is treated as a spouse. The 2004 regulations explicitly stipulate that "non-marital partnerships shall be treated as marriage" if certain conditions are met.

25. *Official Journal of the European Union* L 158 (April 30, 2004): 77.

26. *Official Journal of the European Union* C 12 (January 15, 2001): 1.

27. COM(2005) 649 final. See also the green paper on maintenance obligations, COM(2004) 254 final.

28. COM(2006) 399 final.

29. The International Covenant on Economic, Social and Cultural rights, on the other hand, recognizes the "right of everyone to the enjoyment of the highest attainable standard of physical and mental health" (article 12).

30. See Judith Takács, *Social Exclusion of Young Lesbian, Gay, Bisexual and Transgender (LGBT) People in Europe* (Brussels: ILGA-Europe and IGLYO, 2006).

31. See http://www.salto-youth.net/inclusionLGBT/.

32. Information about the Organization for Security and Co-operation in Europe (OSCE) at http://www.osce.org. The Tolerance and Non-Discrimination Information Centre provides information on hate crime motivated by homophobia, http://tandis.odihr.pl/index.php?p=ki-ho.

33. See http://fra.europa.eu/fraWebsite/material/pub/comparativestudy/FRA_hdgso_part1_en.pdf.

FINLAND

Krister Karttunen

OVERVIEW

Finland is small country in northern Europe, with quite a large area but a small population. There are some five million inhabitants in 130,000 square miles, and the country stretches 690 miles between latitudes 60 and 70. The capital city is Helsinki, with about a million inhabitants in the area. The long coastal line of the Baltic Sea is crowded with small islands and inland areas are covered by conifer forests, peat lands, and innumerable lakes; in the far north there is a large expanse of wilderness and mountains.

Finland has been inhabited since the last ice age, some 9,000 years ago. Christianity arrived mainly from the west in the 13th century, with the oldest stone churches dating from the 14th century. Finland was under Swedish rule until 1809, when Russia occupied it and granted some autonomy in internal affairs. In 1906, near the fall of the Russian Empire, Finland achieved a democracy in which everyone could vote and run for office, including women.

In the melee of revolution in Russia and World War I, Finland opted for independence. This was gained in 1918, but only after a very fierce and bloody civil war between the conservatives and socialists. As usually happens in such conflicts, civilians suffered most. Just before the outbreak of World War II, Russia attacked Finland as a precaution to ward off Nazi Germany. In the Winter War, Finland surprised everybody by holding off the significantly larger Russian army for many months, but eventually had to make peace, giving over large territories. To gain back these areas, and perhaps to acquire some more, Finland made a pact with Germany and attacked Russia, but once again lost when Germany collapsed. However, there was no Nazi party in Finland; Jews were welcomed or compelled to join the army, and only about six refugees were turned over to Germany. Neither Nazi nor Soviet troops occupied Finland.

After the war, Finland had to recognize the power of a huge Communist neighbor and many overtures and pacts of friendships were made. At the same time, private ownership was not in any way limited, and the Finnish economy boomed with commerce both to the Soviet Union and to the West. The Finnish population believes that the country navigated rather smartly and successfully through the years of cold war with its policy of neutrality. In 1994, Finland joined the European Union and in 2003 made a pact with NATO without full membership.

Swedish and imperial Russian control, a severe civil war, and the fights and forced peace with the Soviet Union are ingrained in the collective memory of Finland, and may explain some Finnish peculiarities.

The Finnish economy was agrarian until the 1950s. There are few natural resources except forests, and the paper industry is still very important. Since the 1980s, however, information technology (IT) has gained in importance. The Finnish mobile phone manufacturer Nokia is the emblem of this, but there are many small companies supplying devices and programs for various purposes, from NASA satellites to internet security to game consoles.

Culturally, Finland has been very uniform until quite recently. There is a Protestant Lutheran state church, of which some 85 percent of people are members. They do not, however, take religion very seriously, attending services only about once a year.[1] Protestantism is rather a cultural thing in the nation. Primary education has been free and compulsory since the 1930s, and the fees for higher and university education are nominal. About 50 percent of the people finish high school and about 20 percent of each class attends one of the 10 universities in the country.[2] The biggest and oldest, Helsinki University, was founded 1654.

The Finnish language is fairly unique. Estonian is a close relative, but Hungarian is about as close to Finnish as English is to Sanskrit. As often is the case in small countries, Finns tend to know foreign languages quite well. Almost all young people know English.

There are some small minorities in Finland.[3] The biggest one is only linguistic, the speakers of Swedish. For centuries, Sweden was the language of government, learning, and society, and contrasted with Finnish, which was the language of peasants. After the independence in 1917, Finnish speakers have gained the upper hand, almost without violence. The position of Swedish speakers is guaranteed in the Finnish constitution: they have the right to education and to any public services in their own language anywhere in the country. They constitute some 4 percent of the population. The few thousand Roma people quite frequently face discrimination and suffer stereotyping by the main population; only recently have their cultural rights been recognized to some degree. The Sami people, the only indigenous people in Europe, of the semi-arctic north, numbering some thousands, struggle to maintain their traditional culture of reindeer herding.[4] The government has recognized their cultural and linguistic rights and granted some autonomy, but there is continuing disagreement over land ownership. Presently, over one hundred thousand foreign nationals also live in Finland.

OVERVIEW OF LGBT ISSUES

The general situation in terms of LGBT rights in Finland is about the same as in other Scandinavian countries, though most reforms were achieved some decades later. Government policy, supported by public opinion, has usually been to ignore LGBT issues. Mainly due to activity by human rights and LGBT organizations, LGBT rights are presently fairly widespread, and discrimination is minor. In part, this change has been achieved because of the pressure from the European Union (EU) and European Human Rights Convention (EHRC).

Pressure from Europe has been resented in some nationalistic circles. In some clerical and conservative circles, there is still opposition to gay rights. The most common slogan has been that gay rights ruin family values. In the past decade, new progay legislation has been accepted in the parliament with a two-thirds majority. On the other hand, the government has been quite careful with the proposals to get the majority.

Nowadays, after decades of struggle, the situation for LGBT people is quite good in Finland. There are no antisodomy laws, the age of consent has been standardized, military regulations have been changed to accept open service members, marriage rights have been extended to LGBT individuals, hate crime and antidiscrimination legislation has been passed, the government supports many LGBT organizations, and HIV testing as well as AIDS medication is free. The last bastion of reactionaries seems to be the church, but even this is rapidly changing.

Changes in laws have partly been made possible by the changes in public attitudes, but in many cases the laws have been more enlightened than public opinion. Mostly, opinions have also changed, partly because Finns are quite law-abiding people and partly due to the new visibility of LGBT persons. People have come to notice that lesbians, gays, bisexuals, and transgender individuals, whether in the parliament or living next door, are quite ordinary. This has been confirmed by the growing number of positive stories and interviews about LGBT persons in mainstream television and magazines. This situation can be contrasted with how it was a few decades before, when the few published stories were sex scandals or AIDS horror stories. Today, outing would be quite difficult in Finland because few would care who is gay and who is not.

Some problems remain. The changes in the attitudes have been most prevalent in bigger cities. In the countryside, and especially in more religious districts, there are still problems. The limited adoption rights for gay and lesbian couples, insufficient antidiscrimination laws, and virtual lack of hate crime policies still pose problems. Many people find the church's position offensive, bisexuals feel ignored, intersexuality is hardly recognized, and teenagers do not get the help and support they need.

EDUCATION

In Finland, primary education is free for all, and colleges, vocational schools, and universities charge only nominal fees. Schools are municipal and follow a common curriculum. About 50 percent of the population finish high school and 15 percent acquire university degrees.[5] Finland's school system has been ranked best in the Europe-wide comparisons in several years. There are some dozen universities and several colleges, with the oldest and for centuries the only one being Helsinki University, which was established in 1643.

Violence at schools has not been a very serious problem, but has increased lately. Larger cities have a more diverse population, including some immigrants and refugees, which may lead to conflicts, but smaller residential areas are ethnically very uniform, making life difficult for the few rebellious children. Possession of fire arms is mainly restricted to hunters and arms very rarely figure in violence in schools. However, in 1989, Finland experienced its first school shooting, in which there were two victims; in a 2007 incident, a high school student shot six students and two teachers.

Bullying has been identified as one source of the violence. There are some programs aimed toward easing the situation, especially among the younger children. Students are encouraged to report all kinds of bullying for whatever reason to teachers and parents, and not to regard this as snitching.

In Finland, there is some data on bullying of young homosexuals or children of homosexual families.[6] Abusive vocabulary commonly includes words like homo and lesbian, usually aimed randomly without any idea of the victim's sexual orientation. This practice, however, is not constructive for the self-image of young gays and lesbians. Alarmed by the studies in comparable countries like Norway that indicated that young homosexuals are prone to suicide,[7] some LGBT organizations have unsuccessfully sought a response from the government. The leading national organizations for child protection, however, have recently been quite attentive to the special problems that gay youngsters and families face.

Ironically, bullying and other forms of discrimination may have increased with the greater publicity of LGBT issues. Previously, gays and lesbians and other sexual minorities were invisible and ignored; if mentioned at all, they were treated as psychiatric cases in textbooks. In the school curriculums, homosexuality is still treated quite cursorily. For the gay youth themselves, there are many other ways to acquire information, including the Internet, which is used routinely by young Finnish people.

The gay family is such a recent phenomenon in Finland that little can be said about how children of such families are treated in schools. In the public day care, which is attended by a great majority of young children, there have been some attempts to recognize these special families. In many cases, problems are not due to active discrimination or ill will, but rather ignorance and the prevailing heteronormativity. There have been some efforts in the schooling of teachers and other professionals to address this.

EMPLOYMENT AND ECONOMICS

Finland is a small but modern economy with a gross domestic product (GDP) of 175 billion euros and annual growth of about 5 percent, usually ranking near the top in international comparisons. Roughly one-third of the Finnish labor force is employed in the public sector and 20 percent each in business and industry. Virtually all are members of labor unions and those unemployed are fairly well compensated by insurance and government. Relatively few are self-employed or private entrepreneurs.

Most Finnish women work, but often in less well-paid, minor jobs. Their careers are not as good as men's and occasionally they are paid less for the same position. Solving these problems and fighting sexual harassment have been a high priority of the state for some time. For example, according to the law there must be a plan to promote equality in every workplace. Various ideas about quotas for women and minorities have been hotly debated, but mostly rejected as discriminating.

The latest Equality Act from 2004 is fairly stringent about discrimination at work. It specifically states that discrimination based on an employee's sexual orientation is a criminal offence. This includes employing, distributing work, possible harassment, unfair treatment, promotions, salaries, and so on. In Finnish legislation the burden of proof is reversed in these offenses, a unique practice. If one makes a proper complaint against an employer, the employer must show that no discrimination occurred. There is yet very little evidence of how effective this law has been for LGBT people. In a study, 12 percent of interviewed LGBT persons had encountered or suffered harassment or discrimination at work because of sexual orientation, and 50 percent had been subjected to unpleasant jokes.[8] Half the people interviewed were willing to take the case to a court if discriminated against.

Public officers and private entrepreneurs offering public services, such as restaurants, are further constrained by the criminal code's articles on discrimination. They must serve all customers equally and cannot deny entrance. These articles concern ethnic minorities, the disabled, and LGBT persons. Some people, like the Roma, are forced to evoke these rules routinely, but gays and lesbians very rarely need to demand these legal rights. There are few cases in which the complaints have been successful, including an instance in which a male couple was evicted from a bar because they were kissing.

Perhaps surprisingly, the Finnish Army's official policy has been approving or at least tolerant of gays. In Finland, all male citizens are required to take part in a 180- to 360-day military service in the army or, alternately, they may choose to serve 360 days in a nonmilitary capacity in some public utility. Women may voluntarily partake in the military service. At least since the late 1970s, when homosexuality was decriminalized in Finland, army officers were informing recruits that homosexuality is not a valid reason to be exempted from the service. Nevertheless, those choosing a military career have thought it prudent to keep their same-sex inclinations quiet.

For some years, persecution because of sexual orientation or gender has been recognized as valid reason to earn refugee status or a permanent residence permit.

SOCIAL/GOVERNMENT PROGRAMS

Traditionally in Finland, the state and municipalities have taken care of many social issues. Although charitable or nonprofit-seeking associations, foundations, and cooperatives are quite active, taking care of some health care, for example, they are mainly financed by the state. Part of the budget of many LGBT organizations is covered by government subsidies. Recently, many special programs and studies in various fields, such as gays and lesbians in the workplace and the support of transsexual, gay, and lesbian families, have been funded by the state.

FAMILY

Parenting

According to the official statistics, in 2006 there were 120 registered female and 3 male couples with children living in the same household.[9] Other LGBT families with children do not appear in statistics.

In discussing LGBT families, some legal categories must be defined. Biological and adoptive parents are treated almost equally in Finland. They have some rights and duties, while custodians enjoy some other rights. In most heterosexual families, the parents are also custodians, though after divorce and remarriage the situation may get more complicated. Some rights and duties depend on whether a parent is living in the same household with the children.

In general, a child, biological or adopted, has the right of inheritance, subsistence, and the visitation of a parent, whether living in the same household or not. A custodian may take part in the upbringing of a child, will get all relevant information, and must be consulted in all decisions concerning the child. In Finland, the salaried maternity and paternity leaves are fairly long, and parents staying at home taking care of their children get quite good support from the state, including allowing workers to leave the workplace to care for sick children. These benefits usually concern people living together with the children, parents or custodians or neither, but not those parents living separately from them.

This legal mishmash creates problems for gay and lesbian parents. In divorce from a registered union, children have no rights of visitation or subsistence from a social parent or custodian, regardless of how close their relationship had been or how long it lasted. Custodianship gives no rights to inheritance to the child, and even if there is a will, the taxation may be higher than with biological parents. Further, a biological parent not living with the children does not enjoy the parental leaves and payments.

The award of custodianship is automatic for presumed biological married parents. A female couple with a child without a known father usually gets a shared custodianship without a problem. Although by the law, the number of custodians is not limited, the courts have very rarely accepted more than two. This means that if the father is known, the female partner who is not the biological mother may not be accepted as a custodian.

In most cases, courts have wide powers to assign parenthood, custodianship, visitation rights, and so on. For example, in one case, courts placed a child under the care and custodianship of the deceased mother's female companion, overriding the claims of a biological father.

Marriage

People in same-sex relationships have been able to register their unions since 2002. In 2006, there were 455 registered male couples and 493 female. The legal consequences are almost identical to marriage (see Politics and Law).

Insemination

Artificial insemination and laws relating to it have been debated in Finland for decades. The discussions have mainly been about general principles, but the hottest topic has always been the right of single women to seek the procedure. It has been practiced in private and semi-official clinics since the method became widespread, and the first attempts to regulate it occurred in the 1980s. Since then, many state committees have published reports and proposals to regulate insemination, but only a 2006 Fertility Treatment Act was accepted. The unregulated situation was not wholly unfavorable to lesbians, because clinics could choose their customers and many did not discriminate.

The government proposal to allow single women or female couples to be treated aroused strong opposition, especially from churches and some conservative psychiatrists. The act eventually passed the parliament with a vote of 105 for and 83 against, which is a fairly accurate picture of attitudes toward LGBT rights in the Finnish parliament.

At present, single women and those living in a registered partnership can get insemination. The sperm donors cannot be anonymous. They may give consent to be possibly recognized as legal fathers. If they do not want to accept that kind of legal consequence, their names still must be registered to be given to the child, if he or she asks for it after coming of age. This may be in the best interest of the child, but has led to a shortage of sperm donors.

Some lesbians become pregnant by home insemination by friends or have children from previous heterosexual relationships.

Fathers

Among gay men, there is growing interest in fatherhood. Some men have children from previous heterosexual relationships, often with joint custodianship with the mother, and sometimes living permanently with them. Although single-parent adoption is open to men, this is extremely difficult in practice. In Finland, the use of surrogate mothers is illegal, although it has happened unofficially.

Sometimes gay men have joined lesbian couples or single women to form extended families with children. The legal as well as practical arrangements vary. A problem is that the spouses of the biological parents have rarely been awarded custodianship, leaving them with almost no legal status. This kind of joint parenthood with up to four people is also a challenge to authorities, teachers, relatives, and so on, and may require detailed negotiations between the parties.

Adoption and Foster Care

In general, adoption is possible in Finland only if the biological parent gives his or her consent, and thereby gives up all rights of parenthood, or if the parents are unknown or dead. In practice, there are very few Finnish children given up for adoption, as most orphans are taken in by relatives and single and young mothers take care of their babies. On the other hand, many children are placed in foster care, with or without the consent of the biological parents, but in Finland this almost never leads to adoption.

In May 2009 Finnish parliament amended the Act of Registered Partnership, allowing same-sex partners to legally adopt their spouses' children if the other biological parent consents or is unknown, including cases of artificial insemination in public health care. Unlike married couples, gays and lesbians may not jointly adopt foreign children. Adoption as a single parent is, however, possible, even if one lives in a registered partnership. This possibility is to a large extent theoretical, since married couples are often preferred in the adoption process, both in Finland and in the delivering countries.

Lesbian and gay couples sometimes act as foster parents, with only some of the rights and duties of legal parents. Until recently this has been quite rare, despite the fact that there is a shortage of families to take care of foster children. It seems that Finns are more reluctant to consider gay rights in relation to children than marriage or military concerns.

COMMUNITY

Until quite recently gays, lesbians, and trans persons were quite invisible in Finnish society. Even obviously intimate same-sex relationships were interpreted as something else or ignored.

The first glimmers of gay subculture in Finland emerge during wartime in the 1940s. There were certain bars or public parks where LGBT people could meet. It was obviously difficult for LGBT people to organize when homosexuality was illegal. The first organization that had gay rights in its agenda was established in 1969, though its activities were not quite open. In 1974, SETA (Sexual Equality) was established, and since its beginning it has been politically oriented, fighting for a variety of equality issues. Social programs have been important; SETA started the first and only gay magazine in 1975, and organized the first gay pride parades in the 1980s. The present President of Finland, Tarja Halonen, served as a young liberal lawyer as the president of SETA in 1980–1981, and still sends her greetings to all pride events.

In the 1990s, the LGBT community proliferated. Nowadays, there are organizations in all bigger cities and SETA functions as an umbrella organization. The programs of local organizations are mainly social, but they have some activity in local politics, and usually they are open to people of all sexes and sexualities. There are also LGBT student unions; youth organizations; religious associations; sports clubs; various fetish groups; and so on. Transsexuals, gay and lesbian families, and HIV-positive people have formed their own associations, while actively cooperating with mainstream LGBT organizations.

The commercial scene was fairly quiet for decades. The first openly gay bar opened in 1984. At present, there are a half dozen in Helsinki and a couple in other bigger towns. Otherwise, there are almost no commercial enterprises targeted especially at LGBT people. There are no gay-centric travel agents, hotels, beauty salons, gyms, clinics, or real estate agents. The reasons for this may be that Finland is such a small country, with a population of only 5 million; most mainstream business caters fairly well for LGBT customers; and many needs, including health care, are met by organizations and clubs or by public services.

The change in the culture in the past two decades can be observed in all kinds of research and studies, including analysis of gays, lesbians, and transsexuals in folklore; queer themes in literature; LGTB life in the 1940s; criminal sentences under sodomy laws; and gay dads' self-images. Students in various schools and colleges have been active in writing their theses and essays about LGBT themes. This new activity is also reflected in the growing number of positive stories, news items, and interviews in various magazines and on TV.

HEALTH

The first HIV case in Finland was reported in June1983, making big headlines in all the tabloids. This created a lot of negative publicity for gay men, including threats of violence and killing and public outcry about gay cancer, as it was sometimes called. At first, the state and municipal health officials were quite unable, perhaps unwilling, to cope with the virus or to arrange any counseling or support for those who were infected. The job was taken on by the LGBT organizations and some doctors. Later, health officials and voluntary organizations combined their resources fairly effectively.

There are some dedicated centers for testing and advising people with HIV or AIDS and in any local health center, one can get tested anonymously and free of charge. There is also an organized group for HIV-positive people and another campaign for healthy sexual practices.

By the end of 2007, there had been 2,258 HIV infections, 744 of those from sex between men; there had been 492 cases of AIDS and 281 deaths. In 2007, 184 new infections were detected, 59 from sex between men.[10] These figures must be seen in relation to the number of inhabitants of Finland, totaling a little over five million. In Finland, HIV and AIDS are not especially problematic for the gay community except in popular mythology. Nevertheless, being HIV positive or having AIDS is a stigma both in general society and among homosexuals.

There are no reliable statistics about LGBT people and venereal diseases or other illnesses. There is some indication of growing numbers of sexually transmitted diseases (STDs) among gay men. A slight rise in HIV infections and the proportion of infections resulting from sex between men may indicate carelessness when it comes to proper protection in sex.

Even after the belated removal of homosexuality as a diagnostic criterion in Finland in 1981, there have been some psychologists and psychiatrists, including some that are quite influential, who have considered LGBT people to be disturbed. Many Finnish gays and lesbians have had traumatic and expensive experiences in therapy. At present these represent a small minority. There may be an excess amount of depression among LGBT people, but most psychologists and psychiatrists are quite sympathetic, and the LGBT organizations offer some counseling.

Recently, there have been very few attempts to offer to "cure" homosexuality, mostly by some religious fundamentalists. Likewise, there are no ex-gays (allegedly recuperated), healed gays, or lesbians figuring in public media. At the moment this is only a very minor problem.

There is a state-sponsored universal health insurance system in Finland and all municipalities are required to offer low-price medical services. These systems cover HIV and AIDS medication. A flaw in the public sector system is the sometimes long wait for nonserious cases, and especially for mental problems. Private health care is also widely used and partly covered by the official health insurance.

Since the 2003 transsexuals have enjoyed reasonable legal and social rights in Finland. Transsexual people get full state support for medication and operations, and the state recognizes a person's new sex legally and officially. Any procedure involves interviews and counseling at a special medical unit. The person can determine the scheduling of the operations and a name change. If the person is living in a heterosexual marriage or homosexual registered union, the relationship can carry on without a break with the new appropriate name and status, and the legal status with offspring is not disrupted.

Special issues involving intersexual persons have, on the other hand, been largely ignored.

POLITICS AND LAW

Sodomy

Official sodomy laws, forbidding fornication between persons of the same sex, were established in 1889, but before that other articles of the civil or canonical codes were applied. The law was not reformed until 1971. The punishment under the articles included imprisonment for up to two years. In all, 1,026 men and 53 women were convicted during the 20th century. In the early decades, only a couple of people were convicted annually, but the number rose to over 60 in the 1950s and dropped to 16 in the 1960s.[11]

The new 1971 law was part of a more general reform in the spirit of the 1960s and had been campaigned mainly by nonqueer activists, liberal lawyers, doctors, writers, and so on. In those times it was quite difficult to be openly gay or lesbian in Finland.

There was strong opposition to the reform, and partly to placate those fighting against LGBT rights, the new law included a higher age of consent for homosexuals, which, at 18 years, was two years older than the minimum 16 years considered legal for heterosexual encounters. A new article was introduced, which forbade publicly encourage or promote indecency between members of the same sex. In effect this meant that the distribution of any positive information about homosexuality was criminalized. This article was seldom applied, but it acted as a strong deterrent for television producers, newspaper editors, and publishers. Behind these limitations was the theory that young people especially could be infected by homosexuality.

The information ban was the target of a long campaign by emerging gay and lesbian activist groups in the 1970s. Although it was not abolished until 1999, it had been defunct for decades. Police had refused to deal with any reports or self-denouncements by activists of anyone breaking the rule.

The unequal age of consent law was changed in the same 1999 reform to a minimum age of 16 years for all youths. Only a few individuals had been convicted under the article, but it had been seen as strongly discriminative.

Marriage

Another long debate has concerned civil union and marriage between people of the same sex. The possibility had been discussed since the early 1990s and finally, in 2002, the Act of Registered Partnership was accepted. This law treated official unions between people of the same sex in an almost equal way to heterosexual married couples, although the word marriage was deliberately avoided to appease clerics and other conservative groups. The exceptions concern the right to adopt children and sharing a common family name, which requires a separate application.

Any two people of the same sex may enter into a registered partnership so long as one of them is a resident of Finland. They will receive all the same benefits in taxation, social security, inheritance, and power of attorney, for example, as married couples, and also in turn all the same inconveniences. The union is made publicly before an official registrar and can be dissolved in a court by application of either party after a six-month consideration period or after a separation of two years. The courts require no explanations or reasons. In the last few years, about 200 partnerships have been registered annually and 30 terminated. By the end of 2006, there were about 1,000 registered couples.

Same-sex unions contracted in foreign countries with originally more or less the same legal consequences can be officially recognized in Finland by application to a court. If the union's legal effects in the country of origin are significantly weaker, for example, in regard to inheritance, the union will be treated only as a civil contract under foreign law.

Discrimination

In the recently reformed Constitution of Finland, all kinds of discrimination are denounced. LGBT people and sexual orientation are not mentioned in the document, but in the preparatory works and in the discussions in the parliament, it was understood that LGBT people are covered by the final words, "or other reason that concerns his or her person," of the sixth section of the constitution. This invisibility of homosexuals is a common problem in Finnish as well as international legislation and affects public opinion, making the application of the pertinent articles inefficient.

The Equality Act of 2004 is fairly effective in terms of discrimination at work. The statutes also deal with discrimination more widely(e.g., in housing), but those articles specifically exclude homosexuals. In the criminal code there are some articles about hate crimes and discrimination that have rarely been applied (see Violence).

In Finland, ombudsmen deal with all kinds of complaints by citizens, and may investigate unprompted. They are supposed to pay special attention to discrimination and have considerable powers. There is one ombudsman in the parliament for all kinds of grievances, and dedicated ones for women, children, and ethnic minorities. None of the last three can consider complaints of discrimination based on sexual orientation. It has been argued that there should be one to monitor discrimination against LGBT people, as in Sweden, and to help in the enforcement of the aforementioned legislation.

RELIGION AND SPIRITUALITY

Religiously, Finland is almost a monoculture. The great majority, 85 percent, of people are members of the state Lutheran church. The Orthodox Church, also state-sponsored, and some evangelical and other denominations (Baptists, Mormons, free, etc.) comprise only some 2 percent, while 13 percent are classified as irreligious. Within the Lutheran church, there are, however, various groups differing in their position on women's priesthood and acceptance of LGBT parishioners. There is no special church for homosexuals and no data as to which church, if any, gays and lesbians favor.

Most of the minor churches and some organized groups within the Lutheran church regard homosexuality as a grave sin and actively oppose any changes in legislation that would target discrimination. Although they are supported by very few people, they are very vociferous and have organized demonstrations and campaigns.

The Lutheran church has slowly changed its position.[12] At first, in 1984, the synod of bishops agreed that homosexuals cannot change their nature and should be loved as Christian brothers. Homosexual acts, however, were still condemned, meaning that only celibacy was acceptable to the church. The Lutheran church also officially opposed the Same Sex Union Act in the 1990s, as well as all other moves to end discrimination. Gay and lesbian people have also been fired from their jobs in the church.

Historically, there have been homosexual ministers in the church, but they have carefully avoided any publicity. Some ministers have also been friendly to LGBT people, privately blessing homes and giving absolutions.

All this discrimination and silence has been traumatic to people seeking consolation within the churches or who have felt that they are called to be priests. In this century, the situation is rapidly changing. Many priests and bishops have raised their voices to demand full acceptance of LGBT people in the church. At the same time the state has created new legislation, allowing same-sex unions, banning discrimination in work, and so on, which the church cannot ignore. At the moment, the Lutheran church seems to be in a crisis that may lead to some dispersion. The more conservative elements within the church appear adamant in their condemnation of homosexuality while the more open-minded liberals are losing their patience.

Christian LGBT people have founded some groups for peer support and to alter the policies of the church. They are usually ecumenical in nature. Some of them also produce theological works, meet with other religious organizations, offer counseling, and arrange training for local congregations.

VIOLENCE

There is a certain strong tradition of violence in Finland. Fighting usually occurs among acquaintances in homes and bars while people are drinking, not in streets against strangers, and people fight with their fists or knives, not firearms. Murder is not especially common. There are roughly two murders and homicides per 100,000 persons. The incarceration rate is about 75 per 100,000 persons.

Domestic violence, usually in the form of aggressive husbands, is seen as a serious problem and also occurs among homosexual couples. There are special refuges for victims of domestic violence, including men and LGBT people.

There is no systematic gay bashing in Finland though harassment and name calling occur. Violence expressly against LGBT people is not recorded by the police and is hardly ever reported in the press. By comparison to other Western European countries, it can be alleged that anti-LGBT violence is not infrequent. It can be assumed that people think that they would not get unbiased treatment from the authorities for being gay or lesbian. Minor brutalities are perhaps not reported at all.

There are hate crime prohibitions in Finnish law, although they are not often invoked and were passed without much discussion. Debasement or incitement of violence against minorities is criminalized, and crimes motivated by racism or homophobia can be punished with more severe sentences. These articles, however, have apparently never been applied in relation to LGBT individuals. In regard to the first article, there have been only a few prosecuted cases of slurs against people of color.

Hundreds of racist crimes are recognized yearly under the articles against racial hate crimes. The police or prosecutors, however, are not compelled to recognize the crimes as bias crimes unless the victims report them as such, and even then police and prosecutors have been quite disinclined to respond to homophobic violence. Authorities are not presently under obligation to record and compile statistics, even of reported hate crimes against LGBT people. New European Union regulations may change this.

OUTLOOK FOR THE 21ST CENTURY

It would seem that the life of LGBT people is fairly easy in 21st-century Finland. The major discriminative laws have been amended, the general public is fairly friendly or impartial, and the public and private services are as good and extensive as possible. However, there are gaps in legislation, the courts and public officials are on occasion unsympathetic, and public opinion can change.

At the moment, the most controversial practices and attitudes are found in the church. Although the majority of the parishioners might accept equal rights for gays and lesbians, the minority is usually more active and vocal. Presently, same-sex couples may not be officially blessed, nor are publicly gay or lesbian priests tolerated. Priesthood has been open to women since 1986 after decades of long, bitter discussions, and only now are the bishops forcing out those who oppose the inclusive regulation. Now, LGBT issues are similarly a very controversial and divisive topic in the church.

Adoption rights are a discussed legal issue. For example, new regulations allow same-sex couples to adopt each other's children, but not to jointly adopt non-biologically related children. This inequality has been criticized, but the government does not want to antagonize the opposition.

The existing hate crime and antidiscrimination laws, as such fairly adequate, are rarely or inefficiently applied. There have been no statistics about hate crimes, but this may change because of new Europe-wide practices. One remedy would be more effective training for police, prosecutors, and other officials, since problems are due to ignorance or disinterest rather than malice.

The HIV/AIDS situation seems to be fairly well under control, although much could be done to relieve the social discrimination of people with HIV/AIDS. There is some concern about the slowly rising trend of new infections; gay men and others seem to have relaxed their safe sex practices.

Racism and discrimination among LGBT people are often seen as growing problems. Everyday social issues are receiving more and more attention within the queer community, including poverty, elderly people, and families and children.

RESOURCE GUIDE

Suggested Reading

Jukka Lehtonen, and Kati Mustola, eds., *"Straight People Don't Tell, Do They…?" Negotiating the Boundaries of Sexuality and Gender at Work* (Helsinki, Finland: Ministry of Labour, 2004).

Jens Rydström, and Kati Mustola, eds., *Criminally Queer: Homosexuality and Criminal Law in Scandinavia 1842–1999* (Amsterdam: Aksant, 2007).

Web Sites

FINNQUEER, www.finnqueer.net/.
    Web journal for sexual and gender minorities.
Kimmoliisa, http://kimmoliisa.net/.
    Helsinki gay radio.
Ranneliike, http://ranneliike.net/.
    Internet discussion forum for gay men and information about gay life, night life, pride celebrations, and other happenings.
Sappho Net, http://www.sappho.net/.
    Guide to lesbian life and resources in Finland.

Organizations

AIDS Tukikeskukset, http://www.aidstukikeskus.fi/sivut/.
　　Provides AIDS help centers with offices in many cities. This semi-public institution works to prevent HIV infection while advising the government, arranging confidential testing, and offering support and counsel to HIV-positive persons.
ARCUS, http://www.arcusfinland.net/.
　　An ecumenical group of employees and active members of churches.
HOT, http://www.hot.fi/.
　　Sports club for lesbians and gay men.
MSC Finland, http://www.mscfin.fi/.
　　Union of gay bikers, leather men, and others.
Out 'n loud, http://www.outnloud.fi/.
　　Helsinki's gay men's chorus.
POSITIIVISET, http://www.positiiviset.fi/.
　　The Finnish Body Positive Association, a self support group of HIV-positive people and their friends and family.
SATEENKAARIPERHEET, http://www.sateenkaariperheet.fi/.
　　Rainbow Families, an association for lesbian, gay, bisexual, and transgender families and parents.
SETA, http://www.seta.fi.
　　SETA, Sexual Equality, is a national coalition organization for sex and sexual minorities with offices in Helsinki.
TRANSTUKIPISTE, http://www.transtukipiste.fi/.
　　SETAs support and resource center for transsexuals, transvestites, and intersexual persons.
TRASEK, http://www.trasek.net/.
　　Organization for transsexual and intersexual persons seeking medical treatment, therapy, or legal counseling.

NOTES

1. Church Research Institute, *Church in Change: The Evangelical Lutheran Church of Finland from 2000 to 2003* (Church Research Institute, Publication 55, 2005), http://www.evl.fi/kkh/ktk/english/p55.htm; Kääriäinen Kimmo, Kati, K. Niemelä, and Kimmo Ketola, *Religion in Finland: Decline, Change and Transformation of Finnish Religiosity* (Church Research Institute, Publication 54, 2005), http://www.evl.fi/kkh/ktk/english/p54.htm.

2. Statistics Finland, *Education in Finland 2006* (Statistics Finland, 2006).

3. Statistics Finland, https://stat.fi/index_en.html (accessed May 30, 2008).

4. The Sámi in Finland, http://www.samediggi.fi/images/stories/pdf_tiedostot/saamelaisetenglanti.pdf (accessed May 30, 2008).

5. Statistics Finland, *Education in Finland 2006.*

6. Vappu Sunnari, Jenny Kangasvuo, and Mervi Heikkinen, eds., *Gendered and Sexualised Violence in Educational Environments* (Oulu: Oulu University Press, 2002).

7. Kristin Hegna and Lars Wichström, "Suicide Attempts among Norwegian Gay, Lesbian and Bisexual Youths," *Acta Sociologica* 50 (2007): 21–37.

8. Jukka Lehtonen and Kati Mustola, eds., *Straight People Don't Tell, Do They? Negotiating the Boundaries of Sexuality and Gender at Work* (Helsinki: ESF Research Publications 2004/2b, Ministry of Labour, 2004), http://www.esr.fi/esr/fi/__yleiset/research report2b04.pdf.

9. Statistics Finland, https://stat.fi/index_en.html.

10. National Public Health Institute, HIV and AIDS statistics (2008), http://www.ktl.fi/ (accessed May 30, 2008).

11. Jens Rydström and Kati Mustola, eds., *Criminally Queer: Homosexuality and Criminal Law in Scandinavia 1842–1999* (Amsterdam: Aksant, 2007).

12. Arcus Finland, "Gays and Lesbians in Finnish Society and Churches," http://www.arcusfinland.net/churches.htm (accessed May 30, 2008).

FRANCE

Marianne Blidon and Régis Revenin

OVERVIEW

France, officially known as the French Republic, is a democratic country in western Europe. It shares borders with five countries: Spain to the south, Switzerland and Germany to the east, and Belgium and Luxembourg to the north. France also has an extensive coastline, with access to the Mediterranean Sea in the south, and the English Channel, Bay of Biscayne, and Atlantic Ocean in the north and west. France covers an area of approximately 212,356 square miles in Europe. The French Republic, including its overseas territories, has a population of almost 65 million. Paris, the capital France, is a major world metropolis, with a population of 12 million. Lyons and Marseilles, the second-tier cities in France, each has a population of under 2 million. France is one of the oldest states in Europe, and is highly ethnically diverse. Today, France has a mixed presidential-parliamentary system of government that vests strong powers in the executive branch.

The official language of France is French, but a number of regional languages are also spoken. France has the sixth largest economy in the world, making it a major industrial power. France has a capitalist economy with substantial state intervention. The official currency is the euro, which in 2002 replaced the franc and the currencies of 11 other member states of the European Union (EU). France is a member of the Council of Europe and one of the founding members of the EU, the eurozone, and the Schengen area. It is one of the five permanent members of the United Nations Security Council, and belongs to the Group of Eight (G8), the Organisation for Economic Co-operation and Development (OECD), La Francophonie, and the Latin Union. Militarily, France is a member of the North Atlantic Treaty Alliance (NATO) and has nuclear capability.

France is a secular nation, but influenced by a strong Catholic tradition. It also has a large Muslim population. An estimated 7 million people in France identify with the faith of Islam, and there are roughly 700,000 Jews. France is also home to small Protestant, Evangelical, Buddhist, and Hindu minorities. In addition to social problems such as unemployment faced by all industrialized countries since the 1970s, the issue of racial discrimination in French society has come to the fore since the late 1980s, crystallized recently by the Islamic headscarf debate and the riots in France.

A country with high symbolic value, particularly in the field of culture, France, and especially Paris, is the world's primary tourist destination.

OVERVIEW OF LGBT ISSUES

France is a highly ambiguous country when it comes toattitudes toward sexual orientation. Many French writers, from Proust to Colette, Gide, Cocteau, Jouhandeau, Montherlant, and Genet, established the existence of gays and lesbians in France. In 1791, France was also the first nation to abolish the crime of sodomy, which was considered a victimless crime. On the other hand, France was among the countries that declared homosexuality a psychological disorder in the first half of the 19th century. Homosexuality was only declassified as a disease in the early 1980s, when a left-wing coalition came to power.

French people, especially in the large cities, are fairly tolerant or indifferent toward homosexuality, particularly since same-sex civil unions were passed into law by a left-wing parliamentary majority in 1999. The civil union contract, Le Pacte Civil de Solidarité (PaCS) is open to both same-sex and opposite-sex couples, although it was initially designed and advocated by gay groups in the 1980s.

The City of Paris, a conservative stronghold for more than a century, elected a gay mayor, Socialist Bertrand Delanoé, in 2001.

Gay marriage and same-sex parenting are now the key issues for gay groups in France, whereas the main agenda in the 1990s was combating homophobia, and the chief concerns of the 1970s were sexual liberation and teenage sexuality.

EDUCATION

Sex education has not been a priority for recent French governments. The sex education curriculum remains focused on reproduction, contraception, and sexually transmitted diseases (STDs), neglecting sexual desire, sexual pleasure, and sexual orientation. The issue of discrimination based on sexual orientation or gender is rarely addressed in schools. LGBT associations like SOS Homophobie have shown that schools are rife with homophobia, and advocate that young people should be educated to be more tolerant and accepting of homosexuality from childhood.

There is no official program to combat homophobic or transphobic discrimination in secondary schools or institutions of higher education in France. Some LGBT groups propose actions to raise awareness of homophobic discrimination, but they frequently meet with refusal from school principals and university chancellors who fear homosexual proselytizing.

In French colleges and universities, there is no research unit, department, or program dedicated to research on homosexuality, or sexuality in general. In spite of this, young LGBT researchers are emerging in disciplines such as history, sociology, and geography, but French academia remains unsupportive of this rich, dynamic movement. Ironically, France has been home to many intellectuals of great importance for gay and lesbian studies, such as Michel Foucault, Monique Wittig, and Guy Hocquenghem, and outstanding contemporary writers such as Hervé Guibert, Nina Bouraoui, and Guillaume Dustan.

EMPLOYMENT AND ECONOMICS

France is the world's sixth-largest economy. The French economy combines private enterprise, government programs, and social economy policies. The central government controls most defense, education, police, and security spending. Local governments control spending for infrastructure, the environment, recreation, and culture. The French state is the largest single employer.

France has shifted from an industrial economy to a service economy. The service sector employs three-quarters of the workforce. France is nevertheless the world's fourth-largest exporter overall, and number two for farm and agri-food products, even though those sectors employ fewer and fewer people. Since the oil shock in 1974, French economic growth has slowed, and unemployment hovers around 10 percent. Unemployment is highest among people under 30 years old, low-skilled workers, and women. Various incentive measures have been introduced to tackle the youth unemployment problem.

Aside from the law on equal gender representation in politics, there is no policy to combat discrimination based on gender, race, or sexual orientation in the workplace. The majority of women still come up against the glass ceiling, which keeps them out of positions of power in large corporations and government.

Since 1985, the law (no. 85–772 of July 25, 1985) has prohibited discrimination based on "mores." Sexual orientation in France is considered a private matter. Therefore, there is no official data on the employment of LGBT people or discrimination against LGBT people in the workplace. Some attribute the overrepresentation of gay and lesbian college graduates in surveys to greater investment in education by gays and lesbians, whereas others see the career choices of gays and lesbians as more oriented toward artistic and intellectual occupations.[1] This is the basis for various myths, such as the strong purchasing power of gays, called the pink euro.[2] This image overrides the invisibility and various forms of discrimination suffered by LGBT workers.

Several LGBT groups are active in combating LGBT discrimination in the workplace, and play a consultative role for the public authorities and companies concerned. L'Autre Cercle, founded in 1998, is one of the main national gay groups of France. It has more than 600 working male and female members. The group focuses on combating homophobia in the workplace. Personnel associations are forming to combat discrimination, enhance visibility, and promote equal rights in both the public sector, such as the education system and the police force, and in private corporations such as Air France. *Le syndicat national des entreprises gaies* (SNEG), founded in 1990, provides support and promotion for companies run by LGBT people or catering to LGBT consumers.

SOS Homophobie, which runs a hotline, states in its annual report that one in five reported homophobic incidents occurring in the workplace.[3] The incidents include hurtful remarks, verbal abuse, harassment, or discrimination in hiring or career advancement. As a result, few employees are open about their homosexuality in the workplace.

SOCIAL/GOVERNMENT PROGRAMS

Neither the central government nor local governments fund any social programs specifically designed for lesbians, gays, bisexuals, or transgender people. The EU treaties do not explicitly recognize discrimination based on sexual orientation, and therefore contain no specific provisions for special programs. Social policies in France completely disregard LGBT issues.

SEXUALITY/SEXUAL PRACTICES

Traditional attitudes toward sexuality in France highlighted the fact that sexuality was taboo. The absence of sex education at school and in the family demonstrate this anxiety.

Since the 1980s, the issue of sexuality has been approached primarily from the angle of HIV prevention, and rarely from that of sexual desire or sexual pleasure. This epidemiological approach to sexuality, expressed in terms of risk, has had an obvious influence on perceptions of sexuality and sexual practices. It has prompted numerous surveys on the sexual behavior of gays and bisexuals, and more rarely of lesbians and transsexuals. As HIV and AIDS cases increase again, the debate refocuses on safe sex versus barebacking, endorsed by the writings of Eric Remès and Guillaume Dustan. The renewed popularity of barebacking highlights the changing perception of the connection between homosexuality and AIDS, and challenges the norm of prevention, which is now perceived as a restriction.[4]

Surveys conducted by the French gay media after 1985 show a steep increase in the number of respondents seeking a stable relationship. In reaction to the epidemic, many gay men in relationships initially gave up outside encounters. The 1990s saw a revival of casual sex, an increase in the declared number of partners, and a return to potentially risky sexual practices such as group sex and the use of accessories. Homosexuals adapt their safe sex strategies according to the level of intimacy with their partners, and whether the relationship is stable or casual.[5]

Surveys and prevention campaigns have rarely been directed at lesbians, who are often considered not at risk for HIV transmission. In 2000, the ENVEFF (L'enquête nationale sur les violences envers les femmes en France)[6] survey on violence toward women, however, showed that lesbians tend to become sexually active earlier than heterosexual women, and only 20 percent of French lesbians have their first experience of sexual intercourse with a woman. According to the survey, lesbians have more sexual partners during their lifetimes than heterosexual women. Bisexual women tend to have more male than female partners.[7]

FAMILY

Traditional French culture promotes the idea that the nuclear family, composed of husband, wife, and children, is the preferred family arrangement. That model is based on a naturalist view of the family, which some French psychoanalysts claim guarantees the symbolic order.[8] That dominant model has been challenged since the 1960s, mainly because of the widespread increase in divorce, which has brought single-parent families and blended families into the mainstream. Single-parent families account for 10 percent of households, while blended families make up 8 percent of households. The number of divorces has increased fourfold since the 1960s.

Traditionally, the French family was established through the rite of marriage. Yet, the frequency of marriage—still reserved exclusively for heterosexual couples in France—has declined significantly. In the 1960s, only 10 percent of couples cohabited before marrying. Now the figure is 90 percent. One-third of children are born outside wedlock. Since World War II, the French family has changed profoundly.

The civil code does not explicitly state that marriage concerns only heterosexual couples. In 2004, after the publication of a manifesto for equal rights, Noël Mamère, the mayor of Bègles, a small town, approved a marriage between two men. Mamère was suspended from office for a month and the marriage was annulled by the public prosecutor.[9] The European Court of Human Rights (ECtHR) upheld the conformity of the ban on marriage between same-sex partners even though gay marriage is legal in several member states, namely Spain, Belgium, Denmark, and the Netherlands.

The push for same-sex marriage and for the social recognition of same-sex parents is the expression of social reality in France. Surveys show that approximately half of gay men and lesbians are in stable relationships equivalent to marriage.[10] The number of children of gay or lesbian parents is estimated at between 40,000 and 300,000.[11]

Same-sex couples raising children, as well as gays and lesbians who have children from a previous heterosexual union, highlight a legal void. Same-sex parenthood calls for a redefinition of the model of parenthood along the lines of adoption rather than biology. It also calls for a shift from the dominant model of the nuclear family, already challenged by single-parent and blended families, away from the couple and toward a relationship that can involve between one and four adults.

These social changes meet resistance from the main religious institutions, conservatives, and also some figures considered progressive. The issues of same-sex marriage and the right to adopt children have shaken up the political scene and the traditional opposition between left and right.

The family is also the environment where young LGBT people grow up. For most families, homosexuality is not even considered a possibility, so coming out is often a painful experience. SOS Homophobie reports that 10 percent of calls it receives are from people who have been blackmailed, verbally abused, or physically assaulted by family members. The group reports a few cases of young people thrown out of their homes with no money after they came out, as well as forced marriages, although little else is known about the extent of the problem.[12]

COMMUNITY

The idea of a gay community, similar to any distinct non-French ethnic community, is frowned upon in France. Communities, particularly of minorities, have a negative social, cultural, and political image. In opposition to multiculturalism, considered an American import, France, at least officially, champions universalism *à la française,* underpinned by the ideas of social mix and equality. Social, racial, religious, gender, and sexual discrimination are nevertheless highly prevalent in France, and there is no proactive antidiscrimination policy, particularly in regard to sexual orientation.

Although its roots stretch farther back, the gay community only became visible in France during the 1970s and 1980s with the AIDS epidemic and the formation of activist groups like Act-up Paris. The 1990s saw fairly sterile debates on multiculturalism versus universalism. A wide variety of gay associations emerged, including social clubs, recreational groups, and student associations. Simultaneously, there was an explosion of gay businesses and gay media. Gay bars, restaurants, and clubs are not a new phenomenon, however: gay social venues have existed in Paris since the 1880s.

The first real gay organization in France has been Arcadie, founded in 1954 by André Baudry. It was a homophile movement, and also had a monthly journal. In 1971, the Front Homosexuel d'Action Révolutionnaire (FHAR) was created by radical lesbian and gay people.

Gay and lesbian centers only appeared in the late 1980s and expanded in the 1990s, partly bridging the gap between the activist and commercial spheres. There have been long-running tensions between activists, intellectuals, and gay businesspeople, with leftist activists deriding the gay district as a ghetto.[13] There is also less heated debate among gays about whether the Marais, the gay district in Paris, is a haven or a ghetto. Both in Paris and other large French cities such as Marseilles, Lyons, Bordeaux, Nice, Lille, Nantes, and Toulouse, gay businesses are concentrated in particular districts such as Le Marais in Paris, or particular streets in large provincial cities.

The lesbian community, mainly visible in Paris, has a much lower profile than the male gay community, with fewer than 10 bars and clubs in Paris as of 2008.

Paris, as well as some large provincial cities, has a broad fabric of social and sex businesses, making it probably one of the gayest cities in the world since the late 19th century.

While the first gay pride march in Paris attracted a few hundred activists in 1977, Paris now has one of the most dynamic gay pride marches, recently renamed *Marche des fiertés LGBT* in French, with between 500,000 and 1 million participants in the past few years. A lesbian march and a transsexual march, with a more activist, political focus, are organized alongside the official Gay Pride, now seen by some as too commercial. Marches are also organized in large provincial cities all over France, with between 1,000 and 10,000 participants in each city.

A gay television channel, Pink TV, first went on air in 2004, but recently folded and became a pornography channel. A less ambitious gay Internet television channel started up in 2007 (Free Gay TV).

Several cities in France also host gay and lesbian film festivals. Some feminist lesbian festivals are also emerging. For the past few years, a large gay expo has been held in Paris, with several hundred exhibitors, including activist groups and businesses. Other LGBT-related activist, cultural, literary, and arts events and festivals with gay overtones are emerging in both Paris and the provinces.

Finally, the sudden increase in Internet dating, which has created a kind of virtual LGBT community, is facilitating friendly, romantic, and sexual exchanges, some of which lead to real-life relationships.

HEALTH

Health is a political issue in the French context. Social Security was defined by an order of October 4, 1945, issued by the National Council of the Resistance. Its underlying principle is repeated in the preamble to the constitution: the Fifth Republic "guarantees for all, particularly children, mothers and elderly workers, the protection of health, material security, rest and recreation." However, as life expectancy increases and the proportion of contributors to the system declines, the health care component of Social Security, in deep deficit, is gradually being undermined as patients are asked to pay more.

In this environment, research and prevention campaign choices are influenced by cost concerns and politics. For example, prevention campaigns are rarely aimed at lesbians or transsexuals. Private associations must provide support and information and raise awareness of STDs.

Attitudes toward LGBT health issues are permeated by ignorance and stigma. For example, in its early days, AIDS was called *the gay cancer*. Gays were singled out with drug addicts as the main carriers of the disease while the public authorities delayed launching targeted prevention campaigns. Transsexuals systematically undergo psychiatric evaluation to determine their gender identity in order to decide whether to allow them to receive hormonal treatment or change their gender on identity documents. There are no data available on the number of transsexuals and intersex individuals in France today. Little is known about them and formal organizations are only just emerging.

There are approximately 62,000 AIDS cases in France, 25,000 of which are gay or bisexual people.[14] In 2000, a mortality survey identified 1,600 deaths caused by AIDS per year. STDs that had virtually disappeared, such as syphilis, reappeared in the late 1990s. The number of syphilis cases, as well as the number of cases of other STDs, are no longer systematically recorded in France. There are close interrelationships between STDs and HIV, however, which should therefore be treated together.

POLITICS AND LAW

France is a centralized state, and laws passed apply nationwide, except in rare cases in some overseas territories.

On the legislative front, France decriminalized homosexual relations as late as the 1980s, and has criminalized homophobic language in the 21st century.

The crime of sodomy was abolished in 1791 during the French Revolution. Homosexuality, absent from the penal code until 1942, was not permanently removed until 1982. The legal age of sexual consent is currently 15 years for both heterosexual and homosexual intercourse, whereas for heterosexuals it was 11 years until 1863, and 13 years from 1863 to 1942. Except in cases of rape, there was no legal age of consent from 1791 to 1832.

The criminalization of homosexual intercourse with minors under 21 years of age by the extreme-right Vichy government in 1942 was maintained after the Liberation of France by the provisional government of Christian-Democrats, Gaullists, Socialists, and Communists, while heterosexual intercourse was permitted from the age of 13. The Mirguet Amendment of 1960 extended criminalization to homosexual intercourse between consenting adults, considered an *outrage public à la pudeur* (act of indecency). The law listed homosexuality as a social ill on par with tuberculosis, alcoholism, and prostitution.[15] The amendment was abolished by parliament in 1980 during debates on new provisions to deter rape.

But the Vichy law of 1942 was maintained, prohibiting homosexual intercourse between a minor under 18 years of age (the age of majority was lowered from 21 to 18 in 1974) and an adult, whereas the age of consent for heterosexual intercourse was set at 15. This was finally abolished by a left-wing government in 1982. During debates on reforming the penal code in 1991, however, a parliamentary amendment was submitted to restore the law of 1942, abolished in 1982, on the grounds of protecting youth.

The first antidiscrimination law connected with sexual orientation was passed in 1985 as article 225–1 of the penal code, which punishes discrimination based on mores, a subtle way of referring to homosexuality without naming it. Further antidiscrimination provisions were passed in 1986 and 2001, but since it is difficult to prove that homosexuality was the reason for an employer's rejection of a candidate, these provisions are virtually inapplicable. Moreover, most legislative progress has been driven by European directives, which for more than 20 years have required member states of the European Union to combat inequality in relation to sexual minorities.

Use of homophobic language only became an offense in France in the 21st century. The law of March 4, 2002, officially prohibits all forms of homophobic discrimination in hiring and in the workplace. Several amendments to existing antidiscrimination laws were passed in 2004, punishing the use of homophobic language in public in the same way that xenophobic and racist language is punished. At the same time, the law does not provide a definition of *homophobic*.

An antidiscrimination board, the *Haute autorité de lutte contre les discriminations et pour l'égalité* (HALDE), was established by law on December 30, 2004. HALDE has a mandate to combat homophobia along with other forms of discrimination. The founding law rounds out the provisions of the Press Act of 1881 by making it an offense to insult, defame, incite to hatred, or discriminate against individuals or groups on the basis of their sexual orientation by any means of public expression.

In practice, however, the courts do not always recognize the homophobic aspect of crimes or assaults, even when it is obvious. And HALDE can hardly consider government policy, which excludes gays and lesbians from marriage and parenthood, as homophobic.

Some gay groups criticize the leniency of the French courts.

A conservative member of parliament, Christian Vanneste, recently sentenced by the French courts for use of homophobic language, submitted an amendment to abolish the law of 2004 for consideration by parliament.[16] Vanneste declared that homosexuality was a threat to the survival of humankind and was inferior to heterosexuality, because if it were universalized it would be dangerous for humankind. He added that homosexual behavior was sectarian.

Same-sex marriage is not recognized in France, unlike in other European countries such as Denmark, the Netherlands, Belgium, and Spain. PaCS, the civil union contract passed into law in 1999, confers the status of cohabiting partners on homosexual couples, without granting them any parenting or filial rights. Material benefits, such as joint taxation and inheritance rights, are less generous for PaCS couples than for married couples.

The issue of bisexuality is rarely addressed in France and academic research. There is only one bisexual association: BiCause.[17] There is no recorded bisexual activism in France and few businesses or social venues in Paris or the provinces claim to be bisexual. Bisexuals are virtually invisible in the media, too. A common image of bisexuals is sex-obsessed men who have sex with women and men indiscriminately, or gay men unable to come to terms with their homosexuality. Lesbians and gay men sometimes distrust bisexuals because they refuse to choose.

Transsexuals are more visible than bisexuals, but far less visible than gays and lesbians. Groups such as ASB (Association du Syndrome de Benjamin), PASTT (Groupe de Prévention et d'Action pour la Sante et le Travail des Transsexuel(le)s), and CARITIG (Centre d'Aide, de Recherche et d'Information sur la Transsexualité et l'Identité de Genre) defend transsexual rights. Transphobic discrimination is widespread and persistent in France. Psychiatrization is pervasive, making it difficult to change gender in official documents.

Transsexuality represents a real challenge for French society. Evidence of this can be seen in the recent case of the trans marriage in the Paris suburb of Rueil-Malmaison (2005). The case involved a male-to-female (MTF) transwoman who had undergone sex reassignment surgery and an MTF transwoman who had not had the surgery, and would still be considered a biological man. The French administration and courts refuse to allow them to marry, not on the grounds of their biological sex, as was the case until now, but on the pretext that, in terms of identity, both partners see themselves as women.

Intellectuals such as sociologist Eric Fassin have expressed the view that nonconformity with traditional gender norms, defined by religious precepts, is becoming an obstacle to civil, secular marriage.[18]

RELIGION AND SPIRITUALITY

France is a secular state, which means that the state does not recognize or afford privileges to any particular religion, and that everyone enjoys freedom of belief. The separation of church and state occurred in 1905. Religion is considered a private matter and as such is not recorded in the census. Although the majority of French people are nonpracticing and many are agnostic, an estimated two-thirds of French people identify as Catholic, approximately 7 percent identify as Muslim, and 1 percent as Jewish. Catholicism is an enduring legacy that has left its mark on the calendar of holidays, place names, and French culture in general.

The three main religions of France all condemn homosexuality, partly because it is a type of love that is not aimed at procreation. Religious institutions have often been in the vanguard of opposition to changes to the nuclear family and to rights for same-sex couples. Different religions sometimes issue joint positions on marriage or adoption. During the PaCS controversy, several pro-family groups including Les associations familiales protestantes, l'Union des familles musulmanes and Famille de France formed a federation called Génération anti-pacs. Among the most conservative pro-family groups, Les Associations familiales catholiques cited scripture in its arguments. During the debates prior to the vote on the PaCS bill, a scene alien to France's secular culture took place: a right-wing parliament member, Christine Boutin, brandished the Bible in parliament.[19]

Each religious group, however, has more liberal movements whose positions diverge from the conservative core. Les réseaux du Parvis, founded in 1999, is a federation of some 50 groups from the Catholic reform movement, which defend a more liberal approach, more attuned to the idea that religion must adapt to social change.

Jewish and Muslim gays and lesbians feel threatened by three-way exclusion: exclusion from their religion, which considers homosexuality a transgression of the divine order; exclusion from their families, which often forces them to keep their homosexuality secret; and exclusion from their communities, which leaves them with the choice between silence and rejection. In this environment, an important role is played by religious LGBT groups like David et Jonathan for Christians and Beit Haverim for Jews, which endeavor to reconcile a dual sense of identity in homosexuals who also see themselves as members of a religious faith.

VIOLENCE

There is little information about violence toward LGBT people in France due to a lack of clear statistics on this issue and underreporting. Physical assault is the reason for 11 percent of inbound calls to SOS Homophobie. In 82 percent of cases, the victim was gay. In half of cases, the victims were assaulted in a public place. In 8 percent of cases, the assault occurred within the family.[20]

The French legal system has recognized homophobia as a factor in physical or verbal assault since 2004. Homophobic violence, however, has not disappeared and the courts do not always recognize a homophobic motive. For example, four men who ambushed and assaulted a gay man in a gay meeting place in Reims in 2004 were convicted of a *heinous crime* (*crime crapuleux*) rather than *homophobic acts of violence*.[21]

Homophobic violence is a key factor in influencing the relationship between LGBT people and the world. Every homophobic assault is a collective warning to LGBT people to conform to the heteronormative model. The increase in LGBT bars, clubs, and community centers responds to the need for safety among a collective LGBT community.

Transsexuals in France are highly at risk for violence. There are frequent newspaper reports of murders of transsexual people, to which the media and public opinion are largely indifferent, especially if the victim was a prostitute. In addition to physical violence, there is daily harassment linked to the assertion of their identity. For example, the difference between their appearance and the gender on their identity documents regularly exposes transsexuals to ordinary transphobia, particularly since changing documents is difficult unless the person undergoes surgical sex alteration and agrees to medical and psychiatric monitoring.

OUTLOOK FOR THE 21ST CENTURY

Compared to other nations, France is a fairly gay-friendly country, but the election of Nicolas Sarkozy as president in 2007 has pushed back the likelihood of same-sex marriage and the recognition of homosexual parenting, the most pressing claims of the French gay movement today. In the margins, more radical voices are calling for greater consideration of lesbian, bisexual, and transsexual issues, and a conflation of gender and sexual orientation with race- and class-based relationships of domination and power. The campaigns of the 1970s in favor of sexual liberation and teenage sexuality have been superseded by a hyper-valuation of the couple, and a complete rejection by the gay movement of discussions of pedophilia and male prostitution. Some see this as a heterosexualization of gays, even as the clothing and behavior of heterosexual teenagers is becoming increasingly stereotypically homosexual. Moreover, discrimination based on sexual orientation is still common in the workplace. Homophobia is becoming more insidious: while physical assault and verbal abuse still exist, more indirect forms of rejection are occurring. Being gay in Paris or another large city is not the same as being gay in a small town or rural area.

RESOURCE GUIDE

Suggesting Reading

Nathalie Bajos, and Michel Bozon, eds., *Enquête sur la sexualité en France. Pratiques, genre et santé* (Paris: La Découverte, 2008).

Léo Bersani, *Homos: repenser l'identité* (Paris: Odile Jacob, 1998).

Marianne Blidon, "Les commerces gays entre logiques économiques et logiques communautaires," in *Le choix de l'homosexualité*, ed. Perreau Bruno (Paris: EPEL, 2007).

Daniel Borillo, ed., *Homosexualités et droit: de la tolérance à la reconnaissance juridique* (Paris: PUF, 1999).

Daniel Borillo, *L'homophobie* (Paris, Presses universitaires de France, 2001).

Daniel Borillo and Eric Fassin, eds., *Au-delà du PaCS: l'expertise familiale à l'épreuve de l'homosexualité* (Paris: PUF, 2001).

Christophe Broqua, *Agir pour ne pas mourir! Act up, les homosexuels et le sida* (Paris: Presses de la fondation nationale des sciences politiques, 2005).

Christophe Broqua, *Homosexualités au temps du sida: tensions sociales et identitaires* (Paris: Editions ANRS, 2003).

Hélène Buisson-Fenet, *Un sexe problématique: L'Eglise et l'homosexualité masculine en France: 1971–2000* (Paris: PUV, 2004).

Antony Copley, *Sexual Moralities in France: 1780–1980: New Ideas on the Family, Divorce, and Homosexuality: An Essay on Moral Change* (London: Routledge, 1989).

Carolyn J. Dean, *The Frail Social Body: Pornography, Homosexuality, and Other Fantasies in Interwar France* (Berkeley: University of California Press, 2000).

Catherine Deschamps, *Le miroir bisexuel: une socio-anthropologie de l'invisible* (Paris: Balland, 2002).

Virginie Descoutures, Marie Digoix, Éric Fassin, and Wilfried Rault, eds., *Mariages et homosexualités dans le monde. L'arrangement des normes familiales* (Paris: Autrement, 2008).

Didier Eribon, *Réflexions sur la question gay* (Paris: Fayard, 1999).

Eric Fassin, *L'inversion de la question homosexuelle* (Paris: Éditions Amsterdam, 2005).

Eric Fassin and Clarisse Fabre, *Liberté, égalité, sexualités: actualité politique des questions sexuelles: entretiens* (Paris: Belfond, 2004).

Maxime Foerster, *Histoire des transsexuels en France* (Paris: H & O éditions, 2006).

Guy GrHocquenghem, *Le Désir homosexuel* (Paris: Fayard, 2000).

Martine Gross, ed., *Homoparentalités, état des lieux* (Paris: Eres, 2005).

Martine Gross, *L'homoparentalité* (Paris: Presses universitaires de France, 2007).

Jean Le Bitoux, *Entretiens sur la question gay* (Béziers, France: H &O, 2005).

Frédéric Martel, *Le rose et le noir: les homosexuels en France depuis 1968* (Paris: Seuil, 2000).

Caroline Mécary, *Les droits des homosexuel/les* (Paris: PUF, 2003).

Rommel Mendès-Leite, *Bisexualité, le dernier tabou* (Paris: Calmann-Lévy, 1996).

Jeffrey Merrick and Bryant T. Ragan, eds., *Homosexuality in Modern France* (New York: Oxford University Press, 1996).

Jeffrey Merrick and Michael Sibalis, eds., *Homosexuality in French History and Culture* (New York: Harrington Park Press, 2001).

Janine Mossuz-Lavau, *La vie sexuelle en France* (Paris: La Martinière, 2002).

Laure Murat, *La loi du genre. Une histoire culturelle du "troisième sexe"* (Paris: Fayard, 2006).

Bruno Perreau, ed., *Le choix de l'homosexualité* (Paris: EPEL, 2007).

Bruno Proth, *Lieux de drague, scènes et coulisses d'une sexualité masculine* (Toulouse, France: Octares, 2002).

Régis Revenin, ed., *Hommes et masculinités, de 1789 à nos jours: contributions à l'histoire du genre et de la sexualité en France* (Paris: Editions Autrement, 2007).

Régis Revenin, "Les études et recherches lesbiennes et gays en France, 1970–2006," *Genre & Histoire* 1 (automne 2007), http://genrehistoire.fr.

Vernon A. Rosario *L'irrésistible ascension du pervers: entre littérature et psychiatrie* (Paris: EPEL, 2000).

Marie-Ange Schiltz, *Les homosexuels face au sida: enquête 1995. Regards sur une décennie d'enquêtes* (Paris: Rapport à l'ANR, 1998).

Marie-Ange Schiltz, *Les homosexuels masculins face au sida: Enquêtes 1991–1992* (Paris: CAMS, Rapport à l'Agence Nationale de Recherches sur le Sida, 1993).

Marie-Ange Schiltz, "Un ordinaire insolite: le couple homosexuel," *Actes de la recherche en sciences sociales* 125 (1998): 30–43.

M. Sibalis, "Urban Space and Homosexuality: The Example of the Marais, Paris 'Gay Ghetto,'" *Urban Studies* 41, no. 9 (2004): 1739–58.

Videos/Films

L'homme blessé (109 min.; 1983). Directed by Patrice Chéreau. A young man discovers his homosexuality and begins a relationship with a criminal that he meets at a train station.

Querelle (108 min.; 1982; Franco-German film). Directed by Rainer Werner Fassbinder. A movie adapted from the classical novel by Jean Genet. French sailor Querelle arrives in Brest and starts frequenting a strange whorehouse. He discovers that his brother Robert is the lover of the female owner, Lysiane.

Chouchou (105 min.; 2003). Directed by Merzak Allouache. The love story between a perfect gentlemen and Chouchou, a migrant from north Africa who has just arrived in Paris.

Crustacés et coquillages (93 min.; 2005). Directed by Olivier Ducastel and Jacques Martineau. During the holidays, a family stays in their ancestral house. The father encounters an old friend, his first love.

Le placard (84 min.; 2001). Directed by Francis Veber.

Son frère (95 min.; 2002). Directed by Patrice Chéreau. Two brothers with a problematic relationship in the past come together again when the older one contracts a fatal disease and ask his brother to accompany him to see his doctors.

Jeanne et le garçon formidable (98 min.; 1998). Directed by Olivier Ducastel and Jacques Martineau. The relationship between Jeanne and a young militant from Act-up.

Les témoins (95 min.; 2007). Directed by André Téchiné. Paris 1984, a group of friends contend with the first outbreak of the AIDS epidemic.

Films with Transsexual and Transvestite Characters

Tiresia (115 min.; 2003). Directed by Bertrand Bonello. According to Greek Mythology, Tiresias was both a woman and a man. Here, Tiresias as represented as a Brazilian.

Wild Side (93 min.; 2003). Directed by Sébastien Lifshitz. A transsexual, who survives prostituting herself in Paris, returns to her family home in the countryside with her two lovers to look after her dying mother.

Films with Lesbian Characters

Clara cet été-là (90 min.; 2002). Directed by Patrick de Grandperret. The relationships between two teenagers during holidays.

Coup de foudre (110 min.; 1982). Directed by Diane Kurys. Two married women fall in love and want to run away together.

Oublier Cheyenne (90 min.; 2004). Directed by Valérie Minetto. The relationship between two women who are in love, but one of them wants to live in the country and the other in the city.

L'Homme de sa vie (90 min.; 2005). Directed by Zabou Breitman. During the holidays, a married man falls in love with a gay man.

Web Sites

L'association des parents gays et lesbiens, http://www.apgl.asso.fr.
 Created in 1986 for LGBT people who want to have children.
L'association Act-up Paris, http://www.actupparis.org.
 Famous international association dealing with HIV.
L'association des sœurs de la perpétuelle indulgence, http://www.lessoeurs.org.
 Famous international association dealing with HIV. The French branch was founded in 1991. Local convents.
l'Atelier Genre & Sexualités (association EFiGiES-laboratoire IRIS), http://www.efigies.org.
 Doctoral (PhD) workshop on sexuality, the only one in France, that focuses primarily on two projects: the creation of a peer-reviewed international and interdisciplinary French-language e-journal called *Genre, sexualité et société* and a monthly doctoral seminar in Paris, coordinated by Régis Revenin. The aim is to develop academic studies on sexuality in France.
L'Autre Cercle, http://www.autrecercle.org.
 Work association combating sexual discrimination at work.
Bi'cause, http://bicause.pelnet.com.
 The only bisexual association.
CGL (*centre gays et lesbien*) de Paris, http://www.cglparis.org.
La coordination lesbienne de France, http://www.coordinationlesbienne.org.
 Federation of about twenty lesbian associations, founded in 1997.
La Dixième Muse, http://www.ladixiememuse.com.
 Bimonthly lesbian magazine, published since 2004.
Fédération des CGL de France, http://www.hexagonegay.com/Federation_Centres_LGBT/.
 CGL is an associative community center in all major cities where LGBT people can find information and advice about sexual orientation.
IDAHO (International Day against Homophobia), http://www.idahomophobia.org.
 International Day against Homophobia (IDAHO) is celebrated May 17, and was created by the French academic and militant Louis-Georges Tin, in partnership with ILGA (the International Lesbian and Gay Association). It aims to coordinate international events to call respect for LGBT people worldwide.
l'Inter-LGBT, http://www.inter-lgbt.org.
 Federation of about 50 LGBT associations in France. It organizes several gay pride events (Marches des Fiertés LGBT), as well as working for gay and lesbian rights and against discrimination.
M Mensuel, http://www.mmensuel.com/.
 Gay magazine, monthly since 2007.
Les Panthères roses, http://www.pantheresroses.org.
 Queer radical movement against imposed moral order, patriarchy, sexism, racism, etc.
PASTT, http://www.transmonde.net.

Pref Mag, http://www.prefmag.com.
      Gay magazine, bimonthly since 2004.
SOS Homophobie, http://www.sos-homophobie.org.
      Association created in 1994 to combat discrimination and homophobic aggression.
Têtu Magazine, http://www.tetu.com.
      Gay magazine, monthly since 1995.
The Warning, http://www.thewarning.info.
      New French association combating HIV, with new ideas about prevention.

NOTES

1. Didier Eribon, *Réflexions sur la question gay* (Paris: Fayard, 1999).
2. Marianne Blidon, "Les commerces gays entre logiques économiques et logiques communautaires," in *Le choix de l'homosexualité,* ed. Bruno Perreau (Paris: EPEL, 2007).
3. See http://www.sos-homophobie.org.
4. Michel Bozon and Véronique Doré, *Sexualités, relations et prévention chez les homosexuels masculins. Un nouveau rapport au risque* (Paris: ANRS, 2007).
5. Ibid.
6. This is a representative sample of 6,970 women aged 20 to 59. The data were collected by phone.
7. Bozon and Doré, *Sexualités, relations et prévention chez les homosexuels masculins.*
8. Eric Fassin, "Lieux d'invention. L'amitié, le mariage et la famille," *Vacarme* 29 (2004), http://www.vacarme.eu.org/article457.html.
9. *Le Monde,* "L'annulation du mariage gay célébré à Bègles confirmée en appel," April 19, 2005.
10. SOS Homophobie, http://www.sos-homophobie.org/; Virginie Descoutures, Marie Digoix, Éric Fassin, and Wilfried Rault, eds., *Mariages et homosexualités dans le monde. L'arrangement des normes familiales* (Paris: Autrement, 2008).
11. The figures are extrapolations. The low hypothesis comes from Patrick Festy of INED (ined.fr/) and the high hypothesis from the gay and lesbian parents' association (apgl.asso.fr).
12. Christelle Hamel, *L'amour à l'épreuve de l'exclusion, du sexisme et du racisme* (Paris: La Découverte, 2008).
13. Marianne Blidon, "Prendre la partie pour le tout. Quartier et identité gays, une évidence trompeuse," in *Ces lieux qui nous habitent,* ed. France Guérin-Pace and Elena Filipova (Paris: L'Aube, 2008); Philippe Mangeot, "Communautarisme," in *Dictionnaire de l'homophobie,* ed. Louis-Georges Tin (Paris: PUF, 2003); Michael Sibalis, "Ghetto," in *Dictionnaire de l'homophobie,* ed. Louis-Georges Tin (Paris: PUF, 2003).
14. *InVS Surveillance du sida,* cumulative data to December 12, 2006. Nathalie Bajos and Michel Bozon, eds., *Enquête sur la sexualité en France. Pratiques, genre et santé* (Paris: La Découverte, 2008).
15. Régis Revenin, ed., *Hommes et masculinités, de 1789 à nos jours: contributions à l'histoire du genre et de la sexualité en France* (Paris: Éditions Autrement, 2007); Régis Revenin, *Homosexualité et prostitution masculines à Paris, 1870–1918* (Paris: L'Harmattan, 2005).
16. *Le Monde,* January 24, 2006.
17. Catherine Deschamps, *Le miroir bisexuel: une socio-anthropologie de l'invisible* (Paris: Balland, 2002).
18. Eric Fassin, *L'inversion de la question homosexuelle* (Paris: Amsterdam, 2005).
19. *Prochoix,* February 1998.
20. Rapport de l'association de lutte contre l'homophobie, *SOS Homophobie,* 2006, http://www.sos-homophobie.org.
21. *SOS Homophobie,* http://www.sos-homophobie.org.

GEORGIA

Paata Sabelashvili

OVERVIEW

Georgia is situated at the crossroads of Europe and Asia. It is a country in the southern Caucasus Mountains of the former Soviet Union. Georgia completely borders the Black Sea to the west, and shares borders with Russia to the north, Azerbaijan to the east, and Armenia and Turkey to the south. The territory of the country is 26,911 square miles (69,700 sq. km), slightly smaller than the Republic of Ireland or South Carolina.

Georgia is nestled in between the Greater and Smaller Caucasus mountain chains. Most of its terrain, therefore, is mountainous. Divided into West and East Georgia, its climate varies from Mediterranean, subtropical mild on the Black Sea coast to moderate continental in the east.

Georgia is an ancient country full of history, culture, and tradition. The first states in the land currently known as Georgia date back to 1112 B.C.E., when the kingdoms of Diaukh and Colchis were first mentioned in Assyrian historical inscriptions. The ancient Greeks initially called East Georgians *Iberians.* According to ancient Greek legends, Colchis, now modern day Western Georgia, was the destination

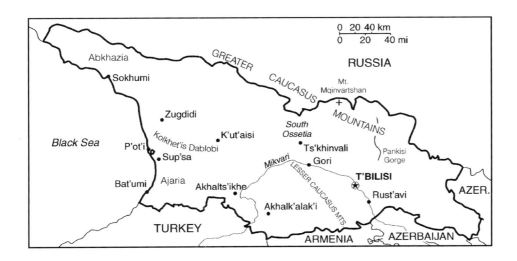

of Argonauts hunting the Golden Fleece. As the legend describes, the Argonauts succeeded in taking the trophy with the assistance of the Colchis princess Medea.

The history of Georgia is a battleground. Situated between the great empires of the Romans, Persians, Arabs, Turks, Mongols, and Russians, Georgia constantly had to struggle for its survival. The 11th through 13th centuries of the Middle Ages are known as the Georgian golden age, when the strongest medieval kingdom occupied the entire Caucasus. During that time, the death penalty was abolished and two universities were established in the territory.[1] After the 13th century, the Georgian state had undergone a consistent decline by being split into feudal princedoms, losing sovereign rule, and finally being annexed by the Russian Empire in 1801.

Georgia enjoyed a brief independence during the First Republic from 1918 to 1921, until it was occupied by the Russian Bolshevik Red Army and eventually joined the Soviet Union. The period of independence, though short, brought many developments. For example, Georgia was the first socialist republic with a leftist government that recognized the voting rights of women. In contrast, the Soviet era resulted in the nationalization of property, mass purges, and significant loss of citizens of reproductive age during World War II. During that time, Georgia lost the largest number of people per capita, and more than the United States did in absolute numbers. Georgia declared independence from the Soviet Union in 1991. Its new period of independence was followed by two territorial conflicts in the breakaway regions of Abkhazia and South Ossetia, both heavily backed by Russia. Loss of territories, civil unrest, and economic collapse provided unfavorable grounds for the transformation of post-Soviet Georgian society into a modern, open society.

After the Revolution of Roses in 2003, Georgia started a rapid reformation in virtually all spheres of public life. The Western-style Georgian government had successfully restructured the police and the military, reformed the education system, targeted rampant corruption, and introduced a liberal business policy. Georgia declared that it aspires to democratic values and the pursuit of integration into Euro-Atlantic systems such as NATO and the European Union (EU).[2] Despite significant progress, the Georgian government is often criticized for its nonindependent judiciary and infringement of civil, political, and property rights.[3]

Georgia mainly produces agricultural products. The biggest share of its gross domestic product (GDP) (purchasing power parity [PPP] US$18.16 billion in 2006)[4] comes from services; its main exports are wine, nuts, and mineral water.

As Georgia aspires to NATO membership, it is undergoing intensive reformation of its armed forces. To meet this end, Georgia allocates the biggest part of its state budget to military modernization. Georgia expected invitation to the membership action plan but the war with Russia in August 2008 seriously hindered this process,

As of a 2007 estimate, the total population of Georgia is 4,646,003, and 83.8 percent of the population is Georgian. The remainder of the population is composed of Azeris (6.5%), Armenian (5.7%), Russian (1.5%), and other ethnic groups (2.5%). Most of the population identifies as Georgian Orthodox Christian (83.9%), while nearly 10 percent identify as Muslim. Armenian-Apostolics (3.9%), Catholics (0.8%), and other religious groups practice in Georgia as well.

The Georgian Orthodox Church enjoys a favored status as a result of constitutional agreement between church and state that recognizes the special role of the Orthodox Church in the history of Georgia.[5] Until recently, the church had not attempted to interfere in the public domain to a significant extent. Recent statements of church spokespersons, however, are more direct and assertive. Church statements are directed toward ongoing reforms in education, the change of the

Georgian state model to a constitutional monarchy with a patriarch appointed as a regent until the monarch is selected, and homosexuality.

OVERVIEW OF LGBT ISSUES

In 1933, homosexuality was criminalized by Josef Stalin—a Soviet dictator of Georgian nationality. It was decriminalized in 2000, thanks to the commitment of Georgia to achieve Council of Europe membership.

Although information on the scale and occurrences of homosexual purges in Georgia is not accessible, one could assume that many gay men were sent to concentration camps in Siberia. The antigay article that prohibited sexual intercourse between adult male persons[6] was often used in suppressing the leaders of dissident movements, even if they were not necessarily associated with homosexuality. In the arts as well, article 141 was often used for blackmailing and censorship. The KGB would use personal data that also would include a record of sexual behavior to recruit spies. The most vivid example of Soviet persecution was the imprisonment of Sergei Parajanov, a prominent Georgian-Armenian movie director, who was sent to prison twice for sodomy. His homosexuality was never a secret to Soviet authorities, though they used the sodomy article when the director's works became alarmingly dissident to Soviet movie censors. Western counterparts of Parajanov pleaded with Soviet authorities to release their colleague and friend from prison. Only when Parajanov was ill with cancer and could no longer continue with his career did Soviet authorities release him.

After the dissolution of the Soviet Union, the sodomy article was not used in independent Georgia to arrest anyone after 1993, but it was still actively used for blackmail and recruitment of agents.

Social attitudes public opinion surveys conducted since 1998 addressed homosexuality in their questionnaires.[7] According to these surveys, homosexuals stand out as the most disliked group in Georgian society. The majority of respondents preferred to have an alcoholic colleague rather than a homosexual person at work.

Homosexuality in Georgia has become a convenient instrument for political struggle. With the decriminalization of male homosexuality, the sexual orientations of politicians moved from gossip to open accusations in the parliament. Many nationalistic political groups would use homosexuality against liberals by claiming that civil equality for LGBT people poses threats to Georgian-ness. Conspiracy theories flooded the pages of the Georgian press, warning the public about the pederasts' mafia.[8]

The Georgian media still remains homophobic. Representation of homosexuals in newspapers would fall into the same sections as crimes and anomalies. Since 2006, there have been attempts to disseminate accurate information on LGBT issues, primarily through *Me Magazine,* published by the only LGBT group in Georgia, which is called the Inclusive Foundation. Few other publications in Georgia devote LGBT-friendly articles to the subjects of homosexuality and homophobia. Those that do are mostly local English language newspapers and expensive glossy magazines that declaredly adhere to basic principles of free and politically correct journalism.[9]

The Georgian media often censors the topic of homosexuality. This was evidenced in 2001, when a prominent journalist was murdered in his own apartment by a person he met in a cruising place. Colleagues of the murdered journalist protested the investigation to confirm homosexual intercourse between the victim and the murderer.

Another act of censorship took place in 2005, when the late prime minister Zurab Zhvania was found poisoned by carbon monoxide along with a young man in an apartment. The Russian media spoke openly of the homosexual relationship between the prime minister and the young man, but the Georgian media never mentioned this version publicly.

Homosexuality in public discourse is very new, and is mostly limited to acts of hate speech. When human rights public officials are asked their opinion, in the best-case scenario, they remain silent.

Another form of censorship was evidenced by another TV event, yet a public one this time. Georgian Public Broadcaster, which is maintained through national tax collection, refused to show a documentary on LGBT rights violations in Europe. A public broadcaster is bound to represent any social group's interest, and homosexuals are openly listed among social groups that broadcasters are obliged to prepare or acquire production about. Inclusive Foundation ensured a free license for screening, and translated and adapted the documentary for the public. Nevertheless, Public Broadcaster returned the video, stating that they were unable to find the airtime. Public Broadcaster had not specified available time to screen the documentary.

The LGBT community never attempted to organize with visible success until 2006, when the first Georgian LGBT nongovernmental organization (NGO), Inclusive Foundation, was formed.

EDUCATION

The main government document to deal with Georgian education policies is the Georgian National Agenda for General Education, signed in 2004 by the late prime minister Zurab Zhvania. The document states that: "the youth should be able to...be a law abiding, *tolerant* citizen"[10] and that "the state will not allow for discrimination of the students based on social, racial, ethnic, religious or political affiliation, physical abilities or other signs."[11]

This document omits sexual orientation, which hampers introducing civil education based on inclusiveness of all social groups. LGBT youth are most vulnerable to discrimination on a daily basis, and the absence of such a provision makes it impossible for human rights groups to lobby for inclusive school policies.

There have not been any attempts to form gay-straight alliances or LGBT support groups in schools at any educational level. It is hard to predict the consequences of this; however, relevant examples suggest that it will not be easy to introduce LGBT-friendly subjects to public schools. There is an ongoing public debate over whether Georgia needs to offer sex education to pupils in schools. The Georgian Orthodox Church is outspokenly against the introduction of sexual education. It insists on bringing Christian subjects to public schools. The Ministry of Education, in turn, opposes the domination of any single religion in schools that receive funding from all citizens of Georgia.

EMPLOYMENT AND ECONOMICS

Georgia mainly produces agricultural products. The biggest share of its GDP[12] comes from services and its most exported goods are wine, nuts, and mineral water.

Georgia has achieved relative economic progress in the last two years since the change of government after the revolution of roses. Collection of tax revenues had improved significantly, and more foreign direct investment (FDI) was attracted. This in its turn derived from the liberal business policy of the government. Georgia has been a fast economic reformer, and consequently moved up to the 18th rank by free business environment criteria.

The new Georgian labor code is the only legal document that explicitly mentions sexual orientation in its antidiscrimination clause. It is hard to determine the rules for applying this provision. The law does not provide for any specific procedures, and does not mention whether the law protects potential employees, new employees, or current employees. In addition, it does not address whether LGBT people would be protected from discrimination during the job interview process or consideration for a raise or promotion.[13]

Interviews and documented cases provide evidence that homosexuality is not only suppressed in society, but in the workplace as well. Direct discrimination cases are rare. Most of the cases refer to concealed discrimination or the creation of invisible obstacles that make people leave their jobs. The methods for manifesting this attitude vary from gossip and ridicule to preventing promotions.[14]

The most serious limitation on freedom of speech—as well as discrimination in the workplace—was imposed when, in October 2007, a gay person publicly outed himself on a live broadcast of one of the private TV reality shows. As the incident was documented, the competitor on the reality show *Bar-4* was selected with the expectation that he would out himself. After he came out on television, the channel management expelled the participant the next morning. Press reports suggest that Patriarch Ilia II called the president of Georgia and protested the appearance of a gay man on a popular TV show. The president, in turn, called the channel management and demanded that the gay participant be expelled from the show.[15] The contestant had a contract with the television company, and had not violated any of the conditions of the contract when he was expelled. By article 2.3 of the antidiscrimination article of the labor code, is a clear case of discrimination based on sexual orientation.

When it comes to public attitudes, it is also apparent that LGBT are the least desired people in the workplace.[16] Qualitative analysis of public perceptions illustrates the attitude in public. The majority of heterosexual people participating in the discussions think that gays belong in the entertainment industry and fashion design. They would not like to see gays in the military or serving in schools, and believe that they could betray the nation and molest children. The Georgian public does not want gays in politics for fear of sexual conspiracies (the idea that if gays are at power they will bring other gays to key position because they are attracted to each other—like sexual nepotism).[17]

SOCIAL/GOVERNMENT PROGRAMS

Since the Revolution of Roses (November 2003), new leadership has rapidly started introducing a reformation policy in virtually every sector. While elaborating policy response to foster the integration of minority groups, the current policy discourse bypasses LGBT people; none of the policy documents mention them. Therefore, the implementation of these policies does not offer anything to the LGBT community in Georgia.

SEXUALITY/SEXUAL PRACTICES

Georgian society is a conservative culture when discussing sexuality as a topic of public discourse. There is no formal sex education in Georgia's schools. When it comes to LGBT issues, the data get even more scarce. In general terms, gender roles determine sexual expression to a great extent. Female sexuality is perceived as subject to male cultural and societal dominance, and women are expected to be virgins at marriage; men are allowed to have pre- and extramarital sexual relationships. No deviation from this model is accepted.[18]

Surveys suggest that most LGBT people are closeted and pursue hidden sexual relationships. Men often meet each other in parks and bathhouses, while women practice very discreet relationships with one person often throughout life, and often both are married. Bisexuality as an orientation is often hard to separate from the widespread bisexual behavior among men. Transgendered persons, on the other hand, rarely have sex in a manner that is conducive to expressing their true gender identity.[19]

FAMILY

Age is one aspect that makes a significant difference in the self-perception as well as visibility of lesbians. Those who are above 40 years old are closeted and live double lives between their heterosexual marriages and a life partner who is often in a similar family situation. Younger women between 30 and 40 years old are independent and more socially active. They are perceived as single women who choose not to marry. The younger the woman, the more personal control she has over her family and the more opportunity to choose a life she finds satisfying.[20]

Age is also an important factor in the self-perception of gay men. Georgian coming out surveys show that older men are rarely out to their families and colleagues. In the majority of cases, they will only come out to very close friends. Gay men between 25 and 40 years old are economically independent and can pursue the life and career that they choose. At the same time, they are not publicly out, as they could lose their career and income. The rate of coming out among gay men aged 25 years and younger is significantly higher, as are their self-esteem and self-awareness.[21]

Both male and female bisexuals in Georgia face dual discrimination. They are targets of prejudice within both the heterosexual and homosexual communities. The lesbian community in particular does not welcome the bisexual behavior of female friends or lovers. Among men, it is hard to determine whether bisexuality is a mere and occasional sexual behavior or an orientation. Many gay men first come out as bisexuals due to the stigma of their homosexual orientation.[22]

COMMUNITY

Until recently, there were very few attempts by the LGBT community to form activist groups, and all initiatives were a result of individual commitment. A few organizations from the local NGO sector have worked on LGBT issues. Tanadgoma NGO works in the HIV/AIDS prevention sector and covers MSM (men who have sex with men). The Georgian Young Lawyers Association (GYLA) is the biggest national advocacy NGO. GYLA has received complaints from homosexual men who were seeking redress. The Women Initiatives' Supporting Group (WISG) has implemented a couple of studies and prepared LGBT-related material in Georgian to post on their Web site. A group of activists started a gay Web site, www.Gay.ge.

The site was targeted by homophobic hackers who damaged the system several times. The Web site is now placed on a secure server and is expanding in terms of both the information offered to the LGBT community and the number of users.

In August 2006, the Ministry of Justice of Georgia officially registered the Inclusive Foundation as the first LGBT rights organization. It acts as an umbrella organization to mainstream LGBT issues in academic research, empower the community, and lobby for the interests of LGBTs.

An LGBT community in a small post-Soviet country is not like the LGBT communities of the West. Most people are not out to their families, even if they are relatively visible and out to friends. Members of the Georgian LGBT community considered to be out make up a small number, only a few hundred in a capital city with a population of over one million. This is explained by a high level of stigmatization of nonheterosexual orientations, low awareness among the population and LGBT community members themselves, a post-Communist legacy, hard socio-economic conditions that foster xenophobia, the Orthodox Christian religion, and the culture and traditions of a patriarchal society.

LGBT people in Georgia do not have exclusively LGBT places to meet. Gay men still seek sexual encounters in old Soviet-style cruising areas and public bathhouses. Younger people, as well as those who can acquire consistent access to the Internet, communicate through international and local Web sites and discussion forums. Even through this confidential medium, LGBT Georgians will hide their real identity or refrain from posting pictures of themselves.

Compared to gay men, lesbians rarely reach out to each other. They undergo double discrimination due to belonging to the female gender in a masculine society and being lesbians. This is the least social group within the LGBT community.

Problems that lesbians face in Georgia are also invisible. Most occur in their relations with family and friends, and in the workplace. Lesbian relationships were never criminalized in the former Soviet Union, yet there were practices of medicalization and institutionalization.[23]

Gay men have always been visible in Georgia, even when male homosexual contacts were punishable under the criminal code. Gay men are also socially active and outgoing. Their social networks often go beyond their areas of residence. This group is noticeable in its high rate of internal and external migration. The visibility of gay men often brings problems in the street and other public spaces. This explains the correlation between their high rate of stigmatization and level of social activity.

The gay community in Georgia is highly segmented based on social class. Those who cruise are rarely welcome in the higher-income community that can afford to go out expensive places, where there are fewer problems than in the street.

Transgender people are not often seen, even among the LGBT community. In Soviet times, transgender people were diagnosed in mental institutions. Nowadays, there is no consistent state policy on transgender issues. People can change their names on forms of identification that do not include gender. If they want to obtain a new passport, however, they will find it almost impossible to do so legally, as the law does not regulate change of the gender marker in passports.

One precedent appeared in 2006–2007, when a postoperational female-to-male (FTM) transgendered person appealed to the court and requested new ID. The court decided in favor of the plaintiff, and ordered the change of all ID according to the new sex of the person. The court made this decision based on the fact that the person had undergone sex reassignment surgery, not simply because he decided that he had a new gender identity.[24]

The number of visible transgender people is very small. As of 2007, the only medical clinic is run by Professor Iva Kuzanov, where transgendered persons seek sex-reassignment surgeries. There have been 18 consultations and only five genital surgeries carried out, all of them MTF.[25]

The process to apply for sex-reassignment surgery is systemized. Transgender people come to the clinic, where a doctor refers them to the State Commission on Bioethics. The commission appoints two independent observation committees, both of which include a psychologist, sexologist, and one or more psychiatrists. After one year of observation, the committees send their evaluations to the commission, which will ultimately decide whether the clinic can carry out the operation.

HEALTH

The first HIV/AIDS case in Georgia was registered in 1989. As of May 2009, there are over 2,005 registered HIV-positive persons in Georgia, of which 2.7 percent are MSM. Gender-specific data regarding the prevalence of the infection among WSW (women who have sex with women) is not recorded. Out of the total number of registered HIV-positive persons, 1,504 have developed AIDS and 435 have died. The real number of infected persons is estimated to be much higher than the number reflected in official statistics. There is also an assumption that the number of cases attributed to MSM sexual contact is probably higher than 2.7 percent.[26] This assumption is based on the fact that homosexuality and sexual contact with persons of the same sex are deeply stigmatized, and registered HIV-positive persons might not disclose the real method of transmission.

Under the support provided by the Global Fund to Fight AIDS, Tuberculosis, and Malaria, HIV testing is free of charge for the groups most at risk. It is also the Global Fund that provides coverage for antiretroviral treatment for people living with AIDS.

Georgia has adopted AIDS legislation. It also had set up necessary institutions to adopt and implement HIV/AIDS prevention intervention. The country coordination mechanism (CCM) is a multistakeholder system that involves state, nongovernmental, and international agencies working in the HIV/AIDS prevention field. CCM has adopted a special action plan that specifies the roles of different stakeholders, and is endorsed by all of them. Funding of the interventions is almost entirely driven by the Global Fund to fight AIDS, Tuberculosis and Malaria.

HIV/AIDS is another reason for being stigmatized in Georgian society. The Georgian law on HIV infection and AIDS prevention obliges infected people to disclose their HIV/AIDS status when accessing medical services. Many persons living with HIV/AIDS often hide this fact from medical institutions and personnel, as these institutions often refuse to treat infected patients.[27]

Surveys conducted among specific segments of the LGBT community reveal that in lesbian and bisexual women, awareness of the risk of HIV/AIDS transmission is mostly low.[28] Gay and bisexual men are more conscious of carrying out safe sexual practices, but overall stigmatization of the entire LGBT community results in low self-esteem, less social interaction, and risky sexual behavior.

There are no discriminatory clauses regarding the access to health care facilities by LGBT persons, aside from the decree against homosexual blood donation. One form of unconscious discrimination that was revealed among lesbians and bisexual women is connected to visiting the gynecologist for regular checkups. Cultural perceptions of female sexuality explain this problem. It is very common to be asked questions such as "Are you married?" by the gynecologist during an exam. Single women who are sexually active remain stigmatized among the older generation, and in addition to the stigma against lesbianism and bisexuality in women, implications of visiting the health professional in these particular circumstances do not encourage lesbians or bisexual women to have regular gynecological exams, making them more vulnerable to women's health problems.

POLITICS AND LAW

Georgian legislation has improved significantly since it joined the Council of Europe in 1999. In 2000, Georgia adopted a new criminal code that did not contain an article incriminating male homosexuality. Georgia is also a signatory of the European Convention of Human Rights (ECHR). Article 14 of the convention provides for nondiscrimination. It lists a wide range of grounds for nondiscrimination, yet omits sexual orientation. This gap was bridged with protocol 12 to article 14, which does specify that, based on the case law of the European Court of Human Rights (ECtHR), sexual orientation is considered an explicit ground for nondiscrimination. Georgia signed the protocol and ratified it in 2005. This is an important international legal instrument for an LGBT Georgian to seek redress if he or she is discriminated against on the grounds of sexual orientation.

The municipal legal system of Georgia avoids mentioning sexual orientation. There is only one exception where the law covers the topic of sexual orientation, in the new labor code of Georgia adopted in 2006. Article 2.3 lists sexual orientation as one of the grounds for nondiscrimination in employment relations. The limitation of this instrument is that there is no further specification of rules of application of this article.[29]

There is the discriminatory clause[30] that prohibits LGBT people from donating blood. The decree of the minister for health, labor, and social affairs explained that this refusal is based on homosexuals belonging to the high risk group for HIV/AIDS. This article is a result of the inability to distinguish between sexual identity and risky sexual behavior.

In other instances, Georgian legislation does not include openly discriminating clauses. The absence of antidiscrimination legislation, definitions of hate speech and hate crimes, and exact punishment for those acts, leaves many gaps that allow for discriminatory practices.

Most LGBT community members are closeted and invisible. Therefore, it is a logical expectation that it will take quite awhile before the Georgian LGBT community will march the streets with demands for equality. The Georgian newspaper *Alia* published an article in July 2007 that informed the public about an upcoming gay pride event in the center of Tbilisi. The event was misconnected with the Council of Europe campaign for civil equality, which was speculated to have concealed the gay pride plan. The reactions from the public, politicians, and the church showed that the freedom of assembly of LGBT people is under a serious threat.

In article 36, paragraph 1 of the Georgian constitution, marriage is defined as "based on equality and consent of spouses." This article is not gender-specific, and therefore does not impose a limitation on same-sex marriage. However, article 1106 of the civil code of Georgia specifies that marriage is the consensual union of a man and a woman. In article 1120, the law states the grounds that prevent marriage. It does not include homosexuality or lesbianism as a legitimate obstacle for marriage. Finally, article 1140 lists the grounds for declaring a marriage as void, and that article does not include marriage to a person belonging to the same sex.

Adoption is covered more clearly in the same civil code. The law asserts the right of any single person to adopt a child when it is in the child's best interest. Two persons are entitled to adopt a child only if they are married. Several clauses that challenge the right of the person to adopt a child use controversial terms such as morality.[31] Therefore, it is unclear what the court decision would be if someone challenged the right of a single LGBT person to adopt a child.

RELIGION AND SPIRITUALITY

Religion has always played a central role in the history of Georgia. After the breakup of the Soviet Union, a considerable part of society went back to church and eventually became more religious. The current tendency of the Georgian Orthodox Church when it is involved in public life has a political nature. The church is also trying to modernize its infrastructure through the creation of religious schools and NGOs.

The head of the Orthodox Church issued a statement in July 2007 by which it condemned an alleged gay pride event in Tbilisi. The Council of Europe's youth campaign, called All Different, All Equal, was in no way connected to the plans to hold a gay pride march; but this connection was made, allowing Patriarch Ilia II to condemn the event with a special statement. The statement condemned the plan to hold the march, and warned organizers and participants that if they did not cancel the march, the results would be fatal.[32] Ever since, the head of the church started addressing issues of sexual orientation and gender identity in every Christmas and Easter epistles, and not in a positive context.

Dogmas of the Georgian Orthodox Church are not favorable to LGBT Christian groups. The church considers homosexuality a sin and calls its followers to confess and return to the true path of religious life in church.

VIOLENCE

Given the degree of homophobia in Georgian society, violence against LGBT persons is often seen as morally justified. The public perceives homosexuality as a problem, but homophobia is not usually questioned.

Violence is a common problem faced by LGBT persons in public. Forms of violence vary from name-calling to physical assault and rape, especially in Georgian prisons. According to a survey conducted among the LGBT community, only two respondents complained to the relevant institutions about violent acts inflicted upon them, and neither of these acts was dealt with in a way that satisfied the victim.[33] This situation once again raises the issue of the absence of hate crime legislation, which makes it extremely difficult to guarantee adequate redress in relation to the rights of LGBT persons.

The number of documented cases of homophobic hate crimes show that it is not always possible to persuade a victim to seek redress of his or her rights due to the stigma, and that available mechanisms do not allow for much advocacy. In 2005, a gay man came out publicly on television. Soon after this he was severely beaten up in the street, while attackers called him names and stressed the connection between the beating and his appearance on television. Because of the lack of hate crime legislation, the investigation agency recorded this as a regular street attack.[34]

OUTLOOK FOR THE 21ST CENTURY

Over the last couple of years, the LGBT community and its concerns has gained significant visibility. Homosexuality is no longer a taboo issue in public discourse, although it is still a very sensitive topic. LGBT rights violations are being studied, documented, and addressed. Alternative information sources such as magazines and Web sites are being developed to disseminate adequate information on LGBT issues. A number of governmental agencies and civil society have started expressing readiness to incorporate LGBT rights in their mandates.

With the further transformation of Georgian society, new threats are emerging. With the advancement of LGBT issues in public discourse, new controversy is being voiced through antigay media sources. Because homosexuality is perceived as a threat to Georgian society, rightist political powers use the issue to magnify the threat and justify their causes, which attracts more supporters. Politicization of the issue involves new risks and targets, meaning that the LGBT community must tackle new problems.

On the other hand, the LGBT community in Georgia is growing, and this irreversible phenomenon is bringing new opportunities to advance LGBT rights in a newly emerging democracy.

RESOURCE GUIDE

Suggested Reading

Ekaterine Aghdgomelashvili, "Representation of Homosexuality/Homosexuals in Georgian Media" (Tbilisi, Georgia: Inclusive Foundation, 2006), http://www.inclusive-foundation.org/home/?page=publications&lang=en.

Ana Dolidze, "Survey of Georgian Legislation Related to LGBT Rights," http://www.inclusive-foundation.org/home/?page=publications&lang=en.

Inclusive Foundation, "Survey on Discrimination Cases of LGBT Group Representatives," http://www.inclusive-foundation.org/home/?page=publications&lang=en.

Inclusive Foundation, GYLA, and ILGA Europe, "Shadow Report on the Implementation of the European Social Charter by Georgia: Employment Issues in Relation to Sexual Orientation," http://www.inclusive-foundation.org/home/?page=publications&lang=en.

Me Magazine (nos. 1–10). Inclusive Foundation, 2006–2009, http://www.inclusive-foundation.org/home/?page=publications&lang=en.

Sheila Quinn, *Report of ILGA-Europe/COC Mission to Georgia* (Brussels: ILGA Europe, 2007).

Organizations/Web Sites

Gay.ge, http://www.gay.ge/.
    The national gateway for the LGBT community in Georgia. This bilingual (Georgian-English) Web resource provides updated news and articles on art, sports, and health issues. The Web site has a discussion board (forum) and chat. It also offers a dating

service. Integrated interface is available for Inclusive Foundation's online consultations with a psychologist and sexologist.

Inclusive Foundation, http://www.inclusive-foundation.org/.

The only national LGBT organization. Fosters the integration of the LGBT community into local society and protect their rights. The bilingual Web site (Georgian and
English) provides information about the organization, its mission and activities. Provides news about the LGBT movement in Georgia and globally, online consultation
services for community members, articles on LGBT topics, glossary, publications
prepared by the foundation, a list of literature available in Foundation's library, and
relevant links.

Lesbi.ge, http://www.lesbi.ge.

Bilingual (Georgian-English) Web site for lesbian and bisexual women in Georgia.
Similarly to gay.ge, this Web site has news, discussions, chat, and dating services. It
offers number of articles on sexual and reproductive health and rights. It also gives
detailed information about lesbian and bisexual women active in arts, literature, and
other cultural fields throughout world history.

NOTES

1. G. Anchabadze, "History of Georgia," http://www.parliament.ge/pages/archive_
en/history/.

2. Parliamentary Assembly of Council of Europe, "Report on Honouring of Obligations and Commitments by Georgia," http://assembly.coe.int/main.asp?Link=/docu
ments/adoptedtext/ta08/eres1603.htm.

3. Parliamentary Assembly of Council of Europe, "Report on Honouring of obligations and commitments by Georgia."

4. CIA, "Georgia," *World Factbook,* https://www.cia.gov/library/publications/the-
world-factbook/geos/gg.html.

5. "Constitutional Agreement between the State of Georgia and the Apostolic
Autocephalous Orthodox Church of Georgia" [in Georgian], http://www.patriarchate.
ge/?action=text/samartali05.

6. Article 141, Penal Code of Georgian Soviet Socialist Republic (1978).

7. Sheila Quinn, *Report of ILGA-Europe/COC Mission to Georgia* (Brussels: ILGA
Europe, 2007).

8. Ekaterine Aghdgomelashvili, *Representation of Homosexuality/Homosexuals in
Georgian Media* (Tbilisi, Georgia: Inclusive Foundation, 2006), http://www.inclusive-
foundation.org/home/?page=publications&lang=en.

9. Ibid.

10. Georgian National Agenda for General Education, Preamble, article H.

11. Georgian National Agenda for General Education, article 4.

12. CIA, "Georgia."

13. Inclusive Foundation, GYLA, and ILGA Europe, "Shadow Report on the Implementation of the European Social Charter by Georgia: Employment Issues in Relation to Sexual Orientation," http://www.inclusive-foundation.org/home/?page=publications&lang=en.

14. Quinn, *Report of ILGA-Europe/COC Mission to Georgia.*

15. Salome Asatiani, "Georgian TV Show Reveals Country's Changing Mores,"
http://www.rferl.org/featuresarticle/2007/10/8D13EFE1–2B1D-4A6A-920D-
476761394AB8.html.

16. Quinn, *Report of ILGA-Europe/COC Mission to Georgia.*

17. Ibid.

18. UNESCO, Cultural and Development Division of Cultural Policies and Intercultural Dialogue, *HIV and AIDS in Georgia: A Socio-Cultural Approach* (Tbilisi, Georgia:
UNESCO, 2005).

19. Inclusive Foundation and Tanadgoma, *Survey of Sexual Behaviour of Gay and Bisexual Men, Lesbian and Bisexual Women and Interview Study of Sexual Behaviour of Transgender Persons in Georgia,* internal report (Tbilisi, Georgia: Inclusive Foundation and Tanadgoma, 2007).

20. Ekaterine Aghdgomelashvili, *Internal Reports on Coming Out Survey among Inclusive Foundation Visitors, and Internal Analysis of Lesbian and Bisexual Women Oral Histories* (Tbilisi, Georgia: Inclusive Foundation, 2007).

21. Ibid.

22. Ibid.

23. Ibid.

24. Sopio Benashvili (Ombudsman's Office of Georgia), interview by Paata Sabelashvili, Tbilisi, Georgia, 2007.

25. Professor Iva Kuzanov, interview by Paata Sabelashvili, Tbilisi, Georgia, 2007.

26. Data updated on May 15, 2009, by the Infectious Deceases, AIDS and Clinical Immunology Research Centre (AIDS Centre), http://aidscenter.ge/epidsituation_eng.html.

27. UNAIDS (Joint United Nations Programme on HIV/AIDS) and UNICEF (United Nations Children's Fund), Georgian AIDS and Clinical Immunology Research Center, *Situation Analysis on HIV/AIDS in Georgia* (Tbilisi, Georgia: UNAIDS and UNICEF, 2001).

28. Inclusive Foundation and Association Tanadgoma, *Survey of Sexual Behaviour of LGBT Community in Georgia,* internal report (Tbilisi, Georgia: Inclusive Foundation and Tanadgoma, 2007).

29. Inclusive Foundation, GYLA, and ILGA Europe, "Shadow Report on the Implementation of the European Social Charter by Georgia."

30. Ministry of Health, Labor and Social Affairs of Georgia, ministerial decree 241/N (2001).

31. Ana Dolidze, "Survey of Georgian Legislation Related to LGBT Rights," http://www.inclusive-foundation.org/home/?page=publications&lang=en.

32. Press Centre of the Orthodox Church of Georgia, statement of patriarch of Georgian Orthodox Church on planned gay pride rally, news release, Tbilisi, Georgia, July 20, 2008.

33. Inclusive Foundation, documentation on cases of discrimination against LGBT persons. Confidential data.

34. Ibid.

GERMANY

Frédéric Jörgens

OVERVIEW

Germany is the most populous country of the European Union, with just over 82.4 million inhabitants as of July 2007. In the north it borders Denmark, in the west the Netherlands, Belgium, Luxemburg, and France. In the south its neighbors are Switzerland and Austria, in the east Poland and the Czech Republic. All of these except Switzerland have joined the European Union (EU). Germany's capital is Berlin, which with 3.6 million inhabitants is also the largest city, followed by Hamburg with 1.7 million, Munich with 1.3 million, and Cologne with just under 1 million inhabitants.

Germany was divided after the World War II when the German army and the Nazi regime were defeated in 1945. The crimes of Nazism and the relationship with the Allied powers (the United States, the Soviet Union, Britain, and France) shaped Germany's geopolitics, society, and culture in the postwar period. Placed in the center of the cold war between the West and the communist East at the end of the 1940s, Germany was split into the German Federal Republic (GFR) in the west and south and the German Democratic Republic (GDR) in the east. Western Germany, with about 60 million inhabitants and its capital Bonn, was under the influence of the Western Allied powers, a liberal democracy, and started the process of European integration with France, Italy, and the Benelux countries (Belgium, the Netherlands, and Luxemburg). Eastern Germany, with about

16 million inhabitants and its capital East Berlin, was under Soviet influence, with a largely nondemocratic communist regime, and was responsible for the building of the Berlin wall in 1962, isolating the Western enclave of West Berlin within the surrounding Communist GDR. In 1989, an uprising in East Germany led to the fall of the wall in Berlin, free elections in the GDR, and less than one year later, in 1990, to the reunification of both German countries. Germany hosts one of the strongest economies in the world, despite strong economic disparities between an increasingly rich south and an economically weaker east and 8–10 percent unemployment nationwide.

Looking further back, Germany was constituted by small independent states for a long period of time, until it was unified in 1870. At the end of World War I, it became a democracy known as the Weimar Republic, and enjoyed an increasing degree of societal freedom that created a boom in literature, theatre, cinema, and art. However, the Weimar Republic lasted only for a short while. In 1933, an economic and political crisis ended in the election of Adolph Hitler. He immediately disembodied the democratic institutions and installed a dictatorial regime that entered history as the worst totalitarian state that ever existed, responsible for the horrors of World War II and the Holocaust. The regime lasted for 12 years, ending with a crushing military defeat in 1945 and leaving the country in ruins.

OVERVIEW OF LGBT ISSUES

The societal acceptance of homosexuality in Germany was fundamentally influenced by the dramatic historical shifts during the 20th century. In 1903, the liberal physician and researcher Magnus Hirschfeld led scientific research on masculine homosexuality. He created a foundation, the Magnus-Hirschfeld-Stiftung, that called for a tolerant societal attitude toward homosexuality, and some argue that this constituted the world's first modern gay movement, For others Hirschfeld's belief in racist eugenics cast an important shadow over his reformist stance concerning homosexuality.

German society, conservative and largely provincial until this time, became a liberal democracy with the onset of the Weimar Republic (1918–33). This republic became world-famous for its tolerance, which left room for a colorful homosexual subculture during the Golden Twenties, which would fall into strict prohibition, cultural censorship, and persecution with the homophobic medical trials in the Nazi period. In the Anglo-Saxon world, the German Golden Twenties became a famous literary reference, especially in British novelist Christopher Isherwood's *Goodbye to Berlin,* which describes the sharp fall of German society from liberal to authoritarian and oppressive in the 1930s.[1]

Homosexuality in West Germany, 1945–1989

After 1945, different societal developments occurred in West and East Germany. In West Germany, with a largely conservative political environment dominated by Konrad Adenauer's Christian Democratic Union (CDU), homosexuality was confined to the margins of society until the late 1960s. Legally, in West Germany, a highly repressive and discriminatory version of the laws homosexual acts was introduced in the period of national socialism, condemning sexual acts between men with a prison sentence of up to 5 and, in special cases, up to 10 years. These laws were left untouched until 1969. Indeed, between 1949 and the legal reform in 1969, about 50,000 men were condemned on the basis of section 175 in the Federal Republic of Germany. In 1957, the West German constitutional court upheld the 1935 version of the law.[2] Homosexual acts thus remained illegal and could lead to formal state prosecution. It should be added that many courts increasingly refrained from implementing anything but symbolic fines on grounds of consenting homosexual acts. After the 1969 reform, scrapping the weaker form of section 175 was an important goal for the West German gay movement. This remaining form of the law stipulated a higher age of consent for homosexual acts than for heterosexual ones, and the aim to eradicate it was achieved only after reunification, in 1994.[3]

Culturally, homosexuality rose from the margins to form an increasingly strong subculture. Cologne, Hamburg, and West Berlin became the centers of West German gay culture. During the 1970s, largely influenced by American hippie culture and politicized after the 1968 student revolts, homosexuality and bisexuality were tolerated and accepted in left-wing subgroups. David Bowie became a queer, bisexual pop icon, residing in West Berlin during the late 1970s; the queer filmmaker and playwright Rainer Fassbinder created a new German cultural avant-garde; and gay film-maker Rosa von Praunheim became the incarnation of the modern German gay liberation movement with his documentary film bearing the bulky title *It is Not the Homosexual Who is Perverted, but the Situation in Which He Lives.*[4]

Subsequently, it was to a large degree the nascent Green movement that channeled claims for political reform and social recognition into an increasingly accepted political position. While West Berlin was the leading location of a 1970s bisexualized hippie culture, Cologne as the West German media capital became the prominent gay capital of the 1980s. Here, personalities such as the cartoon artist Ralf König[5] and the lesbian TV-presenter Hella von Sinnen gained national prominence well into mainstream culture and provided nationwide references for what lesbian and gay life was about. The AIDS crisis of the 1980s, despite individual calls for repressive antigay politics, led to political and societal solidarity with the gay community and prepared the grounds for a new understanding of inclusion. Legally, however, nothing changed as long as the socially conservative Christian Democracy of Helmut Kohl was in power (from 1982 to 1998).

Homosexuality in East Germany

The Socialist/Communist German Democratic Republic lasted from 1949, when it was proclaimed, to 1990, when free elections led to unification with the western part of the country. Concerning human rights and civil liberties, East Germany was clearly more repressive of its citizens than West Germany. This government spied on its citizens by means of an omnipresent information service (the Ministry for State Security, commonly known as the Stasi), did not allow for free elections, and threatened the lives of those who wanted to leave the country. The picture is less black and white, however, concerning the acceptance of homosexuality.

In the legal context, during the postwar period the German Democratic Republic (GDR) had, at least nominally, been more progressive in decriminalizing homosexuality. The discriminatory sections 175 and 175a on homosexual acts were abolished through reforms in 1950, 1957, 1968, and 1988. The decision in 1950 to return to the Weimar Republic version of section 175 implied a lower maximum penalty compared to West Germany (6 months in East Germany, 5 years in West Germany). In 1957, the possibility of nonprosecution was introduced if the homosexual act did not represent "a danger to the socialist society," which in practical terms ended the prosecution of homosexual acts between consenting adults. In 1968, the new penal code of the GDR mentions only a higher age of consent for both male and female homosexual acts, namely 18 years. After a judgment of the East German high court in 1987, the GDR parliament finally abolished this law.[6]

Culturally, however, the East German lesbian and gay scene was far less vibrant, to say the least. There was nothing there comparable to the bars, cafes, clubs, and discotheques that became fundamental experiences in lesbian and gay lives in Hamburg, Cologne, or West Berlin. According to commentators, the absence of a commercial homosexual subculture characterized the main difference between East and West Germany.[7]

There were only very few homosexual bars in East Germany, such as the Schoppenstube in Prenzlauer Berg. Instead, private circles and homosexual associations tolerated within the structures of the Protestant Church constituted a large part of the East German homosexual scene.[8] So did cruising areas. Beyond looking for sex, cruising places arguably had broader social functions, in contrast to those in West Germany.[9] But for many, the existence of a colorful and very visible lesbian and gay culture on the other side of the wall constituted a particular reference point in forging gay identities within East Germany.

Beyond the legally comparatively progressive stance, there had been a real cultural development toward the integration of homosexual perspectives into GDR culture, at least during the 1980s. In the very last years before the wall fell, this effort was symbolized by the production of the GDR film *Coming Out,* which was a state-sanctioned critical review of a young gay teacher's life in East Berlin.[10] The film premiered the night the wall fell, and the East German debate on the cultural acceptance of homosexuality was overtaken by the collapse of the entire Soviet system.

EDUCATION

Germany's education system, generally speaking, is based on a common primary education between the ages of 6 and 10, thereafter branching out into up to four different educational paths, Gymnasium (leading to higher education), Realschule (O-levels), and Hauptschule (manual and practical sectors). Today, about 40 percent of German pupils attain a university-entrance diploma (Abitur). Education lies within the responsibilities of the regions (Länder) and schooling models, based on a strong political divide on the issue as well as historical traditions, differ. The left has criticized the split education model for a long time as socially unjust and restrictive of social mobility and, in a range of regions, has implemented either longer phases of joint schooling or an alternative model of overall joint schooling systems; however, the initial model has not successfully been replaced.

Similarly, a strong political divide has arisen on the question of whether university students should be made to pay for their studies. Traditionally state run and free of charge, a large number of German Länder have recently imposed fees on higher education—although these are still very moderate compared to U.S. standards. The issue remains controversial, and some regions have indeed abolished the student fees after regional elections that have shifted the governing majorities. A large number of German universities now propose LGBTQ studies, most often based on previous gender studies programs. In schools, the inclusion of LGBTQ issues in educational programs has been decided at the regional level, where some but not all left-leaning regions have tended to implement programmatic reforms.

EMPLOYMENT AND ECONOMICS

Germany hosts one of the most powerful and most developed economies in Europe and in the world, leading internationally in the high-tech, transportation technology, and pharmaceuticals industries.[11] Germany's gross domestic product (GDP) comes third worldwide after the United States and Japan, according to current indicators.[12] The country has, however, suffered from a large public debt and structurally high unemployment. Unemployment has recently decreased from 13 percent in 2005 to 7.2 percent in late 2008,[13] but the economy risks an economic downturn in 2009.

SOCIAL/GOVERNMENTAL PROGRAMS

The main basis of the German welfare state was created at the end of the 19th century under the conservative Reichs-chancellor Otto von Bismarck—at the time, the reforms were seen as preempting social movements by implementing basic standards for workers. The postwar model of the (West) German mixed economy—a free market with a strong welfare state—was increasingly put under pressure in the 1990s, mainly due to a systematically high level of unemployment (between 8 and 10%), until a bundle of reforms called Agenda 2010, under the left-wing government of Gerhard Schröder, led to important cutbacks in unemployment benefits, pensions, and social services. Unemployment has fallen since then, but social inequalities have grown, and the sentiment of social exclusion has grown stronger, eventually leading to a shift in Germany's political landscape through the rise of the former Communist Party, renamed Linke (left), which became an important force in both East and West Germany.[14]

SEXUALITY AND SEXUAL PRACTICES

According to an extensive study on sexuality, Germans have sex 139 times a year on average. Just under 40 percent admit to having been unfaithful at least once. (Heterosexual) men, in this study, report having had 10.2 sexual partners on average, and women 6.7.[15] Estimates on the proportion of homosexuals and/or women and men practicing homosexuality tend to differ too widely to be counted as reliable. In the past 5 to 10 years, safer sex habits of gays have dropped significantly, giving rise to increasing worries over a new rise in HIV infections.[16]

FAMILY

Since 2001, Germany recognizes same sex partnerships through the possibility of registered partnership (Eingetragene Lebenspartnerschaft). The law was passed in November 2000 by the left-wing coalition of Social Democrats (SPD) and

Greens (B90/Die Grünen), and was heavily opposed at the time by the Christian Democrats. The two opposition parties (CDU/CSU and FDP) voted against the law. Due to the opposition parties' power of veto over any benefits related to legal change through the high chamber (Bundesrat), a restricted version of the initial project was adopted. Consequently, the law in place falls short of anything close to an equal status to opposite-sex marriage in Germany. In sum, any financial advantages are excluded from the law, while rights concerning citizenship and work and residence permits are included. Thus, the law led to an important symbolic recognition at a societal level as well as to an important tool for securing the bases of couples with one noncitizen partner. In the casual vernacular, registered partnership is often referred to as gay marriage (Homo-Ehe), despite the fact that it is not formally equivalent to marriage. Opinion polls have shown that a majority of Germans today support the existence of not only registered partnership but also of true same sex marriage. In the Eurobarometer 2006, 52 percent were in favor of same-sex marriage—a number that was still under 30 percent in the same Eurobarometer in 1993. A different survey, Gallup Europe 2004, found even more support for same sex marriage, at 65 percent.[17]

The law, however, was heavily criticized by conservatives calling for the defense of marriage as the basis of society, and by the Catholic Church, in particular Joseph Ratzinger (who became pope in 2005), who intervened heavily in the German media debate at the time.

It also had numerous critics on the left who were displeased with the limitations of the reform. Not only are various financial, tax, and pension benefits excluded from the law but also certain symbolic allowances, as same sex ceremonies are often barred from being held in the town hall where many marriages take place, depending on the region. Further, no adoption rights are given to same-sex partners, artificial insemination remains forbidden for a woman unless she is married to a man, and parenthood for the partner of a parent who subsequently enters a same-sex partnership is restricted to a second-order parenthood under the Small Adoption Right (Kleines Adoptionsrecht). Finally, the law was heavily criticized and actively opposed by a significant part of the lesbian and gay movement that advocated a more radical reform of patriarchal, traditionalist societal values and the abolition of marriage. Gay and lesbian groups, particularly left-wing, anarchist, and queer groups in Berlin, grouped in anti–gay marriage demonstrations such as the alternative Christopher Street Day in the borough of Kreuzberg, and accused the author of the law, the Green MP Volker Beck, of social conservatism.[18]

The law took effect on August 1, 2001, and the criticism both on the conservative and on the antimarriage side has practically ceased. Conservative political parties have since included the recognition of same-sex partnerships in their party programs, even the traditionalist Bavarian Christian Social Union (CSU).[19] In addition, a number of queer antimarriage critics have welcomed the reform as to the practical enhancement it represents for non-EU partners.[20] All regional authorities of the Lutheran Protestant Church in Germany have recognized same-sex partnership and propose ceremonial church blessings. The Catholic Church, however, continues to oppose the recognition of same-sex partnerships. This has led to a large source of discrimination due to the fact that the Catholic Church controls a vast amount of employment in Germany, often in state-financed but church-run institutions such as Catholic schools, hospitals, and social services. Thus, in the several million jobs that are controlled by the Catholic Church, lesbians and gays cannot officially identify as homosexual without with the threat of being fired.[21]

Overall, on the societal level, the recognition of same-sex partnerships has led to a deeper acceptance of homosexual lifestyles in Germany. But despite the fact that Germany may well count among the most tolerant countries in the world for LGBTs today, there is still discrimination, homosexuality is still often taboo, and there may even be an increasing amount of homophobic violence in certain areas.

COMMUNITY

Despite the high level of acceptance in Germany, in certain ways homosexuality is still kept secret. Particularly amongst lesbian women, keeping sexual identity a private element of their lives is still very common. It should at least be said that openness about an LGBT identity is carefully weighed against specific social settings, such as family, work, and friends. Dependent on the sector of employment, the workplace traditionally represents a challenging setting for gay and lesbian identities. Whether a woman or a man wants to present her or himself as lesbian or gay or keep it a secret often depends on the potential risks this identity poses to her or his career. Today, some encounter total acceptance in the workplace.

Gay or lesbian identities can be lived publicly in one setting and not in another. The way they choose to reveal their identities in each setting is often based on an experienced or imagined risk. Acceptance is not experienced throughout, and many difficulties remain. Hence, the observed general trend toward greater acceptance does not change the fact that for many people, managing homosexual identities remains the result of a subtle case-to-case judgment. In some of the interviews that were conducted in a study on the social acceptance of homosexuality,[22] specific social settings such as the family, the workplace, and specific cultural groups are singled out. In certain places, or among certain groups of people, some continue to refrain from addressing their homosexuality, even in presumably tolerant large cities like Berlin, where the interviews were held.

Avoiding certain areas or groups of people may or may not be felt as a constraint, but often the area or the group of people in the immediate vicinity has an impact on, for instance, showing affection in public.

This necessity for lesbians and gays to live double lives seems to be the exception in Germany today. But the concept of a case-to-case management of public identity is not entirely absent. This includes careful approaches to being publicly gay or lesbian with certain people, in certain institutions, or in certain areas or neighborhoods. Particularly homosexual women remain largely invisible in Germany's public life.

HEALTH

While at a low level if compared internationally, German HIV infection rates have continued to rise since 1999. The recent rise is particularly significant among homosexuals. Apart from the drawbacks of safer sex campaigns in the gay community, the significant rise in other sexually transmittable infections such as syphilis, which lead to higher infection rates, is seen as a major cause of the recent development. According to 2007 estimates, about 59,000 people in Germany are living with HIV/AIDS.[23]

POLITICS AND LAW

Since 1990, for many, speaking of the difference between East and West German homosexual cultures has lost meaning, and homosexuality, having become largely accepted within mainstream German society, has itself become a nonissue for many. Commentators have pointed to the East German gay and lesbian culture's quick absorption by the West German 1990s culture, in a period that coincided with an increasing acceptance of homosexuality in West German society, politics, media, and law.[24] In the aftermath of German reunification, debates on homosexuality and same-sex marriage were largely dominated by West German media and politicians.

In recent years, Germany has become relatively accepting of homosexuality; in fact, it is among the most tolerant worldwide, together with a range of other European countries.[25] The coming out of national politicians and other prominent public personalities[26] and the introduction of registered partnership for same sex couples in 2000 created a decade of public debate in which the cultural East-West divide had no further significance. It is striking that various surveys indicate no gap between West and East Germany overall in the acceptance of homosexuality.[27] Instead, a city-country divide can be observed.[28] Most prominently, the coming out of the then candidate for Berlin City Hall, Klaus Wowereit, became a national reference for the new self-consciousness of German homosexuals when, during his endorsement speech, he publicly announced: "I am gay, and that's a good thing" (*Ich bin schwul, und das ist auch gut so*).[29] Various lesbian and gay events, such as the gay Christopher Street Day parade and the gay street festivals have become integrated into the main cities' popular culture, particularly in Berlin, Hamburg, and Cologne, and local politicians of all hues are eager to show themselves on the occasion. In the realm of politics, the conservative mayor of Hamburg Ole von Beust and the head of the centrist party FDP count among the most famous openly gay personalities. The coming out of the lipstick lesbian talk show moderator Anne Will constituted a new dimension in lesbian visibility, which had largely lagged behind that of gay men.

RELIGION AND SPIRITUALITY

Although Germany is not formally secular and is politically shaped by a party referring to Christianity, the role of religion has declined sharply. Today, 47 percent of Germans "believe in some sort of God."[30] About 31 percent of Germans are Lutheran Protestant, mainly in the north, and about 31 percent are Catholic, mainly in the south. In eastern Germany and in urban areas such as Hamburg, atheism is dominant.[31] About 4 percent of Germans are Muslims, mostly of Turkish origin.[32]

VIOLENCE

Some studies see homophobia, particularly violent attacks by young men, on the rise. The quantification of homophobic attacks is methodologically very difficult, as they tend to remain unreported. This was precisely the result of a large survey study in Berlin, organized by the gay helpline Maneo together with the sociologist Michael Bochow.[33] The study reported that 90 percent of homophobic attacks that were mentioned in the study had been left unreported.[34] It told of

several violent attacks, including attempted murder, particularly in poorer neighborhoods and in cruising areas such as the Tiergarten Park in the centre of Berlin.
To give the example of Germany's capital, in 2006 police reported 27 homophobic
crimes, while the helpline Maneo reported 200 cases.[35] The survey itself reported
3000 homophobic attacks, including verbal attacks.

OUTLOOK FOR THE 21ST CENTURY

The LGBT fight as a marginal group in German society appears to be history.
But the legal debates on the family and partnership rights are all but settled. Societal advances still have not fully translated into full equal rights and equal respect. In
addition, the focus of antigay discrimination has moved to certain societal groups
(regional, religious, ethnic) but has not disappeared. With the growing inter-
nationalization of societies themselves, the question of homosexuality in Germany
in the 21st century will, to a large and growing extent, depend on the question of
homosexuality in the world.

RESOURCE GUIDE

Suggested Reading

Ilona Bubeck, ed., *Unser Stück vom Kuchen. Zehn Positionen gegen die Homoehe* (Berlin:
    Querverlag, 2000).
Hans-Georg Stümke, *Homosexuelle in Deutschland: Eine politische Geschichte* (München:
    Beck, 1989).

Web Sites

Hinnerx, http://www.hinnerx.de/
    Hamburg's LGBT magazine.
Jugendnetzwerk Lamda, http://www.lamda-online.de/.
    LGBT youth association.
Lesben- und Schwulenverband Deutschland (LsvD), http://www.lsvd.de/.
    LGBT association.
Maneo, http://www.maneo.de/.
    Gay antiviolence network.
Siegessäule, http://www.siegessaeule.de/.
    Berlin's LGBT city magazine.
http://www.queer.de/.
    LGBT internet platform.
http://www.lesweb.de/.
http://www.lesbischleben.de/.
http://www.elles.de/.
    Lesbian internet platforms.
http://www.gayromeo.com/.
    Male gay chat platform.

Films

Ich kenn keinen—Allein unter Heteros (2003). Directed by Jochen Hick.
Was nützt die Liebe in Gedanken (2004). Directed by Achim von Borries.
Sommersturm (2004). Directed by Marco Kreuzpaintner.
Auf der anderen Seite (2007). Directed by Fatih Akin.

NOTES

1. Christopher Sherwood, *Goodbye to Berlin* (London: New Phoenix Library, 1939).

2. Hans-Georg Stümke, *Homosexuelle in Deutschland: Eine politische Geschichte* (München, Germany: Beck, 1989), overview at www.juraforum.de/jura/specials/special/id/15965/.

3. Hans-Georg Stümke, *Homosexuelle in Deutschland*. In 1969 the age of consent for homosexual acts was 21; this was lowered to 18 in 1973.

4. Rosa von Praunheim, *Nicht der Homosexuelle ist pervers, sondern die Situation, in der er lebt* (film; Germany: 1970).

5. E. G. Ralf König, *Der bewegte Mann* (Hamburg: Carlsen Comics, 1987). See also ralf-koenig.de.

6. Hans-Georg Stümke, *Homosexuelle in Deutschland*.

7. As the gay activist Rudolf Klimmer noted in 1968: "Despite this progressive legislation homosexual life in the GDR has not changed…few forms of visibility, no magazines and clubs." See Michael Holy, "Ungelebte Ost/West Beziehungen," in *Schwulsein 2000, Perspektiven im vereinigten Deutschland,* ed. Günther Grau (Hamburg, Männerschwarm-skript, 2001), 58. All translations by the author.

8. Michael Holy, "Ungelebte Ost/West Beziehungen," 60. See also, for example, Rainer Herrn, *Schwule Lebenswelten im Osten* (Berlin: Deutsche AIDS-Hilfe, 1999).

9. Jan Feddersen in group interview, Günther Grau, ed., *Schwulsein 2000, Perspektiven im vereinigten Deutschland* (Hamburg: Männerschwarmskript, 2001), 80.

10. Heiner Carow, *Coming Out* (film; German Democratic Republic [GDR], 1989).

11. André Brodocz and Hans Vorländer, "Deutschland, Wirtschaft," http://www.bpb.de/themen/DZ5640,0,0,Wirtschaft.html.

12. According to 2007 list of the International Monetary Fund, the World Bank, and CIA World Factbook.

13. See http://www.pub.arbeitsamt.de/hst/services/statistik/000100/html/monat/200810.pdf.

14. On the debate and the role of the Linke, see an interview debate at http://www.fr-online.de/top_news/1599593_Agenda-2010-die-Abrechnung.html.

15. See *Focus,* September 17, 2008, http://www.focus.de/gesundheit/ratgeber/sexualitaet/sexstudie-so-liebt-deutschland_aid_334047.html.

16. See *Die Zeit,* November 2, 2004, http://www.zeit.de/2004/49/aids_Deutschland.

17. Eurobarometer 66, 2006. Gallup Europe 2004.

18. For queer antigay marriage positions see Ilona Bubeck, ed., *Unser Stück vom Kuchen. Zehn Positionen gegen die Homoehe* (Berlin: Querverlag, 2000).

19. Since its 2006 party program, see *Tagesspiegel,* October 23, 2006.

20. See, for example, Frédéric Jörgens, "The Individual, the Couple and the Family: Social and Legal Recognition of Same-sex Partnership in Europe," PhD dissertation, Florence, European University Institute, 2007, p. 119f.

21. The constraint imposed by the Catholic Church as an employer is all but fictional: the public registration of a same-sex partnership formally constitutes a reason for terminating the employment even in state-financed institutions if they are administered by the Catholic Church in Germany. This includes a vast number of schools, hospitals and charities. See High Court judgment BVerfGE 70, 138.

22. Jörgens, "The Individual, the Couple and the Family."

23. Robert-Koch-Institut, "Epidemologisches Bulletin," November 23, 2007, http://www.rki.de/nn_205760/DE/Content/Infekt/EpidBull/Archiv/2007/47__07,templateId=raw,property=publicationFile.pdf/47_07.pdf.

24. Holy, "Ungelebte Ost/West Beziehungen," 61–63.

25. In the Pew Global Attitudes Project 2003, Germany comes top of a list of 41 countries surveyed for the study, with 83 percent of respondents saying that "homosexuality

should be accepted by society." It shares this result with the Czech Republic. Pew Global Attitudes Project, http://people-press.org/reports/pdf/185.pdf. Neither Scandinavian countries nor the Netherlands are included in this study. According to the 1999 findings of the World Values Survey 6.1 percent of Swedish, 6.2 percent of Dutch, 8.0 percent of Danish, 11.3 percent of East German, 11.8 percent of West German, 15.6 percent of French, 16.4 percent of Spanish, and 17.4 percent of Belgian respondents mentioned that they would not like to have homosexuals as neighbors, http://www.worldvaluessurvey.org/.

26. Gay public personalities became particularly debated after the controversial *outing* of various politicians and TV presenters by the filmmaker and gay activist Rosa von Praunheim in 1991 in the TV show *Explosiv* on December 10, 1991.

27. See *Datenreport 2004*, Berlin, Bundeszentrale für Politische Bildung 2004, 471–74. For 2002 the report finds that East and West Germans have an equal proportion of respondents judging homosexuality to be "bad" or "rather bad," namely 24 percent. Interestingly, the number is up from 17 percent in East Germany in 2000, and up from 21 percent in West Germany, thus showing a negative trend for both. On other contentious topics, such as abortion, the difference between East and West is significant, arguably because of the more proabortion regime in the German Democratic Republic (GDR): it is bad for 35 percent in East Germany compared to 53 percent in West Germany, with a declining gap since 2000. On East and West Germans' opinions on homosexuality, see also Emnid survey 2001 in *Tagesspiegel*, February 20, 2001.

28. Two regions with a high proportion of rural populations or absence of major cities, Rheinland-Pfalz and Sachsen-Anhalt, come last in the nationwide survey (Emnid survey 2001 in *Tagesspiegel*, February 20, 2001).

29. Klaus Wowereit at the launch of his candidacy for Berlin mayor in June 2001.

30. Eurobarometer poll, 2005.

31. http://www.ekd.de/download/kimi_2004.pdf; http://www.bpb.de/themen/G1RPNN,0,0,Was_ist_Islam.html (Bundeszentrale für Politische Bildung, Berlin, December 2004).

32. http://www.bpb.de/themen/G1RPNN,0,0,Was_ist_Islam.html; http://www.bpb.de/themen/G1RPNN,0,0,Was_ist_Islam.html (Bundeszentrale für Politische Bildung, Berlin, December 2004).

33. Eurobarometer poll 66, 2006; Gallup Europe, 2004.

34. Maneo Report 2007, http://www.maneo-toleranzkampagne.de/index.php?cat=2&sub=2.

35. *Die Welt*, July 2, 2008.

GREECE

Carmen De Michele

OVERVIEW

The Hellenic Republic of Greece has one of the richest cultural heritages in Europe, its history shaped by influences from Europe, Northern Africa, and the Middle East. Western civilization, in turn, has its roots in ancient Greece.

The Greek culture evolved over several thousand years. The earliest civilizations are known to have existed in the Mycenaean (1500–1100 B.C.E.) and Minoan (2700–1450 B.C.E.) eras. Classical Greece (500–323 B.C.E.) and the Hellenistic era (336–31 B.C.E.) were followed by a time of strong influence from the Roman Empire (27 B.C.–393 C.E.). During the Byzantine Empire (330–1453 C.E.), Thessaloniki became its second most important city, after Constantinople. The Ottoman Empire (1299–1923) also had a strong impact on Greek culture until the Greek Revolution (1821–29). The nation won independence from the Ottoman Empire and became a sovereign unified country.[1]

Greece joined NATO in 1952 and the Organisation for Economic Cooperation and Development (OECD) in 1961. In 1975, a referendum abolished the monarchy. According to the Greek constitution of the same year, the nation became a presidential parliamentary republic. On January 1, 1981, Greece became the 10th member of the European Union (EU); it joined the EU's Economic and Monetary Union (EMU) in 2001, adopting the euro as its new currency.

Greece is located in southeastern Europe, on the southern end of the Balkan Peninsula. Its northern neighbors are Albania, the former Yugoslav

Republic of Macedonia, and Bulgaria. Turkey lies to the east, and most of the mainland is surrounded by the sea. The Aegean Sea borders the mainland in the south and east, and the Ionian Sea in the west.

Greece's land boundary is 720 miles (1,160 km) long, while its coastline stretches over 9,250 miles (14,880 km), making it the world's 10th longest coast. About 80 percent of the country consists of mountains and hills, this mountainous territory dominating the mainland. The canal of the Isthmus of Corinth separates the Peloponnesus peninsula from the mainland. The Greek territory also includes about 2,000 islands, such as Crete, Rhodes, and Lesbos, as well as island groups like the Dodecanese and the Cyclades.

Greece's total population is about 11.1 million people. At 1.2,[2] the Greek total fertility rate[3] is steadily declining, and the annual population growth rate between 1994 and 2004 was only 0.4 percent.[4] In addition, infant mortality has declined from 40.07 per 1,000 live births in 1960 to 17.94 in 1980 and 5.34 in 2007.[5] The marriage rate (the number of marriages per 1,000 people) was 5.4, while the divorce rate was 0.9 divorces per 1,000 people. Currently 3.7 percent of live births are to unmarried women.[6] As the infant mortality rate has decreased, so has the life expectancy been increasing substantially in the last decades. The life expectancy in 2006 was 77 years for men and 82 years for women, up from 67.3 and 70.42, respectively, in 1960.[7]

About 35 percent of the Greek population lives in the nation's capital, Athens (3.8 million inhabitants). Thessaloniki, in the northern periphery of Central Macedonia is the second largest city with 1.9 million inhabitants. A total of 61.4 percent of the Greek population is concentrated in urban areas.[8]

Greece is subdivided into 13 administrative peripheries, which consist of 51 prefectures and the autonomous region of Mount Athos. The 240-mile (390 km) peninsula has only 2,250 inhabitants and is geographically part of the Chalcidice peninsula.[9] Female visitors are not permitted to enter the autonomous region. Men are only allowed to visit one of the 20 monasteries, and only with special permission.

The prime minister is the head of government, and holds several executive and legislative functions, as well as performing certain ceremonial duties. However, the Greek government only exercises executive power, while the Hellenic Parliament vests the legislative power. The judiciary power is independent. In the last decades, two parties have continually dominated the multiparty system: the conservative New Democracy and the socialist Panhellenic Socialist Movement (PASOK).

The country has enjoyed substantial economic growth and an increase in living standards, especially in the urban areas. The EU funds large investments in heavy infrastructure. Increased revenues in the shipping and tourism industry, along with a growing service sector, have helped the economy to prosper. In 2004 Athens successfully hosted the Olympic Games, which led to an improved infrastructure in the capital, and specifically the construction of the metro. Major projects commissioned by the EU, like the Via Egnatia road in the north, will connect Greece more closely to its border countries, although Greece's relationship is tense with some of these. The conflict with Turkey over the occupation of Cyprus is still an important issue for many Greeks, as is the dispute with the northern neighbor, Macedonia, about its name, which the Greeks claim for themselves for historical reasons.

OVERVIEW OF LGBT ISSUES

In Greece, the Greek Orthodox Church still plays an important role in shaping society's opinion on issues such as sexuality. Homosexuality is not widely accepted, especially outside the larger urban areas. One of the main struggles of the community is to become more visible within society. Many Greeks still do not admit the existence of lesbians and transsexuals in their country. The family is still considered the nucleus of the society, and many gay Greeks hide behind a pro forma marriage.

On June 3, 2008, the mayor of the small island of Tilos, Anastasios Aliferis, married two homosexual couples, taking advantage of a legal loophole in the 1982 law that legalized civil marriage between persons, without explicit reference to their gender. The church was strongly opposed to this.

The Greek LGBT community has become better organized and more politically active in recent years. LGBT groups have linked themselves closely with other groups in Europe and around the world. Local LGBT groups have established close ties with gay expatriates living in Germany, Italy, the United States, and so on. Furthermore, their activities are not limited to the mainland. In the past decades, Greece has become a very attractive tourist destination for gay travelers. In particular, the small islands of Mykonos and Lesbos have become extremely popular.

Greece's membership in the EU, the large influx of immigrants, HIV/AIDS prevention programs, and increasing tourism are slowly exposing Greeks to the demands of the LGBT groups.

EDUCATION

The adult literacy rate in Greece was 91 percent in 2004, representing male literacy of 94 percent and female literacy of 88.3 percent.[10] Ninety-nine percent of the primary school–aged members of the population were enrolled in primary schools.[11]

Attending primary school and the gymnasium is compulsory for all Greeks. Children start school at about the age of 6 and attend primary school for six years. At age 12, students change to the *gymnasium,* which they attend for three years. Postsecondary education is divided into the *lykeio* (which is similar to the unified upper secondary school), and the technical-vocational schools. The vocational training institutes offer another alternative, and accept students from both the *gymnasium* (lower secondary school) and the *lykeio* (upper secondary education). Improving the educational agenda is an urgent need for the Greek government. The Program for International Student Assessment (PISA), commissioned by the OECD, compares the performance of secondary school children aged 15, and ranks Greek secondary education only as 38th worldwide, which is way below the OECD average.

The state is responsible for education, as determined by the Greek constitution. The Ministry of Education closely supervises all aspects of primary and secondary public education. All schools, private and public, must meet the established curriculum; the state controls the hiring of professors and teachers and is in charge of producing textbooks for students.

There is no sex education in high schools, as it is not permitted by the Greek Orthodox Church. In line with this, neither is there information about safer sex, sexual health, or alternative sexualities. The National Council of Youth, a sub-branch of the Ministry of Education, promotes the European All Different, All Equal campaign in Greece. This program, sponsored by EU funds, is primarily aimed at school children at all levels and should both promote the visibility of LGBT people and uphold their equal rights as Greek and European citizens. It should support teachers in their task of informing all students as appropriate to their ages.

Public higher education is divided into universities, high educational institutions, and high technological institutions. Students must qualify for these institutions through a national examination, which is compulsory after their third year at the *lykeio*. Students aged 22 years are eligible for the Hellenic Open University, which selects its candidates through a kind of lottery.

The constitution allows only state-run universities to provide higher education in Greece. Every year, thousands of students are unable to access the public university system and are forced to emigrate. In 2004, 5,250 students per million inhabitants left their home country to study abroad. This makes Greece by far the world's largest exporter of students, followed by Malaysia, which has 1,780 students abroad per million inhabitants.[12] Since these problems are in part the result of the state's control of higher education, the New Democracy party proposed amending the constitution in the late 1990s. Private universities, the party asserted, should be allowed to operate in Greece as nonprofit institutions. The ruling socialist party, PASOK, rejected the proposal at first, but now also supports a constitutional provision that allows for private universities. Many members of the academic community, professors as well as students, fiercely oppose a change in the system. In 2006, Prime Minister Kostas Karamanlis declared his support of a new amendment to the constitution, which facilitates the creation of non–state-owned universities.

LGBT groups point out that schoolbooks used at universities, especially those used in law schools and at the police academy, present homosexuals as criminals and primary suspects for certain criminal acts like drug addiction and pedophilia.[13]

EMPLOYMENT AND ECONOMICS

Greece's gross domestic product (GDP) per capita in 2007 was $35,167; this comes close to the European Union average. In 2006, the Greek economy produced a total GDP of $305.6 billion.[14] The most prosperous economic sector is tourism, followed by shipping industries. Other important industrial branches include telecommunications, manufacturing and construction, and banking and finance, the last of which has heavily invested in other Balkan countries.

The service industry constitutes 74 percent of the Greek economy, and is the largest and fastest growing sector. In comparison, industry (20.6%) and agriculture (5.1%) are relatively small. Manufacturing accounts for 13 percent of the GDP, and its most profitable and expanding sector is the food industry.[15] Another fast-growing sector is telecommunications. Further important industrial sectors of the Greek economy include textiles, building materials, and electrical appliances.

Over 600,000 Greeks, directly and indirectly, depend on the tourism industry, which accounts for 15 percent of the total GDP and 16.5 percent of total employment. The number of tourists coming to Greece is increasing steadily, from 18 million visitors in 2005 to almost 20 million in 2007.[16]

The unemployment rate in Greece had been increasing drastically in the last decades, from 2.1 percent in 1977 to 9.2 percent in 2006.[17]

In accordance with European Union directive 2007/78, legislation protecting against discrimination in the workplace on the grounds of sexual orientation was adopted in early 2005 (Greek law 3304/05). Victims of discrimination can resort to European courts, but this proves to be difficult and generally too expensive for individuals.

Many single mothers and unmarried couples, homosexual and heterosexual, are disadvantaged. The General Secretariat for Equality in Greece reports that in 1999, the total employment rate of single parents, both male and female, was 63 percent. Since the government fails to support single parents, single mothers have a very high work activity rate; for divorced women with children, it was 77 percent, and for unmarried women, 72 percent. Compared to the average women's activity rate of 36 percent and the average men's rate of 66 percent, the number is strikingly high. Single Greek mothers are often obliged to accept any kind of job and often unfavorable conditions, such as below-average wages, low labor standards, long working hours, and so on.[18]

Military

Greece has universal compulsory military service for all males. Females may serve in the military, but are exempted from conscription.

Officially, gays and lesbians have equal access to the military. However, EOK, an Athens-based LGBT group, reports that homosexuals have been denied access to the military because of their sexual orientation.[19]

A presidential decree signed in 2002 excludes all persons from military service who are "suffering from psychosexual or sexual identity disorders." The country's privacy commissioner had put pressure on the government, so it no longer includes the mental disorder note in the papers of gays discharged from the army, but the papers of older dischargees still have this notation.

SOCIAL/GOVERNMENT PROGRAMS

The government does not provide any kind of support programs for LGBTs, and the information provided by the authorities on antidiscrimination policy is almost nonexistent.

SEXUALITY/SEXUAL PRACTICES

Homosexuality has a long history in the country, even though the term homosexuality, as it is used today, is not readily applicable to ancient Greece. Most Greek men were bisexuals with wives and children. Erotic love between two male adults was considered unusual and even ridiculous. Homosexual love was only socially tolerated between an adult man and a boy, and the Greek word for this kind of bond was *paiderastia*. It was even considered a social duty to engage in intergenerational love affairs. The ideal relationship included an adult man, called the *erastes* (lover) and an adolescent *eromenos* (beloved).[20] There were prominent exceptions, such as the relationship between Alexander the Great and Hephaiston, or between the mythical hero Achilles and his best friend Patroclus.[21] There are several explanations that try to trace the origin of *paiderastia*. In one version, Minos, the King of Crete, imposed this system in order to avoid overpopulation on the island. The love between a man and a young adolescent was considered a rite of passage, and is historically documented in the writing of Ephorus of Kyme.

The bond between man and adolescent was not of an erotic nature. The older lover had a social responsibility for his beloved. He had the duty to provide him, as well as his family and close friends, with valuable presents and facilitate the boy's education. The relationships usually lasted until the end of the youth's education, but in many cases the lover was still considered responsible for the young man until he reached marriageable age. Some male couples were known for their bravery in war, such as those of the Theban Sacred Band, or became known as killers of tyrants, such as Harmodius and his lover Aristogeiton.[22]

Besides the socially desired form of *paiderastia*, prostitution of boys was very common as well. Solon (634–560 B.C.E.) tried to regulate it in his hometown of Athens by enforcing that only *xenoi* (foreigners) who were not Athenian citizens were allowed to work as male prostitutes. Most of the boys offering their services were kidnapped in war or sold off into slavery.[23]

In the classical age of Athens (the fifth century B.C.E.), male love served as inspiration for many important artists, such as Sophocles and Phidias. Many Greek poets, such as Archilochos, Ibycos, Anacreon, and Pindar dedicated a considerable part of their work to the love of young men.

In contrast to the prominent role that male homosexual love played in ancient Greek society, lesbian love remained hidden. The poet Sappho, who was born in 630 B.C.E. in Eresos on the western side of Lesbos, is mainly known for her poems that speak out in favor of lesbian relationships.[24] Only fragments of her nine books remain, the most famous of which are the marriage songs. Her erotic lyrics were addressed to a close circle of female companions. Still today, Lesbos, and particularly Eresos, attracts many lesbians who pay homage to Sappho.

Despite their ancient traditions, many modern Greek LGBTs still feel reluctant to manifest their sexual preference openly. The opinion of many Greeks is still biased when they are asked about LGBT. People living in small villages, in rural areas, or on smaller islands tend to be more homophobic than their urban countrymen. Negative stereotypes are very persistent and gays and lesbians still have to face degrading comments and mockery.

Greek society differentiates strongly between gays and bisexuals, showing more tolerance to the latter. According to the first scientific research conducted by the Athens Medical School in 1992, the majority of homosexual men's sexual activity was masturbation, fellatio, and anal intercourse. In addition, almost all claimed to have heterosexual contacts as well. Many gay men feel forced to marry and behave as heterosexuals, even though they may be emotionally homosexual.[25]

An opinion poll from 1995 captured the feeling of many Greeks: 19 percent of those polled answered that they defined homosexuality as a disease, while about half (50.5%) said that homosexuality is normal; 16.9 percent of them believed that homosexuals are degenerate, and 13.6 percent did not answer the question or said they did not know. Women had a more positive attitude toward the subject than men. For 53.6 percent of the women, homosexuality was normal, while only 47.3 percent of the men said the same.[26]

In polls by age group, the 30-to-39-year-old population had the most positive attitude, 59.9 percent of them finding homosexuality to be normal. The younger groups, aged 14–24 and 25–29, said that homosexuality was normal only at 47.5 percent and 49.8 percent, respectively.[27]

FAMILY

The family constitutes the basis of the Greek social structure. The social pressure on young adults to get married is still felt in both rural and urban areas. Extended family members are expected to help their relatives with both emotional and financial support in times of need. In the absence of a sufficient number of kindergartens or nursery schools, grandparents are often left to take care of the children while their parents are at work. Since the Greek government has not developed a consistent policy for the elderly population, many couples need to take care of their parents. Family ties are very close, and Greek children feel indebted to their elderly parents. Therefore, a considerable number of the elderly receive a lot of help from their relatives, especially from their children, either by sharing the same house with them or by living on their own but receiving informal care and assistance when needed.

Strong family ties also carry over into business relationships. Family businesses are frequent and nepotism is widely accepted. The idea of family honor is still strong and the wrongdoing of one family member can bring dishonor to the whole family.

Same-sex Couples

Same-sex couples are not officially recognized. In theory, same-sex marriages are allowed, since the Greek civil code does not state explicitly that the partners must be of different sex. But the concept of marriage is still popularly considered as the union between a man and a woman.

The law guarantees couples married abroad that their union is valid in Greece, as long as they present their marriage license authenticated by the foreign ministry of the issuing country. So far, there is no record of a same-sex couple married abroad having tried this. As same sex couples are not recognized, they also receive no marital social privileges, no right to visit in hospital, no pension, no shared work insurance, and no inheritance.

George Andreas Papandreou, the leader of PASOK, presented a legislative draft in parliament for the recognition of both heterosexual and homosexual unmarried couples. He proposed to adopt a solution similar to the French *pacte civil de solidarité*. Greek LGBT groups complain, however, that the proposal does not go far enough to ensure equal rights for unmarried same-sex couples.

The National Human Rights Committee proposed to register all unmarried couples, both homosexual and heterosexual. The Coalition of the Left, of Movements and Ecology party (also known as Synaspismós) stated in the Greek media that it will support same sex-marriage. Also, the leader of Synaspismós, Alekos Alavanos, affirmed that his coalition wants to fight all kinds of discrimination and promote the free expression of sexual orientation and same-sex marriages. The ruling New Democracy and Prime Minister Kostas Karamanlis, reelected in 2007, opposes the marriage of same-sex couples.

The Greek Orthodox Church, which holds a very powerful position in Greece, is against all the proposals and recommendations issued so far.

The Eurobarometer opinion poll of December 2006 showed that only 16 percent of the Greek public supports same-sex marriage and 11 percent feel that same-sex couples should have the right to adopt.

These figures are below the 25-member EU average of 44 percent and 33 percent, respectively. According to these numbers, Greece is among the lower ranks of the European Union in this area, together with Poland, Bulgaria, Cyprus, and Romania.[28]

Adoption and Artificial Insemination

The mother and father are still considered the nucleus of the Greek family. In order to adopt a child, the future parents must prove that they are married. Since same-sex couples are not legally recognized by the Greek authorities, they do not qualify for adoption. Even if the proposal issued by PASOK is accepted, this form of partnership explicitly denies same-sex couples the right to adopt children.

A woman cannot be artificially inseminated if there is no man to raise the baby. It is unclear, however, whether this rule is followed by the many private clinics.

COMMUNITY

Media

The law regulating Greek radio and television mentions that "It is forbidden to present people in a way that under the current circumstances, may promote the humiliation, social isolation or negative discrimination against them from part of the audience especially due to sex (gender), race, ethnicity, language, religion, ideology, age, health or disability, sexual orientation or profession." Further, it states that "It is forbidden to promote diminutive, racist, xenophobic (fearing of strangers), or sexist messages and intolerant views and generally ethnic and religious minorities and other sensitive or powerless groups of the population must not be attacked."[29]

But despite these egalitarian intentions, the Greek media do not promote the rights of LGBTs. In many cases, homosexuals continue to be presented as exotic, good to encourage gossip and strong reactions from the audience. The only municipal gay and lesbian radio station in Athens, 94 Epikoinonia FM, was shut down in early 2005, as the Greek National Council for Radio and Television (NCRTV) judged the content of the Athens Gay and Lesbian Radio Show to be degrading.[30]

Local Communities

In Athens, a dynamic gay community is emerging. The capital is developing a gay village in the Gazi neighborhood. In 2007, the Athens Pride march was held in Syntagma Square in the city center. This annual LGBT parade was held for the first time in June 2005. The number of local and international participants has greatly increased since the festival was first held. Despite the growing popularity of the event, the mayor of Athens, Nikitas Kaklamanis, explicitly refused to let the Athens Pride 2007 be held under the auspices of the Athens municipality.

The city is home of the oldest surviving Greek gay organization, EOK, which started around 1989. The gay community in Athens attracts many gays and lesbians from all over the country, who hope to find a more tolerant and open atmosphere in the capital. While the Greek islands such as Mykonos and Sykanthos attract an increasing number of gay tourists, the gay community in Athens is dominated by native Greeks.

Thessaloniki, Greece's second largest city, also has several gay/lesbian venues and two very active LGBT organizations that encourage public discussions: the Cooperation against Homophobia (Sympraxis) and the Homosexual's Initiative against Oppression (POEK). The city is known the be more fashionable, but also more conservative than Athens. The LGBT groups in Thessaloniki are very well linked to other international groups and cover almost all of northern Greece. Sympraxis is one of most active LGBT groups in Greece. They organize public discussions about homosexuality and homophobia, publish the informative *Vitamine O,* and co-organize the annual Homosexual Movies Panorama, in which many other national and international groups take part.

Greece's only LGBT group focusing on transsexuals and transvestites, SATTE (Hellenic Association of Solidarity of Transvestites and Transsexuals), is located in Thessaloniki. There is no official data on these two groups. The Ministry of Health and Social Welfare states that there are 40 to 50 transsexuals living in Greece.[31] Since Greek law does not allow for gender reassignment, they have had their surgeries abroad, mainly in Morocco. Most of those registered work as female prostitutes.

On several smaller Greek islands, local communities have emerged, such as Corfu Lesbians and Gays, Chios Lesbian and Gay Group, and the Cephalonian Lesbian and Gay Group. These groups are trying to provide a discussion platform for the gays and lesbians on their islands. They have established discussion groups and online newsletters for their members, offer support for LGBTs' family members, and write letters to the media. These small LGBT groups also work together with larger groups based on the mainland, such as the Athens Lesbian Group.

Every year, a large number of Greek and international gay tourists visit the island of Mykonos, which is known for its vibrant gay nightlife. Mykonos has a cosmopolitan feel, and has long been known as a favorite gay destination with a gay beach and many small gay-friendly bars. It is one of the few places where gay men show their mutual affection in public, by kissing or holding hands. Many Greek gays visit Mykonos for its international atmosphere. The local population depends on tourism revenue and tries to be tolerant of gay visitors.

The lesbian scene is more focused on the island of Lesbos. In May 2008, the inhabitants of the island planned to go to court in an attempt to stop gay organizations from using the word *lesbian,* as they believed that the natives of Lesbos should be the only ones allowed to use that name. They claim that the dominance of the word in its sexual context violates the human rights of the islanders and disgraces them around the world. Furthermore, they argue that the Greek government is so embarrassed by the term Lesbian that it has been forced to rename the island after its capital, Mytilini.[32]

On the mainland, the Lesbian Group of Athens is among the most active. It was started by a group of women who took part in a discussion that occurred at the Athens Gay Pride in October 2000. Their aim is to make lesbians more visible in Greek society, in which female sexuality outside marriage or a relationship with a male is not supposed to exist. They fight against indirect discrimination and for an adequate public image in the media. In weekly talks, they discuss the potential and the limitations of pursuing lesbian politics, and about the ways in which the lesbian identity constitutes a political identity. The Lesbian Group of Athens is also involved in many events fighting racial discrimination, such as the Antiracism Network.

HEALTH

Health Care System

All Greeks are covered by the Greek health care system. Due to the small population on some of the islands, many islanders have to travel to Athens or Thessaloniki for specialized treatment.

The Greek health care system is complex. Both the national health system (ESY-Ethniko Systima Ygeias) and numerous social insurance funds provide health care. Some of those funds run their own clinics. Arrangements and provisions vary among the different social security funds. These funds require about 25 percent co-payment toward the costs of pharmaceuticals, and if expensive products are needed for chronic illness or a patient is low income, co-payment is limited to 10 percent. In addition, most pharmaceuticals are provided free of charge if related to cases such as maternity, work-related accidents, AIDS, transplants, or certain chronic diseases. In general, the social insurance funds cover the expenses for primary care and prevention, hospital care plus medical tests, and, in exceptional cases, medical treatment abroad in Europe or the United States.

HIV/AIDS

In 2007, around 9,300 people in Greece were living with HIV, of which 2,000 were women aged 15 and up; there were fewer than 100 deaths due to AIDS.[33]

Homosexuals, both gay and lesbian, are considered a high risk group. Blood donors must fill out a form stating that they have not engaged in any homosexual practice in the last 10 years (referring mostly to male homosexuals). LGBT groups report cases of doctors who have refused to see a patient after hearing that he or she was homosexual. Since many homosexual patients decide not to mention their sexual inclination, no statistics about HIV/AIDS infection among LGBTs are available.

By the end of 2004, Greek authorities had reported a total of 7,134 HIV cases. 2,515 people had already developed AIDS, of whom 1,417 had died. For 2004 itself, the authorities reported 434 new HIV cases, 72 new AIDS cases, and 25 AIDS deaths.

For 47.1 percent of the HIV cases, the route of transmission is not indicated. Homosexuals are still the largest group of newly infected, as 30.3 percent of the infected were homosexual males, while heterosexuals account for 19.5 percent. Most of the cases were 25 to 44 years old, with those aged between 30 and 34 the most affected. Sexual transmission was the main route of infection for all HIV cases. By June 2004, 86 percent of the HIV infected were men.[34] According to the statistics, heterosexual contact is the only transmission mode in which women account for the majority of cases.

The annual report of new HIV cases has been relatively low. A peak was reached in 1999, when 1,281 new cases were reported.[35] This can be partly attributed to retrospective reporting of past infections.[36]

POLITICS AND LAW

The Greek constitution prohibits discrimination on the grounds of religion, ethnic origin, and disability. In addition, the EU's gender directive enforces nondiscrimination on the grounds of gender.

Sexual orientation is not included in the Greek constitution as a nondiscrimination category. In 1950, a new criminal code decriminalized homosexual sex. But some provisions that discriminate against homosexuals are still in effect, such as article 347 of the Greek penal code, which states that unnatural debauchery (implying male homosexual sex) is a crime, punishable by three months to five years in prison. It further discriminates in the matter of age of consent, providing for the higher age of 17 years for male homosexuals, as opposed to 15 years for females and 16 for heterosexual males. Further, it gives the police the right to forcibly demand that gay men be tested for sexually transmitted diseases (STDs).

Since 2006, male prostitution has been legal, but not for "acts of unnatural debauchery" as defined in article 347. Lesbians are not mentioned in Greek law. A 1930s law about proselytizing is still valid, and actually forbids anything that could be considered proselytizing by anyone but the Greek Orthodox Church. There is no law protecting gender equality as a whole. The LGBT group SATTE reports frequent harassment.

RELIGION AND SPIRITUALITY

In the Eurostat—Eurobarometer poll of 2005, 81 percent of Greek citizens claimed to believe in God. Only 3 percent responded that they do not believe in any kind of god, spirit, or life force. Sixteen percent[37] answered that they do believe that there is some sort of spirit or life force. The percentage of Greeks asserting that they believe in God was the third highest among EU members, making it the most religious country after Malta and Cyprus.

The Greek constitution mentions Orthodox Christianity as the country's prevailing religion, guaranteeing freedom of religious belief for all; however, proselytism is officially illegal. The Greek Orthodox Church is protected by the state, which is in charge of paying the clergy's salaries. The Greek church remains self-governing, and submits itself to the spiritual guidance of the ecumenical patriarch of Constantinople.

Ninety-seven percent of the Greek population identify themselves as Greek Orthodox and claim to celebrate at least the main religious feasts, especially Pascha (Greek Orthodox Easter).[38]

The Orthodox Church holds the opinion that sexuality is part of the fallen world. Monasticism and marriage are paths to salvation, which is denominated by the Greek word *sotiria,* literally meaning *becoming whole.* The ideal path for monasticism is celibacy, which is obligatory for Orthodox priests. Marriage is blessed under the context of true love. "Man must love his wife as Jesus loved his Church,"[39] as it is repeated during the orthodox marriage ritual. True love as the basis of marriage theoretically means that it is not exclusive of homosexuality. But many members of the church still encourage negative social stereotypes of homosexuals. Several prominent members of the clergy, like the head of the Church of Greece, Archbishop Christodoulos of Athens, have made statements condemning homosexuality.

The Muslim minority is mainly concentrated in the northern province of Thrace and was given legal status by the Treaty of Lausanne (1923). The Muslims are Greece's only officially recognized religious minority. Estimates of the number of Muslims range from 98,000 to 140,000, constituting between 0.9 percent and 1.2 percent of the Greek population. The number of Muslim immigrants is somewhere between 200,000 and 300,000.[40]

Judaism has existed for more than 2,000 years, making it one of most longstanding religions in Greece. This is especially so in Thessaloniki, Greece's second biggest metropolitan area, where Sephardic Jews were an integral part of the city. Their traditional language, Ladino, was also spoken by the non-Jewish population of Thessaloniki. Very few Greek Jews survived the Holocaust, and today the Greek Jewish community has about 5,500 members.[41]

The 50,000 officially recognized Roman Catholics (Byzantine Greek Catholics and Latin Catholics) constitute only a fraction of the general Greek population. Most of them can be found on the Cyclades, an island group that was long under Venetian rule. About 200,000 illegal Roman Catholic immigrants must be added to this number.[42] The increase of immigrants from eastern Europe and the third world has led to a wider spectrum of religious practices.

VIOLENCE

Domestic Violence

The family is the most important element of Greek society. Violence within the family is still taboo, and, in many cases, domestic violence is not reported to the authorities. Victims report that other family members have pressured them to keep silent in order to avoid bringing shame over the whole family. The responsible authorities often offer no real or qualified support for the victims.

In October 2007, the first law concerning violence in the family was introduced. The notion of marital rape was new for many Greeks. Before the change of law, married women had no right to report sexual violence they suffered from their husbands; now, married and unmarried women have the same rights. A new law for the protection of minors was due to be in effect starting in January 2007. It forbids the beating of children for any reason, protecting children from abuse at the hands of educators, religious persons, or other persons with authority over the children. Teachers now are obligated to report signs of physical harm to the school director and the district attorney. The law, however, offers no protection for teachers who get involved in what is considered to be a family matter. The punishment for the aggressor is not very severe, and in many cases he or she can escape any consequences by promising never to commit an act of violence again. The main aim of the new law was to enhance public concern for and visibility of many crimes that were kept secret within families. It mainly targets cohabiting heterosexual couples, both married and unmarried, and their relatives. De facto, the implementation of the law is difficult, as specialized institutions for the victims need to be introduced and the public is still not well-informed about the law.

Abuse among homosexual couples is seldom reported, and the victims mainly have to rely on those organizations that address domestic violence within a heterosexual family. Also, minors who suffer abuse due to their homosexuality cannot expect qualified psychological advice. Greek LGBT groups confirm that many organizations do not offer real support, especially the church-based ones.

Hate Crimes

There is no law describing hate crimes and, according to the Greek statistics, no hate crimes are reported. Human rights groups report violent acts against LGBT persons, but these reports are not made public. Furthermore, Greece has no laws protecting against antigay slogans or hate speech.

OUTLOOK FOR THE 21ST CENTURY

In the 1990s, Greece enjoyed rapid economic growth and a substantial increase in living standards. In 2004, with the Olympic Games in Athens, the country had the world's attention. Even though the country is currently a modern democracy and a fully integrated member of the European Union, certain aspects of it remain conservative. The role of the family as nucleus of Greek society continues to be a strong feature of the culture. But higher costs of living in urban areas, a larger female workforce, and demographic changes are putting pressure on the traditional family model. A large influx of foreigners, tourists as well as immigrants, has forced the Greek population to become more open to new ideas. The increasing popularity of American television programs too, especially among the younger population, may lead to more openness.

The Greek Orthodox Church is still powerful and influences political decisions. An increasing number of immigrants with different religious backgrounds may weaken this position. But the events related to the 9/11 terrorist attack in the United States also caused Greeks to regard their Muslim neighbors in Turkey, Albania, and Macedonia with more suspicion. Many consider traditional values, such as religion and family, to be even more important today than in the late 1990s.

RESOURCE GUIDE

Suggested Reading

P. D. Dagtoglou, "Protection of Individual Rights," *Constitutional Law—Individual Rights—Volume I* [in Greek] (Athens-Komotini: Ant. N. Sakkoulas Publishers, 1991).

International Lesbian and Gay Association (ILGA)-Europe, "Social Exclusion of Young Lesbian, Gay, Bisexual and Transgender People (LGBT) in Europe," ILGA-Europe, April 2006, http://www.ilgaeurope.org/europe/publications/non_periodical/social_exclusion_of_young_lesbian_gay_bisexual_and_transgender_people_lgbt_in_europe_april_2006.

Venetia Kantsa, "Greece," in *Lesbian Histories and Cultures,* ed. Bonnie Zimmermann (New York: Garland, 2000).

Web Sites

AKOE, The Hellenic Homosexual Liberation Movement, http://www.geocities.com/WestHollywood/2225/eok.html/.
    First gay group in Greece. They published the LGBT magazine *Amphi,* which was widely distributed in Greece, and launched a travel guide, the *Lesbian Gay City Guide,* containing information about Athens, Thessaloniki, Mykonos, and Lesbos, in English, German, and Greek.

Greek Helsinki Monitor, http://www.greekhelsinki.gr/bhr/english/index.html/.
    The Balkan human rights Web page gives an overview of human rights groups operating in Greece and neighboring countries. The Greek Helsinki Monitor is part of

the International Helsinki Federation. It frequently reports news concerning LGBT matters.

Greek Sapphites, http://www.SapphoGR.net.

Targets Greek lesbians and LGBT-friendly Greek women. The page gets recent updates and reports news and changes in the Greek lesbian community. Information on Greek LGBT history, a selected bibliography, and a movie list are available in both Greek and English

Omofylofilia Mailing List, http://www.geocities.com/omofylofilia/.

An open mailing list about homosexuality in Greece for people who want up-to-date information about the work from affiliated LGBT organizations. Many Greek homosexual organizations and groups participate, along with organizations supporting LGBT rights in their agenda.

Organizations

SATTE (Hellenic Association of Solidarity of Transvestites and Transsexuals)
Phone/Fax: 210-9214079
E-mail: info@satte.gr

EOK (The Greek Homosexual Community)
Phone: +30 1 3410755
E-mail: eok@nyx.gr

Sympraxis (Cooperation against Homophobia)
Phone: (+30) 6999 249 000
E-mail: sympraxi.thess@yahoo.gr

OLKE
Phone: (+30) 6976550206
E-mail: info@olke.org

Athens Lesbian Group
http://geocities.com/sapphida/loa/
lesbiangroup@hotmail.com

LGBT-Corfu
http://geocities.com/lgbtCorfu/
E-mail: corfulg@yahool.com

NOTES

1. Thomas R. Martin, *An Overview of Classical Greek History from Mycenae to Alexander* (New Haven, CT: Yale University Press, 2000). Also available at http://www.perseus.tufts.edu/hopper/text?doc=Perseus%3atext%3a1999.04.0009.

2. World Health Organization (WHO), *WHO World Health Report, 2006* (Geneva: WHO), http://www.who.int/whr/2006/en/.

3. The total fertility rate of a population is the average number of children that would be born to a woman over her lifetime. It is assumed that she experiences the exact current age–specific fertility rates through her lifetime, and that she survives from birth through the end of her reproductive life. The total fertility rate is obtained by summing the single-year age-specific rates at a given time.

4. OECD, "UN Population Division, 2004," *Science and Information Technology* (Complete Edition) 2004, no. 15 (2004): 1–378.

5. OECD, "National Statistical Service of Greece, 2000," *Science and Information Technology* (Complete Edition) 2004, no. 15 (2004): 1–378.

6. OECD, "Eurostat 2000, demographic statistics," *Science and Information Technology* (Complete Edition) 2004, no. 15 (2004): 1–378.

7. OECD, "National Statistical Service of Greece, 2000; World Health Organization 2000," *Science and Information Technology* (Complete Edition) 2004, no. 15 (2004): 1–378.

8. OECD, "UN Population Division, 2005," *Science and Information Technology* (Complete Edition) 2004, no. 15 (2004): 1–378.

9. OECD, "National Statistical Service of Greece, 2006," *Science and Information Technology* (Complete Edition) 2004, no. 15 (2004): 1–378.

10. OECD, "UNESCO Institute for Statistics, Country Profile (2004)," *Science and Information Technology* (Complete Edition) 2004, no. 15 (2004): 1–378.

11. OECD, "World Bank, Information and Communications for Development 2004: Global Trends and Policies, Countries at a Glance, Greece (2004)," *Science and Information Technology* (Complete Edition) 2004, no. 15 (2004): 1–378.

12. UNDP Human Development Report 2005, "International Cooperation at a Crossroads: Aid, Trade and Insecurity in an Unequal World, Country profile, Greece," http://www.sapphogr.net/news/eg/a04/gr2004.htm.

13. Sappho, Greece, report to the Forumsisters book project of Christian lesbians in Europe, 2005, http://www.sapphogr.net/news/eg/a04/gr2004.htm

14. *The Economist*, "Country Briefings Greece," September 2007.

15. Ibid.

16. "The Greece Tourism Report," *Business Monitor International*, 2007.

17. OECD Statistics Portal, Unemployment Statistics, Standardized Employment Rates for 2007, http://www.oecd.org/dataoecd/51/30/36219429.pdf.

18. OECD, "Social Policy Division, Directorate of Employment, Labour and Social Affairs," *Country Chapter—Benefits and Wages* (Greece: OECD, 2004).

19. EOK, Greek National Gay and Lesbian Association, 2004.

20. Bruce S. Thornton, *Eros: The Myth of Ancient Greek Sexuality* (Boulder, CO: Westview Press, 1997).

21. D. S. Barrett, "The Friendship of Achilles and Patroclus," *Classical Bulletin* 57 (1981): 87–92.

22. Félix Buffière, *Eros adolescent: la pédérastie dans la Grèce antique* (Paris: Les Belles Lettres, 1980).

23. Daniel Ogden, "Homosexuality and Warfare in Ancient Greece," in *Battle in Antiquity*, ed. A. B. Lloyd (London: Duckworth, 1996), 107–68.

24. Willis Barnstone, *Sappho and the Greek Lyric Poets* (New York: Schocken, 1988).

25. A. Hantzakis, "Homosexuality in Greece," in *Homosexual Response Studies. International Report*, ed. Anthony P.M. Coxon (World Health Organization, 1992).

26. *O Pothos*, spring-summer 1995.

27. Ibid.

28. Eurobarometer 66, *Public Opinion in the European Union* (Eurobarometer, 2006).

29. See law 3500/2006—published on FEK 232A' on October 24, 2006, http://www.sapphogr.net/news/index.html.

30. Sappho, Greek Media and Press, http://www.sapphogr.net/news/eg/gr-media.html (accessed September 20, 2009).

31. Ministry of Health, *Social and Cultural Development in Greece*, scientific report Athens, 2002.

32. Malcom Brabant, "Lesbos Islanders Dispute Gay Name," BBC News Athens, May 1, 2008.

33. UNGASS Country Progress Report, Greece, 2008, http://data.unaids.org/pub/Report/2008/greece_2008_country_progress_report_en.pdf.

34. Hellenice Center for Disease Control and Prevention, Ministry of Health and Social Solidarity, *HIV/AIDS Surveillance in Greece,* mid-year report (Ministry of Health and Social Solidarity, 2005).

35. UNGASS Country Progress Report, Greece, 2008.

36. *Epidemiological Fact Sheet on HIV/AIDS and STI* (UNAIDS/WHO, 2006).

37. *Eurostat-Eurobarometer* 63 (2005), http://ec.europa.eu/public_opinion/standard_en.htm.

38. Ibid.

39. Ephesians 5:25–32.

40. General Secretariat of the National Statistical Service of Greece, Census (4), 2001.

41. Ibid.

42. Ibid.

HUNGARY

Judit Takács

OVERVIEW

Hungary is located in the middle of the Carpathian basin in Europe, between western Europe and the Balkan Peninsula. Its neighboring countries are Austria, Slovenia, Croatia, Serbia, Romania, Ukraine, and Slovakia. The land area of Hungary is 35,907 square miles, about 1 percent of the size of Europe, and with 10 million inhabitants[1] it ranks about 80th in the world by population size.[2] According to 2001 census data, only about 5 percent of the population identifies as ethnically non-Hungarian, including identification as German, Slovak, Croatian, Romanian, and Roma or gypsy, the last being the largest ethnic minority in Hungary. Almost 75 percent of the population identifies as religious: 55 percent belong to the Catholic Church and 16 percent to the Reformed Church.[3]

Historically, Hungary was a multiethnic formation: the independent Hungarian Kingdom was established in 1000 c.e. by the descendants of Finno-Ugric tribes, mixed with Turk, Germanic, Slavic, and other peoples. Most of Hungary was occupied by the Ottoman Empire from the early 16th century; this would last for the next 150 years. After the expulsion of the Turks in 1686, the Hungarian Kingdom came under the Austrian Hapsburg Empire, and in 1867 became part of the

Austro-Hungarian Monarchy. As a result of the Treaty of Trianon (1920), which marked the end of World War I, Hungary lost about 60 percent of its land and population, including about 3.2 million ethnic Hungarians. In 1910, 18.3 million people lived in the Hungarian Kingdom (not including Croatia-Slavonia, which the kingdom administered until 1918) on 282,870 square kilometers: 54.4 percent were Hungarians, 10.4 percent Germans, 10.7 percent Slovaks, 16.1 percent Romanians, 2.5 percent Ruthenians, 1.1 percent Croatians, and 2.5 percent Serbs.[4]

After World War II, Hungary was forced to become part of the Soviet sphere. The country was ruled by the Hungarian Communist Party from 1949 until the collapse of the state-socialist system in 1989. Hungary, after regaining its full sovereignty, became a member of the Council of Europe in 1990, NATO in 1999, and the European Union (EU) in 2004.

OVERVIEW OF LGBT ISSUES

Budapest, the capital of Hungary, has always been known for its thermal springs rich in sulfur, and within its bathhouse culture that has flourished for centuries, a distinct bathhouse-oriented gay culture emerged. During the second half of the 20th century, bathhouses, where certain days of the week were reserved for men only, became important social and community spaces, especially for gay men. These provided a hassle-free environment in which they could physically interact with one another without raising suspicion.

During the late 19th century, the city of Budapest provided a home for Károly Kertbeny, the coiner of the terms *homosexual* and *heterosexual*. He lived in the Rudas Thermal Bath for the last seven years of his life. Kertbeny was born in 1924. His mother tongue was German but, as he declared, "I was born in Vienna, yet I am not a Viennese, but rightfully Hungarian."[5] In 1847 he officially changed his original name, Karl Maria Benkert, to Károly Kertbeny—a name at which he arrived by transposing the two syllables of his family name. In Hungarian literary history he is considered a mediocre translator and writer. However, in LGBT history, he is remembered for his inventiveness in sexual terminology and for the theoretical case he made for homosexual emancipation; he was the author of the anonymous pamphlets published in 1869 calling for the legal emancipation of homosexuals by eliminating the Prussian penal code that criminalized same-sex sexual activities. The word *homosexuality* (*homosexualität*), created from the Greek *homo* (same) and the Latin *sexus* (sex), was first openly used in these pamphlets.[6] Kertbeny had already used the terms *homosexual* and *heterosexual* in 1868, in a private letter written to the German gay rights pioneer Karl Heinrich Ulrichs. In this letter, Kertbeny presented a surprisingly modern human rights argument:

> To prove innateness...is a dangerous double edged weapon. Let this riddle of nature be very interesting from the anthropological point of view. Legislation is not concerned whether this inclination is innate or not, legislation is only interested in the personal and social dangers associated with it....Therefore we would not win anything by proving innateness beyond a shadow of doubt. Instead we should convince our opponents—with precisely the same legal notions used by them—that they do not have anything at all to do with this inclination, be it innate or intentional, since the state does not have the right to intervene in anything that occurs between two consenting persons older than fourteen, which does not affect the public sphere, nor the rights of a third party.[7]

The new terms soon became popular, especially in psychiatric literature; they were used as early as 1886 in *Psychopatia Sexualis,* the medical-forensic study of sexual abnormalities, written by the Austrian neurologist Richard von Krafft-Ebing. Today, *homosexual* is perceived by many as a medical term, reflecting the interpretation of same-sex attraction as pathology, degeneration, or illness, while its original context, opposing paternalistic state intervention into people's private lives, has been overshadowed and often rejected as a means of medical control.

In 2002, a new tombstone was erected for Kertbeny by Hungarian gay activists, with the support of national and international LGBT organizations and individuals, in the Fiume Street Cemetery in Budapest,[8] where he was originally buried in 1882. In the same year, near Kertbeny's tombstone, the neglected joint grave of a police constable and a teacher, both men, buried in 1940 and in 1945 respectively, was discovered by accident.[9] Since the discovery of the grave, the Lambda Budapest Gay association had the couple's grave renovated, and each year during the annual LGBT festival a memorial ceremony is organized at both Kertbeny's and the same-sex couple's gravesites. These activities can be interpreted as being part of an LGBT history-making project, an attempt by the Hungarian LGBT people to discover and regain their past.

During the second half of the 20th century, under the rule of the Communist Party, LGBT issues in Hungary were taboo, though consensual sexual activity between same-sex adults had been decriminalized in 1961. The elimination of legal discrimination against LGBT people was accelerated only in the process of preparing to join the EU: in 2002 the difference in age of consent for heterosexual and homosexual relationships was lifted, and in 2003 the Act on Equal Treatment and the Promotion of Equal Opportunities were introduced, protecting both sexual orientation and gender identity. Despite these gains, the social exclusion of LGBT people, homophobia, and transphobia are still visible in many forms in Hungary, providing LGBT organizations and activists with many goals to keep working toward.

EDUCATION

Under the state-socialist system, all schools, from primary grades to higher education, were run by the state, and most school curricula were imbued with the officially prescribed Marxist-Leninist ideology. Since the political system began to change in 1989, private schools, especially higher education institutions, were established or reestablished by private companies and business actors, as well as churches. Between 1990 and 2000, the number of students enrolled in higher education institutions increased from 100,000 to 300,000, and the rate of full-time students in the 18 to 22 age group rose to about 20 percent.[10] In 2005 public education spending was less than 6 percent of the gross domestic product (GDP) and 11 percent of total government expenditure.[11]

Today, a three-level structure, comprised of the National Core Curriculum, the Frame Curricula, and local curricula at the institutional level, provide a framework for teachers to develop syllabi.[12] Based on a central definition of each discipline, the schools and the teaching staff can define and adopt local curricula and syllabi for each class and each subject, but LGBT issues are typically absent or misrepresented in Hungarian schools.

According to a recent survey, half of Hungarian LGBT respondents suffered from discrimination and prejudice in school, especially in secondary school;

90 percent of these cases were instigated by other students, and half of the cases by teachers. Moreover, one-third of the respondents reported a negative or totally missing representation of LGBT issues in school.[13]

With the support of the Phare democracy micro-projects program of the European Union, in 2000 the Labrisz Lesbian Association introduced the Getting to Know Gays and Lesbians educational program for secondary school students and teachers. The main aim of this program is to create a safe and unbiased environment in schools for all students, to help students learn to respect other, to increase teachers' awareness that their students might be gay or lesbian, and to give them ways to help these students. In 2003, the program was expanded to offer a training program on LGBT issues for prospective teachers, psychologists, and social workers. Developing a manual for teachers on LGBT issues was also part of this project.[14]

In 2003, the Károli Gáspár University of the Hungarian Reformed Church, after expelling an openly homosexual student, stated on its homepage that persons propagating and living homosexual lifestyles cannot participate in the church's pastoral and theological teacher training programs. In 2004, the Háttér Support Society for LGBT people in Hungary initiated legal action against the university because of the mistreatment of the homosexual student, applying the *actio popularis* clause of the Equal Treatment Act that had just come into effect that year; this allowed nongovernmental organizations (NGOs) to start cases on behalf of individuals covered by one of the protected categories of the Equal Treatment Act. Though the case was rejected by the court on the grounds of freedom of expression and church autonomy, it was implicitly acknowledged that equal treatment legislation also applies to universities maintained by a church and financially supported by the state.

EMPLOYMENT AND ECONOMICS

After the collapse of the state-socialist system in 1989, dramatic social and economic changes took place in Hungary. Following the one-party system, political pluralism and a market economy had to be created by introducing democratic institutions and constitutional reforms on the one hand, and by privatizing state enterprises and developing the private business sphere (with the influx of foreign capital) on the other. As a result of these structural changes, including the loss of the protected Soviet market, the Hungarian economy (as well as the economies of other postsocialist countries) fell into a deep crisis in the early 1990s. Strong recovery started from the mid-1990s, and the Hungarian GDP reached the 1989 level again by 2000.[15] From 2001 onward, unsustainable fiscal policies have led to a new economic downturn, and progress toward a more developed economy has slowed. One of the major economic problems is the especially low employment rate of the population over age 55, a consequence of the pension system and the health of the population. Since the mid-1990s the Hungarian economy has maintained its dual character: besides the highly competitive, export-oriented manufacturing sector, domestic small and microenterprises suffer from a desperate lack of financial and human resources. In 2006, the rate of unemployment in the economically active Hungarian population between ages 15 and 64 was 7.5 percent; while economic growth in Hungary was among the lowest, the inflation rate was among the highest in the European Union.[16] In 2007, Hungarian economic competitiveness reached 57.6 percent of that of the United States,[17] and was ranked 47th out of 131 countries.[18]

According to a recent survey, more than one-third of Hungarian LGBT respondents had suffered from discrimination and prejudice in the workplace.[19] Most people are afraid to come out as LGBT at their work. Even though equal treatment legislation is in place, requiring public sector employers and businesses with more than 50 employees to develop equal opportunity strategies, LGBT people are not listed among the main target groups. Equal treatment practices are still very rare in Hungary.

SOCIAL/GOVERNMENT PROGRAMS

There is no public funding provided by the state or local governments for any social programs specifically targeting LGBT people. However, a few smaller-scale social health programs have attempted to reach out to at least certain segments of the Hungarian LGBT community, including an AIDS prevention program for gay men in the countryside and a condom machine program for gay bars in Budapest, both implemented by the Háttér Support Society for LGBT People in Hungary and sponsored by the Ministry of Health.

There are two sources of support for civic organizations, including officially registered LGBT organizations. Since the introduction of the 1 Percent Act in 1996, taxpayers can allocate 1 percent of their income tax to a nongovernmental organization of their choice. In 2003, the National Civic Fund was established, which annually announces calls for applications to receive operating grants for NGOs. However, these sources of public support cannot provide a secure background for the functioning of the Hungarian LGBT social and cultural infrastructure.

SEXUALITY/SEXUAL PRACTICES

There has only been limited research on sexual behavior in Hungary, and there is hardly any reliable information available on the sexual practices of Hungarian LGBT people. However, changes in social and cultural norms associated with the rapid transitions of the 1990s have resulted in people starting sexual activity at younger ages, and also an increase in the number of sexual partners, especially among younger age cohorts. According to data from a 2004 national survey of 8,000 Hungarian youths, 54 percent of young people aged 15 to 19 were sexually experienced, as were 93 percent of young people ages 20 to 24. The average age for having a first sexual experience was 17.[20]

During the 1990s, the sexual conservatism of the state-socialist era was replaced by oversexualized media representations and marketing projects, and a flourishing pornography industry started to develop in Hungary. In 1993, individual prostitution was decriminalized and legally interpreted as a petty offense. Since 1999, prostitution has been legalized and considered a form of individual entrepreneurship, but methods of profiting from another's prostitution, such as pimping or running a brothel, are criminalized. In 2000 an association was founded for protecting the interests of Hungarian prostitutes; since 2002 its membership has also included homosexual and transsexual sex service providers.

FAMILY

Until the early 1990s, the concept of family was closely associated with marriage and childbearing, ideally with a married couple raising two children. However, decreasing marriage and fertility rates, marrying at a later age, rising divorce rates, and increasing rates of childless women reflect changes in individual and family lifestyles. Between 1980 and 2004 the total fertility rate decreased from 1.92 to 1.28 in Hungary, while the total divorce rate increased from 29 percent to 42 percent. The amount of childless women ages 15 to 49 increased from 28 percent to 39.6 percent, and the average age of first marriage increased from 22 to 26.5 years for women and from 24.5 to 29 years for men.[21] In 2005, 11.5 percent of the Hungarian population lived in single-person households.[22]

References to these statistics, along with the reality of Hungary's aging population, are regularly used in conservative political discourse as evidence of the death of the nation. Conservatives are calling for a moral revival and the return of the nuclear family. Same-sex families are unimaginable in this context, even though LGBT activists often argue otherwise.

At present, there are no legal institutions allowing same-sex marriage, joint adoption of children by same-sex couples, or second-parent adoption (i.e., adoption of the biological or adoptive child of one's partner). Adoption by LGBT individuals is legal, but national adoption agencies often give preference to married couples. Before 2006, artificial insemination was legally available only for women who were married or cohabiting with a man. Since 1996, single women have been allowed to apply, but only if natural reproduction is improbable because of the woman's age or in the case of medically proven infertility.

For transsexual people, one precondition of an official sex change is being single or divorced, in order to avoid the transformation of an originally heterosexual marriage into a same-sex marriage. In the new Hungarian civil code to be introduced in 2009, a sex change will automatically lead to the dissolution of an existing marriage.

COMMUNITY

While the first homosexual organization, the Homeros Lambda, was established in 1988, the sociocultural infrastructure for LGBT people is still not very well developed in Hungary. Even though there is an increasing number of formally and informally organized groups representing LGBT interests, the number of activists, LGBT social and cultural venues, and LGBT events remains limited. The officially registered LGBT organizations include the Háttér Support Society for LGBT People, which maintains a help line, legal aid service, and several AIDS prevention and other outreach programs; the Labrisz Lesbian Association; the Lambda Budapest Gay Association, which has published the *Mások* gay magazine since 1989; the Szimpozion Association for young LGBT people; the Atlasz LGBT Sport Association; the DAMKÖR Gay Association in southern Hungary; and the Rainbow Mission Foundation, organizing the annual LGBT cultural festivals in Budapest.

All Hungarian LGBT NGOs struggle for survival with the help of volunteers, lacking any kind of regular state support. Most LGBT-related events take place in Budapest, but there are regional LGBT community groups, bars, and parties in several other locales, mainly in bigger cities such as Debrecen, Nyíregyháza, Pécs, Szeged, and Székesfehérvár.

HEALTH

In 2004, Hungary spent 7.9 percent of its GDP on health care. Of the total expenditure on health, 71.6 percent was financed from public sources[23] consisting of revenues from general and local taxation, and more importantly from contributions to the social health insurance scheme, which since its establishment in 1990 has been operating nationwide as a single fund, the Health Insurance Fund. The social health insurance scheme provides nearly universal coverage and a comprehensive benefit package with few exclusions and little or no co-payment except for pharmaceuticals, medical aids, and prostheses. The revenue of the Health Insurance Fund is derived mainly from the health insurance contribution, a proportional payroll tax paid partly by employers and partly by employees. Voluntary health insurance also exists in Hungary, but it is not a significant feature of the health care system. Health care delivery is based on the constitutional obligation of the state to make health services available for all resident citizens.[24]

The collapse of the state-socialist regime was characterized by a marked decline in health status in Hungary. Between 1960 and 2000, the life expectancy increased by only 3.5 years in Hungary, compared to 9 years in the average of the OECD (Organisation for Economic Co-operation and Development) countries. Life expectancy in Hungary is still among the lowest in Europe. The main causes of premature death include cardiovascular disease, malignant tumors, and digestive disorders, as well as external causes, such as suicide; infectious disease seems to be less of a problem, as the incidence of and mortality from most childhood infectious diseases, viral hepatitis, tuberculosis and AIDS continue to occur less frequently in Hungary than in other countries of the central eastern European region.[25]

AIDS is not considered a major health concern in Hungary. The first Hungarian HIV infection was identified in 1985. By the end of 2007, 1,453 HIV infections were officially registered, although the true number is believed to be at least three times higher. In Hungary, the main risk factors for HIV infection are sex between men and unprotected heterosexual sex, while the number of infections caused by intravenous drug use remains very low.[26] There are several anonymous HIV testing facilities in Hungary. However, if a person gets a positive result, his or her identity must be disclosed in order for him or her to receive treatment. All HIV/AIDS-related medical costs are covered by social health insurance.

Hungary's incidence of gonorrhea decreased from 46.9 cases per 100,000 people in 1990 to 8.9 in 2003. Syphilis data show a different tendency: while new syphilis cases steadily decreased from the 1970s until 1990, a sharp increase occurred between 1990 and 2002. In 2002, more than half of new syphilis infections affected people ages 25 to 44, with 21 percent among those under age 24.[27]

Specific health needs of LGBT people are not recognized in Hungary. Safe sex campaigns for LGBT audiences are only conducted by LGBT organizations. According to a recent national survey, 28 percent of 1,122 LGBT respondents encountered discriminative treatment in the health care system, including the rejection of blood donations from people identifying as homosexual based on the alleged risk of HIV infection. Homophobic and transphobic reactions on the part of medical personnel were also common.[28]

Before the 1990s, the Hungarian situation was characterized by the total lack of a health care system for transsexuals. In the early 1990s, when the first sex reassignment surgeries (SRS) took place, the rule was that in order for a person to change his or her birth certificate and other official documents, he or she should have undergone irreversible changes. This unfair arrangement, requiring patients to go through a medical process without any help or recognition, was abandoned because of the high rate of unsuccessful surgeries. Current practice, since 2004, leaves surgery as an option for which the state takes no responsibility. Today, SRS is not a precondition of official sex change, which basically requires permission from the Ministry of Health based on two psychiatrists' expert opinions both stating that it is a case of transsexualism. For a few years, social health insurance could cover, in theory, at least some of the SRS costs of a person, but from 2007 a government decree referred the treatment of transsexuals to private health care; 90 percent of the costs to be paid by the individuals themselves.

POLITICS AND LAW

Criminalization

The medieval practice, death penalty for sodomy, ceased to exist in Hungary following a decree of the Austrian emperor and Hungarian king, Joseph II, in 1787. At the end of the 19th century there was no punishment defined for sodomy or perversion against nature, as it was referred to by the legal terminology used for centuries in the Hungarian penal code, and women could not be prosecuted for this kind of crime at all. The lack of actual penalization was explained by an 18th-century source, which noted that "the Hungarian people have attained virtue and chastity to such a degree that there was no need for a special law like this"; the penalty for acts of sodomy had to depend on the wisdom of the judge.[29]

Between 1878 and 1961, three forms of perversion against nature were distinguished: sex with an animal, sex with a same-sex partner, and any sex act deemed unnatural. Consensual same-sex relationships were considered to be milder crimes and punishable with a maximum of one year of imprisonment, while coerced sodomy was punishable with up to five years of imprisonment.[30]

In 1961, homosexuality was decriminalized;[31] general prosecution of perversion against nature ceased, but different ages of consent were introduced: 14 for heterosexual and 20 for homosexual relationships, and men as well as women could be prosecuted. While perversion against nature with an animal was no longer penalized, two special clauses were introduced: one penalized sodomy conducted in a scandalous manner—that is, causing a public scandal—punishable by three years of imprisonment (the same as for having sex with a same-sex partner younger than 20). The second clause stated that coerced perversion against nature is only applicable if it is committed outside marriage (followed by a clause stating that, in the case of rape, if the perpetrator and the victim get married before the first judgment, the punishment can be mitigated). According to the ministerial explanation of the act, which cited medical arguments, homosexuality was considered a biological phenomenon that could not be handled legally as crime. In addition, it emphasized that the criminalization of homosexuality is dangerous in that it could provide grounds for blackmail.

In 1978, the age of consent for homosexual relationships was lowered from 20 to 18.[32] In 2002, the Hungarian Constitutional Court found this legislation to be unconstitutional and ordered the equalization of the age of consent for same-sex and different-sex partners, which is 14 years of age today.

Antidiscrimination Statutes

In a broad sense, the development of sexual orientation–related antidiscrimination and equal treatment legislation can be traced back to 1989, when article 70/A on the prohibition of discrimination became part of the new Hungarian constitution. Before the introduction of the law on equal treatment and the promotion of equal opportunities in 2003,[33] Hungary already had national laws prohibiting discrimination, such as in the constitution, the labor code, the Act on Public Education, and the Act on Public Health; however, only the last explicitly prohibited sexual orientation–based discrimination. The first Hungarian law explicitly recognizing the necessity of equal treatment on the basis of sexual orientation was the Act on Public Health, introduced in 1997.[34] In all other cases, the question of whether sexual orientation should be included under the heading "any other grounds whatsoever," usually ending the list of discrimination based on "race, color, gender, language, religion, political or other opinion, national or social origin, financial situation, and birth," was a matter for interpretation.

The first general antidiscrimination draft bill, the Hungarian Act on Equal Treatment and the Promotion of Equal Opportunities, was submitted to the Hungarian parliament in April 2001 and included the prohibition of discrimination based on sexual orientation and clear references to the 2000/43 Racial Equality Directive as well as the 2000/78 Employment Equality Directive of the European Union. By the time the draft bill reached parliamentary discussion at the end of 2003, besides the protected categories listed in the employment directive—including race, skin color, ethnicity, language, disability, state of health, religion, political or other views, gender, sexual orientation, age, social origin, circumstances of wealth and birth, and other situations—additional categories, such as family status, motherhood (pregnancy) or fatherhood, gender identity, part-time or limited period employment status, and membership of interest representing bodies, were inserted into the list of protected categories. The bill passed in December 2003 and came into force in January 2004. The Hungarian Equal Treatment Authority, which was stipulated in the act, started to function in 2005.

The Hungarian Act on Equal Treatment and the Promotion of Equal Opportunities was the first national equal treatment legislation in the world that included gender identity, specifically providing antidiscrimination protection for transgender and transsexual people. Another important feature of the act was the possibility of initiating *actio popularis,* providing societal bodies and special interest groups with the opportunity to start legal action without the direct involvement of victims.

Marriage

In 1995, in the constitutional examination of marriage between persons of the same sex, the Hungarian constitutional court denied that the definition of marriage as a communion of a man and a woman can be considered discrimination infringing on the constitution. At the same time, it was also stated that a lasting communion of two persons could constitute such values that they were entitled to legal recognition of their communion based on a fair recognition of the personal dignity of the involved persons irrespective of their sex. Thus, the parliament was ordered to make the changes necessary to recognize same-sex partnerships by March 1996. Since 1996, a legal framework, similar to common-law marriage, exists for same-sex partners who live together, but they must make extra efforts, typically in the form of private legal contracts, if they want to establish a level of family security similar to that inherently enjoyed by married couples. In January 2009 a new legal institution—registered partnership for same-sex and different-sex couples—would have come into effect in Hungary, providing rights similar to marriage but excluding joint adoption of children and the automatic insertion of a partner's family name. However, on December 15, 2008, the Hungarian Constitutional Court found the Act CLXXXIV of 2007 on Registered Partnership to be unconstitutional, arguing that registered partnership for different sex couples would duplicate the institution of marriage, and would thus contradict the special protection of marriage supposedly enshrined in the Hungarian Constitution. Significantly, the Court confirmed that the right of same-sex couples to legal recognition and protection follows from the constitutional principle of human dignity, and the related rights to self-determination and freedom of action. A new bill on registered partnership was submitted to the Parliament in early 2009 and it was passed on April 20, 2009. The Act XXIX of 2009 on Registered Partnership and Related Legislation and on the Amendment of Other Statutes to Facilitate the Proof of Cohabitation came into operation on July 1, 2009, and retains much of the content of the previous bill with one exception: the institution of registered partnership is only available to same-sex couples.

Speech and Association

The right to free speech and association is guaranteed by the Constitution of the Republic of Hungary. Perhaps because of Hungary's state-socialist past, freedom of expression has been held in such high regard that this has prevented efforts to enact hate speech legislation. Hate crimes do exist as a criminal category, but only if the victim is a member of an ethnic or religious minority. A draft bill providing protection on the basis of other grounds, including sexual orientation, was submitted in late 2007.

Transsexuals

There is no consistent legal framework dealing with gender transition in Hungary. Practice tends to abandon medical requirements for complete official gender transition, being relatively easy and costless to achieve, and puts transsexual individuals in a personal status where they have equal rights and responsibilities with people with no experience of gender transition. The lack of legal arrangements regarding accountability, however, can raise concern for the consistency of this practice in the future.

RELIGION AND SPIRITUALITY

Major Christian churches in Hungary follow the "hate the sin but love the sinner" policy, at least in theory. Many LGBT people are religious, but far fewer are active members of a church community. According to the findings of national LGBT social exclusion research conducted in 2007, of 1,122 respondents one-third identified as religious, and 28 percent had experienced prejudice and discrimination within religious communities.[35]

VIOLENCE

As instances of antigay violence and gay bashing are rarely recorded, there is little data on this phenomenon. However, the 2007 July Pride march was marred by openly antigay violent attacks—for the first time in the 12-year history of Hungarian LGBT festivals. Given that antigay violence is typically socially invisible, the violence seen during and after the pride celebration was a great shock.

OUTLOOK FOR THE 21ST CENTURY

The main legal goals to achieve in Hungary in the 21st century are same-sex marriage and joint adoption of children by same-sex partners. However, legal emancipation is only one part of challenging the social heteronormativity still dominating everyday life. In the long run, cultural change can be as effective as legislation. Various aspects of inequality, like discrimination on multiple grounds, also have to be taken into account when raising awareness and working for an inclusive society.

RESOURCE GUIDE

Suggested Reading

Anna Borgos, "Getting to Know Gays and Lesbians in Hungary: Lessons from a Gender-Informed Educational Program," in *Multiple Marginalities: An Intercultural Dialogue on Gender in Education,* ed. Justyna Sempruch, Katharina Willems, and Laura Shook (Königstein/Taunus, Hungary: Ulrike Helmer Verlag, 2007).

Lilla Farkas, "Nice on Paper: The Aborted Liberalisation of Gay Rights in Hungary," in *Legal Recognition of Same-Sex Partnerships: A Study of National, European, and International Law,* ed. R. Wintemute and M. Andenaes (Oxford: Hart Publishing, 2001).

R. Kuhar and J. Takács, eds., *Beyond the Pink Curtain: Everyday Life of LGBT People in Eastern Europe* (Ljubljana, Slovenia: Mirovni Institute, 2007).

Scott Long, "Gay and Lesbian Movements in Eastern Europe: Romania, Hungary, and the Czech Republic," in *The Global Emergence of Gay and Lesbian Politics: National Imprints of a Worldwide Movement,* ed. Barry D. Adam, Jan Willem Duyvendak, and André Krouwel (Philadelphia: Temple University Press, 1999).

Judit Takács, "The Double Life of Kertbeny," in *Past and Present of Radical Sexual Politics,* ed. G. Hekma (Amsterdam: UvA—Mosse Foundation, 2004).

Judit Takács, *How to Put Equality into Practice? Anti-discrimination and Equal Treatment Policymaking and LGBT People* (Budapest: New Mandate, 2007).

Judit Takács, "The Influence of European Institutions on the Hungarian Legislation Regarding LGBT Rights," in *The Gays' and Lesbians' Rights in an Enlarged European Union,* ed. A. Weyembergh and S. Carstocea (Brussels: Éditions de l'Université de Bruxelles, 2006).

Renáta Uitz, "Hungary: Mixed Prospects for the Constitutionalization of Gay Rights," *International Journal of Constitutional Law* 2, no. 4 (2004): 705–15.

Films/Videos

A rózsaszín görény [*The Pink Skunk*] (50 min.; 2003). Directed by Katrin Kremmler. Budapesti Leszbikus Filmbizottság. The first feature film by the Budapest Lesbian Film Committee, a crime parody on a lesbian detective (and her skunk) investigating the disappearance of a female politician.

Egymásra nézve [*Another Way*] (102 min.; 1982). Directed by Károly Makk. Mafilm Dialóg Filmstúdió. The first Hungarian film that referred to the events of 1956 as a revolution (not as a counter-revolution as it was officially regarded during state-socialism), thus being groundbreaking in its portrayal of both sexual and political dissidence. The central theme is the love between two women, Éva and the married Lívia, leading to a disastrous ending in the aftermath of 1956. Polish actress Jankowska-Cieslak, playing Éva's character, won the best actress award at the Cannes Film Festival in 1982.

Eklektika Tánciskola [*Eklektika Dancing School*] (17 min.; 2004). Directed by Mária Takács. Budapesti Leszbikus Filmbizottság. Documentary on the first LGBT classical dancing school, which was opened in 2003 in the backroom of a Budapest café.

Halállal lakoljanak? [*Paying with their Lives?*] (55 min.; 2002). Directed by Bernadett Frivaldszky. Fórum Film Alapítvány. Documentary on the relationship between homosexuality and Christianity as seen by a former theology student.

Mielőtt befejezi röptét a denevér [*Ere the Bat has Flown his Flight*] (91 min.; 1989). Directed by Péter Tímár. Mafilm. Received a CICAE Award from the Berlin International Film Festival in 1989. In the 1980s in Budapest, a single mother, Teréz, falls for a policeman, László, who becomes obsessed with her teenage son, Róbert.

Redl ezredes [*Colonel Redl*] (144 min.; 1984). Directed by István Szabó. Jadran Film. A fictional film inspired by John Osborne's play, *A Patriot for Me,* about the rise and the fall of Alfred Redl, the high-ranking homosexual intelligence officer. For this film István Szabó, the Oscar winning director of *Mephisto* (1981), was nominated for an Oscar and received the Jury Prize at the Cannes Film Festival, as well as a German Film Award in Gold in 1985, and a BAFTA Film Award in 1986.

The Kertbeny Story (10 min.; 2005). Produced by Douglas Conrad, SF CA. Documentary how Károly Kertbeny, who coined the words homosexual and heterosexual, got a new tombstone in 2002 in the Budapest cemetery where he was buried in 1882.

Zarándoklat a Kecskerúzs földjére [*Pilgrimage to the Land of the Goat Rouge*] (35 min.; 2005). Directed by Mária Takács. Budapesti Leszbikus Filmbizottság. Documentary on a Hungarian village, Szatina, where a small lesbian community was formed in the early 1990s.

Web Sites

Annual Hungarian LGBT Festival homepage, http://www.budapestpride.hu.
Budapest Gay Guide, http://www.navegre.hu/index.php?m=guide.
Gay.hu, http://www.gay.hu.
    Forum for gay men.
GayRádió.hu, http://www.gayradio.hu.
Hiv+.hu, http://www.hivpozitiv.hu/.
    Practical information on being HIV positive by people who are HIV positive.
HIV-pozitívak hozzátartozóinak baráti köre, http://www.pozitivtars.tvn.hu.
    Forum for relatives of HIV-positive people.
Magyarországi Meleg Apák, http://www.melegapa.eletmod.hu.
    Forum for gay fathers.
Mások gay magazine online, http://www.masok.hu.
    Meleg vagyok—Coming out campaign.
Műegyetem Meleg Kör, http://www.bbme.uw.hu.
    Gay group of the Budapest Technical University.
Pride.hu, http://www.pride.hu.
    LGBT news portal, forum for LGBT people.
SHIVAMANTRA, http://shivamantra.freeblog.hu/.
    "Being HIV-positive complicates your life, but it is not the end of the world"—Personal blog and counseling for HIV-positive people.

TranSexual Online, http://tsonline.uw.hu/.
    Forum for gay men.
Tranny Baráti Kör, http://tranny.tuti.hu.
    Forum for transvestites.
http://melegvagyok.hu/.

Organizations

Atlasz LMBT Sportegyesület (Atlasz LGBT Sport Association), http://www.atlaszsport.hu.
    Officially registered in 2004. The association has 10 sections: running, rock climbing, soccer, cycling, handball, basketball, dance, badminton, hiking, and swimming.
Budapest Lambda Meleg Baráti Társaság (Budapest Lambda Gay Association), http://www.masok.hu.
    Founded in 1991, this is the oldest Hungarian gay organization that is still functioning. Their main activity has been to publish the monthly gay magazine *Mások,* the first unofficial issue of which came out in 1989.
Dél-Alföldi Meleg Baráti Kör (DAMKÖR Gay Association), http://www.tar.hu/damkor.
    First one of its kind functioning outside the capital of Hungary. It was established in 1999 in Szeged.
Háttér Társaság a Melegekért (Háttér Support Society for LGBT People), http://www.hatter.hu.
    Established in 1995, this group has the largest number of members and most widespread activity in the country. From 1996, information, personal, and telephone counseling services have been operating. In 2000, the Háttér legal aid program was initiated.
Labrisz Leszbikus Egyesület (Labrisz Lesbian Association), http://www.labrisz.hu.
    The only Hungarian lesbian organization was founded officially in 1999 but the core of the organization existed from 1996. Their main goal is to organize community-building activities and increase the social visibility of lesbian and bisexual women in Hungary.
Magyar LMBT Szövetség (Hungarian LGBT Association), http://www.lmbtszovetseg.hu.
    Founded in January 2009, this is the largest Hungarian LGBT umbrella organization with nine member organizations.
PATENT Egyesület (Association of People Challenging Patriarchy), http://patent.org.hu.
    Established in 2006 with the main aim to raise public awareness on violence against women and children, but also deals with sexual minority issues.
PLUSS Magyarországi HIV-pozitívokat Segítő Egyesület (Association for Supporting HIV-positive People in Hungary), http://www.pluss-hiv.hu.
    Established by HIV-positive people in 1989 to represent the interests of people infected with HIV in Hungary. Their goals also include awareness-raising on HIV infection and HIV/AIDS prevention issues.
Szimpozion (Szimpozion Society of Friends, Cultural, Educational and Leisure Time Organization of Gay, Lesbian, Bisexual and Transgender People), http://www.szimpozion.hu.
    Founded in 2002, it organizes the biweekly meetings of the Pocok Club, a youth club with a cultural orientation. In 2006 they started the *Bújj elő!* (Come out!) campaign by launching the www.melegvagyok.hu ('meleg vagyok' = I am gay) internet portal.
Szivárvány Misszió Alapítvány (Rainbow Mission Foundation), E-mail: kurator@gay.hu.
    Established by the Háttér Support Society for LGBT People, the Labrisz Lesbian Association, and the Lambda Budapest Gay Association in 2001 with the primary aim of organizing the events of the annual LGBT Cultural Festival and the Gay Pride Day.

NOTES

1. *Statisztikai tükör* [*Statistical mirror*], July 26, 2007, http://portal.ksh.hu/pls/ksh/docs/hun/xftp/gyor/jel/jel307051.pdf (accessed December 8, 2007).

2. U.S. Census Bureau, "Countries and Areas Ranked by Population: 2007," U.S. Census Bureau, International Data Base, http://www.census.gov/ipc/www/idb/idbr 200707.html and http://www.census.gov/cgi-bin/ipc/idbrank.pl (accessed December 8, 2007).

3. Népszámlálás 2001—Központi Statisztikai Hivatal. Összefoglalás és módszertani megjegyzések [Census 2001—Hungarian Central Statistical Office. Conclusion and methodological notes], http://www.nepszamlalas.hu/hun/kotetek/kotetek.html, http://www.nepszamlalas.hu/hun/kotetek/04/04_modsz.pdf, http://www.nepszamlalas.hu/hun/kotetek/05/tables/load1.html (accessed December 8, 2007).

4. I. Romsics, *Magyarország története a XX. században [History of Hungary in the 20th century]* (Budapest: Osiris, 2001).

5. K. Kertbeny, Kertbeny ismeretlenhez, Országos Széchenyi Könyvtár, Levelestár [Kertbeny's letter to an unknown person], 1880. Original manuscript in the Manuscripts Archive of the National Széchenyi Library, Budapest.

6. M. Herzer, "Kertbeny and the Nameless Love," *Journal of Homosexuality* 12, no. 1 (1986): 1–25; J. C. Féray and M. Herzer, "Homosexual Studies and Politics in the 19th Century: Karl Maria Kertbeny," *Journal of Homosexuality* 19, no. 1 (1990): 23–47.

7. K. Kertbeny, Levéltöredék. Autobiographiai jegyzetek. [Letter sketch. Autobiographical notes], 1868. Original manuscript to be found in the Manuscript Archive of the National Széchenyi Library. Tranlated by J. Takács.

8. "Fiumei Úti Sírkert—34. Parcella" [Fiume Road Cemetery, Plot No. 34], http://www.btirt.hu/terkep/fiumei.gif (accessed December 22, 2007).

9. *Mások*, "Két ismeretlen úr emlékére" ["In Memory of Two Unknown Men"], October 2002, http://www.masok.hu/cikk2.php?sid=104 (accessed December 8, 2007); *Mások*, "Meleg urak száz éve" ["Gay Men a Hundred Years Ago"], December 2004, http://www.masok.hu/cikk2.php?sid=715 (accessed December 8, 2007).

10. Romsics, *Magyarország története a XX. században.*

11. Organisation for Economic Co-operation and Development (OECD), "Education At a Glance 2007," http://www.oecd.org/document/30/0,3343,en_2649_3926329 4_39251550_1_1_1_1,00.html (accessed December 22, 2007).

12. Ministry of Education, "Education in Hungary," http://www.okm.gov.hu/main.php?folderID=68&articleID=454&ctag=articlelist&iid=1 (accessed December 13, 2007).

13. J. Takács, L. Mocsonaki, and T. P. Tóth, *A leszbikus, meleg, biszexuális és transznemű (LMBT) emberek társadalmi kirekesztettsége Magyarországon [Social Exclusion of LGBT People in Hungary]* (Budapest: MTA SZKI, 2007), http://www.socio.mta.hu/kutatasok/LMBT-kirekesztes-2007.pdf (accessed January 6, 2008).

14. B. Sándor, ed., *Már nem tabu. Kézikönyv tanároknak a leszbikusokról, melegekről, biszexuálisokról és transzneműekről [Not a Taboo Anymore: A Manual for Teachers on Lesbians, Gays, Bisexuals and Transgenders]* (Budapest: Labrisz Leszbikus Egyesület, 2002).

15. Romsics, *Magyarország története a XX. században.*

16. *Economic Trends in Eastern Europe* 16, no.3 (2007); KOPINT-TÁRKI Economic Research Limited, Budapest, November 2007.

17. World Competitiveness Scoreboard 2007, http://www.imd.ch/research/publications/wcy/upload/scoreboard.pdf (accessed December 8, 2007).

18. Global Competitiveness Index rankings and 2006–2007 comparisons, http://www.weforum.org/pdf/Global_Competitiveness_Reports/Reports/gcr_2007/gcr2007_rankings.pdf (accessed December 8, 2007).

19. Takács, Mocsonaki, and Tóth, *A leszbikus, meleg, biszexuális és transznemű (LMBT) emberek társadalmi kirekesztettsége Magyarországon.*

20. B. Bauer and A. Szabó, *Ifjúság 2004—Gyorsjelentés* [*Youth 2004—Report*] (Budapest: Mobilitas, 2004), 66–68.

21. E. Bukodi, H. J. Mészárosné, K. Polónyi, and A. Tallér, *Women and Men in Hungary, 2004* (Budapest: Ministry of Youth, Family, Social Affairs and Equal Opportunities—Hungarian Central Statistical Office, 2005).

22. Központi Statisztikai Hivatal [Hungarian Central Statistical Office], "A háztartások a háztartástagok száma szerint, 1960–2005" [Households by Number of Household Members, 1960–2005], http://www.mikrocenzus.hu/mc2005_hun/kotetek/02/tables/prnt1_3_2.html (accessed December 8, 2007).

23. World Health Organization (WHO), "World Health Statistics 2007," http://www.who.int/whosis/whostat2007.pdf (accessed December 22, 2007).

24. P. Gaál, *Health care systems in transition: Hungary* (Copenhagen: WHO Regional Office for Europe on behalf of the European Observatory on Health Systems and Policies, 2004), http://www.euro.who.int/Document/E84926.pdf (accessed January 7, 2007).

25. Ibid.

26. Országos Epidemológiai Központ [National Epidemiological Centre] (Epinfo 2007), 46, 480–83.

27. Központi Statisztikai Hivatal [Hungarian Central Statistical Office], *Egészségügyi Statisztikai Évkönyv* [*Health Statistics Yearbook*] (Budapest: KSH, 2004).

28. Takács, Mocsonaki, and Tóth, *A leszbikus, meleg, biszexuális és transznemű (LMBT) emberek társadalmi kirekesztettsége Magyarországon.*

29. Bodo's *Jurisprudentia criminalis* of 1751 is quoted in T. Pauler, *Büntetőjogtan I* [*Criminal Law Studies I*] (1865), Pest. 110.

30. Act 5 of 1878 (Hungarian Penal Code).

31. Act 5 of 1961 (Hungarian Penal Code).

32. Act 4 of 1978 (Hungarian Penal Code).

33. Act 125 of 2003 (Hungarian Penal Code).

34. Act 54 of 1997 (Hungarian Penal Code).

35. Takács, Mocsonaki, and Tóth, *A leszbikus, meleg, biszexuális és transznemű (LMBT) emberek társadalmi kirekesztettsége Magyarországon.*

IRELAND

Ed Madden

OVERVIEW

Lying in the North Atlantic just west of Great Britain, the island of Ireland is part of western Europe. It covers an area of 32,599 square miles. Though traditionally divided into four provinces (Connacht, Leinster, Munster, and Ulster), the island is now politically divided between the Republic of Ireland, an independent country and a member of the European Union (EU), and Northern Ireland, which is part of the United Kingdom. With 26 counties (including three that were traditionally part of the northern province of Ulster), the Republic of Ireland includes most of the island; six counties of Ulster comprise Northern Ireland. The population of the island is about 6 million, with just over 4 million in the Republic and almost 2 million in Northern Ireland.[1]

Since Northern Ireland is governed, to a great extent, by the laws of Great Britain, the Republic of Ireland is focused on here.

Modern Ireland, as a nation, finds its roots in two profound cultural and historical movements: Christianity and colonialism. Usually linked to St. Patrick's arrival in Ireland in 432 C.E., Christianity developed over the next several centuries in Ireland into an ethno-political sectarianism—as religion became part of the long struggle against British colonial occupation. During the Middle Ages, Ireland saw a flowering of monastic education and culture, which was cut short in part by the Viking raids that began in the early ninth century. Beginning in 1169, Ireland experienced the growing influence of Norman and then English invaders, marked by violent military campaigns and the

immigration of settlers from Scotland and England to English plantations. Through the 17th and 18th centuries, a British-aligned Protestant class solidified its political and economic power, and Irish Catholics were subjected to harsh and restrictive laws governing economic, religious, and political life. This ranged from an exclusion from voting to restrictions on inheritance and occupation, effectively barring them from participation in public life.

After the failed 1798 rebellion of the United Irishmen, Ireland's limited parliament was abolished and direct British rule established by the Act of Union of 1800—setting the stage for a nationalist struggle that would grow into a home rule movement. With anti-Catholic laws repealed in the late 1700s and Catholics allowed to hold public office after the Catholic Emancipation of 1829, the Catholic Church gained strength in tandem with growing Irish nationalism and anti-British sentiment through the 19th century. Nationalism was paradoxically strengthened by the mass starvation and emigration caused by the potato blight of the 1840s, which devastated the native Irish by the steady erosion of the Irish language (through English-language education) and by the continued British suppression of a series of political rebellions. Later, the failure of the 1916 Easter Rebellion set the stage for effective guerilla warfare that led to a treaty with Britain and the creation of the Irish Free State in 1922. Northern Ireland, partitioned off by the agreement, chose to remain part of the United Kingdom. In 1937, Ireland adopted a new constitution and declared its sovereignty, becoming a republic in 1949.

After centuries of struggle, Ireland maintains a position of political neutrality, though its small army[2] participates in multinational peacekeeping operations.

As a result of this history, ethno-political differences were (and, especially in Northern Ireland, sometimes still are) inextricable from sectarian religious difference—Catholicism often linked to nationalist politics and national identity. The Republic of Ireland is predominantly Roman Catholic, with over 87 percent of the population identifying as Catholic in the 2006 census.[3] The influence of the Catholic Church was pervasive in Irish culture, politics, and society. The entanglement of national and religious identity was illustrated by public struggles over divorce and contraception in a series of divisive ballot referenda in the 1980s and 1990s, during which Catholic teaching overwhelmingly influenced discussions of public policy. After a series of very public scandals in the 1990s, however, the church began to lose its moral authority and political legitimacy, and a steady decline in influence and church attendance continues to the present.

From the early 1990s into the first decade of the 21st century—a period of economic growth called the Celtic Tiger—Ireland also experienced rapid economic and social transformations. The sustained economic prosperity, much of it based in the high-tech and information industries, has been marked by increasing urbanization, growing disparities in the distribution of wealth, immigration and the rapid ethnic diversification of metropolitan areas, and the globalization of Irish culture as a consumer culture—radical shifts in traditional Irish society.[4]

OVERVIEW OF LGBT ISSUES

For most of the last two centuries, the language and understanding of sexuality in Ireland has been confined to the language and understanding of the Catholic Church.[5] In practice, that meant a general sense of silence and shame about sexual matters, as well as ignorance about basic sexual and reproductive issues.[6] In theory, this means a focus on genital intercourse in heterosexual marriage as the only appropriate sexual outlet and reproduction as the only purpose for sex. In public policy, this meant that state laws usually affirmed Catholic teachings.[7] The heterosexual, patriarchal, reproductive family was enshrined in the Constitution of Ireland of 1937, which named the family as the fundamental social and political unit.[8]

In such a cultural context, discussions of homosexuality and gay and lesbian identity are constrained by silence and stigma. In the 1920s, Ireland instituted the Censorship of Publications Act and the Censorship of Films Act, in attempts to prohibit the publication or importation of materials seen to threaten Irish Catholic moral teachings. Although focused on foreign influences, censors could single out Irish authors—as Kate O'Brien was for one sentence in her 1941 novel, *The Land of Spices*. The offending sentence read, "She saw Etienne and her father in the embrace of love," a very brief reference to a gay embrace.[9] Although censorship efforts weakened in the 1970s, gay and lesbian texts were still subject to prosecution into the last decade of the 20th century, with the gay-positive children's book *Jenny Lives with Eric and Martin* censored by authorities in 1990.[10]

Ironically, David Norris, a gay activist and openly gay Irish senator since 1987, appealed to the Irish constitution in his 1974 lawsuit challenging Ireland's sodomy laws, grounding his case in a constitutional right to privacy. As was the case in Northern Ireland, however, it would take appeals to European authorities before homosexuality would be decriminalized. Homosexuality was decriminalized in Northern Ireland in 1982, and though Norris won his case in 1988, it was not decriminalized in the Republic of Ireland until 1993.

An earlier pivotal and galvanizing moment was the 1982 murder of a gay man in Dublin's Fairview Park. The youths who beat Declan Flynn to death received suspended sentences, prompting public outrage and a protest march organized by gays, lesbians, and feminist allies—later characterized as Ireland's Stonewall (a reference to the Stonewall Riots of 1969, often seen as a turning point in the U.S. gay rights struggle).[11]

In 1992, the recently elected president of Ireland, Mary Robinson—who as an attorney had earlier helped argue the David Norris case—invited 34 representatives from the LGBT community to her official residence, Áras an Uachtaráin in Phoenix Park of Dublin. The meeting was largely ignored by the media but was celebrated by the community as signaling a turning point in their ongoing struggle for civil rights.[12] The 1993 legalization marked the culmination of two decades of grassroots activism.

Grassroots community organizations struggled to provide resources through the 1970s, looking to both England and the United States for models and information, but working to address the specific cultural and religious constraints of Ireland. While AIDS affected intravenous drug users more than gay men at the beginning of the epidemic in Ireland, it was gay organizers who early on addressed the problems of education and treatment in a country that frowned on all forms of contraception and restricted the sales and distribution of condoms until 1993.

Because of the pervasive association of Catholicism with Irish national identity in both history and culture, the construction of a specifically *Irish* gay identity has been central to the rhetoric of the LGBT civil rights movement in Ireland. As David Norris would remark in the early 1980s, "There remained in the minds of many people until recently a doubt as to whether the terms 'Irish' and 'Homosexual' were not mutually exclusive."[13] Though this theme of identity and the desire to recognize an Irish gay or lesbian identity may be especially evident in emigrant communities (as in the struggles over the inclusion of gays and lesbians in New York St. Patrick's Day parades), it remains a central theme in Irish gay culture and politics.[14] As homosexuality entered Irish public consciousness in the second half of the 20th century, it was often portrayed in political discourse as foreign, a threat or corrupt influence from outside the nation. In contrast, some early LGBT organizers repeatedly connected gay identity to pre-Catholic and precolonial cultures, characterizing homophobia as a product of colonization and thus suggesting that gay rights—despite the long association of Catholicism with Irish national identity—may be part of a continued anticolonial struggle.

EDUCATION

Most of Ireland's primary and secondary schools have denominational affiliations; the state's schools are mostly run by religious organizations and the Department of Education provides funding to all schools as required by the constitution. Religious instruction is permitted by law but not required, and students may be excused at parents' request.

Because of a legacy of religious censorship, repression, and silence, and a subsequent social reticence about sexual matters, until very recently Irish people could reach adulthood knowing very little about sex. For example, when 15-year-old Anne Lovett and her baby died in childbirth in a field outside Granard in the winter of 1984, this tragedy played a critical role in public discussions of abortion and sex education and the Irish government began to consider formal sex education for the secondary school curriculum (although it was frequently opposed and unevenly implemented). Again in the mid-1990s, against considerable opposition, the Department of Education tried to implement a national curriculum on sex and relationships. This came about because a 1994 survey found that Irish sex education was still failing to provide basic information to all students.[15] More than a decade later, sex education still falls short, with many schools refusing to teach the established curriculum.[16]

Although youth services and education are included under the Equal Status Act of 2000, in 2002 the Equality Authority reported a severe lack of resources for LGBT youth. The report found few positive LGBT images in society, hostility from peers toward LGBT students, and the insistent pressure experienced by LGBT students to be normal. Further, because so many youth services are tied to religious institutions or grounded in a religious ethos, church teachings on sexuality make it difficult to meet the needs of LGBT youth.[17] Significantly, in a recent study of homophobic bullying in Irish schools, two of the things listed among those that would make life easier for LGBT youth were challenging Catholic views on sexuality and challenging the silence and taboo around the discussion of homosexuality.[18]

For LGBT youth, inadequate education, institutional silence, and the resulting ignorance of their peers about sexual issues translates into misunderstanding and harassment. A 1998 survey found that the predominant reaction to homosexuality among Irish secondary school boys was one of disgust.[19] Irish youth groups, such as the BeLonG To Youth Project, founded in 2002 and funded by the Department of Education, provide not only individual and group support, but also resources and initiatives directed at schools and other youth institutions—particularly in response to the bullying pervasive in school culture.

EMPLOYMENT AND ECONOMICS

In 1987, the Irish Congress of Trade Unions published guidelines on the protection of lesbian and gay workers. This act signaled one of the primary strategies of early LGBT organizing in Ireland: building alliances with feminists, trade unions, and other progressive organizations.[20]

Equally important to LGBT rights in the workplace has been Ireland's membership in the European Economic Community (EEC) since 1973 and the European Union (the EU, which subsumed the EEC at its creation in 1993). The 1998 Amsterdam Treaty charged the EU with combating workplace and employment discrimination; that same year, Ireland passed the Employment Equality Act, which prohibited workplace discrimination based on sexual orientation. The Equal Status Act of 2000 and the Equality Act of 2004 expanded the reach of Ireland's antidiscrimination laws, extending protection against discrimination in the provision of goods and services, housing, and education. The employment equality acts include an exemption for the religious ethos of schools, an exemption that in effect allows discrimination against openly lesbian and gay teachers.

Of lasting impact has been the creation of the Equality Authority, an independent state body created under the Employment Equality Act to replace the Employment Equality Agency. The Equality Authority has continued to work against discrimination on a number of fronts and, in 2002, released *Implementing Equality for Lesbians, Gays and Bisexuals*—a critical analysis of the status of Ireland's LGBT community with recommendations for policy and action.

While early organizing depended on alliances with progressives, legal reform has also depended on the capital-driven economic imperatives of the EU, which makes tolerance a litmus test for national inclusion, and which hopes to extend antidiscrimination protection into health care, social security, and other areas.

SOCIAL/GOVERNMENT PROGRAMS

As the creation and work of the Equality Authority suggests, some government and institutional support exists for LGBT programs, though it is limited and increasingly imperiled by the most recent economic circumstances. Early responses to HIV education, constrained by the moral views governing most public attitudes about sex, would not have suggested the current status of government funding. Much of this funding is tied to health services and promotion—which includes mental health and suicide prevention—with funds coming from the Health Services Executive and the Department of Education and Science. Dublin's LGBT community center, the Outhouse, receives funding from the Health Services Executive, as does BeLonG To Youth, which provides support services to and advocacy on behalf of LGBT youth. The 2004 annual report for Outhouse, for example, documents funding from the Department of Social and Family Affairs, the Health Board, Dublin City Council, and the Department of Environment.[21]

SEXUALITY/SEXUAL PRACTICES

In a country in which Catholic authorities were incensed by a married woman's suggestion on a 1966 television show that she had not worn a nightgown on her wedding night, condemning this suggestion of marital sexual pleasure as an assault on the nation's morals,[22] and in a country in which, into the early 20th century, women who had given birth were considered impure until they had been to a church—sexuality and sexual pleasure (even in the context of heterosexual reproduction) could still resonate with the shame and silence instilled by Catholic moral attitudes.

Despite the urgency of the AIDS epidemic, Ireland also restricted the sale of condoms until 1993. Previously, condom sales had been allowed in 1978 but were restricted to people over 18 and only in pharmacies or medical clinics. Education about HIV and AIDS was left to struggling gay volunteer organizations in the face of silence and inaction on the part of government and other institutions (which were constrained by religious views on sexuality and contraception). Gay Health Action (GHA) formed in early 1985, years before an AIDS case had been officially diagnosed in Ireland. Although the AIDS epidemic in Ireland would echo situations in eastern Europe (the majority of infections tied to intravenous drug use rather than homosexuality), the bulk of AIDS organizing, education, and support was conducted by gay volunteer groups.

For the first years of the epidemic, GHA was the only organization providing advice on prevention and up-to-date medical information. In contrast, the media consistently offered inaccurate and antigay information and the health department refused to help fund early education efforts. Even still, later efforts excluded useful information about gay sexual practices. The Irish Names Project, Ireland's version of the AIDS Quilt, was started in 1990. The health department committed to working with gay organizations in 1994, and in 2006 the Equality Authority pointed to partnerships between the health department and gay community agencies as an example of good health promotion practices.[23]

Family

The 1937 constitution enshrined a very traditional view of family in law. Article 41 recognized the family as the fundamental unit of society, and as "a moral institution" with natural and "imprescriptible" rights outside of and preceding those granted by law. The family is structurally defined by marriage and marked by patriarchal attitudes about gender roles. The constitution charged the state with protecting marriage—a constitutional ban on divorce was not relaxed until 1995. The constitution further states that the primary role and duties of women are within the home and it charges the state to guarantee that women not "neglect of their duties" by working outside the home. Although the fifth amendment of 1972 removed the Catholic Church from its special position in the document, Catholic teaching about sexuality remains central. The eighth amendment (1983) acknowledges the right to life of the unborn—thus institutionalizing Catholic opposition to abortion.[24]

For several decades, the traditional large Irish family has been in decline, and marriage declined during the 1980s and 1990s. However, the economic boom at the turn of the century saw an increase in both marriages and childbirth. Ireland's divorce rate remains low compared to other nations. Both cohabitation by unmarried couples and childbirth outside of marriage are increasing, however, as are single-parent families.[25]

Only married couples and single people can adopt children in Ireland. Irish gay couples cannot adopt as a couple, though they are allowed to foster children. Until recently, gay and lesbian families in Ireland have had no legal standing or protection. A 2008 High Court of Ireland decision recognized a lesbian couple as a de facto family in a child custody dispute denying the rights of a gay male friend who was the sperm donor. Though the case may be appealed, it will likely help to shape ongoing discussions about the status and rights of gay and lesbian families, as well as unmarried heterosexual couples.[26]

COMMUNITY

The first Irish gay and lesbian community organization, the Irish Gay Rights Movement, was founded in 1974. The organization established a Gay Centre in Dublin's Parnell Square that housed a disco, library, and telephone counseling line. The movement struggled through political, personal, and financial disagreements, with supplemental or sometimes rival organizations arising in the 1970s—such as the National Gay Federation, the Cork Gay Collective, and Liberation for Irish Lesbians. Briefly there were two community centers operating in Dublin, not only duplicating services but also squandering limited resources. In 1981, the first National Gay Conference was held in Cork.[27]

As noted, the formation of a specifically Irish gay and lesbian identity has been central to Irish lesbian and gay culture. In both the Republic and Northern Ireland, homosexuality was frequently portrayed as foreign, a threat, and a corrupting outside influence. And the pervasive association of Catholicism with Irish national identity made it difficult to assert queer Irish identities. This conflict between national and sexual identities is especially evident in Irish emigrant cultures in England and the United States in which ethnic identification sometimes precluded homosexual identification.[28] For example, Irish gays and lesbians were prohibited from participating in the St. Patrick's Day marches in New York (though they were famously welcomed when they first applied to the 1992 march in Cork).[29]

Today, there are visible gay and lesbian communities in most major cities in Ireland with gay pride celebrations held in Belfast, Cork, Dublin, Galway, and even Sligo. There is a growing number of organizations addressing various constituencies and needs in the LGBT community. LGBT people are less visible outside the urban centers, and often lack the resources and community found there. Dublin has also hosted a lesbian arts festival and gay and lesbian theatre and film festivals.

Though transsexuals are included in the common acronym LGBT, and even though a transsexual support group meets at the Outhouse in Dublin, awareness about transgender identity is not widespread. Indeed, some Irish transgender people resist inclusion with lesbians and gays. One transgender organization explicitly separates itself from the LGB communities.[30] Both inside and outside the LGB movement, some activists have begun to use the phrase GID community, drawing on the medical language of Gender Identity Disorder rather than the sometimes confusing terms transgender and transsexual.

HEALTH

Just as religious and political prejudices hampered organizing and education efforts related to HIV and AIDS, prejudice in health care can prove detrimental to lesbian and gay health. Homophobia among health care practitioners is the primary barrier to lesbian health in Ireland. Early accounts of lesbian health reported that lesbians suffered additional trauma in hospitals and clinics, as they faced homophobic and heterosexist responses from hospital personnel.[31] More recently, lesbian service providers have begun to offer advice and information about the particular health risks lesbian women face, including breast cancer, depression, and substance use.[32]

Gender reassignment surgery is not available in Ireland to those diagnosed with Gender Identity Disorder although, in some cases, Irish health services have supported Irish people seeking surgery in England.

POLITICS AND LAW

Sodomy

Until legal reform decriminalized homosexuality, the laws governing male-male sex originated from British laws between 1861 and 1885 and stipulated penal servitude and hard labor for those convicted. (Female sexual behavior was not addressed by the laws.) Working with the Campaign for Homosexual Law Reform, David Norris filed a lawsuit in 1977 challenging the constitutionality of the laws, arguing that they violated constitutional protections—particularly the freedom and dignity of the individual guaranteed by the preamble and a constitutional right to privacy as established in a 1974 case involving marital privacy (which allowed for the legalization of contraception). He also noted that popular and political prejudice was grounded in the laws.

The laws were repealed in England and Wales in 1967, though that repeal did not extend to Northern Ireland. In 1976, after a series of drug raids led to the harassment, arrest, and intended prosecutions of gay men, Jeffrey Dudgeon filed a complaint with the European Commission on Human Rights that year. The European Court of Human Rights (ECtHR) ruled in 1981 that a ban on homosexual conduct violated the European Convention on Human Rights (ECHR) and, in 1982, sodomy was decriminalized in Northern Ireland.

Norris lost his case in both the high court (1980) and the supreme court (1983). He appealed to the ECtHR, winning his case there in 1988. Five years later, the Irish government finally addressed the issue. It not only decriminalized homosexuality but equalized the age of consent for heterosexual and homosexual sex. Irish Catholic leaders opposed the reform, releasing a statement emphasizing the position that homosexuality is morally wrong. Family Solidarity, a conservative advocacy group created in 1984, also opposed divorce and abortion. Before the legalization of sodomy in 1993, many Irish gays and lesbians left Ireland in order to live their sexual identities with more freedom and openness elsewhere. The impact of this reform, which removed not only legal stigma and juridical threat but also social disapprobation, led to rapid and dramatic transformations in the visibility of the Irish LGBT community.[33]

Marriage

As in other nations, there is a growing movement for the recognition of same-sex couples through civil unions or marriage. When Ireland passed a Domestic Violence Bill in 1995, it recognized relationships outside of marriage—effectively acknowledging gay and lesbian relationships in Irish law for the first time.[34] Even still, Ireland does not officially recognize same-sex couples. A recent court decision that described a lesbian couple and their child as a de facto family may affect public policy, as may a pending decision about a lesbian marriage from Canada. An Irish lesbian couple married in Canada in 2003, and filed a lawsuit in 2004 asking that Ireland recognize the legality of their marriage. The case was still pending at the Supreme Court of Ireland as this book went to press, though a 2006 decision of the Irish high court held that Ireland could refuse to recognize same-sex marriages from other nations.

Northern Ireland, as part of the United Kingdom, has offered civil partnerships since 2005 and, in 2006, the Equality Authority argued that the Irish government should provide similar protection. Civil partnerships legislation, which falls short of the attendant status and rights of full marriage equality, was introduced and rejected in 2007, but was introduced again in 2008.

Since the mid-1990s, opinion in Ireland about gay and lesbian families is beginning to shift to more tolerant, even supportive attitudes, with a majority of Irish in recent polls supporting same-sex marriage and over 80 percent affirming that children of lesbian and gay parents should have the same rights as any other children.[35] Further, in recent elections, every major political party supported some form of recognition for same-sex relationships, suggesting the promise of future legislative change.[36]

Transsexuals

The most visible challenge to Ireland's lack of social and legal recognition of transsexual people is the case of Lydia Foy, who tried to get a new birth certificate for 10 years reflecting her change of gender. In 2007, the High Court of Ireland ruled in her favor, arguing that Ireland's refusal to offer her a new birth certificate violated the EHCR. The government of Ireland, however, failed to act on the court's decision and appealed back to the supreme court in early 2008.[37]

RELIGION AND SPIRITUALITY

Religious prejudices—especially those grounded in Catholic moral teachings—have greatly affected lesbian and gay people, communities, and politics in Ireland. This is not only because of the pervasive social, political, religious, and cultural influence of the Catholic Church, and not only because of the majority affiliation with Catholicism, but also because Irish national identity has been consistently—if at times problematically—linked to Catholicism in both culture and history. This is not to indict the Catholic Church as the primary or only opponent of LGBT rights in Ireland. Indeed, other religious groups in Ireland have similar attitudes and, during the debates over legal reform in Northern Ireland, it was the Protestant reverend Ian Paisley of the Democratic Unionist Party who led a Save Ulster from Sodomy campaign.

Regardless, the Catholic position on lesbian and gay issues in Ireland is not monolithic. However, it is important to recognize the pervasive influence of the Catholic Church on social and public policy about sexuality and its effects on LGBT organizing. As a result of the official, institutional homophobia and heterosexism validated by religious attitudes, LGBT advocates in Ireland frequently connected gay identity to pre-Catholic and precolonial cultures in Ireland, suggesting that homophobia is a product of colonization. They portrayed an Irish identity and culture that preceded Catholicism and colonization. In an attempt to counter the frequent perception of the Irish as backward on sexual and social issues, activists cited traditional Irish values of tolerance, fairness, and justice. They might characterize Catholicism's traditional centrality to Irish identity as a historically recent phenomenon, more the product of famine and political struggle than a national sensibility. And they often appealed to early Irish law—the traditional and pre-Christian Brehon laws—as more tolerant of sexual and family diversity. In speaking of justice, they might connect gay rights to a continued anticolonial struggle obviating the historical link of Catholicism to that struggle. It is a strategic and effective appeal to national identity detached from its Catholic supports.[38]

Ireland has recently seen a dramatic shift in the political and social power of the Catholic Church. A series of very public scandals in the 1990s undermined the church's moral authority at the very moment Ireland was experiencing unprecedented economic growth and social change. Among the scandals undermining church authority were: the 1992 revelation that Father Eamonn Casey, bishop of Galway, had both a lover and a child; ongoing revelations about physical and emotional abuse in Irish institutions (the industrial schools for orphans and the Magadalene laundries for unwed mothers); the 1994 death of a priest in a Dublin gay sauna (where he was given last rites by two other priests on the premises); and the ongoing allegations of child sexual abuse and accusations of both church and government cover-ups of the abuse.[39]

At the beginning of the 21st century, the Catholic Church has also seen a marked decline in attendance, with a 2003 survey showing that only 50 percent of Irish adults attended weekly mass.[40]

VIOLENCE

On September 10, 1982, 32-year-old Declan Flynn was beaten to death in Fairview Park by a gang of Dublin youths between the ages of 15 and 20. Fairview Park was known as a cruising area for gay men (where they would meet sexual partners), and the murder was part of a systematic summer campaign of gay bashing and harassment, and represented a small group of youths' attempt to rid the park of queers. The charge against the youths was reduced from murder to manslaughter and, in February 1983, they were found guilty, given suspended sentences, and released. They held their own victory march through the neighborhood upon release.

Public outrage over the ruling and the subsequent march led to a protest march that was organized by gays and lesbians along with feminist and labor union allies. On March 19, 1983, several hundred people marched behind a banner that read, "Stop Violence against Gays and Women." (During that period, lesbian and gay organizations had built alliances with feminist organizations in the campaign against the abortion amendment and the incident also echoed a similar sentence in the murder of a prostitute about the same time.) The march proceeded from Dublin's city center, though the killers' neighborhood, and into Fairview Park.

It was a galvanizing moment for LGBT organizing in Ireland. It solidified coalitions being built, drew national media attention to homophobia and violence against gays and lesbians, marked a turn to direct action on the part of LGBT activists, and focused gay and lesbian energy and anger in a very public statement against violence and discrimination.[41]

In the wake of the Fairview Park murder, Ireland passed the 1989 Prohibition of Incitement to Hatred Act, which addressed written and visual incitements to hatred based on ethnicity, religion, and sexual orientation. Still, Ireland has no specific hate crime laws that would allow courts to consider bias and hatred when handing down sentences.

OUTLOOK FOR THE 21ST CENTURY

Recent studies of Irish public opinion found that Irish views on what are often considered to be moral issues such as abortion, divorce, and homosexuality became more liberal in the 1980s and 1990s. More importantly, the studies found that the liberalization did not reflect simply age difference and population replacement (younger, more accepting generations replacing older, more traditional voters). Instead, opinions actually changed *because of* the very public discussions around ballot referendum campaigns (on abortion and divorce) and *in relation to* institutional and legal reform (divorce and homosexuality).[42] That is, public debate and—perhaps more interestingly—the implementation of progressive social policies resulted in increasing social tolerance. This suggests the ongoing impact of both corporate and governmental policies on diversity and equality, which affect not only workplace environments but also social attitudes.

At the beginning of the 21st century, LGBT organizers had begun to adopt the language of economic success and social well-being rather than that of tolerance and marginality. Although the increasing visibility of the community may belie ongoing problems, particularly those of young people and those living in rural areas, Irish LGBT organizations and their allies are encouraged by changing social and political attitudes.[43]

RESOURCE GUIDE

Suggested Reading

Suzy Byrne and Junior Larkin, *Coming Out: A Book for Lesbians and Gay Men of All Ages* (Dublin: Martello Books, 1994).

Aongus Collins, *A History of Sex and Morals in Ireland* (Cork: Mercier Press, 2001).

Sara-Jane Cromwell, *Becoming Myself: The True Story of Thomas Who Became Sara* (London: Gill & Macmillan, 2008).

Dublin Lesbian and Gay Men's Collectives, *Out for Ourselves: The Lives of Irish Lesbians and Gay Men* (Dublin: Dublin Lesbian and Gay Men's Collectives and Women's Community Press, 1986).

Equality Authority, *Implementing Equality for Lesbians, Gays and Bisexuals* (Dublin: Equality Authority, 2002).

Chrystel Hug, *The Politics of Sexual Morality in Ireland* (New York: St. Martin's Press, 1999).

Brian Lacey, *Terrible Queer Creatures: Homosexuality in Irish History* (Dublin: Wordwell Books, 2008).

Íde O'Carroll and Eoin Collins, eds., *Lesbian and Gay Visions of Ireland: Towards the Twenty-first Century* (London: Cassell, 1995).

Kieran Rose, *Diverse Communities: The Evolution of Lesbian and Gay Politics in Ireland* (Cork: Cork University Press, 1994).

Éibhear Walshe, "Wild(e) Ireland," in *Ireland in Proximity: History, Gender, Space,* ed. Scott Brewter, Virginia Crossman, Fiona Beckett, and David Alderson (New York: Routledge, 1999).

Videos/Films

Breakfast on Pluto (129 min.; 2005). Directed by Neil Jordan. Pathé Pictures International. Based on the novel by Patrick McCabe, the story of an Irish transgender figure living during on political and sexual borders during the violence in Northern Ireland in the 1970s.

Chicken (3 min.; 2001). Directed by Barry Dignam. Bórd Scannán na hÉireann. Two Irish male teens drinking cider and posturing at the shore. A short film that makes complex connections between male vulnerability, adolescent machismo, and sexuality (can be found on YouTube.com.)

Did Anyone Notice Us? Gay Visibility in the Irish Media 1973–1993 (74 min.; 2003). Directed by Edmund Lynch. Documentary. Survey of Irish media coverage of the Irish LGBT movement.

Goldfish Memory (85 min.; 2003). Directed by Elizabeth Gill. Goldfish Films. A gay and lesbian view of contemporary Dublin.

Pigs (78 min.; 1984). Directed by Cathal Black. Irish Film Board and RTE. Early Irish film representation of homosexuality and gay bashing, set in an abandoned house inhabited by squatters in inner city Dublin.

Reefer and the Model (93 min.; 1988). Directed by Joe Comerford. Berber Films. A group of social, sexual, and political outsiders seeking refuge and community on the isolated west coast.

Web Sites

Alternative Parents, http://alternativeparents.com.
Information site for LGBT singles and couples who are or want to become parents.

Bi Irish, http://www.biirish.com.
For Irish bisexuals.

Coalition on Sexual Orientation (CoSO), http://www.coso.org.uk.
Advocacy for LGBT people in Northern Ireland.

Emerald Warriors, http://ewrfc.ie.
Ireland's competitive gay rugby team, founded in 2003.

Gay Belfast, http://gaybelfast.net.
Resource and information site for Belfast and Northern Ireland, includes a summary of Belfast gay history by Jeffrey Dudgeon.

Gay Community News, http://www.gcn.ie.
Ireland's monthly gay magazine, a free publication, founded in 1988 and published under the auspices of the National Lesbian and Gay Federation.

Gay Cork, http://gaycork.com.
Resources and information for Cork and surrounding region.

Irish Queer Archive, http://www.irishqueerarchive.com.
Major collection of LGBT publications and ephemera, recently donated to the National Library.

Irish Queers, http://irishqueers.org.
LGBT activist group based in New York, organizing around Irish queer issues in Ireland and Irish America. Site includes news blog.

KAL Case, http://www.kalcase.org.
Summarizes the lawsuit of Irish lesbian couple Katherine Zappone and Ann Louise Gilligan, asking that Ireland recognize their marriage, which took place in Canada in 2003.

Marriage Equality, http://www.marriagequality.ie.
Initiative seeking civil marriage for gays and lesbians in the Republic of Ireland.

Out In Ireland, http://www.outinireland.net.
Ireland gay and lesbian sports network.

Queer ID, http://www.queerid.com.
>   Social networking and news site for gay men and women in Ireland.

Organizations

BeLonG To Youth Project, http://www.belongto.org.
>   For LGBT young people aged 14–23.

Dublin AIDS Alliance, http://www.dublinaidsalliance.com.
>   Volunteer organization working to improve the lives of people living with HIV.

The Equality Authority, http://www.equality.ie.
>   An independent state body established by the Employment Equality Act of 1998 and replacing the Employment Equality Agency. Addresses discrimination in employment, advertising, education, and the provision of goods and services based on gender, marital or family status, age, disability, race, sexual orientation, religious belief, or membership in the Traveller minority community. Published the essential strategic study on the status of LGBT people in Ireland, *Implementing Equality for Lesbians, Gays and Bisexuals*. Dublin: Equality Authority, 2002.

Gay Lesbian Equality Network (GLEN), http://www.glen.ie.
>   Irish LGBT civil rights organization, focused on legal reform in order to achieve full equality and inclusion and protection from discrimination. Web site includes a number of useful resources and studies related to LGBT issues in Ireland.

Gay Men's Health Project, c/o Outhouse, http://www.gayhealthnetwork.ie.
>   Health project targeting gay and bisexual men, based in Dublin. Sponsors sexual health clinics, personal development courses, outreach, and counseling.

Gay Switchboard Dublin, http://www.gayswitchboard.ie.
>   LGBT information and resource hotline based in Dublin.

Lesbian Advocacy Services Initiative (LASI), http://www.lasionline.org.
>   A lesbian advocacy organization for Northern Ireland.

L.inC (Lesbians in Cork) Community Resource Center, http://www.linc.ie.
>   Network and community resource center for women in Cork.

Northern Ireland Gay Rights Association (NIGRA).
>   Organization focused on gay and lesbian rights, with a special attention to legal issues.

Outhouse, http://www.Outhouse.ie.
>   Dublin's LGBT resource and community center since 1994; Outhouse includes a cafe, library, and Internet access. Home to several local organizations, including the Gay Men's Health Project and support groups for LGBT youth and transgender people.

QueerSpace, http://www.queerspace.org.uk.
>   LGBT volunteer organization for Belfast and Northern Ireland.

Southern Gay Men's Health Project (SGMHP), http://www.gayhealthproject.com
>   Health project targeting gay and bisexual men in the Cork and Kerry regions.

Transgender Equality Network, http://www.teni.ie.
>   Transgender support, education, and advocacy organization based in Dublin's Outhouse.

NOTES

1. Central Statistics Office Ireland, "Population 1901–2006," http://www.cso.ie/statistics/Population1901–2006.htm (accessed November 24, 2008); Northern Ireland Executive, Department of Finance and Personnel, "Northern Ireland Population above 1.75 Million," news release, http://www.northernireland.gov.uk/news/news-dfp/news-dfp-july-2008/news-dfp-310708-ni-population.htm (accessed November 24, 2008).

2. According to the Irish Defence Forces Web site, about 8,500 people serve in the Irish army, http://www.military.ie/army (accessed November 29, 2008).

3. Central Statistics Office Ireland, "Population Classified by Religion and Nationality 2006," http://www.cso.ie/statistics/popnclassbyreligionandnationality2006.htm (accessed November 24, 2008).

4. Mary Corcoran, "Introduction: An Age of Uncertainty," in *Uncertain Ireland: A Sociological Chronicle, 2003–2004,* ed. Mary P. Corcoran and Michel Peillon (Dublin: Institute of Public Administration, 2006).

5. Tom Inglis, *Lessons in Irish Sexuality* (Dublin: University College Dublin Press, 1998).

6. Inglis, *Lessons in Irish Sexuality;* Aongus Collins, *A History of Sex and Morals in Ireland* (Cork: Mercier Press, 2001).

7. Chrystel Hug, *The Politics of Sexual Morality in Ireland* (New York: St. Martin's Press, 1999), 3.

8. The full text of the Constitution of Ireland (1937, 2004) is available from the Department of the Taoiseach, http://193.178.1.117/index.asp?docID=262 (accessed November 23, 2008).

9. Collins, *A History of Sex and Morals in Ireland,* 44–47; Julia Carlson, *Banned in Ireland: Censorship and the Irish Writer* (Athens, GA: University of Georgia Press, 1990); Marie McGonagle, "Censorship Laws Are Out of Date," *Sunday Business Post,* September 10, 2000, http://archives.tcm.ie/businesspost/2000/09/10/story573869038.asp (accessed November 30, 2008).

10. *Gay Community News,* September 1990.

11. Ger Philpott, "Martyr in the Park," *Gay Ireland,* November 2001.

12. Suzy Byrne and Junior Larkin, *Coming Out* (Dublin: Martello Books, 1994).

13. David Norris, "Homosexual People and the Christian Churches in Ireland," *The Crane Bag* 5, no. 2 (1981): 31.

14. Íde O'Carroll and Eoin Collins, *Lesbian and Gay Visions of Ireland: Towards the Twenty-First Century* (London: Cassell, 1994).

15. Inglis, *Lessons in Irish Sexuality,* 3–4.

16. VHI Healthcare Ireland, "Sex Education Falls Short," March 22, 2007, http://www.vhi.ie/news/n220307a.jsp (accessed November 24, 2008).

17. Equality Authority, *Implementing Equality for Lesbians, Gays and Bisexuals* (Dublin: Equality Authority, 2002).

18 Stephen James Minton, Torunn Dahl, Astrid Mona O'Moore, and Donnelly Tuck, *A Report on an Exploratory Survey of the Experiences of Homophobic Bullying amongst Lesbian, Gay, Bisexual, and Transgendered Young People in the Republic of Ireland* (Dublin: Anti-bullying Centre, Trinity College Dublin, 2006), http://www.belongto.org/article.aspx?articleid=84 (accessed November 29, 2008).

19. Inglis, *Lessons in Irish Sexuality,* 144.

20. Kieran Rose, *Diverse Communities: The Evolution of Lesbian and Gay Politics in Ireland* (Cork: Cork University Press, 1994), 25–27.

21. "Annual Report 2004," *Outhouse,* http://www.Outhouse.ie/docs/Annual_Report_2004_v1.pdf (accessed July 24, 2008).

22. On the 1966 "Nightie" episode of *The Late Late Show,* see Collins, *A History of Sex and Morals in Ireland,* 55–56; and Inglis, *Lessons in Irish Sexuality,* 39.

23. Rose, *Diverse Communities,* 22–25; Dublin Lesbian and Gay Men's Collectives, *Out for Ourselves: The Lives of Irish Lesbians and Gay Men* (Dublin: Dublin Lesbian and Gay Men's Collectives and Women's Community Press, 1986), 151–52. See also the Equality Authority, *Implementing Equality for Lesbians, Gays and Bisexuals,* 34.

24. Constitution of Ireland (2004).

25. Department of Social and Family Affairs "Hanafin Launches Report on the Ever-changing Formation of Families in Ireland," news release, 2008, http://www.welfare.ie/

EN/Press/PressReleases/2008/Pages/pr281108.aspx?cssFont=0 (accessed November 24, 2008); One Family, "Definition of Family in Irish Constitution No Longer Valid in Today's Ireland," news release, July 14, 2008, http://www.onefamily.ie/news115.htm (accessed November 24, 2008).

26. Carol Coulter and Mary Carolan, "Lesbian Couple with Child 'a De Facto Family,'" *Irish Times*, April 17, 2008, http://www.irishtimes.com/newspaper/frontpage/2008/0417/1208382316994.html (accessed November 25, 2008).

27. Byrne and Larkin, *Coming Out*; Rose, *Diverse Communities*; Dublin Lesbian and Gay Men's Collectives, *Out for Ourselves*.

28. Máirtín Mac an Ghaill, "Irish Masculinities and Sexualities in England," in *Sexualizing the Social: Power and the Organization of Sexuality*, ed. Lisa Adkins and Vicki Merchant (New York: St. Martin's Press, 1996).

29. Rose, *Diverse Communities*, 31–33.

30. Equality Authority, *Implementing Equality for Lesbians, Gays and Bisexuals*, 32; Dublin Lesbian and Gay Men's Collectives, *Out for Ourselves*, 143.

31. See, for example, the Lesbian Advocacy Service Initiative, "Ten Things Lesbians should Discuss with their Health Care Providers," http://www.lasionline.org/10things.htm (accessed November 28, 2008).

32. Rose, *Coming Out*; Hug, *The Politics of Sexual Morality in Ireland*.

33. Hug, *The Politics of Sexual Morality in Ireland*, 239.

34. Hug, *The Politics of Sexual Morality in Ireland*, 239; also Irish Council for Civil Liberties, "Ireland Fails to Recognise and Protect the Families and Children of Same Sex Couples," Rights Monitor, July 14, 2008, http://rightsmonitor.org/?p=45 (accessed November 25, 2008).

35. Carl O'Brien, "From the Margins to the Mainstream," *Irish Times*, Weekend Review, June 14, 2008.

36. Gender Identity Disorder Ireland, policy statement, http://www.gidi.ie/Gidi_policy_page.htm (accessed November 29, 2008).

37. FLAC, "Briefing Note on the Lydia Foy Case and Transgender Transsexual Cases Generally," October 19, 2007, http://www.flac.ie/news/2007/10/19/briefing-note-on-the-lydia-foy-case-and-transgender-transsexual-cases-generally (accessed November 29, 2008); *Irish Times*, "Sex Change Law Incompatible with ECHR," October 19, 2007, http://www.irishtimes.com/newspaper/ireland/2007/1020/1192820344522.html (accessed November 30, 2008).

38. Kathryn Conrad, *Locked in the Family Cell: Gender, Sexuality and Political Agency in Irish National Discourse* (Madison: University of Wisconsin Press, 2004).

39. Collins, *A History of Sex and Morals in Ireland*, 43, 75–76; Diarmaid Ferriter *The Transformation of Ireland* (Woodstock, NY: Overlook Press, 2004).

40. Tod Robertson, "Catholic Church is Losing Sway in Europe," *Dallas Morning News*, May 8, 2005, http://www.religionnewsblog.com/11159/catholic-church-is-losing-sway-in-europe (accessed November 26, 2008).

41. Dublin Lesbian and Gay Men's Collectives, *Out for Ourselves*; Rose, *Coming Out*, 20–21; Philpott, "Martyr in the Park."

42. Pat Lyons, *Public Opinion, Politics and Society in Contemporary Ireland* (Dublin: Irish Academic Press, 2008), 146–47.

43. O'Brien, "From the Margins to the Mainstream."

ITALY

Michele Grigolo and Frédéric Jörgens

OVERVIEW

Italy is a southern European country and, geographically, a peninsula: its eastern, southern, and western borders are bounded by the Mediterranean Sea (the Adriatic, Ionian, and Tyrrhenian seas). It has an extension of 116,306 square miles and a population of around 57,634,300 (according to the 2000 census). The capital of the country is Rome, though many often refer to Milan as the economic capital. Italy's peak of industrialization occurred during the 1960s, based essentially on the development of small and medium-sized enterprises. Like many other industrialized states, Italy has also been going through a transition toward a service-based economy.

Compared to other western European countries, Italy is a relatively young state. Until the 19th century the peninsula was divided into a number of political entities dominated by major European powers. In 1861, the unification process led by Giuseppe Garibaldi and politically and financially supported by the Kingdom of Sardinia established the Kingdom of Italy. This process was completed in 1871 with the annexation of Rome, which became the capital of Italy. The Vatican was allowed to maintain a formal sovereignty on a small portion of the city land around St. Peter's Cathedral (today's Vatican City State). The country was under the rule of the Fascist regime of Benito Mussolini between 1922 and 1943, when Italy was still fighting on the side of the Nazis against the Allied armies in World War II. Between 1943 and 1945 the

war continued between, on the one hand, the Nazis and the new Fascist Republic of Salò established in Northern Italy and, on the other, the Resistenza (Resistance) movement—led by Communist, Catholic, and liberal groups—and the Allied powers. On April 25, 1945, Italy was finally freed of Nazi Fascism. In 1946, Italians—including, for the first time, Italian women—voted for the establishment of a republic as their form of government. In January 1948, the new constitution entered into force. The constitution represented a compromise between the different political forces of the Resistenza. It guaranteed not only civil and political rights, but also economic and social rights.

OVERVIEW OF LGBT ISSUES

There are a number of social, cultural, and legal issues that LGBT people and the movement that represents them have long considered crucial but that have been relatively invisible in society and the political discourse. These issues are related to violence, discrimination, same-sex relationships, and family rights. Italy has not allowed formal discrimination by state legislation, as is typical of northern European countries such as in the United Kingdom and Germany, as well as the United States. Already in the 19th century, in 1871, the new Italian kingdom decriminalized sexual acts between men. The Italian penal code also set a common age of consent at 14 for both same-sex and opposite-sex sexual acts. With no formal bans or exclusion from educational activities or censorship of LGBT issues ever having been formalized in the public sphere, Italy was at the forefront of tolerant countries in this matter, despite instances of nonlegal persecution of homosexuals during the Mussolini era; even then, homosexuality was not formally criminalized. The status quo of the noncriminalization of homosexuality during Fascism was, however, accompanied by the strong repression of homosexual men through direct police enforcements introduced in 1926.[1] Homosexuality remained legal after the end of World War II.

While Italy has never formally prohibited homosexuality, in the Europe of today the country stands out for not providing any formal protection against discrimination on the grounds of sexual orientation, with the exception of labor legislation, following the transposition of the 2000 European Union Employment Discrimination Directive. It is also one of the few western European countries that have not provided any recognition of same-sex couples or families with same-sex parents. Italy also maintains a dubious position concerning certain practices, such as blood donation, that some may consider discriminatory. Medically assisted insemination is not accessible to single women or same-sex couples.

The combination of these legal and social conditions experienced by LGBT people in Italy has produced an indifferent attitude toward homosexuality, which has guaranteed freedom on the margins, but also a weakness in political organization and scant recognition in mainstream society.

A number of factors account for the invisibility of LGBT issues in Italy. First, the strong social, cultural, and economic influence of the Vatican still exercises its power through a capillary network of churches, schools, seminars, charity institutions, its properties, and its bank. The Catholic Church has a large institutional influence on public life, for instance where millions of workplaces directly depend on church authority. The Vatican has also had a major influence on the entire political system, which is largely focused on controlling the central Catholic vote. The church has used its power not only to condemn nonheterosexual behaviors, but also to censor and silence any debate about LGBT issues in the educational system and in politics at large.

Some would suggest that Italians are less Catholic than the official discourse normally affirms, and that their acceptance of LGBT rights is stronger than the one expressed by the political leadership. Indeed, opinion polls on this matter generally show a tolerant attitude concerning homosexuality, roughly in line with other western European countries. Up to 72 percent of Italians think that homosexuality should be accepted by society.[2] Between 31 percent[3] and 47 percent[4] are in favor of same-sex marriage, while more than half support civil partnerships. But so far the state has not been inclined to adjust to the popular attitude. While in general the LGBT movement has cultivated relations with parties on the left, LGBT issues have never become a priority for any of the center-left governments from the mid-1990s on.

Second, a traditionalist, allegedly macho, and patriarchal cultural background still dominates the country, and the Vatican largely relies on this to enact its silencing policy. The patriarchal culture remains strongest in Italy's southern regions, while the regions of the north have gradually, though not completely, internalized a more western European mindset, based on individual freedom rather than families, clans and communities. The patriarchal culture also clearly accounts for the especially strong invisibility of lesbians in the country.

Third, the LGBT movement has a limited capacity to influence the political system due to its internal differences and divisions. With respect to this, the LGBT movement reflects the many differences and divisions of Italy: it is still largely characterized by localism, a high degree of conflict between left radical and moderate factions, extreme individualism, and, in some instances, the separation of the lesbian and gay movements. While these differences and divisions are meaningful and not without reason, it is indisputable that they have weakened the movement's capacity, for example, to have an impact on policy making. This is especially true at the state level, while at the local and city level LGBT associations have showed a stronger capacity to influence local administrations on LGBT issues.

There have been signs, however, that LGBT issues may gain more weight in Italian politics. In 2000, the Vatican openly requested that the state government prohibit WorldPride from taking place in Rome, claiming its incompatibility with the celebrations for the Great Jubilee in 2000. In response to this open attack, nearly all LGBT associations and networks operating at the national and local levels joined forces to participate in WorldPride. The LGBT movement was also able to involve non-LGBT movements and associations on the left, which considered the Vatican veto to be an unacceptable attack on democratic liberties at large. This event constituted a landmark passage for homosexuality and LGBT issues to find greater public acceptance. Since then, social, cultural, and legal issues related to homosexuality have gained a bit more of attention and visibility in the public sphere, although this has not led to a complete legitimization of homosexuality as a public issue. Since then, there has been a trend toward viewing homosexuality not so much as a value in itself, but as part of the need for a liberal reform of the state, a view shared by at least some of the national elites and represented in some major newspapers and magazines of social-democratic inspiration.

After 2000, homosexuality became more and more present in the Italian media, and some homosexual politicians came out, such as Nichi Vendola, who in 2005 was elected as the president of the Puglia region in the south of Italy. In cities such as Rome and Milan, openly visible gay and lesbian bars, cafes, and club venues have made their appearance since the late 1990s, replacing the mostly hidden bars that relied on insider knowledge, where patrons often had to ring a bell before entering through a locked door. In Rome, this trend, which comes after similar trends in other European countries, can be exemplified by the Coming Out bar opposite the Coliseum, whose visitors are openly visible to passersby.

In Italy today, several cities have a large LGBT scene—some sociologists have called Milan, Rome, and Bologna, among others, gay capitals. Milan is sometimes noted to have the larger gay scene; Bologna, with its tradition as a university town and home to many progressive social movements, is known as the gayest Italian city in relation to its size. Rome is Italy's largest city. It has had a continuously important tradition of homosexual culture in various subcultures, such as the arts scene, associations, outdoor sex, alleged homosexuality in church circles, and, as a rather newer phenomenon, in openly and exclusively gay and lesbian bars and clubs. However, many lesbians and gays attribute a growing social acceptance of homosexuality to an outside influence, as a series of interviews showed:

> Young LGBT women and men in Rome nearly all argued that Italy was behind the times, and that the influence of the Church was an important factor, while they viewed the pressure from the European Union and Italy's interconnectedness with other European countries as a motor for social change toward a greater acceptance of homosexuality in Italy.[5]

Despite generational variations, most Italian lesbians and gays see their country in a phase of progress that stands in contrast with a homophobic past. Homophobic attacks are less frequent in Italy, or at least less reported on, than in some other European countries like the United Kingdom. On the societal level, it is difficult to generalize the degree of homophobia that lesbians and gays experience in Italy, as lived situations differ very radically depending on the region, city, or town, or on the sector of employment. But for most Italian homosexuals, the societal constraints remain important, where they feel strong expectations to confirm to heterosexual society in families, friendships, at the workplace, and the like.[6] And even in very liberal urban environments, despite many signs of a generational change, a "don't ask, don't tell" policy often dominates how LGBT people manage their homosexual identities.[7]

After the 2005 elections in which the center-left government of Romano Prodi took power, the question of recognition of same-sex relationships became the subject of a nationwide debate that has not led to any specific legislative intervention so far, but nevertheless has provided LGBT issues with some visibility. Interestingly, the parliament elected in 2005 includes the first transsexual member of parliament (Vladimir Luxuria), who was also the first transsexual to be elected to a national parliament in any European country. However, because of the relatively higher visibility of LGBT issues compared to the past, the Prodi government has been under attack by the Vatican. Due to the internal divisions of the centre-left coalition, the Prodi government lost its parliamentary majority support in February 2008, and since the newly elected right-wing government took power, cases of antihomosexual violence and racism have surged, and the progression of the past years is being questioned yet again by many observers.

EDUCATION

It is very hard to find anything that resembles gay and lesbian studies, as the subject has recently emerged in other Western countries, in Italy. Some researchers have recently produced studies in sociology, politics, and law concerning LGBT issues in Italy, but these are very few and isolated instances. Even gender studies are largely excluded from mainstream academia, and are left more to the initiative of individual researchers and professors at universities, whose networks are usually informal, but in some cases incorporate attention to lesbian and other issues. This situation reflects the general silence over LGBT issues in the Italian public education system, from primary school to university.

EMPLOYMENT AND ECONOMICS

Employment is certainly one of the areas in which LGBT people have met with most hostility and discrimination. There were cases brought to court by LGBT people who had been fired because of their sexuality. These people won their cases on the basis that private, noncriminal acts cannot be a valid reason for dismissal,[8] although proper case law on the matter of employment discrimination is absent.

Legislative decree 216 of July 9, 2003,[9] guarantees protection from discrimination based on sexual orientation, as is the case for religion and belief, age, and disability. As anticipated, this decree—which has the same value as an act of parliament—transposed the European Union Directive 2000/78/EC concerning employment discrimination.[10] A directive is a type of European Union (EU) legislation that member states have to implement, sticking to some ground rules and principles while remaining free to adapt and adjust other provisions of the directive according to their preference and national priorities.

Although the decree clearly introduced an innovation in the Italian legislation, a 2004 report by Stafano Fabeni[11]—who is part of a network of legal experts funded by the European Union—found several points of the law that were considered not fully in compliance with the directive's main content. The decree condemns both direct and indirect discrimination, and allows for positive actions in the field of antidiscrimination. However, in some points the decree departs from the directive, mainly in the direction of restricting the array of situations in which the law applies.

Special attention, then, should be paid to the question of recruitment in the army. Until a few years ago, military service in Italy was compulsory for all males. Presently, the army recruits only voluntaries and has become a professional army. Despite different attitudes of military districts on admittance of homosexuals to the army, the overall army policy on the matter has been one of rejection. When military service was compulsory, many gay men were reluctant to go into service because of both the homophobic and homoerotic environment of the barracks. On the basis of an informal pact between the army and Arcigay—the biggest gay association—one could be exempted from the service on the ground of homosexuality by presenting a letter from the association declaring that the man in question was a member of the association, supported by a psychologist's statement that the man in question had problems with his sexuality. While aiming to give a practical solution to both sides, this pact was both criticized as homophobic by other gay associations and of course could be abused by anyone.[12]

With the introduction of the professional army, homophobia against those out-side and inside the army has not ended, and occasionally this attitude has appeared to be justified by comments of members of government and center-right-wing parties. In July 2008 Carlo Giovanardi—deputy secretary of the Ministry of Fam-ily of the new Berlusconi government—stated that homosexual men can be part of the army but also that there should not be "an overt, visible, and invasive mani-festation of homosexuality."[13] Giovanardi went on to compare a tolerable type of homosexuality to the attitude of heterosexual men frequenting prostitutes.

SOCIAL/GOVERNMENT PROGRAMS

There is no major program targeting the LGBT communities and their issues at the state level. Occasionally, campaigns against homophobia were organized at the city and regional level out of the cooperation between local LGBT associations and local/regional authorities. In October 2007, the Tuscany region launched a poster campaign portraying a recently born baby wearing a bracelet on which the word *homosexual* was written instead of his or her name. The campaign was criticized by right-wing parties. However, some LGBT activists—including transgender activist Vladimir Luxuria—also raised concerns about the message of the campaign on the ground that it considered homosexuality to be a genetic and therefore immutable factor.[14]

SEXUALITY/SEXUAL PRACTICES

As of 2004, there were about 120,000 HIV-positive people in Italy, largely concentrated in the north-central regions. Since 1982, when the first Italian case of HIV infection was first diagnosed, the dynamics of the infection have changed. While in the early years, transmission of the virus was through drug injection, today it occurs largely via sexual relations, especially through casual sex relations. Both homosexuals and an increasing number of heterosexuals are HIV positive. A study from 2008 revealed that anti-AIDS therapies have reduced the mortality rate for AIDS from 100 percent to 8 percent. At the same time, the study calcu-lated that there are about 40,000 people who ignore being HIV positive, with the consequence that they start therapies late and often put sexual partners at risk of infection.[15]

In light of this situation, many anti-AIDS associations, including LGBT asso-ciations, have advocated state-wide safer-sex campaigns and sexual education in schools. Although some campaigns were in fact organized by the state, these were criticized by many associations for being too reticent to include same-sex relations or to promote the use of condoms for sexual relations.

Another highly controversial topic in the political debate in recent years was that of reproductive rights and the access to new reproductive technologies. Concern-ing reproductive rights, Italy moved from a situation of a certain flexibility and freedom to the imposition of several restrictions following the approval of the first law on medically assisted procreation (*procreazione medicalmente assisitita*) in 2004 by the center-right government of Silvio Berlusconi.[16] The law reserves access to alternative insemination and reproductive services—in both public and private clin-ics certified and authorized by the state—to married and unmarried opposite-sex couples under strict conditions. Heterologous insemination is not permitted by the law. Single men and women and same-sex couples are thus formally excluded from reproductive rights: if a doctor provides alternative insemination to singles and same-sex couples, she or he can be fined between 200,000 and 400,000 euros (US$280,000 and $560,000). Recently, some criticism has been raised about the lack of effectiveness of the law and the fact that those excluded had to travel abroad to access medically assisted procreation in countries with more liberal legislations, especially Spain and some central and eastern European countries.[17] However, an immediate reassessment of the law is not on the political agenda and, in any case, there is little chance that these could ever lead to an opening up of reproductive services to lesbian women, not to mention gay couples.

FAMILY

There is presently a strong tension between the ideology of the family and the practice of family lives. On the one hand, the Italian state—in line with the family doctrine of the Vatican—promotes a family composed of an opposite-sex married couple with children as the cornerstone of society and center of Italian welfare and legislation. On the other, studies have showed the transformation of the Italian family within the wider process of modernization and the secularization of society. The introduction of divorce and abortion legislation in the 1970s and several reforms of the family code contributed to opening the family to a variety of forms and practices of de facto cohabitation and child rearing, which called into question the original model and called for adequate legal recognition. In the last years, the question of families centered on same-sex couples emerged—with children born in previous marriages or, in the case of lesbians, through donor insemination.

However, Italian legislation and public policies have been reluctant recognize new forms of family life. The government has not established any form of recognition of de facto same-sex and opposite-sex couples. In addition, Italian legislation provides that only opposite-sex married couples may adopt children. Therefore, lesbian and gay people have no right to adopt, either as individuals or as couples. There have been cases in which custody (*affido familiare*) has been granted to single people, and in some cases homosexuality was not considered an obstacle to obtaining custody.[18]

COMMUNITY

The LGBT community is highly fragmented and structured above all in cities around local groups concerned with advocacy and/or providing services (health and legal counseling, youth and discussion groups, and so on) to the LGBT community. The community has been particularly divided along political cleavages and priorities and objectives. While usually acting within a center-left political ideology, groups that claim to represent the LGBT community stay within a range that goes from the lobby approach to the grassroots and radical style. While, for example, Arcigay and Arcilesbica—the two best-known national coalitions of gay and lesbian associations—have strong political contacts and affiliations with leftist parties, other radical groups operate more at the margin, with a stronger leftist ideology and in a more oppositional and *movimentist* style.

With respect to radical groups, three years ago some these created the network Facciamo Breccia (which could be translated as something like "Let's break the wall," making reference to the *breccia di Porta Pia,* the passage through which Italian soldiers slipped into Rome and ultimately annexed it in the 19th century, ending the formal Vatican sovereignty over the city). The network was a reaction to the attacks on the LGBT community by the Vatican and the new pope, Benedict XVI.

The relation between these two poles of the LGBT movement has not always been easy due to the fact that lobby-oriented groups privilege mediation and negotiation while groups more on the left have a more provocative style of doing politics.

HEALTH

AIDS, as much as other sexually transmitted diseases (STDs) has always been an issue for the LGBT population in Italy. The state has not produced many national, highly visible information and prevention campaigns on health and safer sex. When it has engaged in such campaigns, it has ignored the specificity of LGBT issues in such matters. However, in many instances, local LGBT groups received funding to print their own informational material. Some of these set up counseling services, providing information on safer sex and other health issues, while at the same time functioning as a link between users and gay-friendly health services. Some lesbian groups—like the association Drasticamente from Padua—focused on women's health issues (such as breast cancer).

POLITICS AND LAW

Sodomy

At the time of the unification of Italy in the late 19th century, only two of the states that became part of the Italian kingdom had criminal legislation concerning sexual activity between men, including the Kingdom of Sardinia. Following the unification, this law was extended to the entire peninsula by the Kingdom of Sardinia. However, private and consensual sexual activity between men was decriminalized with the adoption of kingdom's first penal code (the Codice Zanardelli) in 1889. This decriminalization was largely inspired by the Napoleonic code that was in force in the north of the peninsula before the unification.[19]

Antidiscrimination Legislation

At the moment, there is almost no mention of sexual orientation or preference in any antidiscrimination provision of the civil and penal codes. The Constitution of Italy does not explicitly prohibit discrimination based on sexual orientation in its article on equality (article 3), although the latter does cover factors such as race, gender, and religion.

Law 205 of 1993—the Legge Mancino—contains several antidiscrimination provisions concerning hate crimes motivated by racial, ethnic, national, or religious status. The attention of the LGBT movement to such laws increased between 2006 and 2007 due to the publicity given by the press to episodes of violence against lesbians and bullying against gay youth at school. In 2006, the government committed itself to adding sexual orientation as a protected category in the law.[20]

However, after the fall of the Prodi government, there will probably be no implementation of this in the near future.

Finally, regional antidiscrimination legislation, although not so diffused, may represent a departure from the lack of initiative at the state level in some policy fields. Regions in Italy have extensive autonomy in social policies, including in the areas of education and health. In November 2004, the Tuscany region, which is governed by a leftist majority, approved a regional law banning discrimination based on sexual orientation and gender identity.[21] On the basis of the law, the region targeted LGBT people with respect to inclusion in labor policies and formation, corporate social responsibility, and personnel training. In the area of health, the law also recognized the freedom of any person to indicate another person (outside the family circle) responsible for assisting him or her in case of illness. Designation implies the right of the designated person to make decisions concerning specific therapeutic treatment if the designating person is not in a condition to decide by him or herself. The region also commits itself to promoting cultural events. Finally, it prohibits discrimination by owners of public accommodations.

Same-sex Relations

Neither the Italian constitution[22] nor any law recognizes same-sex marriage. Legal arguments against or in favor of such recognition have usually referred to following constitutional principles. Arguments against recognition usually stress that it is not permitted because article 29 of the constitution stipulates that "the Republic recognizes the rights of the family as natural society founded upon marriage": this statement is interpreted as excluding the legal possibility of any recognition of alternative types of families and relationships. Marriage is assumed to be a union between two people of opposite sexes. Arguments in favor of recognition commonly rely on the supremacy of the equality provision of article 3—intended as implicitly granting equality on all grounds, including sexual orientation. They also make reference to article 2, which states that the republic recognizes "the inviolable rights of the man, both as single and part of those social formations in which he develops his personality" (*sic*). In support of the pro-recognition position, article 9 of the Charter of Fundamental Rights of the European Union—a nonbinding document at the moment—is often referred to as implicitly recognizing the diversity of family lives because it allows in principle for different regulations of marriage in different EU member states.[23]

The recognition of the rights of same-sex relationships gained momentum in Italy early in 2007 during the 15th legislature with the approval of the first official government bill (*disegno di legge*) on the DICO (*diritti dei conviventi*, or rights of cohabitants).[24] Some proposals had already been presented by single members of parliament—especially from parties on the left—starting from the 1990s. However, no such proposal was ever scheduled for discussion and voting.[25] Before the 2005 elections, the center-left coalition of Romano Prodi included in its program the commitment to provide some form of regulation concerning unmarried couples of whatever sex. Between 2006 and 2007, the left and center parties of the governing coalition started a debate on the language to be used in the proposal and the rights to be accorded to the partners: while the left wanted a more advanced proposal, the center parties (and especially the Teo-dem members of the Margherita Party that, in principle, was against any legal initiative on the matter) pushed for the recognition of a minimum set of rights and for the elimination of any possible equation between traditional family rights and the partners of a de facto couple. The mediation of the DICO was carried out by the minister of the family and the minister for equal opportunities.

The outcome was innovative for Italy but well below the prevailing western European standards. The law provided that the partners—of either the same or the opposite sex—must live together: they are actually called *cohabitants* by the law. A DICO must be filed at the civil register office by both or one partner. Each partner can be designated by the other as the person responsible for assisting him or her in hospital or carrying out arrangements after his or her death. The foreign partner can request a residence permit for cohabitation. Although the law recognizes the right of the surviving cohabitant to succeed in the tenancy contract, this right can only be enjoyed after three years of cohabitation (or immediately, if the couple has children). The right to inherit is subject to a nine-year previous cohabitation. Matters related to pension rights are left out of the DICO proposals and assigned to the next reorganization of the entire pension system. No adoption rights are provided under the DICO.

Currently, the DICO proposal is under examination by the Justice Committee of the Senate (the second chamber of the Italian parliament). In July 2007, the proposal was amended and substituted with the Contracts of Supportive Union (*Contratti di Unione Solidale,* CUS).[26] With respect to the DICO, the most relevant differences are that the CUS does not require the cohabitation of the partners, and that the contract must be stipulated by both partners either in front of a justice of the peace or a notary. These elements make the CUS closer to the contractual form of the French PACS (*pacte civil de solidarité*) than the DICO, while at the same time providing a higher public and quasi-marriage status. However, the fall of the Prodi government in February 2008 virtually closed any possibility of pushing either the DICO or the CUS proposal further.

Finally, it is interesting to look at the local registers for civil unions. At the same time as the first civil union law proposals were being presented in the national parliament, some municipalities—like Empoli and Pisa in Tuscany—introduced special registers in which same-sex partners could certify their cohabitation. Since then, other cities have adopted similar initiatives whose values, however, are mainly symbolic. In some cases, litigation started between the local administrations and the CORECO (Regional Supervision Committee) on the issue of the compatibility of these initiatives with national legislation.[27] Some municipalities have opened lists of public housing to cohabiting same-sex couples by relying on the more flexible definition of family according to administrative law.[28]

Asylum

Article 10 of the Italian constitution provides that the stranger who is not permitted to exercise his or her democratic freedom in his or her country of origin has the right to asylum in Italy. However, Italy has no law that specifically defines the criteria on the basis of which asylum can be sought. The right to seek asylum has been recognized as a subjective right by courts, including the Supreme Court of Cassation (Corte Suprema di Cassazione), so that aliens can actually seek asylum by filing a request in the competent tribunal of their domicile. Because of the increasing number of migrants coming to Italy and the national government's effort to distinguish between political and economic immigrants, the matter has become politically sensitive. In a recent 2007 decision that made headlines in Italy, the supreme court ruled that homosexuality is a valid ground upon which asylum can be requested. The court dealt with the case of a man from Senegal who claimed to be gay and did not want to be extradited to his country of origin because, there, homosexuality is punished with imprisonment. The man provided subscription to two gay organizations as evidence of his homosexuality. The court warned of the possible abuse of the general asylum procedure and questioned whether homosexuality per se can lead to imprisonment, or whether it is the overt and public display of homosexuality. At the same time, the court recognized that "sexual freedom is to be intended also as freedom to live without conditionings and restrictions of one's sexual preferences" in line with article 2 of the constitution, and argued that homosexuality is a "condition of the man that deserves protection in conformity with constitutional precepts."[29]

Bisexuals

There is no legal provision in the Italian constitution or legislation that explicitly mentions bisexuals or bisexuality. Bisexuals are never referred to in political debates as a separate category deserving any particular rights, and they are not identified as a specific social or sexual category or group. In Italy, bisexuality is probably more of a practice than a legitimate and established public identity.

Transsexuals and Transgender People

Compared to the legal condition of lesbian and gay people, the recognition of the rights of transsexual and transgender people is relatively progressive. Italy was among the first European countries to legislate on sex reassignment with law.164 in 1982. The law provides that, upon request of the interested person and after the modification of the person's sexual character has been certified, the court orders the rectification of the acts of the civil register. The court also authorizes the medical-surgical intervention if the adjustment of the sexual character of the person is necessary. Following the court's judgment on the rectification of the acts of the civil register, the name and the sex of the person are officially changed. The same judgment causes the dissolution of the eventual marriage of which the person was a part.

However, the law and its interpretation have also showed some limitations and raised criticism and requests for change on the part of the transgender and transsexual movement. In particular, it is unclear in the law whether the medical-surgical intervention is a prerequisite for the rectification of the acts of the civil register and, in particular, for the name change. Case law has almost unanimously upheld the first interpretation, although the word of the law suggests, or in any case does not preclude, the second option. Therefore, the law seems inadequate to meet the need of transgender people who do not want to undergo a surgical change of sex. At the same time, the impossibility of changing names before the operation has been causing both psychological and social problems for transsexuals during the period of transition from one sex to the other. This has been especially true in searching for a job. In some cases, there were also episodes of discrimination in which transsexual and transgender people were accused of breaking an old legislation of 1931 that prohibits people from appearing in public in disguise.

Intersexes

There is no specific legislation in Italy dealing with intersexuality and the rights of intersexual people concerning sex assignment. There are three medical centers in the country specializing in intersexuality. The law imposes that sex assignment must be completed before the baby leaves the hospital. Sex assignment is conducted by a team of experts comprising pediatricians, urologists, geneticists, and legal doctors, together with the parents of the baby. According to transgender parliamentarian Vladimir Luxuria, the final choice is often made on the basis of the wishes of the family. There have been cases of mistakes, in which the Tribunal for Minors has had to intervene to reassign the sex. There have also been cases of originally declared females who sued their parents after discovering that they were actually males.[30]

RELIGION AND SPIRITUALITY

There is no research concerning the relation between religious institutions and homosexual believers. However, anecdotal evidence and information show that a number of people are both homosexual and believers, and have come out as such both as individuals and by establishing groups that tend to be increasingly visible and structured. The Faith and Homosexuality Group of the 2006 Turin Pride committee is one example. Other groups of lesbian and gay believers have been formed locally and with respect to different religions and faiths, especially Christianity. Reactions by the official and organized religious institutions have been mixed. The Baptist, Methodist, and Waldensian Churches and communities of Italy have exhibited different positions among themselves concerning the adoption of a special blessing ceremony for same-sex couples. Waldensians, who have a liberal view on sex and sexuality in general, have been open to homosexual believers and their official recognition in Waldensian churches. Such openness is clearly unlike the Catholic Church, although the Vatican's official position rejects homosexuality but not homosexuals per se. The ambiguity of this position has caused different types of responses from both the church hierarchies and parish churches and dioceses. These have varied from occasional institutional meetings and confrontations between representatives of the church and of groups and networks of homosexual believers to a sometimes more intense dialogue and practical collaboration between the latter and some Catholic communities and associations such as the Abele Group (Gruppo Abele). In November 2006, the Abele Group publicly launched the project of the National Documentation Center on Homosexuality and Faith.[31]

VIOLENCE

Although there are no official statistics concerning episodes of either verbal or physical violence against LGBT people, some surveys have addressed violence against young LGBT people. A 1990 survey by Arcigay and the Institute of Political, Economic, and Social Studies (Istituto di Studi Politici Economici e Sociali, ISPES) showed that 24 percent of lesbian and gay people under age 20 had been the object of some violence. However, interviews were collected by approaching people in gay and lesbian associations, meaning that those interviewed already socialized in a gay and lesbian environment, and therefore not representative of the overall homosexual population. Between 1998 and 2000, the Florentine association Azione Gay e Lesbica collaborated on an Internet survey on violence against LGBT youth as part of the EU Daphne project Who's That Boy? Who's That Girl? About one-third of the replies to the online questionnaires were from Italians, mainly from gay men but with a relatively high percentage of lesbian women (18.1%) compared to other EU countries (5.13%) and non-EU countries (2.6%). The Daphne survey tended to confirm the results of the 1990 survey, with 26.65 percent of people—29.73 percent of women and 25.83 percent of men—declaring that they had been victims of violence.[32] More recently, Arcigay has started an international project on homophobic bullying called Schoolmates.[33] In a survey conducted between 2006 and 2007 on 500 high school teachers and students, Arcigay showed that 53.5 percent of respondents had often or frequently heard offensive words such as *finocchio* (faggot) that were used to address homosexual or perceived homosexual males in the school.[34] Local and national LGBT associations have started projects in schools to try to limit the phenomenon of bullying. These have included training for teachers, who are perceived as underestimating the problem. However, visible and constant public support for these initiatives has been lacking—especially at the national level—due to the usual institutional reluctance to lend visibility to homosexuality.

Not surprisingly, the data also showed a relation between violence and suicide. The Arcigay/ISPES survey revealed that 41.79 percent of the interviewees thought about suicide and 14.07 percent had actually attempted suicide. The Daphne survey showed a positive correlation between being the victim of violence and inclination to commit suicide: among those who were not subject to violence, 33.72 percent thought about suicide and 11.43 percent had attempted it, while victims of violence thought about suicide in 64 percent of cases and attempted it in 21.6 percent of cases.[35]

Although the issue of violence against LGBT people has been largely invisible in the media and has received little attention by state authorities, things could soon change. Several recent episodes of violence were reported by the media and triggered a public debate on the issue of homophobic violence. One concerned physical attacks against lesbians in Torre del Lago, a seaside town that has become known as a place where many lesbians and gay people spend their summer holidays. In August 2006, one of these women was raped by a group of right-wing men.[36] The other incident occurred in April 2007 and concerned a 16-year-old boy from Turin, who was a victim of bullying and who committed suicide.[37] The most recent incident, in November 2007, involved a boy in Finale Ligure: his schoolmates stripped him and wrote the word gay and drew a swastika on his chest. The minister of education sent inspectors to the school.[38] All of these episodes provoked the mobilization of LGBT associations on the specific issue of violence. Gay, lesbian, and transgender members of parliament—Franco Grillini, Titti de Simone, and Vladimir Luxuria—requested the inclusion of sexual orientation among the factors that determine punishable acts of hatred. Sit-ins were launched in early December by Arcigay in support of the amendments to the Mancino law.[39] Again, however, the fall of the Prodi government in February 2008 put an end of all hopes that the law could be amended in the near future.

OUTLOOK FOR THE 21ST CENTURY

Italy is going through a phase of change and mobilization. From the 1990s on, there has been an increase in the visibility of LGBT people in society and the media. LGBT people have also come out at every level of society. Different components of the LGBT movement have been able to coordinate for national pride demonstrations, which, while not duplicating the numbers of WorldPride 2000, have nevertheless seen vast participation and an increased awareness of the need to capitalize on the previous gains in visibility. There are also signs of an increasing radicalization of the movement, as attacks against the politics of the Vatican and the requests to guarantee the secular nature of the Italian state and its institutions have become louder (as demonstrated by the visibility gained by the anti-Vatican "No Vat" movement over the last three years).

This increased visibility and degree of activism, however, have also provoked a negative reaction by conservative parties and forces, including violent groups. There is also little doubt that the Vatican—especially after the election of Pope Benedict XVI—has provided a crucial legitimization of these negative reactions by attacking homosexual behaviors and lifestyles in many instances and public arenas, and by trying to influence Italian politics in a way that hinders any possibility of recognition of LGBT rights. The impression is that, precisely because most western European countries—including a traditionally strongly Catholic country like Spain—have provided an increased recognition of LGBT rights, the Vatican will not easily give up Italy as the last bastion of Catholic civilization. This explains why, although LGBT issues gained some political visibility during the last center-left Prodi government, that same government ended up doing nothing on LGBT issues, and even faced a crisis triggered by its internal (and the external) Catholic political and conservative groups when it tried to pass LGBT-related legislation.

What Italian LGBT people may expect to gain in the future will probably depend on the capacity of the movement to unite and focus on specific political and legal issues, to forge alliances with non-LGBT movements, and to convince the country's intellectual and political elites of the value of its requests. Chances of change will also vary depending on the political composition of any future government. Any movement's claims to Europe may help, but will probably not be decisive.

RESOURCE GUIDE

Suggested Reading

Marzio Barbagli and Asher Colombo, *Omosessuali moderni* (Bologna: Il Mulino, 2001).

Gianni Barilli Rossi, *Il movimento gay in Italia* (Milan: Feltrinelli, 1999).

Matteo Bonini Baraldi, *Le nuove convivenze tra discipline straniere e diritto interno* (Milano: IPSOA, 2005).

Daniele Del Pozzo and Luca Scarlini, *Gay. La guida italiana in 150 voci* (Milan: Mondadori, 2006).

Anna Elisabetta Galeotti, *Toleration as Recognition* (Cambridge: Cambridge University Press, 2002).

Flora Leroy-Forgeot, *Histoire juridique de l'homosexualité en Europe* (Paris: Presses Universitaires de France, 1997).

P. M. Nardi, "The Globalisation of the Gay and Lesbian Socio-Political Movement: Some Observation about Europe with a Focus on Italy," *Sociological Perspectives* 41, no. 3 (1998): 567–86.

Piergiorgio Paterlini, *Matrimoni* (Torino: Einaudi, 2004).

Piergiorgio Paterlini, *Ragazzi che amano ragazzi* (Torino: Einaudi, 1991).

Gioia Scapucci, "Italy Walking a Tightrope between Stockholm and the Vatican: Will Legal Recognition of Same-Sex Partnerships Ever Occur?" in *Legal Recognition of Same-Sex Partnerships: A Study of National, European and International Law,* ed. Robert Wintemute and Mads Andenæs (Oxford: Hart Publishing, 2001).

Sara Tonolo, *Le unioni civil nel diritto internazionale privato* (Milan: Giuffrè editore, 2007).

Kees Waaldijk, "Comparative Analysis," in *More or Less Together: Levels of Legal Consequences of Marriage, Cohabitation and Registered Partnership for Different-sex and Same-sex Partners: A Comparative Study of Nine European countries,* Documents de travail No 125 (Paris: Institut National d'Études Démographiques, 2005).

Kees Waaldijk, "Comparative Overview," in *More or Less Together: Levels of Legal Consequences of Marriage, Cohabitation and Registered Partnership for Different-sex and Same-sex Partners: A Comparative Study of Nine European countries,* Documents de travail No 125 (Paris: Institut National d'Études Démographiques, 2005).

Kees Waaldijk and Matteo Bonini-Baraldi, *Sexual Discrimination in the European Union—National Laws and the Employment Equality Directive* (The Hague, Netherlands: Asser Press, 2006).

Web Sites/Organizations

Antagonismo gay, http://isole.ecn.org/agaybologna/index.php.
>   LGBT/Queer group from Bologna.

Arcigay, http://www.arcigay.it.
>   National network, with list of local Arcigay associations.

Arcilesbica, http://www.arcilesbica.it.
>   National network, with list of local Arcilesbica associations.

Azione Gay e Lesbica, http://www.azionegayelesbica.it.
>   LGBT association from Florence.

Circolo Drasticamente, http://www.drasticamente.it.
>   Lesbian association from Padua.

Circolo Mario Mieli, http://www.mariomieli.org.
>   LGBT association from Rome.

Circolo Maurice, http://www.mauriceglbt.org.
>   LGBT association from Turin.

Facciamo breccia, www.facciamobreccia.it.
>   National network of local associations that organizes the No Vat annual demonstration in Rome.

Movimento Identità Transessuale (MIT), http://www.mit-italia.it.
>   National transsexual/transgender organization.

Open Mind, http://www.inventati.org/openmind/open.htm.
>   LGBT association from Catania.

NOTES

1. Gianfranco Goretti, "Confino Fascista," in Gay, *La Guida Italiana in 150 voci,* ed. Del Daniele Pozzo and Luca Scarpini (Milan: Mondadori, 2006), 65–67.

2. Pew Research Center Report, November 18, 2003, http://pewforum.org/publications/surveys/religion-homosexuality.pdf (accessed September 20, 2009).

3. IGLA-Europe, December 18, 2006. "EU: attitudes towards same-sex marriage & adoption significantly vary," Eurobarometre.

4. Gallup Europe, 2004, "Public opinion and same-sex unions (2003)". *ILGA Europe* (accessed January 29, 2006).

5. Frédéric Jörgens, "The Individual, the Couple, and the Family: Social and Legal Recognition of Same-Sex Partnerships in Europe," PhD dissertation, Florence, European University Institute, Italy, 2007.

6. See Marzio Barbagli and Asher Colombo, *Omosessuali moderni* (Il Mulino: Bologna, 2001).

7. Ibid., 68–85.

8. International Lesbian and Gay Association (ILGA)-Europe, *Equality for Lesbians and Gay Men* (ILGA, 1998), 66.

9. Parlamento italiano, Decreto legislativo 9 luglio 2003 n.216, "Attuazione della direttiva 2000/78/CE per l a parità di trattamento in materia di occupazione e di condizioni di lavoro," http://www.camera.it/parlam/leggi/deleghe/testi/03216dl.htm (accessed November 28, 2007).

10. Council Directive (EC) 2000/78 of November 27, 2007, establishing a general framework for equal treatment in employment and occupation, http://ec.europa.eu/employment_social/fundamental_rights/pdf/legisln/2000_78_en.pdf (accessed November 27, 2007).

11. See the report of the Stefano Fabeni, European Group of Experts on Combating Sexual Orientation Discrimination, *About the Implementation up to April 2004 of Directive 2000/78/EC Establishing a General Framework for Equal Treatment in Employment and Occupation,* chapter 11, http://ec.europa.eu/employment_social/fundamental_rights/policy/aneval/mon_en.htm.

12. ILGA-Europe, *Equality for Lesbians and Gay Men,* 68–69.

13. Author's translation. See "Gay nell'esercito? Si puo' ma con moderazione," *Il Manifesto,* July 5, 2008, http://www.ilmanifesto.it/ricerca/ric_view.php3?page=/Quotidiano-archivio/05-Luglio-2008/art17.html&word=giovanardi;omosess (accessed July 7, 2008).

14. See "Omosessuali si nasce campagna choc con bebè," *La Repubblica,* October 24, 2007, http://firenze.repubblica.it/dettaglio/Campagna-choc-contro-lomofobia/1380214?ref=rephp (accessed July 6, 2008).

15. Dica33, "Malattie infettive," http://www.dica33.it/argomenti/malattie_infettive/aids/1aids04.asp (accessed July 6, 2008); "AIDS: in Italia ci sono 40mila persone sieropositive che non sanno di esserlo," *Corriere della Sera,* June 18, 2008, http://www.corriere.it/salute/08_giugno_18/adis_folla_sieropositivi_d4e73374–3d43–11dd-bfea-00144f02aabc.shtml (accessed July 6, 2008).

16. Parlamento italiano, Legge n.40/2004, Norme sulla procreazione medicalmente assistita, http://www.parlamento.it/leggi/04040l.htm (accessed December 2, 2007).

17. "Bimbi in provetta boom di viaggi all'estero," *Repubblica,* December 1, 2006, http://www.repubblica.it/2006/12/sezioni/cronaca/bimbi-provetta/bimbi-provetta/bimbi-provetta.html (accessed December 3, 2007); "Addio Spagna, ora si punta ad est: I viaggi delle coppie nelle cliniche low cost," *Corriere della Sera,* November 21, 2007, http://www.corriere.it/cronache/07_novembre_21/mete_maternita_low_cost_est_e684134a-9816–11dc-89d7–0003ba99c53b.shtml (accessed December 3, 2007).

18. ILGA-Europe, *Equality for Lesbians and Gay Men,* 66.

19. For more information, see Giovanni Dall'Orto's home page, http://www.giovannidallorto.com/saggistoria/tollera/tolle2.html (accessed December 3, 2007).

20. Titti de Simone, member of the Chamber of Deputies, news release, http://www.tittidesimone.it/comunicati%20stampa2006.htm (accessed December 2, 2007).

21. Regione Toscana, Legge Regionale del Novembre 15, 2004, n.63, "Norme contro le discriminazioni determinate dall'orientamento sessuale o dall'identità di genere."

22. An English version of the Italian Constitution is available at the constitutional court's Web page, http://www.cortecostituzionale.it/eng/testinormativi/costituzionedellarepubblica/costituzione.asp (accessed November 25, 2007).

23. For a more detailed account on these two views, see the petition signed by 23 Italian law professors, "Le famiglie nella Costituzione," http://www.arcigay.it/show.php?2426, (accessed November 21, 2007).

24. Presidenza del Consiglio dei Ministri, Disegno di legge in material di diritti e doveri dei conviventi (DICO). The bill and other type of information on it can be found at http://www.governo.it/GovernoInforma/Dossier/dico (accessed December 2, 2007).

25. ILGA-Europe, *Equality for Lesbians and Gay Men,* 66.

26. Senato italiano, Atto n.589, Disciplina del contratto di unione solidale. The bill and updated information on it can be found at http://www.senato.it/leg/15/BGT/Schede/Ddliter/25585.htm (accessed December 2, 2007).

27. ILGA-Europe, *Equality for Lesbians and Gay Men,* 66.

28. That has been the case, for example, in the Municipality of Venice.

29. AdnKronos press agency, "La Cassazione apre ai gay: 'Ognuno deve vivere senza condizionamenti,'" July 27, 2007.

30. Vladimir Luxuria, "Per una soluzione italiana ai problemi delle/dei INTERSEX," *Liberazione,* May 24, 2006.

31. The news is from November 30, 2006, reported at http://www.popcorn.it/news/print/313.html (accessed December 2, 2007). For further documentation and updated information on the relationship between faith and homosexuality in Italy visit gionata.org.

32. Finisterrae Bertozzo Graziella, "Da internet le voci di quella ragazza, quel ragazzo," http://www.azionegayelesbica.it/daphne/rivista/3bertozzo.htm (accessed December 2, 2007).

33. Official English Web site, http://www.arcigay.it/schoolmates/UK/index.html (accessed December 3, 2007).

34. "Morire di omofobia a 16 anni," *Arcigay,* April 5, 2007, http://www.arcigay.it/show.php?2490 (accessed December 2, 2007).

35. G. Finisterrae Bertozzo, "Da internet le voci di quella ragazza, quel ragazzo."

36. "Giovane omosessuale violentata in Versilia," *Corriere della Sera,* September 2, 2006, http://www.corriere.it.

37. "Tormentato a scuola: 'Sei gay'. Si uccide," *Corriere della Sera,* April 5, 2007, http://www.corriere.it.

38. "Gli scrivono 'gay' con una svastica sul petto," *Corriere della Sera,* November 28, 2007, http://www.corriere.it.

39. "L'aula discute il testo sull'omofobia: sit-in in tante città," Gay.it, December 3, 2007, http://www.gay.it.

KYRGYZSTAN

Anna Kirey

OVERVIEW

Kyrgyzstan is a landlocked, mountainous country in Central Asia bordering Uzbekistan, Tajikistan, Kazakhstan, and China. Its population of 5.3 million people represents over 60 ethnic groups, with 75 percent of the population identifying as Muslims and 20 percent as Russian Orthodox Christians. The predominant ethnic groups are Kyrgyz, comprising 67.4 percent, Russians at 10.3 percent, and Uzbeks at 14.2 percent of the population. Kyrgyzstan is a post-Soviet country with traditions rooted in nomadism, communism, and Islam, which represents a mix that makes Kyrgyz society diverse and unique. After the collapse of the Soviet Union, Kyrgyzstan found itself in dire poverty and slipping into authoritarianism; to this day the political situation is unstable and the inflation rate is high. The majority of the population is literate and the level of higher education attainment remains high due to the influence of the Soviet legacy. Since 1991, nomadic and Islamic traditions have been reviving, and the number of people who practice religion is on the rise despite decades of Soviet atheist policies. The country is divided into two distinct regions, with the north and south of Kyrgyzstan, which follow different cultural paths. While the north of the country was mostly nomadic until the end

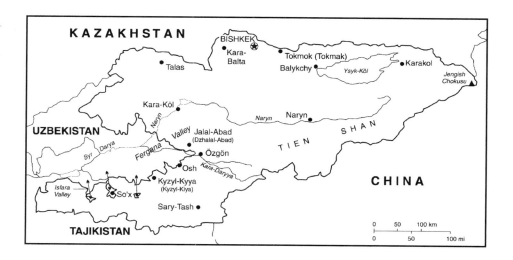

of the 19th century, the south of Kyrgyzstan has been more settled and adheres to Islamic traditions in social relations and everyday practices. In nomadic traditions, women contributed to the well-being of the family and were expected to take an active part in the tribe affairs because of the difficult nomadic life. Men were expected to protect the settlements and hunt. The southern parts of Kyrgyzstan were populated by ethnic Uzbeks. Under the influence of Uzbekistani culture, in which women were expected to stay at home and take care of the house and the family, these regions were different from the other parts of Kyrgyzstan. In the south of Kyrgyzstan, Uzbek traditions were adopted by Kyrgyz families, and some women wore veils in the past and at present are adhering to strict gender roles. Russian (and other non-Asian ethnic minority) women in Kyrgyzstan had a privileged status and do not comply with the norms of the society, due to belonging to a different ethnic group.

OVERVIEW OF LGBT ISSUES

Kyrgyz society perceives the issue of sexuality as taboo, and sexuality is maintained within the marriage context and largely not discussed either inside or outside the family. Muslim and nationalist groups protest open information or education about sexuality for young people, while most of the newspaper kiosks feature adult magazines with explicit photographs. During the years of the Soviet Union, Kyrgyzstan used the Soviet criminal code, which criminalized *muzhelozhstvo* (anal sex between men). The criminal code was changed in 1998[1] and the article about consensual sex between men was dropped from the Kyrgyz criminal code, but the legislation continues to differentiate between homosexual and heterosexual sex in the sphere of sexual violence and assault. The family sphere remains the most dangerous place for LGBT people, due to the prevalent belief that a nonconforming child is a source of shame for the family. Some families send their LGBT children to remote villages to live with relatives; some force them to get married through threatening to stop financial and social support; and some pressure their LGBT children to conform through use of physical and psychological methods.

Despite the high level of intolerance toward LGBT people, Kyrgyz history offers a number of examples of transgender individuals and homosexual behavior. In Kyrgyz ancient epics, there are famous descriptions of two female warriors who were raised as men because their royal families were not able to produce male children. Kyrgyz historians also refer to homosexual relations between men and young boys who were dancers and who dressed in female clothes, a practice that was common in the Fergana Valley (in the south of Kyrgyzstan) in the 19th century. During Soviet times, most gay men were in the closet, and met in small groups to socialize or in cruising areas for sexual encounters. Lesbian women were usually sent to psychiatric hospitals for treatment if their relatives discovered their attraction to other women. Society became more accepting of LGBT people from the time of the collapse of the Soviet Union, due to access to information and the change in gender roles that followed the economic decline.

EDUCATION

No information about LGBT people exists in educational settings, including textbooks and school policies. LGBT people suffer from ostracism and bullying in schools; this is usually not reported and no action is taken to prevent it. Many LGBT people do not complete higher education due to lack of family support and discrimination inflicted by their peers and professors.

EMPLOYMENT AND ECONOMICS

LGBT people are often discriminated against in employment due to their gender expression. There have been cases of firing from jobs on undefined grounds, rejection, lack of promotion, and lack of hiring due to having masculine looks (for women) or not being a man. LGBT people with higher education may end up working in car washes or cafes for years.

SOCIAL/GOVERNMENT PROGRAMS

The only domain where homosexual sexual contacts are part of the state discourse in Kyrgyzstan is legislation on HIV/AIDS prevention. This focus contributes to the stigma experienced by LGBT people by associating them with death and disease. To date, there is only one registered case of homosexual HIV transmission out of 1,800 cases in Kyrgyzstan.

SEXUALITY/SEXUAL PRACTICES

Safe sex has been on the social agenda since the beginning of the HIV epidemic in the 1990s. Numerous nongovernmental organizations (NGOs) in Kyrgyzstan work on providing information to the general public and young people about safe sex practices. The efforts are not systematic due to unstable financial support and the reluctance of the general public to make sexuality part of the public discourse. A teacher's guidebook for teaching about healthy lifestyles was published in 2000. It included information on safe sex and a drawing that depicted how a condom should be used. In May 2003, a number of Kyrgyz NGO activists, mostly from organizations of a nationalist nature, started protesting against state approval for the book's publication and distribution in schools. During one of the protests, the book was publicly burned, and the minister of education and culture decided to withdraw it from libraries and schools. The authors of the book were taken to court for violating the view, customs, and traditions of the Kyrgyz people. This example is indicative of the attitudes toward sexuality in Kyrgyzstan. Due to a lack of information and methods to communicate about sex, sexually transmitted infections (STIs) and HIV are on the rise in Kyrgyzstan.

Bisexuals

Bisexual identities are common among LGBT people in Kyrgyzstan, due to the social pressure to lead a double life (i.e., straight during the day and gay at night). It could be a challenge to define what bisexuality means to them and whether it is a protective or a forced identity.

FAMILY

Kyrgyz families are large, with many relatives (30 to 50) living within the same geographic area and meeting weekly for family events. Kyrgyz people are expected to get married in their early 20s, and a model family has three or more children. Young women are expected to live with their own family until marriage, and then they are passed to the family of their husband and often are not allowed to go back. Most social networks are built on family and clan relations, leaving many LGBT people without social support because they are cut off as a result of leaving their family or being a source of shame for the family. Close and distant family members have the right to comment about the young members of the family and pressure their relatives into following the traditions and customs of the extended family. For LGBT people, this means extra pressure coming not only from the nuclear family, but also from a number of relatives who feel obliged to direct their lost relative to the true path. Men are expected to provide for the family and women to do most of the housework, in addition to holding a full-time job and raising the children. The youngest son has to stay with his parents to provide for them. Due to family pressure, many gay men, especially in smaller towns and villages, get married and lead double lives. In one study conducted by NGOs about the LGBT situation in Kyrgyzstan in 2007, more than 60 percent of the respondents noted that their family pressured them psychologically and emotionally in an attempt to change them, and the same number of respondents said that their main concern was their relations with their family and relatives.[2]

COMMUNITY

The different groups of LGBT people that exist in Kyrgyzstan are usually based on informal networks and are divided by age and ethnicity. Groups of friends spend leisure time together and usually do not communicate with anyone outside of the LGBT communities. The communities interact with each other through participating in leisure events organized by LGBT organizations, and gay men usually meet at one of three disco bars in the capital city. The links within communities represent the extended family in its structure. They are used for emotional and social support, including employment and access to resources and housing. Communities create certain norms for what being LGBT means in the Kyrgyz context, and LGBT people follow these norms, which sometimes resembling heterosexual relations or behavior common for the opposite gender in Kyrgyz society. Many of the LGBT people in Kyrgyzstan experience low self-esteem, feel that they do not deserve to be treated equally with heterosexual people, and do not seek recognition of their rights. This results in apathy, substance abuse, and the inability to secure and maintain a job. Many LGBT people see their difference as a sickness and a cross to bear and do not feel that they are entitled to a family or children. Many LGBT people themselves do not voice their concerns in relation to society's stigma. They believe that hiding and being invisible is the best survival strategy. The communities provide a space where LGBT people can be themselves without having to explain their identity and lifestyle; they can also interact and learn more about each other and the global LGBT movement. There are four organizations in the country working on LGBT issues. Two of them are based in Bishkek—one in Talas (in the northeast) and one in Karabalta (in the northwest); they focus on LGBT empowerment and provide space for social interaction. The community center in Bishkek has a shelter and a referral system for counseling, as well as testing for HIV and other STIs. The organizations based outside of the capital city do their work in secret and mostly focus on gay men who are living with their wives and children due to social pressure to conform. The LGBT organization Labrys documents human rights violations and addresses concerns of LGBT people at the state and international levels through participation in international events and by providing information for various reports.

Transgender people in Kyrgyzstan are the most active group among LGBT people, due to their need to interact with the state to be able to transition medically and legally. A support group for transgender people started in 2005 from informal meetings, and at present is actively lobbying with the Ministry of Health and the Ministry of Justice to develop a system for gender transitioning. Transgender identities present a challenge to the LGBT community, and there is a resistance among other LGBT people when it comes to accepting them.

HEALTH

LGBT health, specifically gay men's and MSM (men who have sex with men) health, is the most researched issue concerning LGBT people in Kyrgyzstan, due to funding of HIV research. In 2007, a report was published on access to health care for LGBT people in Kyrgyzstan that highlighted the following issues as limitations to access to health care for LGBT people: homophobia and transphobia in Kyrgyz society and the medical system, discrimination, fear of discrimination and financial problems, and lack of knowledge among medical personnel about the specific health needs of LGBT people.[3] The most critical health issues are depression and substance abuse. Transgender health is a particularly urgent concern because the majority of medical institutions have no knowledge or expertise when it comes to administering hormones or providing gender reassignment surgeries. Transsexual people can be diagnosed with transsexualism at the Kyrgyz Republican (National) Center of Mental Health, but after the diagnosis is issued there is no medical support for the transitioning process.

POLITICS AND LAW

The Kyrgyz government does not recognize that LGBT people exist and is reluctant to discuss LGBT issues. The only entry point where LGBT concerns have been allowed into the state discourse is through HIV prevention decrees, which specified MSM as one of the key groups for HIV prevention in the country. LGBT issues are only discussed as pathologies in medical programs. Official educational institutions do not offer any information about LGBT issues or sexuality. Another intersection of LGBT lives with the state is within matters concerning transsexual and intersex people. The Kyrgyz civil code has a provision for changing passport sex if a certified medical institution provides a certain document acknowledging that a sex change was performed. In reality, however, the document of certified format does not exist, and transsexual people are not able to change their documents officially.

RELIGION AND SPIRITUALITY

Due to the legacy of the Soviet Union, many LGBT people are atheist and agnostic. There are some LGBT people who are Muslim and Russian Orthodox Christian, but they are usually rejected by the religious institutions. An LGBT-friendly priest of the Russian Apostolic Church offers religious service on Sundays in the community center run by the LGBT organization Labrys. There are no LGBT-friendly or affirming churches or mosques. Religious leaders of both Christian and Muslim congregations have openly expressed their disapproval of LGBT people through the media. When the first brochure on homosexuality in Kyrgyzstan was published by the Labrys, in an interview with the BBC, the Kyrgyz mufti called on Kyrgyz society to react to it. If there was no reaction, he stated, then Kyrgyzstan "has truly sunken below the level of animals."[4]

VIOLENCE

Kyrgyzstani society is a neotraditionalist Islamic post-Soviet society with very specific and fixed gender and social behavioral norms. Lesbian and bisexual women are seen as women who are not getting enough attention from men (due to not following gender roles, such as not being pretty or modest, or being too aggressive) and turning to a perverted lifestyle to fulfill their sexual drives. It is also often the case that when an LGBT person looks masculine or feminine, and people find out that she or he is not a biological man or woman, they mock, harass, and sometimes physically violate the person. Human rights violation cases have been documented by LGBT organizations. The violence can take the form of rape, beatings in the street, domestic violence (including severe beating and rejection from the family), psychological pressure to stay in the closet and change, and treating homosexuality as a disorder and sending the individual to rural areas, where they may be kidnapped for brides or given away in an arranged marriage. Gay men are constantly blackmailed by the police, who stop them near the gay clubs. Feminine men, both gay and heterosexual, are often attacked. The data on violence are mostly anecdotal, because LGBT NGOs started collecting it only recently. However, in the future, reports will be issued about the LGBT situation in Kyrgyzstan by Human Rights Watch and other human rights organizations.

Due to fear of rejection and violence, most LGBT people stay in the closet. They do not demand any recognition of rights, and the general public is hardly aware of LGBT people's existence.

LGBT NGOs are often targeted by the police, and threats of violence against LGBT activists have been documented.

OUTLOOK FOR THE 21ST CENTURY

LGBT issues are not seen as important by the government or human rights organizations in Kyrgyzstan, due to a variety of social and economic issues facing the transitional state. LGBT organizations in Kyrgyzstan will continue to struggle to put LGBT issues on the agendas of human rights organizations and the state. In the near future, transsexual and intersex people will be able to change their gender legally. It will take decades to secure LGBT rights because of social stigma and discrimination. Eventually, the state will acknowledge that LGBT rights have to be secured and protected, largely thanks to the influence of international organizations and LGBT NGO reports.

RESOURCE GUIDE

Suggested Reading

COC-Netherlands, "Kyrgyzstan: The Country of Human Rights...But Not for Homo-
    sexuals," COC-Netherlands, 2004, http://www.iiav.nl/epublications/2004/Kyrgy
    zstan.pdf.
Open Society Institute, "Report on LGBT People Access to Health Care in Kyrgyz-
    stan," Open Society Institute, 2007, http://www.soros.org/initiatives/health/
    focus/sharp/articles_publications/publications/kyrgyzstan_20070731/kyrgyz
    stan_20071030.pdf.

Organizations

Labrys, http://kyrgyzlabrys.wordpress.com.
    Formed in 2004, offers a variety of community events including discos, support
    groups, social gatherings, and movie screenings. Twenty-four-hour shelter, commu-
    nity center, confidential referrals for counseling, STI and HIV testing and treatment.
    Advocacy and lobbying. Resource center on LGBT issues in Russian.
Public Fund Avallon, http://avallon.ucoz.com/, http://www.avallon.web.kg/.
    Formed in 2006, mostly offers STI and HIV testing referral for MSM.
Public Fund Gender Vector, E-mail: gender_vector@mail.ru.
    Since 2006, mostly works with gay men and offers community services.
Public Fund Space, E-mail: atyncha@mail.ru, alfa18@ok.kz.
    Has worked undercover since 2005, mostly with gay men who lead double lives.

NOTES

1. Article 130 (1), Criminal Code of Kyrgyzstan, http://www.legislationline.org/
ru/legislation.php?tid=1&lid=6579.

2. "Access to Health Care for LGBT People in Kyrgyzstan," July 2007, http://
www.soros.org/initiatives/health/focus/sharp/articles_publications/publications/
kyrgyzstan_20070731.

3. Ibid., 35.

4. BBC Report [in Kyrgyz], October 8, 2007, http://www.bbc.co.uk/kyrgyz/
news/story/2007/10/printable/071008_kyrgyz_gays.shtml.

MOLDOVA

Julien Danero Iglesias

OVERVIEW

The Republic of Moldova is located in southeastern Europe between Ukraine and Romania. The only access to the sea is at the harbor of Giurgiulesti on a tiny strip on the Danube River. The population on January 1, 2007, was 3,518,100 people in a territory of 13,000 square miles, giving a density of population of approximately 270 inhabitants per square mile The capital and largest city is Chisinau (Kichinev in Russian), with a population of 780,000. Other main cities include Balti in the north, and Cahul in the south.[1]

The country gained independence in 1991 after the Soviet Union collapsed. Throughout its history, Moldova experienced different invasions and rules, being successively part of the Ottoman Empire, the Russian tsarist empire from 1812, Romania between World War I and World War II, and finally the Soviet Union. After independence, civil war occurred between 1991 and 1992, in which the regular Moldovan Army opposed Transdniestrian secessionists located on the east bank of the Dniester River. The conflict arose mainly for economic reasons, although the Russophile powers in Tiraspol, capital of the secessionist republic, made use of the ethnic argument. The new Moldovan powers were allegedly not recognizing rights for the Russophile minority. Tensions arose at the same time among the Gagauz minority, located in the south of the republic, which was claiming recognition of a particular national identity. A ceasefire was signed in 1992 between Moldova and the 14th Russian Army, but Transdniestria is nowadays a de facto independent republic, only recognized by Russia. The peace resolution process never proved to be efficient and, until now, no agreement has been made between Chisinau and Tiraspol. In the Gagauz case, a solution was found in 1995, when the minority was granted a constitutional autonomous region, which enjoys mainly cultural powers.

The Republic of Moldova is now a parliamentary republic. The official language is Moldovan, while Russian has been granted the status of *language of interethnic communication*. Indeed, the country counts more than 100 different nationalities, among which Moldovans account for 75.8 percent, Ukrainians for 8.4 percent, Russians for 5.9 percent, Gagauz (Christian Orthodox Turks) for 4.4 percent, Romanians for 2.2 percent and Bulgarians for 1.9 percent.[2] Apart from Moldovan, the Russian language is the most highly visible in the country. The main minorities have the right to education in their own language.[3]

Since 2001 a neo-Communist party has been in power, and it appointed Vladimir Voronin as president, making Moldova the first new independent state (NIS) to be ruled by the Communist Party. Moldova is Europe's poorest country, and is generally referred as partly free. The Moldovan authorities have been condemned in more than 100 European courts for human rights violations.[4]

OVERVIEW OF LGBT ISSUES

The situation of the Moldovan LGBT community has to be understood in the context of a poor and newly democratic country. General attitudes toward homosexuals have been highly influenced by Soviet times, when homosexuality did not officially exist. Tolerance of ethnic minorities has been proclaimed since independence, but tolerance of sexual minorities is not yet a priority. The majority of Moldovans exhibit negative attitudes toward homosexuals, mainly due to lack of information about LGBT issues. GenderDoc-M, founded in 1998, is the only LGBT association in the country and its actions are opposed by national and municipal authorities as well as by a powerful Christian Orthodox lobby.

EDUCATION

Education in Moldova is compulsory for children from the age of five. Public education ranges from primary school to higher education. Doctoral and postdoctoral studies are available. In 2007, there were 31 higher institutions throughout the country, among which 17 were public.[5]

The Moldovan educational system is inherited from the Soviet educational system, which ensured an efficient initial formation and detailed databases available for research, particularly in exact sciences. Since 2005, the Moldovan authorities adapted to European educational standards, known as the *Bologna process*. Moldovan students may now pursue three years of bachelor's studies, two years of master's studies, and three of doctoral studies.[6]

The state supports all public high schools but, due to lack of state funding, Moldovan universities developed a system of admission with taxes. The best students may enter universities without paying taxes and the financial costs of their studies are supported by the state, which decides the number of students that will be supported every year. Others may enter university but must pay fees.[7]

LGBT issues are not tackled by the Moldovan educational system. Sexual education in general is not a priority.

Nevertheless, some workshops and information conferences have been organized by GenderDoc-M in partnership with Moldovan universities in order to present LGBT issues and to start a dialogue with the students. For example, in

2006, 15 seminars, in which approximately 15 persons participated per seminar, were held in GenderDoc-M office; the topic was *essential aspects of homosexuality and sexual diversity*.[8] In the context of a general lack of information on the community and on its way of living, these informative sessions have been welcomed by students and professors.

These sessions are generally held without any official permission; they are made possible by a network of professors and psychologists who support the LGBT community.

EMPLOYMENT AND ECONOMICS

Moldova is highly economically dependent on its neighbors. The energy supply depends mainly on Russia. The country lacks mineral resources and is mainly agricultural, exporting fruits, vegetables, and wine. Following the 1991 and 1992 civil war and the secession of Transdniestria, the most industrialized region of the country, Moldova lost a 16th of its territory, reducing the industrial production by 36 percent, the production of electric energy by 87.5 percent, consumption goods by 28 percent, vegetables by 38 percent, and fruits by 24 percent. The total gross domestic product (GDP) was then reduced by 24 percent.[9]

Transition from a socialist economy to a free market economy was hindered by political instability throughout the 1990s, and the country suffered greatly from the Russian financial crisis in 1998. Since the neo-Communists came to power in 2001, the situation proved more stable, but their ambiguous foreign policy did not help the country in finding stable foreign partners.

The average monthly salary was about 1,697 Moldovan lei (approximately US$140 in 2007. It was about 915 Moldovan lei (US$75)in the countryside. The rural population makes up 61.5 percent of the population, and the trend toward a move back from the cities to the countryside is observed because opportunities in the cities are not satisfactory.

No research has been conducted in Moldova on discrimination at work based on sexual orientation. Some LGBT community members have claimed that they were fired because they were gay. Still, this reason was never openly given. Thus, LGBT people tend to live in the closet and prove reluctant to announce their sexual orientation.

SOCIAL/GOVERNMENT PROGRAMS

The Moldovan authorities have not yet implemented any program regarding LGBT issues. In September 2005, the Ministry of Health implemented a national control program for HIV infection and other sexually transmitted diseases (STDs).[10]

SEXUALITY/SEXUAL PRACTICES AND FAMILY

The Christian vision of sexuality and family still predominates in Moldova. Having a gay child is often seen as a cause of despair that could affect the family's reputation. While coming out is nowadays more common among a range of close friends, members of the LGBT community still hesitate in doing so to family.

In vitro fertilization and adoption are possible only in the case of a married couple. Laws on surrogate mothers and sperm donations lack precision, but interpretations of the family code make them possible only in the case of a married couple.

The only LGBT association in the country, the GenderDoc-M Information Center, has been fighting for recognition of the community and for the adoption of an antidiscrimination law by the government. Gay marriage, civil union, and adoption are not yet on the agenda.

COMMUNITY

According to some of the LGBT community members, gay life in Moldova was easier during Soviet times, when homosexuality was forbidden. The LGBT community was forced to meet in cruising areas, like parks and public toilets, avoiding home and public places where they could have been followed or recognized. Many homosexuals married and had families. Officially, homosexuality did not exist, apart from in penitentiary statistics.

Generally speaking, the Soviet era left a strong imprint on the people. Post-Soviet countries show evidence of deep individualism, and any sense of community is hard to create in general. This affects the LGBT community.

Nevertheless, the LGBT community is more visible nowadays, especially among young people. Some of them come out and are no longer ashamed of their sexual orientation. Following the publication of several articles in the Moldovan press and some positive documentaries about sexual minorities on Moldovan television, the population has obtained more information on LGBT issues and has a less negative point of view, even if research shows that the general negative attitudes of the Moldovan population toward homosexuality remain the main obstacle that keeps homosexuals from coming out.

Gay bars have opened and closed in the last 10 years; a few of them are still open in Chisinau. Furthermore, gay evenings take place every week in a club in the capital city. The Internet remains, nevertheless, one of the easiest ways for homosexuals to interact with one another.

GenderDoc-M provides free services for the LGBT community, provides help, and follows members of the community in case of discrimination. The center has a small library in the city center of Chisinau, and organizes public events in order to make the community more visible (such as conferences, an annual gay pride parade, film screenings, etc.).

While gay life is progressing little by little in Chisinau, it is completely absent from the countryside. Another LGBT association, GenderDoc-Ost, opened recently in Bender (Tighina in Romanian) in the self-proclaimed Transdniestran republic, but organizational and staff problems prevent it from being efficient at this moment. ATIS (Activi, Tineri, Informati si Sanatosi [Active, Young, Informed, and Healthy]), a center derived from the TDP association (Tineret Pentru Dreptul la Viata [Youth for Right to Live]), has just started dealing with the local LGBT population.

Compared to Chisinau, gay communities are much more visible in Bucharest, Odessa, and Moscow. Many members of the Moldovan LGBT community left Moldova for these cities.

HEALTH

HIV remains the main concern among the LGBT community in Moldova. Homosexuals in Moldova are often considered as HIV positive and as drug addicts. The Moldovan Center for AIDS Prevention showed that of the 2,780 HIV-positive cases registered in Moldova in 2005, only 10 were contracted by homosexual relations.[11] Nevertheless, this information needs to be balanced with the fact that many homosexuals in Moldova do not want to inform their doctor of their sexual orientation. Thirty-four percent of the Moldovan gays and lesbians thought that their doctor was receptive to LGBT issues, 56 percent did not know, and 10 percent were afraid of visiting a doctor because of their sexual orientation.[12]

In 2002, the Moldovan Ministry of Health expressed in a letter to Gender-Doc-M that homosexuality is not considered a disease. The letter explained that the ministry "is unfamiliar with cases of employees who would have been fired because of their homosexual orientations. A homosexual orientation cannot be taken as a reason to be fired. Homosexual relations are studied in colleges and universities in the realm of psychiatry and are considered as sexual perversions. Persons presenting a homosexual orientation are granted medical assistance in the same way it is granted to every other patient."[13]

Different types of guides (for families, for doctors, etc.) are provided by GenderDoc-M. The center also holds conferences on LGBT medical issues all around the country.

POLITICS AND LAW

In Moldova, the Soviet penal code prevailed until 1995. According to article 106 of this code, in force from 1961, "Homosexuality is an unnatural relationship between two men. The same deed performed with a minor, with implication of either physical or psychological force, or by using the unconscious state of the victim is punished with from two to five years deprivation of liberty."[14]

In 1995, changes were introduced: the former heading of homosexuality was replaced by *forced homosexuality;* the first sentence was deleted; "the same deed" was substituted with "homosexual acts." These particular changes were only a first step for Chisinau to comply with the Council of Europe's standards, and they still kept the door open for abuse. In 2003, article 174 of the new penal code stated: "A sexual act, homosexual act, lesbian act and other sexual behavior with a person, whose age is known to be less than 14 years old, will be deprived of liberty for up to five years."[15] The new age of consent for both homosexual and heterosexual behavior is thus 14 years. Before 2003, discrimination against homosexuals existed, as 16 was the age of consent for heterosexuals and 18 for homosexuals. Furthermore, since 2003, the law mentions lesbian sexual acts and the notion of lesbian rape, which was not interpreted as intercourse before.[16]

These first changes were introduced through a lobbying campaign of Gender-Doc-M and other human rights associations. The LGBT community and others are fighting for real antidiscrimination laws that include sexual minorities as well as the disabled. Indeed, the law against discrimination up until now has concerned discrimination based on race, gender, language, religion, political and other beliefs, national and social origin, and other. This leaves room for interpretation, which could be seen as positive for the LGBT community—at this moment contending with freedom of expression and freedom of assembly—to defend its cause. A law including every kind of discrimination would nevertheless be a real step to the recognition of rights for the LGBT community.

As the Soviet article 106 was abrogated in 1995 to satisfy the Council of Europe, a law against discrimination could be drafted to comply with the European

Union's statements. This law has already been on the government's agenda, but the need for such a law was not completely recognized by the authorities, who argued that the current law was sufficient. Furthermore, Marian Lupu, the speaker of the parliament, stated at a university in Balti in May 2008 that the general opinion of the authorities with regards to LGBT issues was that "homosexuals' demonstrations in public are not possible in Moldova. Orientation does not matter in private. If tomorrow Brussels says that one of the conditions is to institutionalize or to take a law on sexual minorities' parades, this does not mean that we would do it." Lupu added: "This univocal position is shared by every politician in Chisinau, because these are the mentality and the values of the Moldovan society."[17]

RELIGION AND SPIRITUALITY

Moldova is a Christian Orthodox country, and 93.3 percent of the population self-declares as Christian Orthodox.[18] This greatly influences the general view of homosexuality. Some Christian lobbies are promoting a strong anti-LGBT agenda in the republic.

One powerful Christian Orthodox lobby is acting against the LGBT community in the country, holding an Internet forum, sending letters to the national and municipal authorities, condemning any LGBT attempt to receive recognition. The argument of priest Vasile Filat, the leader of the movement, is purportedly based on the Bible and goes against, in his words, what "God calls disgusting practices." Quoting the Bible, the lobby argues first that Moldova is a Christian country, and fears that the country could be lost and suffer from God's anger if homosexuality were tolerated. Second, Filat argues that the LGBT minority goes against families, which are, according to the Bible's vision, composed of a father (man) and a mother (woman).[19] GenderDoc-M is seen as promoting perversion and gay proselytizing. The Christian lobby organizes demonstrations in Chisinau and generally opposes any LGBT action.

Another association called English for a New Life generally opposes the LGBT community in Moldova. One of its leaders in Moldova, Elena Brewer, argues:

> There is an organization in my country of Moldova that has been attacking the family and the country for the past ten years. The organization is made up of homosexuals and lesbians, funded from the highly immoral European Union, who are on a mission to destroy the country. They are attacking the foundation of society, the family, and if they are not stopped then there will be terrible consequences to pay.[20]

This association generally attempts to stop LGBT demonstrations, writes letters, and holds a forum on the Internet.

Prejudices and stereotypes are numerous, mainly due to a lack of information regarding LGBT issues, but the Christian lobbies are expressing a minority opinion.

VIOLENCE

GenderDoc-M has been organizing meetings and festivals in Chisinau for 10 years. The first pride effort, A Rainbow over the Dniester, took place in 2002. Since 2005, the Chisinau city hall, the police, and state agencies expressed their opposition to such events.

In 2006, a report from the International Lesbian and Gay Association (ILGA)-Europe showed evidence "of what appears to be an increasingly concerted campaign by elements in government ministries, the Chisinau City Hall, and the police, co-operating with fundamentalist religious organizations, to deny freedom of assembly to Moldova's principal LGBT organization, the GenderDoc-M Information Center."[21]

Among others, the officials of Chisinau city hall violated the right of peaceful assembly by prohibiting the May 2005 and May 2006 pride demonstrations and the All Different, All Equal youth march, "almost certainly because of the participation of GenderDoc-M"; the Chisinau police exceeded their powers "in insisting that all outdoor activities by GenderDoc-M are impermissible," and infiltrated the organization in a manner likely to intimidate; the Ministry of the Interior failed to exercise fair and nondiscriminatory governance by "absolving a senior police officer of manifestly inflammatory statements with the spurious reasoning that he was protected by the 'religion' ground in the antidiscrimination article of the Labor Code"; the Ministry of Education and Youth pressured GenderDoc-M to accept a compromise that would deny the information center any visibility while "the incidents described took place within the context of Moldova's participation in the Council of Europe's All Different/All Equal Program, a key purpose of which is to combat discrimination, and for which the Ministry has responsibility."

After initially supporting the LGBT information center, the Moldovan courts did not uphold the right of freedom of assembly through the failure of the supreme court to support the appeals court's initial ruling that the ban on the May 2005 pride demonstration was illegal, through the reversal by the appeals court of its initial ruling, and through the support of the supreme court for the appeals court's second ruling upholding the ban on the May 2005 pride demonstration. Moreover, a fair hearing was denied to the president of GenderDoc-M when the appeals court did not allow him to give evidence regarding letters opposing the May 2006 pride demonstration. Finally, the courts did not observe their own time limits for reaching decisions in these cases.[22]

In July 2006, GenderDoc-M organized a festival in Causeni, in eastern Moldova. All minorities were invited, especially the disabled and the Roma. Obtaining the support of a human rights nongovernmental organization (NGO) based in this city, the Causeni Raion Law Center, and the authorization of the local authority, the festival consisted of a roundtable, the screening of a film and an open-air concert. Two religious organizations, English for a new life and Equity, held a press conference and called the city mayor, arguing the festival was "an event for sexual minorities." When the festival took place, the religious organizations interrupted the roundtable, insulted the president of GenderDoc-M, gave leaflets asking *Will Causeni Become Sodom?* and tried to convince the participants of the concert that the event was designed to promote homosexuality. The Causeni police did maintain order in an appropriate manner.[23]

Concerning the 2005 and 2006 Chisinau prides and the Causeni Festival, ILGA-Europe argues that the religious organizations were supported by the government. Indeed, the European LGBT organization considers that "the insignificance of these organizations tends to suggest that the main influence in denying freedom of assembly to GenderDoc-M comes from within the government circles, rather than from these groups."[24]

In April 2007, the sixth pride was called; GenderDoc-M, among other events, inaugurated a new community center, held a pastoral service with communion, organized a meeting in front of the Chisinau city hall building, married two members of the community, and so on. As the city hall had banned the meeting, LGBT community members stood in front of the building with their mouths sealed by rainbow-colored tape. Eggs were thrown at the demonstrators and some people shouted: "Make mud at your place! Get out of here!" The police did not react. Furthermore, the police did not allow the LGBT participants to lay flowers at the monument to repression victims in Chisinau.[25]

In May 2007, Human Rights Watch sent a letter to the president of the Republic of Moldova to express concerns about the ban on gay rights demonstrations in Chisinau and to urge the authorities to respect domestic and European law. The Intergroup on Gay and Lesbian Rights from the European Parliament also expressed such concerns in 2006 and 2007.

In May 2008, the seventh pride was organized by GenderDoc-M and was set to be the first legal gay pride event ever organized in Moldova, as Chisinau city hall did not forbid it. Participants intended to meet in Chisinau's main square in order to ask for an antidiscrimination law and to promote a spirit of tolerance. Fundamentalist religious organizations and an extreme-right organization, Noua Dreapta (New Right), stopped the bus in which the demonstrators were arriving at the square. They blocked it for 45 minutes. The Chisinau police did not react. The tension only lessened when the LGBT activists agreed to give up and destroy the materials they had prepared for the event. The remainder of the scheduled program did not take place due to security measures.[26]

A few days later, another demonstration against homosexuality was organized by Vasile Filat's religious organization in Chisinau's main square. Leaflets asking whether Moldova will become Sodom were distributed.

Apart from these demonstrations and the violent opposition that they sometimes meet, violence against LGBT people in Moldova is not openly expressed. Still, verbal and physical violence against people that has occurred because of their sexual orientation is often reported.

The Scottish newspaper, the *Daily Record,* reported on the case of Andrei Ivanov in February 2008, a young Moldovan who sought asylum in the United Kingdom because he would "face discrimination if sent back to his native Moldova." The newspaper presented his case as follows:

> Police there beat him up after he was seen holding hands with another man, he claimed. He also received death threats. After being warned his home would be torched, he fled and was smuggled into Britain in the back of a lorry, along with his younger sister. His plea to be allowed to stay was rejected when immigration officials said they did not believe his story. They also ruled being gay did not give Ivanov the right to be treated as a refugee because his fear of persecution was not based on grounds of race, religion, nationality, politics or membership of a social group.

The young Moldovan challenged the decision to the Court of Session. Judge Colin MacAulay QC gave Ivanov "a second chance to put his case for staying in Scotland," arguing that "there was evidence of police beatings and general prejudices against gays in Moldova."[27]

There are many stories of young men being arrested by the police in parks or other cruising areas of Chisinau. If citizens do not present their papers, they are asked to follow the officers. On the way to the police office, police officers threaten them with informing their family that they have sexual relations with men. Compromises are generally found by bribing the police officers.[28]

In Transdniestria, despite organized Web propaganda presenting the country as a multiparty democracy with the opposition in control of the parliament, it is commonly seen as a closed authoritarian state, where mafia-controlled economics rule and an illegal weapons industry flourishes.

No information on LGBT issues in the region is available. Article 106 of the Soviet code was abrogated in 2003 and homosexuality was no longer formally punished. The country boasts an ombudsman on human rights and stipulates total tolerance toward sexual minorities. The authorities of Tiraspol would even have offered to host the gay prides that were forbidden in Chisinau.

Nevertheless, diverse reports on human rights in Transdniestria showed evidence that the situation was not as idyllic as presented in the propaganda. In a report from Amnesty International in 2007 about torture and illegal treatment that strongly blamed the Moldovan authorities, a few lines about the region state:

> The report does not include any cases from the self-proclaimed Trans-Dniestr Moldavian Republic (Transdniestria). This is not because of the absence of torture and ill-treatment in Transdniestria, but because of a greater reluctance on the part of those living in Transdniestria to report cases of torture and ill-treatment, a lack of NGOs working on this issue and low awareness among lawyers. In its report on a visit to Transdniestria in 2000, the European Committee for the Prevention of Torture and Inhuman or Degrading Treatment or Punishment (CPT) stated that "a significant number of the persons deprived of their liberty interviewed by the CPT's delegation alleged that they had been ill-treated by the police."[29]

Most of the homosexuals in Transdniestria have left for Chisinau or Odessa. Those who remained in the country are supposed to hide. There is no gay life in Transdniestria or any open LGBT community.

OUTLOOK FOR THE 21ST CENTURY

Tolerance and acceptance of sexual minorities have not yet been achieved in Moldova. The Moldovan LGBT community finds itself in a general context of pauperization and strong social and economic problems, which hinders any positive development. NGO reports in Moldova still show a huge lack of democracy throughout the country. The Communist authorities are often blamed for acting like the authorities did in Soviet times, against freedom of the press and assembly.

As article 106 of the Soviet penal code was abrogated in 1995 when Moldova adjusted to the Council of Europe's statements, a new law against discrimination and any other protection or recognition will probably come from the authorities' adaptation to the European Union's decrees. The relationship between Moldova and the European Union is determined by the European Neighborhood Policy Action Plan. Ensuring openness toward sexual minorities and improving antidiscrimination laws are two of the many conditions for a stable partnership.

Homosexuals in Moldova still suffer from numerous prejudices and stereotypes from the rest of the population. This situation will change only slowly, helped by objective information from the Moldovan mass media. Mentalities are changing, but the process takes a long time. A new generation has fewer negative attitudes toward LGBT issues, which seems positive as the community has begun to fight for recognition and rights, starting little by little to gain visibility.

RESOURCE GUIDE

Suggested Reading

Igor Doncila, *Ghid pentru medici care lucreaza cu persoane de orientare homosexuala* [*Guide to the Doctors Working with Homosexuals*] (Chisinau, Moldova: GenderDoc-M, 2006).

Charles King, *The Moldovans. Romania, Russia and the Politics of Culture* (Stanford, CA: Hoover Institution Press, Stanford University, 2000).

Svetlana Rusnac and Svetlana Klivade, *Minoritatile sexuale: atitudini sociale si informarea populatiei* [*Sexual Minorities: Social Attitudes and Information of the Population*] (Chisinau, Moldova: GenderDoc-M, 2008).

Svetlana Rusnac and Svetlana Klivade, *Particularitatile orientarilor valorice si trebuintelor de baza ale tinerilor din comunitatea LGBT* [*Particularities of the Values Orientations and of the Basic Needs of the Young from the LGBT Community*] (Chisinau, Moldova: GenderDoc-M, 2008).

Dennis Van der Veur, *"We Need Cleaner Places than a Public Toilet": Homosexuals in the Republic of Moldova* (Amsterdam: COC Netherlands, 2001).

Web Sites

European Parliament's Intergroup on Gay and Lesbian Rights, http://www.lgbt-ep.eu.

GenderDoc-M, http://www.gay.md.

> GenderDoc-Information Center in Chisinau publishes a magazine in Romanian and in Russian, including some English features: *Dialog*.

ILGA-Europe, http://www.ilga-europe.org.

NOTES

1. See Biroul National de Statistica al Republicii Moldova, *Moldova în Cifre. Breviar Statistic* (Chisinau: Biroul National de Statistica al Republicii Moldova, 2007), for more details, see http://www.statistica.md.

2. Ibid.

3. Gheorghe Moldovanu, *Politica si planificare lingvistica: de la teorie la practica* [*Politics and Linguistic Planning: From Theory to Practice*] (Chisinau: ASEM, 2007), 207–31.

4. Deca-Press News Agency, "Autoritatile vor depune eforturi pentru a reduce numarul de condamnari a Moldovei la CEDO" ["Authorities Will Try to Reduce the Number of ECHR's Condemnations"], Chisinau, March 21, 2008.

5. Biroul National de Statistica al Republicii Moldova, *Moldova în Cifre*, 30.

6. See Ambassade de France en Moldavie, "Fiche Moldavie," 2007, http://www.diplomatie.gouv.fr/fr/IMG/pdf/Fiche_Moldavie_2007.pdf.

7. Ibid.

8. GenderDoc-M, *Annual Report 2006,* GenderDoc-M Information Center, (Chisinau: GenderDoc-M, 2007), 139.

9. Nicolae Enciu, *Istoria Românilor. Epoca Contemporana* [*History of the Romanians: Contemporary Era*] (Chisinau: Civitas, 2005), 170.

10. Programul National de Profilaxie si control al infectiei HIV/SIDA si infectiilor cu transmitere sexuala pe anii 2006–2010, adopted on September 5, 2005, by the Moldovan Government.

11. Igor Doncila, *Ghid pentru medici care lucreaza cu persoane de orientare homosexu-ala* [*Guide for Doctors Working with Homosexuals*] (Chisinau: GenderDoc-M, 2006), 18.

12. Ibid., 9.

13. Ibid., 42.

14. Article 106 of the former Soviet Penal Code.

15. Article 173 of 2003 (Moldovan Penal Code).

16. Dennis Van der Veur, *"We Need Cleaner Places Than a Public Toilet": Homosexuals in the Republic of Moldova* (Amsterdam: COC, 2001), 14–16.

17. Deca-Press News Agency, "Manifestarile homosexualilor in public nu sunt posibile, sustine spicherul Marian Lupu" ["Homosexuals' Demonstrations Are Not Possible in Public, According to Marian Lupu"], Chisinau, May 26, 2007.

18. Biroul National de Statistica al Republicii Moldova, *Moldova in Cifre,* 10.

19. Vasile Filat, "Va Deveni Moldova ca Sodoma?" ["Will Moldova Become Like Sodoma?"], leaflet (Chisinau: Moldova Crestina, 2008).

20. See Erik and Elena Brewer's blog, *Erik and Elena Brewer's Weblog. An Encouraging Blog for Christians to Express their Ideas,* http://erikbrewer.wordpress.com/.

21. International Lesbian and Gay Association (ILGA)-Europe, "Moldova: Comprehensive Denial to Moldova's Principal LGBT Organization of the Right to Freedom of Assembly," report, Brussels, November 19, 2006, 2.

22. Ibid., 6–9.

23. Ibid., 9–12.

24. Ibid., 4.

25. Galina Pavlova, "VIth Festival 'Rainbow over the Nistru'. How it Was...," April 2007, http://www.gay.md/eng/story.php?sid=121.

26. GenderDoc-M, "Human Rights Violations Alert. Moldovan Police Allows for Preclusion of a Public LGBT Manifestation," May 2008, http://www.gay.md/eng/story.php?sid=129.

27. P. O'Hare, "Gay Asylum Seeker Wins Fight To Stay In Scotland," *Daily Record* (Glasgow), February 1, 2008, http://www.dailyrecord.co.uk/news/newsfeed/2008/02/01/gay-asylum-seeker-wins-fight-to-stay-86908–20305477/.

28. See for example, Van der Veur, *"We Need Cleaner Places Than a Public Toilet."*

29. See reports from Amnesty International, May 2007, http://www.amnestyinternational.be/doc/article10818.html, and October 2007, http://www.amnestyinternational.be/doc/article11903.html.

THE NETHERLANDS

Gert Hekma

OVERVIEW

The Netherlands is a relatively small country of about 13,513 square miles that is located between Germany, Belgium, and the North Sea. A delta, the country is flat with many waterways, lakes, and polders. With close to 17 million inhabitants, it is the most densely populated country in Europe.

The Dutch Republic was the first European republic of modern times. Its foundation is generally considered to have been in 1581, during the 80 year Protestant insurgence against Catholic Spain (1568–1648). The 17th century was the country's golden age, when it was the leading economic power in the world and the arts were blossoming with painters such as Rembrandt and Vermeer. Between 1795 and 1806, it was called the Batave Re-public, which found its inspiration in the French Revolution. In 1806, it be-came a kingdom, and between 1810 and 1813, Napoleon incorporated the kingdom in his French Empire. In the period between 1795 and 1813, many institutions of the modern state were introduced in the Netherlands, for example, a centralized democracy with voting rights for tax-paying men, new penal and civil laws, obligatory education, standardization of valuta, and introduction of the metric system. With the French penal code, the crime of sodomy disappeared in 1811 from the law books, while no new criminal laws specifically condemned homosexual practices. Only public indecencies remained punishable, while no age of sexual consent was mentioned in the law. In 1813, the Netherlands be-came an independent kingdom, being

merged in the period 1815–1830 with Belgium. After a century with no special laws regarding homosexuality, article 248bis, introduced in 1911, punished homosexual relations between minors under 21 with adults above that age. Since 1886, the age of consent for all sexual practices had been set at 16 years. The new article of 1911 was abolished in 1971. Some 5,000 persons (99% men; 1% women) were prosecuted under this article.[1] Between 1940 and 1945, the Germans occupied the Netherlands and introduced the German law against unnatural intercourse, which meant that all male homosexual practices became forbidden. This law was rarely used, most often against minors who were—under the Dutch law—victims and could be seen under the German law as perpetrators. The law was abolished after the occupation. The Netherlands was, in 1957, one of the six founders of the European Economic Community, forerunner of the European Union (EU)— meaning that a growing amount of legislation and regulation now came from Brussels, the capital of the EU.

Since 1971, the major legal changes were the right to serve in the army for gays and lesbians (in 1973) and the Equal Rights Law (in 1993) that pertained to women, ethnic minorities, and gays and lesbians. In 1997, a registered partnership was introduced for same-sex and heterosexual couples that could not (homosexuals) or did not want to (heterosexuals) marry; in 2001, marriage was opened for couples of the same sex.

The main political parties in the Netherlands are the Christian Democrats (CDA), the conservative liberals (VVD), the social democrats (PvdA), the progressive liberals (D66), the Green Left (GL), and the Socialist Party (SP). D66 and GL have especially taken up the cause of homosexual rights, while the other parties have shown meandering politics, with the CDA being most negative and the SP most uninterested in homosexual politics. While in the past, the more liberal and progressive parties supported the gay and lesbian movement, nowadays the right wing has taken its cause, partly because of its Islamophobia. Gay issues have proven to be a good stick with which to beat Muslims.

The religious composition of the Netherlands has changed enormously over the last 50 years. While most Dutch people were Protestant or Catholic until the sexual revolution, since then the number of nonbelievers has grown to about 50 percent of the population with only 20 percent being regular visitors of religious services. Some 27 percent are Catholic and another 16 percent Calvinist, a quarter of these Protestants belonging to orthodox denominations. About 5 percent are Muslim, mainly belonging to the 10 percent of recent immigrants and their offspring.[2] Although there is still opposition against LGBT rights coming from (orthodox) Protestant and Catholic groups, the fiercest opposition stems from Muslims, both in terms of the rhetoric of imams and of the queer-bashing by young men. The main ethnic minorities (from large to small) are Surinamese, Moroccan, Turkish, Antillian, and Chinese, while there is a broad range of refugees from different places (the Balkans, Iraq, Iran, Somalia, and many other countries).

The Dutch have a flourishing and modern economy. The country belongs to the 10 richest nations in terms of per capita income (national income $38,500 per capita). The nation is a member of NATO, and the army participates in UN peacekeeping missions elsewhere in the world. The military is open for gays, lesbians, and transgender persons, and has an active policy to combat discrimination against them. This policy is not always successful. Homophobia in the army is covert and insidious rather than direct and violent.

OVERVIEW OF LGBT ISSUES

The Netherlands was the second country to have a homosexual rights movement, the Dutch chapter of the German Scientific-Humanitarian Committee (NWHK). It was founded in 1912 after the introduction of article 248bis of the penal code. Although some gay-friendly doctors and gay novelists were members of the NWHK, it was mainly a one-person organization of the lawyer Jacob Anton Schorer. The main goals were abolition of article 248bis and greater visibility for homosexuals. Schorer's lobbying remained largely unsuccessful and he stopped his activities with the German occupation, knowing the Nazi attitudes regarding homosexuals. His important library was seized and has never been recovered.[3]

Just before the occupation in 1940, a small group of homosexuals started a monthly called *Levensrecht* (the right to live), which was revived after the war. They began in 1946 in what is now the oldest gay and lesbian movement of the world, first named the Shakespeare club and later the COC (Center for Recreation and Culture). Its leaders, especially the chair Bob Angelo (pseudonym of Nico Engelschman), not only lobbied with politicians, religious leaders, psychiatrists, and police officers, but also published the journal *Vriendschap* (Friendship), organized lectures, meetings, and parties, and later owned their own dancing club that would be the largest gay institution of the Western world in the 1950s and 1960s. Their prudent policy worked, and in the 1960s both Catholics (among them a bishop and a leading psychiatrist) and orthodox Protestants began to support homosexuals, accepting—in their language—the sinners while not yet embracing their sins. Homosexuality, which had been defined as a sin, a crime, and a disease, was no longer any of these, and starting in the 1970s, it was rather considered the sexual orientation of a minority.

The 1960s meant a breakthrough for (homo)sexual rights because the majority of the population changed its mind between 1965 and 1975. Instead of rejecting homosexuality, pornography, prostitution, pre- and extramarital sex, contraception, and divorce, it accepted those sexual practices. Homosexuality went from being an unmentionable sin to something that was visible and could be discussed in polite society. Once article 248bis was abolished and gays and lesbians were allowed into the army, the main issues became sex education, gay and lesbian visibility, and individual and relational rights in the fields of housing, labor, insurance, inheritances, adoption, and asylum. From the late 1970s on, equal rights law was a main theme of contestation, in particular with Christian schools that opposed the possibility that they could be forced to hire homosexual teachers. The conclusion was that all schools had to accept homosexual teachers as long as they endorsed the school's philosophy. With the emergence of the AIDS epidemic, issues of health care, prevention, and research became pivotal. Although the health authorities wanted to close down gay sex places like dark rooms (rooms in gay bars where gay men can have sex, in the past mainly in leather bars but now also in more mainstream gay bars and discos) and saunas, the gay movement successfully resisted such demands.

By the mid-1980s, national and local governments started to give grants for gay and lesbian emancipation activities. Most money went to the Schorer Foundation, which specializes in psychological support for LGBT people and became active in prevention and care activities (such as the buddy system) related to AIDS. The gay and lesbian movement received smaller grants for their activities, for example, for renting offices, festivals, educational activities, and so on. In recent years, most subsidies go to initiatives for the elderly, questioning youngsters, and ethnic minorities. The government has a part-time civil servant who is responsible for its homosexual politics. Many cities created diversity offices that are responsible for minority groups like nonwhites, women, LGBT persons, and the handicapped.

When marriage was opened for same-sex couples in 2001, many people, both gay and straight, thought this was the pinnacle of gay and lesbian emancipation, the struggle had ended, and the LGBT movement could close its doors. But it soon became clear that legal equality did not mean social equality. The Netherlands had remained a heteronormative society where the straight norm continued to marginalize LGBT lives.

Most media have been supportive of the gay and lesbian movement since the 1970s as long as the demands and targets belonged to the realm of the normal. This included issues such as same-sex marriage and entry into the army. Since the political right has become interested in gay issues, the media has paid more attention to them. Movies and documentaries rarely depict gay or lesbian topics. On the other hand, many major comedians are gay men and national celebrities including (the late) Jos Brink, André van Duin, and Paul de Leeuw. They are open about being gay and their shows often make the most of the gay-straight difference for a straight public. The problem of media representation remains, as elsewhere, that the gap between the media and everyday life is enormous. A gay comedian on television is something very different from the gay guy next door.

EDUCATION

The Dutch LGBT movement considers visibility as its main subject of contestation. This issue has been central since the 1970s. The main focus is on education. In secondary schools, sex education is obligatory and should include themes of homosexuality, but because of the large discretionary space for schools, little or no attention is being paid to gay and lesbian issues. The COC offers classes on gay and lesbian themes for schools, but only a small number of the schools make use of this opportunity. In Amsterdam, for example, only 20 percent of the secondary schools incorporate the COC classes. Moreover, most education focuses on biological issues (genitals, reproduction) and the prevention of sexual misery (sexually transmitted diseases [STDs] with a focus on AIDS, teenage pregnancies, sexual abuse), and not on the promotion of sexual pleasure or the acknowledgement of gender and sexual diversity. Topics of sexuality are generally not dealt with in disciplines such as history, citizenship, geography, or religion. The school climate (particularly in schools where ethnic minorities are in the majority) is unfavorable to the coming out of both teachers and pupils. On courtyards and sporting fields the most common slurs still are *faggot, homo,* and *dyke.* School administrations, in most cases, do little to counter this negative climate for all kinds of reasons, for example out of prudery or because they are afraid for the reputation of the school. The first gay/straight alliances to create solidarity across sexual boundaries were only founded in 2008. Although the Dutch government and cities have allocated financial support for initiatives to promote education on homosexuality, the budgets have been far too small to counter the prejudices and discriminations and were given for too little time to be enacted.

EMPLOYMENT AND ECONOMICS

Antidiscrimination legislation forbids discrimination in various fields such as the workplace, housing, and services. Few cases of discrimination based on homosexual orientation have been taken to court or the Equal Rights Commission (which has an advice function). Few gays and lesbians are eager to come forward with such cases. Cases often will prove to be complex and unclear because discrimination often remains hidden in a cloud of injurious jokes or subtle forms of opposition. The last case of straightforward labor discrimination dates back to 1982 when the Royal House rejected a gay social worker. Many gays and lesbians also report that they remain silent at their job, and when they have problems after coming out, they see it as their personal struggle to be accepted by their fellow workers and bosses.

Although some types of work are still largely straight and considered masculine (construction, the army, higher levels of management, male professional sports), stereotypical gay and lesbian jobs have become less so. There are now many straight male ballet dancers, comedians, and hairdressers in Holland. Nonetheless, some professions in the service sector continue to attract disproportional numbers of gays and lesbians, for example police officers for women or stewards and waiters for men. There has, however, never been a representative survey of workplace and sexual orientation conducted in the Netherlands, so these data depend on the hearsay of insiders. Most trade unions and workers deny the importance of questions of sexual orientation in labor relations.

SOCIAL/GOVERNMENT PROGRAMS

The main programs of national, provincial, and local governments target health and education issues. Next to those, special budgets regard projects for LGBT ethnic minority groups, for LGBT visibility, for queer youth, and for LGBT sport organizations. The establishment of the HomoMonument in 1987 and the Gay Games of 1998, both in Amsterdam, were lavishly supported by both local and national government. The EuroGames were held for the first time in The Hague in 1992 and in 2005 in Utrecht. Other cities now compete to organize the games as a way to demonstrate being gay-friendly. Diversity programs that in the past often overlooked queer issues now generally tend to include those, and many major companies now have pride groups as part of such policies.

SEXUALITY/SEXUAL PRACTICES

Public Sex

There is a set of sociopolitical issues that are not generally shared among gays and lesbians. The first is gay public cruising. Over the last 25 years, the Dutch police force has made some efforts to protect gay cruising areas against queer bashers. At the same time, the general population became more and more opposed to these sexual practices. In the past, it was argued that public cruising areas were used by married and closeted gay men who had no other place to go. Now, with the greater acceptance of gay men, many people see no need to endorse public sex. They oppose public sex as being offensive and sleazy. Although most cruising places are hidden and mainly used after dark, the idea of gay men having sex in the bushes or in a public bathroom offers sufficient ground for gay and straight people to feel offended. Because of such opposition, some gay cruising places in urban parks or along highways have been closed down for gay use. Defending such gay public cruising places has become more controversial and the few politicians who did so faced fierce criticism and ugly insults. A contrary argument has become that gays can now marry and enjoy themselves in bars and discos and, as such, there is no longer any need to have cruising places. Some journalists have even argued for the elimination of dark rooms or saunas. The press is more often speaking out against such use of public places while denying that straights also use public space for sexual pastimes (they do, but often in less concentrated areas than gay men because they form the majority and can use sexually unmarked places for their pleasures). The general heterosexualization of Dutch society leads to a growing opposition against and revulsion toward gay cruising.

Doing "Normal"

The long-time exposure to straight norms has led to a growing sentiment among gays and lesbians that they have to behave normally, meaning they have to perform in gender-normative and nonsexual ways.[4] The most common reproach against gays and lesbians is their nonnormative behavior. Gay men are seen as sissies, un-masculine men who talk too much about sex, while lesbians are looked down upon as butches—too masculine for a woman. The negative prejudices internalized by gay men and lesbian women produce personal misery, psychological problems, and rejection of behaviors that are considered extravagant or extreme by both straight and gay people. The norm has become that gay men should behave in masculine and lesbians in feminine ways. This norm leads to revulsion among gays against *faggots* and *sissies* and among lesbians against *butches*. The queer turn in the Netherlands is not a fierce critique of gender and sexual standards, but of people who diverge from such norms. Sexual and gender norms that mutually reinforce one another have led to a heterosexualization and a strict division of gender roles in Dutch society, which is also apparent in gay and lesbian life. Most straight people may continue to see gay men as sissies and lesbian women as butches, and the younger gay generation does everything to prove its behavior is normal—meaning conformist in sexual and gender performance, reproducing the problems they themselves have faced as young queers.

FAMILY

In the Netherlands, one is not allowed to speak of gay marriage because marriage is the same for gay and straight. During the sexual revolution, gays, and even more so lesbians, were opposed to the marital institution because it was viewed as sexist and homophobic. At that time, doctors advised gays to enter into het-erosexual marriage as an effective way to eliminate homosexual desires. Slowly, psychiatrists who took a different and positive stance on homosexuality advised against marriage; they were aware that it would not heal homosexuals of their sexual preferences and would make the partners and children in such marriages unhappy.

For a long time, the COC propagated individualization instead of a focus on couple relations in some kind of marriage—that accumulation of special rights in such diverse fields as housing, sexuality, education of children, insurances, legacies, and dozens of others. The LGBT movement was rather in favor of splitting up the diverse functions of marriage instead of this piling up of straight privileges. In the late 1980s, conservative gay men began lobbying for gay marriage. This was partly because gay men had learned from AIDS that couples needed rights, and lesbian couples wanted to secure parenthood rights for children born either in their own same-sex couple or in previous heterosexual relations. The success in this effort encouraged the gay and lesbian movement to follow suit and embrace the struggle for marriage. The government initially instituted registered partnerships in 1997, but soon realized such arrangements for homo- and heterosexual represented a second-rate marriage that mainly organized rights and rules for couples, whereas marriage had broader functions—in particular in relation to third parties. This halfway solution was repaired in 2001 when marriage was opened up for same-sex couples. The Netherlands became the first country to do so. In a legal sense, most differences between gay and straight were lifted by this legal inclusion. There were three exceptions where homo- and heterosexual couples were still unequally treated. First, the *biological fiction*—meaning that the legislator assumes the husband is the biological father of the child born in wedlock—was not extended to gay and lesbian couples, so they always had to deal with a third person (the biological father or mother of the child). The second difference is that gay and lesbian couples could not adopt children from countries that were opposed to such adoptions. A reparation of this inequality is now under way. The third exception is that the king or queen cannot be married to a person of the same sex. Such a position demonstrates how antigay the royal house is and reinforces in Dutch society that homosexuality is not equal to heterosexuality.

The number of marriages of same-sex couples has been quite low; close to 10,000 same-sex couples had been married by the beginning of 2007. There are no reliable data on the number of homosexuals, but assuming a percentage of 4 percent of the population, this would translate into 500,000 adult gays and lesbians. Comparing this to the 10,000 same-sex marriages, this works out to about 4 percent of all gays and lesbians getting married. This is surprising because there are advantages to marriage in terms of income and inheritance taxes, as well as legalizing a non-Dutch partner. It is thought that the primary reason for same-sex couples to marry may be for the financial or legal benefits, without an attachment to marital ideals. It seems that although the idea of coupling is strong, the eagerness to marry is weak among Dutch gays and lesbians. This is similar to the straight population, which does not show great eagerness to marry. In general, gays and lesbians who marry often report that their families and friends were supportive and sometimes even promoted their marriage. Still, some 20 percent of the general population is unfavorable to same-sex marriages. The only political issue has been resistance by some civil servants to consecrate same-sex marriage; they have asked for exemption from performing them. The exemptions have been allowed. Many in the LGBT movement and liberal parties see this as a continuation of discrimination against homosexuals because no other such exemption exists. If, for example, civil servants refused to marry couples of a different religion or ethnicity, the Dutch would never support such special rights. This shows how exceptional and discriminatory the exemption is. The new center-right government of CDA, PvdA, and a small orthodox Calvinist party (the PvdA is puritanical on sexual issues) supports this exception.

In the past, the stereotypical image of gay men was that they intensely pursued sexual possibilities, whereas lesbians were often seen either as lower-class and violent drunkards or as unhappy wives trapped in marriage. Nowadays, these views are changing as seen by all the successful gay men and lesbian women who often live in quite normal couples, including raising children. Concrete data on gay and lesbian lives are lacking, so the real situation is unknown. However, gay and lesbian lives are not yet completely normalized, as evident from mental health surveys that indicate a higher prevalence of psychological problems among gays and lesbians and of suicide among queer youngsters.

COMMUNITY

In the latest Dutch survey of 2006, 4 percent of the men and 2.6 percent of the women state they are homosexual, and some 3 percent of both claim to be bisexual. Eighteen percent of women feel attraction to and 12 percent have had sex with females, while 13 percent of the men say they feel attraction to males, and a similar number report having had homosexual encounters.[5] What they do sexually has not been studied. From another survey, it seems as if the number of gays, lesbians, and bisexuals is growing from the oldest (65+) to the youngest generation (18–24), from 1.6 percent to 6.3 percent of the population, while the percentage of those who refused to indicate their sexual preference went down from 3.7 to 0.9 percent. Even if all those would be closeted gays and included as gays, there is still a substantial growth in two generations (i.e., from 5.3 to 7.2%).[6] Comparing the surveys of 1991 and 2006, there are seven times more women who indicate a lesbian preference. It remains unclear whether this steep growth indicates a rising number of lesbians or of women who are open about their lesbian preference. Further, the latest survey indicates that gay men generally have more partners than hetero- and bisexuals or lesbians. They also have a bit more sex, masturbate more, and are substantially more active on the Internet than heterosexuals. Little can be said on kinky variations except that 7 percent of all Dutch engage in sadomasochistic behavior and 10 percent have such desires, whereas 10 percent of the men and 4 percent of the women get aroused by fetishes.[7] For various reasons, the visibility of gay sexual variations is higher than those of heterosexuals and lesbians. The gay world has a subculture with leather and rubber shops and bars, sadomasochism, and sport sex parties that are largely not in existence for straights and lesbians. Another impression is that Dutch gay men focus less on anal sex than their North American counterparts, and have a broader sexual repertoire.

Male prostitution is legal in the Netherlands, as are other forms of prostitution, with the provision that only EU-citizens can officially work in the business and they have to be over 18 years of age. Most large cities have some male street prostitution, usually in and around railway stations in the past, and now mainly in parks. There were six bordellos in the country from the 1980s, but only one survives in Amsterdam now. Most of the bars that catered to male prostitutes and their clients have closed. The main reason for this is the growing number of prostitutes working as escorts and using the Internet to find clients. The Web is safe and anonymous, thus protecting hustlers from acquaintances who they would prefer not to know about their job. On the other hand, few hotels nowadays refuse to allow hustlers to visit clients. The escorts are expensive and professional, while prostitution in parks is cheap and incidental—mainly ethnic minority youth who want to earn some pocket money. There have been various unsuccessful efforts to organize male prostitutes, who have been intermittently the object of care and prevention until the late 1990s—as long as AIDS was considered to be a major health risk.

Spaces

The Netherlands does not have gay ghettos or vicinities. At most, one can find a concentration of queer bars and discos, some shops, and gay people living in a certain district, but the concentration is always rather low and, even in the gayest street, LGBT people are at most a tiny majority. Although many cities and towns have gay bars, discos, and saunas, or local chapters of the COC, Amsterdam has by far the biggest gay and lesbian scene in the Netherlands. There is not a strong sense of community among gays and lesbians themselves, who always like to say they is so much more than only gay or lesbian. The problem is that major issues such as marriage, antigay violence, or public sex also divide the gay community. Right-wing politicians who defend gay rights against Muslims are seen by left-wing gays as promoting Islamophobia while doing little to counter the social problems gays and lesbians still face. Conservative gays—now probably the majority among gay men—support the right-wing leaders and parties. The left-wing parties who attract the votes of Muslims have become hesitant to speak in favor of sexual freedoms, afraid to lose these voters, and also because the left never had a clear cut philosophy on sexual issues. In the present day media-democracy, they depend quite a bit on popular opinion. The old and new rifts of Dutch society, even in the gay community itself, hinder gays, lesbians, and transgender persons from feeling united.

Although the feeling of community may be low, there is a wide range of organizations. Next to the COC, the largest one, De Kringen (The Circles), caters to men who come out. These are small groups that gather at someone's home and sometimes continue meeting for decades. There is a wide range of religious groups, varying from an organization of clergymen, groups that organize Catholic, Protestant, and Jewish services, an LGBT group that caters to persons from orthodox Protestant backgrounds to the Foundation Yoesuf for Islam and Homosexuality. The Arab bar Habibi Ana has its own cultural events and an independent group, Nafar, works for the emancipation of Arab queers. One Amsterdam-based Christian organization promises to heal homosexuals of their sinful life and make them happy heterosexuals. Bisexuals are organized, but their activities have by and large remained marginal, invisible for both straight and gay publics. A wide variety of gay and lesbian sport clubs, for example in volleyball, tennis, athletics, self-defense, and swimming provide leisure activities, and some also participate in regular competitions and/or organize their own national and international tournaments. There is no gay organized soccer, the most popular Dutch sport, which is particularly homophobic. Nonetheless, many lesbians have joined it. Some political parties have their own gay and lesbian groups; these were most active in the early 1980s and have recently shown new initiative. Many professions (teachers, soldiers, police officers), as well as big companies, have gay and lesbian groups. There is a lively kinky scene in Amsterdam, mainly organized by the leather and rubber shops in town. However, the major kinky sex place, Vagevuur (Purgatory), is in Eindhoven (although it was recently closed after 25 years of business). The Amsterdam bar scene is divided in two groups who compete for control of the annual canal pride parade, which is the main gay event of the Netherlands, always organized in the

first weekend of August. The second most important event is Pink Saturday, organized each year in a different town during the last weekend of June.

In the past, the gay and lesbian movement had a wide range of specialized
publications. Some still do exist: COC's *Update*, the lesbian *ZijaanZij*, the conservative *Gay Krant*, and the gay glossies *Squeeze* and *Winq*. The low key, artsy, and
semipornographic *Butt* is an English language publication from the Netherlands.
The main media are on the Internet nowadays, the leading one being gay.nl. For
lesbians, the main providers are zijaanzij.nl and femfusion.nl. Most of these sites
provide platforms for profiling and messaging.

Drag Queens, Transsexuals, and Transgender

In 1959, the first bar with drag queen shows was established, Madame Arthur,
after a Parisian example. It catered mainly to a straight public. Cross-dressing was
at that time a popular gay pastime for special parties in the homosexual subculture.
This tradition continues to this day although, since the radical faggot movement
of the 1970s, the transformation of a man into a woman has to be less perfect in
term of gender inversion, aptly summarized in the 1970s term *gender-fuck* or in
the terms of Dolly Bellefleur, one of the leading ladies in the contemporary scene,
gender transformation art.

In 1960, the first transsexual operation took place. After much medical and
political debate, such operations were legalized in 1982: transsexuals could
change their sex legally and the health insurance would pay for the medical costs
if some medical and psychological criteria were fulfilled. Transsexuals had to perform the real life test, living as a person of the other sex for one year; they could
not be married at the time of the sex change (to prevent same-sex marriages);
and they could not be able to reproduce after the operation—which would open
the possibility that a father could mother a child. In summary, the law upheld the
gender dichotomy and the straight norm. Since the 1980s, the Gender Foundation is the main institution to take care of transsexuals. Some other foundations
have emerged that see to social and psychological support for transsexuals.

The first organization in the early 1970s was Travesty and Transsexuality (T&T),
a subdivision of the Dutch Society for Sexual Reform (NVSH). It is functioning to
this day, now also including transgender persons, who began to join in the 1980s.
The political success of transsexuals marginalized the other groups, which have
only become more prominent in the last decade. Transgender persons initiated the
group *Het jongensuur* in 1994 (named after *The Boy's Hour*, a famous transgender
novel written by Andreas Burnier in 1969) and a journal called *Continuüm* in
1996. They mainly cater to females interested in male or boyish gender roles. Since
2001, a biannual transgender film festival has been organized in Amsterdam, which
produced a new transgender group: The Noodles. There is a small but lively transgender community in the Netherlands that publishes a series of quality Internet
journals and newsletters. Transgender themes have also made an entry in the art
world with artists, museums, and galleries occasionally paying attention to gender
blendings and transgressions. In art schools and gender courses, the topic has become popular, but less so on the street or in families. Violence and discrimination
against transsexuals and transgender people remains common in the Netherlands,
with male-to-female transgender people being the main target.

Young Queers

An important question concerns the age of sexual consent. Young people come out earlier and earlier, while their sexual majority is legally set at 16 years. Young queers have no chance to visit gay places like bars, gay organizations, or gay Internet sites because of the set age limits. They are left alone until they turn 16, and remain exposed to the straight institutions of families, schools, and sport clubs where youngsters with homosexual preference face prejudice and have little chance to learn anything positive about gay life. In 2007, LGBT youth became a major news item as, for the first time, they had their own 16-minus boat in the gay canal parade. The LGBT movement fears that any effort to lobby for lower ages of sexual consent so that young people can join the gay and lesbian community will be faced with the critique of supporting pedophile interests. Because of the demonization of pedophilia in the Netherlands, birthplace of the pedophile movement in the late 1950s, such a reproach is lethal. Few people from the gay and lesbian world dare to face such verbal straight terror. In name of the protection of children, sexual diversity is impeded and gay and lesbian youngsters remain exposed to straight norms until they turn 16. But due to the success of the 16-minus boat, a lively movement of young queers, Jong&Out, has been started.

Visibility in Public

Gay men are most visible in popular TV programs and magazines, but much less in newspapers or on the streets except in gay streets. In some gay-friendly workplaces, gays are outed as soon as they start their jobs. Being openly gay entails the condition that they should behave normally—in the sense of gender and sexual performance. This means that gay males have to act in normative masculine and straight ways so as to be invisible. Lesbians are much less visible than gay men in both media and public life. They are made invisible, but also tend to keep themselves invisible. In the absence of a lively street and bar culture, most lesbians dress to fit into mainstream culture. Although visibility is a major issue for the LGBT movement, it is far from being realized, even in the lives of most LGBT people themselves.

Screaming queens are rare birds, even in Amsterdam, where blue jeans have been the pinnacle of fashion for 40 years. Since the extension of the kinky scene from leather to rubber and skinhead and sport clothing, even kinky apparel has become less visible in Amsterdam's streets. Both gay and straight often say that they oppose queer provocation, another way of indicating that homosexual visibility is unwanted. One could reformulate the public visibility of queers in the following way: because straight people, in particular young men, are much more aware of homosexuality nowadays, gays have made themselves less conspicuous to prevent unpleasant situations or insults. Surveys show that although 95 percent of the Dutch consider themselves to be tolerant of gays, 43 percent still object to two men kissing in the streets, and only 8 percent have objections to a straight couple doing the same. Dutch gays wonder how many of the 57 percent non-objectors may change their minds when they see two men kissing in real life instead of reading about it a survey. Thus, it remains streetwise not to make homosexuality too visible.[8]

HEALTH

Although the AIDS epidemic continues, it has come to be considered as a less important issue. AIDS has changed from a mortal into a chronic disease since 1996, so the attention to the epidemic has diminished and the focus is now on other countries, in particular some countries in Africa. In the Netherlands, AIDS has remained largely a gay disease, with virtually all cases related to homosexual behavior. Since 2000, the 200 new annual cases are divided equally between homo- and heterosexuals.

The Schorer Foundation began in 1967 to serve gays and lesbians with specifically homo-psychological problems. Since 1980, it has become the main institution to provide care and support for AIDS patients and prevention for the gay community. Since the emergence of the epidemic, there has been cooperation between the government, health authorities, and the gay movement. Although there were some points of controversy, the epidemic was handled well in general. Two points of debate have been whether condoms should be provided widely—the Dutch believed safe sex would entail no anal sex, with or without condoms—and whether the gay sex places should be closed—something the health authorities very much favor. On the last issue, it was decided not to do so because bedrooms with no third parties present could be more dangerous than a sauna or dark room, and because sex places were the best locations to provide information on AIDS, safe sex practices, and health care.

The main point of controversy remains *barebacking* (engaging in unprotected anal sex). Also in the Netherlands, a group called *poz and proud* has emerged within HIV-positive society (a client organization), suggesting that HIV-positive gay men can engage in unsafe sex among themselves. This organization received full media attention in 2007 after a scandal in which three gay men not only infected each other, but also raped other gay men and injected them with their blood in an apparent crazed effort to enlarge the group of HIV-positive people with whom to have unsafe sex. Surprisingly, health authorities had known of these unsafe encounters for more than a year, and warned the local gay community in Groningen. The raped and infected gay men were so closeted or afraid of the consequences of coming forward that none of the 15 victims who reported the attacks to the police felt the responsibility or had the courage to immediately indict the perpetrators. This case shows the limits of openness for homosexuality in the Netherlands. When it comes to the provision of medical and social support for AIDS patients, the situation has, in general, been positive since the late 1980s.

The physicians of the Gender Foundation now engage in treatments for adolescents who may become transsexual; they can obtain medication to slow down their gender development, so the sex change will be easier once they decide on their sex at 16 years. The foundation is also involved in the treatment of intersexual people, where they take the rather strict position that one sex needs to be determined and medically imposed on the baby soon after the birth.

POLITICS AND LAW

The Netherlands has had an equal rights law since 1993. It has been used successfully by women, ethnic, and religious minorities. Gays and lesbians, however, have rarely used this approach to complain about discrimination. The same is true for lodging complaints to the police about slurs and hate crimes. Dutch gays and lesbians were for a long time too closeted or too complacent to denounce queer bashers or persons who insulted them. According to some surveys, one-fourth of gays and lesbians have been confronted with forms of abuse that merit official attention, but the number of complaints being filed with the police is very small. For example, in a city like Amsterdam, only about a dozen complaints are filed each year.

Since 2007, the police have actively request that the LGBT community lodge complaints about antigay abuse and insults. Further, the police have promised to be more aware of such cases and to register them specifically as antigay violence. The same is true for the Equal Rights Law. There have been few gay or lesbian cases because the concerned persons appear to be too closeted or complacent (e.g., thinking that this is how [gay] life is). LGBT people have internalized the straight norm and have not learned to stand up for themselves and their issues.

RELIGION AND SPIRITUALITY

The main Protestant denomination, The Protestant Church in the Netherlands, allows gay and lesbian ministers and the celebration of same-sex marriage. Local churches, though, have some free space to maneuver around these doctrines. In the 1960s, the Catholic Church was open to homosexuality, accepted the homosexual person, and had an institutional open door policy that catered to homosexuals with personal problems. The main Catholic psychiatrist asked for acceptance of homosexuals, including gay couples. It was a time in which the Catholic Church, especially in the Netherlands, was more engaged with social issues. It was the progressive wind of Vatican II that allowed the clergy some space, but within 10 years, the tables turned and the Dutch province was again under the reign of conservative bishops who kept to the strict morality of the church. One of the results was a massive dropout of Catholics from the church. Since then, bishops have expressed their negative views of homosexuality on several occasions. For example, a bishop declared that homosexuality is a neurosis, and the archbishop declared that Catholics should not rent rooms to homosexuals. The other religions go from very progressive (Remonstrants, Mennonites) to very conservative (orthodox Protestants and Jews). Most of the Muslim imams agree that homosexuality is forbidden in Islam, while some vehemently denounce the tolerance for gays and lesbians and state that Europeans are worse than dogs and pigs because they allow gay marriage.[9]

The influence of religion is strong in the Netherlands, as the social system was traditionally based (and remains so) on a division of the major institutions according to religion, including schools, hospitals, political parties, media outlets, sport clubs, and even economic activity. Although this *pillarization* has been losing ground since the 1960s, there are still important ramifications. For example, half of the schools remain religious, with another half being public. The system continues to be used by orthodox Protestants and is being revived by Muslims. This pillarization and the freedom to decide on the contents of education by schools continue to impede sexual openness in the educational system. It affected the coalitional political system because only in the period 1994–2002 were no Christian parties in government. This is in contrast with all other governments since World War I, which included Christians who used their influence to promote religious values that were most often detrimental to sexual freedom.

VIOLENCE

The issue of antigay violence was initially viewed by police as violence perpetrated by gay men cruising in parks or around urinals, and queer bashing as gay men's fights among themselves or with straight lovers. The latter kind of violence continues to this day in the world of male prostitution. Male hustlers often attack and sometimes murder their clients. Research in Amsterdam from the 1980s indicates that two gay men were murdered each year by young men for whom prostitution often was an irregular trade. At that time, the topic of queer bashing came on the political agenda.

There have never been reliable statistics on the number of such incidents, as neither the police nor the gay movement keeps track of them. There have been some cases where gay men were murdered in cruising places, while less violent incidents have been reported from streets with a high concentration of gay bars. In 2007, a transgendered person was murdered in the streets of The Hague. Gay men or lesbian women holding hands outside gay districts also face violence. Another form of threats concerns gay men, transgendered people, and lesbians in their homes; they face the insults and aggression of neighbors and sometimes move to other districts. The number of cases reported to the Amsterdam police was 15 for 2006 and 24 for the first eight months of 2007. The police believe that the real number is 96 percent, meaning that the real number of antigay incidents would be 25 times higher.

With the gay canal parade of 2007, four gay tourists who visited Amsterdam were beaten up by local youth. The media reported extensively on these and earlier incidents. The Amsterdam City Council, police, and justice showed great indignation and promised stricter measures of control and prevention. This violence was seen as an attack not only on the queers, but also on the reputation of Amsterdam as a tolerant and gay-friendly city. The authorities promised more education on homosexuality, more preventive measures in ethnic minority schools and families (whose male sons are seen as being more prone to this kind of violence than young white men), and to keep a stricter record of such cases while asking gays and lesbians to report experiences of discrimination more often. This violence, however, is not restricted to the city of Amsterdam; furthermore, not only ethnic minority male youth are involved in it, but also young ethnic majority males. Some young straight men feel their masculinity and heterosexuality are threatened by gay men—another example of the continuing lack of social acceptance of homosexuality in Dutch society.

OUTLOOK FOR THE 21ST CENTURY

Although the Netherlands has seen the legal changes that have made homo- and heterosexual citizens nearly equal, the country needs still the social changes to implement this equality throughout the heteronormative character of most of its institutions. Moreover, an effort is needed to counter antihomosexual prejudices that often remain under the surface but sometimes are very visible—such as the hate crimes and insults directed at LGBT people or the utter lack of gay education in schools. The main theme, however, seems to be the broader sexual emancipation of the Dutch. Similar to other Western societies, the perspective on sexuality in the Netherlands remains one sided, which impedes the citizenship rights of different groups, in particular LGBT people. Sexuality is seen as something more typical for men than for women, so it remains not only homophobic but also sexist. The common belief is that sex and love should belong together. This leads to unwarranted criticism of those who like sex but not necessarily in loving relationships. The view is that sex is a private affair that not only leads to discriminatory legislation on public indecencies, but also to an absence of perceptive political debates on sex and of sensible sex education. Sex is seen as an identity, and this hinders a more open sex culture where people are able to experiment beyond their identities. The French utopian socialist Charles Fourier suggested two centuries ago the idea of rallying or plural love as a way to go beyond the egoism of the couple and create social cohesion in society. But the present-day insistence on identities is even impeding lovers from finding common ground because it is sexual curiosity rather than identity that creates bridges between citizens.

RESOURCE GUIDE

Suggested Reading

Thijs Bartels and Jos Versteegen, eds., *Homo-Encyclopedie van Nederland* (Amsterdam: Anthos, 2005).

Jan Willem Duyvendak, "The Depoliticization of the Dutch Identity, or Why Dutch Gays Aren't Queer," in *Queer Theory/Sociology,* ed. Steven Seidman (Cambridge, MA: Wiley/Blackwell, 1996).

Jan Willem Duyvendak, "Identity Politics in France and the Netherlands: The Case of Gay and Lesbian Liberation," in *Sexual Identities—Queer Politics,* ed. Mark Blasius (Princeton, NJ: Princeton University Press, 2001).

Gert Hekma, "The Demise of Gay and Lesbian Radicalism in the Netherlands," in *New Social Movements and Sexuality,* ed. Melinda Chateauvert (Sofia, Bulgaria: Bilitis Resource Center, 2006).

Gert Hekma, *Homoseksualiteit in Nederland van 1730 tot de moderne tijd* (Amsterdam: Meulenhoff, 2004).

Gert Hekma, "How Libertine is the Netherlands? Exploring Contemporary Dutch Sexual Cultures," in *Regulating Sex: The Politics of Intimacy and Identity,* ed. Elizabeth Bernstein and Laurie Schaffner (New York: Routledge, 2005).

Saskia Keuzenkamp and David Bos, *Out in the Netherlands. Acceptance of Homosexuality in the Netherlands* (The Hague: SCP, 2007).

Saskia Keuzenkamp, David Bos, Jan Willem Duyvendak, and Gert Hekma, eds., *Gewoon doen. Acceptatie van homoseksualiteit in Nederland* (The Hague: SCP, 2006).

Pieter Koenders, *Tussen Christelijk Réveil en seksuele revolutie. Bestrijding van zedeloosheid met de nadruk op repressie van homoseksualiteit* (Amsterdam: IISG, 1996).

Harry Oosterhuis, *Homoseksualiteit in katholiek Nederland. Een sociale geschiedenis 1900–1970* (Amsterdam: SUA, 1992).

Judith Schuyf, *Een stilzwijgende samenzwering. Lesbische vrouwen in Nederland, 1920–1970* (Amsterdam: IISG, 1994).

Judith Schuyf and André Krouwel, "The Dutch Lesbian and Gay Movement. The Politics of Accommodation," in *The Global Emergence of Gay and Lesbian Politics,* ed. Barry D. Adam, Jan Willem Duyvendak, and André Krouwel (Philadelphia: Temple University Press, 1999).

Steven Seidman, *Difference Troubles. Queering Social Theory and Sexual Politics* (Cambridge: Cambridge University Press, 1997).

Rob A. P. Tielman, *Homoseksualiteit in Nederland. Studie van een emancipatiebeweging* (Meppel, Netherlands: Boom, 1982).

Alex X. Van Naerssen, ed., *Gay Life in Dutch society* (New York: Harrington Press, 1987).

Video/Film

In dit teken...(45 min.; 1949). Directed by Piet Henneman and Jan Lemstra Documentary on the COC, its views and activities. Not available on DVD.

Two Women (113 min.; 1979). Directed by George Sluizer. Based on a novel by Harry Mulisch. Two women fall in love but one runs off with the ex-husband of the other.

Spetters (105 min.; 1980). Directed by Paul Verhoeven. Movie about three young guys, one of whom discovers he is gay after being raped. Controversial at the time it came out.

The Fourth Man (105 min.; 1983). Directed by Paul Verhoeven. Based on a novel of leading Dutch gay novelist Gerard Reve. A gay writer engages in a sexual relation with an adorer.

For a Lost Soldier (93 min.; 1992). Directed by Roeland Kerbosch. Based on a novel by Rudi van Dantzig about the love between a Canadian soldier and a Dutch adolescent just after the liberation of Holland from the German occupation (1945).

Yes Nurse! No Nurse! (102 min.; 2002). Directed by Pieter Kramer. A campy Dutch movie based on a 1960s television comedy series.

While living in Holland, the Flemish novelist and film critic Eric de Kuyper made four experimental movies with strong queer undertones: *Casta Diva* (1983), *Naughty Boys* (1983), *A Strange Love Affair* (1984) and *Pink Ulysses* (1990).

Organizations

COC, http://www.coc.nl.

National LGBT organization site with news and relevant information on the COC and links to most other Dutch Web sites of professional, religious, political, sport, health, and youth groups, for gay and lesbian parents and community events.

IIAV. International Information Centre and Archives for the Women's Movement, http://www.iiav.nl.

Material on the lesbian movement and other women's sex organizations.

Landelijk Netwerk Biseksualiteit, http://www.lnbi.nl.

National organization of bisexuals.

LKG T&T, http://www.transgendernederland.nl.

National Web site of transgendered people with links to other clubs and newsletters.

NOTES

1. Pieter Koenders, *Tussen Christelijk Réveil en seksuele revolutie. Bestrijding van zedeloosheid met de nadruk op repressie van homoseksualiteit* (Amsterdam: IISG, 1996).

2. Jos Becker and Joep de Hart, *Godsdienstige veranderingen in Nederland* (The Hague: SCP, 2006).

3. Theo van der Meer, *Jonkheer Mr. Jacob Anton Schorer. Een biografie van homoseksualiteit* (Amsterdam: Schorer Boeken, 2007)

4. Saskia Keuzenkamp, David Bos, Jan Willem Duyvendak, and Gert Hekma, eds., *Gewoon doen. Acceptatie van homoseksualiteit in Nederland* [*Out in the Netherlands. Acceptance of homosexuality in the Netherlands*] (The Hague: SCP, 2006).

5. Floor Bakker and Ine Vanwesenbeeck, *Seksuele gezondheid in Nederland 2006* (Delft, Netherlands: Eburon, 2007).

6. Jan Janssens, Agnes Elling, and Janine van Kalmthout, *"Het gaat om de sport." Een onderzoek naar de sportdeelname van homoseksuele mannen en lesbische vrouwen* (Nieuwegein, Netherlands: Arko, 2003), 55.

7. Bakker and Vanwesenbeeck, *Seksuele gezondheid in Nederland 2006.*

8. Keuzenkamp, Bos, Duyvendak, and Hekma, *Gewoon doen.*

9. Gert Hekma, "Imams and Homosexuality: A Post-gay Debate in the Netherlands," *Sexualities* 5, no. 2 (2002): 269–80.

NORWAY

Tone Hellesund

OVERVIEW

As of 2007, Norway has a population of 4.7 million people. It has a total area of 148,709 square miles, meaning that there are approximately 31.6 persons per square mile. Norway shares borders with Sweden, Finland, and Russia, but is mainly surrounded by sea. The capitol is Oslo, with 540,000 inhabitants. The population growth is currently 0.7, well below the replacement value. The average life expectancy in 2005 was 82.5 years for women and 77.7 years for men.

Norway is a constitutional monarchy and the formal head of state is King Harald V. The king mainly has ceremonial functions. The heir to the throne, Haakon, and his wife, Mette-Marit, are explicitly supportive of gay/lesbian/transsexual issues. The prime minister is the leader of the government, and as such the executive leader of the nation. Norway has a multiparty system and had seven political parties represented in the parliament in 2007.

Norwegian is the official language (two versions: Bokmål and Nynorsk), and in some districts, Sámi (spoken by the indigenous Sámi population) is also an official language.

The royal family was reintroduced in Norway in 1905, when the country again became an independent nation after 100 years under the Swedish government and 400 years under the Danish government. The Norwegian constitution was based on the French and U.S. constitutions and was sanctioned while the nation was still under Swedish government on May 17, 1814. May 17 is Constitution Day and a major holiday in Norway.

All men are called to military service when they are 18 years old. They have to serve 12–18 months in the Norwegian armed forces. Women are also allowed to join, but service is not mandatory for women.

Until the 1880s, Norway was a society mainly composed of peasants, farmers, and fishermen. Up until the 1960s, the main part of the population still lived in the countryside. There is no nobility in Norway apart from the royal family, and egalitarian values have been a major component in the national identity.

Between 1825 and 1925, approximately 800,000 people emigrated from Norway to the United States in the hope of a better life. Most left Norway between 1865 and 1910. Considering that the Norwegian population was 1.7 million in 1865 and 2.4 million in 1910, most Norwegian families were affected by the massive emigration.[1] Until World War II, emigration remained high, and then almost came to an end during the economic crisis of the 1930s. According to the U.S. census, there were 3.9 million Americans of Norwegian descent in 1990.

In 1970, a gigantic field of oil was found in the North Sea. Oil has made Norway one of the world's richest countries per capita. In 2006, Norway was the fifth leading oil-exporting country in the world.

During two referendums (in 1972 and 1994), the people of Norway voted against joining the European Union (EU). However, Norway has extensive agreements with the EU on a range of economic and social issues.

Since the end of the 1960s, Norway has experienced new immigration. This represented 1 percent of the population in the 1970s and the early 1980s. In 2007, the immigrant population (persons with two foreign-born parents) in Norway was 8.3 percent, or 386 000 persons, consisting of persons with backgrounds from over 200 different countries. Immigrants live in all the different counties, but Oslo has the largest share with 23 percent of the population. An official ban on immigration was implemented in 1975. This ban remains in effect today, but does not apply to specified refugee groups and asylum seekers. There are small annual entry quotas for these groups. Another way of gaining entry to Norway is through family reunification. Norway is regularly criticized by the UN chief of refugees for being too strict and not conforming to the recommendations of the UN.[2]

While roughly 82 percent of the population belongs to the state Protestant Church of Norway (Evangelical Lutheran), only 10 percent attend church services or other Christian-related meetings more than once a month. Some 8 percent of the population belongs to other religious communities, while about 10 percent do not belong to any religious community at all.[3]

OVERVIEW OF LGBT ISSUES

The modern homosexual movement appeared around 1950. In 1951, the newly started lesbian/gay organization DNF-48 (Norwegian Association of 1948) published the first Norwegian pamphlet about homosexuality. Here they also introduced the concept *homofil* (homophile), much used by liberation movements of the 1940s and 1950s in western Europe and the United States. Norway might be the only country still using this as the main concept for same-sex sexuality.[4] The word *homofil* was created from Latin, *homos* meaning same, and *philein* meaning to love. The term was first used in a Norwegian newspaper in 1965.[5] DNF-48 wanted this word to replace the term *homosexual*, to get rid of the negative sexual connotations of the latter. *Homofil* is the most common and—apart from in (academic) queer circles—also the most politically correct term for same-sex lovers in contemporary Norway.

The term *legning* (inborn disposition) is also almost universally used in Norway, despite its strong links to essentialist views on homosexuality. It is frequently used in public debates concerning homosexuality. It was probably introduced by homophile activists to replace the view of homosexuality as a sin or a diagnosis. *Legning* can also be translated as sexual identity, if *identity* is understood in strictly essentialist terms.

Until 2005, the main organization for trans people was called the National Organization for Transsexuals. At their annual meeting in 2005, they decided to change the name to the National Organization for Transgendered People. This was explained by a wish to move away from a highly stigmatized and sexualized image and to underline that being transgendered is about gender identity, not about sexuality.

The Norwegian language differs from English on important points in terms of intimate life. Although the specific language around homosexuality seems quite traditional or old fashioned from an Anglo-American perspective, public language around intimate life and intimate policy in many other contexts seems quite inclusive of same-sex relationships and same-sex families.[6]

EDUCATION

Norway has 10 years of compulsory elementary and secondary school, starting when the children are six years old. Two percent of Norwegian pupils are enrolled in private schools, the rest in public schools (2005–2006). The private schools also get public funding. To do so, they have to offer particular programs not offered in the public schools (e.g., religious, pedagogy, elite sports).[7] Some private schools have been established in densely populated areas where the children would have a long trip to the closest public school.

As of 2006, 70 percent of the pupils finished the three years of education after secondary schools. After this three year school, depending on grades and chosen subjects, students have access to universities and colleges. Some choose a theoretical high school while others choose to be trained as skilled laborers (electricians, hair-dressers, carpenters, etc).

The Norwegian constitution is linked to the Church of Norway, and until 1997 all pupils in Norwegian schools were educated in Christianity. Non-Christian pupils could get an exemption from these classes. In 1997, a new subject called *Christianity, religion, and philosophies of life* replaced Christianity as a school subject. This was supposed to be a more inclusive subject, and it became harder to get an exemption from these classes. In June 2007, the European Court of Human Rights (ECtHR) judged that this arrangement violated human rights. The government has now toned down the focus on Christianity and renamed the subject *Religion, ethics, and philosophies of life.*[8] Parallel with this debate is a debate over whether Norway should continue to have a state religion and state church. Relevant institutions have been asked to contribute to a hearing both concerning the state church and the constitutional link between the nation and the Christian religion.

There is a national curriculum for the 10-year compulsory school with which all schools must comply. LGBT issues are on the agenda from the fourth grade and in various subjects. Despite the focus in the national curriculum, research has shown that both textbooks and teachers tend to ignore nonheterosexuality or to represent it in negative and problem-oriented ways.[9]

EMPLOYMENT AND ECONOMICS

National laws are established to prevent the LGBT population from being discriminated against in the workplace and in the housing market. Both public and private companies have to comply with the laws, but religious communities have been exempted.

Despite the laws, lesbian, gays, and bisexuals still experience discrimination in many areas of life, and a few discrimination cases have been taken to court.

Several towns and cities have recently developed action programs to promote the living conditions of all lesbian, gay, and bisexuals in their area.

Military

The national defense granted full rights for homosexuals in 1979. Formal acceptance did not mean an end to all discrimination, and several gay/lesbian soldiers have reported problems with being accepted in the organization. In the last couple of years, the national defense has worked to promote softer values and claims to seek diversity among recruits and employees. They particularly underline the need for more lesbian/gays and immigrants among the ranks.[10]

SEXUALITY/SEXUAL PRACTICES

The age of sexual consent is 16 years for both same-sex and opposite-sex sexual contacts. In modern times, there have never been any laws against specific sexual practices (like oral or anal sex). The paragraph on rape in the Criminal Act includes not only intercourse by force but also sexual acts such as masturbation. The law is gender-neutral, both concerning perpetrator and victim, and is also in force if the parties are married to each other. The paragraph expresses that if a person (with certain means) forces the other to sexual relations, this can be treated as rape under the law (section 192). There are no laws making it illegal to make sexual proposals to others—in bathrooms or other places—and no laws making it illegal to sell sex toys.

Two paragraphs in the Criminal Act deal with pornography, one concerning adults and one concerning children under 18 years old. Section 204: It is illegal to publish or sell pornography or to give it to persons under 18 years old. Pornography is here defined "as humanly degrading sexual descriptions such as sexual activity including corpses, animals, violence, or force. Sexual descriptions defined as art, science, or information are not seen as pornography." Section 204a: It is illegal to obtain, own, produce, or distribute sexual descriptions involving children under 18 years old. Gender/sexuality is not an issue in regard to pornography. There are no porn theaters in Norway.

Prostitution is defined as a person having sexual relations (defined to include a wide range of sexual activities) with another person for payment. The law does not mention genders, and the law is equal regarding both male and female prostitution. Until 2009, it was illegal in Norway to promote the prostitution of others, to rent out housing/rooms used for prostitution, and to publicly offer, arrange, or demand prostitution. In 2007, there was a heated public debate around a proposal to make it illegal to buy sex. While most prostitution researchers and organizations for prostitutes were strongly opposed to this (arguing that it would make it much harder and much more dangerous to be working as prostitutes), it became more and more accepted that the general feminist/politically correct standpoint should be prohibition. The new law prohibiting the purchase of sex was passed in the parliament in 2008, and became effective in January 2009.

FAMILY

About 60 percent of the Norwegian population lives with a partner, while 18 percent of the adult population lives alone. Of all couples living together in 2004, approximately 26 percent were cohabitants and 74 percent married couples.[11] Approximately 40 percent of Norwegian children are born to cohabiting parents, approximately 10 percent to single mothers, and approximately 50 percent to married parents. Of children under 18 years old, 75 percent are living with both of their parents.[12] Approximately 12 percent of Norwegian women (at 45 years), and 18 percent of Norwegian men (at 50 years) do not have biological children.

Between 1993 and 2007, 3,404 persons had registered as partners, the lesbian and gay version of marriage.[13] The majority of these were male couples. Female couples living as registered partners were 2.2 times more likely to divorce than male couples.[14] Until 2005, 70 children had been born to a mother living in a registered partnership. In January 2009, a new gender-neutral Marriage Act has come into force, making the Act on Registered Partnership redundant.

The Act on Adoption and governmental regulations and guidelines constitute the legal framework for adoption in Norway. Adoption is managed through cooperation between the state and three private adoption organizations. The Act on Adoption, section 5, states that only married couples can adopt. The marriage should have lasted for a minimum of two years. This excludes both registered partners (lesbian/gay marriages) and the vast number of cohabiting couples (heterosexual and homosexual). The authorities and the private adoption agencies take care of different parts of the adoption process. Potential parents have to apply to the authorities to get approval to go ahead with the process. The authorities determine whether the applicants are fit parents; this is done through interviews and home visits. The applicants must have normal/good health both physically and mentally and a stable financial situation. They must have a good conduct and a clean police record. Single persons have increasingly—although still extremely rarely—been allowed to apply for adoption since 1998. If they are judged as fit parents, one of the adoption agencies can get them a child. An adoption is quite costly for the couple adopting and usually takes several years.

There is virtually no national adoption in Norway. Most of the children who are taken away from their parents are placed in foster care, and only in extremely rare cases are babies born in Norway put up for adoption. It is seen as highly immoral for a mother (or father) in Norway to give up a child for adoption.

The adoption regulations seem to promote a more narrow understanding of family than many other parts of the Norwegian intimate policy arena. There can be several reasons for this, and one of the reasons is an increased focus on parenthood and biology. Another reason is the claims set by the nations adopting away their children. No countries currently allowing children to be adopted in Norway accept same-sex couples as parents. Following increased demand, China has tightened their claims and will no longer accept single applicants. China has been the main source of children for single adoptive mothers in Norway until the present. China will also make it harder for overweight people and people with lower incomes to adopt a child.

Fostering of children is state-regulated and organized by the state. Theoretically, lesbian/gays can become foster parents, but it has proved very hard for same-sex couples to be approved by the authorities.

Since the new Act on Biotechnology from 2003, assisted conception has been allowed for stable cohabitating heterosexual couples as well as for married couples (before 2003, only married couples were allowed). All assisted conception takes place in public hospitals. After the new, gender-neutral Marriage Act was passed, all married couples will have the same right to assisted conception. There are no legal regulations on the private provision of assisted conception, and egg-transplantation is illegal in Norway. Since 2003, the former rule on sperm donors being anonymous has been changed to no option of anonymity. All children conceived from donor sperm are now entitled to the name of the donor when they turn 18.[15] Surrogacy is prohibited in Norway, as in the rest of Scandinavia. The Act on Parents and Children also states that the mother of a child is the woman giving birth to it, thus making surrogate mothers legally impossible.[16]

On one hand, it can be argued that the nuclear family is still strong in Norway, but that the definition of *nuclear family* has been broadened during the last three decades. Neither marriage nor heterosexuality is a necessary condition in many policy contexts, nor are biological bonds necessary to constitute a parent-child relationship. Although the policies supporting single parenthood is quite strong, it is also clear that partners in a romantic relationship are seen as one of the foundations for *family*. These partners are assumed to be living together. Children are also seen as a preferable ingredient in a family. Families with children have been the main target for supportive stately policies.

At the same time, this wide and democratic definition of *family* has competition from another discourse: the increased focus on biology. In some policy areas, biological bonds are highly stressed, particularly in the policy areas concerning fatherhood, national adoption, and assisted fertilization.

Adults not living in romantic relationships and not having children are invisible in the policy field of intimate citizenship. This also seems to reflect a major ideological marginalization of this group. The field of public focus and policy on intimacy in Norway marginalizes all intimacies that fall outside the couple (two partners) or parent-child relation.

COMMUNITY

Different forms of communities around same-sex lovers can probably be traced quite far back in history. Only a few historical studies of same-sex sexuality have been performed in the Norwegian context. The modern homosexual identity movement can be traced back to 1950, when a branch of the Danish homophile organization Forbundet af 1948 was established in Norway. The Danish organization was named as a reference to the declaration of human rights from 1948.[17] In 1952, the Norwegian branch was formalized as a separate organization called the Norwegian Association of 1948 (DNF-48). New forms of activism took place during the radical waves of the 1970s and 1980s, and the lesbian and gay movement experienced major divisions and conflicts, as well as diversity and creativity. After much turmoil during the 1970s and 1980s, different parts of lesbian and gay Norway were reunited in 1992 in the organization now called LLH (Norwegian National Association of Lesbian and Gay Liberation). LLH focuses public and government attention on cases of discrimination against LGBT people by asserting political/diplomatic pressure, providing information, and working with other organizations and national media. Since 1992, LLH has been responsible for a very successful identity politics, with strong ties to powerful political allies. The Norwegian lesbian and gay organizations have a strong tradition of lobbying authorities as the main strategy for gaining support and influence.

LLH is presently the only national lesbian/gay rights organization. It has about 2,000 members, spread out over 15 local chapters. Some of the local lesbian/gay/queer organizations are associated with the LLH, while others are autonomous entities. New forms of LGBT communities can be found on the Internet. The main lesbian/gay Web site gaysir.no has more than 44,000 registered users.[18]

Both on a national and local level, the state provide funding to lesbian and gay organizations and their activities. This includes health work, information work, cultural work, and the running of the national lesbian and gay organization (LLH).

There has been little focus on bisexuality in the Norwegian context, and no lasting organization exclusively for bisexuals has been established.

The main national organization for transsexuals is the Harry Benjamin ressurssenter (The Harry Benjamin Resource Center). The organization has close contact with the authorities and the one state hospital that performs gender-reassignment surgery. It was founded in 2000 and has mainly worked to lobby politicians and medical experts. It emphasizes that it is not an organization for all transpersons, but an organization for transsexuals who have received the ICD diagnosis F64.0.[19]

Until 2005, the Harry Benjamin ressurssenter was called LFTS, The National Organization for Transsexuals. At their annual meeting in 2005, they decided to change their name to The National Organization for Transgendered People, to avoid sexual connotations to their cause. In 2009 they changed their name to the Harry Benjamin ressurssenter. The organization does not want to be included in a LGBT community, and stresses that their cause is related to gender only, and they insist that this is something entirely different from sexuality.[20]

There are patient organizations for the different intersex groups,[21] but there is no intersex movement as such in Norway.

HEALTH

All Norwegian citizens and individuals working in Norway are automatically qualified for membership in the Norwegian National Insurance Scheme, a government insurance program entitling members to pensions (e.g. old age, survivor, disability), as well as benefits in connection with illness, accidents, pregnancy, birth, single parent families, and funerals. Together with the insurance programs for family allowance and the cash benefit to parents of young children (*kontantstøtte*), the National Insurance comprises the most important general insurance program in Norway. It is financed by membership fees from employees, self-employed individuals and other insured parties, employers' contributions, and government allocations.[22]

When admitted to hospital and members of the National Insurance, patients do not pay for treatment, medication, or hospital accommodation. For visiting doctors and psychologists outside a hospital, a fee is paid, but if the fees exceed the annual upper limit (currently approximately US$270), a patient is entitled to a fee exemption card (*frikort*). Expectant mothers do not pay for pregnancy check-ups.[23] Testing for sexually transmitted diseases (STDs) and HIV is also free of charge.

Gay and Lesbian Health Norway (GLHN) was founded in 1983 and has become an important organization in the Norwegian context. Several lesbian and gay organizations as well as individuals joined forces to address health issues relevant to the lesbian and gay community.[24]

To qualify for sex reassignment treatment in Norway, one has to be accepted as a patient by the state hospital Rikshospitalet, which performs the treatment. Surgical treatment started in Norway in 1962. Since then, more than 400 transsexuals have undergone hormonal and surgical treatment. Hormone treatment is not started until the patient is 18 years old.

Intersex conditions in Norway are divided between genital anomalies (atypical reproductive anatomies) and disorders of sex development (Turner's syndrome and Klinefelter syndrome). About 11 children are born each year with atypical reproductive anatomies, about 12 girls with Turner's syndrome, and an unknown number of boys with Klinefelter syndrome (which is underdiagnosed).

POLITICS AND LAW

Sexual relations between men were illegal in Norway from about 1100 until 1972. Sexual relations between women have never been formally illegal.

In the Norse era (700–1350 C.E., also known as the Viking era), accusation of unmanliness was the worst form of defamation. The term *Ergi* was used to describe unmanliness or weakness, and it was often used to describe a man who "let himself be used as a woman," the passive partner in anal intercourse. In the middle ages, the understanding of sex between men as *Ergi* was replaced by a Christian-based understanding of sex between men (and between men and animals) as sodomy or *fornication against nature*. In the late 19th century, this understanding was again replaced by an understanding of same-sex relations as a disease,[25] which again was replaced during the 20th century by an understanding of homosexuality as an inborn disposition (*legning*), no longer seen as a disease.[26] A new law concerning male homosexuality was introduced in 1902. It stressed that homosexuality was only to be prosecuted if the actions performed did public damage.[27] In this regard, the law differed significantly from laws on homosexuality in many other countries (e.g., Sweden), and it meant that only very few cases of homosexuality were taken to court. During the debates around the new law in 1902, some suggested that sex between women should also be included in the new law. A prominent cabinet minister then declared: "Sexual relations between two women—have you ever heard such a thing? It is an impossibility."[28]

When the first organization for homosexuals was founded in 1950 (DNF-48), it immediately started work to remove the paragraph making sexual relations between men illegal. In 1953, the penal code committee suggested removing the paragraph, but then wanted the age of consent set to 18 (instead of 16 as for heterosexual relations) and to prohibit homosexual propaganda. The fear of the spreading of homosexuality was behind these discussions. DNF-48 felt that this was worse than the existing (mostly unused) paragraph, and the work for decriminalization died down. In the late 1960s, it was taken up again, and in March 1972 removal of section 213 was passed in the parliament (*Odelstinget*) with 65 votes versus 13. No new paragraphs on the issue were introduced.[29]

Antidiscrimination Statutes

Norway has one big law on equality, the Gender Equality Act of 1978. The law only set out to hinder discrimination based on gender. Discrimination toward other groups is partly taken care of through:

- An act on prohibition of discrimination on the basis of ethnicity, religion, and so on (the Anti-Discrimination Act)
- The Working Environment Act's equal opportunity chapter (chapter 13)
- The antidiscrimination provisions in the Tenancy Act, Owner-Tenant Act, Housing Cooperative Act, and Home Building Association Act

On its Web site, the Equality and Anti-discrimination Ombuds office claims that, "The Ombuds Office contributes to the promotion of equal opportunity and fights discrimination. The Ombuds Office combats discrimination based on gender, ethnic origin, sexual orientation, physical handicap, and age. The Ombuds Office upholds the law and acts as a proactive agent for equal opportunity throughout society."[30] The current ombudswoman (2009) officially describes herself as a lesbian, and she has focused particularly on lesbians/gays and disabled people.

In the Norwegian law, hate crimes are mainly defined as *utterances*. Hate actions are taken care of in other parts of the law, but section 135 of the criminal code states that it is illegal to utter a hateful or discriminatory statement concerning skin color, national or ethnic origin, religion, "homophile legning," lifestyle, or orientation.

The punishment could be fines or prison up to three years. So far, the law has only been used a couple of times.

The current socialist government (2009) wants to strengthen the work against hate crimes, and has given LLH money to map out the scope of hate crimes against homosexuals.

Marriage

In 1993, the Act on Registered Partnership was passed in parliament. Thus, Norway became the second nation in the world (after Denmark) to grant some sort of marriage rights to same-sex couples. The law gave the same rights for same-sex couples as marriage, apart from the right to apply for adoption and the right to get married in a church. The law gave the same rights and responsibilities concerning tax, social security, and unemployment benefits, pensions, survivor benefits, caregivers' allowances, inheritance rights, and so on. In January 2007, 3,404 persons were registered partners.[31] From 1993 until 2005, there were 70 children born to mothers living in registered partnerships, most of these in recent years.

The Act on Registered Partnership became a reality after a lot of work by individual lesbian/gay activists in an alliance with individual politicians from the Labor Party (AP) and the Socialist Party (SV). Among the conservatives and liberals, the attitudes were also changing in favor of the law. Most parties let their representatives vote individually on this case. Only the Christian Democratic Party (KrF) was 100 percent opposed to the proposal. The public debate around this issue was huge. The debate was mainly progay (in favor of the law) and antigay (opposing the law). There was very little debate, either public or internally in the lesbian/gay community on whether this was something the lesbian/gay movement wanted to prioritize, and very few voices spoke up against marriage in general. An important exception to this was the former president of DNF-48, Karen-Christine Friele, who was against the Law on Partnership. She withdrew from the organization in 1989, after more than 20 years as a strong front figure for the lesbian and gay movement.[32] Many of the lesbian/gay activists working toward this law were also active in the reorganization of the Norwegian lesbian/gay movement into the organization LLH in 1992.

A new Marriage Act, making marriages gender neutral, was passed in parliament in June 2008, and became effective in January 2009. By the new Marriage Act the Act on Registered Partnership was made redundant. The important changes have been that same-sex couples are now included in the symbolic marriage union, and also same-sex couples now have the right to apply for adoption and receive assisted fertilization. The active proponents of the gender-neutral marriage law were mainly the AP, the SV, and the LLH. Several of the other political parties are also mainly in favor of the new law. The visible opponents were mainly Christian conservative groups. The debate on a gender-neutral marriage has, somewhat surprisingly, been a lot less heated than the debate on the Act on Registered Partnership in 1993. In 2009, however, the Norwegian Association of the Freedom of Expression Foundation gave their respected award to the well-known antigay philosopher Nina Karin Monsen for her speaking up against the gender-neutral Marriage Act. The controversial choice of reward recipient gave rise to a heated public debate.

Speech and Association

Free speech and association has not been a big issue in the Norwegian LGBT debates. Discussions concerning restrictions on the Internet or on information about LGBT issues have hardly been heard in the public realm. In some of the religious private schools, this has been an issue, and in some public schools individual parents have reacted negatively to information about LGBT issues. In the few discrimination cases taken to court where extreme conservative Christians have been indicted, they have tried to argue that their hate speech is protected by the freedom of speech. In the most famous of these cases, from 1984, the supreme court judged that antidiscrimination took precedence over freedom of speech in that case.[33]

Transsexuals

After genital surgery has been performed, transsexuals have the right to a new birth certificate and social security number.[34]

The KrF has been among the strongest opponents to lesbian and gay rights in Norway. However, in their political manifesto for the period 2005–2009, they were the only party to strongly support the right of transsexuals.

RELIGION AND SPIRITUALITY

While roughly 88 percent of the population belongs to the Protestant Church of Norway, only 10 percent attend church services or other Christian-related meetings more than once a month. Some 8 percent of the population belongs to other religious communities, while 10 percent do not belong to any religious community at all. The largest religious and lifestyle communities outside the Church of Norway are the humanist movement, represented by the Norwegian Humanist Association (78,000), Islam (79,000, mostly Shia Muslims), the Pentecostal movement (45,000), the Roman Catholic Church (51 000 or more), the Evangelical Lutheran free church (20,000), Methodists (13,000), and several smaller free churches. About 11,000 Buddhists are registered in Norway (mostly of Vietnamese origin), approximately 4,000 Hindus, and 850 Jews.[35]

Norway is generally seen as a largely secular society, and the national identity portrayed in the public sphere is very much one of secularism, modernity, and progress. Despite this, different versions of Christian morality and Christian cultural norms are an important reference in public discourse and in many local communities. After the debate on abortion died out after a law legalizing it in 1979, the debate about homosexuality has been one of the major moral issues within the Christian communities, as well as in the parliament and public discourse.

In 1954, the Diocesan Council of the Church of Norway stated that "homosexuality is a threat of world-dimensions." Since then, the debate on homosexuality has been a hot topic in meeting after meeting in the church and has created divisions both on local and national levels. In 1977, the council decided to accept the inborn disposition to (*legning*) homosexuality, but to condemn the *practice* of this disposition. In 1999, the first female bishop, Rosemarie Köhn, was the first to go against both the Diocesan Council and the National Synod when she let a lesbian theologian be a priest in one of her congregations. At the synod in 2007, 84 members voted for allowing different views on the question of lesbians and gays in ordained positions, while 50 still voted against accepting different views.

The Open Church Group for Lesbians and Gays was founded in 1976, and is an ecumenical Christian organization with national membership. The Open Church Group has been the main organization fighting for the rights and inclusion of lesbians and gays in different Christian communities, particularly the Church of Norway. The Open Church Group in Oslo organizes services every Friday. Chapters of the Open Church Group can also be found in other cities.

VIOLENCE

Violence against lesbians and gays does occur in Norway. Several gay men have been killed because of their sexual orientation, and lesbian and gay adolescents seem to be facing a particularly high amount of discrimination and violence in their everyday lives.[36]

There is no particular focus on domestic violence in nonheterosexual relationships in Norway. In the statistics from the Women's Shelter, 4 percent of the users state that their offender was a woman. There are, however, no statistics to show what kind of a relationship there was between the victim and the offender.

OUTLOOK FOR THE 21ST CENTURY

Heteronormativity is still dominating Norwegian society, but there is no general fear of the LBGT population losing civil rights. After the gender-neutral Marriage Act was passed, there are few formal boundaries left between heterosexuals and homosexuals. Whether the lesbian/gay movement can continue as a civil rights–focused identity movement, or whether it has to open up for alternative frameworks, remains to be seen.[37]

RESOURCE GUIDE

Suggested Reading

Norman Anderssen, *Homofile Menn: Kategorisering og Identitet,* Master's thesis in psychology, University of Bergen, 1986.

Norman Anderssen, "Er Lesbiske Kvinner og Homofile Menn Fortsatt Stigmatiserte i Norge? Notat om holdninger overfor lesbiske kvinner og homofile menn," in *Vite for Å Forstå. 10 Artikler om Homoseksualitet og Homofiles Livsvilkår i Norge i Dag,* ed. V. Benum (Oslo: LLH, 1997).

Agnes Bolsø, "Hvem Sin Identitetskrise? Kronikk," *Blikk* (June 2007): 22.

Agnes Bolsø, "Mission Accomplished? Gay Elitism and the Constant Misery of a Minority," *Trikster* (January 2008).

Agnes Bolsø, "Triangulering av Begjær," in *Når Heteroseksualiteten må Forklare Seg,* ed. T. Annfelt, B. Andersen, and A. Bolsø (Trondheim, Norway: Tapir, 2007).

Gerd Brantenberg, *Opp Alle Jordens Homofile* [*What Comes Naturally*] (London: The Women's Press, 1973).

Marianne Brantsæther, Turid Eikvam, Reidar Kjær, and Knut Olav Åmos, *Norsk homoforskning* (Oslo: Universitetsforlaget, 2003).

Tor Folgerø and Tone Hellesund, Transseksualitet på norsk, "Heteronormering av kjønn og hverdagsliv," in *Norske seksualiteter,* ed. Åse Røthing and Wencke Mühleisen (Oslo: Cappelen, 2009).

Karen-Christine Friele, *Fra Undertrykkelse til Opprør: Om Å Være Homofil—og Være Glad for Det* (Oslo: Gyldendal, 1975).

Karen-Christine Friele, *Troll Skal Temmes* (Oslo: Scanbok, 1990).

Jan Olav Gatland, *Mellom Linjene: Homofile Tema i Norsk Litteratur* (Oslo: Aschehoug, 1990).

Merethe Giertsen and Norman Anderssen, "Time Period and Lesbian Identity Events: A Comparison of Norwegian Lesbians across 1986 and 2005," *Journal of Sex Research* 44, no. 4 (2007): 328–39.

Finn Grodal, *Vi Som Føler Annerledes: Homoseksualiteten og Samfunnet* (Oslo: Aschehoug, 1957).

Martin Skaug Halsos, *§ 213 i Almindelig Borgerlig Straffelov av 1902: Homoseksualitet i Norge og Rettslige Sanksjoner mot den fra Slutten av 1800-tallet til 1972* (Hovedoppgave: University of Bergen, 1999).

Anders Sømme Hammer, "Vil Rekruttere Homoer og Innvandrere," *Dagsavisen* (May 8, 2007).

Tone Maria Hansen, "Treatment in Norway for the Diagnose F.64.0 Transsexualism." Paper presented at the IFGE Conference, Philadelphia, 2003, http://www.lfts.no/?module=Articles;action=ArticleFolder.publicOpenFolder;ID=182.

Kristinn Hegna, "Coming Out, Coming Into What? Identification and Risks in the 'Coming Out' Story of a Norwegian Late Adolescent Gay Man," *Sexualities* 10, no. 5 (2007): 582–602.

Kristinn Hegna, "Ungdoms Seksualvaner—'Homo' og 'Hetero'?" *Tidsskrift for ungdomsforskning* 3, no. 2 (2003): 113–18.

Kristinn Hegna, Hans Wiggo Kristiansen, and Bera Moseng, *Levekår og Livskvalitet blant Lesbiske Kvinner og Homofile Menn.* NOVA rapport 1 (Oslo: NOVA, 1999).

Kristinn Hegna and Lars Wichstrøm, "Suicide Attempts among Norwegian Gay, Lesbian and Bisexual Youths: General and Specific Risk Factors," *Acta Sociologica. Journal of the Nordic Sociological Association* 50, no. 1 (2007): 21–37.

Arne Heli, *Åpen om det Forbudte* (Oslo: Pax, 2006).

Runar Jordåen, *Frå Synd til Sjukdom. Konstruksjonen av Mannleg Homoseksualitet i Norge 1886–1950*. Master's thesis, Universitetet i Bergen, 2003.

Hans Wiggo Kristiansen, *Masker og motstand: diskré homoliv i Norge 1920–1970* (Oslo: Unipub, 2008).

Hans Wiggo Kristiansen, *Kjærlighetskarusellen: Eldre Homoseksuelle Menns Livsfortellinger og Livsløp i Norge*. PhD diss, University of Oslo, 2004.

Hans Wiggo Kristiansen, "Narrating Past Lives and Present Concerns: Older Gay Men in Norway," in *Gay and Lesbian Aging: Research and Future Directions,* ed. G. Herdt (New York: Springer, 2004).

Hans Wiggo Kristiansen, "Når Skeiv Teori blir Levd Liv," *Samtiden* 2 (2003): 79–87.

Hans Wiggo Kristiansen and Willy Pedersen, "Å Gjøre det, å Føle det og å Være det: Homoseksualitet i det Seinmoderne," *Tidsskrift for Samfunnsforskning* 1 (2003): 3–36.

Anne-Lise Middelthon, *Being Young and Gay in the Context of HIV: a Qualitative Study among Young Norwegian Gay Men*. PhD dissertation, University of Oslo, 2001.

Bera Moseng, *Lesbiskes Psykiske Helse*. NOVA Rapport: 4 (Oslo: NOVA, 2002).

Bera Moseng, *Vold mot Lesbiske og Homofile Tenåringer. En Representativ Undersøkelse av Omfang, Risiko og Beskyttelse* (Oslo: NOVA Rapport: 19, 2007).

Turid Noack, "Skilsmisser i Registrerte Partnerskap og Ekteskap. Partnere Skiller seg Oftest," *Samfunnsspeilet* 6 (2005).

Anbjørg Ohnstad, "Den Rosa Panteren eller En i Den Grå Masse. Forståelse av Lesbiske i Terapi," *Tidsskrift for Norsk Psykologforening* 4 (1992): 313–21.

Anbjørg Ohnstad and Kirsti Malterud, eds., *Lesbiske og Homofile i Møte med Helse- og Sosialtenesta* (Oslo: Samlaget, 2006).

Marit Vaula Rasmussen, *Å Gjøre Kjønn: Performativitet og Meningsskaping blant Transkjønn og Andre Kjønn i Norge*. Master's thesis in anthropology, Universitetet i Bergen, 2005.

Øystein Rian, "Mellom Straff og Fortielse. Homoseksualitet i Norge fra Vikingtiden til 1930-årene," in *Norsk Homoforskning,* ed. Marianne Brantsæther, Turid Eikvam, Reidar Kjær and Knut Olav Åmos. (Oslo: Universitetsforlaget, 2001).

Åse Røthing, "Homonegativisme og Homofobi i Klasserommet. Marginaliserte Maskuliniteter, Disiplinerende Jenter og Rådville Lærere," *Tidsskrift for Ungdomsforskning* 7, no. 1 (2007): 27–51.

Åse Røthing, "Kjønn og Seksualitet i Grunnskolens Læreplaner. Historisk Tilbakeblikk og Aktuelle Utfordringer," *Norsk Pedagogisk Tidsskrift* 88 (2004): 356–68.

Åse Røthing and Stine Helena Bang Svendsen, *Seksualitet i skolen. Perspektiver på undervisning* (Oslo: Cappelen, 2009).

Jens Rydström and Kati Mustola, eds., *Criminally Queer: Homosexuality and Criminal Law in Scandinavia 1842–1999* (Amsterdam: Aksant, 2007).

Bjørn Smestad, ed., *Ressurspakke for Undervisning om Homofili i Profesjonsutdanningene,* versjon 1.04, http://homoproff.blogspot.com/.

Dag Stenvoll, *Politisk Argumentasjon: en Analyse av Norske Stortingsdebatter om Seksualitet og Reproduksjon 1945–2001*. PhD dissertation, Universitetet i Bergen, 2003.

Lars Wichstrøm and Kristin Hegna, "Sexual Orientation and Suicide Attempts. A Longitudinal Study of the General Norwegian Adolescent Population," *Journal of Abnormal Psychology* 112, no. 1 (2003): 144–51.

Organizations

Bergen Beans, http://www.bergenbeans.com/.
   Soccer, handball, and volleyball teams for lesbians and gay men in Bergen.
Blikk, http://www.blikk.no/.
   LGB newspaper,
Den norske bjørneklubben (Norway Bears), http://www.norwaybears.com/.
   Club for gay men.

Fhiol, http://home.hio.no/fhiohl/.
>   For lesbians and gays at Oslo University College.
Fjellgruppen (The Mountain Group), http://www.fjellgruppen.no/.
>   Men who like men who like mountains.
Foreningen for partnerskapsbarn, http://www.partnerbarn.no/.
>   Organization working for the rights of children born to parents living as registered
>   partners.
Freedom of Personality Expression (FPE), http://www.fpenorge.no/default.asp?sec=3.
>   Organization for transgendered people (transvestites, transsexuals, cross-dressers,
>   and other trans-types) in Norway.
Gaysir, http://www.gaysir.no.
>   Norway's largest LBG Web forum, news, discussions, dating, shop, and so on. More
>   than 44,000 members (July 2009).
Harry Benjamin ressurssenter [Harry Benjamin Resource Center], www.lfts.no.
>   The main organization for transsexuals (ICD diagnosis F64.0) in Norway.
Helsestasjon for lesbisk, homofil, bifil og transkjønnet ungdom, http://www.bydel-gruner
>   lokka.oslo.kommune.no/helse/helsestasjon_for_lesbisk_homofil_og_bifil_ungdom/.
>   Public health clinic for lesbian, gay, bi, and trans youth
Helseutvalget—Gay & Lesbian Health Norway (GLHN), http://www.helseutvalget.no/.
>   Works on health issues among men who have sex with men (MSM) and women who
>   have sex with women (WSW).
Nettverk for forskning om homoseksualitet (Network for Research on Homosexuality),
>   http://www.jus.uio.no/ikrs/nettverket/.
>   Extensive Web site on Norwegian lesbian/gay/queer research. Also a monthly
>   research forum.
Norwegian National Association of Lesbian and Gay Liberation (LLH), http://www.llh.
>   no/English/.
>   Works for the equality of lesbian, gay, and bisexual (LGB) people and their liberation
>   from all forms of discrimination. A wide variety of social groups are also a part of the
>   LLH organization.
Open Church Group, http://www.apenkirkegruppe.org/index2.htm.
>   Ecumenical Christian organization, part of LLH, with national membership. The
>   group was established in 1976 and currently has 210 members.
Raadgivningstjenesten for homofile og lesbiske, http://www.zinus.no/rt/rtjenesten.htm.
>   Counseling service for gays and lesbians.
Rosa Rebell (Pink Rebel), http://rosarebell.wordpress.com/.
>   News blog launching news related to lesbian, gay, and bi life in Norway.
Scandinavian Leather Men, http://www.slm-oslo.no/index.php.
>   Club for gay men.
Skeiv Ungdom (Queer Youth), http://www.skeivungdom.no/.
>   The youth organization of the LLH, although largely independent and focusing on
>   queer rather than lesbian/gay.
Skeivt Forum—skeiv studentforening, E-mail: skeivtforum@gmail.com.
>   Student organization, University of Oslo.
Trikster, http://www.trikster.net.
>   New Nordic Web magazine. Offering queer perspectives on politics and culture.
UgleZ—skeiv studentorganisasjon i Bergen, http://uglez.blogspirit.com/.
>   Queer student organization in Bergen.

NOTES

1. Digitalskolen, Historisk institutt, Universitetet i Bergen, http://web.hist.uib.no/
digitalskolen/oe/noemi.htm.

2. Norwegian Organization for Asylum Seekers, "Tema: FN's anbefalinger," http://www.noas.org/?p=news&news_id=79.

3. SSB, "Kirkelige handlinger og medlemmer i Den norske kirke. 2005–2006," SSB, http://www.ssb.no/trosamf/.

4. Runar Jordåen, *Frå Synd til Sjukdom. Konstruksjonen av Mannleg Homoseksualitet i Norge 1886–1950*, Master's thesis, Universitetet i Bergen 2003, p. 91.

5. Riksålsordboken refers to Morgenbladet 1965/14/10/2.

6. Norman Anderssen; Tone Hellesund. 2008. "Heteronormative consensus in the Norwegian same-sex adoption debate?" Kilden: Information Centre for Gender Research in Norway. http://eng.kilden.forskningsradet.no/c52781/publikasjon/vis.html?tid=61339&strukt_tid=52781 (accessed September 20, 2009).

7. The Act on Private Schools and their Right to Public Funding.

8. Kunnskapsdepartmentet, "Foreslår endring av KRL-faget," news release 87–07, July 12, 2007.

9. Åse Røthing, "Kjønn og Seksualitet i Grunnskolens Læreplaner. Historisk Tilbakeblikk og Aktuelle Utfordringer," *Norsk Pedagogisk Tidsskrift* 88 (2004): 356–68; Åse Røthing, "Homonegativisme og Homofobi i Klasserommet. Marginaliserte Maskuliniteter, Disiplinerende Jenter og Rådville Lærere," *Tidsskrift for Ungdomsforskning* 7, no. 1 (2007): 27–51; Åse Røthing and Stine Helena Bang Svendsen, *Seksualitet i skolen. Perspektiver på undervisning* (Oslo: Cappelen); Bjørn Smestad ed., (August 14, 2009) *Ressurspakke for Undervisning om Homofili i Profesjonsutdanningene*, versjon 1.04, http://homoproff.blogspot.com/.

10. Anders Sømme Hammer, "Vil Rekruttere Homoer og Innvandrere," *Dagsavisen*, May 8, 2007.

11. SSB, "Folkemengd, etter sivilstand, kjønn og alder," January 1, 2007.

12. SSB, "Befolkningsstatistikk. Barn, 1. januar 2007: Tre av fire barn bodde med begge foreldrene," http://www.ssb.no/barn/.

13. SSB, "Folkemengd, etter sivilstand, kjønn og alder."

14. Turid Noack, "Skilsmisser i Registrerte Partnerskap og Ekteskap. Partnere Skiller seg Oftest," *Samfunnsspeilet* 6 (2005).

15. Act on Biotechnology, http://www.lovdata.no/all/hl-20031205–100.html#2–2.

16. Act on Parents and Children, http://www.lovdata.no/all/hl-19810408–007.html#map002.

17. Arne Heli, *Åpen om det Forbudte* (Oslo: Pax, 2006).

18. See http://www.gaysir.no/, July 2009.

19. Tor Folgerø and Tone Hellesund, "Transseksualitet på norsk. Heteronormering av kjønn og hverdagsliv," in *Norske seksualiteter*, ed. Åse Røthing and Wencke Mühleisen (Oslo: Cappelen, 2009).

20. "Transgenders Want Out of Homoplan," *Blikk*, October 8, 2007, http://www.blikk.no/nyheter/sak.html?kat=1&id=9259.

21. Turner Syndrome Association, http://www.turnersyndrom.no/hoved.htm; Klinefelter Association, http://klinefelter.no/; Association for Genital Anomalies, http://www.cah.no/AGSCAH.html.

22. Norway, the Official Page in the United States, Facts and Figures, Published by the Norwegian Embassy in the USA, "National Insurance Scheme," http://www.norway.org/facts/living/insurance/insurance.htm.

23. Norway.no, "Your Gateway to the Public Sector in Norway," http://www.norway.no/oss/#a3173.

24. Gay and Lesbian Health Norway, http://www.helseutvalget.no/.

25. All the above from Jordåen, *Frå Synd til Sjukdom*.

26. For example, Jordåen, *Frå Synd til Sjukdom;* and Dag Stenvoll, *Politisk Argumentasjon: en Analyse av Norske Stortingsdebatter om Seksualitet og Reproduksjon 1945–2001*, PhD dissertation, Universitetet i Bergen, 2002.

27. Jordåen, *Frå Synd til Sjukdom*, 38–46.

28. Jordåen, *Frå Synd til Sjukdom,* 39.

29. Ibid., 93–97.

30. The Equality and Anti-discrimination Ombud, http://www.ldo.no.

31. SSB, "Folkemengd, etter sivilstand, kjønn og alder," January 1, 2007.

32. Karen-Christine Friele, *Troll Skal Temmes* (Oslo: Scanbok, 1990).

33. The case against pastor Hans Bratterud.

34. Tone Maria Hansen, "Treatment in Norway for the Diagnose F.64.0 Transsexualism," paper presented at the IFGE Conference, Philadelphia, 2003.

35. SSB, "Medlemmer i trus- og livssynssamfunn utanfor Den norske kyrkja, etter religion/livssyn, January 1, 2005–2007. Absolutte tal og prosent"; SSB, "Medlemmer i kristne trussamfunn utanfor Den norske kyrkja, Per January 1, 2005–2007."

36. Bera Moseng, *Vold mot Lesbiske og Homofile Tenåringer. En Representativ Undersøkelse av Omfang, Risiko og Beskyttelse* (Oslo: NOVA, 2007).

37. Agnes Bolsø, "Mission Accomplished? Gay Elitism and the Constant Misery of a Minority," *Trikster,* January 2008.

POLAND

Joanna Mizielinska

OVERVIEW

The Republic of Poland, a country in eastern central Europe, has an area of 120,728 square miles. It borders Germany to the west, the Czech Republic and Slovakia to the south, and Ukraine, Lithuania, and Belarus to the east. The Baltic Sea and Kalingrad Oblast, a Russian exclave, are to the north.

Poland has a population of 38.5 million, with a density of 47 people per square mile, most of whom live in big cities. The capital, Warsaw, has about 3 million inhabitants.

Poland is a relatively ethnically homogenous state: 99.3 percent of its population is Polish. It has small minorities of Germans, Belarusians, and Ukrainians. The Jewish community of almost 3.5 million was almost entirely exterminated by Nazis during World War II and the subsequent emigration. According to the 2002 census, there are only about 1,000 Jewish people living in Poland.

Approximately 92 percent of Poles are Catholic (46% of the country). The most important religious minorities include Polish Orthodox, Jehovah's Witnesses, Orthodox Catholics, and Lutherans.

Poland's history as a state began in 966 C.E. when its first ruler, Mieszko I, was baptized. Since then, Polish history has experienced a golden age where Poland built a commonwealth with the Grand Duchy of Lithuania (1569–1795) and partitions (1795–1918) where Poland was divided between Russia, Prussia, and Austro-Hungary. In 1918, after World War I, Poland regained its independence but

only for a short time. It lost it again by being divided between Nazi Germany and the Soviet Union during the World War II. After World War II, Poland was part of the Soviet Bloc. When Communism collapsed in 1989, thanks in part to the solidarity movement, Poland regained its full independence.

Poland has been a member of the European Union (EU) since May 1, 2004.

OVERVIEW OF LGBT ISSUES

Poland, contrary to some other post-Communist countries, has had a long tradition of not criminalizing homosexual activities. That practice dates back to the Napoleonic code that was in force in Poland from 1832 and prevailed when Poland regained its independence in 1918 (the Polish independent criminal code of 1932 was silent on homosexuality). Meanwhile, under Russian rule, the imperial law was introduced, according to which homosexuality (but only between men) was illegal, the same as it was in the parts of Poland that belonged to Prussia and Austro-Hungary. In the new Polish constitution of 1997, sexual orientation is not mentioned among the factors that demand special protection from the state (contrary to gender or ethnicity, for example), but the equality of all citizens is guaranteed by article 32, which states the following: "All are equal before the law. All have rights to be treated equally by public authorities. Nobody can be discriminated against in political, social and economic life for any reason."[1]

However, behind this superficial tolerance lies deeply rooted homophobia that is strongly influenced by the teaching of the Catholic Church. LGBT people are discriminated against in their daily life at work, in school, and in families. Also, when one looks at how the issue of legislation of same-sex partnership is discussed, in the Polish constitution, marriage has been very strictly defined as a union between a woman and a man. This narrow and discriminating definition of marriage was introduced due to the strong pressure of the Catholic Church long before this issue was discussed publicly by the Polish LGBT movement. As a consequence, any attempts to legalize same-sex partnership could be considered as unconstitutional.

In addition, in a country where 92 percent of the population is Catholic, public opinion about LGBT issues is strongly influenced by Roman Catholic teaching. In a poll conducted in July 2005, 89 percent of respondents considered homosexuality a deviance and only a few (4%) considered it as normal behavior. Among the first group, 55 percent (a growth of 8% comparing to the poll results from 2001) thought that homosexuals should be tolerated; 34 percent (7% less than four years before) thought the opposite. Regarding same-sex partnership law, 46 percent support legalization but almost the same number (44%) are against it. However, same-sex marriage is accepted by 22 percent of respondents, whereas 72 percent are against this idea.[2]

Asked their opinion about lesbians, almost 43 percent declare that they do not accept them at all, whereas 40 percent say that that they do not accept gays at all. Forty-two percent believe that the law should not allow homosexuals to engage in sexual encounters. Forty percent support private homosexual practices.[3]

According to the poll, the majority of Poles would accept a gay or lesbian person as their neighbor (56% and 54 %). A relatively large percentage of respondents would accept a gay or lesbian person as a boss (41% and 42%) or a coworker (45% and 42%). Thirty-seven percent would accept gays or lesbians as members of parliament.

Poles very strongly resist any contact between homosexuals and children. Only about 20 percent of them would accept a gay or lesbian teacher. Even fewer would accept homosexuals as child care worker (11% for gays and 14% for lesbians). A gay priest would be accepted only by 13 percent of Poles.[4]

Lately, there have been changes in Polish attitudes toward LGBT issues, as well as more activity on the part of LGBT people, who are slowly regaining their own voice and are fighting for their rights in the public sphere. These changes are due to several important factors discussed here, and underlined by the fact that Poland joined the EU in 2004; the latter development has had a strong impact on Polish LGBT politics. One of the fundamental principles of the EU is nondiscrimination on the grounds of sexual orientation. Additionally, Polish LGBT people can bring/ discuss issues of Polish homophobia on an international level and, in this way, influence the state's policy by achieving visibility and the voice they had lacked before.

EDUCATION

The Polish education system could serve as an illustration of the promotion of homophobia and intolerance toward all nonnormative sexual and gender behaviors. There are no programs in Polish schools that provide useful information about human sexuality in general or LGBT issues in particular. One of the subjects where students/pupils are introduced to the realm of sexuality, called *family life education,* presents homosexuality, transsexuality, and bisexuality in a very prejudiced way. Moreover, this subject is not obligatory and has been very often taught by teachers who do not have any training in sex education. In the school textbooks designed for this subject and approved by the Ministry of Education, there is a very strong influence of Catholic teaching. Where homosexuality is discussed at all, it is included in a discussion about sexual deviance, along with pedophilia, incest, and/ or bestiality. Homosexuality is presented as an exception from the rule/norm, as a mental disorder, or as something that should and can be cured. Following the Catholic Church's teaching, authors very often differentiate between homosexual tendencies and homosexual acts. Whereas the former can be tolerated under the condition of not acting upon them, the latter should be condemned. They present homosexuality as culturally conditioned and are strongly opposed to any genetic explanation.

Introduced this way, information about nonnormative sexual behavior is not only against the International Classification of Diseases (ICD) published by the World Health Organization (WHO) in 1991, which does not consider homosexual or bisexual orientation as a disease, but also reproduces social fears and prejudices that might harm LGBT people. The result is a kind of indoctrination that produces students who lack good information about sexual minorities, are against any kind of otherness, and feel free to express homophobia and intolerance openly. Thus, the majority of LGBT people choose to conceal their preferences in schools and universities. They also avoid discussing sexuality in public. According to the LGBT organizations' report from 2005–2006, 79 percent of the poll respondents hid their sexual orientation and private life in schools and universities. Among them, 27.4 percent kept it from everyone, and 51.6 percent from only some people. They hid it both from teachers (77.8%) and schoolmates (82.7%).[5]

The fear and silence were strengthened while the right wing was recently in power in Poland.[6] In November 2005, the Law and Justice Party (a mix of nationalism, populism, and Catholic conservatism), run by the Kaczynski twins (Jaroslaw and Lech), won the parliamentary election and built a coalition with the extremist League of Polish Families and conservative populist party Samoobrona. For the first time during the campaign, right-wing candidates often appealed to their voters using homophobic language warning against the "promotion of homosexuality" in the public and presenting themselves as defenders of traditional values. For instance, Jaroslaw Kaczynski described homosexuality as an abomination and said that, in his opinion, homosexuals should not be allowed to be teachers. What followed was openly expressed homophobia that had a very important political impact on political decisions in everyday life. For instance, in June 2006, Miroslaw Sielatycki, the director of the Center for Teachers' Improvement, was fired by the Ministry of Education's Roman Giertych, who was also the leader of the League of Polish Families. The main motive given to the public was the promotion of homosexuality in schools by the publication printed by the center. This publication was an official guidebook sponsored by the Council of Europe titled *Compass—Education of Human Rights in Working with the Youth,* and included an introduction by Terry Davis, the general secretary of the Council of Europe. The book contains scenarios for conducting classes on women's rights, domestic violence, and sexual discrimination. It also encourages teachers to invite representatives of LGBT organizations to speak.

In his international speech at the European conference in Heidelberg, Roman Giertych openly expressed his homophobic views, asking all EU ministers of education to condemn/ban both abortion and homosexual propaganda in Europe. He said that homosexual propaganda must be limited so children will have the correct view of the family. Although he did not receive any support in the international forum, he did at the national level. In March 2007, the deputy minister of education, Miroslaw Orzechowski, stated that new legislation against the promotion of homosexuality in schools would soon be introduced. It was supposed to "punish anyone who promotes homosexuality or any other deviance of a sexual nature in education." He also claimed that "teachers who reveal their homosexuality will be dismissed." Although the legal changes have not been introduced so far, this kind of policy induces fear and intimidation among students and teachers, preventing them from coming out.

EMPLOYMENT AND ECONOMICS

One of the consequences of Poland becoming an EU member in 2004 was an obligation to fully implement its national antidiscrimination legislation, including the regulations protecting equal treatment on the basis of sexual orientation. On January 1, 2004, a new labor code was introduced, with amendments imposing a ban on discrimination against employees based on sexual orientation. The amendment brought into effect the provision of the Council of Europe directive from December 2000 establishing a general framework for equal treatment in employment and occupation. The labor code was implemented with such provisions as a ban on direct/indirect discrimination and sexual abuse, and a reversal of the burden of proof in proceedings on equal treatment (i.e., the employer has to prove that there was no discrimination).

Many organizations working in the field of equal treatment for the LGBT population have used these provisions in bringing cases into the court and successfully collected compensation for discrimination based on sexual orientation. However, few mainstream employees are aware of the existence of such provisions. In consequence, most gay and lesbian people conceal their sexual orientation and private life at work. According to the LAMBDA report, 84.6 percent of their respondents do conceal their sexual orientation at work.[7] More than one-third of them felt the need to hide from all coworkers or be silent about their sexual orientation. Half of the respondents had come out to some coworkers, and only 10 percent could talk openly about their private life at the workplace. What is very telling is that the majority of respondents kept their orientation from their employers and supervisors (61.9%). However, according to the report, there was no difference in the level of experiencing discrimination between those who concealed their sexuality at work and those who came out. Among the latter, 13 percent have experienced worse treatment compared to 9.6 percent of those who hide their sexuality.

Because discrimination in the workplace in general is still a barely researched topic, unequal treatment is very difficult to prove. There is little data about how many Poles bring cases to the court accusing employers of discrimination based on sexual orientation, and how many of them just accept unequal treatment to keep their jobs. Poland still has a high unemployment rate, which may prevent many employees from coming out. At the same time, as a result of entering the EU, many Poles have started to emigrate and look for work abroad. One may speculate that one of the reasons workers decide to work in England or Ireland, which host the biggest population of Polish migrants nowadays, is that in those countries LGBT people can be more open about their sexual orientation. According to the Campaign against Homophobia, almost 100,000 Polish gays and lesbians have left Poland because of discrimination based on sexual orientation.

SOCIAL/GOVERNMENT PROGRAMS

The attitude of the Polish government after 1989 toward LGBT issues has depended on whether right- or left-wing parties are in power. Whereas the former represent an openly hostile homophobic approach, the left tries to be more open and supportive of the LGBT community. It is possible to quantify these differences by analyzing the funds (or lack of them) that have been distributed among different NGOs and social programs designed to fight sexism and homophobia within given years. For instance, the right-wing government that was in power from 1997–2001 gave grants according to the political preferences of the plenipotentiary for family, Kazimierz Kapera, to all initiatives that strengthened family, had a Catholic background, and were highly conservative. In 2002 when the left-wing government was in power (2001–2005), its plenipotentiary for the equal status of men and women (notice the important change in the title), Izabela Jaruga-Nowacka was responsible for fighting discrimination based not only on gender but also sexual orientation, age, ethnicity, and religious beliefs. The plenipotentiary at that time cooperated very closely not only with feminist but also with LGBT organizations, distributing funds for their activities, sponsoring conferences that aimed to fight prejudice and hate, and publishing leaflets and co-organizing social campaigns. One of the most important social campaigns cosponsored by the plenipotentiary was the project by the Polish LGBT organization Campaign against Homophobia titled Let Them See Us. This was initiated in the autumn of 2002 by Karolina Bregula, a graduate of the Stockholm University School of Photography. Let Them See Us consisted of an exhibition of 30 pictures, portraying 15 gay and 15 lesbian couples, all of them holding hands in winter scenery. The pictures, exhibited in art galleries in Warsaw, Cracow, Gdansk, and Sosnowiec, were only part of the project, which also involved an outdoor poster campaign, as well as an information campaign. The project generated a heated discussion on gay and lesbian rights, especially the right to public space, revealing a great deal of prejudice. In the streets, posters were destroyed, and many galleries refused to host it after the whole initiative became publicized. Moreover, the plenipotentiary was highly criticized by politicians from opposition parties for promoting the depravation of the Polish nation.

One of the first political decisions after the Law and Justice Party won the parliamentary election in 2005 was a decision to fire the current plenipotentiary of equal status, changing the name and status of the office to the vice-minister of women and family and redefining its policy by symbolically dissociating from the politics of promoting tolerance and fighting against homophobia. Although Joanna Kluzik-Rostkowska, who performed this function, did not fully agree with the government view of homosexuality or abortion, she worked under strong pressure from its homophobic opinion and her funding was very limited.

Since 2005, almost all social campaigns that fight homophobia and promote tolerance toward the LGBT community have been refused state funding. Moreover, even the EU funding that is controlled by the Polish government is very limited. For instance, the Ministry of National Education criticized the project Do we Need Gender? put forth by the Campaign against Homophobia and accused it of the moral corruption of teenagers, stating that there would be no more money spent on the organization. Do we Need Gender was a youth exchange project financed by the European Commission's youth program with funding distributed by the National Agency. It aimed at the informal education of young people and overcoming prejudices and stereotypes concerning gender and sexual orientation; in this way, it realized specific priorities of the European Commission. Despite the fact that the Campaign against Homophobia wrote a special protest letter to the Ministry of National Education demanding a clarification, it was excluded from gaining EU subsidies from the youth program. In the explanation of its decision, the ministry declared that no organizations that promote homosexuality among youngsters can ever count on its support.

SEXUALITY/SEXUAL PRACTICES

Little research has been done on LGBT sexual practices in Poland. All existing research deals with male homosexual behavior and has been conducted in the context of HIV prevention work. There are not enough studies on nonnormative female sexuality, not to mention transgender or transsexual studies.

A good source of information about sexual practices of men who have sex with men (MSM) is the broad research done by Professor Zbigniew Izdebski in the context of HIV prevention.[8] The research included 400 men who had had a sexual encounter with another man within the last six months and consisted of a very precise set of questions concerning not only their past and present sexual practices but their opinion about family life, community, coming out, relations with parents and friends, experience of discrimination, and so on. According to the report, 70 percent of its respondents had sexual contacts exclusively with men; and 29 percent said that they had had sex with women. Eighty percent defined themselves as homosexuals, 17 percent as bisexuals, and 2 percent as straight. Thirty-four percent had their first sexual encounter at the age of 16–18. Thirty-sex percent reported that they had had no more than 10 sexual partners in their lifetime; 2 percent had only one partner; 33 percent had between 11–50 partners; 10 percent between 50–100 partners; and 10 percent more than 100. Fifty-two percent reported that they had had at least one sexual contact with a woman. Regarding the place where men seek sexual encounters, respondents mentioned private apartments (88%), bars (72%), discos (74%), saunas (19%), and parks (16%). Ninety-five percent used the Internet in looking for information and contacts with other men.[9]

The author of the report underlines the *temporal faithfulness* of MSM. Seventy-four percent of them declared that, within the last 12 months, they had one partner. Ninety-nine percent of the respondents had had at least one instance of manual sexual contact with a noncommercial partner (i.e., not a prostitute), 94 percent oral contact, and 87 percent anal. Regarding safe sex practices, more than half of the respondents (58%) had never used condoms in their noncommercial oral sexual contact, 24 percent used condoms very seldom or sometimes, 18 percent used condoms often or almost always, and only 7 percent always used them. Interestingly, the younger generation is much more reluctant to use condoms: 63 percent of the respondents aged 18–24 declared that they never used a condom in contact with noncommercial oral partners. Although those numbers differ for anal contact (i.e., 14 percent declared that they never used condoms, 32 percent always used them), the results clearly show a huge need for a social campaign regarding safe sex and HIV prevention in Poland.[10]

There are no similarly extensive studies on lesbians, female bisexuals, or transgender people. This is not only due to the fact that there is much less interest in female sexuality in general, but also that female sex has always been more tamed and privatized in the whole process of the socialization of gender roles. Therefore, the majority of lesbian sexual encounters take place in private spaces, although dark rooms in Polish gay bars are very often non–gender specific. Also, the Internet plays a very important role in establishing contacts and looking for sexual partners. However, contrary to gay men's sex advertisements on the Internet, lesbians have a strong tendency to romanticize relationships and look for a long-term partner and love more often than exclusively sexual contacts. According to research by Alicja Dlugolecka, who interviewed 70 lesbians, while they are in relationships lesbians usually do not cheat on their partners; they want and believe in relationships that last forever. They create partner relationships and avoid role division or role playing. Their most popular sexual contact in adolescence is kissing, then petting, mutual masturbation, and then whole body contact. Other techniques such as using dildos or anal contact are very rare. In their lifetime, they have sexual encounters with men, but those contacts usually do not last long and are usually related to negative feelings. They usually have few lesbian relationships, and those they do have last longer and do not have an exclusively sexual character. They emphasize romantic feelings and the sense of safety playing important roles in their relationships.[11]

Even less research has been done regarding the sexual practices of transgender people in Poland. The main concern of transsexuals nowadays is to have the cost of the sex operation refunded by the Ministry of Health. The first such operation in Poland took place in 1963. Contrary to the rest of the world, where there are more male-to-female transsexuals, in Poland the tendency is the opposite and the majority of transsexuals are female-to-male. In addition, as Imielinski and Dulko, two main sexologists in Poland working on transsexuality report, the majority of transsexuals have homosexual contacts (i.e., consistent with their body structure), while about 15 percent of both homo- and heterosexual transgender people have exclusively heterosexual encounters. The rate of their suicide attempts ranges between 70 and 90 percent. This rate could be a result of the fact that transsexuals are excluded from the rest of society, very often mistreated by professionals, and 90 percent of them cannot even count on the support of their families. They also experience great difficulty in finding a life partner and building a satisfactory family life.[12]

FAMILY

The family life of LGBT people is still a relatively unknown topic. In the official statistics, for instance, in the recent census from 2002 in the part concerning family, LGBT families are not officially included. They are hidden under the category of *partnership families,* which according to the census comprise 2 percent of all Polish families.

Although the overall situation of LGBT people has worsened in Poland since 2006 and many of them experience violence and prejudice in their public life, in the private sphere they lead quite a satisfactory life, being mostly out to their friends and having many social encounters with straight and LGBT people. In the 2005–2006 report, almost 60 percent declared that they are in a monogamous relationship. Most of their relationships last between three and five years (24.4%) or between one to two years (22.9%). Such data undermine a common belief that homosexual people cannot build long-lasting relationships. More and more bi- and homosexual people are out in their family life. Seventy percent of respondents declared that their sexual orientation is known by their parents, mostly by mothers (80.7% compared to 55.2% known by fathers). Half of those who have come out feel completely accepted by their families. According to the report, 5.4 percent of the respondents have children. This means that approximately 57,000 gays and lesbians in Poland bring up children in homosexual relationships.[13] Moreover, in Izdebski's research, 84 percent of the respondents (MSM) think that Poland should legalize same-sex partnerships. Mostly respondents were in favor of the social benefits that this kind of recognition would give LGBT people, but only 22.3 percent were in favor of adoption rights.[14] However, despite some attempts toward the legalization of same-sex partnerships (i.e., the bill proposed by Senator Maria Szyszkowska in 2003), such families still remain unrecognized by Polish law and Polish society, of which the majority is against such recognition.

Regarding transsexual families, there are no studies that document their life after a sex change operation. One of the main reasons for this is that, after the operation, most transsexuals want to forget about their past, conform to gender norms, and live their new lives with their new partners. In addition, little research has been done on partners and spouses of those who are in the process of changing their biological sex. According to statistics, transsexuals conforming to the social pressure very often marry and have children, but those relationships do not last. What is interesting, more female-to-male transsexuals leave their previous relationship before consulting the sexologist. Marriages of male-to-female transsexuals are much more indissoluble. Many biological fathers stay in them because of their children. Very often, their wives know about their specific needs and support them.

COMMUNITY

According to the Campaign against Homophobia, there are two million homosexuals and two million transsexuals in Poland. The LGBT community is represented by large numbers of different formal and informal groups. Of note is the increasing role of the Internet in building a sense of belonging and helping people find important information and establish contacts.

The beginning of the Polish LGBT movement dates back to the early 1980s. However, due to the fact that Communist government was against of any kind of civil organization at that time, it mostly consisted of informal groups, mostly gay men whose role was enabling people to meet, help one another, and find partners. In the late 1980s, the first gay magazines were published: *Filo* in Gdansk and *Efebos* in Warsaw. Their distribution was still unofficial. Moreover, Polish Communist authorities tried to put the gay community under surveillance. In 1985, in different Polish cities, police launched a secret operation called Hyacynt that aimed at collecting records on all homosexuals. The collected data served as a means to threaten and blackmail the gay community into collaboration with the Communist regime. The result of this action was that many gay men left the country.

The transition to democracy in 1989 helped in building the LGBT community and movement, finally that could leave the underground and enter the public sphere. In addition, instead of small informal marginal groups, many LG(BT) organizations have been created with very specific targets and diverse aims. The first LGBT organization formally recognized and registered by the court was LAMBDA in 1990. This group works toward widespread social tolerance of homosexuality and to build a positive consciousness among female and male homosexuals. It also leads AIDS/HIV prevention campaigns. One of the most important organizations nowadays is the Campaign against Homophobia, established in 2000. There is only one specifically lesbian organization, Lesbian Coalition LBT, that widely cooperates with the feminist movement and tries to track lesbian genealogy within Polish culture. In 1990, the first gay magazines, *Filo* and *Efebos,* began to be officially distributed. In 1997–2000, the lesbian magazine *Furia Pierwsza* was published by the now defunct lesbian organization OLA Archive. It aimed at fighting against lesbian invisibility in both the gay and feminist movements. Its seventh and last issue was the first Polish publication fully devoted to queer theory. Furthermore, after 1989, many gay-friendly places started to operate in different Polish cities, and gay issues appeared more broadly in the media. In 1995, the first gay pride parade was organized in Warsaw.

Although almost all Polish gay and lesbian organizations now call themselves LGBT, bisexuals and transgender people are underrepresented in their membership. The same is true concerning places that specifically target transgender people. As mentioned, one of the main problems that transsexuals experience in Poland is solitude and difficulties in finding life partners. That was one of the main reasons for establishing four clubs for transsexuals that also aim to help them to find partners. However, today the main source of information and support for transsexuals is the Internet. There are transsexual groups that cooperate with gay and lesbian organizations—for instance, two of them meet at LAMBDA sites in Warsaw and Szczecin—but there are no specific transsexual organizations in Poland so far that can represent transsexuals and fight for their rights in the public sphere. Recently, there have been talks about creating one among Polish transgender people.

HEALTH

Poland has a universal health care system. However, since the fall of Communism, the system has not functioned very well and there is a constant threat that citizens will have to pay for more complicated medical procedures, leaving only the basic ones covered. There is more and more private medical coverage for those who can afford it.

As far as the problem of AIDS/HIV is concerned, there is a constant lack of sufficient preventive actions at the state level by governmental authorities. The common strategy by the government (no matter the political option) is to use the existing LGBT NGOs by giving them some small subsidies for such actions. However, as statistics show, there is little knowledge about AIDS and other sexually transmitted diseases (STDs) among ordinary citizens, and there is a constant need for developing prevention, education, and awareness programs.

According to the National AIDS Centre,[15] the state institution established by the Ministry of Health and Social Care in 1993, since the beginning of the epidemic in 1985 through the end of August 2007, there were 11,131 people registered as living with HIV, 1,970 AIDS cases, and 878 deaths due to AIDS. But experts estimate that those numbers are much higher, that is, 20,000 to 30,000 HIV infections. The main methods of disease transmission in those years were intravenous substance use (54%) and sexual contact between men. While recently, the former has been diminishing, the latter has increased, probably due to the decline of condom use in this group. In addition, there is a growing number of infections through heterosexual intercourse (in 2005, 8 percent compared to 5 percent through homosexual acts and 21 percent infected by intravenous substance use), and a growing number of infected women.[16]

All medical care concerning people with AIDS/HIV is covered by the state health care system, but there is a lack of funding for more expensive and effective therapies. Furthermore, the medical staff in Polish hospitals lack fundamental knowledge about AIDS/HIV transmission and very often deny ordinary treatment to patients with AIDS, sending them to an AIDS specialist instead. Discrimination toward gay and lesbian people in the health service system ranges from the refusal to provide information about a homosexual partner's health or refusal of visitation to exclusion of a partner in the decision making process concerning medical therapy, and refusal by the blood donor centers to collect blood from openly homosexual men and women. One of the most common problems suffered by lesbians is the lack of lesbian-friendly gynecologists who recognize the specific needs of this group. In addition, in terms of AIDS/HIV prevention programs, lesbians and their specificity are hardly taken into account by specialists or by gay and lesbian organizations dealing with this issue.

POLITICS AND LAW

The first Polish criminal code of 1932 was based on the Napoleonic code that was in force during the Duchy of Warsaw (1807–1813) and did not criminalize homosexual behavior. Before that (1794–1918), Poland was a dependant country divided between Russia, Prussia, and Austro-Hungary, and their laws prevailed on the occupied territory. For instance, under Russian rule, homosexuality was illegal.

Poland regained its independence in 1918 and, during the interwar period, many reformers worked to remove the existing foreign laws criminalizing homosexuality. Thanks to their effort, the 1932 Polish criminal code was silent on the issue of homosexuality. Lesbians were not mentioned in the Russian criminal code or in the new Polish criminal code.

During Communist Poland (1945–1989), homosexual activity was not criminalized; however, police kept records on homosexuals, and there were no gay and lesbian organizations and no legal meeting places or press.

After a return to democracy in 1989, freedom of speech and association allowed the LGBT community an institutional form for fighting for their rights. Many gay and lesbian organizations were immediately established. Contemporary Polish law does not refer to the question of homosexuality. However, there are no antidiscrimination statutes based on sexual orientation, which by necessity is very often stressed by LGBT organizations. The exception is the Polish labor code of January 1, 2004. While joining the EU, Poland was obliged to implement national legislation on discrimination, including a ban on discrimination toward an employee based on sexual orientation.

In the lack of more general antidiscrimination statutes based on sexual orientation, the only one that is binding for all Polish citizens is article 32 from the Polish constitution, which secures equality for all and states that "nobody can be discriminated against for all kinds of reasons." However, it does not specify those reasons. And the same constitution can be an example of discrimination because of its very strict and exclusionary definition of marriage as a heterosexual relationship only (article 18), which was repeated in the family and care code. As a consequence, marriage between same-sex partners is formally precluded by any law in Poland (i.e., tax law, administrative law, succession law). Stable and long term same-sex relationships cannot be accepted as a legal form of concubinage.

Therefore, one of the aims of the Polish gay and lesbian movement is to fight for legal recognition of same-sex relationships. In August 2003, Senator Maria Szyszkowska publicly presented the motion on registered same-sex partnership that was prepared in cooperation with gay and lesbian representatives. On November 21, 2003, the motion was submitted to the Senate and was signed by 36 senators, mostly from left-wing and central parties. The bill guaranteed a host of rights and benefits for same-sex couples, including tax benefits, pension benefits for widowed spouses, the right to inheritance, and social insurance, but openly excluded the right to adoption. The motion was backed to the Polish parliament one year later but no legislative procedure on the bill was initiated. The draft was not even sent to any of the parliamentary committees that could give it a final form. In the following parliament, when the right wing parties had gained power (2005–2007), the question of the bill was never discussed again. During the last parliamentary election that took place two years earlier on October 21, 2001 (when the Law and Justice party could not maintain power after their coalition with the League of Polish Families, and the Self-Defence Parties collapsed and were forced to organize new elections), the Law and Justice Party lost power. The neo-liberal Civic Platform, the clear winner of the elections (with 41.4% of the vote) has built a governing coalition with a moderate Polish Peasants' Party. It is hard to predict the future of the discussed bill and the policy toward LGBT issues by the new government. However, many Poles describe this change of power as a return to normality. Also, the well-known Civic Platform commitment to improve

relations with the EU allows LGBT people in Poland to hope that their rights will
be better supported.

One of the main recent concerns of Polish LGBT organizations has been to
fight for their rights to free speech and to assembly. In recent years (2004–2006),
several bans of LGBT parades took place in different Polish cities. On November 15, 2005 the mayor of Poznan banned the march organized by the Committee
on Equality and Tolerance. The justification of his decision was "fear of destroy-
ing the peace of a public space." Despite the ban, several hundred people gathered. Their peaceful manifestation met with aggressive harassment by members of
the All-Polish Youth Organization. Police intervened rather violently and arrested
those who protested illegally. As a reaction to dispersing a peaceful manifestation
in Poznan in November 2005, rallies took place in several Polish cities for freedom
of speech and assembly.

In 2004 and 2005, the mayor of Warsaw Lech Kaczynski (currently president of
Poland) banned the Equality Parade in Warsaw, justifying his decision by the presumed obscenity of the demonstration and possible injury to the religious beliefs
of other citizens. Despite his ban, on June 10, 2005, a spontaneous parade took
place, which could be described as an act of civil disobedience, that hosted more
than 2,500 people. The Equality Foundation, which organizes equality parades in
Warsaw, filed an appeal to the European Court of Human Rights. Its verdict was
announced in May 2007, and stated that the banning of the Warsaw parade violated human rights. Furthermore, as a reaction to what had happened in Poland
in recent years, the European Parliament issued a resolution on homophobia in
Europe, dated January 18, 2006, calling all member states to prevent homophobic speech and acts of violence. This resolution proceeded the one from June 15,
2006, on the increase of racism, xenophobia, and homophobia in Europe and the
necessity to fight against them. This document listed specific cases of intolerance in
Europe, including those in Poland. Both resolutions were strongly criticized and
opposed by Polish politicians and Polish EU representatives, regardless of their
political affiliations.

RELIGION AND SPIRITUALITY

In a country where 92 percent of people are Catholics, the influence of the
Roman Catholic Church and its stance on homosexuality is enormous. In its teaching, the church condemns homosexuality and opposes any LGBT efforts to achieve
acceptance and tolerance. It was under this pressure that the very rigid and exclusive definition of marriage as a union between a man and a woman was introduced
in the Polish constitution. The church also condemns all kinds of LGBT manifestations and supports their ban. It tries to influence social, legal, and political life and
puts a lot of pressure on right-wing Polish politicians to block any antidiscrimination legislation and the acceptance of same-sex relationships.

In addition, the Catholic Church supports Catholic groups that aim to help/
cure homosexuals. It is strongly emphasized in Roman Catholic teaching on homosexuality that homosexual orientation is not inborn (natural) but chosen, and
therefore it could (and should) be changed. These Catholic groups want to help
individuals either to stay celibate or reject a homosexual lifestyle and choose to
be heterosexual instead. One of the best known of these groups is called Odwaga
(Courage), and it is run by the Light-Life Movement in Lublin. The therapy that

is carried out there consists of three stages of healing and maturing, and its main task is to help homosexual people recover from their *sick* condition and to establish *normal* relationships in the future.

Catholic organizations in Poland are not only active in their reparative attempts but also in their ideological fight in the public space. The most active in this field is the group from Cracow called the Father Piotr Skarga Association for Christian Culture, established in 1999. During the public debates on LGBT manifestations in Cracow, Warsaw, and Poznan, the group delivered leaflets to people's mailboxes with the statement, "Say NO to the promotion of homosexuality," and included pictures of men in drag and a preaddressed protest letter that one could sign and send to local authorities. The association proudly admits its connection with an international organization, Tradition, Family, and Property, that aims to protect tradition. In spring 2006, the association sent a 50-page brochure to schools titled "Hidden Problems of Homosexuality," which describes homosexuality as a deviation. The brochure was based on materials from the American organization, the Family Research Institute.

The Catholic Church is partly responsible for public homophobia in Poland. Moreover, it refuses any kind of priesthood service for homosexuals, although the representatives of Catholic homosexuals do appeal to church authorities for such services. Many LGBT people are deeply religious despite all the prejudices in the teachings of the Catholic Church. In 1994, a group of gay Christians, Berith, was established. They meet at Lambda several times a week. Its aim is for members to support one another in their faith and show that one can be homosexual and religious.

VIOLENCE

Polish LGBT people are the target of all kinds of hate crimes. And the statistics on anti-LGBT violence have been increasing systematically. Most of the incidents are not even reported to the police. According to a 2005–2006 report, 17.6 percent of respondents (bi- and homosexuals) had experienced physical violence in recent years (14% of women and 20% of men). Among those who experienced physical violence, 41.9 percent had experienced three or more attacks. The majority of this crime (55.8%) happened in public places such as on the streets or in parks. Other venues for violence included shops or public transport (28.4%), at school/university (24.4%), and in their own apartments (15.9%).[17]

The majority of respondents who experienced physical violence were kicked, pushed, or hit. The second most frequent type of violence was sexual harassment (32.4%); almost 25 percent were battered, and 4 percent experienced sexual violence. In most cases, respondents did not know the perpetrators (59.7%), but in 29.5 percent of cases they were their own school/university colleagues. In 85.1 percent of cases, the police were not informed, mostly because of the lack of trust.[18]

LGBT people also suffer because of psychological violence. The most common form is verbal harassment (75% have experienced this). The respondents were also offended, ridiculed, and humiliated (55.8%), or negative opinion was spread about them (44.6%). In 15.3 percent of cases they were threatened, 5.9 percent received hate letters, and 6.5 percent were blackmailed. In most cases, the perpetrators were unknown (57.7%), but in 29 percent of cases they were schoolmates. Acts of psychological violence are almost never reported to the police (96.1%).[19]

One of the most common places for disseminating biases, intolerance, and hate speech targeting LGBT people is on the Internet, starting with homophobic comments on any articles that touch on LGBT issues through jokes about LGBT people, which one can easily find on Polish Web sites linked to neo-Nazi and religious groups. Also, Polish LGBT organizations (and their leaders) receive many threatening and hate-filled e-mails.

OUTLOOK FOR THE 21ST CENTURY

Concerning the level of intolerance, bias, and violence that Polish LGBT people experience, the main focus of their activity is fighting homophobia in their daily life, both publicly and privately. Lots of work must be done in order to let LGBT people really become equal citizens. One of the main concerns is to fight prejudice and public hatred. This could be aided by decent sex education programs that show human sexuality in all its diverse forms. Furthermore, some legal changes, such as antidiscrimination statutes that could guarantee more protection, are some main aims of LGBT organizations. The fight for same-sex partnership law is at the top of the list, as well. However, regarding the Polish political situation and the popularity of right-wing and populist parties, the possibility of decent debates over this issue is very dubious. The fact that Poland is an EU member will help in the case of any violation of LGBT human rights in the future. What cannot be achieved on the national level can be achieved at a supranational level, and one can expect that this international forum and international legislation will matter more and more for Polish LGBT organizations fighting for equal rights.

RESOURCE GUIDE

Suggested Reading

Tomasz Basiuk, "Queerowanie po Polsku," *Furia Pierwsza* 7 (2000): 28–36.

Tomasz Basiuk, Dominika Ferens, and Tomasz Sikora, *Mniejszościowe orientacje seksualne w perspektywie gnder/A Queer Mixture. Gender Studies Perspectives on Minority Sexual Identities* (Warsaw: Wydawnictwo Bellona, 2002).

Agata Engel-Bernatowicz and Aleksandra Kaminska, *Coming Out* (Warsaw: Anka Zet Studio, 2005).

Kazimierz Imieliński and Stanislaw Dulko, *Przeklenstwo Androgyne. Transseksualizm: Mity i Rzeczywistosc* (Szczecin: Glob, 1989).

Jacek Kochanowski, *Fantazmat Zroznicowany. Socjologiczne Studium Przemian Tozsamosci Gejow* (Cracow: Universitas, 2004).

Ireneusz Krzemiński ed., *Wolność, Równość, Odmienność. Nowe Ruchy Społeczne w Polsce Poczatku XXI wieku* (Warszawa: Wydawnictwo Akademckie I Profesjonalne, 2006).

Joanna Mizielinska, *Gender/Body/Sexuality: From Feminism to Queer Theory* (Cracow: Universitas, 2007).

Joanna Mizielinska, "Lesbianism in Poland—Between Consciousness and its Lack," *Furia Pierwsza* 1 (1997): 7–34.

Joanna Mizielinska, "The Rest Is Silence . . . : Polish Nationalism and the Question of Lesbian Existence," *European Journal of Women's Studies* 8, no. 3 (2001): 281–297.

Krystyna Slany, Beata Kowalska, and Marcin Smietana, eds., *Homoseksualizm. Perspektywa Interdyscyplinarna* (Cracow: NOMOS, 2005).

Zbigniew Sypniewski and Blazej Warkocki, eds., *Homofobia po Polsku* (Warsaw: Sic! 2004).

Web Sites

Amnesty International—LGBT, http://www.amnesty.org.pl/lgbt.
  Polish Amnesty International group devoted to LGBT rights.
Berith, group of Christian gay and lesbian people, http://berithprzymierze.republika.pl.
  Information about the main issues and concerns of Christian lesbians and gays.
Crossdressing, http://www.crossdressing.pl.
  Resource on the Polish cross-dressing scene.
Inna Strona, http://www.innastrona.pl/.
  Lesbian and gay portal.
Jestem Gejem, Jestem Lesbijką (I Am Gay, I Am a Lesbian), http://www.homoseksualizm.pl.
  Accompanies the project I am Gay, I am a Lesbian organized by the Campaign against Homophobia.
Kampania Przeciw Homofobii/Campaign Against Homophobia, http://www.kampania.org.pl.
  Official Web page of the organization.
Kobiety—Kobietom—Portal Lesbijski (Women for Women—Lesbian Portal), http://kobiety-kobietom.com.
  Lesbian portal with lots of information about lesbian and feminist activities.
Lambda, http://www.lambda.org.pl/.
  Information about the organization and its activities, including some publications.
Lesbijka.org, http://www.lesbijka.org.
  Lesbian portal.
Moje Prawa (My Rights), http://www.mojeprawa.info.
  Includes information about the legal status of LGBT people. It is a part of a project led by the Campaign against Homophobia.
National AIDS Centre, http://www.aids.gov.pl.
  National AIDS program.
Porozumienie Lesbijek (Lesbian Coalition), http://porozumienie.lesbijek.org/.
  Lesbian organization founded in 2004.
Transfuzja, http://transfuzja.wroclaw.pl/.
  Transgender group from Wroclaw.
Transseksualizm, http://www.transseksualizm.pl.
  Information about Polish transsexuals.

NOTES

1. Konstytucja Rzeczpospolitej Polskiej/Polish Republic Constitution, Warsaw 1997.
2. Public Opinion Research Center (CBOS) poll, July 2001.
3. Ibid.
4. Ibid.
5. Marta Abramowicz ed., *Situation of Bisexuals and Homosexual Persons in Poland: 2005–2006 Report* (Warsaw: Lambda, Campaign against Homophobia, 2007), http://warszawa.lambda.org.pl.
6. In October 2007, Poland had a new more liberal government, based on the coalition of neoliberal party Platforma Obywatelska (Civic Platform) and Polskie Stronnictwo Ludowe (Polish Peasant Party). The two most extreme parties and erstwhile coalition partners for the Law and Justice Party, that is, the League of Polish Families and Self-Defence, have fallen the below 5 percent minimum threshold for representation in parliament.
7. LAMBDA is the the first registered gay and lesbian organization in Poland. See Abramowicz, *Situation of Bisexuals and Homosexual Persons in Poland*.
8. Piotr Sztabinski, *Raport z badania w grupie mezczyzn majacych seks z mezczyznami* (Warsaw: TNS OBOP, 2005).

9. Ibid.

10. Ibid.

11. A. Dlugolecka, *Pokochac kobiete*...(Warsaw: Elma Books, 2005).

12. Kazimierz Imieliński and Stanislaw Dulko, *Przeklenstwo Androgyne. Transseksual-izm: mity i rzeczywistosc* (Szczecin: Glob, 1989).

13. Abramowicz, *Situation of Bisexuals and Homosexual Persons in Poland*.

14. Sztabinski, *Raport z badania w grupie mezczyzn majacych seks z mezczyznami*.

15. National AIDS Centre, the Agenda of the Ministry of Health, http://www.aids.gov.pl.

16. Ibid.

17. Abramowicz, *Situation of Bisexuals and Homosexual Persons in Poland*.

18. Ibid.

19. Ibid.

PORTUGAL

Ana Cristina Santos

OVERVIEW

Portugal is a southern Mediterranean country with a population of approximately 10.5 million (51.8% women). Life expectancy is 81.4 years for women and 74.9 for men. With a total area of 35,580 square miles, its territory is divided into 18 districts on the mainland and the two autonomous regions of Azores and Madeira. The capital city is Lisbon.

Portugal had the longest dictatorship in western Europe (1926–1974). From 1933 until 1968, António de Oliveira Salazar, a conservative and Catholic, led the country. During this period, sexual and reproductive rights were disregarded (e.g., abortion and divorce were forbidden, and homosexuality was criminalized). The right-wing regime was overturned by a military coup in 1974, which became known worldwide as the Revolution of Carnations. The red carnation is still a national symbol of democracy, and the revolution is celebrated on April 25th (a national holiday). After 1974, Portugal's former colonies in Africa (Angola, Cape Verde, Guinea-Bissau, Mozambique, São Tomé, and Principe) gained independence.

The political system in Portugal is a parliamentary democracy and governments have shifted between two major political parties: the Democrat Social Party (PSD) and the Socialist Party (PS). Portugal has been a member of the Council of Europe since 1976 and became a European Union (EU) member in 1986. The euro currency replaced the *escudo* in 2002.

Azores and Madeira Islands are not shown.

OVERVIEW OF LGBT ISSUES

There is no antidiscrimination law as such, but discriminating based on sexual orientation is prohibited by the constitution. This constitutional ban exists parallel to other pieces of legislation that still reinforce difference and discrimination: same-sex civil marriage is illegal, same-sex couples cannot adopt children, and only married women or women in a heterosexual de facto union can have access to assisted conception. Same-sex civil marriage is the most controversial issue, but also the one that has gathered more public support as well as activist initiatives.

The LGBT movement is very active and successful in pushing for legal reform, and therefore there is a social expectation that all discriminatory laws will change in the near future, similar to what happened in Spain. Moreover, since 2007, the ages of consent have been equalized and hate crimes based on sexual orientation have been included among the aggravating grounds in the revised penal code. Both of these were long-term demands of the LGBT movement. Therefore, Portugal constitutes an example of the potential of social movements in generating political, legal, and social change in the sphere of LGBT issues.

EDUCATION

In 2001, 10 percent of the population could not read or write. In the 2004–2005 academic year, the total number of individuals with a university degree was over 70,000, of which 65 percent were female.

Concerning LGBT issues, sex education is one of the most debated issues. In 1984, after a period of social and political debate, the parliament passed a law on sex education (law 3/84). However, the specific regulations that would determine how the law would come into force were never established, and therefore law 3/84 was never fully applied. In September 2007, the final report of the state Working Group on Sex Education was launched, suggesting that schools should implement sex education. In this report, the link between sex education and health and biology was reinforced, with very little being said about preventing discrimination and combating bullying.

There are LGBT organizations doing youth work, namely facilitating discussions with students and teachers. The youth organization *rede ex aequo* is the most active in the field of education, setting up workshops and publishing specific materials. However, there is no regularity in these activities and therefore no guarantee that the educational system will consistently and formally address issues of sexual orientation and gender identity.

EMPLOYMENT AND ECONOMICS

In 2005, the activity rate (percentage of people over 15 years old, both employed and unemployed, compared to the overall population) was 52.5 percent. The unemployment rate hit 7.6 percent, being more prominent among women (8.7% against 6.7% among men) and among the age group of 15–24 years old.[1]

Many stories of discrimination in employment against LGBT employees have been reported over the years by LGBT organizations and the media. However, to date there have been no formal complaints in the courts on these matters. Such absence of formal complaints is justified to a great extent by fear of an unwanted coming out or a general lack of confidence in the national judicial system.

In 2003, the new labor code came into force, responding to EU demands to include directive 2000/78/CE into national legislation. Clearly stating that no employee should be discriminated against based on sexual orientation, the labor code became the first piece of national legislation mentioning sexual orientation. It also changed the rules concerning pressing charges based on discrimination; before the labor code, the burden was on the employees to prove they had been discriminated against, whereas after 2003 it is the employer who needs to prove the company has not discriminated against the person pressing charges.

SOCIAL/GOVERNMENT PROGRAMS

Drawing on EU policies, the language of equality and nondiscrimination gradually became part of the political ideology aiming to transform Portugal into a modern state in the eyes of its counterparts. Signing the Amsterdam Treaty in June 1997, Portugal became symbolically obliged to enforce the principle of nondiscrimination, which mainly targeted gender equality. As a result, the Portuguese government started to invest resources in preparing experts in the field of equality and nondiscrimination between women and men, namely by subsidizing training courses, the first of which took place in 2001. Nonetheless, there are no state-funded social programs targeting the LGBT population or specifically addressing issues of sexual orientation or gender identity.

In terms of social attitudes, there has been some change. Today, the Portuguese people recognize that current discrimination based on sexual orientation is more widespread than it was five years ago (45%, compared to the average of 31% in the rest of the EU), as it is also more widespread today in terms of gender (41%, compared to the EU average of 27%).[2] These figures represent a move away from data collected by a study in 1998, according to which 48.5 percent of the respondents believed sexual relationships should only be allowed between men and women.[3]

SEXUALITY/SEXUAL PRACTICES

The Portuguese penal code reform of 1982 decriminalized sexual acts practiced in private by consenting adults. These included adultery, incest, prostitution, and homosexuality, which had figured in previous penal codes as crimes against decency or crimes against custom.

In terms of sexual practices, according to a survey by Eurosondagem in 2005,[4] 52.2 percent of interviewees said AIDS did not affect their sexual activity. 60.2 percent of all women interviewed and 44 percent of all men admitted they never changed their behavior in order to prevent AIDS. One-third never used condoms (33.5%) and 28.8 percent used condoms only on certain occasions. Concerning sexual orientation, 1 in 10 Portuguese identify themselves as gay/lesbian (7%) or bisexual (2.9%). Half the interviewees had come out as gay/lesbian (50.8%) and the vast majority of bisexuals were still in the closet (85.7%). Nearly half of gay/lesbian interviewees had a stable partner (49%), whereas that number decreased to 33.3 percent in the case of bisexuals and increased to 72.3 percent in the case of heterosexuals.

FAMILY

Compared to the 1991 census, in 2001 there were more married people with no children (30.9%, compared to 28.8% in 1991), single parents (11.5% compared to 9.2%), and lone mothers (10% compared to 7.9%). In contrast, there was a decrease in the percentage of married people with children (56.7% compared to 60.9%). The percentage of families of grandparents with grandchildren is very low (0.5%).[5] In 2005, the marriage rate was 4.6 per 1,000 habitants and the divorce rate was 2.1 per 1,000 habitants. The average age for getting married is 31.3 for males and 28.9 for females, and the average age for getting divorced is 39.8 years old.[6] There is no statistical information about same-sex families.

Marriage is defined in the Family Law, which is included in the civil code. According to this law, marriage is a "contract between two different-sex people who wish to start a family in a full sharing of life" (article 1577). The same code also states that a marriage between two same-sex persons is legally nonexistent (article 1628). Faced with this obstacle, for a long period of time family related LGBT claims focused on the recognition of same-sex cohabitation. This was achieved in 2001, with the approval of a de facto union law that does not discriminate based on sexual orientation.

According to the 2001 census, between 1991 and 2001 there was an increase of 96.1 percent in cohabitation ("marriage without registration"), with 194,000 people living in a de facto union relationship in 1991 increasing to 381,000 in 2001. However, because this law included both same-sex and different-sex couples, there is no specific information about same-sex cohabitation.

Since 2005, the major banner of the LGBT movement in Portugal is the right to same-sex civil marriage. This claim leads a series of other family related demands, such as specific regulation for the de facto union law, recognition of same-sex adoption, and access to assisted conception techniques for lesbian women.

COMMUNITY

The first Portuguese LGBT organization emerged in 1991. Since then, several other groups emerged in the country, most of them in Lisbon. Today, there are 10 LGBT organizations, some of which have subgroups and satellites in other regions of the country. Most organizations are self-identified as LGBT. There are only three exceptions to this, which consist of more specific targeted organizations: Clube Safo (lesbian-oriented), Ponto Bi (bisexual-oriented), and AT (transgender-oriented). Organizations play an important role in social visibility and political struggle, not only in the field of LGBT rights but also in the field of women's rights. Pride (locally called *Arraial* and consisting of a festival that has followed the LGBT march since 2000) has been celebrated since 1997. In 2000, there was the first LGBT march in Lisbon, which attracted more than 500 people. These numbers have increased over time—up to 3,500 people in more recent parades. Other important initiatives include Porto Pride and the LGBT March of Porto, both taking place in the north after 2001 and 2006, respectively.

LGBT community services are scarce. There is an online publisher (Zayas), bookshop (Esquina Cor de Rosa), travel agency (Saga Escape), magazine (*Korpus*), radio show (*Vidas Alternativas*), and a few bars, hotels, and clubs.[7] These are mostly situated in the two main cities, Lisbon and Porto.

HEALTH

Portugal has the second highest rate of teenage pregnancy in Europe, with an estimated average of 6,000 a year. Preventing teenage pregnancy is considered a priority by family planning and reproductive health services, and there are free contraceptives available to everyone, regardless of age, in health centers. Since 2007, abortion is also available upon request to women who are up to 10 weeks pregnant.

Until 1995, sex reassignment surgery was forbidden by the Portuguese Deontological Medical Code. In May 1995, a resolution of the Medical Council determined that sex reassignment could be possible in cases of transsexuality or gender dysphoria. The criteria include being over 18 years old and not being previously married. The process is long, requiring several doctors' authorizations and a two-year period on hormones before surgery can be done. Surgeries concerning breasts (mastectomy or enlargement) and genitals are paid for by the National Health System, which, however, does not pay for other aesthetic procedures, like hair or Adam's apple removal. The transgender community has several claims in this respect, some of which relate to a call for a gender recognition law and freedom from compulsory psychiatric dependency.

HIV and AIDS in Portugal are mostly found among drug users (47.5%) and heterosexual people (34.4%). Homosexual and bisexual people corresponded to 12.9 percent of all cases of HIV and AIDS between 1983 and 2007. Despite these figures, HIV organizations played a key role as embryos for LGBT visibility in Portugal. In fact, many LGBT activists were first drawn into activism through HIV-related campaigning.[8]

POLITICS AND LAW

Homosexuality was decriminalized in 1982, eight years after the democratic revolution. Cohabitation has been legally recognized for opposite-sex couples since 2000 and for lesbian and gay couples since 2001, but this law does not include the same rights ascribed to straight couples such as adopting children.

On April 22, 2004, Portugal became the first European country and the fourth worldwide to include sexual orientation among the unacceptable reasons for prejudicial treatment (article 13) in the constitution. However, there is still discrimination in the law (e.g., adoption and same-sex civil marriage). Furthermore, in 2006, the parliament approved a law on assisted conception that granted exclusive access to married women or women in a heterosexual de facto union, thus excluding lesbian women from accessing assisted conception techniques. Until the revision of the penal code in 2007, there were still different ages of consent (14 for heterosexual relations and 16 for same-sex relations). Finally, there is no specific law protecting transgender people from discrimination, as gender identity is not mentioned among the unacceptable reasons for prejudicial treatment, and there is no gender recognition law such as exists in the UK (2004) or Spain (2007).

Few court cases have addressed LGBT rights in Portugal. The first of them was *Mouta versus Portugal*, in 1998, and it created a case law in the European Court of Human Rights (ECtHR). After being denied custody of his only daughter because of his sexual orientation, Joao Mouta (the father) took his case to the ECtHR. The Portuguese state was found guilty of discrimination and violation of the right to respect for private and family life.[9] In 2004, Opus Gay and Anabela Rocha started judicial proceedings against Cesar das Neves, an academic and columnist. The claimants alleged there was homophobic content in some of das Neves' articles published in the newspaper *Diario de Noticias*. The case never went to court. Finally, there is an ongoing court case initiated by two lesbian women who are demanding the right to be allowed a civil marriage based on the fact that the Portuguese constitution states that no one can be discriminated against because of sexual orientation. Presently, the case is awaiting sentence from the highest court of appeal in the country, the Constitutional Court.

RELIGION AND SPIRITUALITY

Catholicism is the dominant religion in Portugal: 72 percent of the population is religious and, among those, 97 percent self-identify as Catholic. In 2001, 63 percent of all weddings celebrated in Portugal were Catholic.[10]

On several occasions, Catholic authorities have expressed their public views against the recognition of LGBT rights. Due to the symbolic power it holds, the Catholic Church is one of the main powers blocking the advancement of LGBT claims, namely those that are family or child related.

There is no tradition of religious LGBT groups in Portugal. However, there are two recent religious LGBT groups. One is called the Portuguese Group of Social Intervention, whose members are self-identified as lesbians and gay men, and former members of the religious Jehovah's Witness movement. The other one is called Rumos Novos (New Paths) and is self-defined as a Catholic homosexual group.

VIOLENCE

There have been several reported cases of homophobic and transphobic violence, including death threats and the beating of gay men in public toilets in the northern rural city Viseu, in 2005. This mobilized the movement to organize a major petition against violence, to give legal support to the victims, to denounce the attacks in the media, and to organize several initiatives such as debates and demonstrations in the streets. Furthermore, these attacks were politically legitimized by the city mayor, who asked for the authority's intervention in order to prevent homosexual encounters in public toilets in the city. This request was at odds with article 13 of the constitution, which forbids discrimination based on sexual orientation. Furthermore, the request is not supported by any other law, as homosexuality and prostitution are not considered crimes according to the Portuguese penal code. The mayor, later on, joined the *stop-homophobia* demonstration in Viseu, organized by the LGBT movement in May 2005.

In February 2006, Gisberta, a transgender woman, was repeatedly tortured, raped, and beaten, thrown into a well, and left to die. The aggressors were a group of teenage boys and the court sentence dated August 1, 2006, stated that Gisberta died not from injuries but because she had drowned in the well water. This case stirred international support, and for the first time the transgender movement achieved some visibility concerning discrimination and the specific measures required to combat it. This case led to a change in the penal code in 2007, whereby sexual orientation was included among the aggravating grounds for hate crimes (article 132).

There have been debates around same-sex domestic violence. In December 2006, the Union Association of Portuguese Judges issued a document stating that there could not be a legal recognition of same-sex domestic violence because same-sex civil marriage was not allowed. Furthermore, it was also stated that domestic violence presupposed a physical strength difference, which was absent from same-sex relationships, and that same-sex families were nothing but ideological banners, for advocacy purposes.[11] In spite of this statement, the new penal code, which came into force in September 2007, included among potential victims of domestic violence a person—either same-sex or different-sex—with whom the aggressor has or has had a relationship similar to married partners, regardless of whether they are cohabiting or not (article 152).

OUTLOOK FOR THE 21ST CENTURY

LGBT issues in Portugal are rich and complex. The early years of the LGBT movement date to the 1990s, and there were many social and cultural struggles and legal achievements in very few years. However, some areas remain less visible than others, as is the case with bisexuality, intersexuality, and—to a lesser extent in recent years—transgenderism.

Another underestimated group is queer-straights, who remain a minority inside another minority. But there is an increase in the numbers of people that, despite their self-perceived heterosexuality, engage in praxis of public support of LGBT issues. This is obvious in recent LGBT marches, where self-identified heterosexual celebrities and other people join the event, demonstrating a public commitment against heteronormativity.[12]

There are no lesbian and gay studies or queer theory modules taught either at the undergraduate or postgraduate level in Portuguese universities. Nevertheless, LGBT issues in academia are an area in expansion, as demonstrated by the growing interest on the part of students and researchers.

RESOURCE GUIDE

Suggested Reading

Ana Brandão, "Ser e Saber—(re)visitações do passado e construção das identidades (homo) sexuais," *Actas do V Congresso Português de Sociologia,* Associação Portuguesa de Sociologia, May 12–15, 2004.

Clara Caldeira, *A Representação das Minorias Sexuais na Informação Televisiva Portuguesa* (Lisbon: Livros Horizonte, 2006).

Nuno Santos Carneiro and Isabel Menezes, "From Oppressive Languages to Affirmative Identities: Lesbian and Gay Political Participation in Portugal," *Journal of Homosexuality* 53, no. 3 (2007): 65–82.

Nuno Santos Carneiro and Isabel Menezes, "La construction de l'identité des jeunes homosexuels au Portugal," *L'Orientation Scolaire et Professionnelle* 35, no. 2 (2006): 225–49.

Nuno Santos Carneiro, *Homossexualidades: Uma Psicologia Entre Ser, Pertencer e Participar* (Porto: Livpsic, 2009).

António Fernando Cascais, "Como Quem Não Quer a Coisa," *Fenda (In)Finda* 7 (1983): 9–17.

António Fernando Cascais, "Portugal," in *Dictionnaire de l'Homophobie,* ed. Georges-Louis Tin (Paris: Presses Universitaires de France, 2003).

António Fernando Cascais, ed., *Indisciplinar a Teoria: Estudos Gays, Lesbicos e Queer* (Lisbon: Fenda, 2004).

Octávio Gameiro, *Do Acto à Identidade: Orientação Sexual e Estruturação Sexual.* Master's thesis, ICSUL, Lisbon, 1998.

Carlos A. M. Gouveia, "Assumptions about Gender, Power and Opportunity: Gays and Lesbians as Discursive Subjects in a Portuguese Newspaper," in *Feminist Critical Discourse Analysis. Gender, Power and Ideology in Discourse,* ed. Michelle M. Lazar (London: Palgrave Macmillan, 2005).

Inês Meneses, *Espaços Públicos, Vidas Privadas: Identidade Gay em Lisboa.* Master's thesis, ICSUL, Lisbon, 1998.

Inês Meneses, "Intimidade, Norma e Diferença: a Modernidade Gay em Lisboa," *Análise Social* 153 (2000): 933–55.

Maria Gabriela Moita, *Discursos sobre a Homossexualidade no Contexto Clínico: A Homossexualidade de Dois Lados do Espelho.* PhD dissertation, Instituto de Ciências Biomédicas Abel Salazar, Universidade do Porto, 2001.

Ana Cristina Santos, *A Lei do Desejo: Direitos Humanos e Minorias Sexuais em Portugal* (Porto: Afrontamento, 2005).

Ana Cristina Santos, "Cidadania Sexual na Democracia Portuguesa," *Revista de Psicologia Política* 4, no. 8 (2004): 253–74.

Ana Cristina Santos, "Direitos Humanos e Minorias Sexuais em Portugal: o Jurídico ao Serviço de um Novo Movimento Social," in *Indisciplinar a Teoria. Estudos Gays, Lésbicos e Queer,* ed. Fernando Cascais (Lisboa: Fenda, 2004).

Ana Cristina Santos, "Entre a academia e o activismo: sociologia, estudos queer e movimento LGBT em Portugal" ["Between Academia and Activism: Sociology, Queer Studies, and the LGBT Movement in Portugal"], in *Queer Studies: Identities, Contexts and Collective Action* (special issue, *Revista Crítica de Ciências Sociais*) 76 (2006): 91–108.

Ana Cristina Santos, "Feminismos e Lesbianismos: notas para uma tradução (ou alicerces de uma ponte por reconstruir)" ["Feminism and Lesbianism: Contributions to a Translation"], in *Feminismos 80 Anos Depois,* ed. Lígia Amâncio, Manuela Tavares, and Teresa Joaquim (Lisboa: D. Quixote, 2007).

Ana Cristina Santos, "Heteronormatividades: formas de violência simbólica e factual com base na orientação sexual e na identidade de género" ["Heteronormativities: Forms of Symbolic and Physical Violence Based on Sexual Orientation and Gender Identity"], in *Forms and Contexts of Violence* (special issue, *Revista Portuguesa de História*) 37 (2006): 281–98.

Ana Cristina Santos, "Heteroqueers contra a heteronormatividade: notas para uma teoria queer inclusiva" ["Straight-queers against Heteronormativity: Towards an Inclusive Queer Theory"], *Oficina do CES* 239 (November 2005), http://www.ces.uc.pt/publicacoes/oficina/239/239.php.

Ana Cristina Santos, "Portuguese Law and Sexual Orientation," European Union Accession Monitoring Program, 2002, http://www.eumap.org/journal/features/2002/april02.

Ana Cristina Santos, "Sexualidades politizadas: o activismo nas áreas da sida e da homossexualidade em Portugal" ["Politicised Sexualities: AIDS and Gay Activism in Portugal"], *Cadernos de Saúde Pública* 18, no. 3 (2002): 595–611.

Ana Cristina Santos, "Sexual Orientation in Portugal: Towards Emancipation," *South European Society and Politics* 9, no. 2 (2004): 159–90.

Ana Cristina Santos and Fernando Fontes, "O Estado português e os desafios da (homo) sexualidade" ["The Portuguese State and the Challenges of (Homo)sexuality"], *Revista Crítica de Ciências Sociais* 59 (2001): 173–94.

Ana Cristina Santos and Paulo Jorge Vieira, "Do outro lado da ponte: movimentos sexuais e direitos humanos no século XXI" ["From the Other Side of the Bridge: Sexual Movements and Human Rights in the 21st Century"], in *Os direitos humanos na sociedade cosmopolita* [*Human Rights in the Cosmopolitan Society*], ed. César Augusto Baldi (Rio de Janeiro: Editora Renovar, 2004).

Miguel Vale de Alemida, *A Chave do Armário: Homossexualidade, Casamento, Família* (Lisbon: ICS, 2009).

Paulo Jorge Vieira, *aeminiumqueer: Quadro Teórico e Estudo Exploratório*. Bachelor's thesis, Instituto de Estudos Geográficos, Coimbra, 2005.

Organizations

Associação Cultural Janela Indiscreta, http://www.lisbonfilmfest.org/.
> Cultural organization responsible for the Lisbon Lesbian and Gay Movie Festival since 1997.

AT—Associação para o Estudo e Defesa dos Direitos à Identidade de Género, http://a-trans.planetaclix.pt/.
> Created in 2003, in Lisbon, it is the only transgender-only organization in Portugal.

Clube Safo, http://www.clubesafo.com/.
> Created in 1996. It is the only women-only LGBT organization. Besides co-organizing national events, they organize annual women's camps and edit a bi-monthly bulletin called *Zona Livre*.

ILGA-Portugal, http://ilga-portugal.oninet.pt/.
> Created in 1995, in Lisbon, they run the only Lesbian and Gay Communitarian Centre, a space that was given by the Lisbon municipality in 1997. ILGA-Portugal has organized the Annual Lisbon Pride Party since 1997.

não te prives—Grupo de Defesa dos Direitos Sexuais, http://www.naoteprives.org/.
> Created in 2002, in Coimbra, it is a youth organization and the only one that is simultaneously feminist and LGBT in its self-identification.

Opus Gay, http://www.opusgay.org/.
> Created in 1997, in Lisbon. They run a LGBT weekly radio show (since 1999) and they co-edited the *First Anthology of Portuguese Homoerotic Literature,* and edit the magazine *Korpus.*

Panteras Rosa—Frente de Combate à LesBiGayTransfobia, http://www.panterasrosa.com/.
> Created in 2004, in Lisbon, they mainly organize direct action initiatives.

Ponto Bi, http://www.pontobi.org/.
> Created in 2006, in Porto, it is the only bisexuality-only organization.

PortugalGay.PT, http://portugalgay.pt/.
> Created in 1996, in Porto, they have organized the Porto Pride since 2001 and have co-organized the Porto LGBT March since 2006. They also launched the Porto Gay and Lesbian Guide in 2000. Their regular activities center on a Web site that, as they report, receives 75,000 visits per month.

rede ex aequo, http://ex-aequo.web.pt/.
> Youth organization created in 2003, in Lisbon, with branches in most regions of the country. They organize youth camps and run an education observatory designed to collect data on and monitor bullying in schools.

NOTES

1. Instituto Nacional de Estatistica (INE), *Indicadores Sociais 2005* [*Official Statistics on Social Trends, 2005*] (Lisbon: INE, December 22, 2006).

2. Eurobarometer, "Discrimination in the European Union" (Lisbon: INE, January 2007).

3. José Machado Pais, ed., *Gerações e Valores na Sociedade Portuguesa Contemporânea* (Lisbon: Secretaria de Estado da Juventude, 1998).

4. *Expresso*, December 30, 2005.

5. INE, *Census 2001* [Official statistics on social trends], 2001.

6. INE, *Indicadores Sociais 2005*.

7. For example, Bar 106, http://www.bar106.com/; Bar O Bico, http://www.obico. org/; Bar Pride Bar, http://www.pride-bar.net/index2.html; Club Boys'R'Us, http:// portugalgay.pt/pub/boysrus/; Club Trumps, http://www.trumps.pt/; Hotel Anjo Azul, http://www.cb2web.com/anjoazul/index-en.php; Hotel Pouso dos Anjos, http://www. pousodosanjos.com/.

8. António Fernando Cascais, "Diferentes como só nós. O associativismo GLBT português em três andamentos," *Revista Crítica de Ciências Sociais* 76 (2006): 109–26; Ana Cristina Santos, "Sexualidades politizadas: o activismo nas áreas da sida e da homossexualidade em Portugal" ["Politicised Sexualities: AIDS and Gay Activism in Portugal"], *Cadernos de Saúde Pública* 18, no. 3 (2002): 595–611.

9. The sentence of the European Court of Human Rights dates to December 21, 1999.

10. INE, *Census 2001* (Lisbon: INE).

11. *Diario de Noticias,* December 20, 2006.

12. Ana Cristina Santos, *Enacting Activism: The Political, Legal and Social Impacts of LGBT Activism in Portugal,* PhD dissertation, Centre for Interdisciplinary Gender Studies, University of Leeds, 2008.

ROMANIA

Sinziana Carstocea

OVERVIEW

Situated in southeastern Europe, Romania[1] is the largest country in the Balkans and the 12th largest in Europe. With a total surface area of 91,892 square miles, the territory stretches 319 miles from north to south and 447 miles east to west. The Danube River is a natural border on the south and southwest, separating the country from Serbia and Bulgaria. The Black Sea borders it on the southeast, while to the northeast the river Prut marks the border with the Republic of Moldova. Romania's other neighboring countries are Ukraine to the north and Hungry to the west.

The country features the entire range of geographical configurations, with the Carpathian Mountains (also called the Transylvanian Alps) dominating the center of Romania, reaching 8,346 feet at the highest altitude and covering roughly one-third of the territory. Hills and plains cover most of the remaining area, and the Danube forms a delta when meeting the Black Sea. The geographical heterogeneity and the temperate climate support habitats for a wide variety of fauna and flora.

Romania has a population of approximately 21.6 million people, with the majority being ethnic Romanians (89.5%). Other ethnicities include Hungarians and Roma (Gypsies) (6.6% and 2% of the population, respectively), while a small percentage (1.4%) are Ukrainians, Germans, Turks, Serbs, Bulgarians, Lipovans, Greeks, Russians, Poles, or other ethnic groups. The official language is Romanian, a Romance language with primarily Slavic, but also Turkish, Greek, and Hungarian

influences. Hungarian and Romani are the main minority languages spoken, followed by German.

The country is administrated in 41 counties (*judet*) and the capital is Bucharest, a booming commercial, industrial, and cultural center, and the richest city in Romania. The currency denomination is the leu.

December 1989 marked the end of Nicolae Ceausescu's dictatorship in Romania and almost half a century of Communism. Over the 1990s to the present, the country has been undergone extensive but arduous development, also referred to as a period of slow transition toward a market economy and democracy. The years of transition are marked by significant reforms that have had a great impact at all levels of society, with most aiming to meet European Union (EU) recommendations for admission to the EU. Romania succeeded in becoming a member of the EU on January 1, 2007.

OVERVIEW OF LGBT ISSUES

Romania is generally considered to be one of the most homophobic countries in Europe, characterized by a lack of legal provisions regarding LGBT persons, an adverse social climate translating into a weak LGBT subculture, and a poor mobilization around LGBT rights. Gay and lesbian issues rarely enter the public discourse in Romania; only in recent years has public attention come to focus on homosexuality, with European-oriented activists facing opposition from conservative factions of society, such as the political parties affiliated with the Orthodox Church, and right-wing organizations.

Although Romania is a secular state, the Romanian Orthodox Church (ROC) claims a special place in domestic affairs and actively defines itself as the moral compass of society, using the allegiance of 87 percent of Romanians as the basis for its involvement in the political arena. Church intervention has had significant consequences for the progress of reforms concerning LGBT issues.

Indeed, a complete ban on homosexuality, including the criminalization of association and expression related to homosexuality, persisted until 2001. The decriminalization of homosexuality was only possible due to European pressure and conditionality in view of the country joining the EU, together with an intense international lobby mediated through a local organization (Accept, the main Romanian nongovernmental organization [NGO] defending LGBT rights). The topic of gay partnership was only mentioned in 2006, at the press conference launching Gay Fest, an annual event organized by Accept. Prompt opposition from Orthodox and nationalist voices followed in the media.

As in many other regions of the world, there is no information available concerning the general characteristics of the LGBT population in Romania. Inheriting a long history of active criminalization reinforced by social stigma, Romanian homosexuals remain very discreet, with no public personality openly embracing his or her homosexual orientation.

EDUCATION

Following the collapse of the Communist regime in 1989, the education system in Romania went through a continuous process of reconfiguration, with several contradictory reforms and a number of partial legislative acts meant to adjust and reconcile the previous changes. The education system makes a distinction between preuniversity and higher education. Only eight years of school are mandatory, from first grade to eighth grade. Children start school between the ages of six and seven. Government funding for education differs from year to year, reaching 5.2 percent of the gross domestic product (GDP) in 2007, funds used for different governmental programs aimed at encouraging attendance and improving the quality of education.

For example, students are given a monthly allowance on the condition of full attendance in classes. In 2006, a government ordinance[2] modified the conditions of this provision, making any child under 18, whether enrolled or not, able to receive this monthly allowance. By the same logic, another measure, the milk and croissant (*laptele si cornul*) program, established in 2002, consisted in providing a daily glass of milk and a croissant to all students attending primary schools classes. Scholarships rewarding high achievement or in support of economically disadvantaged students, aid in terms of supplies, and technology (including computers) are also provided to students.

A parallel network of private schools has developed since the mid-1990s, mostly for kindergarten and university students. The private university system had to respond to great challenges concerning quality of training, being considered of a lower caliber than public schools, even though all schools have to follow the ministerial guidelines, programs, and curricula.

Religious education in schools is a sensitive matter. Mandatory in primary school, religion is an optional class in secondary schools. Given that a large percentage of Romanians are Orthodox, along with the lack of resources and the impossibility of providing classes on different religions, the Orthodox religion is the predominant religion taught throughout preuniversity schools. In most classes, one can find a religious icon displayed on the wall.

The Romanian school system leaves little room for socialization outside the usual hours of classes. There is no lunch break; classes finish for some students at noon, while for others they start at noon. Usually, there is no transportation provided to and from school. Some schools have extracurricular clubs, but not many. There is no evidence of any LGBT groups on campuses, and most gay and lesbian students are not open about their orientation at school.

Sex education is not a priority of the educational system in Romania. The curricula include limited information on sex, focusing mainly on the reproductive system. Since the early and mid-1990s, sex education topics have been covered in schools by representatives of NGOs dealing with reproductive health, or by multinational companies advertising their products. Since 2004, the national curriculum has included health education, but only as an optional class. In addition, a new figure is beginning to make its way into the school universe: the school psychologist (*psiholog scolar*). His or her role and responsibilities are yet to be defined; for the moment, the counselor has broad liberty to organize activities.

In 2005, however, the publication of a comprehensive and accessible brochure on sexual orientation designated for use in schools was a great accomplishment in setting the framework for a neutral approach to the topic.[3] This is especially important since almost 50 percent of discriminatory incidents are reported to happen in education-related institutions.[4]

EMPLOYMENT AND ECONOMICS

From an economic point of view, Romania is among the most problematic countries in Europe, with slow progress toward an open economy. The GDP per capita for 2006 was estimated at $10,661, and GDP growth at 7.7 percent, while inflation was estimated at 6.5 percent.[5] The process of transition initially brought about a period of economic instability and decline in Romania, which lasted for over a decade. Nonetheless, since 2000, signs of evolution and stability are apparent: there is growth in the private sector, increased foreign investment, and decreased rates of inflation and unemployment. Exports have developed significantly over the last few years, but there is still an important trade deficit since Romania imports more goods than it exports.

There are no available figures describing discrimination in the workplace or in other spheres dealing with public services, and such figures would be hard to obtain. A large number of LGBT Romanians live in the closet, choosing not to publicly announce their sexual orientation, thus avoiding the very real threat of discrimination. A legal framework protecting LGBT people against discrimination has existed since 2000, as the implementation of a European directive: ordinance 137/2000 explicitly bans any discrimination on the basis of sexual orientation (along with other criteria) across public and professional fields, such as employment, access to goods and services, education, health, and justice. Even though this legal provision is not extensively used in everyday life, there have been a few cases of prosecution based on it, ruling in favor of LGBT people.

SOCIAL/GOVERNMENT PROGRAMS

The Romanian government does not provide funding for any social programs specifically targeted to LGBT people. Nevertheless, the Ministry of Health is involved in social health programs addressing sexually transmitted diseases and particularly AIDS and its impact on this segment of the population. Also, the Ministry of Education has offered a brochure for teachers about sexual orientation in schools across the country (this agreement occurred only after the LGBT organization Accept sued the ministry for not making the content of the program for health education classes available; the ministry lost the case based on the law of access to public information).

SEXUALITY/SEXUAL PRACTICES

The Communist era left a strong imprint on the LGBT way of life. Having been denied for so long the basic right of recognition (all same-sex relations, even consensual and private, were forbidden and could result in five years of imprisonment), gays and lesbians adopted a set of behaviors, attitudes, and codes aimed at minimizing the risk of being caught. Anonymous and random socialization did take place in public places such as public toilets and parks, as opposed to private apartments or exclusive parties, where the risk of being identified was too high. This social history is reflected in the current manners of socializing: Romanian homosexuals still hide under the veil of secrecy and seclusion. Therefore, information concerning common practices is poor and fails to describe behaviors extensively. Yet, some information is emerging. A 2005 Internet survey[6] of men who have sex with men (MSM) shows that condom use is generally low (56.7%) and depends on the type of relationship, being slightly higher in the case of casual sex than in the case of monogamous relationships. Meanwhile, a different study[7] on the LGBT population concludes that only 24.2 percent of respondents always use condoms when engaging in anal sex, while 8.7 percent say they never do.

FAMILY

Romanian society gives great importance to the traditional family; the patriarchal family, with predefined roles for men and women, is considered the cement that holds Romanian society together. Even today, success is defined as having a family with children, and this is the ultimate goal of many people's lives. Family ties are powerful and long lasting, not only within the core family, but in the extended family as well. Children are expected to obey their parents until adulthood, and dependence often continues beyond that point; grandparents assume a very pivotal role in raising children. However, recent developments in society since the end of Communism have brought about transformations in family life—for example, delays in starting a family, a lower marriage rate, and smaller family units. In 2002, a large proportion of Romanians families were couples without children (30.9%) and single-parent families (12.9%), and there were fewer couples with children (56.2%).[8]

The Romanian legal system does not allow civil unions or full marriages to LGBT people. The debate over same-sex unions was launched in 2006, as an initiative of the main LGBT organization in Bucharest. The issue led Orthodox, nationalist, and right-wing representatives to mobilize and call for a referendum on the matter. Their initiative also calls for an intervention on the constitutional law in order to define marriage as union between a man and a woman.

The Romanian legal system prevents LGBT people from adopting children. Yet, the law opens adoption to single parents (along with heterosexual parents). It is known that gays and lesbians could take advantage of this loophole and adopt children as single parents, disguising their homosexuality from the authorities; however, it is unclear what the consequences would be of disclosing an adoptive parent's homosexuality.

COMMUNITY

The lack of a sense of community often applies to Romanian society at all levels; the deficit in participation, affiliation, and collaboration is evident all over Romanian civil society, to the point of being virtually nonexistent. The poor organization of gays and lesbians into some kind of community follows directly from this more general pattern; the fact that same sex relationships were illegal in Romania and the explicit interdiction of expression and association for LGBT people until very recently also contribute to this.

The Internet constitutes the main arena for LGBT people to interact with one another, and is the most reliable space for networking and communication. Only in recent years have gay bars and nightclubs appeared, along with LGBT associations and social circles, mainly in the capital and in a few other big cities.

One organization for LGBT people that has been operating since 1996 is Accept, which is registered as an NGO defending human rights. Accept has become the main Romanian organization protecting LGBT interests, accumulating more and more influence at international levels and gaining credibility at the national level. Beside their activities of lobbying and advocating for LGBT rights, the association's aim is to develop the LGBT community. Different programs have been established, such as support groups, a small library, counseling, and more, along with a gay festival every spring for the last four years, including artistic events and culminating with a pride march. However, the structure of Accept is considered too rigid and official, detached from the day-to-day lives of gays, lesbians, bisexuals, and transsexuals; it has been successful in terms of legal accomplishments, but so far has failed to be representative of the Romanian LGBT community.

HEALTH

Regarding the health issues of LGBT people, sexually transmitted diseases (STDs) and in particular HIV are the main concerns. Two different studies conducted in 2005[9] concluded that risk perception for both STDs and HIV is very low. Only about one-half of gay men and lesbians (57.1%) or MSM (47.4%) have ever been tested for HIV, and only 1.8 percent and 2.2 percent, respectively, tested positive. Moreover around 5.3 percent from the respondents did not know the result or did not want to declare it. In the case of STDs, the numbers are comparable for getting tested, but over 25 percent declare having tested positive for an STD.

An important aspect of health issues for LGBT people in Romania is mental health; it is common in Romania to associate homosexuality with a mental or emotional disorder, and to consider that it could be cured by treatment. Furthermore, these beliefs are shared by a number of counselors, psychologists, and even medical personnel working directly with LGBT people. From this point of view, transsexuals are often exposed as such when it comes to medical assistance, mainly because there is no standard procedure for their treatment. The first sex reassignment surgery in Romania took place in 1994, and since then there have been only six such procedures, with an equal distribution between male-to-female (MTF) and female-to-male (FTM) surgeries. However, even the surgeon performing these surgeries, in an interview for a national newspaper,[10] referred to the transsexuals' condition as a psychological disorder.

POLITICS AND LAW

Homosexuality was illegal in Romania until 2001. The legal provisions against homosexuality were first introduced in Romania in 1936. Then, in 1968, the Communist ideology called for a reformation of the law. Even though the word homosexuality was not mentioned in any law, a specific article of the Romanian penal code, article 200, criminalized all consensual homosexual acts between males or females. Under this article, "sexual relations between same sex persons will be punished by a prison sentence of one to five years." This statute remained on the books and as a part of Romanian legislation until 1996, when a first reform succeeded in modifying this article: same-sex relationships became punishable "if performed in public or resulting in public scandal." Moreover, a new clause has been added to the text, explicitly denying the right of free speech and association to LGBT people: a new paragraph was added to the legal text, stating, "The impulsion or lure of another person in the viewing of the practice of sexual relations between persons of the same sex, as well as propaganda or any other acts of proselytism committed for the same purpose are punishable with a prison term between one and 5 years."

These modifications, even though they were meant to symbolize a democratic reform, in fact did not bring significant change: the definition of *public scandal* is obscure, leaving much room for interpretation; in addition, gay men and lesbians were compelled to invisibility. Article 200 was finally repealed in 2001 by government ordinance, while the last case of imprisonment based on this legislation was reported in 1997.

Discrimination

Romania benefits from an extensive legal framework concerning discrimination, also introduced by government ordinance in 2000. The law refers to discrimination as any distinction, exclusion, restriction, or preference made on the basis of a series of criteria, including sexual orientation, along with race, nationality, religion, and so forth, with the purpose or result of denying human rights and fundamental freedoms. Based on this legal provision, an agency was created, the National Council against Discrimination; its mission is to solve complaints about violations of antidiscrimination stipulations.

For over one year, the legal system contained two contradictory stipulations: article 200 was repealed only in 2001, while the antidiscrimination provisions were introduced in 2000. Nevertheless, the parliament adopted the two ordinances at the same time and they both became law in early 2002.

Transsexuals

There is no special legal provision concerning transsexuals in Romania, and there is no specific regulation for sex reassignment surgery. Transsexuality remains a vague term, with no specific definition. Therefore, several fundamental aspects related to transsexuality remain unclear, for instance, the civil status of a transsexual, or the conditions for sex reassignment surgery. This gap in the legislative corpus has resulted in endless contradictions and interpretations, with variable results depending often on the subjectivity of specific decision makers involved in particular cases. Furthermore, Romanian surgeons performing such interventions specifically ask for legal expertise and a judicial decision before executing the surgery.

RELIGION AND SPIRITUALITY

Romania is a secular state, and therefore officially neutral in matters of religion. In reality though, the Orthodox Church identifies itself as a national church, with over 87 percent of the Romanian population declaring it as their religion. Moreover, the ROC benefits from the highest rate of confidence from the population compared to other institutions of the state.

Relations between religion and politics are problematic, as in any society. The case of the ROC and its place in Romanian society is not exceptional, but presents some particularities. Orthodox representatives over the centuries have claimed Romanian Orthodoxy to have a strong relationship with the Romanian people, not only in matters of spirituality and faith, but also as the cement of the nation itself; Orthodoxy is considered the constituent and the identity of the Romanian community. Democratic transition challenged the Romanian Orthodoxy on a number of issues, but the main difficulty was redefining its role in a changing society. After the Communist period (a time of declared atheism with strong persecutions of priests, demolition of churches and monasteries, and also an affirmed allegiance to the state), the church has constantly tried to affirm its role as a unique and incontestable moral reference. To this end, the ROC participates in political debates, negotiating with the state over matters of political interest, while claiming to preserve the nation's health and integrity.

In this context, the subject of decriminalizing homosexual relations constitutes for the ROC a handy instrument in exercising its influence on the political scene, to affirm the role of religion in society. Therefore, the government's initiative to repeal article 200 encountered strong opposition from the majority of the political parties, apprehensive about introducing unpopular reforms that would contradict the majority Orthodox spirit.

Because of the strong incompatibility between faith and homosexual behavior, Romanian gays and lesbians experience great distress, struggling to accept themselves despite their behavior, which is defined as sinful; sometimes they fight the temptation, and sometimes they give up their faith. However, an alternative choice came from the collaboration between Accept and the Metropolitan Community Church, mainly through the work of Canadian bishop Diane Fisher, the elder of this congregation in central and eastern Europe. Over the last couple of years, Accept has hosted religious services and support groups for LGBT people in search of spirituality.

VIOLENCE

The overall climate in Romanian society is predominantly characterized by homophobia and rejection of differences. However, the adverse reaction to LGBT people does not usually include beatings, killings, or violent aggression. Mostly, LGBT people have to face rejection in terms of verbal aggression, mockery, exclusion from social groups, and threats. A study[11] revealed that 66.6 percent of LGBT people who came out to their family or friends did not experience negative reactions. However, the same study points out that over 61 percent of the persons questioned did not come out to their family at all, and over 32 percent did not come out to their friends. It would not be difficult to conclude that LGBT people avoid possible violence by hiding their sexual orientation.

Cases of violent treatment of homosexuals by the police were extremely common before the repeal of article 200 and shortly after. Arrests, interrogations, and harassments were conducted without any consideration for human rights and dignity.

Today, the most violent incidents have happened in Romania during the gay festivals organized in Bucharest over the last three years, especially during the marches. Several incidents marked each event, mainly counterdemonstrations, hate slogans, and homophobic messages on banners, culminating with attacks using firecrackers, eggs, or stones. From one year to the next, the police have ensured a more strict control of the route of the marches and mobilized more personnel for the event. On one occasion, though, after the march was over, a group of participants was attacked while leaving the setting and were beaten up in a subway car, in front of indifferent commuters. Among the opponents of gay marches were later identified right-wing extremists and football (soccer) supporters.

OUTLOOK FOR THE 21ST CENTURY

With legislation explicitly specifying sexual orientation among the criteria of discrimination, and a national agency (National Council against Discrimination) responsible for investigating cases of discrimination, Romania has the basis for building a more tolerant environment for LGBT people. There is evidence of an emerging LGBT community, with bars and clubs and a number of organizations defending LGBT rights; different social circles have been established following the repeal of criminalizing legislation. The conditionality for European Union membership offered the occasion for judicial level change. Membership in the EU offers the opportunity to experience European values and the hope of more openness toward difference. Still, nationalistic voices will always be heard in Romanian society, and the Orthodox Church will continue to intervene in the political process as an influential actor.

Aside from the legal issues waiting to be solved (partnership and adoption legislation, the status of transsexuals, and the procedures for sex reassignment interventions), many other social aspects need improvement in Romanian society. Still, with an annual gay festival, more and more visibility for LGBT people through art events and movies, with antidiscrimination legal provisions, there is hope for a more tolerant climate and acceptance of otherness.

RESOURCE GUIDE

Suggested Reading

Accept, *Despre noi. Minoritati Sexuale in Romania* [*About Us. Sexual Minorities in Romania*] (Bucharest, 2003).

Amnesty International, *Romania: A Summary of Human Rights Concerns* (EUR 39/06/1998, March 1998), http://www.amnesty.org/.

Ingrid Baciu, Vera Câmpeanu, and Mona Nicoara, "Romania," in *Unspoken Rules: Sexual Orientation and Women's Human Rights,* ed. Rachel Rosenbloom (San Francisco, CA: International Gay and Lesbian Human Rights Commission, 1995).

Sinziana Carstocea, "Une identité clandestine: l'homosexualité en Roumanie" ["A Clandestine Identity: Homosexuality in Romania"], *Revue d'histoire moderne et contemporaine* 53–54 (2006): 191–210.

Human Rights Watch and the International Gay and Lesbian Human Rights Commission, *Public Scandals. Sexual Orientation and Criminal Law in Romania.* Report (New York: Human Rights Watch and the International Gay and Lesbian Human Rights Commission, 1998).

Scott Long, "Gay and Lesbian Movements in Eastern Europe," in *The Global Emergence of Gay and Lesbian Politics: National Imprints of a Worldwide Movement,* ed. Barry D. Adam, Jan Willem Duyvendak, and André Krowel (Philadelphia: Temple University Press, 1999).

Mona Nicoara, "Silenced and Silent—Lesbians in Romania," *Canadian Women Studies / Les Cahiers de la Femme* 16, no. 1 (1995): 43–46.

Denise Roman, *Fragmented Identities. Popular Culture, Sex and Everyday Life in Post Communist Romania* (Oxford: Lexington Books, 2003).

Lavinia Stan and Lucian Turcescu, "The Orthodox Church and Post-Communist Democratisation," *Europe-Asia Studies* 52, no. 8 (2000): 1467–88.

Catalin Augustin Stoica, "An Otherness that Scares: Public Attitudes and Debates on Homosexuality in Romania," in *National Reconciliation in Eastern Europe,* ed. H. Carey (Boulder, CO: Eastern Europe Monographs, 2003).

Carl F. Stychin, "Same Sex Sexualities and the Globalization of Human Rights Discourse," *McGill Law Journal / Revue de droit McGill* 49 (2004): 951–68.

Anne Weyembergh and Sinziana Carstocea, eds., *The Gays' and Lesbians' Rights in an Enlarged European Union* (Brussels: Éditions de l'Université de Bruxelles, 2006).

Organizations

Accept, http://www.accept-romania.ro.
> First NGO defending human rights for LGBT people in Romania, established in 1996.

Be An Angel, http://angelicuss@go.ro.
> Gay organization functioning in Cluj.

PSI (Population Services International) Romania, http://www.psi.ro/.
> Nonprofit organization founded in 1998 as an affiliate of the Global PSI Network.

Web Sites

Gay Bucuresti, http://www.gaybucuresti.ro.

Gay One-Portal Gay Romanesc, http://www.gayone.ro.

Noua Dreapta, http://www.nouadreapta.org/.
> Antigay, New Right, extremist organization established in 2000.

Queer.ro, http://www.queer.ro.

Total Gay, http://www.totalgay.ro.
> General news and information on LGBT lifestyle, events, classified ads, and online sex shops.

2G, http://www.2g.ro.

NOTES

1. For a comprehensive presentation of Romania see the National Institute of Statistics, "Statistical Yearbook 2006," http://www.insse.ro, particularly chapter 1, Geography, Meteorology and Environment, and chapter 2, Population.

2. Ordonanta de Urgenta Guvernamentala–Goverment Emergency Ordinance (OUG) 44, June 14, 2006.

3. See Accept, *Sexual Orientation: A Guide for Teachers* (Bucharest: Maiko Publishing House, 2005).

4. See the Accept report, *Barriers in the Social life of LGBT People* (Bucharest: Accept, 2005), 18.

5. See World Bank, http://www.worldbank.org.ro.

6. PSI Romania, "Romania (2005): HIV/AIDS TraC Study among Men Who Have Sex with Men," The PSI Dashboard, January 2006, http://www.psi.ro.

7. Accept, *Barriers in the Social life of LGBT People,* 12.

8. Institutul National de Statistica [National Institute of Statistics], http://www.insse.ro.

9. PSI Romania, *Romania (2005): HIV / AIDS TraC Study among Men who have Sex with Men.*

10. Ioan Lascar, interview for the national newspaper *Libertatea,* December 14, 2006.

11. See Accept, *Barriers in the Social life of LGBT People.*

RUSSIA

James Dochterman

OVERVIEW

Russia, also known as the Russian Federation (Rossiyskaya Federatsiya), is the largest nation in the world when measured by landmass. Russia encompasses 10,610,162 square miles, covering both the European and Asian continents, and is home to more than 141 million people.[1] Russia's population has declined over the last decade. In addition to its enormous size, Russia claims some of the richest natural resources of any country, with substantial petroleum and natural gas reserves, as well as large quantities of diamonds and precious metals.[2] Extensive exploitation of these natural resources has resulted in making Russia's capital city, Moscow, one of the most expensive cities in the world.[3] Russian is the official language, although 30 other languages are officially recognized and spoken throughout Russia's vast regions.

Russia inherited the military industry and structure of the former Union of Soviet Socialist Republics (USSR), also known as the Soviet Union. As the political control center of the USSR, 70 percent of the former Soviet Union's military resources resided in Russia, and remained in Russia's control after the dissolution of the Soviet Union in December 1991. Russia's current military budget is a

state secret, but is estimated at 2.7 percent of the gross domestic product (GDP), roughly $31 billion dollars.[4] This military inheritance leaves Russia in possession of one of the largest modern military forces, including the world's largest stockpile of nuclear weapons and the only strategic bomber force other than that of the United States.[5] Russia maintains six independent coequal combat arms, covering land, sea, air, and space combat areas. Russia is second only to the United States in military spending, although exact figures are unknown and official Russian figures are widely regarded as artificially deflated.[6]

Despite its enormous natural resources and military force, the Russian economy is still in a developing stage. Throughout the 1990s, Russia experienced numerous economic challenges following the collapse of the Soviet Union and its centralized five-year economic plans. These crises included the near collapse of the burgeoning banking industry, skyrocketing unemployment, and the devaluation of the ruble, Russia's official currency. In 2007, Russia was still addressing the aftermath of the post-Soviet economy, when the new government imposed brutal free market reforms. Precious natural resources were distributed to political insiders and former Soviet bureaucrats (*aparatchnikii*). As a result of this transfer, astonishing amounts of wealth and power became concentrated among a small group of industrialists known as the oligarchs. The overwhelming majority of Russians, who were accustomed to a Communist state that purported to advocate community ownership (among other liberal ideals), never benefited from this dissemination and reapportionment of wealth. Nearly 18 percent of Russians live below the poverty line, while Russia's per capita GDP ranked 59th in the world in 2006.[7]

Russia began as Kievan Rus in the year 862 A.D., and became one of the first principalities to declare Christianity its official religion, in 988 A.D. Over the next 600 years, Russia endured multiple invasions and foreign rulers. Modern Russia has its beginning in the 12th century with the founding of the Principle of Moscuvy, born out of the demise of the Byzantine Empire. A Mongol invasion in 1223 and subsequent occupation of Russia lasted for 200 years until the Mongols were run out of Russian lands by Ivan III (Ivan the Great) in 1380. Ivan IV (Ivan the Terrible) was declared the first Russian tsar in 1547. Under his rule, Russia expanded its borders and established its first formal legal code, as well as its first representative legislative body.[8] Despite these social advances, Ivan the Terrible earned his moniker by ushering in an age of severe brutality. Following another period of foreign invasion and conflict in the early 1600s, known as the *time of troubles,* Tsar Michael Romanov solidified the nascent Romanov dynasty's power.

Under the stringent westernization efforts of Tsar Peter I (Peter the Great), who ruled from 1682 to 1725, Russia established itself as a true European power. Peter the Great founded Russia's new northern capital, Saint Petersburg, on the model of a European city, and introduced dramatic social and cultural reforms. These reforms were continued by Tsarina Catherine II (Catherine the Great), who ruled from 1762 until her death in 1796. Catherine's rule gained notoriety in Europe for its purported liberalism and support for the arts, including the creation of the renowned Hermitage Museum. In spite of European admiration for Catherine II, she subjected the Russian people to censorship and state control of publications, and was largely inattentive to the deplorable conditions under which the vast majority of Russians lived. Saint Petersburg remained Russia's capital until the Russian Revolutions of 1917, when political power was returned to Moscow and the governmental fortress, known as the Kremlin.

Under tsarist rule, Russia survived many subsequent wars and invasions, including Napoleon Bonaparte's unsuccessful French invasion during the War of 1812. Russians are proud to point to Alexander II's abolition of serfdom in Russia in 1861. However, additional reforms were few and far between. Continued social oppression led to a brief revolution in 1905.

Ultimately, the greatest threat to Russia's political and social stability lay within Russia itself. Unrest grew within Russia as the tsarist regime of Nicholas II grew increasingly conservative, dictatorial, and incompetent in its management of the military campaign in World War I. Peasants and laborers organized under a burgeoning Marxist ideology, at first voicing simple discontent, but evolving into a revolution. Led by Vladimir Ilyich Lenin and his Bolshevik (Majority) party, Russia experienced two revolutions in 1917. The first revolution occurred in February 1917, which overthrew the Russian monarchy and executed Tsar Nicholas II and his family. The subsequent, more renowned October 1917 revolution established the first-ever Communist state.

Following the 1917 October Revolution, Russia entered a tumultuous period. Although Russia reached a peace treaty during World War I in which it ceased hostilities with the Central Powers and forfeited former territories, civil war continued after the revolution. Conflict between the Bolshevik and White (counterrevolutionary) armies caused mass starvation, widespread atrocities, and devastation to the Russian economy. In response to the internal struggle, Lenin instituted a policy of war Communism, which, while helping the Bolsheviks prevail in 1921, also became the model for future Soviet totalitarian rule. A combined 16 million Russians died during World War I, the subsequent October Revolution, and the civil war.[9] Russia's society and economy was devastated.

Reconstruction of the Russian economy and society began when Russia and three local republics formed the Soviet Union on December 20, 1922. From this moment, Russia's history and that of the Soviet Union are inexorably intertwined. Following a brief experimentation with limited free-market reforms, known as the new economic policy (NEP), Communist control over the country became increasingly onerous.

Lenin died in 1924. After intense intraparty struggle, Lenin was succeeded by the ruthless Joseph Stalin. Stalin later introduced the Soviet Union's first economic five-year plan which instituted forced industrialization and collectivization of agricultural resources, to devastating effect. Until Stalin's death in 1953, Russia, and by extension the entire Soviet Union, suffered the dual horrors of World War II, during which the USSR lost nearly 27 million lives, and a political ideology enforced with labor camps, mass relocation, and executions.

In the intervening 74 years between the revolution and the collapse of the Soviet Union, Russians suffered extreme restrictions on their freedom to criticize the Communist party or to choose with whom and how they would associate in society. This control effectively frustrated any attempt by homosexuals to form their own social or political organizations for most of the 20th century. But, as at other times in Russia's history, a radical shift in government soon created a brief opportunity for social development.

In 1985, Mikhail Gorbachev became general secretary of the Communist Party, ushering in a momentary relaxation of social control known as *glasnost* (openness) and *perestroika* (restructuring). While these programs were meant to reinvigorate and modernize Communist rule, they instead precipitated the downfall of the Communist Party and the Soviet Union's collapse. Communist party rule of Russia lasted until the fall of the Soviet Union in 1991.

Since the collapse of the Soviet Union, Russia has undergone a period of social upheaval and political turmoil. Following the first Russian president Boris Yeltsin's lackluster leadership and resignation on December 31, 1999, Prime Minister Vladimir Putin ascended to the Russian presidency. Over the subsequent eight years, President Putin endeavored to recentralize control over Russian society. Putin's leadership of Russia was marked by antagonism toward the West and a relentless focus on reestablishing Russian international power. In particular, Putin's efforts are attributed to the burgeoning growth of Russian ultranationalist sociopolitical organizations, such as United Russia (Yedinaya Rossiya) and Ours (Nashi, or Youth Movement—Ours!). It remains to be seen whether the 2008 presidential inauguration of former attorney and Putin protégé Dmitry A. Medvedev will usher in another period of Russian social liberalism, or extend the Soviet-style politics of the Putin presidency.

The social struggles of LGBT Russians cannot easily be compared to Western experiences. There is precious little evidence of a historical, organized legal effort focused on LGBT liberation, as there is in the West. Although there are modern legal efforts to hasten tolerance and civil rights, they stand in sharp contrast with Russia's historical trends. Furthermore, Russia's social history and culture has long resisted transparency. Russian government policies, whether Tsarist, Communist, or Soviet, historically focused their efforts on secrecy, disinformation, and outright hostility toward the existence of LGBT people in Russia.

While the Russian Orthodox Church played a critical role in Russian society under tsarist rule, nearly a century of Communism severely restricted direct Christian influence, which is historically common in Western societies. Communist ideology is overtly hostile to religious institutions. Because organized religions often compete with governments for influence among national citizens, Russian Communists were particularly determined to excise the Russian Orthodox Church from Russians' daily lives. This campaign was particularly intense in the early 20th century, when Communists destroyed classic Orthodox churches, often the center of village life in the vast Russian countryside. Among those buildings destroyed was the enormous Cathedral of Christ the Savior, in Moscow. The cathedral (*khram*) was demolished to make way for an enormous Soviet monument, but when engineers determined that such a structure could not be built, a large municipal pool was built in its place. Among the structures that survived Communist rule is Saint Basil's Cathedral. Saint Basil's sits in Red Square (Krasnaya Ploshed) alongside the Kremlin.

The preservation of Saint Basil's is important to note. Although Communists greatly reduced the Russian Orthodox Church's role, some church icons and elements of church ideology outlived the Soviet Union. After the Soviet Union disintegrated, many Russians searched for some form of ideology or leadership to replace the Communist Party. In recent years, the Russian Orthodox Church has experienced a resurgence of believers, as well as higher levels of influence in the Russian government and among Russian ultranationalist political organizations. Even the *khram* has been rebuilt on its former site in Moscow.

The Russian monarchy and the Russian Orthodox Church have coexisted since the birth of the Russian state. The monarchy served under the moral authority of, and drew its legitimacy from, the Orthodox Church. But where prohibitions against homosexual behavior grew increasingly harsh in European societies, Russia's geographical and religious isolation allowed it to evolve along a different path.[10] Punishment for homosexual behavior was similar to that for drunken or disorderly behaviors. In fact, it was under Communism that Russians developed a more pronounced sense of homophobia. Led by party ideologues such as Maxim Gorky, what was considered deviant behavior became the subject of vitriolic attacks. From the Communist perspective, all nonheteronormative behavior was aberrant, and associated with Western or even Nazi influences. Thus, homosexuals became scapegoats for all of Communism's postrevolution failings, and a principal target of the Stalinist establishment.[11]

OVERVIEW OF LGBT ISSUES

Most Russian citizens do not respect or tolerate homosexuality, bisexuality, or transgenderism. Following the collapse of the Soviet Union, Russia experienced a brief surge in LGBT activism. This activism was centered in Russia's large urban areas, particularly the capital city Moscow and the pre-Soviet capital Saint Petersburg. Recent political and social upheavals in Russia present a more difficult atmosphere in which to develop LGBT communities and civil rights organizations.

HIV and AIDS constitute a severe health crisis in Russia. Worldwide organizations offer continual assistance to Russia, but in Russia's modern political climate, this assistance is often treated as interference. HIV/AIDS prevention and treatment programs in Russia are typically administered by local governments. It is difficult to determine which programs are administered centrally by the Russian government, and to what extent these programs are successful. As in most societies, there is a tremendous stigma attached to HIV/AIDS, and health care services can be extremely difficult to attain.

Russia has no national employment discrimination protection for homosexual, bisexual, or transgender people. Although a 2005 court decision in Saint Petersburg ruled that the plaintiff, known only as VP, could not be denied work because he was gay, this was the first and only such known ruling. In addition, the LGBT community does not have access to same-sex marriage, or any governmental support or education programs.

Recent attempts by LGBT activists to express free speech and associative activities in the form of a gay pride parade in Moscow have been met with fierce legal opposition and physical violence. As with local attempts to address the AIDS crisis, modern Russia sees LGBT activism as Western interference with Russian society. Modern polling reveals that many Russians support the internment or killing of gays and lesbians.[12]

Due to deficiencies in Soviet recordkeeping and the short history of independent native Russian LGBT organizations, much of what is known about the lives of LGBT Russians is assembled from anecdotal evidence.

EDUCATION

Russia provides no social programs focused on LGBT education, civil rights, or employment protection. On the contrary, there has been a recent resurgence of nationalist organizations that operate as quasi-governmental bodies and openly advocate against LGBT people.

Russia is currently experiencing a net population loss that has prompted other regions (*oblasti*') to institute fertility incentives. These incentives are both monetary and political, in some cases recalling old Soviet propaganda. As a result of these programs, nonprocreative behavior, such as homosexual sex, is considered anathema to the country's economic and social stabilization goals. This opposition has historic parallels to the early Communist Russia, where abortion was outlawed in 1936 to facilitate the repopulation of Russia following extensive war and famine.

EMPLOYMENT AND ECONOMICS

Antidiscrimination Statutes

In 2005, a Saint Petersburg court ruled that a gay man cannot be denied employment simply because he is gay. The plaintiff, known only as VP, had been denied military service in 1992 due to his homosexuality. At the time, homosexuality was still treated as a mental disorder, and his official documents listed him as mentally ill. As a result of the military's mental illness designation, VP was denied subsequent employment with a railroad that refused to hire a mentally ill person. Absent this court ruling, there are no currently known laws that protect Russian LGBT citizens.

Military

Currently, the Russian Federation does not exclude homosexuals from military service. Russia has compulsory military service for all men 18 to 27 years old. The Russian military is known for its harsh treatment of recruits under the hazing system known as *dedovshchina* (rule of the grandfathers), whereby young recruits are beaten mercilessly. As a result, draft avoidance, through bribery or hiding, is widespread.

SOCIAL/GOVERNMENT PROGRAMS

There are no official Russian government programs tasked with increasing acceptance, tolerance, or acknowledgement of homosexuals, bisexuals, or transgender peoples. To the contrary, many nationalist political parties, high-profile politicians, and Russian Orthodox priests publicly condemn nonheterosexual behavior. These denouncements lead to tacit approval of gay bashing, known as *remont* ("fixing" or "repair") and pervasive discrimination and harassment.

SEXUALITY/SEXUAL PRACTICES

Russian is in the midst of a severe health crisis. Although the country largely dismissed the severity of the burgeoning HIV/AIDS epidemic throughout the past two decades, it has recently improved its response and coordinated its outreach with the Joint United Nations Programme on HIV/AIDS (UNAIDS). Russians attribute most HIV infections to intravenous drug use, rather than sexual behavior. While safer sex education programs exist in Russia, it remains to be seen whether there will be long-term beneficial results.

FAMILY

Russians adhere to very conservative, strict models of the family unit, intertwined with a fierce nationalistic pride. Russian family law does not recognize variations on the nuclear family, and adoption is uncommon. Children with developmental or physical disabilities often end up institutionalized.

COMMUNITY

Homosexual art and literature enjoyed a brief blossoming during the early 20th century. In 1906, Saint Petersburg–based author Mikhail Kuzmin published his bathhouse coming-out novel *Wings* (*Kryl'ia*). *Wings* was met with severe criticism, but the LGBT community, such as it was at the time, embraced the novel for "its decidedly unmedical view of male love as an exalted experience, superior to the love of men for women, mediated by classical learning and mentorship."[13] One year later, the lesbian-themed novel *Thirty-three Monsters* was published by Lidiia Zinov'eva-Annibal.

Communist rule of Russia severely restricted the organizational methods and means available to LGBT Russia citizens. Once sodomy was recriminalized in 1933, all facets of LGBT life became the subject of Communist ideology and oppression. Communists used nonheteronormative behaviors as ideological scapegoats identified with decadent, bourgeois societies. Throughout the 20th century, LGBT Russian communities existed primarily as subcultures in Soviet prisons (*gulag*) and institutions. Any attempt to create unapproved communities contrary to Soviet norms would be crushed, often with the involvement of the Soviet internal security apparatus. Only recently have LGBT Russians been able to begin assembling the rudimentary foundation of what Western scholars would generally refer to as community.

With the assistance of the International Gay Association and Finnish organizations, Aleksandr Zaremba assembled a small group of gay men and women in Leningrad in 1983.[14] Known as the Gay Laboratory (Gei-laboratoriia), the organization soon disbanded under pressure from the KGB and Zaremba's imprisonment. Within two years, the *glasnost* and *perestroika* period in the mid-1980s saw the first beginnings of LGBT open speech and association.

In 1989, the Moscow Association of Sexual Minorities was formed in Moscow by Roman Kalinin, who later cofounded the International Gay and Lesbian Human Rights Commission. The group established the gay-themed newspaper, *Tema*, or *The Theme*, which was gay slang referencing homosexuality.[15] By the mid-1990s, the group had split into two factions, with the newly named and radicalized Moscow Union of Homosexuals eager to gain media attention. A more conservative faction calling itself the Association for Equal Rights (ARGO) was created in 1990. ARGO published their own newspaper, titled *RISK*, which intended to educate fellow homosexuals about homosexuality.

Because LGBT Russians face tremendous religious, social, historical, and governmental roadblocks, it is unreasonable to expect that Russia should have or develop Western-style gay communities. The LGBT community in Russia is developing slowly, at its own pace. In 2008, LGBT organizers made significant progress toward developing a cohesive plan to organize and advocate for Russian gays and lesbians.

HEALTH

Life expectancy for Russian males has declined since the collapse of the Soviet Union. Currently, a Russian man may expect to live for 59 years. The life expectancy for Russian women is 72 years.[16]

HIV/AIDS and STDs

Russia is currently experiencing a full-blown HIV/AIDS crisis, accounting for the majority of all new HIV infections worldwide. While infection rates peaked at the end of the last century, recent infection rates have slowed in Russia from a peak of 87,000 in 2001, to a low of 34,000 in 2003. According to UNAIDS, 39,000 cases were reported in 2006. As of November 2007, there were over 940,000 cases of HIV infection in Russia, although official Russian figures count roughly 400,000 cases.[17] Approximately 30,000 new cases were reported in 2007.[18] It is widely assumed by world health organizations that cases of HIV infection in Russia are dramatically underreported.[19]

According to the Russian State Sanitary Department, 2007 registered a 12 percent increase in HIV infections over the previous year. Saint Petersburg has the largest share of HIV infections, totaling over 33,000. Russia continues to face difficulty maintaining antiviral treatments for HIV-positive patients.[20]

Intravenous drug use accounts for 66 percent of all new HIV infections in Russia. Thirty-two percent of all new infections result from heterosexual intercourse, a figure which has been slowly increasing since the turn of the century. Only 1 percent of newly registered HIV cases in 2006 were attributed to unsafe sex between men.[21] However, the accuracy of this low figure is questionable, as sex between men carries an enormous social stigma in modern Russia, and may cause some Russians to attribute their infection to nonsexual origins. According to official reports, HIV infection in Russia stems overwhelmingly from sex workers and intravenous drug users.

Russia recorded its first case of HIV infection in 1986. Soviet policy did not recognize the health threat. Given the difficulty of keeping records in Russia, the exact number of HIV infections during the precollapse period may never be known. After the 1991 collapse of the Soviet Union, Russian HIV/AIDS prevention and education was in disarray. A centralized governmental response was almost nonexistent. Only by the mid-1990s did nongovernmental organizations (NGOs) gradually form to address the epidemic. When the Russian government did address HIV/AIDS, it was without pronounced sensitivity to the populace's privacy. It was common practice for the State Committee on Epidemiology and Sanitary Surveillance (SEC) to test for HIV without patient consent and have patients inform on sexual partners.

Since the turn of the century, Russia has made dramatic improvements in its approach to fighting HIV/AIDS. In October 2006, the Russian Federation established a Governmental Commission on AIDS. According to UNAIDS, "coverage of prevention and treatment programs for people whose behaviors are likely to put them most at risk are still low, i.e., a significant impact of the increased efforts has not yet been observed."[22] The Russian government's recent commitment stems in part from the recognition that spiraling HIV/AIDS infection rates endanger Russia's current economic and social security.

Ninety percent of Russians infected with HIV will not know they are infected until they develop full-blown AIDS. Although Russia offers universal health care, the system has been the subject of much international concern and improvement efforts. In 2004, a consortium of NGO outreach organizations joined efforts to form GLOBUS ("Globalnoye Ob'yedinyeniye Usilii Protiv SPIDa," or "The Global Association of Efforts against AIDS"), a five-year plan to combat the AIDS epidemic in Russia.

Educational programs regarding HIV transmission and AIDS are in their infancy in Russia. These programs face extraordinary ignorance and prejudice within the general population. A 2004 survey in Moscow found that 70 percent of people interviewed felt "fear, anger, or disgust towards those living with the virus."[23] In 2008, coordinated Russian and United Nations efforts may prove substantially more effective than past programs. The Russian Ministry of Health and Social Development continues their ILO/USDOL HIV/AIDS Workplace Education Programme, primarily involving Moscow trade unions. A successful HIV/AIDS workplace education program, targeted at increasing understanding and tolerance of HIV/AIDS, would be a turning point in Russian social and educational policy.[24]

Forced Medical Treatment and Lesbians

The rhetoric of pathology defined LGBT Russian sexual identities throughout the 20th century. Whether under tsarist or Soviet rule, Russian lesbians were far more likely than gay men to be subjected to various medical and psychological treatments by Russian doctors to cure female homosexual behavior. Beginning in the 1920s, Communist desires to build what would become ideal Soviet gender models targeted women for treatment. Those subjected to medical treatment endured drug therapies, aversion therapies, shock therapy, and morbid endocrinological experiments where donor, often nonhuman, testes or ovaries were surgically attached to a patient in an effort to fix the subject's supposed hormonal imbalance.[25]

It is not known how many women were subjected to psychological therapies because Soviet psychologists did not record lesbianism as the disease being treated. Instead, they identified lesbians as having "sluggishly manifesting schizophrenia" (*vialotekushaia shizofreniia*). This diagnosis was not restricted to lesbianism, but could apply to an astonishingly broad, undefined set of behaviors deemed contrary to Soviet law and ideology. The mere threat of institutionalization and social stigma was sufficient to ensure general compliance with nationalist and Communist ideals of women as dutiful wives and mothers.[26]

From both Russian and Soviet perspectives, nonconforming male behavior, especially sodomy, was treated as a criminal activity. For much of Russia's political history, nonheteronormative gender behaviors were considered symptoms of a bourgeois decadence and perversion. This was due, in part, to the concept that sodomy resulted from a character defect, brought about either by alcohol abuse or social corruption, whereas a woman who misbehaved violated not social convention, but nature itself. Male homosexuality was treated and punished as simple misbehavior, while female homosexuality was treated as a biological deviation from the natural female state. There were rare, unsuccessful attempts by Russian criminologists and doctors to decriminalize sodomy, based on the medical theory that because homosexuality was a disease, the individual should not be held criminally liable for behaviors that they could not naturally know to be wrong.[27]

It is only within the past 30 years that Russia, and by extension the former Soviet Union, ceased forcibly institutionalizing gays and lesbians. Homosexuality is no longer officially classified as a mental disorder.

POLITICS AND LAW

Legal constructions of homosexual, bisexual, and transgender identities are vital to understanding the development, or lack thereof, of the Russian LGBT community. Throughout Russian history, construction of a homosexual social identity has been almost entirely male and criminal. Lesbian invisibility in Russian history is exceeded only by the severe lack of bisexual references. In addition, the Soviet Union treated transgenderism as a medical disorder; as a result, "Russian experts are more likely to categorize individual bodies as incorrectly sexed, rather than forcing every body into the hetero/homosexual divide of [Western] society."[28]

Sodomy

Despite occasional historical moments of pronounced liberalism, if only manifested by good intentions, sodomy became a secular criminal offense under tsarist rule. When Peter the Great instituted European social standards in Russia, he included a new criminalization of sodomy in 1716, as well as prevailing European condemnations of homosexual behavior.[29] Although the military legal code applied only to the military service, it became the basis for the 1835 expansion of criminalized sodomy into civilian society by Tsar Nicholas I.

Known as article 995, the 1835 antisodomy law applied only to anal intercourse among men (*muzhelozhstvo,* or "men lying with men").[30] Traditionally, Russian legal constructions regarding sodomy were focused exclusively on male behavior. Female homosexuals were instead regarded as suffering from psychological or physical aberrations. As such, lesbians were not eligible for prosecution under article 995.

While there have been laws prohibiting sodomy, enforcement of these laws has varied widely throughout Russian history. After Peter the Great criminalized sodomy in the military, Catherine the Great made a point of instructing judges to "exercise 'the utmost clemency and mercy' in sodomy cases, since 'the victims must be considered to have been more temporarily out of their wits, than really criminal.'"[31] Catherine's statement is a precursor to future Russian conceptions of homosexuality as a psychological affliction or disease better treated by medicine than criminal law. Russian treatment of nonheterosexual identities as psychological deviance reached its zenith during Communist rule, when untold numbers of lesbian, gay, bisexual, and transgender peoples were forcibly institutionalized.

In 1922, Bolshevik Communists instituted a new penal code that repealed the tsarist antisodomy law. Although the 1917 revolution withdrew the entire tsarist penal code, no substitute code was made available, and courts continued to follow tsarist law, which did not conflict with revolutionary ideals.[32] Although sodomy was no longer a criminal activity, there is debate as to whether this repeal was an enlightened deliberate act, or instead part of a broader, wholesale abrogation of tsarist law. Radical changes to the legal environment and code structures are not uncommon in Russian history.[33] In a similar vein, the Soviet Union developed a pattern of altering historical documents, monuments, and even public artworks so as to constantly readjust and control public perceptions of official Soviet policies.

In 1933, Stalin enacted article 154 of the penal code for the Russian Federation, which recriminalized male homosexual consensual behavior. Once the Soviet Union was formed, this code became known as article 121.1 and was enforced throughout the Soviet Union. Violations of articles 154 and 121.1 were punishable by up to five years of hard labor.[34] Although article 121.1 applied to all Soviet citizens, scholars note that citizens in the more far-flung corners of the Soviet Union, particularly non-Russians, were treated differently than Russian Soviet citizens. Whereas Russian men were more likely to be convicted of criminal offenses under article 121.1, citizens of the other regions who committed sodomy were more likely to be treated as sexual deviants suffering from an inferior cultural heritage.[35]

Soviet-era secrecy frustrates any attempt to report the exact number of Russian citizens prosecuted for sodomy during Communist rule.[36] Following the recriminalization of sodomy, the Communists stirred up public hatred of homosexuals by associating homosexuality with decadent Western perversion and a supposed homosexual-led conspiracy against Russia's social revolution.[37] Like other minorities considered threatening to the Communist party, homosexuals were subjected to mass arrest and imprisonment. Following this antihomosexual campaign, homosexuality as a nonmedical subject matter largely disappeared from all official Communist materials.

During the 1960s, approximately 1,414 male Soviet citizens were sent to jail annually for committing sodomy.[38] Of these citizens, an estimated 560 men were from the Russian Federation.[39] From 1970 until the fall of the Soviet Union, an estimated 462 to 831 Russian citizens were convicted, with the lower figures representing the beginning of the collapse of the Soviet Union. It is not known exactly how many Russian citizens were prosecuted, but not convicted, subjected to prosecution under other similar criminal statutes, or forcibly institutionalized.[40]

Lesbians, bisexuals, and transgender people are practically invisible in the criminal histories, but are overwhelmingly more likely to have been forcibly institutionalized or subjected to Soviet medical treatments. Men convicted of sodomy joined an abused prison underclass, known as the *opushcheny* (the degraded). This social stigma followed them even after their eventual release from prison.

Criminalized sodomy changed little in Russia until April 1993, when President Boris Yeltsin signed a bill that repealed article 121.1. The repeal occurred without LGBT activist involvement and caught the community by surprise.[41] However, this repeal did not affect a similar law, article 121.2, which criminalized sodomy with a minor. It is not known how many Russian men were imprisoned under other criminal statutes used to persecute homosexuals.[42] By comparison, tsarist-era convictions for male-on-male rape (article 996, similar in concept to the modern article 121.2), occurred four times as often as convictions for sodomy.[43]

While modern Russia no longer criminalizes sodomy, it does maintain a criminal code that singles out homosexual sexual activity. Enacted in 1996, "Article 132, 'Violent Acts of a Sexual Nature,' allows prosecution for 'sodomy, lesbianism, or any other acts of a sexual nature which use force or the threat of force to the victim or any other persons or take advantage of the helpless position of the victim.'"[44] The loose language of this statute allows for the possibility of further harassment of LGBT Russians, should the state ever require it. In addition, this is the first instance in Russian legal history where lesbianism is explicitly referenced in law.[45]

Antidiscrimination Statutes

Russia has no antidiscrimination statutes protecting homosexuals, bisexuals, and transgender people.

Marriage

Russia does not recognize same-sex marriage. A same-sex marriage was attempted in the early 1990s as a publicity stunt. More recently, an activist attempted to draw attention to the Russian family code by applying for a same-sex marriage license in Moscow. The activist claimed not to be gay himself, but merely a gay-rights supporter, further illustrating the difficulties inherent in identifying and developing LGBT communities in Russia.[46]

Speech and Association

Soviet deconstruction of public and private space had a tremendous effect on the formation of homosexual identities and communities in Russia. Under the tsarist regime, urban men were able to meet same-sex partners in local bathhouses (*banya*). However, once Communism took hold and the Soviet Union was established, these quasi-private spaces came under government control. The result of Communist regulation, as in many other areas of life under Soviet rule, was to force homosexuals to carve out semi-private spaces in public areas, such as public toilets, subway stations, and parks.[47]

Whereas some Western societies had access to forms of private space necessary for developing sustainable homosexual communities and organizations, this access was fundamentally impossible for Russians under Communist rule. All forms of private space became public under the eyes of the Communist party. To accommodate concentrated urban populations, most housing was converted to communal apartment living, known as a *kommunalka*. Russians were not even permitted to rent a hotel room without presenting a multitude of documents, including an internal passport, and obtaining special permission from a Communist Party bureaucrat.

With the advent of Communism, Russian LGBT citizens' identities were most often formed in secret. Public LGBT identities were the purview of the Communist party. The Soviet Union inherited Russian legal and medical prejudices of the late 19th century. Whereas, over time, Western societies developed tolerance-based legal and medical strategies to oppose discrimination, Communist Russia institutionalized pathology-based definitions of homosexual, bisexual, and transgender identities. Without an identity separated from Soviet ideology, LGBT Russians were unable to form social or advocacy organizations. Instead, Soviet ideology defined the LGBT community, often through imprisonment (for men) or psychological cures applied to women.[48]

In Leningrad, Olga Zhuk founded the Chaykovskiy Fund for Cultural Initiatives and Aid to Sexual Minorities. Closely aligned with the activist Moscow Union, Zhuk successfully advocated for the rights of Russian citizens imprisoned under article 121.1, convincing Russian prison officials to allow a visitation with these prisoners by a delegation of American activists.[49] As the end of the Soviet Union approached, tiny activist groups formed as far away as Siberia. On the whole, these smaller groups were extremely short lived, accomplishing little in comparison to the more organized groups in Moscow and Leningrad. No Russian group could properly organize and advocate without official state recognition, which was never granted, and by the time the Soviet Union collapsed, so did the few Russian LGBT organizations.

As in the West, the ability to hold public gatherings such as parades is an integral part of LGBT community building. Furthermore, like past Western governmental opposition to gay pride parades and festivals, this has been strongly manifested in modern-day Russia. Russia's capital city, Moscow, is the most public modern battleground in the effort to establish LGBT rights to free association.

On May 27, 2006, gay rights activists, led by Nicholas Alexeyev, attempted to conduct the first gay pride parade in Moscow, and the first such event in Russia. Moscow mayor Yuri Luzhkov refused the group permission to march, on the grounds that it was offensive to Russian values and would provoke violence. Mayor Luzhkov's ongoing criticism of homosexuality and a hostile police presence resulted in brutal attacks on the activists by skinheads, and the arrest of 120 people.[50] Parade organizers filed a legal challenge to Moscow's ban on sexual minorities' parades. In August 2006, Moscow's Taganka court validated the ban within the city's Central Administrative District prefecture. Subsequent organizer appeals fared no better, and attempts to change the parade's location within Moscow were met with additional bans.

In November 2006, the Moscow Central Prefecture Court upheld Moscow's gay pride parade ban on the grounds that security concerns were sufficient to deny a parade permit. The organizer's final appeal was denied in June 2006, when the Supreme Court of the Russian Federation upheld the ban. The court found that the ban was legal under both Russian law and the European Convention on Human Rights, due to the government's interest in protecting public safety and security. A second attempt to hold a gay pride parade in May 2007 was also blocked by Moscow mayor Yuri Luzhkov. Activists attempted to march in defiance of the ban, and were met by physical attacks and arrests, repeating the events of May 2006.

RELIGION AND SPIRITUALITY

Since the collapse of the Soviet Union, the Russian Orthodox Church has enjoyed a recent resurgence in membership and political influence within Russia. In particular, the church condemns homosexual behavior as perverted and sinful. The church's influence in Russian homosexual life became more pronounced as it vigorously opposed the recently attempted LGBT parade in Moscow.

VIOLENCE

Accurate statistical evidence regarding violence against the LGBT community in Russia is difficult, if not impossible, to uncover. International LGBT rights organizations have documented the consistent hostility faced by the LGBT community, which occasionally escalated into raw hatred and severe violence. As most Russians consider homosexuality to be a perversion, there are no social disincentives that serve to prevent violence against homosexuals. In fact, antigay discrimination and its concurrent violent byproduct are considered by some to be traditional aspects of Russian history and culture.

OUTLOOK FOR THE 21ST CENTURY

Recent political and economic developments have made it extremely difficult to determine with any accuracy the future of the LGBT community in Russia. As recently as 2004, the Russian duma (parliament) considered a proposal by ultranationalist leader of the Liberal Democratic Party, Vladimir Zhirinovsky, to introduce the death penalty for sodomy. No further action was taken by the duma, but that such a proposal would be made indicates a dangerous atmosphere in which to conduct LGBT activism.

The upheaval and mild liberalization of the mid-1990s parallels earlier moments in Russian history, which brought about exuberant social changes. However, Russian history is replete with pronounced, nationalistic backlashes against any liberalizing forces. Any deviation from the historical self-image of an aggressive, independent, and self-sufficient Russian state may be confronted with violence and abuse. The best opportunity for an LGBT community to thrive in Russia is to operate within the parameters of the Russian historical psyche. Liberation of LGBT Russian people will be a long, slow process proceeding well into the 21st century.

RESOURCE GUIDE

Suggested Reading

Laurie Essig, *Queer in Russia: A Story of Sex, Self, and the Other* (Durham, NC: Duke University Press, 1999).

Dan Healey, *Homosexual Desire in Revolutionary Russia: The Regulation of Sexual and Gender Dissent* (Chicago: University of Chicago Press, 2001).

Daniel P. Schluter, *Gay Life in the Former USSR: Fraternity without Community* (New York: Routledge, 2002).

David Tuller, *Cracks in the Iron Closet: Travels in Gay and Lesbian Russia* (London: Faber and Faber, 1996).

Video/Film

Kiev Blue (1992). Directed by Heather MacDonald.
    Documentary about gay men and lesbians in pre-coup Kiev.
To My Women Friends (1993). Directed by Natalia Sharandak.
    Frameline. Six Russian lesbians discuss issues that touch their lives.
Moscow Fags [*Moskovskie golubye*] (25 min.; 1995). Directed by Iakov Poselski.
    Underground documentary about U.S.-Russian gay couples and the harsh realities of gay life in Russia.
Creation of Adam [*Sotvorenie Adama*]. Facets Video.
    Heterosexual marriage faces trouble when the husband is perceived to be gay.
Hammer and Sickle (1994). Directed by Sergei Livnev.
    Transgendered social fantasy about a woman transformed into a man by a Soviet experiment.
You I Love (2004). Directed by Ol'ga Stolpovskaya and Dmitry Troitsky.
    Bisexual love triangle in modern Moscow.
Far from Sunset Boulevard (2006). Directed by Igor' Minaev, *unreleased*.
    Love triangle involving famous Soviet filmmakers in a gay relationship.
Pushkin: The Last Duel (2006). Directed by Natalia Bondarchuk.
    Homophobic conspiracy film about the man who killed Pushkin in a duel.

Web Sites

Gay.ru, http://www.gay.ru.
    News and resource information for LGBT Russians. Includes English translations of some articles.

GayRussia.ru, http://www.gayrussia.ru.

> News and resource information for LGBT Russians.

Gay Russian Culture, http://community.middlebury.edu/~moss/RGC.html.

> Academic overview of modern Russian LGBT cultural issues.

Infoshare.ru, http://www.inforshare.ru.

> Russian HIV/AIDS health portal.

Poz.ru, http://www.poz.ru/.

> Extensive health and social service resources for HIV+ Russians.

UNAIDS, The Joint United Nations Programme on HIV in the Russian Federation, http://www.unaids.ru/.

> News and organizational resources for the United Nations' HIV/AIDS health programs in Russia.

NOTES

1. CIA, "Russia," *World Factbook,* https://www.cia.gov/library/publications/the-world-factbook/geos/rs.html (accessed November 12, 2007).

2. World Bank, "Country Brief 2008, Russian Federation," http://web.worldbank.org/WBSITE/EXTERNAL/COUNTRIES/ECAEXT/RUSSIANFEDERATIONEXTN/0,contentMDK:21054807~menuPK:517666~pagePK:1497618~piPK:217854~theSitePK:305600,00.html (accessed May 29, 2008).

3. Jeanne Sahadi, "Moscow Remains the World's Most Expensive City while London Moves Up from Fifth to Second Place," CNNMoney.com, http://money.cnn.com/2007/06/15/pf/most_expensive_cities/index.htm.

4. See http://www.globalsecurity.org/military/world/russia/mo-budget.htm.

5. Federation of American Scientists, "Status of Nuclear Powers and their Nuclear Capabilities," http://www.fas.org/nuke/guide/summary.htm.

6. CIA, "Russia."

7. Ibid.

8. Sergey Solovyov, *History of Russia from the Earliest Times* (AST, 2001), 562–604.

9. Vadim Erlikman, *Poteri narodonaseleniia v XX veke: spravochnik* (2004).

10. Daniel P. Schulter, *Gay Life in the Former USSR: Fraternity without Community* (New York: Routledge, 2002), 118.

11. Laurie Essig, *Queer in Russia: A Story of Sex, Self, and the Other* (Durham: Duke University Press, 1999), 6.

12. Cathy Young, "Anti-Gay Russia: Why Is a Former Communist Country so Homophobic?" 2007, http://www.reason.com/news/show/120638.html.

13. Dan Healey, *Homosexual Desire in Revolutionary Russia: The Regulation of Sexual and Gender Dissent* (Chicago: University of Chicago Press, 2001), 106.

14. Healey, *Homosexual Desire in Revolutionary Russia,* 247; Daniel P. Schulter, *Gay Life in the Former USSR: Fraternity without Community* (New York: Routledge, 2002), 129–30.

15. Schulter, *Gay Life in the Former USSR,* 130.

16. UNAIDS (Joint United Nations Programme on HIV/AIDS), "Report on the Global AIDS Epidemic," 2006, http://www.unaids.org/en/HIV_data/2006GlobalReport/default.asp.

17. Ibid.

18. Poz.ru, "Sait dlya lyudei, zhivushihk s VICH/SPIDom novosti" ["A News Web Site for People Living with HIV/AIDS"], http://www.poz.ru.

19. UNAIDS, "AIDS Epidemic Update," 2007, http://www.unaids.org/en/HIV_data/2007EpiUpdate/default.asp; 2007_epiupdate_en.pdf.

20. V. Andrey, "Saint Petersburg had Most HIV Cases so far in 2007," Gay.ru, 2007, http://english.gay.ru/news/rainbow/2007/09/21–11022.htm.

21. UNAIDS, "AIDS Epidemic Update."

22. UNAIDS, "2008 Progress Reports Submitted by Countries," http://data.unaids.org/pub/Report/2008/russia_2008_country_progress_report_ru.pdf.

23. Avert.org, "HIV/AIDS in Russia, Eastern Europe and Central Asia," http://www.avert.org/ecstatee.htm.

24. UNAIDS and the Joint United Nations Programme on HIV in the Russian Federation, "Learn about it at Work: Summing up HIV/AIDS Education Programme in Russia," 2008, http://www.unaids.ru/en/presscenter/news/2008/03/20/.

25. Laurie Essig, *Queer in Russia: A Story of Sex, Self, and the Other* (Durham, NC: Duke University Press, 1999), 29.

26. Essig, *Queer in Russia*, 29.

27. Healey, *Homosexual Desire in Revolutionary Russia*, 248.

28. Essig, *Queer in Russia*, 38.

29. Healey, *Homosexual Desire in Revolutionary Russia*, 22.

30. Essig, *Queer in Russia*, 4.

31. Schulter, *Gay Life in the Former USSR*, 119.

32. Ibid., 120.

33. See foreignlawguide.org.

34. Essig, *Queer in Russia*, 6.

35. Healey, *Homosexual Desire in Revolutionary Russia*, 97–98.

36. Schulter, *Gay Life in the Former USSR*, 122–23.

37. Essig, *Queer in Russia*, 6.

38. Ibid., 8.

39. Ibid.

40. Schulter, *Gay Life in the Former USSR*, 123.

41. Healey, *Homosexual Desire in Revolutionary Russia*, 249.

42. Essig, *Queer in Russia*, 13.

43. Healey, *Homosexual Desire in Revolutionary Russia*, 95.

44. Essig, *Queer in Russia*, 14.

45. Healey, *Homosexual Desire in Revolutionary Russia*, 250.

46. See http://www.gay.com/news/article.html?2005/01/18/4.

47. Healey, *Homosexual Desire in Revolutionary Russia*, ch. 1.

48. Essig, *Queer in Russia*, ch. 2.

49. Schulter, *Gay Life in the Former USSR*, 131.

50. Peter Finn, "Moscow's First Gay Pride Parade Disrupted by Police and Hecklers," *Washington Post Foreign Service,* May 28, 2006, http://www.washingtonpost.com/wp-dyn/content/article/2006/05/27/AR2006052701002.html.

SLOVENIA

Roman Kuhar

OVERVIEW

Slovenia has a population of two million[1] and is located in southern central Europe. It shares borders with Italy, Austria, Hungary, Croatia, and the Adriatic Sea to the southwest. After Finland and Sweden, Slovenia is the third most forested country in Europe, as around one-half of the country is covered by forests. The total area of Slovenia is a little more than 7,700 square miles, which is slightly smaller than New Jersey.[2]

In the seventh century, the Slavic Duchy of Carantania was established in the territory of the present day Slovenia. The Habsburgs took over most of this territory in the 14th century, and the area remained under their rule for over 600 years, until the end of the World War I.

In the 16th century, the Reformation movement established the foundations of the Slovene literary language. In 1550, the first two books in the Slovenian language—*Catechism* and *Abecedary*—were published by the Protestant Primož Trubar (his image is now commemorated on the Slovenian 1 euro coin). Thirty-four years later, the first Slovenian translation of the Bible was published. Even though most Protestants were expelled from Slovenian lands in the beginning of the 17th century, when the Catholic Church suppressed Protestantism by burning books in the Slovenian language, the importance of the Reformation for the Slovenian culture is indubitable.

Empress Maria Theresa introduced compulsory primary education in the territory of present-day Slovenia in

1774. After the short-lived Napoleonic rule between 1809 and 1813, Slovenian land became part of the Austrian empire and later, in 1867, the Austro-Hungarian monarchy. In 1848, a movement aiming at the political unification of all Slovenes emerged as part of the Spring of the Nations movement, but the idea was never implemented. After World War I, Slovenes joined the Kingdom of Serbs, Croats, and Slovenes, which was renamed the Kingdom of Yugoslavia in 1929 (Yugoslavia meaning "the country of South Slavs"). After World War II, Slovenia became part of the new Yugoslavia, which broke up with the Soviet Union in 1948 and introduced its own specific version of socialism, based on common property (private property had been nationalized by 1947) and self-management. In 1963, Yugoslavia became known as the Socialist Federal Republic of Yugoslavia, which was comprised of six federal republics (Croatia, Serbia, Bosnia, Macedonia, Montenegro, and Slovenia) and two autonomous provinces, Vojvodina and Kosovo. In the context of former Yugoslavia, Slovenia was known for its high level of economic development. In 1990, its gross domestic product (GDP) was two times higher than the state average.[3]

After the public referendum in December of 1990, when over 88 percent of Slovenian citizens voted in favor of it, Slovenian independence was declared on June 25, 1991. The next day, Slovenia was attacked by the Yugoslav army, but a truce was called after 10 days (the conflict is now known as 10-day war for independence). The European Union (EU) recognized Slovenia in 1992, when it also became a member of the United Nations.

In 2004, Slovenia joined the EU and NATO. In 2007, it joined eurozone[4] and adopted the euro, becoming the first transition country in the European Union to introduce the euro as a national currency. In 2008, Slovenia was the first postsocialist country to hold the Presidency of the Council of the EU.

Unlike some postsocialist countries, Slovenia did not suffer from extensive social differentiation after the transformation from a communist to a capitalist system at the beginning of the 1990s. Its relatively good economic situation within the former Yugoslavia helped to quickly accommodate it to the world market economy and to begin significant economic growth. Today, Slovenia has around 91 percent of the EU average gross domestic product (GDP) per capita. According to the Global Competitiveness Index 2007–2008, which measures the level of prosperity the country offers to its citizens, Slovenia ranks 39th among 131 countries in the world.[5]

According to the 2002 census, 83 percent of the population identifies as Slovenian, followed by nearly 2 percent identifying as Serbs, 2 percent Croats, and 1 percent Bosnians. According to the same census, 58 percent of the population self-declares as Roman Catholic. Other religious groups include Islam (2.4%), Eastern Orthodox (2.3%), and Protestant (0.8%). Ten percent of the population self-declared as atheist.[6]

The political transition and the introduction of democracy in the 1990s did not automatically establish a better position for the LGBT population in Slovenia. Even though homosexuality was criminalized until 1976 (the punishment was one year of imprisonment), there are no known cases of legal prosecution of homosexuals since the early 1950s. The 1980s saw the beginning of a vibrant gay culture and LGBT movement. Even though their political demands were not met, the socialist government did not try to prevent or ban the movement. However, the introduction of democracy and a quest to respect EU standards on human rights—as part of the process of preparation for joining the EU—offered new opportunities for the gay and lesbian movement. Still, with better visibility of the gay and lesbian minority, the 1990s also saw the raise of hate speech, homophobia, and increased ostracism of homosexuals. According to the Slovenian public opinion polls during the 1990s and early 2000s, some 55 percent of Slovenian citizens did not want a homosexual to be their neighbor. That percentage dropped to 35 percent in 2005.[7]

OVERVIEW OF LGBT ISSUES

The Slovenian gay and lesbian movement started in 1984. In April of that year, the first festival of gay culture, Magnus (after Magnus Hirschfeld, the German sexologist), was organized in the capital city of Ljubljana. Today, the festival is known as the Ljubljana Gay and Lesbian Film Festival.

In December 1984, the first Slovenian gay organization was established. Together with feminist, peace, and other movements, the gay movement became an important part of the new social movements of the 1980s in Slovenia. Like the festival, the organization was called Magnus. In 1987 the first Slovenian lesbian organization, LL (which stands for Lesbian Lilith), was established. These were the first gay and lesbian organizations in former Yugoslavia and in eastern Europe.

Despite the fact that they originated in Slovenia, they both had an impact on a broader cultural and political level in the former Yugoslavia. They helped to relocate the issue of homosexuality from the medical context of the 1970s and early 1980s to a cultural and political context. For example, in 1986, Magnus issued a public manifesto demanding an amendment to the Yugoslav constitution so that discrimination on the basis of sexual orientation would be prohibited. They also demanded that homosexuality be decriminalized in Serbia, Bosnia, and Macedonia, and that the Yugoslav government should stage a protest against Romania, the Soviet Union, Cuba, Iran, and other countries where homosexuals were persecuted at the time. None of their requests were fulfilled. However, such interventions into the political sphere contributed to increased attention to the LGBT community from the media and the general public.

Homosexuality became a household issue in 1987, when the fourth annual festival of gay culture was supposed to take place in Ljubljana. It was scheduled to start on May 25, which was late Yugoslavian president Tito's birthday (Marshal Tito died in 1980). The Serbian and Bosnian media took this fact as another Slovenian provocation and proclaimed that a world festival of queers would take place in Ljubljana.[8] A scandal erupted, and under pressure from the Yugoslav government, the local Slovenian government issued a public statement, saying that the organization of such a festival would represent a threat to a healthy society. Homosexuals were thought to be solely responsible for the spread of AIDS. While the festival was never officially banned, the gay organization decided to prepare workshops on safe sex instead. In a broader context, homosexuality was abused as a tool of political revenge between Ljubljana and Belgrade—at the time Slovenia was already suspected of having aspirations to exit from the Yugoslav federation.

Another notorious scandal occurred in 2001 when two gay poets—Slovenian Brane Mozetič and Canadian Jean-Paul Daoust—were stopped at the bar Café Galerija. The bouncer prevented them from entering the bar, which used to be known as gay friendly. He said, "they should get used to the fact that this pub is not for *that kind* of people."[9] The scandal—widely reported on in the media—led to the organization of the first gay pride parade in Ljubljana in July 2001.

It was primarily through such scandals, which resulted in extensive media coverage, that the general public in Slovenia became acquainted with the homosexual minority.

With the diversification of the media in the 1990s, when the change of the political system contributed to the emergence of new newspapers and magazines, the frequency of media reports on homosexuality intensified. While there were a few more than 80 articles published on homosexuality in the Slovenian media from 1980 to 1990, the '90s saw hundreds of articles on the topic.[10] In media representations, gays and lesbians became normal citizens, just like anyone else. The normal image—a step forward, but not necessarily an unproblematic one—was reinforced by global gay images: *Ellen, Will and Grace, Queer as Folk,* and other television shows with gay and lesbian characters were all shown on Slovenian national television or commercial channels.

The issue of nondiscrimination on the basis of sexual orientation and the debate on same-sex registered partnership intensified in the process of preparing to join the EU. The transposition of EU directives forced Slovenian legislators to introduce several antidiscrimination provisions, including on the ground of sexual orientation.

EDUCATION

In 1980, health education was introduced into the secondary school curriculum. According to the health education textbook, teachers should briefly address homosexuality under the chapter "Unusual Sexual Behavior" along with exhibitionism, fetishism, promiscuity, prostitution, incest, and rape.[11]

At the time, the guidelines for teachers provided by the Ministry of Education explicitly stated that the goal of health education is "to bring a young person towards a satisfactory heterosexual partnership."[12]

The short chapter on homosexuality in the health education textbook changed slightly over the years. At first, homosexuality was defined as the "result of a wrong education."[13] Since 1988, the textbook has claimed that "there is no proof that homosexuals are severely unadjusted" and that one should get rid of any prejudices about homosexuality.

In 1991, with the reform of the public school system, health education was removed from secondary schools and no substituting course was introduced. Since then, it has been up to the teacher to start a debate on homosexuality. According to recent research, slightly more than 79 percent of gays and lesbians surveyed do not recall homosexuality being discussed in schools, or if it was, not much was said about the topic. Eighteen percent of those who remember homosexuality being discussed reported that discussion was mainly negative toward homosexuality.[14]

Another channel through which debate on homosexuality entered secondary schools was courses conducted by extracurricular teachers, such as representatives of nongovernmental organizations (NGOs). In 1998–1999, the Association against Violent Communication conducted a series of lectures on nonviolence and tolerance in several secondary schools in Ljubljana. The set of lectures consisted of one lecture on homosexuality, which was conducted by a gay man who came out of the closet during the lecture. After one of these lectures, four parents complained to the headmaster that the school was agitating for homosexuality. The headmaster therefore asked the Association against Violent Communication to remove the lecture on homosexuality from their list. The association refused to do so, but the set of lectures was no longer requested by any of the secondary schools in Ljubljana.[15]

In the contemporary curriculum for the compulsory nine-year elementary schools (introduced in 2003–2004), homosexuality is not explicitly mentioned, except in one instance. In the fifth grade society course, pupils are supposed to learn about differences among people in society, which include differences in gender, age, religion, ethnic origin, social and cultural differences, and sexual orientation. Still, the textbooks for this course do not address sexual orientation. Similarly, textbooks do not address same-sex families in their discussion of different types of families.

In the past few years, several NGOs have produced didactic tools such as CD-ROMs and booklets for teachers aimed at facilitating classroom discussions on homosexuality. Sporadically, an NGO (such as the LGBT organization Legebitra or Amnesty International Slovenia) would be invited to prepare a workshop on homosexuality for the secondary school pupils, but most of the schools still fear that talking about homosexuality is promoting it, or they do not see any need for such discussions.

Gay bashing in the school setting is not often discussed or even recognized. However, according to recent research, nearly 23 percent of gays and lesbians who have already suffered violence due to their sexual orientation (53% of the entire sample) mentioned that perpetrators of the violent acts were schoolmates. They were ridiculed, teased, insulted, or avoided altogether, and 10 percent mentioned being physically beaten in school because of their sexuality.[16]

EMPLOYMENT AND ECONOMICS

Slovenia had a relatively prosperous economy before gaining independence in 1991. Although the population of Slovenia represented a 13th of the total population of Yugoslavia, the Slovenian economy accounted for one-fifth of Yugoslavia's total GDP and one-third of Yugoslavia's export at the time.[17] Since independence and transformation to a market economy, the country has enjoyed economic stability.

Among the 10 countries that joined the EU in May 2004, Slovenia had the highest GDP per capita. The fact that inflation declined from nearly 200 percent in 1992 to 2.3 percent in 2006 helped contribute to the opening of the eurozone for Slovenia in 2007. The employment rate in August 2007 was 7.4 percent. More women (9.3%) than men (5.9%) are unemployed.[18]

In 2002, the Employment Relationship Act was adopted, transposing the EU directive on nondiscrimination in the workplace. The act explicitly prohibits discrimination on the grounds of sexual orientation in any place of employment. While the latter includes the military (gay men and women may serve in the armed forces), religious institutions are exempt. The latest Vatican prohibition (2005) on "active homosexuals and supporters of gay culture" becoming priests applies to Slovenia as well.

There are no officially documented cases of discrimination on the grounds of sexual orientation in Slovenia. This can be attributed to the fact that many gays and lesbians are not out in the workplace or would not report such discrimination. According to the latest research, 50 percent of gays and lesbians are not out at work, or they have come out to only one or two coworkers.[19] Gays and lesbians fear insults, ridicule, and the obstruction of promotion or even dismissal from work. The same research showed that one percent of people surveyed reported explicit discrimination in the workplace, and five percent reported implicit discrimination due to their homosexuality.[20]

The nongovernmental initiatives to fight discrimination in the workplace (such as Škuc LL's Partnership for Equality[21]) showed that trade unions and employers are often not aware that implicit or explicit discrimination on the grounds of sexual orientation is taking place. Several manuals were produced in order to inform trade unions and employers about the problem. As part of the same project, the first television advertisement calling attention to the discrimination against gays and lesbians in the workplace was aired in 2007 on national television and some other channels.[22]

There are also some examples of good workplace practices. A few companies— such as Telekom Slovenia (a telephone company) and RTV Slovenia (a national broadcasting company)—introduced antidiscrimination measures on the basis of sexual orientation in their internal codes of practice.[23]

SOCIAL/GOVERNMENT PROGRAMS

There are no specific governmental programs in Slovenia aimed at the LGBT community. Exceptions are the occasional AIDS and STD-related programs (programs concerning sexually transmitted diseases), which are aimed at either the general public or specifically at men who have sex with men (MSM). Nevertheless, national and local governments do fund LGBT NGOs through their social, health, antidiscrimination, and similar programs. Another source of funding comes from the EU programs. As of 2007, each taxpayer can allocate 0.5 percent of his or her tax return to the NGO of his or her choice.

In 2007, the LGBT organization Legebitra sued the Ministry of Work, Family, and Social Affairs, claiming that their application for the funding of preventive programs for children and youth was rejected for homophobic reasons. The court ruled in favor of Legebitra.[24]

SEXUALITY/SEXUAL PRACTICES

The most comprehensive research on sexual behavior and the sexual practices of Slovenian citizens has been conducted by Irena Klavs in 1999–2001 on a sample of 1,752 respondents aged 18 to 49. Male respondents (median value) had the first sexual intercourse at the age of 17 and women at the age of 18. About two percent of female respondents and seven percent of male respondents had their first sexual intercourse before the age of 15. In the past five years women on average had 1.5 heterosexual partners and men 3.2 heterosexual partners. The median value of sexual partners in a lifetime is two for women and four for men. About 28 percent of male respondents and a bit less than 6 percent of female respondents reported 10 or more sexual partners in their lifetime. About 34 percent of women and 32 percent of men did not use any contraception methods during their first sexual intercourse. About 32 percent of men and 22 percent of women reported having had heterosexual anal intercourse at least once. Twelve percent of women reported having been forced into sexual intercourse at least once in their lifetime and 4.4 percent of men reported having paid for sex with a woman. One percent of male respondents and 0.9 percent of female respondents reported having had a sexual experience or contact with a person of the same sex.[25]

Recent research among secondary school students aged 17 and 18 on the topic of their first sexual experience[26] showed that the average age for a first sexual encounter is 15.9 for women and 15.5 for men. However, 45 percent of those in the sample had not yet had any sexual experiences. The research also found that self-declared religiosity is negatively correlated to number of sexual experiences; those adolescents who are more religious have fewer sexual experiences. More women (80%) experienced their first sexual intercourse with a steady partner compared to men (60%). This also explains why significantly more male (44%) than female (17%) respondents reported having had their first sexual experience during the summer holidays. Some 55 percent of respondents used birth control (including coitus interruptus) during their first sexual intercourse, which is less than what similar research on youth in western European countries has shown.[27]

Prostitution in Slovenia was decriminalized in 2003. From the 1970s on it was legally defined as a lesser offense against public order. The first initiatives to decriminalize prostitution came in the 1980s, but the issue was more seriously tackled only in the 1990s, when prostitution started to flourish with the growth of nightclubs.[28] Currently, the most widespread forms of prostitution are cell phone prostitution, apartment prostitution, and classical hotel and bar prostitution.[29] There is no street prostitution in Slovenia.[30]

No research on the sexual behavior or sexual practices of LGBT people has been conducted in Slovenia.

FAMILY

In family composition, Slovenia generally follows western European trends. While the traditional nuclear family is still prevalent, it is on the decline. According to the 2002 census, nuclear families represented 53 percent of all family types (a 6% decrease compared to the 1991 census, and a 10% decrease compared to the 1981 census). The number of unmarried couples with children increased from 2.2 percent in 1991 to 5 percent in 2002. Every fifth family in Slovenia is a single parent family—in 86 percent of cases the parent is a mother.[31]

Despite the diversification of family forms, the Resolution on the Foundations of Family Policy, adopted by the government in 1993, does not reflect this diversity. Even though the resolution recognizes different types of families, it is aimed at preserving the traditional nuclear family. Same-sex families are not mentioned or addressed in the resolution.

The number of marriages has decreased since 1972, when 9 people per 1,000 were married. The marriage rate had dropped by nearly three times by 2006. On the other hand, the age at which individuals first get married is increasing. In 1972 a bride was 24 years old on average (and 30 years old in 2006), while the average age of a groom was 27.5 in 1972 and 32.8 in 2006.[32] The number of divorces is also increasing. In 1972 there were nearly 117 divorces per 1,000 marriages. In 2006 this number increased to nearly 367. However, 2006 saw the first decrease in the number of divorces (a 13% decrease) in 10 years. The divorce rate in 2006 was 1.2 divorced people per 1,000 inhabitants, which places Slovenia among the European countries with the lowest divorce rates (with Greece, Italy, and Ireland).[33]

There are no official statistics on homosexual families in Slovenia. Recent research has shown that some 40 percent of gays and lesbians surveyed would like to have children, 38 percent do not want to have children, and the rest do not know or cannot decide. When asked how they want to have a child, adoption was the most often mentioned possibility.[34]

While gays and lesbians can theoretically adopt children in Slovenia (as single people, not as same-sex couples), in practice this is not common. The number of children available for adoption is much lower than the number of heterosexual couples wanting to adopt. On average, there are 30 children adopted per year, while 250 heterosexual couples are waiting for adoption. Another option is foster parenting. In 2007, there were 1,189 children in foster care. While fostering is not explicitly prohibited for homosexuals, there are no publicly known gay foster families.

For lesbian couples, artificial insemination is one of the most common ways to have children. However, since 2001, medically assisted insemination has not officially been available for single women or women who are not in a heterosexual partnership. Since 1977, when the first medically assisted insemination was performed in Slovenia, the Health Measures in Exercising Freedom of Choice in Childbearing Act granted the right to artificial insemination to all adult women. In 1994, a committee of genealogists decided to stop performing medically assisted insemination, as the 1977 act was outdated and did not address new technical and medical advancements in artificial insemination. An amended act on medically assisted insemination was prepared by 1999 and adopted by the parliament in 2000. The new act did not grant the right to artificial insemination to all women. Instead only women who are either married or are living in a heterosexual relationship and need artificial insemination for medical reasons are now entitled to procedures of fertilization with medical assistance. In 2001, the act was brought to the subsequent legislative public referendum, but a majority of Slovenian citizens confirmed the parliament's decision to exclude single women from being entitled to artificial insemination. One of the key arguments used in the public debate was the fear that lesbians might want to exercise this right and get artificially inseminated.

At present, same-sex marriages are not allowed, nor are joint adoptions by same-sex couples or second-parent adoptions.

COMMUNITY

The gay and lesbian movement in Slovenia lived through a condensed adolescence. While similar movements in the West gradually progressed from assimilation movements toward identity and queer politics, the gay and lesbian movement in Slovenia established itself by immediately demanding political equality, skipping the assimilation phase.

In Slovenia, there are no gay or lesbian districts or quarters. The gay and lesbian social life is organized around two clubs in the autonomous cultural zone, *Metelkova mesto,* in the capital, Ljubljana (Tiffany, the gay club, and Monokel, the lesbian club). *Metelkova mesto* was a military barracks of the former Yugoslav army. Nowadays, it is the center of alternative culture in Ljubljana.

Other referential points for the gay and lesbian community are the gay-friendly bar Café Open and the disco club K4. Since the early 1980s, Sundays (and more recently also Saturday nights) in K4 are known as Roza K4—a disco for gays and lesbians.

An annual meeting point for the gay and lesbian community is the gay and lesbian film festival, which takes place in Ljubljana every December. It has been operating for 25 years, which makes it the oldest LGBT film festival in central and eastern Europe.

There is no such gay and lesbian infrastructure in other towns in Slovenia.

The infrastructure of the community has been constantly developing. While certain initiatives have died out over the years (for example, a gay and lesbian magazine called *Revolver*), new ones are turning up. Nowadays, there are five LGBT organizations in Slovenia (Magnus, LL, Legebitra, Dih, and Lingsium). In 2007, Galfon, the gay and lesbian telephone helpline, ceased to operate after 12 years, but it has now been replaced by two other help and counseling centers and telephone lines (operating within Legebitra and Dih). There is a gay book series, *Škuc-Lambda,* and a lesbian book series, *Škuc-Vizibilija,* where Slovenian and translated LGBT prose, poetry, and theory are published.

An important LGBT resource is the Lesbian Library (operating under LL). There are also several media initiatives: the radio show *Lesbomania* (broadcast on Radio Študent) and the magazine *Narobe.*

In the past few years, the virtual gay and lesbian community has grown extensively. There are several LGBT forums available—while some of them are general, several are more specific (only for women, for gay parents, and so forth).

None of these initiatives are commercial in nature. It seems that investing money into gay- and lesbian-related private businesses is still too risky or too stigmatized. However, there are two commercial initiatives in Slovenia: a gay sauna called Gymnasivm, and gay-owned accommodations in Ljubljana and Piran.

There are also several initiatives and self-help groups for HIV-positive people. Some of them are not exclusively gay.

Most of these initiatives depend on the volunteer work of activists, of which there are not many.

HEALTH

Slovenia has a universal health care system with a compulsory insurance scheme. The system was reformed in 1992, when the Health Insurance Institute of Slovenia was established as a nonprofit institute. It operates with compulsory health insurance, which replaced previous direct funding from the Ministry of Health to primarily employment-based financing. On the other hand, the reform also enabled privatization of parts of the public health network.[35] Even though the Slovenian health system is generally considered good, some experts warn that the progressive privatization and commercialization of health services is potentially damaging for the health care system.[36]

AIDS is not considered a major health concern. Since 1986, when the first two HIV-positive patients were recorded in Slovenia, 349 people have been identified as having the HIV virus. In 136 of the cases, full-blown AIDS has already developed, and 78 people have died because of AIDS-related diseases. The actual number of HIV-positive people is probably higher, as only 1.3 people per 100 were tested in 2006.[37]

MSM represent over 85 percent of all HIV-positive people. There are also some HIV-positive people among intravenous drug users. However, due to prevention programs originating in the early 1990s (including information and the distribution of needles) this group has low levels of HIV infection.

Slovenia remains among the countries with a low incidence of HIV/AIDS, with fewer than 1 HIV-positive person per 1,000 inhabitants. However, the number of newly identified HIV-positive people has doubled in recent years (from an average of 15 to 35 new infections in 2005 and 2006). Experts mention cheap airfare and the Internet (both of which have facilitated sexual contacts), homophobia, and the lack of prevention programs in recent years as the reasons for the increase in HIV infection. Still, according to the World Health Organization (WHO), the risk of an explosive spread of the HIV virus in Slovenia is low.[38]

Retrovirus treatment is available to all HIV-positive people. The expenses are covered by compulsory health insurance.

In 1983, the federal Commission for Aids was established in the former Yugoslavia. In 1985, the first prevention program was adopted, HIV testing started, and the gay organization Magnus published the first informative leaflet on AIDS, titled "Everything You Ever Wanted to Know about AIDS, but Were Afraid to Ask." In the following years, a variety of information leaflets, posters, television advertisements, school prevention programs, and prevention actions were organized by NGOs, student organizations, and governmental institutions.

Since 1986, all donated blood has been tested for HIV, and there has been no recorded case of HIV transmission through blood donation. However, MSM are still not allowed to donate blood in Slovenia.

The first nationwide campaign on safe sex and AIDS prevention was organized in 1988. Since 1989, the Clinic for Infection Diseases has performed free and anonymous testing for AIDS. The results are available four days after testing. Similar free testing is also available in other parts of Slovenia.

In 1996, the Ministry of Health established an expert group on AIDS, which also consisted of representatives of LGBT NGOs. Later that year, the national action plan against AIDS was adopted by the government. It aimed at reducing HIV infection, providing information on safe sex, and reducing the use of non-prescription drugs.

HIV-positive people are virtually invisible in Slovenia, and the stigma of HIV/AIDS is very high. According to the Slovenian public opinion poll from 2000, 46 percent of people surveyed would not want an HIV-positive person to be their neighbor.[39]

In recent years there have been several scandals connected to AIDS. When the fourth Magnus cultural festival in 1987 was notoriously presented as a world festival of queers in the Bosnian and Serbian media, one of the concerns was that gay people from abroad would transmit AIDS to Slovenia and endanger a healthy society. In 1993, when Magnus issued the information leaflet "Sexuality and Aids," which featured naked male and female bodies without faces on its cover, several Catholic groups and organizations protested, claiming that such leaflets promote group sex and homosexuality. Professor Anton Dolenc from the medical school at the University of Ljubljana claimed that homosexuals are degenerates and "a dead bough on a tree of life."[40] The WHO later issued an opinion that the leaflet was not problematic.

The year 2004 saw the first AIDS patient come out on national television. However, the 24-year-old gay man lost his job the next day due to his HIV-positive status.

In 2005, one HIV-positive person was prevented from entering his flat when his neighbors learned that he was HIV-positive. He had to move to another town.

In the past few years, the number of other STDs, primarily chlamydia and human papilloma virus (HPV) infections, are remaining constant. The most affected group is MSM.[41]

POLITICS AND LAW

Article 186 of the Yugoslavian penal code criminalized "unnatural acts of unchastity between people of the male sex." Lesbian sex was never criminalized. The penalty for unnatural acts was three years of imprisonment. Later, in 1959, the penalty was reduced to one year. Homosexuality was decriminalized in Slovenia (and in Croatia and Montenegro) in 1976, but not in the other former Yugoslav republics. In the same year, the age of consent was set at 14 (and in 1999 to 15) for both heterosexual and homosexual relations. Janez Šinkovec, a supreme court judge in the Socialist Republic of Slovenia, had already called for the decriminalization of homosexuality in 1974, claiming that "intimate lives of adults, who don't hurt anyone by their actions, are truly their personal matters. There is no need for society to believe that it has a right to interfere in this area."[42]

As the Slovenian political sphere started to change at the end of the 1980s, expectations for democracy, human rights, and equality intensified. However, the first disappointment came with the first legal document of the independent Slovenia—its constitution. Article 14 of the constitution ensures legal equality as one of the basic human rights regardless of any personal circumstances. While race, gender, religion, national origin, and similar conditions are mentioned explicitly in the article, sexual orientation is not. While the liberal bloc called for the explicit protection of sexual orientation, right-wing conservative parties refused to support the article in such a form.

A compromise with the right-wing parties was worked out; sexual orientation was replaced by the term *personal circumstances*. Article 14 now reads: "In Slovenia everyone shall be guaranteed equal human rights and fundamental freedoms irrespective of national origin, race, sex, language, religion, political or other conviction, material standing, birth, education, social status, disability or any other personal circumstance."[43] The explanatory note to the constitution states that "personal circumstances" include sexual orientation.

The first explicit mention of sexual orientation in the Slovenian legal system came in 1995 with the adoption of an amended penal code. Discrimination on the grounds of sexual orientation is prohibited. With the amendments to the penal code in 2008, incitement to hatred or intolerance on the basis of sexual orientation, including hate speech, is also criminalized. Similar provisions are included in several other laws, primarily as a result of the obligatory transposition of the EU nondiscrimination directives into the national legislation. This is most notable in the Employment Relationship Act of 2002 and the Implementation of the Principle of Equal Treatment Act of 2004. The latter prohibits discrimination or harassment on the grounds of sexual orientation. The act stipulates that the government and self-governing local communities are responsible for providing the conditions for equal treatment regardless of—among other things—sexual orientation.

After continued public debate on same-sex partnership in the late 1990s, and after several initiatives to establish a legal framework for same-sex partnership—the first one dates to 1993—the Ministry of Labor, Family, and Social Affairs established an expert group for preparation of a bill in 1998. However, the bill was never sent to the parliament. In 2003, the same ministry, in cooperation with gay and lesbian organizations, prepared another bill. It proposed complete equalization of the rights of heterosexual and homosexual couples, with the exception of adoption rights. In 2004, the bill received the first of three readings in the parliament. However, after the parliamentary elections in autumn 2004 and the subsequent change of government, the new right-wing government rejected the 2003 bill. Instead, they prepared their own bill, which did not have support from the gay and lesbian organizations because they believed that the bill is discriminatory. The right-wing government, however, was not willing to consider annotations to the bill submitted by the left-wing parties and the gay and lesbian organizations. The legislation was passed on June 22, 2005, with two left-wing parties obstructing the vote.

Slovenia was the 18th country in Europe to introduce the regulation of same-sex partnerships into its legal system. It was also the first country in the world where such legislation was prepared and adopted on a national level by a conservative center-right-wing government.

The main deficiency of the act—which primarily regulates property relations between partners (inheritance rights)—is that it does not recognize the status of next of kin to the registered partners. As a result, registered same-sex partners are not considered close relatives. For that reason, they are not entitled to any rights deriving from social, health, pension, and other insurances. Registered partners also lack all other rights related to the status of next of kin, such as social and pension rights, disability benefits, adoption or parenting rights, and others. The only exception is the right to visit one's registered partner in a hospital and to decide upon his or her medical treatment if he or she is unable to do so. The law obliges the registered partners to take care of each other (for example, if one partner is ill), but it does not provide any rights for the implementation of these obligations (for example, a registered partner is not entitled to leave from work when his or her partner is ill, while heterosexual partners have such a right).

Another problem with the Same-sex Registered Partnership Act arises at a more symbolic level. The term *to register* is used in the Slovenian language for such activities as registering cars; it is not generally used when talking about humans. Additionally, same-sex partners are not allowed to be registered in wedding halls. The registration is instead reduced to a simple administrative procedure: signing the form at the counter of the administrative unit. In such a way, the legislators drew a clear symbolic and legal distinction between marriage and registered partnership.

Despite the downsides of the Same-sex Registered Partnership Act, it contributed to the recognition of same-sex partnership as a social institution. Several laws, adopted after the act, now recognize such unions as one form of partnership. For example, the recent bill on domestic violence (2007) explicitly states that family members include partners in registered partnership.

The gay and lesbian community has showed little interest in registered partnership as it is now enacted. Some gay and lesbian organizations have called on the LGBT community not to use the law, as it is discriminatory. About 20 same-sex couples have been registered since the adoption of the law, while research on the everyday lives of gays and lesbians—conducted before the act was passed—showed that 62 percent of gays and lesbians want to register their partnership for primarily pragmatic reasons (such as social security and tax relief) rather than for ideological reasons (registration as a sign of true love).[44] The low level of interest in the law is due to its emphasis on property relations rather than social, health, or other issues.

One registered gay couple, Mitja Blažič and Viki Kern, appealed to the constitutional court in 2006, claiming that the law is unconstitutional. In July 2009 the constitutional court ruled that the law is in fact unconstitutional as it puts registered same-sex partners and heterosexual partners on different footing in regard to inheritance rights. The parliament has to change this provision in six months time. The Minister of Labor, Family, and Social Affairs has already announced the modernization of the law. The aim of the current government is to completely equalize the rights of homosexual and heterosexual partners, including adoption rights (primarily the legal recognition of social parenting and the right to adopt a partner's child).

RELIGION AND SPIRITUALITY

The Roman Catholic Church, with 58 percent of the population being self-declared Catholics, is the most influential religious institution in Slovenia. It follows the Vatican's moral condemnation of homosexuality. Their official view is that some people are born gay, but their homosexuality is seen as a burden they have to carry through life, and on which they should not act. For the Slovenian Roman Catholic Church, homosexuality is a moral problem when it results in a sexual act. Or, as the Slovenian bishop Franc Kramberger claimed in one interview: "The Church cannot accept homosexuals, but it may never sentence them. The Church has to stand by them and help them get rid of their burden."[45] As recent research has shown, 30 percent of gays and lesbians are religious, and 51 percent of them belong to the Roman Catholic Church.[46]

After World War II, the Slovenian constitution introduced church-state separation. Before the war, the Roman Catholic Church played an important role in society. Its values were often presented as national values and, at least symbolically, membership in the church meant membership in the nation.

The introduction of Communism as a political system in Slovenia after the World War II further diminished the Church's influence, although the Catholic tradition was (and still is) embedded in the Slovenian value system and has managed to coexist throughout the socialist period.

The position of the Roman Catholic Church was revised in the beginning of the 1990s with the introduction of political pluralism in Slovenia. The church was enabled to launch its agenda, which aimed at reestablishing traditional values in Slovenian society. However, the rehabilitation of the Church was also accompanied by the secularization of Slovenian society. While nearly 72 percent of people declared themselves to be Roman Catholics in the 1991 census, the 2002 census showed that the number of self-declared Catholics had dropped by nearly 14 percent.[47]

One of the topics the Roman Catholic Church often plays on is the demographic situation in Slovenia. Basing their arguments in demographic statistics, they claim that the Slovenian nation is dying out. Therefore, the right to abortion (which is constitutionally granted) and homosexual rights are seen as contributing to the decline of the nation. Furthermore, supporting abortion and homosexual rights runs against theological teaching about sexuality and family. When the political and public debate on same-sex registered partnership reached its peak in 2003, church representatives often participated. For example, Archbishop Franc Rode addressed these issues in his sermon during the feast of the assumption in 2003, asking

> what is our attitude towards life? The birthrate is declining and endangers the existence of the nation. We are at the top of the scale by the number of suicides in the world. We act irresponsibly towards conceived lives, which are often ended by an abortion. The spread of drugs and other sorts of addiction is alarming. All of this signifies that we do not have a healthy approach to life. At the same time, the left-wing government, pressured by the overzealous ideologists, adopts more and more permissive legislation. It fosters public immorality and devaluates family, which is the only guarantor for the future of the nation.[48]

A few days later he commented on his sermon in a television interview, arguing that homosexuality is disgusting and claiming that same-sex unions are "harmful to society, since they destabilize family and accustom people, whose sexual identity is not clear, to such a determination."[49]

Not all church representatives' views are as radical as Rode's. Some of them did not oppose the legal recognition of same-sex partnership as long as the rights and obligations of same-sex partners were not equated with those of heterosexual partners and the institution was not called a marriage. They claimed that the state is obliged to protect the importance of family for the Slovenian nation. That means that what they have called the homosexual way of life should not be elevated to a social value. These views were later embedded in the 2005 bill on registered same-sex partnership.

VIOLENCE

The murder rate in Slovenia is 1.5 per 100,000 inhabitants.[50] Every year there are around 20 to 25 murders in Slovenia. Most of them take place within the family. Slovenia has a high rate of suicide—25 people per 100,000 inhabitants. This places Slovenia among the top 10 countries in the world in terms of suicides. Every year, around 600 people in Slovenia commit suicide.[51] There are 65 people in prison per 100,000 inhabitants, 4 percent of whom are women.[52]

None of these acts are officially known to be related to homosexuality. There are also no statistics available on gay bashing and hate crimes related to homosexuality. After several years of peaceful pride parades, gay bashing occurred after the pride parades in 2006 and 2007. However, few people were injured.

On the evening of June 25, 2009, the Slovenian Independence Day, a group of eight masked young men attacked about 30 people attending the gay and lesbian literature reading in the gay-friendly pub Café Open. They threw fire into the bar and physically injured gay activist Mitja Blažič, who was standing outside the bar at the moment of the attack. Besides Blažič, who was mildly injured, nobody suffered any physical injuries. The incident attracted huge media attention and politicians from the right- and the left-wing parties condemned the attack. As a sign of solidarity the Minister of the Interior Katarina Kresal marched in the Pride Parade, which took place two days after the attack. Within a week, three perpetrators were traced down by the police. The 18-, 21-, and 22-year-old men confessed with no regret to attacking Café Open. They face several years imprisonment.

Two available studies on violence against gays and lesbians in Slovenia pointed to high levels of violence and harassment on the basis of sexual orientation. Both studies showed that one in two respondents has already been the victim of violence due to his or her homosexuality.[53] The most common form of violence suffered by gays and lesbians is verbal violence (91% of gays and lesbians who reported having experienced violence due to homosexuality suffered from it), followed by physical violence (24%) and sexual assaults (6%). In 61 percent of cases the perpetrators of the violent act were strangers, and the violent acts often took place in public (such as in bars or on the street). The research also suggests that while the public sphere is the most dangerous for both gays and lesbians, the location of homophobic acts is also gendered: lesbians have experienced violence in private life more often than gays.[54]

The recent study on homophobic discrimination and violence showed that 92 percent of respondents who have suffered from homophobic violence have not reported the violence to the police. The main reason for not reporting is the minimizing of violence: about 36 percent of respondents claimed that the homophobic violence they had experienced had not been worth reporting, while 27 percent thought that reporting such violence made no sense.[55]

OUTLOOK FOR THE 21ST CENTURY

While most of the antidiscrimination legislation is already in place, the struggle for full marriage and the right to joint adoption will surely stay at the top of the political agenda of the Slovenian gay and lesbian movement in the 21st century. However, even more important than legal victories are social victories; endeavors for social visibility and inclusion should remain an important part of the struggle.

RESOURCE GUIDE

Suggested Reading

Tatjana Greif, "The Social Status of Lesbian Women in Slovenia in the 1990s," in *Sexuality and Gender in Post-Communist Eastern Europe and Russia,* ed. A. Štulhofer and T. Sandfort (New York: Haworth Press, 2005).

Roman Kuhar, "Homosexuality as a Litmus Test of Democracy and Post-modern Value Orientations," in *Democratic Transition in Slovenia,* ed. S. P. Ramet and D. Fink-Hafner (College Station, TX: Texas A&M University Press, 2005).

Roman Kuhar, "The Impracticability of Active Citizenship beyond the Closet in Slovenia," in *The Gays' and Lesbians' Rights in an Enlarged European Union,* ed. A. Weyembergh and S. Carstocea (Brussels: L'Université de Bruxelles, 2005).

Roman Kuhar, *Media Representations of Homosexuality: An Analysis of the Print Media in Slovenia, 1970–2000* (Ljubljana, Slovenia: Peace Institute, 2003), http://mediawatch.mirovni-institut.si/eng/mw13.htm.

Bogdan Lešnik, "Melting the Iron Curtain: The Beginnings of the LGBT Movement in Slovenia," in *New Social Movements and Sexuality,* ed. M. Chateauvert (Sofia, Bulgaria: Bilitis Resource Center, 2006).

Alenka Švab, "Do They Have A Choice? Reproductive Preferences among Lesbians and Gays in Slovenia," in *Beyond the Pink Curtain. Everyday Life of LGBT People in Eastern Europe,* ed. R. Kuhar and J. Takács (Ljubljana, Slovenia: Peace Institute, 2007).

Alenka Švab and Roman Kuhar, *The Unbearable Comfort of Privacy: The Everyday Life of Gays and Lesbians* (Ljubljana, Slovenia: Peace Institute, 2005), http://www2.mirovni-institut.si/eng_html/publications/pdf/MI_gay_eng.pdf.

Suzana Tratnik, "Lesbian Visibility in Slovenia," *The European Journal of Women's Studies* 8, no. 3 (2001): 373–80.

Video/Film

Just Happy The Way I Am (45 min.; 1998). Film by Klaus Müller, camera by Miha Lobnik. East/West Film Production. Slovenian/Dutch documentary portrays the lives of young gays and lesbians who met at the Homophobia and Fascism conference in Italy in 1997.

Guardian of the Frontier (98 min.; 2002). Belafilm. The movie explores political and mental frontiers. Three girls canoe down the river Kolpa, where the border between Slovenia and Croatia is located. Their adventure takes a violent twist that changes their lives forever. A love affair develops between two of the girls, challenging the border between the permissible and the forbidden in their own minds.

Web Sites

Annual Pride Parade, http://www.ljubljanapride.org.
> Cultural center Q, http://www.kulturnicenterq.org/.
> Provides general information on what is going on in the gay and lesbian clubs Monokel and Tiffany

eL magazin (Lesbian magazine), http://www.elmagazin.com.
Gymnasivm—gay sauna, http://www.klub-libero.si.
Lambda—the gay book series, http://www.ljudmila.org/siqrd/lambda.php.
Lesbo (Lesbian magazine), http://www.ljudmila.org/lesbo/lesbo.htm.
Ljubljana's gay and lesbian film festival, http://www.ljudmila.org/siqrd/fglf.
Mavrični forum—Rainbow forum, http://www.mavricni-forum.net.
> Forum for gays and lesbians.
Monokel—the lesbian club, http://www.klubmonokel.com.
Narobe—Wrong (LGBT magazine), http://www.narobe.si.
> The site provides an electronic version of the magazine and *Narobe blog* with the latest news on LGBT life in Slovenia.
1XY (Gay magazine), http://www.1xy.biz.
Slovenia for Gay Travelers, http://www.sloveniaforgaytravelers.com.
Slovenian Queer Resource Directory, http://www.ljudmila.org/siqrd.
> Provides general information on what is going on in the LGBT community in Slovenia.
Tiffany—the gay club, http://www.ljudmila.org/siqrd/tiffany.
Vizibilija—the lesbian book series, http://www.ljudmila.org/lesbo/vizibilija.htm.

Organizations

DIH, http://www.dih.si.
> DIH started as Out in Slovenija in 2000 as an informal LGBT sports group; sport is still part of DIH's activities. DIH was officially established in 2003. Like Legebitra, it is involved in political activism, counseling, organizing social, cultural and sport activities, and AIDS prevention.
> Društvo Parada ponosa, http://www.ljubljanapride.org/.
> Društvo Parada ponosa was established in 2009 in order to organize annual Pride parade. In previous years the Pride Parade was jointly organized by all GLBT organizations in Slovenia.

Legebitra, http://www.drustvo-legebitra.si.

Legebitra was established in 1998 as the first Slovenian LGBT youth group. Over the years it has expanded its activities to political activism, counseling, and organizing social, cultural, and sport activities, as well as AIDS prevention and other programs. It publishes the LGBT magazine *Narobe* (*Wrong*).

Lingsium, http://www.lingsium.org.

Lingsium, established in 2004, is the only LGBT group operating outside Ljubljana. It is a youth LGBT organization.

LL, http://www.ljudmila.org/lesbo.

LL was established in 1987. It is the oldest Slovenian (and eastern European) lesbian organization and plays one of the crucial rules in political activism in Slovenia. It runs the Lesbian Library radio show Lezbomania, lesbian club Monokel, lesbian book series *Vizibilija,* and occasionally publishes the lesbian magazine *Lesbo.*

Magnus, http://www.ljudmila.org/siqrd/magnus.

Established in 1984, it is the oldest Slovenian (and eastern European) gay organization. In the past years it has primarily dealt with AIDS prevention.

NOTES

1. "Countries and Areas Ranked by Population: 2008," 2008, http://www.census.gov/cgi-bin/ipc/idbrank.pl (accessed January 13, 2008).

2. CIA, "Slovenia," *World Factbook,* https://www.cia.gov/library/publications/the-world-factbook/geos/si.html#Geo (accessed January 13, 2008).

3. World Bank, *World Development Report 1991,* Statistical Annex (World Bank, 1991).

4. The *eurozone* refers to the union of those countries within the European Union that adopted the euro as their official currency.

5. World Economic Forum, "Global Competitiveness Index 2007," http://www.weforum.org/pdf/Global_Competitiveness_Reports/Reports/gcr_2007/gcr2007_rankings.pdf (accessed January 13, 2008).

6. Statistični urad Republike Slovenije [Statistical Office of the Republic of Slovenia], *Census (2002),* http://www.stat.si/popis2002/si/rezultati/rezultati_red.asp?ter=SLO&st=8 (accessed January 13, 2008).

7. Niko Toš, ed., *Vrednote v prehodu II. Slovensko javno mnenje 1990–1998 [Values in Transition II: Slovenian Public Opinion 1990–1998]* (Ljubljana: FDV IDV, CJMMK, 1999); Niko Toš ed., *Vrednote v prehodu III. Slovensko javno mnenje 1999–2004 [Values in transition III: Slovenian Public Opinion 1999–2004]* (Ljubljana: FDV IDV, CJMMK, 2004).

8. Roman Kuhar, *Mi, drugi. Oblikovanje in razkritje homoseksualne identitete [We, the Others. Formation and Disclosure of Homosexual Identity]* (Ljubljana: Škuc-Lambda, 2001), 92–95.

9. Roman Kuhar, "Homosexuality as a Litmus Test of Democracy and Postmodern Value Orientations," in *Democratic Transition in Slovenia,* ed. Sabrina P. Ramet and Danica Fink-Hafner (College Station: Texas A&M University Press, 2006), 233–58.

10. Roman Kuhar, *Media Representations of Homosexuality: An Analysis of the Print Media in Slovenia* (Ljubljana: Peace Institute, 2003).

11. Anton Gradišek, Hubert Požarnik, and Dušan Repovž, *Zdravstvena vzgoja [Health Education]* (Ljubljana: Državna založba Slovenije, 1991), 145.

12. Kuhar, *Mi, drugi,* 162–63.

13. Gradišek, Požarnik, and Repovž, *Zdravstvena vzgoja,* 137.

14. Alenka Švab and Roman Kuhar, *The Unbearable Comfort of Privacy: The Everyday Life of Gays and Lesbians* (Ljubljana: Peace Institute, 2005).

15. Sebastijan Ozmec, "Homofobija po srednješolsko" ["High-school-style Homophobia"], Mladina, 2001, http://www.mladina.si/tednik/200120/clanek/m-homo/ (accessed January 13, 2007).

16. Ibid.

17. U.S. Department of State, "Slovenia," http://www.state.gov/r/pa/ei/bgn/3407. htm (accessed January 13, 2007).

18. Metka Drnovšek, "Labour Force, Slovenia, August 2007," Statistical Office of the Republic of Slovenia, 2007, http://www.stat.si/eng/novica_prikazi.aspx?id=1209 (accessed November 13, 2007).

19. Švab and Kuhar, *The Unbearable Comfort of Privacy.*

20. Ibid.

21. See http://www.ljudmila.org/lesbo/EQUAL/index.htm.

22. See http://www.ljudmila.org/lesbo/EQUAL/FILMER/homofobija.wmv.

23. Mirovni inštitut project, "Diversity Makes Us Richer: Not Poorer," http://www2. mirovni-institut.si/razlicnost/ (accessed January 13, 2007).

24. Roman Kuhar, "Učim se 'zmernega aktivizma'. Intervju z Mihom Lobnikom" ["I Learn How to Conduct a 'Moderate Activism': An Interview with Miha Lobnik"], *Narobe,* July 2007, http://www.narobe.si/stevilka-2/lobnik.html (accessed February 15, 2008).

25. Irena Klavs, L. C. Rodrigues, K. Wellings, H. A. Weiss, and R. Hayes, "Sexual Behaviour and HIV/Sexually Transmitted Infection Risk Behaviours in the General Population of Slovenia, a Low HIV Prevalence Country in Central Europe," *Sexually Transmitted Infections* (2009): 85, 132–38.

26. Ivan Bernik and Valentina Hlebec, "How Did it Happen the First Time?: Formative Sexual Experiences of Secondary School Students in Seven Post-Socialist Countries," paper presented at the Sexualities in Transition conference, Dubrovnik, June 12–16, 2001. The study results apply to Ljubljana and Koper—two cities where the research was conducted.

27. Bernik and Hlebec, "How did It Happen the First Time?"

28. Majda Hrženjak, Vlasta Jalušič, Birgit Sauer, and Karin Tertinegg, "Framing Prostitution Policies: A Comparison of Slovenia and Austria," *Greek Review of Social Research* 117 (2005): 93–118.

29. Cell phone prostitution refers to prostitution where the initial contact with the prostitute is made using a cell phone. The meeting place is agreed over the phone. The cell numbers are usually posted on the Internet. Apartment prostitution takes place in private apartments in residential areas. Hotel and bar prostitution refers to picking up the prostitute in bars or hotels.

30. Mojca Pajnik and Urša Kavčič, *The Demand Side of Sex: Perspectives on Trafficking and Prostitution (The Case of Slovenia)* (Ljubljana: Peace Institute, 2006).

31. Tina Žnidaršič, *Ob mednarodnem dnevu družin: Družine v Sloveniji* [*International Day of Families: Families in Slovenia*], Statistical Office of the Republic of Slovenia, 2006, http://www.stat.si/novica_prikazi.aspx?ID=169 (accessed November 13, 2007).

32. Milena Ilič and Darja Šter, *Podatki o sklenitvah in razvezah zakonskih zvez, podrobni podatki, Slovenija, 2006* [*Data on marriages and divorces, Slovenia, 2006*], Statistical Office of the Republic of Slovenia, (2006), http://www.stat.si/novica_prikazi.aspx?ID=1279 (accessed November 13, 2007).

33. Statistical Office of the Republic of Slovenia, http://www.stat.si.

34. Švab and Kuhar, *The Unbearable Comfort of Privacy.*

35. Tit Albreht, Marjan Cesen, Don Hindle, Elke Jakubowski, Boris Kramberger, Vesna Kerstin Petric, Marjan Premik, and Martin Toth, "Health Care Systems in Transition: Slovenia," 2002, http://www.euro.who.int/document/E76966.pdf (accessed November 13, 2007).

36. "Gibanje za ohranitev in izboljšanje javnega zdravstva" ["The Movement for the Preservation and Improvement of Public Health Care"], http://www.ohranimo.si/index. php (accessed April 29, 2008).

37. Irena Klavs, Tanja Kustec, Nejc Bergant, and Zdenka Kastelic, "Okužba s HIV v svetu, Evropi in v Sloveniji" ["HIV Infections in the World, in Europe and in Slovenia"],

2007, http://www.ivz.si/index.php?akcija=novica&n=1429 (accessed November 13, 2007).

38. World Health Organization (WHO), "Slovenia—HIV/AIDS Country Profile," 2007, http://www.euro.who.int/aids/ctryinfo/overview/20060118_40 (accessed November 13, 2007).

39. Toš, *Vrednote v prehodu III*.

40. Quoted in Nataša Velikonja, *Dvajset let gejevskega in lezbičnega gibanja* [*Twenty Years of the Gay and Lesbian Movement*] (Ljubljana, Slovenia: Škuc, 2004), 33.

41. Boštjan Mlakar, "Humani virusi papiloma (HPV)," *Narobe* (December 2007), http://www.narobe.si/stevilka-4/zdravje.html (accessed April 29, 2007).

42. Nataša Velikonja ed., *20 let gejevskega in lezbičnega gibanja* [*20 Years of Gay and Lesbian Movement*] (Ljubljana, Slovenia: Škuc, 2004), 7.

43. Constitution of Slovenia, http://www.servat.unibe.ch/icl/si00000_.html (accessed April 29, 2007).

44. Švab and Kuhar, *The Unbearable Comfort of Privacy*.

45. Quoted by the Slovenian Press Agency Online, http://www.sta.si (accessed December 24, 2002).

46. Švab and Kuhar, *The Unbearable Comfort of Privacy*.

47. Statistični urad Republike Slovenije [Statistical Office of the Republic of Slovenia], *Census (2002)*, http://www.stat.si/popis2002/si/rezultati/rezultati_red.asp?ter=SLO&st=8 (accessed January 13, 2008).

48. Quoted in *Delo, Sobotna priloga*, August 23, 2003, 11.

49. TV Slovenija 1, *Aktualno*, August 19, 2003.

50. United Nations Office on Drugs and Crime, *Human Development Report 2007/08*, 2007, http://hdrstats.undp.org/indicators/263.html (accessed November 13, 2007).

51. *Mladina Online*, "V Sloveniji zaradi samomora letno umre 600 ljudi" ["In Slovenia 600 People Die Because of a Suicide Every Year"], http://www.mladina.si/dnevnik/69270/ (accessed November 13, 2007).

52. United Nations Development Programme, "Slovenia," *Human Development Reports 2007/2008*, http://hdrstats.undp.org/countries/data_sheets/cty_ds_SVN.html (accessed November 13, 2007).

53. Nataša Velikonja and Tatjana Greif, *Anketa o diskriminaciji na osnovi spolne usmerjenosti* [*A Questionnaire on Discrimination on the Basis of Sexual Orientation*], (Ljubljana: Škuc-LL, 2001); Švab and Kuhar, *The Unbearable Comfort of Privacy*.

54. Švab and Kuhar, *The Unbearable Comfort of Privacy*.

55. Roman Kuhar, "Nič manj homofobičnega nasilja" ["No Less Homophobic Violence"], *Narobe*, December 2008, http://www.narobe.si/stevilka-8-december-2008/nasilje-raziskava.html (accessed July 14, 2009).

SPAIN

José Ignacio Pichardo Galán

OVERVIEW

The Kingdom of Spain is situated in the southwest of the European continent, with an area of 194,897 square miles. In 2008, its population was 46,063,511 inhabitants. The main cities are Madrid, Barcelona, Valencia, and Seville. After Francisco Franco's dictatorship (1939–1975), the country went through a transition to democracy, which concluded with the ratification of the 1978 Spanish constitution. Since then, Spain has been a democratic country with a parliamentary monarchy. There is periodic voting to elect representatives at four different levels: the European Parliament, the Spanish parliament (Congress and Senate), regional parliaments, and local parliaments. The country joined the European Union (EU) in 1986, along with Portugal.

Spain is defined in its constitution as a plurinational country committed to respecting and protecting cultural diversity. The state became decentralized with the recognition of the diverse nationalities and regions that, in the form of independent communities or regions, make up Spain. The national government controls the regulation of marriage, registries, nationality and migration, labor and social security, among others. The autonomous regions, on the other hand, have their own parliament, laws, and president. Among the ample jurisdictional areas assumed by these autonomous regions are health, education, and social assistance.

Six out of the 17 autonomous regions and two autonomous cities into which Spain is divided have a series of their own historical *fueros* (areas of

jurisdiction) that allow them to have their own legislation regarding matters of civil rights, especially those related to family law, inheritance, and succession; in some cases (as in Navarre and the Basque Country), these rights include the tributary system.

Socioeconomic data situate Spain among the group of developed countries: it is the 9th economy in the world according to gross domestic product (GDP), the average annual income has risen to $27,400, the life expectancy at birth is among the highest in the world (80.23 years), and the infant mortality rate is among the lowest (4.54 deaths/1,000 live births). *The Economist*'s 2005 quality-of-life index ranked Spain tenth, ahead of countries such as France, the United Kingdom, the United States, and Canada. Spain is a welfare state with social security, retirement pensions, and public systems for health and education.

Spain has a mixed economy—capitalist with the intervention of the state. It boomed from the mid-1980s until the mid-1990s, and has had moderate growth since then that is higher than the average for countries in the EU. The official currency is the euro, and the main labor activities are services (65%) and industry (30%), with Spain being the world's second most popular tourist destination. Unemployment, inflation, and a large underground economy are the main economic weaknesses.

Spanish is the official language, as well as Catalan, Basque, and Galician in some regions. About 10 percent of the people living in Spain come from other countries. Many of them are economic and social migrants coming mainly from Latin America, eastern Europe, and Africa, but one-fifth of the non-Spanish residents come from western European countries such as Germany or the United Kingdom, probably attracted by the sun and good weather.

OVERVIEW OF LGBT ISSUES

Homosexual love and sexuality can be found throughout the history of Spain.[1] The sexually permissive Phoenician civilization, the homosexual Roman emperor Hadrian that came from Hispania, and the hedonistic and tolerant of homosexuality of Islamic Al-Andalus are only a few examples. And yet, within the same territory, the Spanish Inquisition and many Catholic kings and queens made the repression of sodomy and homosexuality one of their main signs of identity. The documents of this prosecution do establish that same-sex relations have been present in the Iberian Peninsula for centuries. Even some of the major Spanish intellectuals and artists, such as the writer Cervantes or the painter Goya, are supposed to have had homosexual relations.

Still, it was not until the beginning of the 20th century that same-sex relations appeared more or less openly in the public sphere. In the 1930s, French writer Jean Genet wrote about a group of 30 faggots demonstrating in a public urinary destroyed by a bomb in Barcelona.[2] In these years, one of the most important Spanish poets, Federico García Lorca, had an affair with the bisexual painter Salvador Dalí. But these small appearances of homosexuality were cut off by the national Catholic dictatorial regime of Fascist Franco.

During the different stages of Franco's dictatorship, homosexuality in Spain was synonymous with persecution, exile, and even murder. In 1971, the Law of Dangerousness and Social Rehabilitation took effect. This statute considered homosexuals dangerous people and stipulated their separation from the society in an attempt to rehabilitate them. During the period in which this law was enforced

(1971–1979), approximately 1,000 homosexual men were locked up. They were taken to jails or to special disciplinary centers for homosexual men.[3] At the same time, lesbians suffered repression in private spaces: if the police found two amorous women, they would report the case to the families, and their parents, husbands, or brothers would be in charge of the punishment, and could elect to send the women to a mental institution.[4]

During the transition to democracy, Spanish society showed an important tolerance and openness to sexuality and sexual behaviors. This tolerance was restricted solely to heterosexual behaviors, since homosexual behavior remained strongly stigmatized for about two more decades. The first gay pride demonstration in Spain took place in 1977 in Barcelona. The event was strongly repressed by the police. Five thousand people participated in the gathering. By the 1980s, the LGBT movement's primary goals were achieved (the abolishment of the Law of Dangerousness and Social Rehabilitation and the legalization of homosexuality) and it suffered a decline in activism.

As occurred in other countries in the region, the AIDS epidemic brought the gay and lesbian movement back to life in Spain, largely because the epidemic placed homosexuality at the center of social and mass media attention and made the needs of same-sex couples visible. In the late 1980s and early 1990s, activism and participation in organizations increased. This is most likely the foundation upon which the boom in the Spanish LGBT movement after 1995 was based.

During the 1990s, equality for homosexual people surfaced as a question in political debate. In 2005, Spain became the third country in the world to legalize same-sex marriage, as most of the parties in the parliament voted for reforming the civil code in order to recognize the right of same-sex couples to contract marriage. In 2007, the parliament approved a law that allows transsexual[5] people to legally change their sex without having genital surgery.

EDUCATION

Spain has a free public education system. Parents can choose to send their children to a public school, a private school funded by the state, or a completely private school. A significant percentage of private schools are managed by the Catholic Church through agreements with the state. One-third of all students of primary and secondary education attend Catholic schools. The Catholic Church has teachers of the Catholic faith in all public schools that are paid by the state but hired and controlled by the dioceses. This explains the influence of the hierarchy of this religion in everything that has to do with education in the country.

Sex education was intended to be implemented with democracy, but it did not find a place in the official class schedule. It was supposed to be taught alongside other subjects, but most teachers were not trained to conduct sex education during their classes and almost no one did it. Sometimes, outside experts visit classes and spend a couple of hours explaining the basics of sexuality. During these lessons, same-sex relations are usually not discussed, and when they do, only male homosexuality in relation with HIV/AIDS is addressed.

In 2006, a new Law on Education was implemented. This law explicitly states in its preamble that respect for sexual and familial diversity has to be taught at school. It even created a new subject, *education for human rights and citizenship,* in which the fight against homophobia and the recognition of diverse forms of families must be considered. This new subject elicited strong resistance from conservative groups and the Catholic Church.

These new legal instruments and some others, such as the proposition approved by the national parliament in 2006 to fight homophobia in schools, have had no impact yet because of the resistance of the Catholic Church, fears of parental re-actions, the lack of resources for teachers, and the normalization of homophobic discrimination in the educational system.

Students continue to perceive schools as especially homophobic spaces for LGBT teenagers. According to studies conducted by the Spanish LGBT Federation,[6] students who have a sexual desire for same-sex people or who are questioning their sexual orientation are at least three times more likely to be bullied than heterosexual students. About one-third of students show homophobic attitudes, but these rates are much higher among boys than among girls, marking the gendered reality of homophobia and the connection of heteronormativity with the sex-gender system. Lesbian, bisexual, and, especially, transsexual students are more vulnerable in the education system than gay males.

Lesbian students are more often exposed to sexual harassment from their male classmates (15% of secondary male students would come on to a lesbian classmate). This percentage is lower among younger students and increases to 33 percent among older groups. This means that in a class of 30 students, a lesbian could face harassment from 5 male classmates.[7]

The impact of homophobic bullying means higher school failure and attrition rates among LGBT students, but there are no official rates and almost no official programs to fight homophobia in schools. Most of the initiatives that support respect for sexual diversity in Spanish schools come from individual teachers (who face much resistance), from LGBT organizations, and from trade unions, which use funds to train teachers and to publish didactic materials.

A teacher cannot lose his or her job in the public school system for being openly LGBT, but many prefer not to come out in order to avoid being bullied or mocked by students or faculty. If he or she teaches at a private school, the chance of being fired because of sexual orientation is higher. This prevents students from having adult LGBT references at school. In the country of García Lorca, or gay Nobel Prize winners such as the writers Benavente or Alexaindre, most students cannot name an LGBT person.[8]

In Spanish universities, there are no specific diplomas or departments of LGBT or queer studies. Some universities are beginning to conduct research and provide summer courses on the subject.

EMPLOYMENT AND ECONOMICS

As in many other areas concerning LGBT rights in Spain, the EU has had a major impact in terms of equality at work with its directive for establishing a general framework for equal treatment in employment and occupation, which entered into force at the end of the year 2000. Nonetheless, there is no concrete plan for fighting discrimination at work for lesbian, gay, bisexual, transsexual, or HIV-positive people. There are no official data on the subject, but Toni Poveda, president of the Spanish LGBT Federation and former trade unionist, has declared that only 15 percent of gay males and 7 percent of lesbians come out in their workplace. The great majority fears negative consequences if they do come out: being fired or harassed, having no access to promotions, or experiencing problems with colleagues. Lesbian women, for example, are more exposed to sexual harassment at work than heterosexual women, according to one Spanish trade union.

Some people who marry same-sex partners are being pressured by their bosses not to take the 15 days off that they are owed after marriage according to Spanish law, something that would never happen to a heterosexual person. Other couples voluntarily give up their right to take a honeymoon vacation from their job because they do not want their boss, colleagues, or clients to know about their same-sex wedding. Some will say they were sick the day of their marriage because they do not dare to ask for a day off and they prefer not to explain the absence. Legal equality is certainly not social equality, and homophobia is still an enormous threat for many queers in Spain.

Transsexual women confront significant problems concerning employment. Exclusion of transsexual women usually begins at school, when they are bullied for challenging gender frontiers. There is a link between transphobic harassment and higher rates of school failure among transsexual women. Some have to quit school and cut off ties with their family, complicating their position in the labor market. In this context, sex work appears to be the only possibility for many of these women. Transsexual women are probably the most vulnerable sexual minority in terms of discrimination, which is why activists demand that they be recognized as a group that suffers significant social and juridical prejudices at work. They demand positive action for transsexual women.

Openly nonheterosexual people can legally serve in the Spanish army. In 2000, Lieutenant Colonel Sánchez Silva publicly came out on the cover of *Zero*, an important LGBT magazine, creating a great controversy. Since then, many others have followed. There have already been same-sex marriages between soldiers, and transsexual women have fought to be recognized as women in the barracks.

SOCIAL/GOVERNMENT PROGRAMS

After the legalization of same-sex marriage, the challenge for LGBT groups is the transformation of legal equality into real equality. Public policies are one of the main tools to achieve this objective.

At the national level, some laws are beginning to incorporate sexual diversity. One of the most important ones, as mentioned, has been the Law on Education. Several other new laws also take into account respect for LGBTs, including the Law Against Violence, Racism, Xenophobia and Intolerance in Sports (2007), which considers declarations, gestures, insults, and any other conduct implying discrimination of a person or group of persons because of his or her sexual orientation (among other personal characteristics) as a very serious infraction that can be punished with a temporary closure of the sports facility.

Another important milestone was the inclusion of homosexuals and transsexuals as priority groups when assuring equality of opportunity in the frame of the national plan of action for social inclusion (2005–2006). Nevertheless, this plan did not become a reality since there are no funds, department, institute, or directorate of the national government specifically dedicated to working against discrimination of gays, lesbians, bisexuals, and transsexuals in Spain.

On the contrary, regional governments are the leaders on this issue. The Basque government, for example, has a program called Berdindu dedicated only to the fight against homophobia and to creating the means for social inclusion of LGBT people. The Catalonian government has a plan in all departments with similar objectives and, in 2007, joined the International Gay and Lesbian Association (ILGA), making it the first government to do so. Other regional governments, such as those of Madrid and Extremadura, prefer to fund associations that provide psychological or juridical support for LGBT people.

Different municipalities have specific programs for LGBT, usually related to their gender equality policies. Indeed, one of them, Vitoria, became the first public institution to recognize same-sex couples in 1994, and has created a psychological support program for nonheterosexual people. Maspalomas and Coslada have funded research on homophobia. Other local authorities such as Rivas-Vaciamadrid, Sagunto, Tarrasa, Elche, and Barcelona also have public policies for sexual diversity.

The major Spanish trade unions, Unión General de Trabajadores (UGT) and especially Comisiones Obreras (CCOO), are leading the struggle for social equality of LGBT not only at work, but also in society at large, with specific programs for sexual equality.

SEXUALITY/SEXUAL PRACTICES

Today, Spain is an open country in terms of sexuality. After 40 years of national Catholicism, any censorship on sexuality is considered a backlash and after the transition to democracy, sex is presented without a problem in most public spaces (advertising, movies, conversations, TV shows) except in the educational system.

Still, this openness toward sexuality was limited to the desires and practices of heterosexual people during many years after the arrival of democracy in 1978. In 1996, a scandal commonly known as the *caso Arny* significantly changed attitudes toward gay men and homosexuality. Some 49 men, among them well-known public figures, were accused by a minor of having had paid sex with him at a bar (the Arny) in Seville. Most charges were proved false, but the affair had a relevant impact on the gay public image and many famous people came out as gay in its wake. One of them was Jesús Vázquez, a famous and successful TV presenter who since then has become a positive gay icon for both homosexual and heterosexual Spaniards, and who married his long-time boyfriend and has even kissed him on the mouth in some of his widely seen TV appearances.

There are many places to find sex partners in Spain, especially for gay adult men, including specific neighborhoods, bars, discos, sex clubs, parks, cinemas, bath houses, and cruising areas in most cities and towns. The Internet revolution has meant a sexual revolution for most queers in Spain, as in many other countries. Not only do many LGBT sites have Spanish versions (such as gaydar.es) but local Web sites also stay very busy for finding sex partners because they are free and allow explicit sexual images like, for example, bakala.org or chueca.com. This means that anyone, no matter if they live in a big city or a small village, has access to other LGBTs from all over Spain (or the world) as long as they have an Internet connection.

Thanks to HIV prevention programs, there is now much more information about sexual practices among men who have sex with men (MSM), but less available information relevant to lesbians. According to some studies,[9] the most frequent practice is not anal penetration (15–20% never do it) but oral sex and masturbation, practiced by 85 percent of gay males when having sex with someone. Although more people prefer to be identified as a top than as a bottom, more than one-third define themselves as "versatile," and the division between top and bottom identities does not seem to be very strict. More than half of gay males reported having more than 6 sexual partners in a year, and 15–20 percent (depending on the age) had more than 20 sexual partners in the past year.

There is not much information available about sexual practices between women, as research is never focused on this group. The National Survey on Sexual Habits, carried out in 2003 by the Spanish Ministry of Health, only considered *sexual relations* to involve a penetration of the penis in the vagina, mouth, or anus, completely concealing lesbian sex and preventing researchers and policymakers from gathering information about sexuality between women.

FAMILY

The Spanish family has changed from the Catholic conception (legal and cultural) that prevailed during Franco's dictatorship in accordance with the legal transformations derived from Spain's newly democratic 1978 constitution. Under Franco, the notion was: "no sex without children and no children without sex"; today, however, people can have sex without children and children without sex, too. The Spanish Law on Assisted Reproductive Techniques (ART) of 1988, for example, considered that any woman over 18 years has the right to use these techniques regardless of her civil status. That is, any woman, married or not, heterosexual or homosexual, can use ART. Ten percent of the women who use these techniques are not married and began this process without a partner, but how many of them are lesbian is unknown.

With the Adoption Law of 1987, any heterosexual couple (married or not) can adopt jointly. At the same time, any single person, heterosexual or not, is allowed to adopt a child individually. This created a way for many homosexual people to adopt children, although, legally, only one person could be the adoptive parent. Today, Spain ranks as the country with the second most international adoptions, a phenomenon that is creating new multiracial and multiethnic families. These children come mainly from China, Russia, and various countries in Latin America and Africa.

After the changes that took place immediately following the transition to democracy, Spain is experiencing a second wave of legal adjustments in the 2000s that reflect the social changes people have performed in their lives and that update the legal system to a new familial reality. These adjustments include regional laws recognizing same-sex partners (1998–2005), the Law against Gender Violence (2004), the legalization of homosexual marriage (2005), a new divorce law (2005), a new reproductive techniques law (2006), the Gender Equality Law (2007) and the Dependence Law (2007).

The most significant transformation that has taken place has been to give same-sex couples the possibility of marrying. This change could not have been possible without the evolution that took place in Spanish public opinion regarding the acceptance of homosexual marriage. According to various polls, in 1973 only

3 percent of society accepted homosexuality, whereas in 2004, two-thirds of the population was in favor of gay marriage.[10]

In the 2001 Spanish census, homosexual couples could declare themselves as such. Only 10,474 couples did so, that is, 0.11 percent of all homosexual couples and 0.051 percent of the Spanish population at that time. LGBT associations interpreted these data as indicating that most cohabiting homosexual couples did not identify themselves during that census because of the homophobia still present in our society. Within these 10,474 couples, the number of male couples (6,996) is double the number of female couples (3,478).

In June 2006, the Spanish National Statistics Institute published the 2005 demographic data, including for the first time marriages between same-sex couples. The number of marriages celebrated during the last six months of the year, when the law was enforced, totaled 1,275, that is, 0.61 percent of all marriages celebrated in 2005. The following year, 4,574 same-sex marriages were celebrated. In 2007 the number of same-sex marriages decreased slightly to 3,250, and in 2008 there were 3,549 marriages (2,299 between men and 1,250 between women), which equals 1.77 percent of all marriages celebrated in 2008. This seems insignificant in quantitative terms, but homosexual marriage has had a huge cultural, legal, and political impact. This would explain, for example, the strong resistance coming from the Catholic Church.

According to data offered by the Spanish LGBT Federation (FELGTB), by the end of July 2006, more than 150 same-sex couples had begun the process for joint adoption. Since same-sex marriage was approved, as of the end of 2007 only 42 couples had divorced.[11] The first divorce had a great media impact, especially in the conservative newspapers.

The people who are getting married are mainly: people in long-term relationships with common possessions; couples in which one member is ill or about to die; couples with offspring (in order to adopt the other partner's son/daughter); or couples in which one of the partners needs to stabilize immigration status. Indeed, the number of marriages between Spaniards and foreigners is higher in percentage among same-sex couples, especially in male-male marriages, where 4.5 out of 10 are held between a Spaniard and a foreigner.

Homophobia is still a widespread attitude in Spain. Some same-sex unions are being celebrated without the presence of any or some of the relatives of the spouses because family members are not aware of the couple's sexual orientation. Indeed, many same-sex couples prefer not to marry because it makes the fact that they are gay or lesbian completely public and visible: all legal documents will indicate that one is married to a person of the same sex and not everybody can afford such an outing. For some people who want to adopt, it is preferable not to be married, because most countries that accept adoptions from one-parent homes would never accept a homosexual couple as adoptive parents.

Gays and lesbians can also face difficulties with child custody after a divorce from a heterosexual partner, should a homophobic judge deny them custody due to their homosexuality. There have been several cases of homophobic sentences in recent years against same-sex couples, such as the one from a judge in Murcia preventing a woman from adopting her wife's child—conceived through ART—using the argument that a baby has the right to have a mother and a father. The judge was later suspended and fined, but the family had to confront a great deal of public controversy.[12]

COMMUNITY

According to the National Survey on Health and Sexual Habits conducted by the National Statistics Institute for the Spanish Ministry of Health in 2003, the rate of persons that declared having had homosexual relations at some time in their life has risen to 3.3 percent. This low rate can be explained by the fact that, in this survey, sexual relations among women were not considered, showing an important lesbophobic bias. Another study carried out among adolescents in 2007 revealed that around 5 percent declared themselves to be nonheterosexuals.[13]

Due to the repression of homosexuality during the dictatorship, it was not until 1971 that the first Spanish liberation group was created. In that year, the Movimiento Español de Liberación Homosexual (MEHL) was born. This group became the Front d'Alliberament Gai de Catalunya during the democracy. Since then, many other LGBT groups have been set up throughout Spain. Some of the most important ones, such as Cogam in Madrid, Xega in Asturias, or Nos in Granada, are confederated with almost 50 other associations in FELGTB. In Catalonia, the Coordinadora Gai-Lesbiana plays the same role as a regional federation. The organizations gathered within these two groups led the political and social fight to achieve same-sex marriage during the 1990s and 2000s. Other national LGBT Federations are the Fundación Triángulo and Colegas.

Most Spanish cities have some bars or gathering places for LGBT. Chueca in Madrid, Eixample in Barcelona, and Alameda in Seville are the main examples of neighborhoods where a high concentration of discos, bars, shops, saunas, or sex clubs for gays and lesbians can be found. Other Spanish cities such as Murcia, Bilbao, and Valencia (with an important lesbian community) also have very busy scenes.

Businesses targeted at an LGBT public have been crucial in the introduction of gay and lesbian identities in the country. There is even an association of LGBT entrepreneurs (AEGAL) that co-organizes the National Gay Pride in Madrid, one of the biggest gay prides in Europe, with more than half a million participants. This gay pride event is considered at once a celebration and a political demonstration: there is always a slogan and manifesto demanding rights for sexual minorities. Indeed, the presence of hundreds of thousands of people in the streets was one argument used to demand same-sex marriage. On the other hand, this demonstration in Madrid and other major cities in Spain is a way of gathering and celebrating community.

Gay and lesbian life is not only visible in big cities. In a country where tourism has traditionally been a way of life, there are some major international meccas for gay tourism: Ibiza, Sitges-Barcelona, Maspalomas, and Torremolinos. All along the coast, nudist and cruising areas can be found. Because cruising in beaches, parks, cinemas, malls, or gas stations is not illegal in Spain, many tourists come to Spain looking for a society with a tolerant attitude toward same-sex sexual encounters.

The coming out of many men and women, their visibility and pride, and the creation of a pink market were made possible in part by the dramatic increase in the number of LGBT media outlets, including independent radio programs and especially magazines (*Shangay Express, Zero, Odisea, Nois, Gai Inform, Gay Barcelona,* among others). The Internet has meant a sexual revolution for LGBTs in Spain. There are plenty of Spanish Web sites used to advocate or to chat, to find information, documents, support, friends, or sexual partners. There are some gay

TV programs on regional and local TV stations. Some nationwide television channels have broadcast American TV series for gays and lesbians or incorporated LGBT characters into their major sitcoms. There are reality shows that have cast LGBT participants who have subsequently become public referents of sexual diversity. *Big Brother,* for example, has made lesbians or transsexuals (both female to male [FTM] and male to female [MTF]) famous in the country. Indeed, TV showmen such as Jesús Vázquez or Boris Izaguirre are the main LGBT referents in Spain, together with some artists: the gay filmmakers Pedro Almodóvar and Alejandro Amenábar, and the transsexual woman and actress Bibi Andersen.

Since 2005, Madrid has held an annual festival of LGBT art and culture called Visible, as well as an important LGBT film festival, with an audience of more than 12,000 people. LGBT film festivals are also held in other cities and regions in Spain: Barcelona, Bilbao, Extremadura, and the Canary Islands.

HEALTH

The Spanish social security system provides universal health coverage for anyone living in Spain. This means that anybody living with HIV/AIDS has the right to treatment and medicine, with costs covered by the public health system.

The situation is very similar for those with sexually transmitted diseases (STDs): their treatment is part of the social security system, and most major cities have public health units specializing in STDs and HIV/AIDS where anyone can obtain anonymous and free testing.

The main channel of transmission of HIV/AIDS in Spain has traditionally been intravenous drugs use, but this tendency has changed significantly in the last years, and sexual (heterosexual and homosexual) transmission is on the rise. The rates of transmission among MSM are steadily increasing. The official numbers only reflect the rates of people living with AIDS, and there are no official national percentages for people living with HIV. In 2007, only Spain and Italy were unable to offer national data on new cases of HIV infections, despite the fact that Spain is one of the countries in Europe with higher rates of HIV infections.[14] Still, some studies say that almost 25 percent of gay men are HIV positive in Barcelona.[15] Cities such as Madrid and Barcelona and the Balearic and Canary Islands have higher rates of HIV-positive gay men than the national average.

The health system is decentralized in Spain and the autonomous regions are in charge of HIV/AIDS prevention campaigns, which means 19 different regional HIV prevention programs, each with its own objectives and campaigns. There exists a National Plan against AIDS with the objective of coordinating these public policies, and though it has led to some nationwide campaigns, they are usually generalist and not targeted at MSM. In 2007, the Ministry of Health launched its first advertising campaign targeting specifically at MSM, but the Minister of Health banned an image of two men kissing. Sex workers, transsexuals, and migrants are the focus of some other specific campaigns.

The health of lesbian women is an invisible reality. They do not exist for the public health system as lesbians and are not taken into account in any health program or research.

In 2007, the government included sex reassignment surgery in the list of public and free public health services. Previously, some regions, such us Andalusia and Asturias, had provided this public service, but the waiting list was so long that many transsexual men and, especially, women, preferred to travel to southeast Asia and pay for their surgery.

Although genital surgery is no longer compulsory for legal sex change, some transsexual groups disagree with the fact that a psychiatrist has to certify gender dysphoria after at least two years of medical treatment (such as being injected with hormones). They consider these procedures to be a medicalization of gender.

Intersexuality is a medical reality, unknown to most people in Spain. If a child is born intersexual, he or she will be considered ill and will undergo clinical surgery and treatment.[16] There are no public intersexual activists and the great majority of LGBT groups do not consider intersexuality to be an issue.

POLITICS AND LAW

One of the main objectives of the first LGBT groups created in the 1970s was the abolishment of the Law of Dangerousness and Social Rehabilitation in order to decriminalize homosexual relations. When this happened at the end of 1979, the associations emptied and the dance floors filled with people. In 1993, some LGBT groups began a campaign demanding registered partnership for heterosexual and same-sex couples, and equality for homosexual people then surfaced as a question in the political debate. It was then that the Spanish Workers Socialist Party (Partido Socialista Obrero Español, PSOE), in power since 1982, began to establish relations with the LGBT movement, but they lost the national elections of March 1996 and were unable to fulfill the promise of approving a law that would give homosexual couples certain rights. The conservative Popular Party, in government for eight years, restrained numerous initiatives presented in the Spanish parliament for the regulation of homosexual couples.

Since 1997, the Spanish LGBT Federation, together with the Coordinadora Gai-Lesbiana asked for the legalization of homosexual marriage, abandoning their fight for legal recognition of registered partners. Since then, 12 of the 17 autonomous regions have passed laws giving same-sex couples the possibility of contracting legal rights and duties, including the right to adopt jointly in 4 regions.

In the national elections of March 2004, gay marriage happened to occupy the center stage during the election campaign. All parties were forced to make their position on the matter clear, and most of them (except the conservative Popular Party) stated in their electoral platform that they were in favor of legalizing same-sex marriage. In the new parliament, the Socialist Party and its allies (former Communists and progressive nationalists from Catalonia) formed a majority and could pass any law. The new prime minister, Rodríguez Zapatero, announced in his inaugural speech to the parliament that:

> The moment has finally arrived to end once and for all the intolerable discrimination which many Spaniards suffer because of their sexual preferences....Homosexuals and transsexuals deserve the same public consideration as heterosexuals and they have the right to live freely the life they have chosen. As a result we will modify the Civil Code to recognize their equal right to marriage with the resulting effects over inheritance, labor rights and social security protection.[17]

For the first time, a president spoke about homosexuality to the parliament in the context of an inaugural discourse.

In the meantime, the Popular Party was the only representative political opposition to gay marriage. They proposed an alternative law giving extensive rights to homosexual couples, excluding both the right to adopt and to call homosexual unions *marriage*. The rest of the parties and the activists rejected this alternative law with the argument that only 100 percent equality is equality.

The Spanish debate about same-sex marriage aroused moral panic, but media, visibility, and social acceptance paved the way to making it legal. With the political opportunity open, activism, with a unified discourse and action, supported government approval with the arguments of equality, democracy, citizenship, and human rights. Spain became the third country in the world to recognize homosexual marriage nationwide, and the first one to give these couples the same rights that heterosexuals have.

Another significant milestone for LGBT rights in the country was the approval of the Gender Identity Law in 2007, which allows transsexual people to legally change their sex and name without having genital surgery, but with a report of gender dysphoria from a psychiatrist. Prominent transsexual activists had to go through hunger strikes before the socialist government would fulfill this electoral promise. At the end of the same year, the national government passed a law compelling all autonomous regions to conduct free genital surgery for both male and female transsexuals in the public health system.

Some politicians, especially gay males, have publicly come out as nonheterosexuals: the mayor of Las Palmas de Gran Canaria and former minister, Jerónimo Saavedra, and the city supervisor of Madrid and leader of the Spanish LGBT Movement, Pedro Zerolo. Manuela Trasovares, a transsexual who was elected as councilwoman in her little village but was isolated by the rest of the elected political officers in the town for transphobic reasons. Some well-known women in significant Spanish cities are known to be lesbians but have never openly disclosed themselves as such. This shows that transsexual and lesbian women face more difficulties in a political career than gay males in Spain.

RELIGION AND SPIRITUALITY

Spain is usually considered to be a Catholic country: 76.1 percent of Spaniards define themselves as Catholic, 13.3 percent say they do not believe in any religion, and 7 percent define themselves as atheist.[18] Nonetheless, religion was considered an important aspect of their lives by only 34 percent of the Spanish population, Spain being one of the less religious countries in Europe:[19] the numbers of Catholic marriages and baptisms are steadily falling and only 19.6 percent of the population attends mass weekly.[20] Although Spain is a nondenominational state, a concordat with the Vatican regulates ecclesiastical matters and allows Catholic priests and teachers to be paid by the Spanish government. At the same time, the Catholic Church has the means to spread its ideology in the country: its own TV and radio network, churches and schools, and plenty of general media attention whenever it gives an opinion on any subject.

The Catholic ecclesiastical hierarchy has been the most important opponent to same-sex marriage in Spain because of its factual, historical, political, and moral power in Spanish society, opposing any alteration that departs from the traditional notion of family. Nonetheless, there has been a social detachment from Catholic morality in Spanish society, at least when it comes to issues regarding sexuality and family. People might tend to relate Catholic notions of family with the past and, by extension, with the dictatorship.

There is almost no research on the relationship between religion and attitudes toward homosexuality in Spain, but if three out of four Spaniards define themselves as Catholic and two out of three people in Spain are for same-sex marriage, then a definite incongruity exists between what the Catholic Church says and what Catholics think. Indeed, in a survey of adolescents, the percentage of homophobic attitudes was only slightly higher among Catholic students than those who were not religious at all. The highest percentages of homophobic attitudes came from students who declared themselves Evangelic, Adventist, and Muslim.[21]

On the other hand, there are many Catholic and religious groups in LGBT associations, but no significant confession in Spain has recognized same-sex couples or homosexual people.

VIOLENCE

There is no official data about homophobic aggression in Spain. Police do not record the specificity of this kind of violence whenever a formal complaint takes place. Most aggressions, anyway, are not reported to the police, because many victims do not want to disclose their sexual orientation. LGBT associations periodically document homophobic and transphobic violence all over the country, but there is almost no research about homophobic violence, as this is not yet officially considered a social problem.

In the last years, several cases have become public thanks to media attention. This might be a symptom of greater interest in this kind of violence or, most probably, just reflects a backlash increase in homophobic violence since the approval of same-sex marriage. Before this law, there were no specific groups against homosexuality or homosexuals, but during the legislative process, some antigay political and associative groups were formed. These groups are well funded by conservative sectors and operate mainly over the Internet, nourishing feelings of hate.

Although queer activists are demanding a specific law to protect LGBT people against homophobic and transphobic aggression, there is no special law in Spain to prevent hate crimes. The penal code does address crimes committed based on the sexual orientation of the victim. However, for this to apply, the judge must consider the aggression a crime, and not a misdemeanor, a distinction which may not be made by a homophobic judge. In Catalonia, there is a special public prosecutor for homophobic or transphobic crimes, as well as an association of gay and lesbian policemen and policewomen that trains LGBT people on how to avoid and deal with these kinds of assaults.

Cruising and public sex are not illegal in Spain (except if scandalous), but most homophobic attacks take place in public spaces such as parks, streets, or public toilets. In some cases, the private security employees of train/bus stations or malls perform these assaults against gay males having sex there. Transsexual women are the primary victims of transphobic aggressions, especially if they are sex workers on the street. Violence against lesbians usually takes place in the private sphere and is perpetrated by their families or close circles, such as colleagues or neighbors.

OUTLOOK FOR THE 21ST CENTURY

There are still many challenges for queer and LGBT activism in Spain, most of them related to the goal of achieving not only legal equality, but also social equality. New public policies being implemented for homosexual people are not backed with the budget to implement them, and such policies face strong resistance from the Catholic Church and the most conservative groups in the country. The power of the church in education makes schools one of the main strongholds of homophobia in Spain. Some homophobic elements in the Spanish judicial system hinder the effective defense of LGBT rights when they are violated or when homophobic bashing or attacks take place.

Although many LGBT groups in Spain argue that this civil code reform means homosexual and heterosexual marriages get 100 percent the same rights, that is not completely true: the law modifying the Spanish civil code to allow same-sex marriage makes an exception and does not modify the articles related to filiation of children born inside the marriage (article 116, 117, and 118). That is, if a child is born in a heterosexual marriage, filiation rights are automatically granted to, and recognized of, the mother's spouse; but if that child is born in a homosexual marriage, the filiation rights of the spouse are not automatically recognized or granted. This is only the case for lesbian women, who get two different family books: when this happens, the mother's spouse is obligated to adopt her spouse's child if she wants filiation rights. These problems also appear in the New Assisted Reproduction Law. This law, approved in 2006, (i) does not take into account that a marriage can be between two women; and (ii) has a heterosexist bias. The Spanish government, however, changed and eliminated the heterosexist conceptions of this law in 2007.

New conceptions of family appear in other laws that have been implemented in the last decades in Spain. For example, the new Catalan law for adoption allows unmarried and unregistered couples (homo- or heterosexual) to adopt jointly, basing the decision on psychological and social characteristics of the couple, not on their legal status.

Although a nationwide registered partners law was in the electoral program of the Socialist Party and its allied parties in parliament (along with homosexual marriage), no one has spoken about it since the recognition of homosexual marriage: not the parties, politicians, LGBT groups, or feminist groups. Nobody is demanding it, not even within the gay and lesbian community. A new national law for registered partners could not only unify the different regional laws on the issue, but would go further because of the more extensive competences the national government has on the subject.

New challenges have arisen with the demands of some small LGBT groups—mainly in Catalonia and mainly lesbian feminist—that are fighting for the abolition of civil marriage and for the recognition of personal rights outside family or kinship relations. For example, they argue for the right to have work or resident visas, to receive a pension, to have a house to live in, and, especially, to care and be cared for. These groups argue that it is neither necessary nor desirable for such rights to rest solely on an institution such as marriage, but rather that these rights must be assumed both collectively and provided for individually through the state, not necessarily through marriage.

Thus far, these demands have only been presented by these groups and have not been actively defended by other political groups (nonlesbian feminist, anarchist, etc.). And, as of yet, they have had almost no social impact.

RESOURCE GUIDE

Suggested Reading

Juan Vicente Aliaga and José Miguel G. Cortés, *Identidad y diferencia. Sobre la cultura gay en España* (Madrid: Egales, 1997).

Arturo Arnalte, *Redada de violetas: la represión de los homosexuales durante el franquismo* (Madrid: La esfera de los libros, 2003).

Josiah Blackmore and Gregory S. Hutcheson, eds., *Queer Iberia: Sexualities, Cultures and Crossings from the Middle Ages to the Renaissance* (Durham: Duke University Press, 1999).

Xosé M. Buxán ed., *ConCiencia de un singular deseo* (Barcelona: Laertes, 1997).

Kerman Calvo, *Ciudadanía y minorías sexuales: la regulación del matrimonio homosexual en España* (Madrid: Fundación Alternativas, 2005).

Alberto Cardín, *Guerreros, chamanes y travestis: indicios de homosexualidad entre los exóticos* (Barcelona: Tusquets, 1989).

David Córdoba, Javier Sáez, and Paco Vidarte, eds., *Teoría Queer: Políticas bolleras, maricas, trans, mestizas* (Madrid: Egales, 2005).

Armand Fluviá, *El moviment gai a la clandestinitat del franquisme (1970–1975)* (Barcelona: Laertes, 2003).

Jesús Generelo, José Ignacio Pichardo, and Guillem Galofré, eds., *Adolescencia y sexualidades minoritarias: Voces desde la exclusión* (Alcalá la Real, Spain: Formación Alcalá, 2008).

Beatriz Gimeno, *Historia y análisis político del lesbianismo* (Barcelona: Gedisa, 2006).

María del Mar González, *El desarrollo infantil y adolescente en familias homoparentales* (Seville: Departamento de Psicología Evolutiva y de la Educación, Universidad de Sevilla, 2002).

Grupo de Trabajo Queer, ed., *El eje del mal es heterosexual. Figuraciones, movimientos y prácticas feministas queer* (Madrid: Traficantes de sueños, 2005).

Óscar Guasch, *La sociedad rosa* (Barcelona: Anagrama, 1995).

Oscar Guasch and Olga Viñuales, eds., *Sexualidades. Diversidad y control social* (Barcelona: Bellaterra, 2003).

Juan A. Herrero Brasas, ed., *Primera plana—La construcción de una cultura queer en España* (Madrid: Egales, 2007).

Ricardo Llamas, ed., *Construyendo Sidentidades: Estudios desde el corazón de una pandemia* (Madrid: Siglo XXI, 1995).

Romero Martín, *La transexualidad: diversidad de una realidad* (Madrid: Comunidad de Madrid, 2006).

Norma Mejía, *Transgenerismos: una experiencia transexual desde la perspectiva antropológica* (Barcelona: Bellaterra, 2006).

Alberto Mira, *De Sodoma a Chueca: Una historia cultural de la homosexualidad en España en el siglo XX* (Madrid: Egales, 2004).

Alberto Mira, *Para entendernos. Diccionario de cultura homosexual, gay y lésbica* (Barcelona: Llibres de l'Índex, 2002).

José Antonio Nieto, ed., *Transexualidad, transgenerismo y cultura. Antropología, identidad y género* (Madrid: Talasa, 1998).

Fernando Olmeda, *El látigo y la pluma. Homosexuales en la España de Franco* (Madrid: Oberon, 2004).

Raquel Osborne and Gracia Trujillo, "Sessualità periferiche: una panoramica sulla produzione GLBT e queer in Spagna," in *Omosapiens: studi e ricerche sull'orientamento sessuale*, ed. Domenico Rizzo (Rome: Carocci editore, 2006).

Ferran Pereda, *El cancaneo: diccionario petardo de argot gai, lesbi y trans* (Barcelona: Laertes, 2004).

Begoña Pérez Sancho, *Homosexualidad: Secreto de familia. El manejo del secreto en familias con algún miembro homosexual* (Madrid: Egales, 2005).

Jordi Petit, *Vidas del arco iris: Historias del ambiente* (Barcelona: Random House Mondadori, 2004).

Raquel Platero, ed., *Lesbianas. Discursos y representaciones* (Barcelona: Melusina, 2008).

Beatriz Preciado, *Manifiesto contra-sexual* (Madrid: Ópera Prima, 2002).

Félix Rodríguez and Angie Simonis, eds., *Cultura, Homosexualidad y Homofobia* (Madrid: Laertes, 2007).

Gil Soriano and Manuel Ángel, *La marginación homosexual en la España de la transición* (Madrid: Egales, 2005).

Sonia Soriano, *Cómo se vive la homosexualidad y el lesbianismo* (Salamanca: Amarú Ediciones, 1999).

Laurentino Vélez-Pelligrini, *Minorías sexuales y sociología de la diferencia* (Barcelona: Editorial Montesinos, 2008).

Paco Vidarte, *Ética marica* (Madrid: Egales, 2007).

Fernando Villaamil, *La transformación de la identidad gay en España* (Madrid: Catarata, 2004).

Olga Viñuales, *Identidades lésbicas* (Barcelona: Bellaterra, 2002).

Films

20 centímetros [*20 Centimeters*] (112 min.; 2005). Directed by Ramón Salazar. The main character, Marieta, is saving money for surgery in order have her penis removed. Meanwhile, she falls in love with a boy.

A mi madre le gustan las mujeres [*My Mother Likes Women*] (96 min.; 2002). Directed by Inés París and Daniela Fejerman. Three women learn that their mother is in love with another woman.

Amic, amat [*Beloved/Friend*] (90 min.; 1999). Directed by Ventura Pons. The story of a male professor in love with a same-sex student.

Cachorro [*Bear Cub*] (100 min.; 2004). Directed by Miguel Albadalejo. A gay man takes care of his young nephew for several weeks. This film depicts the Spanish bear culture and deals with other issues such as LGBT families, coupling, sex, social life, and HIV/AIDS.

El diputado [*Confessions of a Congressman*] (110 min.; 1978). Directed by Eloy de la Iglesia. A gay politician is set up with a male hustler by political opponents for sexual entanglement.

Electroshock [*A Love to Keep*] (98 min.; 2006). Directed by Juan Carlos Claver. During Franco's dictatorship, a lesbian woman is confined by her family in a mental institution in order to cure her with electroshock treatment.

Krámpac [*Nico and Dani*] (91 min.; 2000). Directed by Cesc Gay. Dani is a teenager who wants physical contact with Nico, his school friend who is spending the summer with him.

La ley del deseo [*Law of Desire*] (102 min.; 1987). Directed by Pedro Almodóvar. A gay writer and director with a transsexual sister is strongly desired by Antonio, who stalks him.

La mala educación [*Bad Education*] (106 min.; 2004). Directed by Pedro Almodóvar. Sexual abuse, same-sex sexuality and love, drugs, friendship, and, overall, the effect of the Catholic and Franco's dictatorship educational system on the lives of a group of young men, are the main plot lines of this film.

Las cosas del querer [*The Things of Love*] (98 min.; 1989). Directed by Jaime Chávarri. A musical depicting life for Spanish homosexuals in the 1940s after the civil war. The plot is based on the life of the singer Miguel de Molina, who was incarcerated and exiled because of his homosexuality.

Ocaña, un retrato intermitente [*Ocana, an Intermittent Portrait*] (85 min.; 1978). Directed by Ventura Pons. A documentary not only about the life of painter Ocaña, but about his time and the places where he lived, revealing what happened after Franco's death.

Perdona bonita, pero Lucas me quería a mí [*Excuse Me Darling, but Lucas Loved Me*] (92 min.; 1997). Directed by Dunia Ayaso and Félix Sabroso. A camp comedy in which three gay housemates are involved in a murder.

Reinas [*Queens*] (107 min.; 2005). Directed by Gómez Pereira. Gay marriage is legal in Spain and this movie deals with the issue when presenting five mothers whose sons are getting married.

Web Sites

Organizations and Federations

Ambiente G, http://www.ambienteg.com.
   Commercial blog with news from the LGBT community.
Asociacion de Familias de Gays y Lesbianas con Hijos y Hijas, http://www.galehi.org.
   This association is a gathering point for all gays and lesbians who have children or want to have them. They provide information and counseling, and organize meetings and visits, especially for families with children.
Associació de Mares, Pares y Familiars de Gais y Lesbianes, http://www.ampgil.org.
   Parents of LGBT organized to protect their sons and daughters and themselves against homophobia. They have national meetings and workshops and organize information campaigns.
Asociación Española de Transexuales - Transexualia, http://www.transexualia.org.
   Spanish Association of Transsexual and Intersexual People Web site, with plenty of information and links concerning transsexuality and, to a lesser extent, intersexuality.
Bakala.org, http://www.bakala.org.
   Most successful local Web site for gay dating or just to find sex partners.
Chueca.com, http://www.chueca.com.
   Main Spanish LGBT Web site with news, chat rooms, surveys, blogs, personal profiles, Web dating, and more.
Colectivo de Transexuales de Cataluña, http://www.transsexualitat.org.
   Catalan Transsexual Association Web site that displays links, videos, documents, and other data about transsexuality.
COGAM, http://www.cogam.org.
   Madrid's main group is not only devoted to defending LGBT rights, but has extensive and specific programs for the community, including youth, lesbians, migrants, the elderly, deaf people, and transsexuals, as well as education and counseling programs, among others.
Coordinadora Gai-Lesbiana (Catalonia), http://www.cogailes.org.
   Catalonia LGBT Federation that works coordinately with FELGTB. For nationalist reasons, Catalan LGBT associations prefer not to join the Spanish federation.
Diario Digital Transexual, http://www.carlaantonelli.com.
   Everything concerning transsexuality.
Dos Manzanas, http://www.dosmanzanas.org.
   Daily updated blog with news for the LGBT community in Spanish. There are always plenty of discussions on controversial issues.
FELGTB (Spanish LGBT Federation), http://www.felgtb.org.
   More than 50 local LGBT associations are members of this federation to conduct political activism, HIV/AIDS prevention, campaigning for LGBT rights, and many other activities.
Fundación Triángulo, http://www.fundaciontriangulo.es.
   This foundation works in several regions of Spain (Madrid, Extremadura, Valladolid, Andalusia, and Valencia). Fundación Triángulo is behind the main LGBT film festivals throughout the country and in Latin America. They have specific programs for young LGBT and sex workers.

Federación Colegas, http://www.colegaweb.org.
> Federation of LGBT associations from southern Spain. They have campaigned for lesbians and transsexual rights and put a strong emphasis on fighting homophobia with a specific Web page, http://www.stophomofobia.com.

Grup de Lesbianes Feministes (Lesbian Feminist Barcelona), http://www.lesbifem.org.
> With background in both the LGBT movement and the feminist movement, this Catalan group works for lesbian women's rights, giving special importance to creating spaces for reflection and action.

El Hombre Transsexual, http://www.elhombretransexual.es.
> FTM transsexuals can use this site to contact other FTM and get legal and health information.

Kamasutra Lésbico, http://www.kamasutralesbico.net.
> Lesbian girls' site providing erotic images of sex between women.

HIV/AIDS

Coordinadora Estatal de VIH/SIDA, http://www.cesida.org.
> Spanish Federation of Organizations working in HIV/AIDS issues.

Gaispositius, http://www.gaispositius.org.
> Gay men living with HIV/AIDS.

Stop Sida, http://www.stopsida.org.
> HIV/AIDS prevention for MSM.

NOTES

1. Daniel Eisenberg, "La escondida senda: homosexuality in Spanish History and Culture," in *Introduction to Spanish Writers on Gay and Lesbian Themes: A Bio-Critical Sourcebook,* ed. David William Foster (Westport, CT: Greenwood Press, 1999), 1–21.

2. Armand Fluviá, *El moviment gai a la clandestinitat del franquisme (1970–1975),* (Barcelona: Laertes, 2003); and Ricardo Llamas and Fefa Vila, "Spain: Passion for life. Una historia del movimiento de lesbianas y gays en el estado español," in *ConCiencia de un singular deseo,* ed. Xosé M. Buxán (Barcelona: Laertes, 1997).

3. Kerman Calvo, "Polítiques d´(homo)sexualitat a Espanya. Les respostes de la democràcia davant d'un dilema moral," in *Sociologia de la sexualitat. Una aproximació a la diversitat sexual,* ed. Óscar Guasch (Barcelona: Fundació Bosch i Gimpera, Universitat de Barcelona, 2002).

4. Arturo Arnalte, *Redada de violetas: la represión de los homosexuales durante el franquismo* (Madrid: La esfera de los libros, 2003).

5. *Transsexuals* is the word used in Spain for transgender people.

6. Jesús Generelo and José Ignacio Pichardo, eds., *Homofobia en el sistema educativo* (Madrid: COGAM, 2005); José Ignacio Pichardo, Belén Molinuevo, and Pedro Rodríguez, *Actitudes ante la diversidad sexual de la población adolescente de Coslada (Madrid) y San Bartolomé de Tirajana (Gran Canaria)* (Madrid: FELGTB, 2007).

7. Pichardo, Molinuevo, and Rodríguez, *Actitudes ante la diversidad sexual de la población adolescente de Coslada (Madrid) y San Bartolomé de Tirajana.*

8. Ibid.

9. Luis Mitjans, Vicent Bataller, and Rubén Sancho, *Sexualidad y conductas sexuales preventivas en varones homosexuales de la comunidad valenciana* (Valencia: Generalitat Valenciana, Conselleria de Sanitat, 2003).

10. Centro de Investigaciones Sociológicas (CIS), *Barómetro de junio,* Estudio no. 2.568 (Madrid: CIS, 2004).

11. *ABC,* December 19, 2007.

12. *El País,* February 20, 2008.

13. Pichardo, Molinuevo, and Rodríguez, *Actitudes ante la diversidad sexual de la población adolescente de Coslada (Madrid) y San Bartolomé de Tirajana.*

14. *El País,* March 19, 2007.

15. Stop Sida, *Es cosa de hombres* (Barcelona: Stop Sida/CEESCAT, 2004).

16. José Antonio Nieto, "La intersexualidad y los límites del modelo 'dos sexos/dos géneros'" in *Sexualidades. Diversidad y control social,* ed. Oscar Guasch and Olga Viñuales (Barcelona: Bellaterra, 2003); and Nuria Gregori, "Los cuerpos ficticios de la biomedicina. El proceso de construcción del género en los protocolos médicos de asignación de sexo en bebés intersexuales," *AIBR Revista Iberoamericana de Antropología* 1, no. 1 (2006): 103–24.

17. *Diario de sesiones del Congreso de los Diputados,* April 15, 2004.

18. CIS, *Barómetro de abril,* Estudio no. 2.640 (Madrid: CIS, 2006).

19. European Commission, *European Social Reality,* Eurobarometer special no. 273, 2007.

20. CIS, *Barómetro de abril,* Estudio no. 2.672 (Madrid: CIS, 2007).

21. Pichardo, Molinuevo, and Rodríguez, *Actitudes ante la diversidad sexual de la población adolescente de Coslada (Madrid) y San Bartolomé de Tirajana.*

SWITZERLAND

Natalia Gerodetti

OVERVIEW

Switzerland is a land-locked country in the heart of Europe. It shares borders with France to the west, Italy to the south, Liechtenstein and Austria to the east, and Germany to the north. The Swiss territory encompasses approximately 16,216 square miles, and currently has an estimated 7.5 million inhabitants. Although its mythical origins and traditions go back to 1291 when William Tell famously defied the landlords, it has been a modern nation since 1848. Today, Switzerland is a complicated federalist state composed of central government, cantons, and communes with referendums and initiatives underpinning its political system, and has three official and four national languages (German, French, Italian, and Rumantsch).

Switzerland is characterized by an institutional balance between consensus democracy and pluralism, and celebrates its fundamental political institutions—neutrality, federalism, and direct democracy—as sacrosanct. These institutions are responsible for political, linguistic, confessional, and other compromises and conflicts in Switzerland.[1]

With few natural resources within its territory, a specialized economy has evolved in Switzerland, generating income from financial institutions, technology, and leisure and tourism, as well as the export of food products such as cheese and chocolate. It has astonishing wealth but is also hugely reliable on its huge proportion of foreign workers. Switzerland has always been a country of emigration as well as immigration; its present multicultural society comprises further languages, cultural traditions, and ethnicities than its four national languages would suggest. While Switzerland has been a progressive pioneer in areas such as technology, education, and psychology, it is also known for some of its discriminatory practices, such as its exclusion of women from the vote until 1971.[2]

In terms of the rights of citizens, Switzerland may have been the first nation to enfranchise all its male citizens in the late 1900s, but for many years this has obscured the limited political rights of other groups such as women and migrants. In other areas, however, the Swiss have produced legislation and policies that compare much more favorably with those of its European neighbors. In contrast to formal political rights, women gained an early access to higher education in Switzerland from the 1860s,[3] before any other European country. Inclusive education, it appears, has a longer and stronger tradition in Switzerland than political equality. This is probably not least due to educational pioneers such as Jean-Jacques Rousseau, whose ideas were well received among the French-speaking population, and Johann Pestalozzi, whose plea for compulsory education of boys and girls was implemented in German-speaking Protestant cantons even before the foundation of the nation state.

OVERVIEW OF LGBT ISSUES

Switzerland was a pioneer in relation to its criminal law, which legalized consenting same-sex relationships in 1942, before other European countries did so.[4] While the age of consent was set at 20 years in 1942 for both sexes, a more recent revision of the criminal law lowered the age of consent to 16 years in 1991.[5] In 2005, the ILGA (International Lesbian and Gay Association) World Conference was held in Geneva and registered partnerships became a legal option on a cantonal basis. Since January 1, 2007, registered partnerships have been legal under federal law. Political activism in the LGBT movement in Switzerland now centers not only on international equality issues but also on education, which is seen as an important location of intervention because the rate of suicide is still considerably higher amongst LGBT youths than their heterosexual peers.

As for religion, the predominant religion of Switzerland is Christianity, and the country is evenly balanced between Protestants and Catholics with a complex patchwork across the nation. There are also sizeable minority religions such as Islam and Eastern Orthodox Christianity due to the immigrant populations, and there are a significant number of atheists. Religion has a historical importance and a personal importance for Swiss individuals, but it is less overtly found in the majority of public discourses. The campaign for marital rights and recognized same-sex partnerships has invoked some reactions from religious leaders who spoke out against them, yet their opinions found no majority.

As for the Swiss military, the gays in the military debate has been largely absent in Switzerland, not least because the Swiss Army is largely based on conscription. All males are conscripted at the age of 19 years for introductory and then annual short training courses, and women can join the army on a voluntary basis. The army has not been involved in war or combat for a long time, and it is largely involved in peacekeeping or civic activities. What has shaken the Swiss military most in its foundation recently was an initiative to abolish the army, which received support from 35.6 percent of the electorate. This has been taken to mean that the army is no longer the national icon it perhaps once was. Nonconformist identities, therefore, no longer pose a strong threat to national identity, as they once did. In contrast to civil life, the military penal code had outlawed same-sex activities.

EDUCATION

Within the federal state, education remains, somewhat controversially, a cantonal matter. Because of this, names of schools, subjects, and the starting age of students and duration vary significantly. Textbooks are under no obligation to address sexuality, although efforts to address sexuality are intensifying with regard to both sexual education and institutional support of diversity in the education system. A number of organizations (Pink Cross, LOS [the Swiss Lesbian Organization], and FELS [Friends and Parents of Lesbian and Gay People]) actively lobby the cantonal education authorities to support gay and lesbian pupils in schools. While the last 30 years have seen remarkable success in relation to the visibility of sexual minorities, schools do perpetuate forms of discrimination or isolation. Lesbian and gay youth have a suicide rate four to seven times higher than that of heterosexual youth.[6] Organizations such as Pink Cross, LOS, and FELS want to encourage lesbian and gay teachers to be visible role models without fear of recrimination, and they also want education about sexual orientation incorporated into the curriculum.

With regard to these issues, Swiss organizations call for the state to adopt official support of the International Day against Homophobia on May 17, which is already supported by 50 states. The date was chosen because the World Health Organization (WHO) crossed homosexuality off the list of pathologies on that day. Various forms of awareness-raising and direct action campaigns are also used to bring lesbian and gay issues into the education agenda. For example, an organization called RainbowLine posts advertisements in the form of stickers in school restrooms for support groups for gay male students in vocational training and further education. In recent years, campaigns to promote sexual education that includes a portrayal of homosexuality in a neutral way and that constitutes part of the curriculum have been increasing. With the increasing use of the Internet as a tool of education, and with public funding to support the inclusion of Web-based knowledge in schools, LGBT organizations have been critical of schools and Internet providers that deny access to lesbian and gay support and information sites. This effort to police access to sexual information, while targeted at pornography, deploys such a wide definition of indecency that it has a severe discriminatory effect on lesbian and gay issues. Several organizations, beyond the national lobby groups, work in school environments with students, teachers, parents, and educational authorities to address issues that affect LGBT students.

There has been an increasing interest in LGBT issues in academic contexts and although there are no LGBT studies or queer theory programs in Switzerland, courses on these subjects are being taught by interested academics as part of their modules within existing undergraduate or postgraduate programs, particularly at universities where there are gender studies departments or programs available.

EMPLOYMENT AND ECONOMICS

Switzerland has few natural resources and has traditionally fostered a highly qualified labor force that performs highly skilled work in areas such as microtechnology, hi-tech, biotechnology, and pharmaceuticals, as well as banking and insurance. Like many industrialized countries, the service sector is the biggest employer where many people work in small and medium-sized enterprises, which are crucial to the Swiss economy. Situated within a geographical region that has a fragile environment, the Swiss have long been concerned about the environmental impact of economic activity, and energy and transport policies in particular have been trying to be environmentally friendly.

While concern for the environment has been long established, policies regulating and safeguarding employment relations are somewhat slower to emerge. In relation to gender, employment relations are safeguarded by federal legislation mandating equal pay for men and women, maternity insurance, and retirement benefits. The principle of gender equality has been part of the constitution since 1981, and in 1996 the Gender Equality Act came into effect. Legislation addressing LGBT issues has existed since 2000, when it was laid down in the constitution that it is illegal to discriminate on the basis of *lifestyle,* meaning sexual orientation. In reality, this legislation has been slow to take effect. In relation to pension systems for same-sex partners, for instance, varied practices existed until registered partnerships became a legal reality.

Gay and lesbian organizations demand greater efforts to safeguard the rights of lesbian and gay employees, who continue to experience discrimination in the workplace. LGBT people can face nonemployment because of their identity, harassment at work, being prevented from promotion, or even termination. While there is some legal protection, it is often hard to find evidence that would hold up in court for these discriminatory practices, and victims of discrimination might simply choose to move away from the troublesome workplace.

Other strategies have been found to strengthen the position of LGBT people in employment, such as the creation of networks. The conservative gay manager organization network is concerned about educational issues as well as employment issues, and demands more respect and recognition of homosexual rights, particularly in the context of cultural diversity. Demands are made for better federal protection and policies that address citizenship issues, including sexual citizenship. Network is an organization of 270 male managers in Switzerland and explicitly excludes women. A female equivalent, WyberNet, was thus created to address the particular issues of lesbian women in management and executive positions. Wyber-Net serves to establish a wide range of connections between lesbians and aims to have a strong public presence to contribute to the recognition of a gay women's community in society, economy, culture, and politics. Another lobby group, Fachgruppe Arbeitswelt, aims to deal with employment issues and a wider recognition of diversity across the gender divide.

PinkRail, on the other hand, has been campaigning successfully on employment and public service issues in relation to public transport and, in particular, to the national railways. Most notably, they have been successful in obtaining equal recognition of same-sex partnerships for the purpose of discount rail season tickets. Given the centrality of the railways to transport and to Swiss national identity, this has been seen as an important milestone. In addition, as a public sector employer, upper management has since been supportive of a number of demands and has publicly supported gay and lesbian events.

SOCIAL/GOVERNMENT PROGRAMS

Funding for LGBT projects can be obtained from publicly funded organizations. In addition, there are specific funding opportunities for LGBT issues such as the nongovernmental organization (NGO) Respect The aim is to secure long-term funding for projects and services that assist in promoting nondiscriminatory views and practices in society, but that also help to strengthen the identity of lesbians and gay men.

SEXUALITY/SEXUAL PRACTICES

The Swiss moral fabric is as complex as anywhere else but could be placed somewhere along the liberal continuum. The decriminalization of consenting homosexuality in 1942 was an early indicator that what is done in private is not of particular interest to the public or the state. In 1991, the age of consent for same-sex sexual practices was lowered to 16 years, equalizing it with the age of consent for heterosexual sex. This has meant that teenagers' sexual intercourse was no longer threatened by legal prosecution. Leading up to this change in law was a much stronger presence of the lesbian and gay movement, which has campaigned since the 1970s, together with the women's movement, on changing the law in relation to sex-related offenses. This Swiss respect for privacy, on the other hand, has also meant that public figures are rarely outgoing about their sexual identities.

Part of a new visibility in relation to sexuality was prompted by HIV/AIDS and, in 1985, the Swiss Aids Federation (SAF) was founded. While a public profile and campaigns around HIV transmission that treated all routes of transmission equally was rapidly established, sex education and the free distribution of condoms in schools was rather slower to happen if at all. While adults could reasonably easily access information and free condoms, there was a marked difference in the treatment of young people. With the lowering of the age of consent and a more general change in society and popular culture in regard to sexuality, this could be expected to change in future.

FAMILY

LGBT people in the West have gone some way to redefining the traditional nuclear family that has been upheld in the postwar era as a social ideal. Given the relative social, political, and cultural parallels across the West, in Switzerland as elsewhere LGBT people have formed couples, families with children, extended families including blood family and/or extended family, and a variety of other understandings of *family* to which individuals see themselves as belonging. The sociological literature, which attests that understandings of love and intimacy, which can be found amongst LGBT people, have an increasingly wider impact, also holds true for Switzerland in general, where people are engaged in a variety of relationships.

This variety of practices is, to some extent, under threat from the metanarrative of legally recognized and registered partnerships as they are increasingly available to people. The registration of same-sex partnerships has become a widely recognized and debated form of same-sex intimacy. From January 2007 to April 2008, 2,300 partnerships were registered, of which 1,600 were between men.[7]

While Swiss law and the constitution hold that that people should have the right to privacy and a protected family life,[8] the federal court has decided that this does not apply to same-sex partnerships. Partners of Swiss nationals or of foreign nationals with permanent residency in Switzerland face severe difficulties to obtain a permit to stay, and decisions are left with cantonal authorities, which decide whether non-Swiss partners will receive residence permits.

Since 1998, 557 permits have been issued for same-sex couples when SLAP was founded in 1998, on the one hand to support same-sex couples of different nationalities in their pursuit to obtain residency status, and on the other hand to carry out public promotional and educational work to raise awareness about the difficulties that same-sex couples face in that situation. SLAP stands for Gay and Lesbian with Foreign Partners (Schwule & Lesben mit ausländischen PartnerInnen), but the English meaning of the acronym is equally invoked to signify waking up the authorities.

It is legal in Switzerland for transsexuals to alter their birth certificate and marry following surgery.

COMMUNITY

The LGBT community has had a long history in German-speaking countries. Germany, for example, had seen quite outspoken gay organizations before the destruction of Magnus Hirschfeld's Institute for Sex Research and the Scientific Humanitarian Committee in 1933. In Switzerland, the organization and the international magazine *Der Kreis* continuously promoted the legal and social rights of gay men from 1932 until 1967. *Der Kreis* was the only continuously existing gay organization bridging the first and second wave of cultural and political activism.

The decriminalization of consensual adult same-sex relations in 1942 was an important legal step not just for lesbian and gay people in Switzerland, but also for those migrating during the war years. The border canton of Basel had been renowned for its liberal law on same-sex relations since 1919, and had been an attractive city for traveling homosexuals. At the same time, early access for women to higher education had already attracted many international sapphists to Swiss university towns since the late 1800s.

The New York Stonewall riots claim their place in Swiss LGBT history, although it was an event that was mostly known through the media. They were a catalyst for changing perceptions of community and the secrecy under which gay clubs operated beforehand. The 1970s witnessed activism to change the criminal law in regard to the age of consent; although Swiss criminal law did not penalize consenting homosexual relations from 1942, it set the age of consent at 20 years of age. Integral to the gay liberation movement of the 1970s were the newly emerging social understandings of homosexuality, which were also fuelled by pride marches. The first Gay Pride march in Switzerland took place in Zurich in 1978. Since then, an annual Gay Pride event takes place in different cities or towns each year, with some locations proving more contentious than others.

Criticizing the institutions of heterosexuality, marriage, and the family allowed distinct, positive gay and lesbian identities to emerge. In the 1980s, various local urban homosexual pressure groups (*Homosexuelle Arbeitsgruppen*) emerged that had a political as well as a social purpose. In 1989, the LOS was founded. The removal of homosexuality from the list of pathologies by the World Health Organization (WHO) spurred more local organizations to emerge, such as the Pink Cross in 1993, the Fondation d'Alpagai in 1994, and the Fondation de Vogay in 1997.

Most groups have always had a larger male membership and continue to do so. Lesbians who were politically engaged in Switzerland would more likely join feminist groups. At times this proved to have its own problems when the women's movement, which only just had a major success with the women's vote in 1971, did not want to engage in the politics of sexuality. From the 1970s to 1989, lesbians struggled to have their distinct voices heard. LOS was founded in 1990, and aimed to specifically represent lesbian interests. Some social movements in Switzerland continue to operate with membership and statutes. Social and political organization in Switzerland works overwhelmingly through groups with statutes, attesting perhaps to a notable adherence to social order and rules. Direct public action mostly adheres to sanctioned campaigns. Nevertheless, less formal, non-mainstream LGBT political movements also emerged in the late 1980s through the youth movement and its urban manifestations in cultural centers and cultural politics.

HEALTH

HIV/AIDS has received public attention since the early 1980s, and the federal government has worked together with organizations engaged in preventative work. The SAF (Swiss AIDS Federation), established in 1985, is a national AIDS organization. AIDS campaigns in Switzerland were deployed early on and have had a relatively high profile without stigmatizing particular populations. The three main aims of the SAF remain the prevention of HIV infection, the defense of a good quality life for people with HIV/AIDS, and legal representation and the promotion of solidarity. In addition, SAF generally strives to prevent the spread of other STDs (sexually transmitted diseases) such as hepatitis, as well as to promote good sexual health.

Currently, about there are about 25,000 people living with HIV and AIDS in Switzerland. With regard to the cumulative number of AIDS patients in Switzerland, it is regularly one of the highest in Europe. Since 1996, fewer Swiss people have developed AIDS due to the newly developed medicines, but challenges still face those living with HIV to deal with the impact on their career and social prospects. Life quality includes social integration in addition to from physiological and mental health, and it is recognized that many HIV-positive people have to deal with discrimination at work and difficulty in finding partners.

In addition, between 70,000 and 90,000 people in Switzerland have a form of chronic hepatitis B or C, and many others do not know their status. The notion of sexual health with which SAF operates is derived from the WHO definition, which sees sexuality as an important aspect of health and as part of sexual and reproductive rights.[9] From the start of the epidemic to the end of December 2006, more than 8,600 cases of AIDS have been recorded, and 5,738 people have died of the consequences of AIDS. In 2007, 761 new positive HIV test results were recorded and, of these, 30 percent were women. Approximately 45 percent of all infections in Switzerland are due to heterosexual contact. In 2006, 60 percent of the men acquired HIV/AIDS through sex with men, while 29 percent acquired it through sex with women, and 8 percent through intravenous drug use. Meanwhile, 83 percent of female HIV/AIDS patients acquired the disease through sex with men, 7 percent through intravenous drug use, and 10 percent through unknown means.[10]

Health needs of lesbians or bisexuals are acknowledged by organizations such as LOS and advice and support given. Though health needs may not directly relate to sexual identity per se, such that breast cancer is not thought to occur more frequently amongst lesbians, health needs may be exacerbated by sexual identity. Mental health issues tend to be greater amongst all minorities concomitant with society's lack of acknowledgment of diverse identities. Similarly, domestic violence may pose an even bigger problem to lesbians, as same-sex domestic violence is rarely mentioned in domestic violence support documentation.[11]

POLITICS AND LAW

As of 2000, the new federal constitution prohibits discrimination on the basis of sexual orientation, paving both the way for better employment protection and same-sex partnership recognition acts, first on a cantonal basis then on a national basis. Since 1996, the Gender Equality Act has provided a legal framework against discrimination on the basis of gender. In terms of the treatment of sexual violence in the Swiss criminal law, rape is treated differently according to gender. The traditional paragraph dealing with rape defines it explicitly as "forced sexual intercourse of a woman" because sexual intercourse has always been defined as a heterosexual act in law. Nevertheless, there are provisions to prosecute sexual violence against men, although the perpetrators of these crimes are less severely penalized. Rape within marriage has only been acknowledged since 1992 in Swiss law.[12] Violence against people is punishable without making specific provisions for gender or sexual orientation.

Switzerland introduced registered partnerships first on a regional and cantonal basis, creating a fragmented patchwork that largely made this form of legal recognition available in the bigger cities. Geneva was the first city to allow registered partnerships in 2001, followed by Zurich in 2003, then Neuchâtel and Fribourg in 2004. The French-speaking cantons, regardless of religious influence, were thus the first to make provisions for partnership recognitions.

Since January 1, 2007, a federal law has come into force that allows nationally recognized registered partnerships. Registered partnerships give same-sex couples some of the same rights and responsibilities under the law as heterosexual married couples, except for rights related to adoption, fertility treatment, and taking the same surname. Thus, registered partners are considered as one economic unit with the duty of financial support between the partners. Taxes are paid on the same basis as married couples, and public and private pension provisions are also calculated the same way as for married partners.[13]

There has been some opposition to both the cantonal and the national legislation by the Federal Democratic Union, which collected enough signatures to force a national referendum. Given that the national legislation was put to a public vote and gained majority support, however, it is reasonable to conclude that those lobbying against registered partnerships were a vocal but ultimately insignificant minority.

Lesbian and gay organizations have been slow to incorporate further sexual and gender diversity initiatives into their cultural and political efforts, although in recent years this can increasingly be seen in urban centers. Opportunities for transgender and intersex people to organize, campaign, and socialize have thus been vastly increased by virtual and online technologies that allow for anonymity and communication across great distances. The French-speaking Intersex Network of Europe (FINE) is an important site for local, national, and international connections, publications, and blogs for intersex communities. The Swiss German intersex group intersex.ch has named four demands that overlap between health issues and social and political demands: no forced operations on intersex children who have not given informed consent; policies on respecting intersex children's particular needs, including fostering contact with other intersex children; information and support for parents of intersex children; and the dissemination of information to society in general and health professionals in particular about intersexuality.[14]

Gender reassignment is legal or openly performed without prosecution. Upon surgery, all personal documents such as the birth certificate, driving license, passport, social security, and so forth, can be reissued to reflect the change. Consequently, transsexuals are also allowed to marry.[15]

Nevertheless, transgender and intersex politics, communities, and identities continue to suffer from discrimination and acts of violence. Transgender Association Switzerland (TAS) is a group that works on both transgender and intersex issues in an attempt to combine efforts despite differences. TAS campaigns against the exclusion of transgender and intersex people from social, cultural, and institutional life in Switzerland. In addition, it offers a platform for discussion, provides a social space, and organizes self-awareness groups.

Transgender and intersex people often face a lack of understanding and exclusion from lesbian and gay communities and organizations. Some continue to use the acronym of LGBT in their documents and programs without specifically taking account of the specificities of either transgender or intersex people, while other groups consciously restrict their aims and goals to lesbian and gay people, in an effort to gain ground and acceptance within society for lesbians and gay men.

RELIGION AND SPIRITUALITY

LGBT people are active members of many churches, but at the same time, do not receive complete acceptance from their churches. The Catholic Church in particular, which has a stronghold in some cantons in Switzerland, has been generating public discourse about the dangerousness of LGBT people, casting them as child abusers who endanger the health of the population. Calling the 2001 pride events in the Catholic canton Wallis a "devilish game," the Catholic Church was most vocal in denouncing these public manifestations, and also raised opposition to the registered partnership act.

In terms of being included in religious communities, LGBT people also face marginalization or exclusion, despite the efforts of groups such as COOL (Christliche Organisation von Lesben) and ADAMIM (Verein Schwule Seelsorger) are the lesbian and gay groups within the Swiss Christian church that work to combat LGBT discrimination and exclusion from religious life.[16] It is acknowledged that the choice between partner and faith can lead to pressures that can in turn lead to physical and mental health difficulties, and that more lobbying is necessary before the churches acknowledge homosexuality as an equal lifestyle.

VIOLENCE

Violence towards LGBT people exists in Switzerland in subtle as well as more overt forms. There were more reports of antigay violence in 2007 than ever before,[17] though it is unclear whether this is due to the efforts of gay organizations to encourage more people to report or whether actual incidents have increased. In addition to encouraging people to report all incidences of homophobic violence, Pink Cross has also launched a campaign to address antigay violence in the public sphere more widely. Agencies seem to address a variety of forms of violence, such as sexual abuse during youth and antigay violence during adulthood, and a number of support services are available. It appears, however, that these agencies have not yet acknowledged and addressed the existence of abuse or domestic violence within same-sex couples.

Men's bureaus (*Männerbüros*) exist in all bigger Swiss cities, and they address wider issues in relation to masculinity and identity. They work with men who are violent, men who have been abused, and gay men who have experienced antigay violence.

OUTLOOK FOR THE 21ST CENTURY

Awareness of LGBT issues in Switzerland will increase in years to come. The presence of LGBT people and their concerns in the public sphere, both in terms of legislative protection and cultural expression, will continue to be an issue for campaigners. Bisexuals, transgender people, and intersex people still remain invisible to the mainstream Swiss population, and they are just beginning to promote their issues to the mainstream as well as the lesbian and gay communities.

RESOURCE GUIDE

Suggested Reading

Beat Gerber, *Lila ist die Farbe des Regenbogens, Schwestern, die Farbe der Befreiung ist rot: Die Homosexuellen Arbeitsgruppen der Schweiz (HACH) von 1974–1995* (Köniz, Switzerland: Edition Soziothek, 1998).

Natalia Gerodetti, *Modernising Sexualities: Toward a Socio-historical Understanding of Sexualities in the Swiss Nation* (Bern, Switzerland: Peter Lang, 2005).

Rudolf Jaun and Brigitte Studer, eds., *Weiblich—männlich. Geschlechterverhältnisse in der Schweiz. Rechtssprechung, Diskurs, Praktiken* (Zurich: Chronos, 1995).

Hubert Kennedy, *The Ideal Gay Man: The Story of "Der Kreis"* (Binghamton: Haworth Press, 1995).

Ilse Kokula and Ulrike Böhmer, *Und die Welt gehört uns doch! Zusammenschluss lesbischer Frauen in der Schweiz der 30er Jahre* (Zurich: eFeF-Verlag, 1991).

Rüdiger Lautmann, ed., *Homosexualität. Handbuch der Theorie- und Forschungsgeschichte* (Frankfurt am Main: Campus, 1993).

Helmut Puff, ed., *Lust, Angst und Provokation. Homosexualität in der Gesellschaft* (Göttingen and Zürich: Vandenhoeck und Ruprecht, 1993).

Udo Rauchfleisch, *Schwule—Lesben—Bisexualle. Lebensweisen, Vorurteile, Einsichten* (Göttingen, Germany: Vandenhoeck and Ruprecht, 1994).

Web Sites

ADAMIM (Organization of Gay Curates in Switzerland), http://www.adamim.ch/,
E-mail: info@adamim.ch
> Open to all who are active within the church, interconfessional.

Cool—Christliche Organisation von Lesben, http://www.cool-schweiz.ch/ Religious organization for lesbians.

CSD-Zurich, http://www.csdzh.ch
> Organizer of pride events, taking its acronym from Christopher Street Day in New York.

Frauenraum (Women's Room), http://www.frauenraum.ch/reitschule/frauenag/index.shtml.
> Frauenraum is an alternative cultural space for sociopolitical work as well as a party space.

HAZ, Homosexuelle Arbeitsgruppen Zürich, http://www.haz.ch/
> Local network and campaign group for the Zurich region.

ImMigration, SLAP *Schwule & Lesben mit ausländischen PartnerInnen,* http://www.swiss-slap.ch/
> Network and support forum for binational couples.

Lesbische und Schwule Basiskirche Basel, http://www.lsbk.ch/
> Lesbian and gay ecumenical community in northern Switzerland, bordering onto France and Germany.

Lestime, http://www.lestime.ch/
> Geneva-based lesbian organization and network.

LOS (Lesbian Organization Switzerland), http://www.los.ch/
> National lesbian organization with local regional and national events, campaigning groups, and much more.

Pink Cross, http://www.pinkcross.ch
> National gay organization with local regional and national events, campaigning groups, and much more.

Spot 25, Gay Youth Group Zurich, http://swix.ch/spot25/ (German), http://swix.ch/spot25/englisch/index.html (English)
> Youth group in the largest Swiss city.

Health

Swiss AIDS Federation, http://www.aids.ch/
> NGO working on HIV/AIDS issues.

Sport

Gaysport Zürich, http://www.gaysport.ch/
> Gay sports organization and network for Switzerland's biggest city.

Education

French-speaking Intersex Network of Europe (FINE)
intersex.ch, http://www.intersex.ch
> Online support and campaigning network.

Männerbüro Bern, http://www.mumm.ch
> Network, support, and campaign initiatives for men.

RainbowLine, http://www.rainbowline.ch
> Phone helpline and Internet support for LGBT teenagers and people working in education.

GLL—*das andere schulprojekt Gleichgeschlechtliche liebe leben,* http://www.gll.ch
    Educational promotion materials and training.
Réseau des Intersexué-e-s Francophones d'Europe (RIFE), rife@webglaz.ch
    Online intersex network.
Transgender Association Switzerland, http://www.tas-org.ch/
    Transgender support network.

Film Festivals

http://www.pinkapple.ch/
    Schwullesbisches film festival in Zurich and Frauenfeld.
http://www.queersicht.ch/
    Lesbisch-schwules Filmfestival Bern.

NOTES

1. Deconstructing this mythology, it has been argued that rather than happy to-gether, the Swiss live happy apart, and that, indeed, Switzerland is highly compartmen-talized. As Kriesi says: "The Swiss get along because they don't understand each other," Hanspeter Kriesi, *Le Système Politique Suisse* (Paris: Economica, 1998).

2. For good introductions to the Swiss social, historical, and political context, see for example Jonathan Steinberg, *Why Switzerland?* (Cambridge: Cambridge University Press, 1996) or Frederick William Dame, *A History of Switzerland,* vols. 1, 2, and 3 (New York: Edwin Mellen Press, 2001).

3. Nadescha Suslowa was the first woman to get a doctorate from Zürich University in 1867 (see, Beatrix Mesmer, *Ausgeklammert—Eingeklammert: Frauen und Frauenorgani-sationen in der Schweiz des 19. Jahrhunderts* [Basel: Helbing & Lichtenhahn, 1988]), but women were allowed into the auditoriums of the University of Zürich from the early 1860s. It was upon a petition of Swiss mothers, amongst them Marie Goegg, that women were allowed to graduate from Swiss universities from the 1870s onward, albeit with massive resistance from some universities such as Basel, see Elisabeth Joris and Heidi Witzig, eds., *Frauengeschichte(n). Dokumente aus zwei Jahrhunderten zur Situation der Frauen in der Schweiz* (Zürich: Limmat Verlag, 1986). However, restrictions remained in place as to the professional possibilities available to these women.

4. Natalia Gerodetti, *Modernising Sexualities: Toward a Socio-historical Understand-ing of Sexualities in the Swiss Nation* (Bern: Peter Lang, 2005).

5. See Gerodetti, *Modernising Sexualities,* or Beat Gerber, *Lila ist die Farbe des Re-genbogens, Schwestern, die Farbe der Befreiung ist rot: Die Homosexuellen Arbeitsgruppen der Schweiz (HACH) von 1974–1995* (Köniz: Edition Soziothek, 1998).

6. See the Bernese Coalition against Depression, which draws on research by Han-sruedi Völkle and has worked hard to combat the high rates of suicide amongst LGBT teenagers, "Suizid bei jungen Homosexuellen. Berner Bündnis gegen Depression," http://www.zugerbuendnis.ch/buendnis/docs/s46_47.pdf (accessed May 28, 2008).

7. Swiss Office for Statistics, *Bevölkerungsbewegung—Indikatoren. Eingetragene Partnerschaften,* 2008, http://www.bfs.admin.ch/bfs/portal/de/index/themen/01/06/blank/key/07.html (accessed May 28, 2008).

8. BV Art. 13 Abs. 1 and EMRK Art.8.

9. The World Health Organization's (WHO) definition of sexual health is "A state of physical, emotional, mental and social well-being related to sexuality; not merely the absence of disease, dysfunction or infirmity. Sexual health requires a positive and respectful approach to sexuality and sexual relationships, as well as the possibility of having pleasur-able and safe sexual experiences, free of coercion, discrimination and violence. For sexual health to be attained and maintained, the sexual rights of all persons must be protected,

respected and fulfilled," http://www.lho.org.uk/LHO_Topics/Health_Topics/Determi
nants_of_Health/Lifestyle_and_Behaviour/SexualHealth.aspx (accessed July 8, 2009). Or
see World Health Organization (WHO), for more information, http://www.who.int/en/
(accessed May 28, 2008).

10. See Swiss Aids Federation, http://www.aids.ch/d/fragen/zahlen.php (accessed
July 8, 2009).

11. See also International Lesbian and Gay Association (ILGA), *Lesbian and Bisexual
Women's Health: Common Concerns,* local issues report 121, ILGA, March 2006, http://
doc.ilga.org/ilga/publications/publications_in_english/other_publications/lesbian_and_
bisexual_women_s_health_report (accessed May 28, 2008).

12. See StGB (Schweizerisches Strafgesetzbuch [Swiss Criminal Code]) but also Peter M.
Leuenberger, Vergewaltigungsmythen in der Literatur von 1980–2000 zum Thema Verge-
waltigung, Semesterarbeit, Fachhochschule Solothurn Nordwestschweiz, 2002.

13. Although female partners are treated the same as widowers, a remaining female
partner will only receive a pension when there are children younger than 18 years present
who are also entitled to a pension. By contrast, a regular widow will receive a pension if she
is 45 years or older and was married for at least five years, http://www.vpod-ssp.ch/vpod/
berufe/infoblatt_partnerschaftsgesetz.pdf (accessed May 28, 2008).

14. See www.intersex.ch for a more extensive discussion.

15. See Press for Change, which campaigns for respect and equality for trans people.
Integrating Transsexual and Transgendered People, http://www.pfc.org.uk/node/345,
and for an International comparison see *Sexual Minorities and the Law: A World Survey* (updated 2006), http://www.asylumlaw.org/docs/sexualminorities/World%20SurveyAIho
mosexuality.pdf.

16. ADAMIM are an active networking group of gay men from different confessional
denominations who work within religious settings. See the link and archival material on the
media debate through ADAMIM's Web site, http://www.adamim.ch/archiv_verzeichnis.
htm.

17. See support and reports on www.pinkcross.ch, which is the umbrella association
of gay organizations in Switzerland, as well as queeramnesty.ch, the Swiss Amnesty International LGBT-group, fighting against identity-based discrimination and for the rights of
lesbians, gays, bisexuals, and transgender people in Switzerland, http://www.queeramnesty.
ch/index.htm.

TURKEY

Emrecan Özen

OVERVIEW

The Republic of Turkey has an area of 300,948 square miles. One of the few transcontinental countries, 291,772 square miles of Turkey's land is in Anatolia (in Asia), while 9,175 square miles is in southeast Europe. The Marmara Sea lies between the two continents, and is connected to the Black Sea by the strait of Bosphorus, and to the Aegean Sea by the Dardanelles. Turkey's neighboring countries are Greece and Bulgaria in Europe, and Georgia, Armenia, Azerbaijan, Iran, Iraq, and Syria in Asia. The Anatolian peninsula is surrounded by four seas: the Black Sea to the north, the inland Sea of Marmara to the northwest, the Aegean Sea to the west, and the Mediterranean Sea to the south.

The country has a rapidly growing population. As of December 2007, Turkey's population was 70,586,256,[1] while the official 2000 census showed 67,803,927 people,[2] with a density of 40 people per square mile. The growth rate is 1.5 percent per year. Over 10 million people live in Istanbul. Ankara is the capital city, and is the second largest city after Istanbul, followed by Izmir on the Aegean coast.[3] The country is divided into 7 regions and 81 provinces.

The republic was proclaimed on October 29, 1923, following the fall of the Ottoman Empire and the Turkish War of Independence. After 22 years of a single-party system, the republic is now a multiparty, parliamentary representative democracy. It is a secular, unitary state. It is also currently a candidate to join the European Union (EU), and the negotiations for this started in late 2004.[4]

Turkey has been described as a bridge between the East and the West, not only because of its geographical position, but also thanks to its immensely diverse cultural heritage. All over the country, it is possible to find, side by side, the modern and the traditional, the West and the East, the European and the Islamic, the wealthiest and the poorest. While life in big cities is relaxed enough to let sexual minorities thrive, smaller cities and rural areas are still steadfastly traditional. Istanbul—renowned throughout the world as a popular vacation destination, an industrious business hub, and a center of culture and entertainment—remains the safest and easiest place to live for LGBT people in Turkey.

OVERVIEW OF LGBT ISSUES

While gay life and the gay scene are flourishing in contemporary Turkey, legal rights and LGBT visibility suffer greatly from censorship and invisibility. With a modernization process in full force, progress in gay rights has been swift, but rarely solid enough to keep the momentum going. The media pays little attention to gay and lesbian issues, and when it does, it is threatened with legal action due to ambiguous regulations about public order and morals. Therefore, almost all developments in the LGBT world—legal battles, hate crimes, pride parades, and all other negative or positive news—go unacknowledged or censored in the media, and the biggest challenge that faces the country's LGBT rights organizations is to find a mechanism by which to bring important matters into public view to create an active gay rights discourse.

At the same time, LGBT-related issues generally cause tension and controversy when brought up in a public forum. Man-boy love (pederasty) was very prevalent in the Ottoman culture, and contemporary Turkish gay culture has made this a pivotal point in the fight for gay rights.[5] However, the official history books rarely, if ever, mention this, and hard-line nationalists strongly oppose discussions of what they see as an insult to their ancestors.

Almost all gay rights organizations in Turkey have histories full of legal battles against public prosecutors who try to close them down, with many, though not all, pride parades and other demonstrations obstructed.

EDUCATION

The Ministry of National Education controls matters of education in Turkey. The Council of Higher Education of the Republic of Turkey was formed as an autonomous body in 1981, to preside over all the universities in the country. Whether the council of higher education should exist is highly contested by many, its far-reaching duties questioned and criticized, with frequent demands to grant universities autonomy.

There is no government or nongovernmental organization (NGO) program working specifically against homophobic bullying in schools. However, two gay rights groups exist in universities. The Üniversitelerarası Lezbiyen ve Gey Topluluğu, also known as LEGATO (Lesbian and Gay Interuniversity Organization), was formed at the Middle East Technical University in Ankara in 1996. Shortly there-after, other branches were opened in other universities, and in 2002 all branches were merged to form the biggest gay and lesbian organization in Turkey.

Additionally, the Bilgi Gökkuşağı LGBT Kulübü (Bilgi Rainbow LGBT Club) was formed in early 2007 and became the first LGBT group in a Turkish university with an official authorization from the university rectorate and the council of higher education. News about the club caused an outrage where reported, and members of an education union filed an official complaint to the chief prosecutor's office against the council and the rectorate for giving authorization for the club.[6] The rectorate has also been criticized by the club members, who have alleged that the university gave permission to the club only as a superficial gesture to seem liberal and Western, while the activities of the club have been unofficially suppressed.

EMPLOYMENT AND ECONOMICS

In Turkey, the private sector's involvement has drastically increased in the past couple of decades, and the country's economy has been growing rapidly. Industrial growth has been swift, and the agricultural output is dramatically higher, while the service sector is expanding. At the same time, the public sector still enjoys consid-erable size and influence. The country's per capita gross domestic product (GDP) is $10,737.

There is no antidiscrimination law in Turkey regarding sexual minorities, and discrimination in the workplace forces many gay men and women to stay in the closet. Coming out can cause homophobic bullying, or can even be grounds for dismissal. Virtually no workplace offers jobs for transsexuals, and almost all trans-gender persons are forced into some form of sex work, where they are harassed by the police and the public.

The biggest problem facing male LGBT persons when joining the workforce is closely related to the mandatory military service for all male citizens of a certain age. (This age is fixed at 20, but the service is postponed for university students until they graduate.) With an official application, gay men can get exemptions from mandatory military service.

While getting an exemption might mean getting out of a 15-month service at a strongly and openly antigay institution where homophobic abuse and assault is very likely, it also substantially lessens one's employability. As with all others ex-empted from mandatory military service, exempted gay men are deprived of the right to work for any institution that is owned by the state (including public of-fices, the government, some universities, and banks), because they are registered as mentally unfit for service.[7]

At the same time, the necessity to provide details of personal military history in job applications (because employers rarely hire people who will soon be recruited) is another obstacle for exempted gay men who are looking to find a job in the private sector. The required disclosure of the details of exemption works as a forced coming out, and employers are likely to choose not to hire gay men—especially considering that there is no law that prohibits discrimination based on sexual orientation.

SOCIAL/GOVERNMENT PROGRAMS

There are no social or government programs that are directed to reach out to LGBT persons in Turkey.

SEXUALITY/SEXUAL PRACTICES

Even in big cities, masculinity is ardently treasured, and machismo is very strong. At the same time, strict gender-based understandings of sexuality are very prominent. Therefore, homosexuality is considered a sort of feminization—a loss of manhood, a failure in one's masculinity. Similarly, a man can retain his masculinity as long as he remains solely the penetrative partner. Therefore, the active-passive distinction in homosexuality is very prevalent, with one partner irreversibly assuming the feminine role, and the other, the masculine.

LGBT rights organizations have been working hard to challenge this understanding. In the last decade, they successfully put the word gay into everyday use (sometimes spelled *gey*) to distinguish between the traditional understanding of the emasculated homosexual and a more modern identity. However, gay bars and traditional Turkish baths (*hamam*s) are still frequented by heterosexual men who are looking for a quick fling with homosexuals. On the other hand, a Turkish gay identity in the Western sense has been developing in bigger cities, leading to a more egalitarian relationship within gay encounters.

FAMILY

Family values are highly esteemed everywhere in the country. The crude marriage rate was 6.43 in 2002,[8] while the crude divorce rate has remained lower than 1 per thousand per year, which is much lower than international rates.[9] A religious marriage ceremony is not legally valid on its own; however, couples may choose to have both a civil and a religious ceremony.

Rural and urban areas of the country show great diversity in how family life is conducted. In eastern and rural parts of the country, arranged marriages are very common, young women are still sold into marriages, and honor killings are still an unsolved problem, while in western and urban areas, single motherhood and children out of wedlock are not unheard of, albeit definitely not the norm. Similarly, the divorce rate in eastern Anatolia is much lower than in the western part of the country.[10]

Domestic violence is still very much an issue that is actively combated by feminist organizations and the Turkish Family Health and Planning Foundation.[11]

No legally recognized civil union or other legal partnerships exist between same-sex partners. However, postoperative transgender persons can marry a partner of the opposite sex without any legal obstacles. At the same time, many gay men and women end up having to marry a partner their parents choose for them, in order to conceal their homosexuality.

The supreme court ruled in 1982 that the custody of a female child cannot be given to a lesbian mother, and this ruling is still in effect.[12]

COMMUNITY

Organized gay activism is still in its preliminary stage. Gay activist organizations are small and invariably local in scope. Due to censorship in the media, these organizations have little or no political power. Therefore, they function mainly as cultural centers and help lines for sexual minorities. While these local organizations largely work together, there is no centralized entity that covers the whole country.

Arguably the strongest organization is Kaos GL in Ankara, founded in 1994. It mostly works as a cultural center, devoted to the education and self-awareness of LGBT persons. Its magazine, also called *Kaos GL,* is published biannually. It also owns the first LBGT library of Turkey. As of 2007, Kaos GL has organized two international antihomophobia meetings in Ankara to great success, with activists, journalists, academics, and lawyers from all over the world. Since October 2005, Kaos GL has worked as a legally registered association.

Lambdaistanbul was established under the name Gökkuşağı (Rainbow) in 1993, after the Governor's Office obstructed the planned gay pride celebrations. The organization rapidly grew. In 1996 and 1997, it hosted and broadcasted on Açık Radyo the first radio program to take up issues of LGBT people. In 2003, it organized the first pride parade in Istanbul. By 2007, the parade had become very popular among sexual minorities, with politicians, singers, authors, and journalists attending. Lambdaistanbul also runs a switchboard to provide immediate help and answers for anyone who has questions about LGBT issues. The group retains its strong antimilitarist stance and continues to work with women's rights groups. A May 2008 court verdict ruled that Lambda should close down, but the group's lawyers stated that they will take the case to the appeals court.

Other than these very salient groups, there are many smaller communities that are sometimes formed around specific identities. Pembe Üçgen Topluluğu (the Pink Triangle Group) is an LGBT organization in Izmir. Pembe Hayat (Pink Life) in Ankara is a foundation that provides assistance to transgender people. Antalya Gökkuşağı Eşcinsel Oluşumu (Antalya Rainbow Gay Group) is a small group that works in the coastal city of Antalya in southwest Turkey. Piramid GL was formed in Diyarbakır and is the first gay rights group that works in the southeastern part of Turkey, with an emphasis on the Kurdish culture in that region. *Gacı Istanbul* is a magazine published by transsexuals, transvestites, and sex workers. Türkiye Ayıları (Turkish Bears) is a community with an emphasis on bear culture. Homoloji.com, a newly formed but already prolific online community, is a forum in which information on sexual minority cultures is compiled by LGBT users and moderators.

HEALTH

According to the World Health Organization (WHO), life expectancy at birth in Turkey has risen from 65 to 73 years between 1990 and 2006.[13] According to 2003 WHO estimates, Turkey is among the countries with higher child mortality rates, with 35 to 41 children under the age of five dying per 1,000 live births, following the rate in the Turkic republics of the former Soviet Union. Ten percent of government expenditure is on health.

In Turkey, AIDS is not necessarily considered a gay disease. After the Soviet Union's dissolution, many immigrants from Russia, Moldova, and Ukraine came to the big cities of Turkey and the northern region of Anatolia. With not many choices in employment for these immigrants, there was a considerable rise in prostitution in the late 1980s and early 1990s in Turkey. Unsafe sex acts gave rise to many sexually transmitted diseases (STDs) like HIV/AIDS in men, women, and children, with men often transmitting STDs to their families. According to the Ministry of Health figures, there have been 2,711 reported HIV infections in Turkey between 1985 and June 2007, and most (50 to 60%) of infections occur through unprotected heterosexual intercourse.[14]

In the past couple of decades, the Ministry of Health has been working to raise public awareness about STD prevention. However, a research study of married women, carried out as part of the Turkey Demographic and Health Survey in 2003, proved that one in three married women is not informed about HIV/AIDS or methods of prevention.[15]

Another research study done with the help of Kaos GL points out that over 50 percent of sexually active gay men and women are aware of the fact that they are in a risk group for HIV/AIDS and that, despite this awareness, only one-third of the male respondents use condoms.[16]

POLITICS AND LAW

Homosexual conduct was never a criminal offense in Turkey. Age of consent for all people is 18. Gender reassignment surgeries with medical approval were legalized in 1988. There are, however, no laws that protect sexual minorities from discrimination.

In 1999, Demet Demir, a male-to-female (MTF) transsexual and activist, became the first transgender person to run for public office.

In 2002, women's and LGBT rights groups started a campaign to change the Turkish penal code; part of their campaign was to criminalize discrimination based on sexual orientation. The year 2004 saw the first visit of a delegation of sexual minorities to the Justice Commission; however, the draft of an antidiscrimination reference was dropped the same year. Although ultimately discrimination against LGBT people was not criminalized, the campaign is still considered a very important step in securing legal rights for sexual minorities, thanks to the public debates resulting from it.

After the elections of 2007, the new government started to work on a draft for a new constitution with the intention of replacing the much criticized constitution of 1980, which was written after the military coup of September 12, 1980, and was ratified in 1982. Kaos GL sent a letter to the government officials, demanding the addition of sexual orientation and gender identity to article 10, which prohibits discrimination based on "language, race, color, sex, political opinion, philosophical belief, religion and sect."[17] Members of many LGBT rights groups and associations all over Turkey (Antalya Gökkuşağı Eşcinsel Oluşumu, Kaos GL Derneği, Kaos GL İzmir, KAOSİST Eşcinsel Sivil Toplum Girişimi, Lambdaistanbul LGBTT Derneği, Pembe Hayat LGBTT Derneği, and MorEL Eskişehir LGBTT Oluşumu) gathered together to form the Constitution LGBT Commission (Anayasa LGBTT Komisyonu). When the LGBT Commission chairman Burhan Kuzu from the parliament apathetically mentioned in a newspaper that "naturally, we won't grant them [any rights]," the LGBT Commission started a campaign that involved sending rainbow postcards to the parliament.

After years of NGO work, Lambdaistanbul became a registered association in May 2007. After a short while, the Governor's Office of Istanbul moved to close down Lambda, on the grounds that "No association may be founded for unlawful or immoral purposes."[18] The prosecutor rejected the case, but the Governor's Office went to a higher court, and the case was opened in July 2007. In May 2008, after six hearings, the judge ruled to close down the association, to the shock and dismay of many national and international human rights groups. Lambda's lawyers took the decision to the appeals court and in late 2008 the decision was overruled.

In a final hearing in April 2009, the local court decided that the association will not be closed, finalizing the lenghty legal battle. Lambdaistanbul again applied to the appeals court to get a homophobic statement amended in the final decision, however, the decision remains in favor of the association.

By law, gay men are not allowed in the military. Article 17 B/3 of the Compilation of Ailments and Defects (part of the Turkish Armed Forces Health Requirement Regulation) lists homosexuality, transsexuality, and transvestitism as "psychosexual disorders," alongside "chronic antisocial behavior, substance abuse," and "mental deficiency."[19] Should a gay man want to be exempted from mandatory military service, he is required to prove his homosexuality to the psychiatric facility of a hospital appointed by the headquarters. The procedure is not standardized, varies greatly from hospital to hospital, and is highly ambiguous: the proof of homosexuality almost always calls for highly invasive methods such as an anal examination and photos taken while the candidate for exemption is having passive anal sex with another man.[20]

RELIGION AND SPIRITUALITY

Ninety-nine percent of the Turkish population is said to be Muslim.[21] Though the practice may be merely nominal in the secular state, Islam is certainly the predominant religion in the country.[22]

Islam's holy book, the Quran, strictly bans extramarital affairs, and modern interpretations of this ban are strongly conservative. Despite the fact that homosexuality is only frowned upon in the Quran and not forbidden per se, due to readings of hadith (unwritten rules of Islam, based on sayings attributed to the prophet Mohammed) and fatwas (judgments made by Islamic scholars under the sharia), it is traditionally accepted as a sin.

That said, it might be safely claimed that the dynamics of homophobia in Turkey are very different than the strongly religious homophobia of Islamic countries like Iran, Saudi Arabia, and Egypt. Turkey has been a firmly secular country since the declaration of the republic in 1923. However, the highly secular governmental institutions and the army, although they distance themselves drastically from religion, remain extremely homophobic.

VIOLENCE

Violence against sexual minorities is still a very big problem in Turkey, with many gay bashing incidents and open hostility from the police, directed especially toward transgender people. Due to police brutality, many incidents go unreported, unless there is a fatality.

The violent events at Ülker Street in Istanbul in 1996 and the evacuation of the transgender population in the area is widely accepted as the epitome of this phenomenon, likened by many members of the local LGBT community to the Stonewall riots in New York. It has been speculated that the district's police force instigated and participated in the incidents.[23]

A decade later, similar events occurred in the Eryaman district of Ankara, when a group of vigilantes carried out a series of violent assaults on the transgender population in what seemed to be a systematic attempt to cleanse the area.

Both events were large enough to get relatively extensive media coverage and inspire sociological studies, but the majority of singular incidents of hate crimes still go largely unnoticed. LGBT rights organizations have rightly criticized the media for ignoring these problems. At the same time, the murder of openly gay author and journalist Baki Koşar in February 2006 generated considerable media attention, due to his friendships in media circles.[24]

In 2007 the Commission for Monitoring the Human Rights of LGBT Individuals and Law, which was assembled by several local LGBT rights organizations, collected first-hand retellings of human-rights violations against LGBT persons and prepared a report about media coverage of the hate crimes perpetrated against sexual minorities between January and October 2007. The report warned the media against fostering a hostile environment against sexual minorities and drew attention to the fact that nonrecognition of sexual minorities in hate crime law facilitates violent attacks on LGBT persons. In 2008 the Commission for Monitoring the Human Rights of LGBT Individuals and Law changed its name to LGBT Rights Platform, and compiled and published a similar report for that year. The 2009 report will be published by the end of the year.

Similarly, the Human Rights Watch report on LGBT issues in Turkey, released May 2008, includes many cases of gay bashing and police brutality.

OUTLOOK FOR THE 21ST CENTURY

By the late 1990s and the beginning of the 21st century, gays all over Turkey have come a long way, swiftly moving from a gender-based understanding of homosexuality to a more egalitarian interpretation. At the same time, a distinct gay identity has rapidly taken root, especially in big cities. With these social advents, the Turkish gay rights movement has started to parallel similar movements in Western countries.

Still, there is a long way to go before LGBT people are granted total equality—or even acceptance—and controversial issues such as gay marriage will be debated for years to come. However, the new century has been a good start for the Turkish gay rights movement, and it has brought about a clearer view of the problems at hand. NGOs addressing gay issues have been better organized, and with the help of all other NGOs working for a more advanced democracy in Turkey, one can expect a brighter future for LGBT people there.

RESOURCE GUIDE

Suggested Reading

Tarık Bereket and Barry D. Adam, "The Emergence of Gay Identities in Contemporary Turkey," *Sexualities* 9, no. 2 (2006): 131–51.

Selin Berghan, *Lubunya: Transseksüel Kimlik ve Beden* (Istanbul: Metis Yayınları, 2007).

Pınar Çekirge, *Yalnızlık Adasının Erkekleri* (Istanbul: Arma Eğitim Gereçleri Yayıncılık ve Tic. Ltd. Şti., 1999).

Commission for Monitoring the Human Rights of LGBT Individuals and Law, "LGBTT Bireylerin İnsan Hakları Raporu 2007" (Ankara: LGBTT Haklari Platformu, 2008).

Murat Hocaoğlu, *Eşcinsel Erkekler: Yirmi Beş Tanıklık* (Istanbul: Metis Yayınları, 2002).

Human Rights Watch, "We Need a Law for Liberation: Gender, Sexuality, and Human Rights in a Changing Turkey," Human Rights Watch, http://hrw.org/reports/2008/turkey0508/turkey0508web.pdf (accessed May 31, 2008).

KAOS GL, "Türkiye'de Eşcinsel Olmak" (Ankara: KAOS-GL, 2008).

Lambdaistanbul Eşcinsel Sivil Toplum Girişimi, "Ne Yanlış Ne de Yalnızız! Bir Alan Araştırması: Eşcinsel ve Biseksüellerin Sorunları" (Istanbul: Bianet, 2006).

LGBT Rights Platform, "LGBTT Bireylerin İnsan Hakları Raporu 2008" (Ankara: LGBTT Haklari Platformu, 2009).

Cenk Özbay and Serdar Soydan, *Eşcinsel Kadınlar: Yirmi Dört Tanıklık* (Istanbul: Metis Yayınları, 2003).

Doğu Perinçek, *Eşcinsellik ve Yabancılaşma* (Istanbul: Kaynak Yayınları, 2000).

Ali Kemal Yılmaz, *Erkek ve Kadında Eşcinsellik* (Istanbul: Özgür Yayınları, 1998).

Devrim Yılmaz, *Bir Eşcinselin Sıradan Hikâyesi* (Istanbul: An Yayıncılık, 2002).

Arslan Yüzgün, *Türkiye'de Eşcinsellik: Dün, Bugün* (Istanbul: Huryuz Yayınları, 1986).

Organizations/Web Sites

Kaos GL, Gazi Mustafa Kemal Bulvarı, 29/12, http://www.kaosgl.org.
   Leading local LGBT rights organization in Ankara that reaches LBGT persons all over the country thanks to its monthly magazine and big events like the international antihomophobia meeting.

Lambdaistanbul, Katip Mustafa Çelebi Mah. Tel Sok, 28/5, http://www.lambdaistanbul.org.
   Leading local LGBT rights organization in Istanbul.

LEGATO, http://www.unilegato.org.
   Online community of lesbian and gay university students.

Pembe Hayat, http://www.pembehayat.org.
   Local transgender rights group in Ankara.

Pozitif Yaşam Derneği (Positive Life Foundation), http://www.pozitifyasam.org.
   Not solely an LGBT organization, it aims to raise HIV/AIDS awareness.

Türkiye Ayıları, http://www.ayilar.net/en/bearsofturkey.htm, info@ayilar.net.
   Community for the bear culture. They also publish an online magazine, *Beargi*, devoted to bear culture, http://www.beargi.com.

Videos/Films

Beyaz Atlı Prens Boşuna Gelme [*Prince Charming, Don't Come In Vain*] (30 min.) 2009. Directed by Aykut Atasay, İzlem Aybastı, Zeliha Deniz.
   Documentary about representation and visibility of lesbian and bisexual women in Turkey.

Çürüğüm, Askerim, Reddediyorum [*Trilemma: Rotten, Soldier, Objector*] (29 min.) 2009. Directed by Aydın Öztek.
   Documentary about gay men and male-to-female transsexuals who have declared conscientious objection, have done their compulsory military services, or have opted to get exempted from the service on the basis of their sexual orientation or gender identity.

Esmeray: Bir Direniş Öyküsü [*Esmeray: A Story of Resistance*] (16 min.) 2009. Directed by Aydın Öztek.
   A short documentary about Esmeray, a transsexual woman, who is trying to build a life for herself outside the compulsory sex work that the Turkish society imposes on transgendered women.

Travesti Terörü [*The Transvestite Terror*] (18 min.) 2005. Directed by Aykut Atasay.
   A short documentary illustrating how transgender sex workers are depicted in the Turkish media.

Travestiler (*Transvestites*) (26 min.) 2008. Directed by Aykut Atasay.
Documentary about Turkish transvestites.

Yürüyoruz (*We Are Marching*) (26 min., 50 min. Director's Cut) 2006.
Directed by Aykut Atasay.
Documentary depicting the police and civilian brutality that led to the cancellation of a protest march in the city of Bursa by LGBT individuals in 2006.

NOTES

1. State Institute of Statistics, *Results of the Census of Population 2007,* Prime Ministry, Republic of Turkey, http://www.tuik.gov.tr/PreHaberBultenleri.do?id=3894 (accessed May 31, 2008).

2. State Institute of Statistics, *Census of Population 2000: Social and Economic Characteristics of Population* (Ankara: Prime Ministry, Republic of Turkey, 2003).

3. State Institute of Statistics, *Results of the Census of Population 2007.*

4. Brussels European Council, "Presidency Conclusions," http://ue.eu.int/ueDocs/cms_Data/docs/pressData/en/ec/83201.pdf (accessed May 31, 2008).

5. Murat Bardakçı, *Osmanlı'da Seks* (İstanbul: Gür, 1993).

6. " 'Gay Kulübü' nedeniyle YÖK'e suç duyurusu," *Hürriyet,* http://www.hurriyet.com.tr/egitim/anasayfa/6526399.asp (accessed May 31, 2008).

7. The OECD defines the crude marriage rate as "the number of marriages occurring among the population of a given geographical area during a given year, per 1,000 mid-year total population of the given geographical area during the same year." Human Rights Watch, *"We Need a Law for Liberation": Gender, Sexuality, and Human Rights in a Changing Turkey,* Human Rights Watch, 2008, http://hrw.org/reports/2008/turkey0508/turkey0508web.pdf (accessed May 31, 2008). The reports and legal opinions about this matter are rather mixed. Because the Turkish military's procedures are very arbitrary, whether an exempted person can work for a state institution or not is unclear, although the widespread understanding is that state employment is out of the question.

8. Turkish Statistical Institute, "Number of Marriage and Crude Marriage Rate, 1932–2002," TurkStat, http://www.die.gov.tr/tkba/t048.xls (accessed May 31, 2008).

9. "Turkey—Family Life and Structure," *Marriage and Family Encyclopedia,* http://family.jrank.org/pages/1718/Turkey-Family-Life-Structure.html (accessed May 31, 2008).

10. Haber3, "TÜİK'ten Evlilik İstatistikleri," http://www.haber3.com/haber.php?haber_id=289974 (accessed May 31, 2008).

11. Some of these organizations and foundations are Turkish Family Health and Planning Foundation, http://www.tapv.org.tr/; Amargi Kadın Akademisi, http://www.amargi.org.tr/; Uçan Süpürge, http://www.ucansupurge.org/; Filmmor, http://www.filmmor.com/; Ka-der, http://www.ka-der.org.tr/.

12. The supreme court decision of June 21, 1982, which set a precedent, states that "The grounds for divorce [in this case] is homosexuality, namely lesbianism, which could never be tolerated by the society. Giving custody of a girl child to a woman with such pathological habits could endanger the child's future development. In such situations, the custody should be given to the father." See LGBT Rights Platform, "LGBTT Bireylerin İnsan Hakları Raporu 2008" (Ankara: LGBTT Haklari Platformu, 2009).

13. World Health Organization (WHO), "World Health Statistics 2008," http://www.who.int/whosis/whostat/EN_WHS08_Full.pdf (accessed May 31, 2008).

14. Ministry of Health of Turkey, *Basic Health Newsletter,* December 12, 2007, http://www.saglik.gov.tr/TR/dosyagoster.aspx?DIL=1&BELGEANAH=25383&DOSYAISIM=14.pdf (accessed May 31, 2008).

15. Hacettepe University Institute of Population Studies, "Turkey Demographic and Health Survey," Hacettepe University Institute of Population Studies, 2003, http://www.hips.hacettepe.edu.tr/tnsa2003/data/English/chapter13.pdf (accessed May 31, 2008).

16. Veli Duyan, "Gey ve lezbiyenlerin AIDS konusundaki bilgileri ve AIDS'e yaka-lanan kişilere yönelik tutumları: Kaos GL örneği," *Kaos GL 13,* December 2002–January 2003, http://www.kaosgl.org/node/738 (accessed May 31, 2008).

17. Direct quote from the Constitution of the Republic of Turkey, http://www.tbmm.gov.tr/develop/owa/anayasaeng.maddeler?p3=10.

18. Turkish Civil Code, Article 47/2, http://www.tbmm.gov.tr/kanunlar/k4721.html (translation mine).

19. The Turkish Ministry of Justice, "Türk Silahlı Kuvvetleri Sağlık Yeteneği Yönetmeliği" ["The Turkish Armed Forces Health Requirement Regulation"], http://www.mevzuat.adalet.gov.tr/html/20176.html (accessed May 31, 2008).

20. Human Rights Watch, *"We Need a Law for Liberation."*

21. Bureau of Democracy, Human Rights, and Labor, "International Religious Freedom Report 2006: Turkey," http://www.state.gov/g/drl/rls/irf/2006/71413.htm (accessed May 31, 2008).

22. Every person born in Turkey is automatically registered as Muslim, unless he or she is born into a family of a different religion. This is why the official percentage of Muslims in Turkey is said to be 99 percent, whereas the number of actual followers is widely accepted to be much less. There has been no research into how many Turkish citizens consider themselves Muslims.

23. Pınar Selek, *Maskeler Süvariler Gacılar, Ülker Sokak: Bir Altkültürün Dışlanma Mekânı* (Istanbul: Istiklal Kitabevi, 2007).

24. Many articles and obituaries by Baki Koşar's journalist friends were collected in Doğan Hızlan, Reyhan Yıldız, Baki Koşar, Fikri Nazif Ayyıldız, Arif Arslan, Avni Yanıkoğlu, Ayşenur Yazıcı, et al., *Diclenin Gözyaşları: Baki Koşar'ın Anısına* (Istanbul: Erko Yayıncılık, 2006).

UNITED KINGDOM

Zowie Davy

OVERVIEW

The United Kingdom of Great Britain and Northern Ireland (UK) has a land-mass of approximately 81,081square miles. The population at present is about 60,000,000, and population density is approximately 110 people per square mile. The United Kingdom consists of England, Scotland, Wales, and Northern Ireland, as well as a number of small islands, such as Jersey, Guernsey, and the Isle of Man. However, the islands and states have various political relationships with the main UK government in London. England, Scotland, and Wales are connected lands, whereas Northern Ireland is separated by the Irish Sea and lies at the northeast of the island of Ireland. The United Kingdom's west coast faces the Atlantic Ocean and Irish Sea, the east coast faces the North Sea, and the south coast faces the English Channel.

In the 13th century, Wales became a principality of England and was integrated under English rule in the 16th century. In 1999, Wales was granted limited self-governance from Britain. From the 17th century, there has been a political union between England and Scotland of various types, which formed the United Kingdom of Great Britain. Scotland was granted home rule in 1999. Ireland, through the implementation of the Act of Union in 1801, became a part of the United Kingdom, which resulted in the name change to United Kingdom of Great Britain and Ireland. In 1922, the Irish Free State was formed, which consisted of 26 counties. In 1937, the Irish Free State, through legislation, removed most of the constitutional powers of the government and monarch of the United Kingdom, and was renamed Eire. This national break left only counties in Northern Ireland under the United Kingdom's rule until 2007, when power was restored to the Northern Ireland Assembly, which was established as part of the Belfast Agreement.

While most laws are similar, if not equal, in each part of the United Kingdom, there are cultural variations. In some of the smaller islands, such as the Isle of Man situated in the Irish Sea, and Jersey, Guernsey, Sark, and Alderney, which are collectively known as the Channel Islands, some aspects of the legislature have minor differences and they have their own governments. The islands are situated off the northwest coast of France; they are Crown Dependencies, and although not strictly a part of the United Kingdom, owe allegiance to the British Crown. Each of the islands has its own primary legislature and is not represented in the UK parliament.

0   50 100 150 km

0   50   100   150 mi

The Island of Rockall not shown.

North Atlantic Ocean

Voe — Shetland Islands

Orkeny Islands

Hebrides

Scotland

Aberdeen

Dundee

North Sea

Grangemouth

Edinburgh

Glasgow

Newcastle upon Tyne

Londonderry

Northern Ireland

Belfast

Middlesbrough

Isle of Man (U.K.)

Kingston upon Hull

Irish Sea

Manchester

IRELAND

Liverpool

England

Wales

Birmingham

Cardiff

LONDON

Bristol

Dover

Portsmouth

Southhampton

Channel Tunnel

Celtic Sea

English Channel

Guernsey (U.K.)

Jersey (U.K.)

FRANCE

These state governments are known as the States of Guernsey, States of Jersey, and States of Alderney. In Sark, the government is known as Chief Pleas. Laws passed by the states are given Royal Sanction by the UK's Monarch in Council, to which the islands' governments are responsible. Acts of the UK parliament may, however, be extended at any time, to any of the Channel Islands (as with the Isle of Man) by Order-in-Council, thus giving the UK's government the ultimate responsibility for governance in the islands. On the Isle of Man, laws are debated in the House of Keys.

The British Empire was the largest empire in history and for many years was an immense global power. Following World War II, most of the territories of the empire became independent. However, many territories and former colonies went on to join the Commonwealth of Nations, which makes up one-third of the population of the world. The UK's imperial past has given the states of the Commonwealth of Nations a legacy of shared language, and similar legal and political systems. Many people were invited to the United Kingdom from the former colonies and the Commonwealth countries to fill in the worker shortage after World War II. This met with hostility from some of the British public, and much racial discrimination was evident. The Race Relations Act came into force on December 8, 1965, making racial discrimination unlawful in public places. The act forbids discrimination on the grounds of skin color, race, or ethnic and national origins, and covered both UK residents and overseas visitors. The law was strengthened in 1968 when racial discrimination was extended to include legislation on employment and housing provision.

Initially, there were three separate equality commissions in the United Kingdom: the Commission for Racial Equality, the Equal Opportunities Commission, and the Disability Rights Commission. On October 1, 2007, the three commissions merged into the Commission for Equality and Human Rights (CEHR). The Discrimination Law Review in 2005[1] was initiated by Tony Blair's Labour government to put an end to all forms of discrimination, whether based on disability, gender, age, race, religion or belief, or sexual orientation. Furthermore, this review was intended to help simplify and modernize the discrimination law and ultimately make it more effective. The Labour government at the time wanted a single equality act, which would later be used to secure LGBT rights, among other groups of people deemed at risk of prejudice. The Equality Act of 2006, which established the CEHR, was granted Royal Assent on February 16, 2006.

In the 2001 census 92 percent of the population was recorded as white. South Asians were the largest of the other ethnic minority groups, followed by people with mixed ethnic backgrounds. The next largest groups were black Caribbean and black Africans. These figures, however, do not fully represent the UK population in 2007. Following the breakup of the Soviet Union and the inclusion of some of the newly independent states into the European Union (EU) and the lessening of controls over movement in the EU, migration to the United Kingdom has increased. Polish and Portuguese migrants have been the largest groups to migrate to the United Kingdom in recent years.

The Treaty of Rome established the Economic European Community (EEC). The treaty was signed in Rome on March 25, 1957, and entered into force on January 1, 1958. After being refused entry in 1963 and 1967, the United Kingdom joined the EEC in 1973. This political unification enhanced trade relations. The United Kingdom also has strong economic links with the Commonwealth of Nations. This is also the case with the United States, and investments between the two countries are very high. The United Kingdom is the largest foreign investor in the United States and the United States is the largest foreign investor in the United Kingdom. Approximately 45 percent of the UK's outward investment goes to the United States, and 40 percent of overseas direct investment in the United Kingdom comes from the United States. The service sector accounts for about 66 percent of the gross domestic product (GDP) in the United Kingdom, and the United Kingdom has the largest financial services trade surplus in the world. London remains the largest center in the world for international financial services. London's command in Europe's financial service sector is also increasing. The *Pink Pound*, a term describing the spending power of the LGBT community in the United Kingdom, is estimated to be worth 70 billion pounds ($113.3 billion).[2] The UK's defense budget between 2005 and 2006 was 30.1 billion pounds ($48.5 billion). In terms of government expenditure, this puts the United Kingdom second in the world on defense spending. This expenditure is, however, a long way behind the biggest spender, the United States. Defense represents approximately 5.4 percent of the total government expenditure.

OVERVIEW OF LGBT ISSUES

More than ever, LGBT people are prominent in the news and media; LGBT issues are debated in parliament, and LGBT concerns are the focus of many legal reforms. There have been great legal gains in recent times, such as the Gender Recognition Act of 2004 for transsexuals, civil partnerships for lesbians and gay men, the institution of a Single Equality Act that awards LGBT people greater legal protection at work and in public places, and the allowance of LGBT people in the armed services.

These gains have helped community organizations to refocus their efforts toward aspects that are still causes of concern. For example, transsexual organizations are highlighting the long waiting lists for sex reassignment surgery in the National Health Service (NHS). Gay and lesbian organizations are highlighting bullying in schools, drawing attention to homophobic violence and hate crimes that are not abating. In addition to these concerns, there is also an effort to produce positive representations in film, television, and the media.

HIV continues to be a major concern. Various community organizations are combining HIV, AIDS, and sexual health awareness campaigns alongside local authority mandates to inform young people about the benefits of safe sex, hence lessening their chances of being infected. Health screenings and vaccinations have been widened to include other sexually transmitted diseases (STDs), such as hepatitis B, syphilis, and gonorrhea, due to the rising numbers of infections.

EDUCATION

In the UK education system there are different types of state schools, partly state-funded schools, and private schools. County schools are owned and funded by local education authorities. These schools provide primary and secondary education. Voluntary schools are mostly established by religious denominations and can be financially maintained in full or in part by the local education authority. The content of worship is in accordance with the religious character of the school. Those with greater financial independence and more control over admissions policies are known as *voluntary aided schools*. These schools are funded in a similar way to other categories of school, but the governing body must pay at least 10 percent of the costs of capital work, which is necessary work on school design and buildings. *Voluntary controlled schools* are funded in full by local education authorities. There are also special arrangement schools. In the aftermath of section 28, which made it illegal to support LGBT issues in the curriculum, and its subsequent repeal, teachers are still wary of approaching LGBT issues in the classroom. The reluctance to intervene is also witnessed when dealing with homophobic or transphobic language and behavior.

A survey about homophobic bullying in 2007,[3] which received 1,145 responses from young people at secondary school, suggested that almost two-thirds of young lesbian, gay, and bisexual people experience homophobic bullying in school.[4] Almost 58 percent of those experiencing homophobic bullying never report it, and if they do the survey shows that 62 percent of the time nothing is done about it. One-half of teachers fail to respond to homophobic language when they hear it being used. Many teachers who took part in the survey thought that they could not talk about sexuality or deal with this kind of bullying because of section 28. However, addressing issues of sexuality and homophobic bullying was never articulated in the legislation.

The Department for Children and Families, working in partnership with Stonewall and Education Action Challenging Homophobia, has recently launched an awareness week that highlights the extent of homophobic bullying and the harm that it can create. The government department has also produced a document that offers guidance on the legal framework that currently exists. This document also covers areas such as how to recognize, prevent, respond to, and monitor homophobic bullying in schools. This information is aimed at teachers and school staff, head teachers, and senior management and school governors.

EMPLOYMENT AND ECONOMICS

The Equality Act (Sexual Orientation) Regulations of 2007 outlaws discrimination in a range of important areas in the public and private sectors. These range from health care providers, such as hospitals, and education providers to other public sector agencies, and from hotels to banking in the private sector. It is recognized that LGBT people pay taxes, and so service providers are obliged to treat everybody equally and without discrimination. It is now illegal for businesses including banks, estate agencies, and hotels and bars to turn away LGBT customers. The new legislation will make a huge difference in schools. It is now illegal for a school to refuse to place students because they are gay or lesbian, or because their parents are. A school that does not take homophobic bullying seriously could also be brought before the law. In the public and private health care sectors, general practitioners can no longer turn anybody away or refuse lesbian, gay, bisexual, and transgender people treatments they would offer anybody else. Council services are also affected by the new legislation. Councils have a duty to recognize that homophobic behavior toward a tenant is reason to start an investigation and to begin gathering evidence for the rehousing of the victim or the eviction of the perpetrators of abuse. LGBT people no longer have to tolerate being treated differently from anyone else.

In the private sector, hotels and bed and breakfast establishments can no longer refuse double rooms to same-sex couples. LGBT businesses also have to abide by the legislation and cannot discriminate against heterosexuals who wish to enter and use the services on offer.

Religious organizations have argued that they should be exempt from these regulations. Regulation 14 of the Equality Act provides an exception for organizations relating to religion and belief. It continues to allow a religion to advance a belief and teach the principles of the religion. Any activity within the structure of the religion, such as marriage, is not included in the legislation. However, the law does extend to those people who act on behalf of a religious organization whose goods and services are commercial or those who provide welfare services on behalf of the government—for example, religious-based adoption and fostering agencies. Religious groups providing publicly funded welfare services to the community, like Meals-On-Wheels or drug rehabilitation, have no right to discriminate against LGBT individuals.

SOCIAL/GOVERNMENT PROGRAMS

The Equalities Review is a government-led program set up to widen ways of understanding how to implement institutional strategies for the advancement of equality in British society. As part of this initiative, LGBT people in the United Kingdom have been included. The initiative is underpinned by understanding *equality* as something more than economic parity. Equality initiatives in the past have focused mainly on LGBT people gaining economic and financial benefits, rather than recognizing legal, social, physical, and political restraints working to constrain equal opportunities. Various research reports have been commissioned by the government in a bid to garner practical recommendations for social policy implementations and best practice guidelines for government and public sector employers and employees. These guidelines will also be utilized for bringing equity within voluntary sector organizations, trade unions, and those working for and receiving services from civic society organizations. The reports for governmental consideration have been produced by nongovernmental organizations (NGOs), such as Stonewall[5] and Press for Change.[6]

There are a number of contemporary pilot schemes to integrate LGBT people into mainstream society. These range from sexual health programs, training, and workshops for employers on the diversity and integration of LGBT people. A controversial pilot was implemented as part of the No Outsiders program, which teaches children about same-sex relationships. Various books depicting gay and lesbian relationships are being used in teaching school children. The program's purpose is to support schools in meeting their requirements of equal access for and equal treatment of LGBT people under the newly implemented Equality Act 2007.

Stakeholders are currently working with the government's Department of Health in developing a strategy to highlight inequality in relation to gender identity and sexual orientation. The Sexual Orientation and Gender Identity Advisory Group (SOGIAG) is assisting the Department of Health on three tiers: health inequalities, better employment of LGBT people, and transgender health provision. This program is to ensure both LGBT users and providers are ensured opportunities to offer their experiences to improve the services available and direct training standards related to sexual orientation and gender identity.

SEXUALITY/SEXUAL PRACTICES

Since the decriminalization of male homosexuality, sexual practices such as sodomy were also decriminalized. Sodomy still retains a certain amount of cultural taboo in the United Kingdom. Often, gay male sex is ridiculed within popular culture as part of British humor. Sex acts between men are often thought of as not falling under equality and human rights legislation, and thus no recourse to defamatory language has been tried in a court of law. CEHR works to combat discrimination against sex, sexual orientation, and gender reassignment by providing support to individuals bringing claims.[7] Although there are such safeguards in place, it does not stop people from making jibes. For example, in 2008 a rector from the Church of England published a post on his blog suggesting that "sodomy can seriously damage your health" and "fellatio kills."[8] A church spokesperson did condemn the jokes; however, these forms of discrimination often go on without denunciation.

There was no equal legislation for lesbians in the United Kingdom and, therefore, lesbian sexual acts have always been legal. The *tribade,* an old name for a lesbian, appears in English texts from circa 1600. The term comes from the Greek word *tribein* (to rub), suggesting the rubbing of the genitals.

FAMILY

The notion of citizenship has been historically colored by its familial and exclusively heterosexual connotations. The citizenship models embodied in the postwar welfare state were explicitly built around the nuclear family and a traditional division of labor between men and women. Changes in family life, combined with other social, cultural, and demographic changes, had an impact on family relations. For example, women's participation in the labor market has increased, children are financially dependent for longer, and kinship relations have changed because families sometimes move away, so that grandparents, aunts, and uncles are not living as closely to their family members as they would have in the past. A multicultural society also makes for diverse family traditions and care commitments. There is also greater acceptance of same-sex relationships, or at least greater acknowledgement of same-sex partnerships, and there has been a marked shift in the acknowledgement of family diversity. A smaller proportion of the population is living as the heterosexual nuclear family of the idealized mid-20th century form. There are fewer people who are choosing or who are able to construct their relationships according to the traditional. In 2003, only 22 percent of households in the United Kingdom were made up of a heterosexual couple with dependent children.

COMMUNITY

Within the LGBT community in the United Kingdom, political actions are widespread, from grassroots activism, attending vigils, demonstrations and local, national, and international forums, to highly publicized legal cases, from naming and shaming health provision and psychiatric gatekeepers to transsexual surgery, helping to fundraise and raise awareness about various issues, and so on. The Internet has provided a valuable community tool, which enables LGBT people worldwide to discuss global and local politics in the United Kingdom.

Positive cultural representations are high on the political agenda within the community.

Homosexuality and transgender had only rarely been represented in popular culture up until the 1990s. When it *was* a focus of television, film, or plays, it was represented as something to fear, something to laugh at, or something to pity. For example, the British Carry On films and comedy series, such as *Are You Being Served?* poked fun at homosexuality, with actors portraying homosexual men with stereotypical, overt campiness. Transgender people have fared no better with representations that are decidedly psychotic in nature. Transgender characters are normally portrayed as assassins, murderers, or sexual deviants. For example, in *Thunderball, Cruising,* and *Silence of the Lambs,* transgender people are represented as something to be feared, if not from violence then from disease. Lesbian and bisexual people were rarely represented at all. Present day television series, including gay-, lesbian-, bisexual-, and transgender-themed material on primetime TV, discuss sex and sexuality-related issues in a more balanced way. There are many shows that have begun to feature homosexual characters alongside heterosexual characters as part of the social milieu. In the past few years, there have been a number of television shows that concentrate predominantly on LGBT people and represent their lifestyles rather than representing them as a deviant member of society. These shows have been much more matter-of-fact in their representation of homosexual lifestyles. Many have included contentious issues, such as gay family adoption, artificial insemination, civil partnerships, coming out, safe sex, HIV-positive status, and so on. Series such as *Queer as Folk* feature explicit sex scenes and reflect upon previously taboo aspects of gay lives in an explicit and forthright way. Lesbians have had much less exposure; however, this imbalance has just started to be rectified, with miniseries such as *Tipping the Velvet.* Another show, *The L-Word,* has also been screened in the United Kingdom. Furthermore, in the Liverpool-based soap opera, *Brookside,* actress Anna Friel, who played Beth, became a household name when her character had an affair with nanny Margaret Clemence, played by Nicola Stephenson. The soap screened the first lesbian kiss to be shown on primetime British TV in 1993. However, Beth and Margaret's kiss was edited from the teatime omnibus edition, highlighting the ongoing uneasiness that producers felt when engaging with issues of LGBT representation.

In the United Kingdom, LGBT History Month is held annually in February. The month provides an exceptional chance to bring to light the lives and histories of LGBT people, their families, and their friends. It is a month when representations are offered about all aspects of the lives LGBT people lead. It is also a month when LGBT people celebrate their diversity through increased visibility.

HEALTH

Gay men and men who have sex with men (MSM) remain the group at greatest risk of becoming infected with HIV in the United Kingdom. Throughout the 1990s, there was a fall in the number of new HIV diagnoses among this group. This was due in part to the work of the NGOs that have campaigned and provided safe sex information about sexual conduct through outreach work on the gay scene and cruising areas. Since 1999, however, the figures have consistently risen. This trend is mainly due to an increase in HIV testing. The Terrence Higgins Trust is campaigning to raise money to provide tests for the estimated 33 percent of people living with HIV in the United Kingdom today who do not know they have contracted the virus. Another contributory factor may be a rise in high-risk sexual behavior, which is indicated by the rise of some STDs such as gonorrhea and syphilis. As of the end of June 2007, almost 40,000 MSM have been diagnosed with HIV in the United Kingdom. This figure includes those who have died from AIDS-related illnesses. The number of heterosexually acquired HIV infections diagnosed in the United Kingdom has risen sharply over the last 15 years. For the first time, the rate of heterosexually acquired HIV diagnoses overtook the rate of diagnoses in MSM. According to one report, in 2006, "there were 3,430 reports of heterosexually acquired HIV, and a total of 36,603 had been reported by the end of June 2007."[9]

There is very little known about the sexual health of lesbians and bisexual women. The political group Stonewall in the United Kingdom has commissioned a survey that will attempt to find out about the health care needs and experiences of these groups. Stonewall hopes that these issues will be better understood, rather than ignored in the future. This is the first survey of its kind in the United Kingdom.

POLITICS AND LAW

In December 1953, the government set up a Royal Commission to investigate the Offenses against the Person Act of 1861 relating to homosexual offenses. The committee was convened because of the publicity about homosexuality as a result of high-profile prosecutions. In 1952, there had been 5,443 prosecutions in England for sodomy, attempted sodomy or indecent assault, and gross indecency.[10] Many homosexual men were the targets of blackmail, and cases at that time were widespread. The committee comprised 3 women and 14 men, of which 13 served for all three years of the committee's considerations. The committee was chaired by John Wolfenden, a former headmaster of boarding schools for boys. In 1957, he was the vice chancellor of Reading University. Wolfenden's son was a gay man. The Wolfenden report, formally known as the *Report of the Departmental Committee on Homosexual Offences and Prostitution*,[11] was published on September 3, 1957, over three years after the committee was set up. The report recommended that homosexual acts should no longer be a criminal offense between adults in private. It took 10 years for the report to influence the passage of the Sexual Offences Act of 1967, which replaced the Offenses against the Person Act of 1861. The 1861 act had criminalized homosexual behavior and homosexual sexual acts.

In 1967, Lord Arran and Leo Abse MP (member of parliament) introduced identical Sexual Offenses Bills to the House of Lords and the House of Commons, respectively. The House of Commons passed the law with a majority of 244 votes to 100 on July 27, 1967. This was after the third reading. The Sexual Offenses Act decriminalized homosexual activity in England and Wales. There were still inequalities within the act in relation to heterosexual activity, because the age of consent was 21 years of age for two consenting men as opposed to 16 years of age for heterosexuals. Also, the notion of *private* was not the same for heterosexual and homosexuals; for example, a hotel room was still understood as a public space for homosexuals, and if two men were found having sex in one, there could still be a prosecution. Even though Lord Arran had presented the bill in the House of Lords, he was not totally comfortable with the legal gains and suggested that homosexuals should accept these legal changes as progressive and not ask for more. At the end of the speech that introduced the bill, Lord Arran said: "Homosexuals must continue to remember that, while there may be nothing bad in being a homosexual, there is certainly nothing good."[12] This decriminalization act did not affect Scotland and Northern Ireland. It took until 1980 to decriminalize homosexuality in Scotland and until 1982 in Northern Ireland. Northern Ireland did, however, attempt to decriminalize homosexuality in 1977, but the Loyalist politician Ian Paisley formed a campaign called Save Ulster from Sodomy, which gained much support and stopped the decriminalization process. It took Jeff Dudgeon's case in the European Court of Human Rights (ECtHR) to sway Northern Ireland to equate their law with England, Wales, and Scotland.

LGBT issues have, in the past few years, been taken up by Tony Blair's Labor government. The repeal of section 28, equal ages of consent for homosexuals and heterosexuals, gender recognition for transsexual people, civil partnerships for lesbian and gay couples, and LGBT people in the armed forces have all been debated and assented in law. These legislative moves in the United Kingdom have usually occurred following rulings from the ECtHR. Many LGBT community groups, such as Stonewall, Press for Change, Liberty, and the Equality Network have all worked closely with the government in the consultation processes during the implementation of new LGBT citizenship rights.

There are an estimated 5,000 transsexuals in the United Kingdom. The United Kingdom was one of four countries in Europe, alongside Andorra, Albania, and Eire, that did not recognize the acquired gender and civil rights of transsexuals prior to 2004. For the previous 34 years transsexuals, were legally considered to be the sex they were at birth. The case that set the legal precedent for what constituted a man and a woman was the infamous *Corbett versus Corbett* case, when transsexual April Ashley and Arthur Corbett, who was the third Baron Rowallan, wanted to divorce. The United Kingdom at that time did not recognize the mutual consent agreement between the two parties as a reason enough to grant a divorce. Lord Judge Ormrod ruled that, because of this, the case's primary issue had to be the actual validity of the marriage between April Ashley, who was known to be a transsexual, and Arthur Corbett. The divorce was dependent on the *true* sex of the respondent April Ashley, because if, through a medical test, she was determined to be male, then the marriage would have been void in the first place. Determining the true sex of the person was based on four factors: chromosomal factors, gonadal factors (i.e., the presence of testes or ovaries), genital factors (which includes internal sexual organs), and psychological factors.

The Gender Recognition Act of 2004 (GRA 2004) became law in June 2004. It enables transsexuals to apply for gender recognition in their acquired gender. The Gender Recognition Panel (GRP) began work on April 1, 2005, deciding who can or cannot gain recognition. Those transsexuals who wish to have all their personal documentation changed to their acquired gender may do so as long as the GRP is satisfied with the evidence the transsexual supplies. At first, this only applied to people who had been living in their new gender for more than six years. This was reduced to two years in April 2007.

The precedents set in the GRA 2004 are regarded as progressive by many political activists and advocates of gender recognition. This is due to the changing legal ideas of what actually constitutes a transgender man versus a transgender woman. The law describes two main paths by with the transsexual obtain acceptance by the GRP: having been diagnosed with gender dysphoria, or planning to have surgery that changes sexual characteristics. The information submitted by a doctor is judged by at least one medical expert in the field of gender dysphoria and a legal expert. The surgical option requires the transsexual to show confirmation of surgical treatment for the purpose of modifying sexual characteristics, for example, genital modification or sex reassignment surgery (vaginoplasty, orchiodectomy, etc.). This is by far the easiest way to apply, because a general practitioner should be able to certify this by looking at the notes and correspondence in the individual's medical record. For diagnosis of gender dysphoria, the evidence needs to be given by a qualified practitioner from a gender identity clinic. This option allows someone who has not undergone genital surgery to obtain recognition. Transsexuals who are married prior to applying for gender recognition must divorce first, because same-sex marriage is not allowed.

The Civil Partnership Act of 2004 came into operation on December 5, 2005, and enables same-sex couples to register as civil partners. The civil partnership does not apply to heterosexual couples or unions between family members, such as siblings, as can be attained through similar legislation in some European countries such as Portugal. It is a legal requirement to give notice of intention to register a civil partnership and, once given, notices are publicized by the registration authority for a period of 15 days. A civil partnership notice states each person's name, date of birth, occupation, nationality, and the place of formation of the union. Once the notice is given it is valid for 12 months. The minimum age for registering a civil partnership is 16 years old, but as with marriages in England and Wales, written consent from a guardian or parents is necessary up until the age of 18.

The local Government Act of 1988, section 28, prohibited local authorities in England, Wales, and Scotland from promoting homosexuality. Margaret Thatcher's Conservative government, who were the drafters of this legislation, also labeled gay family relationships as "pretended family relationships." The existence of section 28 caused much confusion as to what could be said in relation to LGBT issues. Section 28 also created confusion as to the services that could be offered to lesbian, gay, and bisexual members of the community.

Section 28 is often remembered as the legislation that stopped the teaching of gay, lesbian, and bisexual issues in schools. It did not apply to schools directly. It did, however, apply to the local authorities that were responsible for schools. Nonetheless, the media added to these misleading interpretations and stymied the debate about LGBT issues in schools, especially in sex education. Since 2000, section 28 had been a superfluous law due to the implementation of the Learning and Skills Act of 2000, which detached any responsibility from local authorities in offering sex education. However, in 2000, the Department for Education and Employment (DfEE) (now called the Department for Children, Schools, and Families) sent out a circular to schools, which said that it was the responsibility of the schools to make sure that the needs of all pupils are met in their schooling programs, regardless of the student's developing sexuality. The DfEE further suggested that there was still a need, regardless of sexuality, for any student to feel that sex and relationship education is relevant to them and sensitive to their needs. The secretary of state was unambiguous about the fact that teachers should be able to deal sensitively and honestly with issues surrounding sexual orientation. This included the answering of suitable questions, along with providing support about sex and relationship education. However, ambiguity arises when teachers interpret what the protocols mean. Furthermore, there should be no direct promotion of sexual orientation, either homosexual or heterosexual.[13]

The repeal of section 28 had been supported by various organizations, which included local authorities, trade unions, health experts, lesbian and gay groups, and teachers and school governors. In 2000, Scotland's equivalent to section 28, the Section 2a clause, was removed from the statute books. On July 10, 2003, the House of Lords voted overwhelmingly to repeal section 28 of the Local Government Act in England and Wales. This followed the House of Commons vote in March 2003 in favor of a repeal of the statute. The Local Government Bill received Royal Assent on September 18, 2003, and section 28 was removed from the statute books to the relief and jubilation of many LGBT organizations that had campaigned to put this issue back on the agenda.

LGBT people were denied the right to serve in the armed services prior to 1999, based on the findings of the Homosexual Policy Assessment Team (HPAT) report, commissioned in September 1995. The debate took into account an internal assessment of attitudes within the armed services toward homosexuality. The issue of homosexuality in the armed forces was debated in parliament on May 9, 1996. When the Blair government came to power in 1997, they made it clear that the policy would be reviewed during the tenure of their parliament. The ECtHR ruled in 1999 that the Ministry of Defense (MoD) was breaking European law in relation to the right to a private life, freedom of expression, and freedom from discrimination. The ruling followed the case of four service personnel who were discharged after revealing their homosexuality. The armed forces were forced to lift the longstanding ban on homosexuality in the services. Later, the MoD confirmed that a new inclusion policy would also apply to transgender and transsexual people. The ban on homosexuals, transgender people, and transsexuals in the armed forces was not legally sustainable due to Britain's involvement with European law. The new MoD policy recognized sexual orientation and gender expression as a private matter and was formulated with full consultation of the three Service Chiefs. The policy is underpinned by a Code of Social Conduct that applies to everybody's sexual orientation and gender expression, including bisexuals and heterosexuals. The Royal Air Force (RAF) has been at the forefront of recognizing this policy and promoting diversity in its ranks. The RAF marched in Manchester's Gay Pride and a similar event in Brighton. In addition to the armed forces, the police, fire brigade, and ambulance services have also shown support and joined LGBT pride events.

RELIGION AND SPIRITUALITY

The UK population is more culturally diverse than ever before, and people are free to practice their faiths. White Christians remain the biggest single religious group. Christianity is the largest religious group overall, and the majority of black people and those from mixed ethnic backgrounds also identify as Christian. Among the other faiths, the largest groups are Muslims, Hindus, Sikhs, and Jews. In the 2001 census, 15 percent of the UK population reported having no religion. There are mixed views about LGBT issues in the many different faith groups in the United Kingdom. The conservative Christians and Muslims have been the most outspoken on issues of gay marriage, adoption of children by gay and lesbian couples, and transgender rights. There has been a call for nondiscrimination of, and support for, LGBT people from some faith groups; however, this support has come with reservations about homosexual sexual acts and the marriage of transsexuals in places of worship.

Recently, there has been a split within the Anglican Church around the ordination of priests who are practicing homosexuals. While there are no institutional proclamations surrounding this debate, the archbishop of Canterbury, Rowan Williams, advocates for noncelibate priests and bishops to be ordained. At the Anglican synod, there have been mass boycotts of the annual meeting by traditionalists, whose position states that this inclusion goes against the Bible's teachings.

The secularization of Britain has reduced the influence of the various churches in civil life. Islamic and Christian groups are the most vocal defenders of a traditionalist reading of their respective scriptures. Most religions in the United Kingdom comment on legal or societal moves towards tolerance and equality of LGBT people. However, the liberal religious groups who identify as Islamic, Christian, Judaic, and so on, have adapted to the wide tolerance of LGBT people and their concerns. Occasionally there is an outcry by religious leaders on specific issues that arise, such as the teaching of LGBT issues to children.

VIOLENCE

The definition of hate crime in the United Kingdom is "any incident, which constitutes a criminal offense, and which is perceived by the victim or any other person as being motivated by prejudice or hate."[14] The range of hate crimes covers everything from verbal abuse to murder. The British crime survey (BCS) in 2006, which was based on interviews with a wide sample of people and which can expose crimes that are not always reported to the police, indicates that the number of hate crimes offenses could be as great as 260,000. The Metropolitan Police in London reported 11,799 incidents of racist and religious hate crimes and 1,359 incidents of homophobic hate crimes. The police estimate that 90 percent of homophobic crime goes unreported.[15] This underreporting is believed to be because victims are too frightened or embarrassed to let someone know that they have been a victim of homophobic crimes and think that little can be done about the incidents. The police also believe that the typical homophobic hate offender is a young white male. Most homophobic offenders are between 16 and 20 years old. The perpetrator usually lives near the victim, and many hate crimes happen near the victims' homes while they are going about their daily business. This suggests that the gay, lesbian, bisexual, and transgender individual and community are still viewed as someone or something to be regulated through violence and exclusion.

OUTLOOK FOR THE 21ST CENTURY

In the United Kingdom, the global politics that influence how LGBT people are viewed, protected, or unprotected rests very much on the notion of human rights. Nonetheless, in the past few years the government has introduced legislation that partially protects the rights of LGBT people. Huge gains have been made by the numerous grassroots organizations and activists that have been at the forefront of awareness campaigns, attending vigils, demonstrations, and pride marches, as well as local, national, and global forums. These political groups, and other members of the LGBT community, have been concerned with assimilation into social arenas that were previously closed to LGBT people. The gains in most are equal; however, civil partnerships, as opposed to marriage, the continuation of violent homophobic and transphobic attacks in the streets, and bullying in schools continue to be at the forefront for LGBT people. An attempt to break down institutionalized prejudice in public places is another important focus, along with achieving positive and non-justificatory representations in popular culture, medicine, and politics.

RESOURCE GUIDE

Suggested Reading

Sara Ahmed, Orientations: Toward a Queer Phenomenology. *GLQ: A Journal of Lesbian and Gay Studies* 12 (2006): 543–74.

Richard Ekins and Dave King, *Blending Genders: Social Aspects of Cross-Dressing and Sex-Changing* (Routledge, London, 1996).

Tracy Hargreaves, *Androgyny in Modern Literature* (Basingstoke, UK: Palgrave Macmillan, 2005).

Joan Nestle et al., eds., *Genderqueer: Voices Beyond the Sexual Binary* (Los Angeles: Alyson Books, 2002).

Ken Plummer, *Telling Sexual Stories: Power, Change and Social World* (London: Routledge, 1995).

Diane Richardson and Steven Seidman, eds., *Handbook of Lesbian and Gay Studies* (London: Sage, 2002).

Brian Tully, *Accounting for Transsexualism and Transhomosexuality* (London: Whiting and Birch, 1992).

Jeffrey Weeks, *Invented Moralities: Sexual Values in the Age of Uncertainty* (Cambridge: Polity Press, 1995).

Jeffrey Weeks, *Making Sexual History* (Cambridge: Polity Press, 2000).

Video/Film

The Crying Game (112 min.; 1992). Directed by Neil Jordan. British Screen Productions. Psychological thriller set against the backdrop of tensions between the IRA and British army. Following the kidnapping of a British soldier (Jody) by an IRA member (Fergus), a friendship between the captor and the captive flourishes. The film then moves to London where the IRA member searches for the partner (Dil) of the soldier to fulfill his promise to him. When the IRA member eventually finds her they begin a love affair. Dil is transgendered. The film explores sexuality, race, and nationality.

Breakfast on Pluto (135 min.; 2006). Directed by Neil Jordan. Pathe Pictures International. This comedy is a lighthearted look at the life of Kitten, who is a transwoman. Kitten leaves home and meets a sugar daddy who is a singer in a glam rock band and has links to the IRA. Kitten then moves to London where she becomes a prostitute. She is also trying to find her biological mother.

My Beautiful Laundrette (97 min.; 1985). Directed by Stephen Frears. Channel Four Films.
> This is the unlikely story of a meeting between two old school friends in Thatcher's Britain. Johnny, who is white and is involved with a neo-Nazi group, starts to work for his Asian friend in a launderette. Despite the political divisions, the two friends become lovers.

Web Sites

FtM Network, http://www.ftm.org.uk/.
International Lesbian and Gay Association-Europe (ILGA-Europe), http://www.ilga-europe.org/.
OutRage, http://www.OutRage.org.uk.
Press for Change, http://www.pfc.org.uk.
Stonewall, http://www.stonewall.org.uk/.
Yorkshire MESMAC, http://www.mesmac.co.uk/.

NOTES

1. The final report of the Equalities Review was published on February 28, 2007, and was named *Fairness and Freedom: The Final Report of the Equalities Review,* http://archive.cabinetoffice.gov.uk/equalitiesreview/upload/assets/www.theequalitiesreview.org.uk/equality_review.pdf.

2. "Out Now," *Diva and Gay Times* readers survey, 2005.

3. The report "The Experiences of Young Gay People at School" can be found at http://www.stonewall.org.uk/documents/school_report.pdf.

4. Stonewall's Education for All is a call to action to eliminate homophobic bullying from schools. This campaign is also aimed at homophobic language being used, such as "that's so gay" and "you're so gay," which are commonplace slurs in the United Kingdom.

5. See Stonewall's 2007 report "Sexual Orientation Research" review at http://archive.cabinetoffice.gov.uk/equalitiesreview/upload/assets/www.theequalitiesreview.org.uk/sexor.pdf.

6. See The Equalities Review's report "Engendered Penalties: Transgender and Transsexual People's Experiences of Inequality and Discrimination" at http://archive.cabinetoffice.gov.uk/equalitiesreview/upload/assets/www.theequalitiesreview.org.uk/transgender.pdf.

7. See http://www.cipd.co.uk/subjects/dvsequl/sexdisc/sexdiscrimination.htm.

8. See http://www.independent.co.uk/news/uk/home-news/rector-condemned-for-sodomy-remarks-953134.html.

9. See http://www.avert.org/uksummary.htm.

10. GLBT inc. provides an extensive encyclopedia of gay, lesbian, bisexual, transgender, and queer culture. For more information on the Wolfenden report see http://www.glbtq.com/social-sciences/wolfenden_report.html.

11. Sir John Wolfenden, *Report of the Committee on Homosexual Offences and Prostitution* (London: Her Majesty's Stationery Office, 1957).

12. Andy Stuart, ed., "Ourstory," *PCS Proud Magazine,* 2005.

13. Department for Education and Employment (DfEE), *Sex and Relationship Education Guidance* (London: DfEE, 2000).

14. The government Web site provides extensive information about hate crimes, which suggests that they take this seriously, http://homeoffice.gov.uk/crime-victims/reducing-crime/hate-crime/.

15. The UK Home Office provides extensive information and policy documents, which can be found at http://homeoffice.gov.uk/crime-victims/reducing-crime/hate-crime/.

VOLUME INDEX